AMERICA'S
ANCIENT
TREASURES

AMERICA'S ANCIENT TREASURES

A Guide to Archeological Sites and Museums
in the United States and Canada

FOURTH REVISED, ENLARGED EDITION

Franklin Folsom
Mary Elting Folsom
Illustrations by Rachel Folsom

University of New Mexico Press : *Albuquerque*

Folsom, Franklin, 1907–
    America's ancient treasures: a guide to archeological sites and museums in the United States and Canada/Franklin Folsom, Mary Elting Folsom: illustrations by Rachel Folsom.—4th rev., enl. ed.
        p.   cm.
    Includes index.
    ISBN 0-8263-1449-X (cloth).—ISBN 0-8263-1450-3 (paper)
    1. Indians of North America—Museums—Guidebooks.
2. Indians of North America—Antiquities—Guidebooks.
3. United States—Antiquities—Guidebooks.
4. Canada—Antiquities—Guidebooks.
5. Archaeological museums and collections—United States—Guidebooks.
6. Archaeological museums and collections—Canada—Guidebooks.
7. United States—Description and travel—1981—Guidebooks.
8. Canada—Description and travel—1981—Guidebooks.
I. Folsom, Mary Elting, 1906–
II. Title.
E56.F64   1993
92-32120
CIP

Designed by Emmy Ezzell

This book about their roots
is dedicated to
the indigenous peoples
of the United States and Canada,
past and present

CONTENTS

PREFACE
TO THE FOURTH EDITION

Five hundred years after 1492, this guide is an attempt to direct people to the amazing variety of life that Columbus and his followers would have seen if they had been a little more curious and a lot less greedy. What remains of the pre-Columbian Western Hemisphere is only a shadow of what could have been seen five centuries ago; but far better that than nothing.

For the many millions of people who lived in what Europeans called the New World, 1492 was a year that marked the beginning of a terrible crisis. All that they had developed in more than 14,000 years, began—very suddenly—to disappear. The human beings who had filled a great variety of ecological niches in the western hemisphere began to die in vast numbers. They had no immunity to diseases that had not afflicted their ancestors in all the millennia during which they had been separated from their homeland in Siberia.

In addition, the military actions of European invaders killed and killed and killed those who had escaped the strange new epidemics. At the same time missionaries from various forms of an imported religion insisted to the surviving aboriginal people that their beliefs were evil and worthless. And the massive importation of an addictive drug—alcohol—played a destructive role. For all these reasons and others, after 1492 the strength to continue life on its unique courses of development dwindled with great speed.

One result of the collapse has been this: It is not easy for us to know the history of life on the land we inhabit.

Nevertheless, much has been done to fill the great gap in our knowledge of those on whose experience we have built. Archeologists have provided a great deal of this knowledge, and the volume of their findings has greatly increased since 1971 when the first edition of this guide book appeared. In 1974 and 1983 it was necessary to revise and update what we had written. Now, a fourth edition is needed because since 1983 more than a hundred new sites have been prepared for public viewing. A number of new museums now interpret prehistory for us, and dozens of older museums have revised their exhibits.

This expansion reflects a tremendous increase in the volume of work done by archeologists, aided in a great many cases by funding the federal government has provided. The enlarged activity also reflects a greatly increased interest on the part of the general public. Included in the growth has been participation by Native Americans in reclaiming—and protecting—their long and rich heritage.

In response to Native Americans insistence, museums have been returning religious artifacts and human remains to the tribes to whom they belong. Museum exhibits have changed as sensitivity to their concerns has become effective.

This book honors the feeling of Native Americans that the skeletons of their ancestors should not be publicly exhibited. It also honors the search of archeologists for truth—a search that has given back to Native Americans many elements of their past that would otherwise have been lost.

Digging up the grandmothers and grandfathers of today's tribal people has been a shock to those people. On the other hand it has helped everyone to see how creative the inhabitants of this continent have been for thousands of years. It is possible, because of archeologists, to see the lives of the past as more admirable than we could otherwise have realized. One source of knowledge has been the study of skeletons. We do not hide this fact, although we do honor the dead by not showing them in our illustrations. As we do this we look forward to the day when the religions of Native Americans and the science of archeologists will both contribute to a sense of mutual respect that will benefit everyone.

Nineteen ninety-three, the year of the publication of this book, has been declared by the United Nations Commission on Human Rights to be the International Year of the World's Indigenous People. As we note this, we observe that increasingly the descendants of the first inhabitants of this hemisphere wish to be known as indigenous or aboriginal. The world *Indian,* reminiscent of the hated invasion of their homeland by Europeans, still cannot be avoided completely. For example, one of their important organizations is the Association on American Indian Affairs. Another is the American Indian Movement (AIM). To a degree *Native American* has replaced *Indian* as the term preferred by indigenous people, but it suggests that they are properly named after an Italian navigator who once saw some of their ancestors.

Because the language that one group of human beings uses about another group often lags behind changing reality, readers will find the old familiar terms *Indian* and *Native American* in what we have written. This is meant simply as an aid to those who are used to those terms. We hope that by the time a fifth edition of *America's Ancient Treasures* is needed, the general public will habitually refer to the oldest inhabitants by the words preferred by those whose ancestors were the real discoverers of what is now the homeland of us all.

It has not been easy to catch up with all the new exhibits and new sites. We hope we have not missed any, but if we have, we invite our readers to write to us with data that will be needed for another edition of this book sometime in the future.

In our search for up-to-date information we have been greatly aided by federal, state, provincial, academic and self-employed archeologists and by good leads that have been sent in by readers of earlier editions of this book. We thank them all.

Readers of earlier editions have asked for mail addresses and phone numbers of those responsible for sites or museums. The present edition provides these, when available. With this information prior to a visit, it will be possible to learn about exact visiting hours or fee policies both of which often change.

The entries about most sites and museums have been checked for accuracy with those in charge of them. In some cases, we have had to rely on other sources.

America's Ancient Treasures tries to open doors to those who are curious and who want to dig metaphorically into the past. But it is also meant to be a wall against those who are thoughtless or who, motivated by greed are only interested in digging for profit or to collect souvenirs. Accordingly, the road directions lead only to places where digging *cannot* be done, or can be done only under expert guidance. Also, we have tried not to direct visitors to sites that Native Americans regard as sacred and where religious ceremonies take place. It is for the First Americans—and no one else—to decide who should be present as they worship.

Franklin Folsom
Mary Elting Folsom
Boulder, Colorado

PREFACE
TO THE THIRD EDITION

Prehistoric Americans north of Mexico had not yet developed their own symbols for the sounds of speech at the time when writing arrived from Europe, only a few hundred years ago. The early Indians could not set down in lasting words any account of the richness of their experience. They could not record in unmistakable form the problems they faced or describe the solutions they worked out. This meant that the First Americans could not communicate fully with their present-day descendants—or, for that matter, with those later Americans with whom their descendants were forced to share their land. The ancient ones have scarcely been able to whisper across the centuries. As a result, the million or so Native Americans living north of Mexico today have not been able, as many other peoples have been, to draw a full measure of strength from their forebears. And other Americans have often not known and valued the creativity of those who for thousands of years elaborated life on this continent. Both Immigrant Americans and Native Americans were deprived as long as there was no breach in the wall of silence between the Indian past and the industrial present.

Archeology has assumed the task of doing what can be done to break down this barrier. Here and there, archeologists have given some voice to a few of the millions of people who once were a part of the life on this land. Using a variety of techniques, borrowed from a dozen other sciences, they have recalled fragments out of the past.

They have literally recreated dwellings and places of worship and indeed whole villages, and in the United States they have done so under a variety of auspices. On the federal level the National Park Service, the Bureau of Land Management, the Forest Service, and other agencies have all joined in the work of protecting and presenting what Indians once built and archeologists have now studied and rebuilt. Certain state, county, and city agencies also have joined in the work of preservation, as have some privately financed institutions. All are saving some of the fast-disappearing past for the benefit of present and future generations. Thanks to these efforts we can move toward the world created by our predecessors and enjoy moments of close proximity to the people of yesterday while we listen to what they have to tell us. In archeological parks and monuments we can stand where Indians once built their dwellings or cooked their meals or said their prayers or made love. We can visit their ancient villages, revived for our delight. We can see the implements of their daily life, their works of art, their games, their religious paraphernalia.

Here, in the pages that follow, you can find your way to archeological sites that have been prepared for public view in the area north of Mexico. Here, too, are the museums which tell with some clarity about America's aboriginal yesterdays. However, you will not find any road directions to sites for which adequate protection does not exist.

There are, of course, many more museums that you will find listed here. A considerable number have good Indian exhibits. However, some of these have been omitted because they lack displays which illuminate *prehistoric* Indian life. By prehistoric is meant that period before the art of writing came to North America and made possible the keeping of written records.

There are also many archeological sites which reflect human experience after European and Indian met. These places, often called historic sites, are not included here, nor are museums devoted solely to materials recovered by workers in historic archeology. Another guidebook will have to be prepared to cover them.

This, the third edition of *America's Ancient Treasures,* appears at a time when archeology has been booming, thanks in good part to new federal legislation. A great many sites have recently been excavated, and a number of these new ones, and some older ones, too, have been prepared for visitation by the public. Museum curators have revised many exhibits to reflect the increased knowledge we have about what life was like when Native Americans were the sole human occupants of this continent. At the same time, a few sites once open to the public have been closed for one reason or another. Some museums have ceased operation or transferred their prehistoric holdings to other institutions. At least one has been burglarized and had its collection stolen.

Because museums, parks, and monuments often make minor adjustments in their fees and the hours and even days when they are open, we have tried to give the information on these points in terms that should remain valid for some time. And as we have brought entries about sites and museums up to date, we have also tried to make the text as a whole consistent with the current understanding of prehistory.

Finally we must point out that we have not been able to resolve confusion about the spelling of a word that is central to our endeavor. We have compromised and followed the *United States Government Printing Office Style Manual* in using the spelling *archeology* in our text and wherever it appears in that form in the writings of others. Where *archaeology* is used by others in titles or in quotations that we make use of, we have kept that form of the word.

August 1981   Franklin Folsom
                                                    Mary Elting Folsom

Keet Seel Ruin in Navajo National Monument lies under a great,
overhanging sandstone cliff at the end of a trail eight miles beyond the end of
the road. Tree-ring dates show that trees for ladders were cut between A.D.
1274 and 1284. National Park Service photo by George A. Grant.

INTRODUCTION

Human beings have been trying to manage life on planet Earth for upwards of two million years. For much of that time their complex and uncertain venture seems to have taken place in Africa. Only recently, on the geological time scale, did they expand their effort at survival onto the Eurasian land mass, and it was only yesterday on that scale that they moved their enterprise into the Americas.

When did the oldest immigrants reach this continent? The experts don't agree on the answer. Some say no solid evidence exists that they arrived more than 13,500 years ago. But if you had asked the late Dr. L. S. B. Leaky, he would have said, "at least 200,000 years ago." His evidence? Stone objects that he believed were tools shaped by men in the Calico Hills in California.

Ask Dr. Christy Turner of Arizona State University the same question and he will tell you that immigrants came from Asia in three waves, the first 14,000 or more years ago, the second between 12,000 and 11,000 years ago, and the third between 11,000 and 10,000 years ago. From the first wave, which may have been a small wavelet, are descended most of the native peoples of North and South America. From the second wave came the Athabaskans of Canada and Alaska and the Navajos and Apaches of the southwestern United States. The third wave produced the Eskimo (Inuit) and the Aleuts. Turner's evidence? Teeth. He has examined teeth in the oldest skeletons in the Americas and in Asia. The American teeth differ distinctly from the teeth of people of Europe or Africa, but are identical with the teeth of certain peoples in Siberia.

Ask Dr. Johanna Nichols of the University of California at Berkeley what she finds by studying the vast number of native languages in North and South America. She says there were perhaps ten migrations that began at least 30,000 years ago.

Ask Cindy Wood of the Denver Museum of Natural History and she says that a date "up to 15,000 years ago is certainly accepted."

Ask Dr. J. M. Adovasio, who excavated Meadowcroft Rock Shelter in Pennsylvania, and he will say that evidence indicates Native Americans were present there by 14,000 to 14,500 years ago.

Ask Dr. Richard MacNeish of the Andover Foundation for Archeological Research and he will tell you that in 1990 he discovered, in a cave in New Mexico, that human beings lived there at least 28,000 years ago. His evidence? Among other things a hand print baked in clay and fire pits that have been carbon dated. Some archeologists who have seen his evidence agree. Others believe there are other possible explanations for this early date and that there is no clear proof of human habitation of the cave.

No matter which date turns out to be right, one thing is clear: people learned and invented a great deal after they settled in the Americas. Largely without teachers, they became experts at living among the wonderfully varied environments in what Europeans later called the New World.

This learning went on, slowly at first, then often at a quickening pace. It continued until a wave of immigrants from Europe, bringing a different experience in life, overwhelmed the American continents. Then much of what had taken 14,500 years or more to evolve was destroyed in a short 400 years.

While two great water barriers separated American Indians from the learning attained by other people, a land bridge linked people around the Mediterranean to energy developments in Mesopotamia, in Africa, in China. People in Mesopotamia and Africa discovered that the energy released by fire could separate certain metals from rock. They also discovered that tools and weapons shaped from those metals could multiply human muscle power many times over.

People around the Mediterranean also learned from China that a certain mixture—a powder—could be made to explode. By combining this powder with tubes made of metal, inventors made guns. Here was a new way of bringing together and concentrating certain new energies. Those who possessed this technology found that they could impose their will on others, who did not happen to be present when someone brought iron and gunpowder together to form weapons. The possessors of guns could force people who had not yet obtained them to do their bidding—and their bidding was to provide land or labor or the products of both.

All this meant that the possessors of the new forms and products of energy could also possess capital, and capital itself became a source of great power on the social scene. Together with material power, this social power made it possible for European culture to displace the culture of Native Americans who had been decimated by disease. It was not a question of the greater serviceability in the American environment of European culture, which as a whole in 1492 was very little more advanced than the high Indian cultures of Mexico and Central America and Peru. Energy and power, and the social cohesion they imposed, basically determined the outcome of the struggle which still affects all of us—including the nearly two and a half million Indians who survive in the United States and Canada.

The losers in the unequal contest were largely silenced. Their voices have generally not carried to present day ears. This has meant that what people learned in millenia about living where immigrant Canadians and Americans now live has been lost. The heirs of the conquerors have had to learn anew how life can be carried on richly among the great resources of a great part of the surface of the earth. The conquered find it difficult to remember.

Belatedly, a search has started to find the essence of the experience of Native Americans, who managed so well on the terrain that others now occupy. The search is not really to find something more to be borrowed from Indians. It is simply for knowledge. Perhaps by understanding a form of humanity that is different from the one that now prevails, the prevailers will better know themselves. At the very least the gain can be something at which to marvel. For Indians the search can be for their roots—and it is from roots that strength can come.

In one sense, this search for Indian roots is the business of American archeology, and more and more fragments of the pre-European past of America are being rescued and returned to view. For a long time the interpreters of archeological materials did not look for any overall meaning in the history of Native Americans. It seemed enough to classify and try to date the artifacts of each region, and when change or development appeared, it was generally attributed to fresh ideas from somewhere else. Recently, however, the study of cultural change in the Americas has itself been evolving. The New Archeology (capital letters indicate the importance its practitioners attach to their work) is concerned with the dynamics of change and development.

For these scientists really to achieve their purpose it is necessary to bring sympathetic imagination to the potsherds and ruined walls and spent projectile points that have come out of the soil. From these products of skill and planning must be inferred the activities of societies that were full of intelligence and striving and love and sorrow.

The search has not been easy or simple. Excavation destroys the very clue the archeologist is looking for, and if he or she makes a mistake, there is no going back to correct the error. Moreover, tomorrow there may be new techniques which will make it possible to squeeze more information out of dry fragments of the past. So, paradoxically, diggers want to dig as little as possible. Although they are all greedy for facts, they feel they must give tomorrow's excavators a chance to use new methods that will gain better results than are possible today.

In an effort to get the maximum of data with a minimum of destruction, the New Archeologists began in the 1960s to use a variety of mathematical devices for learning a lot from a little evidence. These same investigators were bent on discovering as much as they could about the processes of social change that went on yesterday. They tried to find action in the inactive artifacts that came from the earth, and they sought all they could learn about the relationships of human beings to the plants and animals and soils and climates among which they lived. "Cultural ecology," they called it, because they paid much attention to the interrelationships of people with all the rest of nature—and with each other.

The reports that some of the New Archeologists issued often seemed very remote from the humanity they sought. Mathematical formulas, computer printouts, statistical tables and charts, abstractions, and a bewildering variety of jaw-breaking terms littered their pages, tripping up unwary professionals and stopping amateurs dead in their tracks. But this always contentious, sometimes uncommunicative, new group had moved a long way from the early days of archeology, when the main goal of excavators was to recover handsome objects to put on display in museums. With the aid of an ever-growing battery of devices from other sciences, the New Archeologists were discovering something about people, not just accumulating things or tabulating types or traits. And in an age which offers fewer and fewer sites to dig, they were producing more and more ideas.

Even the most refined search for past ways of living and changing will never bring searchers as close as they would like to be to those who have gone before us, but thanks to the abstractions—and to the insistence of the New Archeology on democratic study of the ancient lowly as well as the ancient rich—we do know much more each year about past groups of people. One device of the New Archeology has given notable help. The practitioners of this form of science have put great store on forming hypotheses, then checking the facts to see if their trial theories make sense. The New Archeologists have also learned a great deal from the Old Archeologists. Thanks to both, the search for understanding of human beings has gathered momentum, and it certainly has become more exciting to watch.

Probably the ancestors of the first human beings who made the western hemisphere their home had already learned to deal with Ice-Age climate, when glaciers covered much of the northern hemisphere. Bordering the ice sheets was a treeless zone of tundra, and in this zone lived enormous herds of mammals. Caribou grazed there. So did the huge elephants called mammoths. A male mam-

What Was It Used For?

How can archeologists be sure what stone tools were used for, thousands of years ago? They started with educated guesses based on the shapes of tools and the contexts in which many of them were found. A sharp flint object between the ribs of a bison certainly indicated it was a projectile point. Then in 1962 the Russian scientist S. A. Semenov reported that, under a microscope, even the hardest stone revealed traces of the use to which it had been put. Americans doubted his results until they realized they did not have good enough microscopes to duplicate Semenov's findings. Later experiments with modern replicas of tools convinced them that each kind of work produces its own kind of polish on the stone—and the polish is permanent. A knife used to cut wood takes on a bright polish; bone gives a bright, but less smooth polish than wood, and different from that made by cutting into antler. Sawing shows up in polish, striations, and wear on the edges of a tool. The effect of cutting hide is bright polish with characteristic wear on the edge.

Examination of projectile points found at a buffalo kill site in Colorado indicated that, in addition to bringing down the animals, some of the points had then served as knives for butchering.

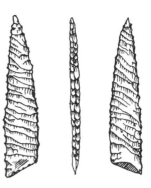

The three views above show a flint blade that has been turned into a point only 1⁵/₈ inches long. This delicate workmanship was done by pre-Eskimo craftsmen at Cape Denbigh, in Alaska. After Giddings.

---

moth could achieve a weight of six or seven tons, living on a diet of arctic herbs and grasses.

Far to the south, extensive prairies also furnished nourishment for mammoths, for giant bison, and for bands of horses and camels. Ground sloths and mastodons grew to great size near the edges of forests, where they lived on a diet of leaves and twigs. Smaller game, too, was abundant—deer, elk, antelope, rabbit, and most of the other animals we know today. Apparently men hunted all these creatures but found it most efficient to kill the largest ones whenever they could. One spear thrust into the heart or lungs of a mammoth produced thousands of times as much meat as one spear that brought down a bounding rabbit.

To reap the harvest of Ice-Age meat, men needed good spears, tipped with ivory or bone or stone, that could pierce the thick skins of large mammals and reach the vital organs. For butchering, hunters found various ways to put sharp edges on certain kinds of stone, thus shaping knives. These stone knives would cut easily though hides that were far too tough for fingers to tear or for teeth to pierce.

Besides food, families needed fire and shelter against the cold, as well as clothing that would produce a miniature warm climate close to their bodies. To make animal-skin clothing, they needed special tools: scrapers of stone or bone to remove from the inside of a skin the tissue that would make it unmanageable when it dried and hardened, awls for punching holes, and needles for sewing.

By burning animal fat and the long bones of mammals, which were rich storehouses of marrow, people could keep warm, even when there was no wood for fires. They could make shelters from the skins of most of the large animals they hunted, although mammoth skins, as thick as automobile tires, were quite unusable. However, in treeless country in Eurasia, mammoth ribs and the leg bones as big around as tree trunks could take the place of wooden frameworks, over which skins could be spread to make houses. With similar inventions and a few others, human beings learned the trick of living under arctic conditions. And having learned it, they wandered far, following the herds of big game that were a good source of food.

This wandering, according to the prevailing theory, took some of them from Siberia into Alaska at a time when a vast stretch of prairie joined Asia to North America. In those days the ocean was lower than it is today because there was actually less water in it. Billions of tons of water had evaporated from the earth's seas, had then fallen in the form of snow, and remained unmelted. Each year more snow piled up on the land. There it was compressed into ice, which formed enormous ice sheets. Deprived of water, the oceans shrank, and land which had been close to the surface was now exposed.

One such area, known as the Bering Land Bridge, or Beringia, between Siberia and Alaska, was sometimes more than 1,000 miles wide, covered with arctic vegetation which fed game animals. Getting to Alaska was no special problem for hunters, and it was possible to live there because much of the land was never covered by ice, although most of Canada was.

No one knows how many people moved into Alaska during the Ice Age, or how long they remained there. Possibly some of these people went south along the edge of the ocean, where seafood was plentiful. Sea level was lower than it is today, and the coastline was different. During the times when glaciers did not reach the water, migration along the edge of the land might have been easier than it would be today. More likely, at least once, perhaps more than once, the ice sheet which covered Canada melted, until a long strip of land, just east of the Rocky Mountains, became ice-free all the way from Alaska and northern Canada to the Great Plains. Vegetation invaded the strip. Then animals followed the plants, and at least once, perhaps many times, a band of hunters passed through this corridor, following game southward. After reaching the Great Plains they remained. The hunting was good, and it didn't matter that the glaciers grew again and met, closing the corridor behind them.

Because the food supply was ample, each band grew in size until it had to subdivide. On the Plains the number of bands steadily increased, and from this central starting point people spread out over all of North and South America.

In the heartland of North America the Big-Game Hunters, who are called Paleo-Indians, continued to use tools of the kind they had brought with them. But in time they made innovations and

In 1927, when excavators near Folsom, New Mexico, found this projectile point between two bones of an extinct bison, they left it in position and summoned experts to observe it. Here was proof that people had lived in America at the same time as animals that had been extinct for about 10,000 years. This Folsom point opened new vistas to archeologists. Denver Museum of Natural History photo by Robert R. Wright.

improvements. One very distinctive tool became popular—a type of spearpoint which the hunters fashioned from certain kinds of stone, such as flint, chalcedony, jasper, and chert. With great skill a point-maker thinned a fragment of hard rock and chipped its edges precisely. Then, striking two perfectly aimed blows, he knocked off flakes to form a groove, or channel, down its front and back. The groove, called a flute, set the point apart from others, and for this archeologists are grateful. Such an easily identifiable tool is almost a fingerprint of Early Man. Early Woman's creations, including Early Children, were less able to survive the ravages of time than were the stone tools that males made. Furthermore, the introduction by men of the term Early Man has proved exceedingly durable and pervasive. We all have to use it as if we were ignoring woman's role in human prehistory.

One kind of fluted point has been named the Clovis point because archeologists first excavated it near Clovis, New Mexico. The excavation offered clear proof that hunters had used points of this kind to kill mammoths about 9220 B.C. In excavations elsewhere evidence has appeared that people worked in groups when they hunted the huge elephants.

Wherever mammoth hunters went, they left points of the Clovis type. Literally thousands have been found in Kentucky, Tennessee, and Alabama, an area in which Paleo-Indians were relatively numerous. Between the years 11,500 B.P. (meaning Before Present) and 11,000 B.P., a thin film of humanity spread over most of the United States and part of Canada. In the next thousand years

(11,000–10,000 B.P.) a different kind of fluted point, called the Folsom point, replaced the Clovis point in popularity. Then fluting went out of fashion, and for 2,500 or 3,000 years Big-Game Hunters brought down their quarry with points that were not fluted. All these hunters were Paleo-Indians, and all seem to have lived in much the same way. Their activities did not vary a great deal whether they lived in southern Arizona or the southeastern states or Massachusetts or Alberta or Nova Scotia.

Perhaps the most famous Paleo site is one near Folsom, New Mexico. Here a spearpoint was found between the ribs of a bison of a type that has long been extinct. It was this find, made in 1927, that established beyond a doubt the great antiquity of human beings in America. Up to that time most scientists did not dare to think that people had arrived here more than 3,000 years ago. The Folsom spearpoints pushed the date back to 10,000 years ago, and subsequently the Clovis point discoveries pushed it back even further. The state of New Mexico made the Folsom Site into a State Monument, but the monument has now been closed to the public. Too many visitors dug there in the portion of the site that had not been scientifically excavated. Pending further professional work, it has been placed off limits to the public.

From time to time a Paleo dig is open to the public while excavation is going on, and there are a few Paleo sites that are permanently open. Fortunately the museum exhibits are numerous and illuminating—perhaps more rewarding even than a visit to a site itself would be. Paleo-Indians left few tools or weapons in any one place, and really fine examples of such artifacts (archeologists call them "goodies") don't turn up every day in a dig.

On the archeologist's calendar, the Paleo-Indian Period came to an end about 6,000 B.C. By that time the great glaciers of the Ice Age had disappeared. So had most of the great animals. The mammoths of North America were all gone. A little later the mastodons disappeared. Then the ground sloth and the giant bison that roamed the prairies vanished, as did the horses and camels.

Scientists disagree among themselves about the causes of this extinction. Some believe the animals could not adjust to the changes in vegetation that came when the ice melted and the land grew warmer. Other investigators think that the reproductive cycle of larger animals was geared to Ice-Age seasons, and when the length of the seasons changed with warmer weather, offspring may have been born at times of the year when they could not survive. Still others believe the Paleo-Indians developed hunting techniques so efficient that they killed off the largest of their quarry.

At any rate people could no longer make use of food that came in the biggest units. They had to depend on smaller game. Men and women both began a more intensive search for things to eat. They developed new lifeways and fashioned new tools to provide a livelihood. To supplement their meat diet more than in the past, they gathered berries and plant food of various kinds, particularly seeds. By now the population had increased from a few bands to

About A.D. 850 Indians at Mesa Verde lived on the mesa top in dwellings built in a row. From a diorama in the museum at Mesa Verde National Park, Colorado.

many thousands of individuals. All over America it had become necessary to exploit even the smallest kinds of food resource. This new stage, with its new developments, has become known as the Archaic. It began in some places before the last vestiges of Paleo culture had disappeared, and in parts of the continent it continued right up to historic times.

In the beginning, as now, the East differed greatly from the West. In the East heavy rains flowed off in numerous streams filled with fish and shellfish. Forests grew thick, and they sheltered smaller animals which were relatively fewer in number than the grazing herds on the grass-rich prairies. Nevertheless, ingenious fish weirs, extensive use of shellfish, or one-man hunting methods geared to the tree-congested forest all produced an ample food supply in certain places. There the people of the Archaic could live in larger groups than had been possible in Paleo times.

One Eastern Archaic site open to the public is Russell Cave National Monument in Alabama, where people first began to live 8,500 or 9,000 years ago. Another Eastern Archaic site is Graham Cave State Park in Missouri. But most Archaic artifacts, like those of Paleo times, are best displayed in museums.

The Archaic lifeway in the Southwest has been called Southwestern Archaic. At one time it was known as the Desert Culture. The region had grown more arid as the Ice Age ended. Large areas had very little rainfall in the course of a year, and this lack of water shaped the kinds of plant that grew there. The plants determined the kinds of animal that lived on them, and these creatures differed markedly from those which lived on and amid lusher vegetation to the east. In turn, the people who lived on both animals and plants in the West worked out patterns of behavior that differed from those in the East. Men whose predecessors had hunted mammoths came more and more to depend on small animals, even the smallest, such as crickets and grasshoppers. But meat of any kind was scarce, and plant food became very important, particularly small seeds. People invented baskets for holding seeds and tools for grinding them.

Out of the Southwestern Archaic developed a number of different and highly specialized ways of living. None of them, of course, followed the modern political state lines, and some in northern Mexico extended into the United States. As time went on, many ideas and institutions flowed from Mexico into the southern parts of the present states of Arizona and New Mexico. Some experts believe it was primarily the ways in which people lived that shifted northward. Others believe that immigrants from the south filtered in, bringing ideas and inventions that affected patterns of local life.

A variety of Southwestern Archaic culture which has been named the Cochise (ko-CHEES) developed in that area before 5000 B.C. Most important of the ideas the Cochise may have received from Mexico was the concept that by planting seeds in garden patches people could create food, not just find it. The result was that several hundred years before the Christian era there began a series of changes toward settled village life.

In what is now northern Arizona, northern New Mexico, and southern Colorado and Utah, there seems to have been an independent and different sort of development. Excavation and research by archeologist Cynthia Irwin-Williams in one part of this area have yielded a continuous picture of evolution from a hunting-and-gathering culture to a sedentary, town-dwelling way of life. In this area, too, the origins of settled communities go back at least 7000 years, and it has been possible for the archeologist to trace through stage after stage an almost unbroken record of human occupation up to Pueblo Indian times. This cultural development has been given the name Oshara Tradition, to distinguish it from the cultures that arose farther south.

Many prehistoric sites throughout the Southwest are open to the public, and finds from these sites may also be enjoyed in museums all over the country.

AMERICA'S ANCIENT TREASURES

More than 600 years ago 12 or 15 families lived in this 19-room, five-story apartment house at Montezuma Castle National Monument.

SOUTHWEST

North of Mexico no places offer more abundant archeological remains than do Arizona, New Mexico, southwestern Colorado, and southern Utah. Millions possibly billions, of pottery fragments lie in and on the soil. Surveys have revealed thousands of habitation sites. All these are reminders that creative people have long lived here, and all have a common history. The changes that led people to shift from the life of hunter-gatherers may have been gradual at first. People who had been collecting seeds may have discovered that they could increase their food supply by scattering or planting some of the seeds they collected. Once they had garden plots, it was necessary for them to be near those plots at least at harvest time. Life became more settled.

Then, villages, of which countless potsherds are an evidence, came into existence, following a development that took place six or seven thousand years ago. At that time people in the Tehuacan Valley of present-day Mexico, and possibly elsewhere, began to domesticate a certain wild grass. The discovery that they could plant its seeds in garden plots changed their lives and the whole of Indian life in large sections of the American continents.

As this wild grass was cultivated, it changed greatly and evolved into the grain we call corn, or maize. It developed husks that wrapped more and more tightly around the seed-bearing cob, until at last maize could no longer sow its own seeds. It could not live from year to year unless humans removed the husks and planted the corn kernels. At the same time, people became so accustomed to eating corn, prepared in many ways, that their lives revolved around planting, cultivating, and harvestig the helpless but nourishing cereal. Corn and humankind became mutually dependent.

The idea of gardening spread northward. So did a knowledge of how to make long-lasting pots for cooking and storing the new food. With the ability to keep food in reserve, diet changed. Dwellings, too, changed under influences that swept into northern Mexico, then into New Mexico and Arizona. Along with corn there came a whole constellation of customs and ceremonies, such as corn dances and other planting and harvest-time rituals. Some of these are still observed today.

Perhaps as early as 1000 B.C. the Western Archaic people known as the Cochise had begun to add corn to their diet. They also added squash and beans. The beans were most important because they furnished protein which would have been lacking if farmers had tried to depend entirely on corn. People could not live by maize alone. Although life changed greatly with the arrival of this extraordinary plant, the changes were not identical throughout the Southwest. They varied from place to place, as communities learned the new ways of creating food while continuing to be a part of the special kind of ecological system in which they had already found a place for themselves. In one sense, of course, all farmers were alike. They could give up the wandering existence of the hunter or gatherer and build more or less permanent dwellings. The differences in the details of how they built and created and elaborated on life are among the things that make Southwestern archeology fascinating to both the scientist and the lay person.

Broadly speaking, four different lifeways developed: The Mogollon (MOH-goh-YOHN), the Hohokam (ho-ho-KAHM), the Patayan (PAH-tah-YAHN), and the Anasazi (AHN-ah-SAH-zee). Eventually there developed several variations or combinations of these four basic cultures.

The Mogollon Culture

By about 100 B.C. the new agricultural way of life had taken on a distinct identity in the highlands of the Mogollon Mountains, which lie across the present border between Arizona and New Mexico. In certain places the slopes of these mountains were ideal for raising corn. They duplicated to a considerable extent the conditions in the part of Mexico where corn was domesticated. Here in the mountains the Cochise had long based their pattern of existence on plant food. They were accustomed to grinding wild seeds in order to make them easy to chew and digest, and it was no problem for women to begin grinding corn as well. We know that the Cochise began to raise corn at a very early date; archeologists have excavated the tiny cobs and husks and even a few seeds of extremely ancient corn in Bat Cave and Tularosa Cave in New Mexico.

After the Cochise settled down and developed the characteristics now called Mogollon, they began to live in dwellings known as pithouses. To make such a house, they dug a circular pit two or three feet deep and set a strong, upright post in the center. Then over the pit they made a cone-shaped roof of saplings which leaned against the center pole from around the upper edge of the pit. Over the saplings they laid or wove small branches, and on top of the branches they spread a thick layer of mud. On one side of the pithouse a ramp led from ground level down to the floor inside.

A pithouse, part below ground and part above, and covered with a thick, insulating layer of earth, was relatively cool in summer and warm in winter. As time went on, its shape changed from circular to oval to rectangular, and it came to be roofed in various ways, but it remained the standard home until very late in Mogollon history.

The pottery that Mogollon people made was at first red or brown without decoration. Later they invented or borrowed many different designs, and those who lived along the Mimbres River developed a unique style. They painted sophisticated, often humorous representations of animals, insects, fish, birds, and human beings on the white surface of their dishes.

The Hohokam Culture

People who lived along the Salt, the Gila, and the San Pedro rivers in southern Arizona also felt the influence of Mexican ideas and inventions. There is no doubt that a great deal of trade went on between Mesoamericans and these Cochise desert dwellers, and much of it passed through a large community in northern Mexico now known as Casas Grandes.

Excavation at Casas Grandes revealed that by the fourteenth century A.D. there were enormous warehouses for goods that people to the north wanted in exchange for turquoise and other gemstones. Copper bells made by a process that had not reached the Southwest, millions of small shells for beads, and large ones for trumpets were stored in the mud-brick rooms of the trading center. Parrots and scarlet and green macaws, much in demand farther north, were actually raised in breeding pens at Casas Grandes.

Before the days of intensive trade, probably as early as 300 B.C., people in the area near present-day Phoenix were developing a special way of life. Known now as the Hohokam (a Pima word for "those who have gone"), they grew corn and other plants from seeds that had come from Mexico, and they brought water to their crops through irrigation canals—a Mexican invention. Later they and neighbors along the rivers diverted water to fields far out on the semiarid land. Rich harvests resulted from irrigation, and the River Hohokam not only had enough to eat, they also had time to spare. Some of them became adept at crafts, making lovely jewelry and figurines. The early Hohokam pottery was buff colored, with red geometric decorations. Later potters made designs in the forms of birds or animals or people.

Early Hohokam houses were somewhat like Mogollon pithouses, except that the builders did less excavation. Later they

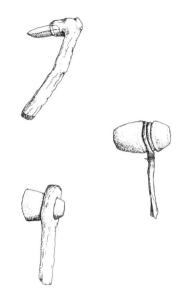

Top to bottom: An adze. A grooved ax. An ungrooved ax, or celt. After Linda Murphy in *Indians of Arkansas,* by Charles R. McGimsey III.

Ax, Adze, and Celt

Prehistoric Indians cut and shaped wood with all three of these tools, which they fashioned from stone. Each was attached to a handle in its own special way. The ax was shaped by chipping, or by chipping and grinding and polishing. It was sometimes sharpened on one end, sometimes on both ends, and it had a groove which made it easier to attach a handle. (This is called hafting.) The groove goes all the way around the ax or only partway.

A celt was usually polished, had no groove, and was hafted as the illustration shows.

Although neither an ax nor a celt looks very efficient to anyone who is used to steel tools, both work surprisingly well. Archeologists who have tried stone axes found they could chop down a six-inch tree in less than twenty minutes.

The cutting edge of an ax or a celt is parallel to the handle; the cutting edge of an adze is at right angles to its handle. An adze is not designed for chopping down trees, but it is effective, for example, in hollowing out logs to make dugout canoes.

---

made large structures several stories high, possibly for storage or defense. They also built ball courts, where they played a kind of ceremonial game with a solid rubber ball, apparently derived from a similar Mexican game.

Did descendants of the ancient Cochise simply adapt ideas and technology that came with traders from the south? Many—perhaps most—archeologists think so. Others, who have done a great deal of work in the Hohokam areas, believe that the Hohokam culture resulted from the actual immigration of people from Mesoamerica. At any rate traces of Mexican interaction with Southwesterners can be clearly seen in such things as food crops, irrigation, building styles, and evidence of religious beliefs.

In the days of the Hohokam there was apparently somewhat more rainfall than there is today in southern Arizona. With more moisture people had more to eat with less work. So life was a little easier than it is for the present-day Pima and Tohono o'dham (Papago) Indians, who may be the descendants of the ancient Hohokam.

The Patayan Culture

In the valley of the Colorado River, which includes the western part of Arizona, lived a people to whom agriculture came later than it did to the Mogollon and the Hohokam. Here farming began only about A.D. 600. In the lowlands on the banks of the great

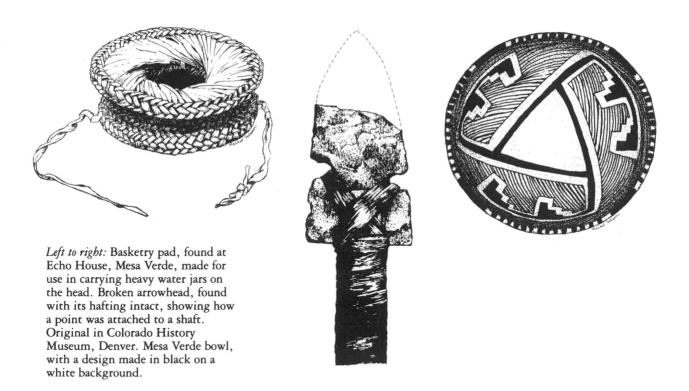

Left to right: Basketry pad, found at Echo House, Mesa Verde, made for use in carrying heavy water jars on the head. Broken arrowhead, found with its hafting intact, showing how a point was attached to a shaft. Original in Colorado History Museum, Denver. Mesa Verde bowl, with a design made in black on a white background.

river, and in the high plateau country through which the Colorado had cut its deep channel, distinct lifeways developed.

Not a great deal is known about these prehistoric people, who are called Patayan, the Yuman word for "old people." The reason is simple: much evidence of life along the riverbanks has been buried under layers of silt brought down by the Colorado River. Other sites have been washed away and now lie, lost forever, in the Gulf of California.

At the time when corn reached them from Mexico, the Patayan lived in flimsy shelters made of poles covered with brush. Later they began to make more permanent structures covered with mud. Finally some of them borrowed an architectural idea from neighbors to the north and began to build stone dwellings.

People who live along the Colorado River today—the Havasupai, the Maricopa, and the Yuma, among others—are probably descendants of the ancient Patayan people.

The Anasazi Culture
Still farther north of Mexico lies rugged country where high plateaus are cut by deep canyons and rimmed with steep cliffs. Here, through the southern part of Colorado and Utah and the northern part of New Mexico and Arizona, still other groups of Western Archaic people made their homes, beginning about 7000 years ago. In one region of northwestern New Mexico, the late Cynthia

These pinnacles, known to Navajos as Spider Rock, are near White House ruins in Canyon de Chelly National Monument. National Park Service photo by Fred Mang, Jr.

Irwin-Williams and her colleagues studied a group whose lifeways belonged to what is now called the Oshara Tradition. Like other prefarming, preceramic peoples, they hunted and harvested wild crops, moving about in roughly this one area in an annual round. Sometime after 2800 B.C. these people learned about the maize plant and began to grow it in small patches on the floors of canyons. A more settled way of life was now possible, and with it more structured social and ceremonial customs, which finally evolved into the fully sedentary lifeways now called Anasazi.

As the Anasazi culture developed, changes were so very marked that archeologists have given special names to each of the stages. The first stage is usually called Basketmaker II or simply Basketmaker. There is no Basketmaker I; the archeologists who named it have been disappointed. They expected some day to find evidence of a stage they could call Basketmaker I. They never did. At any rate these first Anasazi corn farmers tended to live in caves or recesses in the cliff walls, where their nomadic ancestors had often camped. Sometimes they may have put up brush shelters in the caves, and they certainly stored food in slab-lined pits in cave floors. Later they learned to build pithouses for their own use. These resembled in many ways the pithouses of the Mogollon, but in Anasazi country the half-subterranean dwellings had an interesting later history, which is best told at the museum in Mesa Verde National Park.

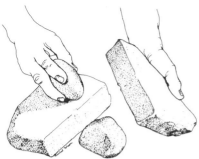

Ancient masonry methods: First, with a sharp-edged blade of chert, a deep groove was scratched on the surface of a slab of sandstone. Next the slab was placed over a pebble. Then, the groove was tapped with a hammerstone, directly above the pebble, to break the slab cleanly in two. *Photo:* Section of a wall built of stone shaped by this method, in Aztec Ruins National Monument. National Park Service photo by George A. Grant.

The Basketmakers did indeed make marvelous baskets. Thanks to the dry climate and their taste for living in caves, a great deal of their fine handiwork was protected from the weather and has survived for nearly 2000 years. For the same reason we also know what these people looked like. They buried their dead in empty storage pits, and in the dry air bodies became desiccated. Men wore their hair long, sometimes in braids; women cut theirs from time to time and used the hair to make bags or rope.

By A.D. 700 the Anasazi had learned more about farming and had drawn together in larger groups than before. They were building houses of stone, one against another in communal dwellings. The Spanish word for these apartment-house villages was pueblo, and so archeologists have given the name Pueblo to the next stages in Anasazi culture.

In the next 600 years the Anasazi grew more and more skilled at building and potterymaking and other crafts, such as the creation of jewelry and fine cloth. Even at this distance, trade brought influences from Mesoamerica. Dams and ditches conserved water for crops. Shell beads and ornaments, macaw and parrot skeletons have turned up in excavations at Anasazi sites.

Within the large, general region where they lived, there began to appear three major centers of development. Each had a style of pottery and masonry and architecture that distinguished it from the others.

An Anasazi jar lid. Museum of Anthropology, University of Missouri, photo.

One center was near present-day Kayenta, in Arizona. There the finest achievements of the Kayenta Anasazi are preserved in the Navajo National Monument. A second center was at Mesa Verde, in Colorado. The third was in Chaco Canyon, in New Mexico. From all these developments among the Anasazi one important fact emerges. Using corn, beans, and squash as sources of energy in an area that was far from ideal for agriculture, people managed to shape lifeways that became more and more sophisticated with the passage of time. They gathered together in villages and seemed to be approaching urban life, just as the agriculturists did in the Tigris-Euphrates Valley at the beginning of the era of Middle Eastern Civilization. Then change affected the Anasazi world. Perhaps a series of dry periods made it impossible to store a food surplus for use in bad times. Whatever the cause, the population scattered.

Archeologists do not agree on what caused the change that left most Anasazi pueblos deserted forever, but certainly there was a change.

The Sinagua people built these
houses in Walnut Canyon, Arizona,
and farmed nearby until they
abandoned the site for reasons still
not understood. National Park
Service photo by Hubbard.

A Park Ranger shows how an Indian
woman pushed a mano back and
forth on a metate to crush hard
kernels of corn, making corn meal.
National Park Service photo by
Robert W. Gage.

Carbon-14 Dating

An archeologist can often learn the age of a site if it contains charred wood or bone. He or she sends samples of the charred material to a laboratory where radiocarbon, or carbon-14, or C-14, dating is done.

Carbon is part of the nourishment of every living thing. Plants get it by taking in carbon dioxide from the air; animals and people get it from food, which may be either plants or plant-eating animals. Among the carbon atoms that living things take in, some are radioactive. These radioactive atoms, called carbon-14, or C-14, are not stable. They decay, giving off tiny bursts of energy, which can be detected in a laboratory.

When a plant or animal dies, it ceases to take in food, and therefore it ceases to take in C-14 atoms. But it continues to lose them. The C-14 atoms in a dead object decay at a steady pace. By measuring the number of radioactive bursts produced by C-14 atoms as they decay in a given quantity of dead plant or animal material, a scientist can calculate how long ago the plant or animal died. Since the method does not reveal the exact year of death, allowance is made for error. Therefore a C-14 date is usually written this way: $5,000 \pm 250$. This means that the date of death falls between 4,750 and 5,250 years ago.

The original C-14 method had its flaws. It could not date back more than 50,000 years, and in order to get a date for an object it was necessary to destroy a large sample of it. As much as ten ounces of a unique bone had to be burned in order to tell how old it was. Archeologists also discovered that they had to regard all C-14 dates with caution, because research had revealed that the C-14 content of the atmosphere varied at different times in the past. Checking against dates obtained from other sources showed that C-14 dates tended to be more recent than they should have been. Archeologists had to develop a mathematical formula for use in correcting all C-14 dates obtained before 1971.

Now another method exists that enables archeologists to measure the C-14 atoms that remain in a sample, not the number of atoms that have left it. This new method, called accelerated mass spectometry (AMS) finds a date by comparing the amount of unstable C-14 in a sample to the amount of stable C-12 and C-13 that is there. The method has advantages. It extends the range of radiocarbon dating from about 50,000 years to about 100,000. A date can be obtained much more quickly, and the AMS method destroys much less of the object being tested. It is, however, more expensive.

To check the accuracy of a radiocarbon date, archeologists can sometimes compare it to a date of the same object obtained by the use of tree-ring dating (dendrochronology). The date obtained by this checking process is said to be calibrated. Accurate calibration of radiocarbon dates cannot be carried back much more than 6000 years anywhere. In most of North America tree-ring dates do not go back nearly that far.

Advanced technology helps archeologists to get C-14 dates for prehistoric remains. In this laboratory materials containing carbon are first cleansed, then converted by combustion to carbon dioxide in the sytem shown in the foreground. The carbon dioxide is then further purified and stored for analysis in the system shown in the background which operates at very low temperatures. Teledyne Isotopes photo, Westwood, New Jersey.

Carbon-14 dating can reveal the age of things made of plant material, such as this Anasazi hairbrush.

Perpendicular sandstone walls tower above small clusters of masonry
buildings in niches or on the canyon floor in Canyon de Chelly. National Park
Service photo.

These effigy vessels came from Snaketown, a large Hohokam village site in southern Arizona. National Park Service photo.

Arizona

AMERIND FOUNDATION, INC.

From Tucson (TOO-sahn) drive 64 miles east on Interstate 10 to the Triangle T-Dragoon exit (318). Proceed east 1 mile and turn left at the sign. Mail address: P.O. Box 248, Dragoon, AZ 85609. Phone: 602/586-3666. Open daily except major holidays. Admission charged.

Amerind (a contraction of American Indian) is a private, non-profit archeological research facility and museum. Prehistoric and historic Native American cultures from the Arctic Circle to northern South America are presented in exhibits here. Visitors are welcome to use the nearby scenic picnic grounds.

ARIZONA STATE MUSEUM
(*See University of Arizona*)

ARIZONA STATE UNIVERSITY MUSEUM OF ANTHROPOLOGY

In the Anthropology Building, on the campus, Tempe, AZ 85282. Phone: 602/965-6213. Open free, Monday–Friday.

Exhibits, which are designed and installed by university students, contain a wide variety of material from the collection of the anthropology department and borrowed from other institutions. A number of displays emphasize archeological techniques for studying artifacts and the material culture of prehistoric people.

Special Interest. Dr. Christy G. Turner II of the anthropology department has examined the special characteristics of thousands of teeth, both in the New World and in the Old, and has concluded that there were three migrations of people from Asia, beginning at least 14,000 years ago and perhaps earlier. First the ancestors of all Paleo-Indians crossed into North America from the area of the Lena river in Siberia; then the ancestors of some Northwest Coast people and of the Navajos and the Apaches moved from a forested area of Siberia across the Bering Landbridge before it was covered by the sea; and finally the ancestors of the Aleut and Inuit (Eskimo) arrived by a route close to the ocean shore.

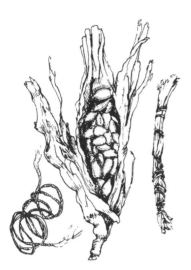

Squash seeds were found in Canyon de Chelly, wrapped tightly in corn husk. Drawn from a National Park Service photo.

BESH BA GOWAH
ARCHEOLOGICAL PARK

150 North Pine St., Globe, AZ 85501. Phone: 602/425-0320. This park and visitor center, situated on a ridge 1.5 miles from downtown Globe, is operated by the City of Globe and is completely handicap accessible. Admission charged. Prearranged tours are available.

Salado people, who at one time numbered about 1,400, lived in this 200 room town from A.D. 1225 to 1400. The residents raised corn, beans, squash, and possibly cotton along the banks of Pinal Creek. However, their main occupation seems to have been trading. They obtained copper bells and feathers from Mesoamerica, shells from California and the Gulf of Mexico, and pottery from many places. The Salado people also made pottery for their own use, wove baskets, sandals, and mats from sotol and yucca fibers, and made cotton cloth.

Following a long drought, people gradually abandoned the town and moved to other areas, By 1400 no one remained in Besh Ba Gowah.

Another Salado village has been preserved in Tonto National Monument about 40 miles northwest of Globe.

Special Interest. This large site has been excavated at two diferent times. Between 1935 and 1940 Irene Vickery directed the excavation as part of the Works Progress Administration program that was designed to provide work for the unemployed. Archeologist Vickery overheard Apaches who worked for her using the term Besh Ba Gowah and she thought they were referring to the ruin, and so she called it Besh Ba Gowah. Actually the Apaches were using words that meant "place of metal" which was their name for Globe—a copper mining center.

The second excavation, which prepared the site for the public, lasted from 1980 to 1988.

CANYON DE CHELLY
NATIONAL MONUMENT
(CANyuhn duh SHAY)

From Gallup, New Mexico, drive north 8 miles on US 666, then 52 miles west on New Mexico-Arizona 264 through Ganado, then 33 miles north on US 191 to monument headquarters and the Visitor Center at Chinle (chin-LEE). Mail address: Box 588, Chinle, AZ 86503. Phone: 602/836-2223. Open free daily, all year. Camping.

Protected by spectacular red sandstone walls, prehistoric Indians built hundreds of small villages and cliff dwellings in this canyon over a period of nearly a thousand years. Visitors can walk to a cliff dwelling called White House Ruin, following a trail that winds down from the canyon rim for about a mile. Other ruins can be seen only when visitors are accompanied by a park ranger or other official guide.

The Story. Beginning about A.D. 350, the canyon was occupied by people now known as the Anasazi, ancestors of the present-day Pueblo Indians. Then about A.D. 1300 the Anasazi moved out, leaving the canyon to occasional visits from their descendants or from the Navajo Indians, who began to take possession of the area. During their thousand-year stay, the Anasazi gardened in small plots on the canyon bottom, where there was flowing water at certain times each year. At other

Rings, bracelets, bone whistle, pottery sculpture, and carved stone found at Casa Grande. National Park Service photo by George A. Grant.

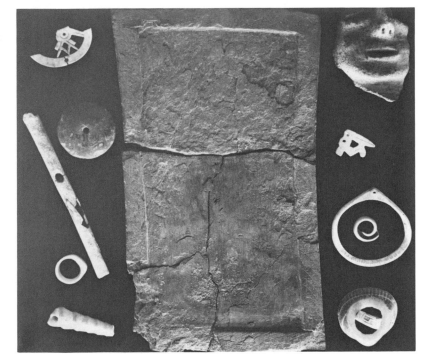

Opposite:
A Park Ranger examines the demolished walls of an ancient pueblo in Canyon de Chelly. This ruin had stood for perhaps a thousand years before it was destroyed in a rock slide caused by a sonic boom. National Park Service photo.

seasons the stream bed must have seemed completely dry, although there was usually enough moisture beneath the surface for crops of corn and squash.

The Anasazi also hunted—at first with spears, then with bows and arrows. Over the years house structures changed as much as hunting methods. Early inhabitants of the canyon lived in houses built partially underground. Their later dwellings, made of stone and entirely above ground, were joined one to another, so that the whole village was one big apartment house. Still later they built some of their apartment houses in large, dry caves in the cliffs.

About A.D. 1300 the Anasazi abandoned Canyon de Chelly, just as they moved out of other villages in the Four Corners area—the area where Arizona, Utah, Colorado, and New Mexico meet. Why they left is still something of a mystery. Archeologists have discovered that there was a severe drought at about this time, and for many years before they moved away the Anasazi had great difficulty raising crops. Quite possibly this was not their only reason for deserting the canyon. Internal dis-

sension may have caused villages to break up. Or pressure from outsiders may have induced people to migrate elsewhere.

Little groups of Navajos settled in the canyon nearly 300 years ago, and some of the paintings they made on its rock walls can still be seen.

The Museum. Contains exhibits of Southwestern archeological finds in the Four Corners area and also artifacts from later Navajo culture.

The Name. De Chelly (duh SHAY) is a mispronunciation in English of a mispronunciation in Spanish of the Navajo word *tsegi,* which means "a rocky canyon."

Special Interest. Here, in January of 1864, Colonel Christopher "Kit" Carson directed a military expedition that destroyed all food supplies and forced large numbers of Navajos to choose between death by starvation and surrender. The United States Army then drove the Navajos to Fort Sumner, New Mexico, over 300 miles away. There, for four years, about 8000 Navajos were confined in what amounted to a prisoner-of-war camp. In the end, their insistence on returning to their home-

land prevailed, and they came back to Canyon de Chelly and the surrounding area. This traumatic episode in their history is known to the Navajos as the Long Walk.

Fort Sumner, also known as Bosque Redondo, is one of the New Mexico State Monuments, located 2 miles east of the town of Fort Sumner on US 60.

CARLING RESERVOIR SITE

From Arizona 389 in Colorado City drive on a dirt road to Carling Reservoir at the southwest end of town. Mail address: Bureau of Land Management, Vermillion Resource Area, 225 N. Bluff, St. George, UT 84770. Phone: 801/628-4491.

Here several pithouses dating to A.D. 180 have been excavated together with another structure that dates at A.D. 1300. A second site, called the Corncob or Kiva Site, is on Academy Ave. at the north end of Colorado City across from the community center. Here seems to have been a kiva and rooms lined up in a row.

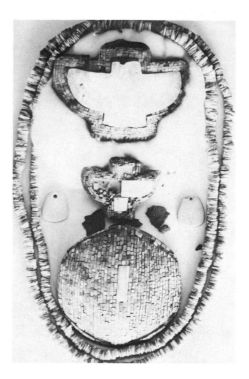

Hohokam craftsmen at Casa Grande glued tiny bits of shaped turquoise onto seashells with mesquite gum. These are in the museum at the site. National Park Service photo by George A. Grant.

CASA GRANDE RUINS NATIONAL MONUMENT (KAH-suh-GRAHN-day)

Halfway between Phoenix and Tucson, 1 mile north of Coolidge on Arizona 87. (Note: the National Monument is *not* in the town of Casa Grande.) Mail address: 1100 Ruins Drive, P.O. Box 518, Coolidge, AZ 85228. Phone: 602/723-3172. Open daily, all year. Admission charged. Camping nearby.

This site offers an excellent introduction to the lifeway of the ancient irrigation farmers now known as the Hohokam. A leaflet provides information for a self-guided tour. During winter months a ranger gives guided tours at scheduled intervals throughout the day.

The Story. The impressive, four-story structure that gives the site its name (*Casa Grande* means big house) was probably built about A.D. 1350 and was used until 1450. It may have been a ceremonial center or fortress or both. Its massive walls, made from a special kind of clay, are not typical of the Ho-

hokam. The building is much more like those seen farther south, in Mexico. The usual Hohokam dwellings were separate, single-room houses, made of brush and mud.

Throughout the semiarid Gila River Valley, the Hohokam managed to raise crops by irrigation. They built more than 250 miles of canals, which were between two and four feet wide and about two feet deep. Some can still be seen today.

The Museum. Here may be seen artifacts of the Hohokam people and panels that explain their life.

The Name. The ruins were visited in 1694 by Father Kino, a Spanish explorer-priest, who named the place Casa Grande. The great size of the main building made it a landmark for later visitors, and the name has remained in use.

CASA MALPAIS

318 E. Main St. (Highway 60), Springerville. Mail address: P.O. Box 390, Springerville, AZ 85938. Phone: 602/ 333-5375. Drive first to the museum.

From there, in summer, visitors will be taken on guided tours three times daily. Admission charged.

The museum serves as Visitor Center for the Casa Malpais National Landmark Site which is located about two miles north of Springerville. Guided tours of the site start at the museum several times a day. Visitors who want to see the entire site are urged to wear boots for a hike to the top of cliffs and to bring a canteen of water.

The Story. Sometime between A.D. 1250 and 1400 Mogollon people built stone houses and religious structures here at the foot of a 150-foot basalt cliff. The land between the village and the Little Colorado River was good for farming, and the site was not abandoned until some time after most of the Mogollon people's little-understood migration to other places.

The rock that these farmers used for buildings was not the easily worked sandstone that villagers found in many other Southwestern places. The basalt in the cliff was of volcanic origin—hard and irregularly shaped when it broke. Nevertheless the builders em-

This massive structure at Casa Grande Ruins National Monument is made from a kind of clay that contains a cement-like material called caliche. The builders shaped the mud by hand in a layer about two feet thick, let it dry, then added another layer. A protective roof now covers the building to prevent erosion. National Park Service photo by George A. Grant.

bedded small chunks of it in mud and put up dwellings and a unique great kiva which unlike most Anasazi kivas was above ground. Cracks in the volcanic rock, sealed with stones and mud, served as burial tombs. A spiral staircase made from slabs of basalt led from the foot of the cliff to the mesa above.

Vandals have robbed the tombs of the beautiful Mogollon pottery and other burial goods, but excavation has salvaged a few things the thieves missed.

Archeologists plan an ongoing program to interpret the site and explain its relation to other Mogollon communities. As this book went to press it seemed possible that the site might become affiliated with the National Park Service.

The Name. The site has sometimes been called Casa Malapais, meaning "house of basalt," but an elderly resident of Springerville assured archeologists that *Malpais* was the word used by early Spanish settlers. So the name probably means "house of the volcanic badland."

EASTERN ARIZONA COLLEGE
(*See Museum of Anthropology*)

EASTERN ARIZONA COLLEGE
EXTENSION
(*See Gila Pueblo*)

EASTERN ARIZONA MUSEUM
AND HISTORICAL SOCIETY

Main and Center streets, Pima. Mail address: #2 N. Main St., Pima, AZ 85543. Phone: 602/485-9400. Open free, Monday–Friday.

Salado and Hohokam artifacts from the vicinity of Pima are on display here, together with some material from northern Arizona, which is not identified.

Volunteers at work helping excavate Elden Pueblo at the edge of Flagstaff, Arizona. National Forest Service photo.

ELDEN PUEBLO

In Flagstaff. Drive northeast on Interstate 40 to Page exit, then north 1.5 miles on US 89 to entrance. Mail address: Coconino National Forest, 2323 E. Greenlaw Lane, Flagstaff, AZ 86004. Phone: 602/556-7410.

At this site, once inhabited by Sinagua people, a summer program for adults and children is conducted by the Coconino National Forest in partnership with the Northern Arizona Natural History Association, the Museum of Northern Arizona and Northern Arizona University. For information about programs and tour, call or write Coconino National Forest (see above).

FORT LOWELL CITY PARK MUSEUM

2900 North Craycroft Rd., near intersection with Fort Lowell Rd., in Old Fort Lowell County Park. Mail address: 2900 North Craycroft Rd., Tucson, AZ 85712. Phone: 602/885-3832. Open free, daily. Closed certain holidays.

Twelve outdoor panel exhibits tell the story of the Hardy Site, a prehistoric Hohokam village that now lies beneath the park and the surrounding neighborhood. Partial excavation of the site revealed the remains of pithouses, outdoor roasting pits, work areas where stone tools were made, and pits where calcium carbonate was mined for mixing with mud and water to form plaster for house floors and walls. For other Hohokam sites, see Index.

GATLIN SITE

On Stout Road, off Old US 80, 3 miles north of Gila Bend. Mail address: c/o Gila Bend Museum, P.O. Drawer #1, Gila Bend, AZ 85337. Phone: 602/683-2002.

This National Historic Landmark is a thousand-year-old Hohokam Indian village consisting of a platform mound associated with pithouses, numerous middens, and prehistoric canals. Contact the Town of Gila Bend at 602/683-2255 (Phoenix line, 256-7856) for information about hours.

GILA PUEBLO

In Globe follow signs along Broad Street to turnoff for Eastern Arizona College. Mail address: Globe, AZ 85501. Phone: 602/425-3151. The site is the actual campus of the college. Open free, Monday–Friday.

This large village was occupied by Salado people from A.D. 1225 to 1400. Many of its more than 200 rooms were excavated and some were restored in the 1920s by archeologists Harold and Winifred Gladwin whose home on the site is now headquarters of Eastern Arizona College. Visitors may take a self-guided tour of the site. There is a small exhibit of artifacts in the Gladwin house, but the main collection is at the University of Arizona.

In Grand Canyon National Park, Tusayan Ruin, built about A.D. 1185, was occupied for less than 50 years. Then, for some unknown reason, it was abandoned. National Park Service photo by J. M. Eden.

GLEN CANYON NATIONAL RECREATION AREA

Headquarters and Visitor Center in Page, 134 miles north of Flagstaff on US 89. Mail address: Box 1507, Page, AZ 86040. Phone: 602/645-2471. Visitor Center open daily, all year. Closed certain holidays.

After construction of the Glen Canyon dam across the Colorado River, the waters of Lake Powell destroyed hundreds of archeological sites dating from A.D. 500 or earlier to the late 13th century. Extensive surveys, conducted before flooding, led to the discovery of many Anasazi ruins and also of many petroglyph and pictograph sites.

The rock art turned out to be particularly interesting to archeologists. Some of their studies made use of the help of modern Hopi Indians whose ancestors probably drew or pecked or scratched many of the pictures on boulders and on the walls of canyons in the Recreation Area. The meaning of these petrographs (a term that includes both petroglyphs and picto-

graphs) is obscure. The numerous representations of sheep very likely had to do with hunting. Some abstract designs probably represent patterns in woven cloth, since it is generally supposed that men were the rock artists and it was men who did Hopi weaving. In some places, where rather crude work appears low down on rock surfaces, children were possibly copying older people's designs.

Fortunately there are three stabilized ruins on the shoreline of Lake Powell: One is Defiance House in Forgotten Canyon near Bullfrog Marina; another is Three Roof Ruin in the Escalante area; and the third is Widow's Ledge, in Slickrock Canyon, south of the Halls Crossing Marina. These are accessible by boat.

Most of the archeological sites that were covered by Lake Powell have remained intact, and in some cases have become attractive to scuba divers who, of course, are warned not to disturb anything they find.

GRAND CANYON NATIONAL PARK
A World Heritage Site

The park is divided by the canyon into two parts, reached by very different routes. For the South Rim drive 59 miles north from Williams on Arizona 64 to park headquarters. Mail address: Box 129, Grand Canyon, AZ 86023. Tusayan Museum phone: 602/638-2305. For the North Rim drive 30 miles south from Jacob Lake on Arizona 67 to the park entrance, then 12 miles farther to the rim. Open (South Rim) all year; (North Rim) mid-May to mid-Oct. Admission charged. Camping.

Prehistoric people lived in and around this incredible canyon for a very long time. Some climbed into caves in the cliffs and left artifacts there. Dr. Robert Euler has explored the canyon walls and bottom lands by helicopter and has found a great many archeological sites. (About half a million acres in the Grand Canyon have still not had an archeological survey.)

A ruined village called Tusayan (too-say-YAHN) on the South Rim may be

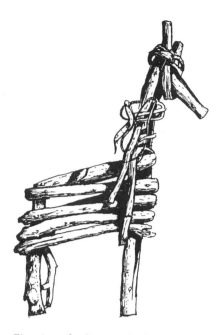

Figurine of a deer, made from split twigs about 3000 years ago in the Grand Canyon area. Original in the Arizona State Museum, Tucson.

The Southwest

Only from the point of view of *norteamericanos* (Spanish for people north of Mexico) is the southwestern part of the United States "the Southwest." From the point of view of Mexicans the area lies to the north. Moreover, in prehistoric times the area received attention from people in Mexico and was influenced by Mexican culture.

To prehistoric Mexicans, and also to the later Spanish *conquistadores,* the region was part of a large area that was known as the Gran Chichimeca, which extended northward from the Tropic of Cancer to the vicinity of present-day San Francisco, California, on the northwest, and to Wichita, Kansas, in the northeast. The *chichimeca* was descriptive. It meant, among other things, "nomad." It also meant "son of the dog," or "outlander." Gran Chichimeca was the Great Land of Nomads— people who were barbarians from the point of view of the more sophisticated inhabitants of the Valley of Mexico. Some United States archeologists want to revive the name Gran Chichimeca and apply it to both northern Mexico and the southwestern United States. Other archeologists, having no less respect for ancient Mexican culture and for present-day Mexican sensibilities, believe that the term "Southwest" is so deeply imbedded in usage that it is practically impossible to substitute the older name. So, bowing to current custom in the United States, this book calls the Gran Chichimeca the Southwest.

visited all year. There are guided tours in summer.

On the North Rim a site called Cape Royal Ruin (G.C. 212) has been excavated and is open to the public.

A third site, Bright Angel Pueblo (G.C. 624) on the canyon bottom near the Colorado River, may be visited all year. The eight-mile Bright Angel Trail leads to the site from the South Rim. Hikers are advised to make the trip in two days. Camping reservations required. Mule trips are also available.

The Story. People of the Western Archaic culture moved into the Grand Canyon area three or four thousand years ago. They lived by gathering wild plant food and by hunting, and they did what other hunters have sometimes done— they made figurines of deer or mountain sheep and left them in caves, apparently in the hope that this practice would bring them luck. A figurine was fashioned of a single long willow twig, split down the middle and bent in an ingenious way into the form of the animal. Sometimes the figurines were pierced by a twig spear, for good measure. Archeologists have found a num-

ber of these split-twig animals in caches in now almost inaccessible caves in the limestone cliffs. Radiocarbon dates indicate that they were left there between 3100 and 4100 years ago. Almost no other artifacts were found with the figurines, so the culture of their makers has remained something of a puzzle.

More than 370 specimens have now been found, not only in the Grand Canyon, but also in Nevada, Utah and California, and at some of these latter sites they were associated with artifacts of various kinds, such as projectile points, sandals, and skin bags. These sites appear to have been used at a later date than were the Grand Canyon caves. The differences in time and the associated material have led to speculation that the non-cave figurines may have served a different purpose. Perhaps they may even have been playthings rather than ritual objects.

Certainly people of the Grand Canyon area changed their patterns of living and, in time, became more like the Anasazi farmers who lived to the east and north. Some found their way

down the canyon's high walls, built small villages, and raised their crops close to the thundering Colorado River. Others made their homes along the canyon rim. Tusayan, built between A.D. 1185 and 1200, housed about 30 people, but they did not stay long. By 1250 they had moved away, probably to the Kayenta region. One by one the other villages down near the river were also abandoned, and by the time the first Spanish explorers arrived the only Indians living in the canyon were the Havasupai, who have remained there to this day.

There is some evidence that conflict may have accounted for abandonment on the South Rim, and curious settlements on so-called islands in the canyon indicate pressure of some sort. The islands are large areas on top of sections of rock that have been isolated by erosion all around them. These almost inaccessible spots may have been chosen as habitation sites when it became necessary to defend hoards of food at times when bad weather restricted crops. Study of the islands is being continued.

Helicopter rides take visitors close up to canyon walls. At one point below Point Sublime on the North Rim, it is possible to see a former settlement, so protected from weathering that the original roofing on the dwellings appears to be intact.

Visitors to the Tusayan Ruin can take a self-guided tour, aided by a pamphlet that tells about the life and culture of those who built this small village.

The Museums. At Tusayan Ruin the museum has exhibits with special emphasis on the culture of the people who lived there. Displays show how artifacts and pottery vessels were made. There are also exhibits of artifacts made and used by Patayan people called the Cohonina, who lived on the South Rim about A.D. 750 to 1100. The museum is open 8 a.m. to 5 p.m. in summer.

At the Visitor Center the museum is open all year, 8 a.m. to sunset. Displays here show artifacts of most people and periods in the area. Of special interest are the split-twig figurines.

This excavated mound at Snaketown was probably a dance platform. National Park Service photo.

Kokopelli with dog. A petroglyph in Many Cherries Canyon, Canyon del Muerto, Canyon de Chelly National Monument. Photo by Bob Powell; copyright by Bob Powell.

GRASSHOPPER RUIN

The University of Arizona conducts a field school in archeology at Grasshopper Ruin which is ten miles from the Apache town of Cibecue and 52 miles from Show Low. For information about the field school, which gives college credit, address inquiries to: J. Jefferson Reid, Director, Archaeological Field School, Department of Anthropology, University of Arizona, Tucson, AZ 85721. Phone: 602/621-6297 or 8546.

HARDY SITE
(*See Fort Lowell City Park Museum*)

HEARD MUSEUM OF NATIVE CULTURES AND ART

22 E. Monte Vista Road, Phoenix, AZ 85004. Phone: 602/252-8840. Open Monday–Saturday; afternoon, Sunday. Closed certain holidays. Admission charged.

Collections in this museum are built around the artifacts and life of Native Americans of the Southwest.

HOMOLOVI RUINS STATE PARK

From Winslow drive 5 miles southwest on Arizona 87. Mail address: 523 West 2nd St., Winslow, AZ 86047. Phone: 602/289-4106. Open Monday–Friday, all year. Admission charged. Camping.

As this book went to press this park was scheduled to open. Six archeological sites in the park were occupied between A.D. 1250 and 1600. The area was a stopping place for the Hopis when they were migrating toward the mesas where they now live.

KEET SEEL
(*See Navajo National Monument*)

Dogs and Prehistoric Americans

No one knows when dogs first appeared in North America. They had already been domesticated by people who camped at the Koster Site in Illinois, about 5000 B.C. They may have been used by hunters to help in pursuing game, but there is no doubt that they were companions for adults and playmates for children. Among some tribes they had an important place in religious ceremonies. Occasionally they were sacrificed, in somewhat the same way that animals were sacrificed in biblical times, and were ritually buried. Sometimes they were eaten ceremonially—or simply as food in some areas, particularly in the Southwest. On the Northwest Coast people raised a special, long-haired breed and used the hair in weaving blankets and belts.

Dogs were known throughout much of America, especially where men were hunters. In some farming areas archeologists have found no skeletons at all to indicate their presence, but wherever they existed they were the most important domesticated animal—often the only domesticated one. In the Plains area they carried loads on special pole frames called travois (truh-VOY).

One curious fact: In many places the very earliest dogs were very small. Later, dogs in the warmer parts of the continent were small, but farther north they were large, and the largest of all lived farthest north.

Pottery in the form of a dog made by an artist of the Mississippian culture in Tennessee. Original in the Peabody Museum, Harvard University.

KINISHBA PUEBLO

Mail address: White Mountain Apache Tribal Headquarters, Box 507, Fort Apache, AZ 85926. Phone at Apache Culture Center: 602/338-4625. The site is 3 miles from Fort Apache. Open free, all year.

This partly restored Mogollon-Anasazi pueblo housed a thousand or more people between A.D. 1100 and 1350. It is one of the largest ruins in the Southwest. Despite its importance, the pueblo can only be viewed through a barbed-wire fence, which the White Mountain Apache Tribe has put up for the safety of visitors and for the protection of the site. When funds become available the tribe hopes to stabilize and restore the entire town, which includes two enclosed courtyards, and to reestablish the museum it once operated here.

Special Interest. An early excavator at Kinishba found the skeleton of a child around which was wrapped a necklace almost six feet long, made of 2,534 carefully polished turquoise beads. This astonishing piece of work is now in the Arizona State Museum at Tucson. Also in the necklace were 11 larger beads made of catlinite (pipestone), which may have been brought by traders from far-away Minnesota. Many other necklaces at Kinishba included coral, which came from either the Gulf of Mexico or Baja California, and shells from the Pacific Coast. Trade was obviously extensive in prehistoric America.

KINLICHEE TRIBAL PARK

On the Navajo Indian Reservation, drive west from Window Rock 22 miles on Navajo 3 (Arizona 264) to Cross Canyon Trading Post, then 2.5 miles north on a gravel road to Kinlichee and Cross Canyon Ruins. Mail address: Parks and Recreation Department, P.O. Box 308, Window Rock, AZ 86515. Phone: 602/871-6436. Open free, at all times. Camping nearby. Fee for camping charged.

Anasazi people lived in this area for more than 500 years. Today, in a Tribal Park, the Navajo Indians are preserving the ruins of Anasazi dwellings, the oldest of which is a pithouse dated at

Paleo and Archaic

Paleo-Indian is the term used for the First Americans. They got their subsistence from various sources, but their special achievement seems to have been as hunters of herding animals, which were often very large. The Paleo way of life ended as the herds of big game disappeared. By 6000 B.C. it was necessary to exploit every available food resource to the maximum.

Smaller animals, edible plants, fish, and shellfish now became the fare of people who followed what is called the Archaic lifeway. They hunted and foraged characteristically in forested areas in the East and in semiarid regions in the West, but their lifeways spread over the entire continent.

Out of the Archaic, beginning about 1000 B.C., or perhaps a little earlier, there developed cultures that practiced gardening. People in many places began to create at least part of their food supply, and this meant that they became more and more settled village dwellers. The older lifeways persisted in areas not suited to food growing, but Indian farms and towns were widespread by the time Europeans mistakenly labeled them Indian.

Montezuma Castle ruin was given its name by early white settlers, who mistakenly guessed that Aztec Indians had built the cliff dwellings here. Santa Fe Railway photo.

about A.D. 800. Other ruins belong to the various Pueblo periods up to about 1300, when the large, apartment-house villages were abandoned. Wayside exhibits and a trail take the visitor on a self-guided tour, which gives an opportunity to see how Anasazi architecture evolved. To help visitors visualize the life of the past one of the ruins has been completely reconstructed.

MARANA MOUND

In the vicinity of Phoenix, AZ. Earthwatch is under the direction of Dr. Paul Fish, Suzanne Fish and Dr. Curtiss Brennan of the Arizona State Museum. The University of Arizona conducts excavation at this Hohokam ceremonial mound and the surrounding area. For information about fees and how to participate in this dig apply to: Earthwatch, 680 Mount Auburn St., Box 403, Waterton, MA 02272. Phone: 617/926-8200.

MESA SOUTHWEST MUSEUM

53 North Macdonald, Mesa, AZ 85201. Phone: 602/644-2230. Open Tuesday–Saturday; afternoon, Sunday. Admission charged.

Full-size replicas of Hohokam and Salado dwellings form part of the museum's permanent exhibits which tell the story of the farming people who lived in the Salt River Valley from about A.D. 400 to 1450.

MONTEZUMA CASTLE NATIONAL MONUMENT

From Flagstaff drive 50 miles south on Interstate 17, then 2.5 miles east to the Visitor Center. Mail address: P.O. Box 219, Camp Verde, AZ 86322. Phone: 602/567-3322. Open daily, all year. Admission charged.

The monument is in two sections— Montezuma Castle and Montezuma Well, 9.5 miles apart. Footpaths from headquarters building lead toward the beautifully preserved "castle," a cliff dwelling built a hundred feet above the valley floor. Along the walk is a

Montezuma Castle. National Park Service photo by Dave Roberts.

diorama with audio tape that explains what life was like in the dwelling more than 600 years ago. The ledge that supports the buildings has weathered so greatly that visits to the castle itself are no longer permitted. Ruins of other dwellings at the foot of the cliff, farther along the trail, may be visited.

At Montezuma Well two ruins overlook a sunken lake, about 400 feet across and 55 feet deep. The well is fed by a huge spring, from which flow 1 1/2 million gallons of water every day.

The Story. Farmers with different customs contributed to the development of a distinct way of life in the valley of the Verde River. About A.D. 600 a group of Hohokam people moved into the valley from the desert country near modern Phoenix, where they lived in one-family, one-room houses made of poles covered with brush and mud. The Hohokam were farmers who dug irrigation canals to water their crops of corn, squash, beans, and cotton.

A second group of farmers lived north of the Verde Valley. These people, who raised crops without irrigation, have been named the Sinagua (sin-AH-wah), Spanish for "without water."

About A.D. 1150 rainfall increased and water-conserving practices improved. Trade in copper and cotton also increased, and the population grew. People began to build stone houses in the cliff overhangs, Anasazi-fashion. Then by about A.D. 1250 the people left these buildings, no one knows why, and moved off to the southeast.

The Name. Early white settlers in the Verde Valley mistakenly thought that Aztec Indians had built the dwellings at this site. So the five-story apartment house and the well, several miles away, were both named in honor of Montezuma, last Aztec emperor. The name, although misleading, has stuck.

Special Feature. The prehistoric farmers here built irrigation canals from Montezuma Well to their garden plots. Because the water contained lime, the ditches became lined with a hard cement-like crust, which has survived to this day.

Could a Clovis Point Kill a Mammoth?

Because mammoths are extinct there is no way to experiment on them. However, some of these prehistoric elephants have been preserved in a frozen state in Siberia, so we know that a mammoth hide was about as thick as a present-day elephant hide and that the two animals were very similar in other ways.

Fortunately for archeologists, officials in a national park in Zimbabwe in southern Africa decided it was necessary to reduce the size of the elephant population. They allowed George C. Frison of the University of Wyoming to help them, using replicated Clovis points. In 1984 and again in 1985 Frison established that Clovis points on darts propelled by atlatls could indeed kill the largest of land mammals.

In 1990 archeologists found blood on an 11,000-year-old Clovis point excavated in the state of Washington. Tests showed that this blood did not come from a mammoth but from a human being. Did a mammoth hunter cut his finger when he was making a Clovis point or is this blood evidence of prehistoric warfare? We are not likely ever to know the answer to that question.

MONUMENT VALLEY NAVAJO TRIBAL PARK

From Kayenta drive 24 miles north on US 191 to directional sign, then 5 miles east on local road to Visitor Center. Mail address: P.O. Box 360289, Monument Valley, UT 84536. Phone: 801/727-3287. Open free, all year.

At the Visitor Center in this Navajo Tribal Park arrangements can be made for guided four-wheel drive trips to prehistoric ruins in the Monument Valley area.

MURRAY SPRINGS CLOVIS SITE

San Pedro Project Office, Bureau of Land Management, Rural Route 1, Box 9853, Huachuca City, AZ 85616. Phone: 602/457-2265.

Paleo-Indians camped here and killed and butchered mammoth and bison. The site was not yet open as this book went to press. Inquire about opening date and road directions at the address above.

MUSEUM OF ANTHROPOLOGY

Eastern Arizona College, 345 College Ave., Thatcher, AZ 85552. Phone: 602/428-1133, ext. 310. Open free Monday–Friday. Closed in summer.

Exhibits here specialize in the archeology of southeastern Arizona and include a stratigraphic depiction of Gila Valley prehistory, functional replicas of Indian weaponry and a diorama of late Ice Age Arizona. The museum offers visitors a chance to grind corn, drill shells and start a fire with a bow drill. Guided tours are available.

MUSEUM OF NORTHERN ARIZONA

Fort Valley Rd. (US 180), Flagstaff. Mail address: Rte 4, Box 720, Flagstaff, AZ 86001. Phone: 602/774-5211. Open free, Monday–Saturday; afternoon, Sunday. Closed certain holidays.

Excellent displays on prehistoric and contemporary native cultures of the Colorado Plateau cover all periods from the Paleo-Indian, Anasazi and Pueblo, through present-day Hopi and Navajo cultures.

Clovis points, named for the site near Clovis, New Mexico, where they were first found, appear in a very wide area. These parts of Clovis points are from a site in Virginia. Thunderbird Research Corporation photo.

NAVAJO COMMUNITY COLLEGE NED HATATHLI CENTER

On the college campus. From US 191 at Round Rock drive 22 miles south on Navajo Route 12 past Lukachukai, then right on Navajo Route 64 and first left on spur leading to the college. Mail address: Tsaile, AZ 86556. Phone: 602/724-3311. Open free, Sunday–Friday; morning Saturday, during the college year.

Displays contain Navajo sand paintings and other materials, together with artifacts from other Indian cultures. This college was the first to be located on a reservation and controlled by Native American people.

NAVAJO NATIONAL MONUMENT

From Tuba City drive 56 miles northeast on US 160, then 9 miles northwest on a paved road to the Visitor Center. Mail address: HC 71, Box 3, Tonalea, AZ 86044-9704. Phone: 602/672-2366. Open free, daily, all year. Camping.

Here several superb cliff dwellings may be visited. Tours are conducted in spring, summer, and fall to the most accessible ruin, Betatakin (be-TAH-tah-kin), which means "ledge house" in the language of the Navajos, who inhabit the region today. This is a village of 135 rooms, built in an immense cave, which reaches 500 feet in height.

Another ruin, one of the largest in Arizona, is Keet Seel, which means "broken pottery" in the Navajo language. An eight-mile trail leads down into a canyon and along a stream to this splendid cliff village, which has a remarkably new appearance, although its 160 rooms have not been lived in for more than 600 years. A visit to Keet Seel takes a full day on horses, which can be rented from Navajos, or two days on foot, with an overnight stay in the campground near the ruin. Only 1500 visitors a year are allowed at Keet Seel. Tours of the ruin are conducted by a park ranger. Make advance arrangement for horses and/or a tour by writing to Monument Headquarters.

Betatakin is one of three well-preserved Anasazi cliff dwellings in Navajo National Monument. National Park Service photo by Natt N. Dodge.

The Story. About 1500 years ago a special way of life began to develop in northern Arizona and New Mexico and in southern Colorado. People there had learned to farm, and so they could settle in small, permanent villages, which were scattered over a very large area. Little by little these communities joined to form bigger ones, and finally the population became oriented around three distinct cultural regions. One centered at Mesa Verde in Colorado, another at Chaco Canyon, in New Mexico, and the third near Kayenta, in Arizona. All of these people shared certain characteristics, and they have been given the general name Anasazi.

The Kayenta branch of the Anasazi built Betatakin, Keet Seel, and a dwelling called Inscription House (not open to visitors). Like many Anasazi villages these were abandoned in the late 1200s for reasons that are little understood.

Modern Navajo Indians, for whom the monument is named, avoided the ruins because they feared all things dead. Then in the nineteenth century John Wetherill, a trader with the In-

dians, and Byron Cummings, an archeologist, visited Betatakin and Inscription House. John Wetherill's brother Richard later discovered Keet Seel.

Special Feature. In the museum at the Visitor Center an audio-visual program shows how the Anasazi lived and what they made. In summer there are campfire programs, which introduce visitors to the history and archeology of the monument.

NAVAJO TRIBAL MUSEUM

Navajo Arts and Crafts Enterprise Bldg., on Arizona 264, Window Rock. Mail address: P.O. Box 308, Window Rock, AZ 86515. Phone: 602/871-6673. Open free, Monday–Saturday; afternoon Sunday, May–September. Closed national and tribal holidays. Donations accepted.

Exhibits in the museum include both Navajo artifacts and prehistoric Anasazi artifacts. Group tours can be arranged by appointment.

A view in the Keet Seel Ruin,
Navajo National Monument.
National Park Service photo by Fred
E. Mang, Jr.

Inscription House Ruin, in Navajo
National Monument, is not open to
the public. National Park Service
photo by Fred E. Mang, Jr.

Betatakin Ruin, in Navajo National Monument. National Park Service photo by Fred E. Mang, Jr.

Kachinas

When the Spanish invaders arrived in the Southwest in 1540, every Indian pueblo except one had what the Hopis called kachinas. These were men, costumed, masked, and painted with elaborate symbolism, who participated in ceremonies in the village plazas or in the kivas. They represented supernatural spirits that were themselves called kachinas, and the dancers were believed to have supernatural powers. Some of the dancers were very earthy clowns. Others were impersonators of spirits both good and evil. Occasionally paintings of kachinas were made on the walls of prehistoric kivas.

To teach children all the symbolism of the costumes, and to help them learn the stories about supernatural beings, men often carved and painted wooden dolls in the form of kachinas. Today the Pueblo Indians still have kachina dancers, and they make kachina dolls for children—and for anyone interested in buying them. Archeologists sometimes find kachina dolls in excavations.

Nokachok kachina doll from the Keams Canyon area. These dolls are made by Hopi and Zuni Indians. Field Museum of Natural History photo.

NEWSPAPER ROCK PETROGLYPHS
(See Petrified Forest National Park)

OLD ORAIBI
(oh-RYE-bee)

From Tuba City at the junction of US 164 and Arizona 264, drive southeast 50 miles on Arizona 264. Mail address: Hopi Indian Agency, Keams Canyon, AZ 86034. Phone: 602/738-2228. Visitors are asked to check in at the Community Building. Photography only with permission. Camping nearby. Open free daily.

Old Oraibi has been inhabited continuously since A.D. 1100. When scientists were working out a way to date ruins by studying tree rings, some of the most important information came from the wooden beams in ancient buildings in Oraibi. Visitors should respect the desire of the Hopi people for privacy in their homes.

PAINTED ROCKS STATE PARK

Drive 13 miles west of Gila Bend on Interstate 8, then 12 miles north on access road. Mail address: Arizona State Parks, 800 W. Washington, Phoenix, AZ 85007. Phone: 602/683-2151. Open daily, all year. Admission charged.

Within the park is a group of Indian rock-art drawings of snakes, lizards, men and geometric figures. The meaning of the drawings is uncertain, but they may represent a system of record keeping.

PARK OF THE CANALS

1700 North Horne, Mesa. From AZ 360, Exit 9, drive north to Brown Road, then right to Horne. Mail address: Mesa Southwest Museum, 53 Macdonald, Mesa, AZ 85201. Phone: 602/644-2351. Open free, sunrise to sunset.

In the city park are preserved a remnant of the 500 miles of irrigation canals built by the Hohokam people throughout the Salt River Valley, where as many as 20,000 farmers once flourished. Across the park the volunteer Southwest Archaeology Team works at excavating a Hohokam village every Saturday morning. Visitors are invited to observe and even to dig after a training session.

Petroglyphs in Petrified Forest National Park. National Park Service photo by George A. Grant.

PETRIFIED FOREST NATIONAL PARK

From Gallup, New Mexico, drive 69 miles southwest on Interstate 40 to northern park entrance and Visitor Center. Or from Holbrook drive 19 miles southeast on US 180 to Rainbow Forest entrance and museum. Mail address: Petrified Forest National Park, AZ 86028. Phone: 602/524-6228. Park open daily. Visitor centers closed certain holidays. Admission charged.

This area, notable for its deposits of petrified wood and paleontological resources from the Triassic period, also contains over 550 archeological sites. These sites demonstrate almost continuous occupation from the Paleo-Indian through historic Navajo periods. Two of the sites are easily reached by the 28-mile park road.

The Puerco Indian Ruins, 11 miles south of the Painted Desert Visitor Center, contained about 150 rooms when it was occupied up to 600 years ago. In addition, hundreds of petroglyphs—pictures and symbols pecked into the area's sandstone boulders—are found adjacent to the ruins.

A reconstructed ruin called Agate House is located adjacent to the Long Logs Interpretive Trail in the park's Rainbow Forest District. Here the Anasazi builders used blocks of petrified wood to erect a small structure.

Another prehistoric site, Newspaper Rock, is located off the main park road one mile south of Puerco Ruins. Here, a large sandstone boulder covered with dozens of petroglyphs can be viewed from an overlook.

The Rainbow Forest Museum, near the park's southern entrance, contains several exhibits that interpret the area's prehistory.

PICTURE ROCKS RETREAT

From Interstate 10 at north edge of Tucson turn west on Ina Rd. At intersection with Wade Ave., turn left and drive about a mile to entrance. Open free, daily, during daylight hours. Inquire at office for directions to site.

A short, well maintained path leads to a tall exposed rock area on which a variety of petroglyphs can be seen. The Redemptorist Fathers maintain the site and welcome visitors.

PIMERIA ALTA HISTORICAL SOCIETY MUSEUM

223 Grand Avenue, Nogales, AZ 85628. Phone: 602/287-4621. Open free, Monday–Saturday; afternoon Sunday. Closed certain holidays.

A large area of southern Arizona and northern Sonora in Mexico was once known as Pimeria Alta. The story of its people from the days of the Hohokam to historic times is told in exhibits in this museum.

PUEBLO GRANDE MUSEUM

4619 E. Washington St., Phoenix, AZ 85034. Phone: 602/495-0900. Open Monday–Saturday; afternoon Sunday. Closed certain holidays. Admission charged.

Here, inside the city of Phoenix, is a large archeological site with an accompanying museum, which illuminates the life of the Hohokam from about A.D. 500 to 1400. Trails with explanatory signs lead to a large platform structure—a mound built of earth—upon which small buildings once rested. They may have served cer-

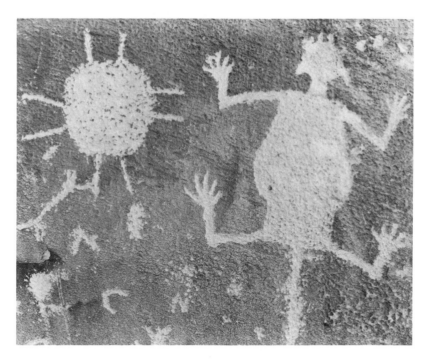

Petroglyphs made by Indians long ago on a sandstone cliff in Petrified Forest National Park. National Park Service photo by George A. Grant.

emonial functions and for storage of food. Around this structure is a village spread over a 2-mile diameter area.

From the mound it is possible to see remnants of irrigation canals. A whole system of canals, totaling possibly 500 miles in length, once made the Phoenix area a very productive farming region. Corn, jackbeans, lima beans, kidney beans, tepary beans, amaranth, two kinds of squash, cotton, and possibly tobacco grew well here. Besides raising crops, the Hohokam people of Pueblo Grande gathered wild plant food and hunted desert animals of many kinds. They produced beautiful pottery and other artifacts, and made ornaments of shell, imported from the Gulf of California.

Irrigation farming began about A.D. 100 in and around Phoenix. No one knows whether the Hohokam invented this practice themselves or borrowed the idea from Mexico, but as soon as water flowed onto the dry land, food increased greatly and so did population. This abundance, however, brought problems. The irrigation necessary for dependable crops may have caused the ground to become waterlogged and salt saturated.

In addition to waterlogging, other problems beset the Hohokam around Phoenix. Salt in the water damaged the walls of their buildings. Occasional floods on the Salt River destroyed the irrigation canals. Frequent floods occurred during the late 1300s. Life became increasingly difficult, and by A.D. 1450 the residents of Pueblo Grande and the surrounding area had all migrated from the Salt River Valley. Probably the Pima and the Tohono o'dham (Papago) Indians of today are descendants of the ancient Hohokam.

The Museum. Exhibits consist of materials recovered from this large site. Much of the excavation was done with the help of crews who were on work relief during the Depression. The museum building was designed after the truncated pyramids of Mexico, reflecting the influence of Mexico on the ancient Southwest. The structure incorporates sophisticated equipment and research laboratories, which will contribute to continuing investigation of the Hohokam. The museum and the archeological site are maintained by the city of Phoenix.

Special Feature. Visible here is a court in which the inhabitants may have played a ball game that was popular in prehistoric times in much of Mexico and Central America.

This logo is used to indicate a World Heritage Site.

Passport in Time

Responding to the growing interest of the public in archeology, the Forest Service of the Department of Agriculture has developed a program in which people may take part as volunteers. Called *Passport in Time* (or PIT), the program is spreading to national forests throughout the United States.

Passport in Time makes it possible for volunteers to work under professional supervision in actual digs and in a variety of other archeological activities. For information apply to Passport in Time Clearinghouse, P.O. Box 18364, Washington, D.C. Phone: 202/293-0922.

SHARLOT HALL MUSEUM
(SHAR-lot)

415 West Gurley, Prescott, AZ 86301. Phone: 602/445-3122. Open free, Tuesday–Saturday; afternoon Sunday. Closed holidays except Memorial Day, Independence Day and Labor Day.

One room in this museum is devoted to prehistoric cultural material from Arizona, particularly from the area around Prescott.

SMOKI MUSEUM
(smoke-eye)

126 North Arizona St., Prescott, AZ 86301. Phone: 602/445-1230. Open free, June–September, weekdays except Wednesday; winter by appointment.

A group of non-Indians, calling themselves the Smoki, have devoted a great deal of energy to the study and preservation of Native American cultures in the Southwest. They have gathered in this small museum some prehistoric Arizona artifacts, together with ethnological material.

SUNSET CRATER NATIONAL MONUMENT

From Flagstaff drive 15 miles northeast on US 89, then follow directional signs on the paved loop road. Mail address: 2717 North Steves Blvd., Flagstaff, AZ 86004. Phone: 602/427-7040. Visitor Center open daily. Closed certain holidays. Admission charged. Camping.

Although archeological sites that have been excavated here are not visitable, Sunset Crater is of archeological interest because of the volcanic eruptions that took place between the growing seasons of A.D. 1064 and 1065. Indians who followed the Sinagua way of life, living in pithouses in the vicinity of the volcano, moved to the southern margin of the cinder fall where they resumed farming. A little later a group of the Sinagua people moved to the cinder-covered Wupatki area and began farming there. The stone pueblos they built can be seen in Wupatki National Monument.

Artifacts made by the Salado people at Tonto National Monument. National Park Service photo.

THREE TURKEY RUIN TRIBAL PARK

From Chinle, at the edge of Canyon de Chelly National Monument, drive south 5 miles on Arizona 7 to directional sign, then 5 miles west on a primitive road to the Three Turkey Overlook. Open free, daily, except in bad weather.

This Anasazi site was occupied for only a little more than 50 years, apparently by people who came from Mesa Verde at about the time that area was being abandoned. The ruin can be viewed from the overlook and is accessible by a hiking trail into the canyon.

TONTO NATIONAL MONUMENT

From Globe drive 4 miles west on US 60, then 28 miles northwest on Arizona 88 to the monument entrance, then 1 mile to the Visitor Center. Mail address: Box 707, Roosevelt, AZ 85545. Phone: 602/467-2241. Open daily. Closed certain holidays. Admission charged. Camping nearby.

Visits to the Upper Ruin can be made only by guided tours, October–April, which must be arranged four days in advance.

On a self-guided tour to the Lower Ruin, which closes at 5:20 p.m. in summer and at 4:20 p.m. in winter, visitors follow a trail to cliff dwellings in which people lived 600 years ago. These ruins are particularly interesting for the richness of the details they have revealed about the lives of those who inhabited them.

The Story. At about A.D. 1100, farming people from the north and east moved into Tonto Basin—the area around Tonto Creek, which flows into the Salt River. Here they lived peacefully with the Hohokam, who already farmed on irrigated land along the stream. The newcomers and the old-timers quickly learned from each other, and the result was vigorous development. Pottery-making flourished. Expert weavers made cloth in intricate patterns, with fancy designs of colored stripes, and they used some dyes not found anywhere else.

For some reason, perhaps for defense, some of the people moved from

These dwellings in Tonto National
Monument were built in the middle
of the fourteenth century. National
Park Service photos.

Mimbres women painted these fish on pottery, although their desert home was far from any fish-producing body of water. Redrawn from Gladwin.

A "mobile" painted on a pot by a Mimbres woman in southern Arizona. Redrawn from Gladwin.

the lower land about the year 1300. They built dwellings in several caves in the cliff, using chunks of very hard rock, which they embedded in mortar of adobe clay. The outside was then plastered with clay to give a smooth finish. The cliff villages were lived in for only about 50 years, and then inhabitants moved away—no one knows where or why.

The unique lifeway of these people, and especially their pottery style, extended over much of the valley of the Salt River, and so archeologists have called them the Salado (sah-LAH-doh), the Spanish word for salty.

The Museum. At the Visitor Center can be seen many of the things that the Salado people made and used—pottery, beautiful cloth, tools, and weapons.

Special Feature. Those who lived here apparently remodeled their houses during cold weather, when farming was over. In several places the wet clay they used to plaster the walls shows clear imprints, at shoulder height, of the fabrics in clothes worn for warmth.

TOPOC MAZE
National Register of Historic Places

From Needles, in California, drive south on Interstate 40 to Park Moabi exit, then west one half mile on a gravel road to its end. There turn left on a second gravel road; at the Y keep left, then left again 200 yards to a parking lot.

This curious huge artifact consists of parallel rows of gravel, which prehistoric people scraped into heaps a few inches high, forming paths three to four feet apart. Some of the paths cross each other although they do not form a real maze. They originally covered about 18 acres, almost half of which have been vandalized.

The meaning of the lines can only be guessed. Some archeologists think they may have been made by people who shared the later Mojave Indian belief in the need for running along certain paths as part of a purification rite.

TUSAYAN RUIN
(See Grand Canyon National Park)

At Tuzigoot National Monument the ancient town covered a ridge that rose 120 feet above the floor of the Verde Valley. In places the building was two stories high. National Park Service photo by Paul V. Long, Jr.

TUZIGOOT NATIONAL MONUMENT
(TOO-zee-goot)

From Flagstaff drive 49 miles southwest on US 89A to Cottonwood, then 3 miles northwest to Monument entrance. Mail address: P.O. Box 68, Clarkdale, AZ 86324. Phone: 602/634-5564. Open daily. Admission charged.

Visitors follow a trail on a self-guided tour of this prehistoric hilltop town, which once consisted of nearly a hundred rooms.

The Story. The earliest settlers of Tuzigoot were related to the Hohokam farmers, who lived more than a thousand years ago near Phoenix. Later, about A.D. 1125, they were joined by people called Sinagua, who also settled at Montezuma Castle. The newcomers, and others who arrived later, built a village of stone houses along a ridge, with a square, two-story structure on the hilltop. The village flourished and grew until the 1400s, when for some unknown reason it was abandoned. Perhaps there was an epidemic, or the land may have ceased to

be productive. Archeologists think that some of the people migrated northward, because modern Hopi and Zuni legends say that some of their families came from the neighborhood of Tuzigoot.

The Museum. Here are displays of artifacts recovered during the excavation of the site.

The Name. Tuzigoot comes from a modern Apache word meaning "crooked water," referring to Peck's Lake, an oxbow lake caused by a meander in the nearby Verde River, which winds back and forth through the valley.

UNIVERSITY OF ARIZONA, ARIZONA STATE MUSEUM

On the campus, N. Park Ave. at University Blvd., Tucson, AZ 85721. Phone: 602/621-6281. Open free, Monday–Saturday; afternoon Sunday. Closed certain holidays.

This remarkable museum has exhibits that illuminate the life of Paleo-Indian hunters of 10,000 years ago and of the Hohokam and Mogollon cul-

On the ridge in the distance stand the ruins of a village in what is now Tuzigoot National Monument. National Park Service photo by Parker Hamilton.

tures dating from A.D. 1 to 1450. Displays include artifacts from Ventana Cave, which was occupied for almost 10,000 years, and from the Naco and Lehner Paleo sites.

The latter site was discovered when a rancher in the San Pedro Valley saw some large bones exposed in an arroyo. He reported the find to Emil Haury of the Arizona State Museum. Haury excavated and found evidence that hunters, more than 10,000 years ago, killed nine mammoths and roasted some of the meat nearby.

Artifacts from the Hohokam site at Snaketown give insight into the subsistence living, clothing, housing and daily life of these desert farmers. Another exhibit explores the use of rock shelters by human beings and features a life-size replica of a Mogollon cliff dwelling.

In another exhibit are mammoth bones and the tools of mammoth hunters exactly as archeologists found them in the earth.

Temporary exhibits feature special collections and research topics by members of the museum staff.

The museum also has a rich collection of materials from the Native American tribes that have lived in Arizona in historic times.

WALNUT CANYON NATIONAL MONUMENT

From Flagstaff drive 7.5 miles east on Interstate 40 to directional sign, then 3 miles southeast to Visitor Center. Mail address: Walnut Canyon Rd., Flagstaff, AZ 86004-9705. Phone: 602/526-0571 or 3367. Open daily. Closed certain holidays. Admission charged.

Visitors can take a self-guided tour along the rim of Walnut Canyon, then down to 25 cliff-dwelling rooms. From the trail about 100 other dwellings can be seen.

The Story. Very few people seem to have lived in this beautiful spot before the eruption in A.D. 1065 of Sunset Crater, a volcano about 15 miles to the north, near present-day Wupatki National Monument. Fifty or sixty years later groups of farmers called Sinagua moved into Walnut Canyon and built

their stone houses in recesses in the cliffs. Here they lived for almost 200 years. Then, like their neighbors in this part of Arizona, they abandoned their homes and moved elsewhere. Possibly some of their descendants are now members of Pueblo Indian groups.

Special Feature. In addition to the cliff house, visitors can see a pithouse, which shows a way of life that was common before people began to build multiple dwellings of stone in the canyon.

Wupatki. About 20 years after the eruption of a nearby volcano, now called Sunset Crater, Sinagua people built a village here and began to plant crops in soil that was mulched by volcanic ash. National Park Service photo by George A. Grant.

WALPI
(WAHL-pee)

From Keams Canyon on Arizona 264 drive 11 miles west, then north at directional sign. Mail address: Hopi Indian Agency, Keams Canyon, AZ 86034. Phone: 602/738-2228. Camping nearby.

Walpi is a Hopi Indian village, built on top of a high mesa. Some of the dwellings go back at least to 1680, and remains of prehistoric houses lie on the slopes below the present village. They are not open to exploration by visitors. No photographing is allowed in Walpi, and visitors are requested not to enter private homes.

Special Feature. Visitors may see at Walpi the Snake Dance ceremony, in the late summer of odd-numbered years. This ceremony had its origin in prehistoric times. Information about the exact date and the place where the dance is held in even-numbered years may be obtained at the Hopi Indian Agency, Keams Canyon, or at Tribal Headquarters, Kykotsmovi.

WUPATKI NATIONAL MONUMENT
(woo-POT-key)

From Flagstaff drive 32 miles north on US 89 to the Wupatki-Sunset Crater Loop Rd. entrance, then 14 miles east to the Vistor Center. Mail address: Wupatki and Sunset Crater National Monuments, 2717 N. Steves Blvd., Flagstaff, AZ 86004. Phone: 602/427-7040. Open daily, all year. Closed certain holidays. Admission charged. Camping in a nearby Forest Service campground, May–Sept.

There are about 800 ruins in the monument, nearly 100 of them within an area of one square mile. Visitors can take self-guided tours to the largest site, Wupatki, which has been partially excavated, and to one called the Citadel, which has not been excavated. At Wupatki archeologists have uncovered an ancient ball court, one of several in northern Arizona.

The Story. In A.D. 1064 a great volcano exploded and formed what is now called Sunset Crater. Volcanic cinders spread over 800 square miles. Instead

Ball Courts

The Spanish who came to Mexico and Central America in the sixteenth century saw Indians playing a game with a solid rubber ball that weighed about five pounds. The players, divided into teams, tried to keep the ball in the air and scored points by bouncing it off the sloping side walls of a specially built court. The biggest score in the game seems to have been made when a player bounced the ball through the hole in one of the doughnut-shaped stone rings that were fixed high in the wall on either side of the court. Players were forbidden to hit the ball with their hands or feet. They could direct it only with blows from their hips or knees or elbows. Apparently the game had ceremonial significance, although it is not known exactly what this was.

In Arizona archeologists have found in Hohokam settlements a number of large areas of hard-packed earth with sloping side walls which somewhat resemble the ball courts of Mexico and Central America. Excavation near one of the Arizona courts turned up a large ball similar to those used in Mexico.

of devastating the land, the cinders formed a kind of mulch, which may have conserved moisture, kept the ground warm, and so somewhat prolonged the growing season. This may have encouraged the Sinagua people to move into the area north of the volcano. Increased rainfall probably helped to make their new farms successful.

At one time archeologists thought that the Sinagua led a rush of Mogollon and Anasazi settlers to exploit this productive land. Artifacts and architecture characteristic of various peoples seemed to indicate that Wupatki became a sort of melting pot. Recent opinion, however, is that the Sinagua became great traders and that it was trade, not immigration that accounts for the traits that had been thought to show a mixture in population. One structure, the idea for which was certainly imported, was the circular ball court of the kind usually found much farther south and originally brought from Mexico.

People remained at Wupatki for about 150 years. Perhaps by then the land was exhausted. For whatever rea-son, the last inhabitants left about A.D. 1225.

The Museum. Exhibits here show methods that prehistoric Indians used in making artifacts.

The Name. Wupatki, a Hopi Indian word, means "tall house." It refers to a multi-story dwelling which, during the 1100s, had more than 100 rooms, housing perhaps 150 people.

Special Feature. Eighteen miles from Wupatki National Monument headquarters, by the Loop Road, is Sunset Crater National Monument. Here may be seen the dead mouth of the volcano that spewed out cinders to cover the surrounding area.

Pot Hound and Grave Robber

A rock hound is a collector of rocks and minerals and harms no one. A pot hound is a collector of pots and other prehistoric Indian artifacts and harms everyone. Usually a pot hound is a grave robber, because Native Americans often buried their honored dead with beautiful vessels as well as ornaments and tools. Whether or not graves are desecrated, the pot hunter is always a vandal, and a collector who buys artifacts from a pot hunter encourages vandalism which destroys forever information that may help us understand other human beings.

Amateur archeologists rightly object to pot hunters, but amateurs and professionals are no better than vandals if they dig without keeping careful, complete records of everything they do and find. Each object, no matter how seemingly insignificant, that is encountered in the ground should be recorded fully, so that all relevant detail will be available when needed.

Collecting artifacts from the surface of privately owned land is not illegal if the landowner gives permission, but such collecting can be harmful from a scientific point of view. Clues on the surface may lead to important evidence beneath the surface. The best thing an amateur can do when he or she finds any ancient object anywhere is to notify a museum or the state archeologist, giving as much exact information as possible about what was found and where. Artifacts left in place can be useful. The same objects moved can be useless.

Pot hunting—grave robbing—on public land has been forbidden since 1906 by the federal Antiquities Act. In addition many states have had their own laws to protect cultural resources. In 1979 a new federal law with more teeth was passed. It is the Archeological Resources Protection Act, which provides that pot hunters can be imprisoned for up to ten years and fined up to $10,000. In the single year in which the law was passed, government agencies estimated that more damage was done to ancient sites than had been done in the preceding 600 years. In spite of the law, and successful prosecutions under it, vandalism still continues.

Another recent law affecting archeological material is the Native American Graves and Repatriation Act, passed in 1990. Under this act skeletal remains and religious objects must be returned to the tribes to whom they rightfully belong. This act has required changes in many museum exhibits and is a reflection of increased sensitivity to the concerns of Native Americans.

A. Some of the pots that came out of
excavations on Wetherill Mesa in
Mesa Verde National Park. National
Park Service photo by Fred Mang.
B. Mogollon people who lived in the
Mimbres Valley, in southwestern
New Mexico, decorated their pottery
imaginatively with figures of animals
and human beings. C. An Anasazi
woman made this bowl about 700
years ago. Original in the museum at
Mesa Verde National Park. D. An
unusual black and white jar found at
Mesa Verde. Original in the
Colorado History Museum in
Denver. E. A Mogollon pottery
canteen made in the Tularosa style in
Arizona about A.D. 1200. Original
in the Southwest Museum, Los
Angeles.

B

C

D

E

A

Classifying the Anasazi Cultures

The culture of the Anasazi people in the Southwest developed in rather clearly defined stages. You will often find these stages referred to according to what is called the Pecos Classification, a set of names agreed to at Pecos, NM in 1927. Here it is:

A.D. 1700 to the present	Pueblo V
A.D. 1300 to 1700	Pueblo IV
A.D. 1100 to 1300	Pueblo III
A.D. 800/850 to 1100	Pueblo II
A.D. 750 to 900	Pueblo I
A.D. 450 to 750	Basketmaker III
A.D. 1 to 500	Basketmaker II
pre-A.D. 1	Basketmaker I

Basketmaker mothers carried babies in cradles made of fiber. The child's head rested on the round pillow, and a pad of soft, shredded cedar bark served as a diaper. After a Mesa Verde photo by Faha.

Colorado
(southwestern)

For additional Colorado listings see Great Plains

ANASAZI HERITAGE CENTER

Three miles west of Dolores on Colorado 184. Mail address: 27501, Highway 184, Dolores, CO 81323. Phone: 303/882-4811. Open free, daily, April 15–October 31; call for schedule for the remainder of the year. Closed certain holidays.

This large museum was built by the Bureau of Land Management to house almost 2,000,000 artifacts that came from excavations called the Dolores Project that preceded the construction of nearby McPhee Dam and Reservoir. The exhibits reveal Anasazi history by tracing changes in technology, architecture and land use patterns. They also illlustrate farming methods, food preparation, crafts and trade. Hands-on exhibits give visitors a chance to weave and grind corn in the Anasazi way. Displays show the methods that archeologists use to gather information.

The Dolores Project employed 500 people to excavate the 120 sites that produced the materials to be seen here. It was the largest government-funded archeological project in U.S. history.

ANASAZI NATIONAL PARK

As this book went to press the Park Service was considering plans to create a large new national park northwest of Cortez to include a great number of sites in the area.

For information about how plans for this new park are progressing, inquire at the Cortez CU Center or at Mesa Verde National Park (see below).

CANYON PINTADO HISTORIC DISTRICT
National Register of Historic Places

From the junction of Colorado 64 and 139 near Rangeley, drive south 2 miles on Colorado 139. Mail address: Bureau of Land Management, P.O. Box 928, Meeker, CO 81641. Phone: 303/878-3601. Open free, all year. Camping.

In this canyon, which has been occupied for 11,000 years, are 30 examples of rock art left by Fremont people who lived here from A.D. 600 to 1300. The first Europeans to see this art were Fathers Dominguez and Escalante who traveled through the area in 1776.

CENTER OF SOUTHWEST STUDIES

Fort Lewis College, Durango, CO 81301. On the campus, third floor of the library. Phone: 303/247-7210. Open free, afternoons Monday–Friday. Closed certain holidays.

In a display area there are exhibits of Anasazi pottery and other artifacts, together with modern Indian rugs and baskets.

This museum also preserves a collection of ceramics from the Yellow Jacket area in southwestern Colorado.

CHIMNEY ROCK

Reached by an access road off Colorado 151 west of Pagosa Springs. Open free, during the summer, only to guided tours. The ruins are not accessible without a guide. Tours are conducted daily between May 15 and September 15 each year. Groups larger than 7 persons should make reservations; smaller groups may attend tours without prior notice. Visitors should contact the San Juan National Forest, Pagosa Ranger District, P.O. Box 310, Pagosa Springs, CO 81147 or phone: 303/264-2268 to make reservations and to confirm tour schedules. The number and timing of tours may vary during a season. The tour enters a protective peregrine falcon habitat closure on two half-mile trails. One trail is moderately challenging, the other is an easy walk. Wheelchair facilities are under construction: contact the Pagosa District for more information about barrier-free access.

Here, a thousand feet above the valley floor, on a ridge with a magnificent view in all directions, perhaps as many

as 500 Anasazi people lived between A.D. 925 and 1125. The population of neighboring related villages may have been 1500. Archeologists believe that a colony of male priests from Chaco Canyon, 90 miles away joined this community about A.D. 1076 and found wives among the resident villagers. After the colonists arrived, in the spring or fall of the year, construction was begun on a Chacoan Great House and kiva. The building was laid out carefully in an L shape, with the kiva to one side of a block of rooms. Tons of rock were then brought in to be chipped and fitted together in fine, even courses.

A great deal of archeological detective work recently done in the Southwest makes this Chimney Rock scenario likely. It is clear that the colonists came from Chaco Canyon, because the construction of new buildings at the site is typical of Chaco towns. The place was laid out according to a predetermined plan characteristic of Chaco, and the beautiful masonry was Chacoan, much finer than that of local buildings near by. The details of the kiva could only have been engineered by peo-

The Bureau of Land Management-Anasazi Heritage Center is located just downhill from Escalante Ruin, a 12th-century Anasazi site, and adjacent to McPhee Reservoir. Bureau of Reclamation photo by Joan Fleetman.

People sharing the Chaco culture built rooms and circular kivas a thousand feet above the surrounding valley here at Chimney Rock, in Colorado. Photo by Frank W. Eddy.

ple—most likely priests—who were familiar with religious architecture. The pottery that was found at the site gives evidence of intermarriage with local women. None of it was made in the Chacoan style. Since women in Pueblo societies were traditionally the potters, it is safe to assume that women did not accompany the colonists from Chaco.

The unusual, even improbable, location for the town, high above the valley and, during the summer months, a mile or more from the nearest drinking water, may have been chosen for religious reasons. Ample snow decreased the water problem in late fall and winter, and this leads to the idea that building must have been done in fall or spring, when water for making mud mortar and plaster did not have to be carried in jars uphill from valley streams. Additional evidence for the religious aspect of the prehistoric Chimney Rock settlement is a historic Taos Indian legend. The two spectacular pinnacles, or chimneys, which rise beside the site were supposedly dedicated to deities known as the Twin War Gods.

A recently discovered connection between the Chaco Great House and an astronomical phenomenon called the northern lunar standstill shows that Chimney Rock may have been an important Chaco ceremonial site. Every 18.6 years, the full moon rises exactly between the twin pinnacles of Chimney rock, as viewed from the Great House, and the dates of this striking moonrise coincide with the construction dates of the Great House: A.D. 1076 and 1094. Chaco priests and worshippers may have made pilgrimages from Chaco Canyon to visit Chimney Rock during these standstill years.

The Chimney Rock community was one of a number of outliers or colonies related to the large center in Chaco Canyon (see New Mexico listing). Among other outliers were the Salmon Ruin, in New Mexico, and the Dominguez and Escalante Ruins, in Colorado. The motivation for the colonies is still not fully understood. Some ar-

cheologists believe they were established to encourage production of resources for the center. Others think they may have served to relieve overpopulation at the center.

COLORADO NATIONAL MONUMENT

Four miles from Grand Junction via Hwy. 340 and Monument Road. Mail address: Fruita, CO 81521. Visitor Center open daily, all year. Admission charged in summer.

A panel in the Visitor Center gives information about the Fremont culture and displays some artifacts.

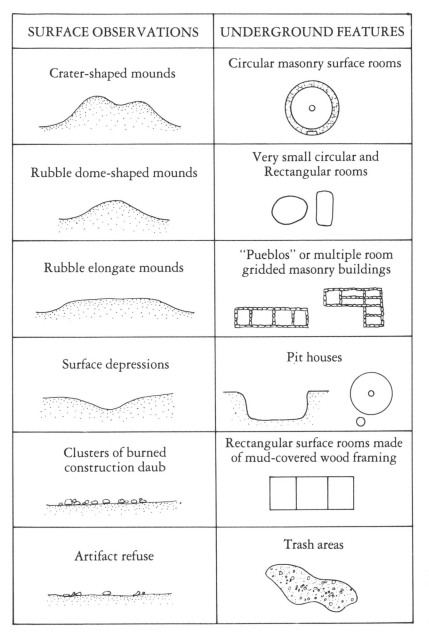

SURFACE OBSERVATIONS	UNDERGROUND FEATURES
Crater-shaped mounds	Circular masonry surface rooms
Rubble dome-shaped mounds	Very small circular and Rectangular rooms
Rubble elongate mounds	"Pueblos" or multiple room gridded masonry buildings
Surface depressions	Pit houses
Clusters of burned construction daub	Rectangular surface rooms made of mud-covered wood framing
Artifact refuse	Trash areas

Redrawn from *Archaeological Investigations at Chimney Rock Mesa: 1970–1972,* by Frank W. Eddy. Boulder, Colorado Archeological Society, 1977.

Surface Surveys

When archeologists walk over an area, they often find evidence that tells them what lies below the surface. This diagram shows (left) features of the kind found on the surface near Chimney Rock and (right) what lay hidden in the ground below.

Right, and opposite: Excavation and stabilization of the Great Kiva in the Escalante portion of Dominguez and Escalante Ruins.

THE CORTEZ CU CENTER

25 North Market, P.O. Box 1326, Cortez, CO 81321. Phone: 303/565-1151. Open free, daily during summer months and on a part time scheudle in other months.

The museum, with the cooperation of the University of Colorado and the Cortez community, has exhibits from the Anasazi Heritage Center, the Ute Mountain Ute Park and the Yellow Jacket site. It also has displays on the archeology that has been done by the University of Colorado.

Special Feature. Commercially operated tours to the many archeological sites in the area originate here. The tours include visits to any digs in progress. Professional guides at each site give talks.

CROW CANYON ARCHAEOLOGICAL CENTER

From Cortez drive north on US 666, then left on County Road L, then south on County Road 23—a total distance of four miles. Mail address: 23390 County Road K, Cortez, CO 81321. Phone: 303/565-8975. Open free, summer months.

This very active educational institution operates a variety of hands-on programs open to the public for various fees. One week-long program is designed for high school students who want to do actual excavating. Full information about the programs can be obtained by writing or phoning the Center. When excavation is in progress at an Anasazi site known as Sand Canyon Pueblo, visitors are invited to come and observe. There is a self-guided tour.

CURECANTI NATIONAL RECREATION AREA, NATIONAL PARK SERVICE

From Gunnison drive 16 miles west on US 50 to entrance and Visitor Center. Mail address: 102 Elk Creek, Gunnison, CO 81230. Phone: 303/641-2337, or 0406. Open free, daily, early June to end of September. Camping.

Surveys and excavation here have led to some unusual finds. Sites in the area

show continued re-occupation for an enormously long period—the earliest with a Carbon-14 date of 10,100 before the present, the most recent about A.D. 1500. Obviously the resources along the nearby banks of the Gunnison River (now partially flooded by a dam) brought people back time after time. But what were the special attractions of the place? Archeologists are not quite sure.

Another intriguing puzzle has been the discovery of several kinds of structure made of poles and mud—a method known as wattle and daub. These have been dated at the Archaic period (between 6000 and 4000 years ago), but exactly what kind of structure they were has not been determined.

At a site more than 200 miles north and east of Curecanti similar structures were unearthed in 1981 by salvage archeologists and dated at about 8000 years ago, amazingly early for wattle and daub.

Testing, excavation, and study of Curecanti will be ongoing, and visitors are welcome to watch the work. Interpretive displays in the Visitor Center give an idea of discoveries at the site, and some days of the week a guide will lead interpretive walks. For information about dates and hours of walks, phone the Visitor Center.

DINOSAUR NATIONAL MONUMENT

From Jensen, Utah, on US 40, drive north 7 miles on Utah 149 to Visitor Center. Mail address: P.O. Box 210, Dinosaur, CO 81610. Phone: 303/374-2216. Open daily, all year. Admission charged. Camping.

Prehistoric people may have been in this area as early as 11,000 years ago, although archeological excavation has revealed few details about them. Fremont people made their homes from 100 B.C. to A.D. 1200 along rivers and creeks, hunting, gathering and farming in the monument area. Their petroglyphs (rock carvings) and pictographs (rock paintings) may be seen in several places. The best and most accessible are east of the dinosaur quarry on a monument road. For information about their location, inquire at Dinosaur Quarry Visitor Center.

More recently, Ute Indians lived in one part of the monument area, Shoshone Indians in another, known as Browns Park. Descendants of the Utes now occupy a reservation nearby.

DOMINGUEZ AND ESCALANTE RUINS

From Dolores drive 3 miles west on Colorado 184 to the site entrance marker adjacent to the Anasazi Heritage Center. Mail address: 27501 Hwy. 184, Dolores, CO 81323. Phone: 303/882-4811. Open free, daily, all year. Closed certain holidays.

This Anasazi site intrigues archeologists because it seems to have been occupied simultaneously by people from two different cultural backgrounds. On top of a hill are the ruins, called Escalante, of a large, pre-planned village, built in the style of Chaco Canyon, in New Mexico. Dominguez, downhill from Escalante, is one of half a dozen small, rather simple sites in the neighborhood, built in the tradition of Mesa Verde, which is much closer by.

Shifting sands at Great Sand Dunes National Monument sometimes reveal artifacts and campsites buried as long as 10,000 years ago. National Park Service photo by Robert Haugen.

Some archeologists believe that colonists from Chaco came here as traders in the late eleventh century and built their four-sided village of large masonry rooms surrounding a ceremonial kiva, with another kiva just outside the walls. Since few articles of trade were discovered in the excavation, another theory is that the Chacoans may have moved here because the population had increased too much at home.

Dominguez Ruin consists of a kiva and four rooms, one of which was small and not very well constructed. These dwellings seem to have been occupied by no more than two or three families. Yet excavation of one room in the modest site revealed the burial of a woman, together with grave goods of extraordinary quality and quantity. Among other things were three elaborate pendants, turquoise and shell mosaics, ceramic vessels, and thousands of beads made from turquoise, jet, and shell. Burials of this sort were not characteristic of Mesa Verde people. Is it possible that a woman of wealth and high rank from Escalante was buried at more humble Dominguez? If so,

what were the other relationships between the two different peoples? Perhaps the Chacoans brought to the area more elaborate religious and social patterns than the indigenous people were used to, and they in turn provided the Chacoans with surplus food or other things that could have been taken back to Chaco Canyon to supply the people there.

The large-scale interaction—here and elsewhere in the region—between Mesa Verde people and those of Chaco Canyon is still not entirely clear, and archeologists hope that the study of Dominguez and Escalante Ruins will lead to solving some of the puzzles.

The Name. In 1776 two Franciscan explorers, Father Dominguez and Father Escalante, set up camp near the present town of Dolores. Dominguez was ill, and while he rested Escalante climbed a hill and came upon the ruin which, he said, "was . . . of the same form as those of the Indians of New Mexico." The site was later named for him, and in 1976 the neighboring site was named for his partner, Dominguez.

GREAT SAND DUNES NATIONAL MONUMENT

From Alamosa drive 14 miles north on Colorado 17, then 18 miles east on 6 Mile Lane to Visitor Center. Mail address: Great Sand Dunes National Monument, Mosca, CO 81146. Phone: 719/378-2312. Open at all times. Admission charged. Camping.

People have been leaving tools and weapons around the Sand Dunes for 10,000 years. Two archeological sites in the area have revealed the campgrounds of people who hunted giant bison, which are now extinct. Bones of the animals have been excavated together with special spear points that Paleo-Indians used when they hunted these huge animals. Points of this kind were first found near Folsom, New Mexico, and are called Folsom points.

Later, hunters, belonging to various groups including some Pueblo Indians, followed great herds of bison, antelope, deer and elk which roamed the San Luis Valley near the Sand Dunes. Archeologists have discovered indications that whole families traveled along definite routes on these

The painted kiva, Lowry Pueblo Ruins, as it once appeared.

hunting expeditions from the south into the valley.

Special Feature. Winds blowing across the San Luis Valley for thousands of years deposited sand at the foot of the mountains along the valley's eastern side, forming some of the world's highest dunes. Hiking is allowed on the dunes, which shift constantly and from time to time uncover a spot where Indians once lived and left artifacts. Visitors may look at but not loot such sites.

One of the authors of this book has written a mystery-adventure story for young readers that tells of the discovery of an archeological site here. The book *Sand Dune Pony* by Troy Nesbit (pseud.) is available at Monument headquarters.

HOVENWEEP NATIONAL MONUMENT
(*See Utah*)

LOWRY PUEBLO RUINS

From Cortez drive north 18 miles on US 666 to Pleasant View, then 9 miles west on a gravel road. Mail address: Bureau of Land Management, Federal Building, 701 Camino Del Rio, Durango, CO 81301. Phone: 303/247-4082. Open free, at all times.

About A.D. 850, possibly earlier, people began to garden at this site. Then for some reason the village was abandoned. Around 1090 it was reoccupied, and eventually it grew to be a community of 40 rooms, in part three stories high, with eight small kivas in addition to a great kiva. In the next 30 years villagers repeatedly altered, rebuilt and added to their dwellings. They filled old rooms with trash and constructed new ones adjoining. The last remodeling was done by masons whose stonework was different from that of earlier builders. Possibly they were newcomers from Chaco Canyon. Soon they, too, deserted the pueblo for what reason archeologists have not determined. People may have left because the land was not able to support the increased population. They seem to have moved without pressure from hostile invaders or from any catastrophe such as fire or drought.

Special Feature. During their first 20 years at the site, villagers built a kiva with a plastered wall on which they painted designs. At least four subsequent coats of plaster were added and decorated. Later this ceremonial room was filled in and a new one built on top of it. Archeologists discovered the painted kiva in the course of excavating the ruins, and the Bureau of Land Management, which administers the site, has built a shelter over it to protect the paintings while continuing to allow visitors to observe them. Despite (or perhaps because of) several efforts to preserve the mural in the Painted Kiva, it is almost totally gone. Only about 6 square inches of the pattern remain.

Cliff Palace, in Mesa Verde National Park, seen from about the place where two cowboys first saw it in 1888. National Park Service photo by Leland J. Abel.

Richard Wetherill (third from right in background), discoverer of Cliff Palace in Mesa Verde, sometimes conducted tourists into the area. Here he rests with some of them in Cliff Palace. National Park Service photo.

Before: When archeologists began excavation in Long House, on Wetherill Mesa, this is what it looked like. *After:* As Long House appears now, cleared of debris, walls stabilized. National Park Service photo.

MESA VERDE NATIONAL PARK
(MAY-suh VER-day)
A World Heritage Site

Midway between Cortez and Mancos on US 160 turn south to park entrance, then drive 21 miles on the park road to Headquarters and museums. Mail address: National Park Service, Mesa Verde National Park, CO 81330. Phone: 303/529-4461 or 4475. Open all year. Admission charged at park entrance. Camping, May 1 through Oct. 14, within the park, 5 miles from entrance. *Note:* The hours for tours, museum, and other visitor services are subject to change. For the latest information consult Park Headquarters.

Mesa Verde is really a huge outdoor archeological museum, which contains many different sites. The park occupies a stretch of high tableland, or mesa, which is cut by deep canyons with steep cliff walls. In many of the canyons prehistoric people found alcoves and rock shelters, and there they built some of the most beautiful and interesting villages to be found in the Southwest. On the mesa top other ruins can be visited. Because there is such

a large number of visitable sites, each with its own special interest, each will be discussed separately in the following pages. All, however, share the same general history.

The Story. At about the beginning of the fifth century A.D., people started to cultivate small gardens in the semi-arid Mesa Verde area. For 800 years they lived here, improving their farming techniques, eventually building dams and storage ponds and irrigation systems. Through one stage after another they developed a special style of architecture, and their pottery took on a beauty and quality that distinguished it from other pottery made in the Southwest in prehistoric times. Now and then the women, who did the work of shaping and decorating pots, adopted new ideas or fads, and these changes in fashion were often very marked. As a result archeologists have been able to use pottery types as an aid in determining the dates of certain events in the region.

Mesa Verde was one of the three regions where Anasazi culture reached a very high point before A.D. 1276. (The others were Chaco Canyon and

One of the striking architectural features of Cliff Palace, in Mesa Verde National Park, is the square tower with its t-shaped doorway in the fourth story. National Park Service photo by Fred Mang.

Kayenta.) The year 1276 was important. At about that date people began to abandon the mesas and the canyons where they had been living. Experts disagree on the reasons for the wholesale migration away from this ancient homeland. Some say that a 23-year-long drought set in; others believe raiders began to attack the villages, seeking the food stored there. Possibly the Mesa Verde people began to have quarrels among themselves and to develop rival factions. They may have moved to other regions because of a breakdown in the general social structure on the mesa.

For whatever reason, everyone did move away over 600 years ago, and what you see now is the evidence of achievement in a far from lush environment, over a period of eight centuries. For glimpses of the life led by descendants of the Mesa Verde people, visitors can go to present-day pueblos along the Rio Grande River and to the Hopi villages on the Hopi mesas. It was in these areas that the emigrants made their homes after they left Mesa Verde.

For a clear and detailed picture of Mesa Verde life at each of its stages, visitors should start at the museum in Park Headquarters.

The Museum. Here well-arranged displays give an orderly and illuminating introduction to prehistoric life in the Mesa Verde area. Exhibits lead the visitor on a journey through time, beginning with the days when Basketmaker women ground corn kernels into usable cornmeal by rubbing them between a small stone called a mano and a large stone called a metate. For cooking, these women used baskets in special ways. Corn or other dry food might be placed in a broad, flat basket along with heated rocks and stirred till it was parched. Some baskets were so finely woven that they could hold water. To cook food in such a vessel, a woman dropped hot rocks into the water to make it boil.

Later at Mesa Verde women continued to weave baskets, but they also learned to make pottery. Men hunted with bows and arrows instead of depending on spears and spear-throwers as their ancestors had done. They were adept at manipulating fibers—yucca fibers, dog hair, human hair—all of which they made into cord. Using the cord they wove sandals, bags, belts, and nets for catching game. Combining cord and strips of rabbit fur they wove blankets. (The magnificent dog-hair sashes in the museum were not found at Mesa Verde but in Obelisk Cave, in nearby northeast Arizona.)

By A.D. 600 people had begun to live in the kind of dwelling called a pithouse. This was a pit two or three feet deep, roofed over with branches and mud and entered by a ladder through a hole in the roof.

From this half-underground house, Anasazi architecture evolved in two different and fascinating ways, as an exhibit in the museum shows. Step by step, people learned to build homes of stone entirely above ground, but still with entrances through the roof. At the same time they dug deeper rooms entirely underground, and these they used as ceremonial chambers, now called kivas.

For a long time the stone houses clustered together in villages on the mesa top. Then people began to build in caves in the cliffs. For 75 or 100 years they lived in the cliff dwellings

Spruce Tree House is usually the first ruin seen by visitors to Mesa Verde National Park. National Park Service photo.

and tossed their trash down over the side. Refuse piled up, and very often it was entirely sheltered by the overhanging rock. In the dry Southwestern air the refuse did not decay, and the result was that archeologists found the trash heaps a mine of relics from the past. Many of their finds can be seen in the museum.

Spruce Tree House

Open daily, summer, self-guided trip; three guided tours per day, winter.

From the museum a good trail (walking time 45 minutes to one hour) leads to the Spruce Tree House ruin in the canyon nearby.

This is an unusually good place to examine a kiva, a type of ceremonial room which was hollowed out of the rock or dug into the earth. Such underground chambers were common at Anasazi sites in the Southwest.

Entrance to a kiva was by ladder through a hole in the courtyard floor. This entrance hole also allowed smoke to escape from the fire, which furnished heat and some light. Fresh air

came down into the chamber through a ventilator shaft, built at one side. In front of the opening to the shaft inside the kiva, an upright slab of rock deflected the incoming air and kept it from scattering ashes and smoke across the room. At intervals around the wall of the kiva stood masonry columns called pilasters.

The roof of a kiva rested on these pilasters, and it was ingeniously built. First, a row of logs, with their ends supported by the pilasters, was laid around the room. Then another row of logs was laid on top of this. In this second row the ends of each log were placed in the middle of the logs below them. On top of this second row another was similarly placed. The result of this cribbing was a dome-shaped structure. After the logs were all in place, they were covered with earth which was leveled off to serve as part of the courtyard floor.

In the kiva members of a clan or a society held their ceremonies. Here also they lounged and sometimes worked at their looms. Apparently it was the men and not the women who did the fine Mesa Verde weaving. In many

The archeologist at the left is using surveying instruments as he maps a site on Wetherill Mesa, in Mesa Verde National Park. Atop the tripod the photographer is recording with care every stage of the excavation of the site. National Park Service photo by Al Hayes.

places in the Anasazi Southwest there were also great kivas, each large enough to serve a whole community.

The history of the kiva seems to be something like the following. Early people lived in semi-subterranean pithouses. They may have conducted certain clan or society ceremonies in these dwellings. Or they may have had special large pithouses for community-wide ceremonies.

Then among the Anasazi the type of house changed. People began to build their dwellings entirely above ground. At the same time, following a conservative impulse, they continued to hold their ceremonies in the old-fashioned type of pithouse. Later apparently, they got the notion that if holding ceremonies partly underground was a good idea, it would be an even better idea to hold them in rooms that were all the way underground. So, fully subterranean kivas were built.

Ruins Road

(Two loops totaling 12 miles in length.) Open 8 a.m. to 8 p.m. in summer; closed in winter. If you follow this road, which runs along the mesa top, you will see ruins in the order in which development took place during the course of Mesa Verde history.

1. A pithouse built in the A.D. 500s.

2. Pithouses built in the A.D. 600s and 700s.

3. Pueblos built A.D. 850, 900, 950, 1000 and 1075.

4. Sun Point Pueblo, built A.D. 1100 to 1300 before people moved down into the canyon, taking with them material from the roofs and walls of their old homes to use in building new ones.

5. Sun temple, a large ceremonial center.

6. Cliff Palace. Open 9 a.m. to 7 p.m. summer; self-guided tours. Ranger-guided tours in spring and fall start at the Viewpoint on the road. (Inquire about hours at Park Headquarters.) Total walking distance, one-

Two kivas in the south courtyard in Mesa Verde's Balcony House. National Park Service photo by Jack E. Boucher.

quarter mile; time required, 45 minutes to one hour.

In this alcove and at other cliff dwellings during the 1200s, the arts of weaving and pottery making reached their peak. When Mesa Verde was abandoned, people left most of their possessions behind and the vacant dwellings were undisturbed by white settlers until one snowy winter day in 1888 when two cowboys, Richard Wetherill and Charles Mason, discovered the pueblo and named it Cliff Palace. Although many walls had tumbled and dust had filled some rooms, Wetherill and Mason found treasures of pottery and other artifacts in the ruins.

7. Viewpoints. Along Ruins Road are a number of turnouts from which it is possible to see structures of several kinds in the canyon walls. Some are small granaries, or storerooms. Others are pueblos of various sizes. One is a ceremonial site. These sites are not now accessible. To enter and leave many of them, the Mesa Verde people had to use small handholds and footholds they had chopped in the rock with hammerstones or axes made of harder rock.

8. Balcony House. Ranger-guided trips start at the Viewpoint sign in the Balcony House parking area on the hour and half-hour from 9 a.m. to 5 p.m. in summer. The total walking distance is one-half mile. The trip takes one hour.

In this village there is a second-story walkway or balcony, left intact from prehistoric times, which suggested the name for the ruin. Visitors may walk today through the courtyards, high above the canyon floor, protected by the original wall, which has been reinforced for safety. However, archeologists have found evidence in the ruins that cliff dwellings were not alway safe for those who lived in them. Skeletons of people whose bones had been broken have turned up in burials, as have crutches and splints.

9. Cedar Tree Tower. After leaving Balcony House, visitors should stop at Cedar Tree Tower on the drive back toward the park entrance. A road one-half mile long on the mesa top leads to this curious structure, which was

Before: This photograph, taken by one of the Wetherill brothers, probably in the early 1890s, shows Cliff Palace as it looked when Richard Wetherill and Charles Mason discovered it in 1888. Courtesy of Library, State Historical Society of Colorado.

After: Cliff Palace, in Mesa Verde National Park, as it looks today, after archeologists excavated and stabilized the structures. National Park Service photo by Jack E. Boucher.

used for ceremonial purposes. From the round tower an underground passage led to a circular kiva, which is also connected to a small niche under an overhanging rounded rock.

No one knows exactly what ceremonies went on here—or elsewhere in Mesa Verde. Archeologists do know that among the Anasazi there were people who practiced healing and magical arts. A kit used by one of them has been excavated and is on display in the museum. Archeologists also know how such kits are used in modern times, for they have studied the ceremonies of present-day Pueblo Indians, some of whom are descended from Mesa Verde people. It seems likely that ancient ceremonies resembled in some ways the modern Pueblo ceremonies. If so, they expressed the desire to have all the elements of the world working together in harmony.

10. Far View Ruins. Between the park entrance and the museum, a short side road leads to this group of ruins on the mesa top. The pueblos here were inhabited before people moved down into cliff dwellings.

Near the ruins is Mummy Lake, which can be reached by a short trail leading past the ruins of another small pueblo. Some archeologists think the dry basin called Mummy Lake was once an artificial reservoir. In ancient times a series of barriers or dams higher up on the mesa collected rainwater and channeled it into ditches which ultimately led into the reservoir. The water in the ditches was muddy, and to keep some of the silt out of the reservoir, the stone-age engineers who designed this facility worked out an ingenious device. They made a sharp curve near the end of the last ditch. The curve slowed the flow of water, and some of the silt settled out before the water entered the reservoir. From Mummy Lake a bypass ditch ran along the sloping mesa, carrying water several miles to the area where Park headquarters is now located.

Not all archeologists agree with this theory. Some believe that Mummy Lake was a dance plaza.

Mug House, one of the ruins on Wetherill Mesa, Mesa Verde National Park. National Park Service photo by Fred E. Mang, Jr.

Close to Far View Ruins another group of dwellings, with a round tower next to a kiva, has been excavated.

Wetherill Mesa

This area of the park, first opened to the public in 1973, is reached by private car from the Far View Visitor Center, then by minitrain to the top of the cliff. Guided tours are offered daily, June 9 through Labor Day. Inquire about hours at Park Headquarters.

Several ruins in the Wetherill Mesa area have been excavated. One of them, which has been prepared for visitors, is Long House. Built in an enormous rock shelter, it has 150 rooms and 21 kivas. Only Cliff Palace is larger.

Pictograph Point

Hikers who register with the ranger on duty in the park office near the Chapin Mesa Museum may follow a trail to a place where Mesa Verde people made paintings on rock surfaces.

Campfire Programs. The last stop on any day in Mesa Verde should be at the campfire program in the Morefield Campground. Nightly at 9:00, from early June through Labor Day, a ranger talks on some aspect of Mesa Verde life.

The Future. The Park Service has a large site at Yucca House National Monument about 10 miles northwest of Cortez, in Montezuma Valley below Mesa Verde. When funds become available this site will be developed and open to the public.

MUSEUM OF WESTERN COLORADO

258 South Fourth St., Grand Junction, CO 81501. Phone: 303/242-0971. Open free in winter Tuesday–Saturday; in summer also open Monday. Closed certain holidays.

In addition to historic Ute material, this museum has a collection of Mimbres pots and Fremont material from both Colorado and Utah.

PAINTED HAND PUEBLO

For directions to this back-country site that can be reached year round in dry weather by vehicle and a short hike, apply to Bureau of Land Management, San Juan Resources Area, 433 N. Main St., P.O. Box 7, Monticello, UT 84535. Phone: 801/587-2141.

In this 13th century Anasazi ruin is a masonry tower that may have been part of a prehistoric communication network that used fire by night and mica or pyrite mirrors by day for signalling.

RANGELY MUSEUM

434 S. Main St., P.O. Box 131, Rangely, CO 81648. Phone: 303/675-2612. Open free (donation appreciated), daily, June–August; Friday–Sunday, April–May, September–October; afternoon, Sunday. Camping nearby.

This museum, which has a small collection of local artifacts, sponsors tours to rock art sites, including those in the Canyon Pintado Historic Dis-

Top to bottom: Anasazi double mug. The original is in the Mesa Verde National Park museum. Mesa Verde women used the beveled edges of bone tools to scrape flesh from hides. Originals of these fleshers are in the Colorado Historical Museum, Denver. A black-on-white pottery ladle. A pot made in the shape of a duck by a woman at Mesa Verde, between A.D. 750 and A.D. 1100. The ladle and the pot are in the Mesa Verde National Park museum.

Left:
Archeologists photograph artifacts in situ, meaning in exactly the situation in which they are found. Here is a bowl, broken by a fallen rock, in a cave on Wetherill Mesa, Mesa Verde National Park. National Park Service photo.

Right:
The routes used by ancient Anasazi people at Mesa Verde as they entered and left alcoves have often weathered so much they are not usable today. Here an archeologist descends into an alcove on Wetherill Mesa by rope ladder. National Park Service photo by Al Hayes.

To aid in the study of prehistory, archeologists often put back together things that have been broken. On the left, a laboratory technician reconstructs a large, corrugated cooking pot found on Wetherill Mesa, in Mesa Verde National Park. On the right, the pot restored, with its yucca-fiber harness and sitting on its original doughnut-shaped rest. National Park Service photos by Fred Mang.

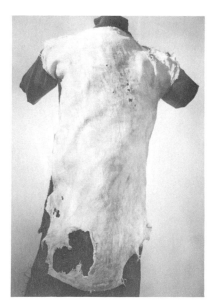 

Left:
This finely woven cotton shirt was found on a mummy in Mesa Verde National Park. National Park Service photo by Fred E. Mang, Jr.

Right:
A crew of University of Colorado students digging a test trench in the trash heap beside a Pueblo II ruin on the mesa top in Mesa Verde National Park in 1968.

Tree House Site in Johnson Canyon, Ute Mountain Tribal Park. Photo by Bob Powell; copyright by Bob Powell.

trict (see above). Some of the sites are of particular interest to those who seek information about archeoastronomy. The museum also sells a 24-minute video, *Rock Art of the Painted Canyon*.

SAND AND EAST ROCK CANYONS

Twelve miles west of Cortez, adjacent to County Road G, McElmo Road. Mail address: Bureau of Land Management, San Juan Resource Area, 433 N. Main St., P.O. Box 7, Monticello, UT 84535. Phone: 801/587-2141.

Here self-guided day hikes and back-country camping trips lead to small Anasazi ruins. Minimal interpretation is provided.

UTE MOUNTAIN TRIBAL PARK

Near Towaoc (TOY-akh), 15 miles south of Cortez on US 666. Mail address: Towaoc, CO 81334. Phone: 303/565-3751, ext. 282. Tours guided by members of the Ute Tribe leave daily at 9 a.m. from the Ute Mountain Tribal Pottery Building. Those taking the tours are asked to bring their own vehicles (with plenty of gas) and to come with lunch, water, sun screen, insect repellent, and sturdy hiking boots. Fees are charged according to the length of the tour taken. Day hikes, overnight camping and backpacking can be arranged. Some roads in the park are dirt. Others are gravel surfaced.

A back-country trip in this colorful, 125,000-acre park includes visits to many surface sites, cliff dwellings, and sites of rock art. Ancient settlements here were Anasazi, similar to those adjacent in Mesa Verde National Park.

At the tribally owned Ute Mountain Pottery it is possible not only to see finished pottery for sale, but to watch the entire process of manufacture.

Special Interest. As this book went to press, newspapers reported the discovery in this immense park of a Chaco-type roadway (see Chaco Culture National Historical Park entry below).

UTE MOUNTAIN UTE TRIBAL PARK MUSEUM

This museum, partially funded by the federal government, is scheduled to open in 1996 at the junction of US 666 and US 160 south of Cortez. In addition to exhibiting materials that illuminate Ute life of the historic period, the museum will display an extensive collection of prehistoric Anasazi perishable artifacts recovered from the Ute Mountain Tribal park. Some of this material has been turned over to the tribe by the University of Colorado Museum. For information phone 303/565-3751, ext. 282.

Prehistoric Cosmology

One of the intangibles that an archeologist cannot dig up is the world-view—the cosmology—of a vanished, preliterate people. However, it is sometimes possible to make an educated guess about how some ancient people saw their place in the universe. For instance, an archeologist in the Southwest can draw a number of conclusions when a small hole appears in the floor of an underground chamber that he or she calls a kiva. This hole, known as a sipapu, resembles holes found in kivas that are still in use today in Pueblo societies near the ancient ruins.

To the Hopi and other descendants of the Anasazi, a sipapu is a passageway from the underworld through which their ancestors emerged long ago. The world that people found when they came up from the underworld radiated out from a home village in six major directions. One direction was to the northeast where the sun rose on the horizon on the longest day of the year—the summer solstice. Another was to the northwest where the sun went down over the horizon on the same day. The southeasterly direction was marked by the point on the horizon over which the sun rose on the shortest day of the year, the winter solstice, and so on for the southwest. The fifth and sixth directions were straight up and straight down. With each direction certain symbols were associated—colors, animals, plants. Using these symbols, people created ceremonies, often focusing on the sun on which life depended.

From a little hole in the floor of an ancient pit, an archeologist can learn a great deal, and the same is true of other discoveries that resemble objects that have spiritual significance to Native Americans today.

Above: A jar used in kiva ceremonies. The design was painted with a brush of yucca fiber and paint made of boiled plant juices. Original is in the museum at Mesa Verde. *Below:* The ground plan of a kiva. After a drawing in the trail guide to Spruce Tree House, Mesa Verde.

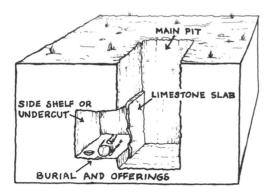

Diagram of an undercut grave at Montezuma Castle National Monument. After Schroeder and Hastings.

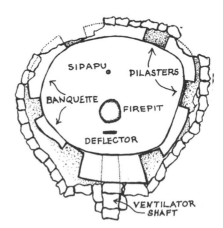

This kiva, at Casa Rinconada in Chaco Canyon, had a special entryway from an adjoining building. The woman in the foreground is standing in what was formerly a covered tunnel that led to an opening in the floor seen in the background. Photo by Julia M. Johnson; copyright by Julia M. Johnson.

Inside the Great Kiva at Aztec Ruins National Monument, after restoration. The t-shaped doorway in the center was popular in many Anasazi pueblos. The pits to the left and right may have been covered with boards and used as dance platforms or foot drums. National Park Service photo by George A. Grant.

New Mexico

ABÓ
(ah-BOH)
(Unit of Salinas Pueblo Missions National Monument)

Drive 9 miles west of Mountainair on US 60 to a directional sign, then .6 mile north on New Mexico 513. Mail address: Salinas Pueblo Missions National Monument, P.O. Box 496, Mountainair, NM 87036. Phone: 505/847-2400. Open free, daily, all year.

Here, in addition to a seventeenth-century Spanish mission, is an unexcavated prehistoric pueblo adjacent to an unexcavated historic pueblo. The people who lived here are recorded in historical documents as speaking the Tompiro language, which was also the language of Gran Quivira (see entry below). The Tompiro were related to the Piro who lived in the area near Socorro, New Mexico.

The pueblo, built on a pass leading into the Rio Grande valley, was a center for trade in such things as salt, hides and piñon nuts between the people of the Plains and those of the Acoma, Zuni and Santa Fe areas. After the arrival of the Spanish the prosperity of the pueblo finally declined and by 1678 the inhabitants had left to settle in other towns in the valley.

Formerly a New Mexico state monument, Abó has become part of the Salinas Pueblo Missions National Monument (see entry below). A self-guided tour leads through the site. Visitors should note that there is no drinking water at the Contact Station here.

ACOMA PUEBLO
(AH-koh-mah)

Between Albuquerque and Gallup leave Interstate 40 at Casa Blanca and drive south 14 miles on New Mexico 23. Mail address: Pueblo of Acoma, NM 87034. Phone: 505/252-1139. Open daily, all year. Closed for certain religious activities. Admission charged.

Acoma, often called Sky City, is on top of a high sandstone rock. About A.D. 900, people began to live on or near the site of the present village. Ever since A.D. 1075, the pueblo has been continuously occupied. This means that visitors at Acoma are seeing a lived-in prehistoric site, although most of the structures that are visible are obviously of recent origin.

Visitors should respect the privacy of the people of Acoma and should obtain permits from the governor of the pueblo if they wish to take photographs or do painting or drawing. The graveyards, the kivas and the waterholes are out of bounds to tourists.

AZTEC RUINS NATIONAL MONUMENT

From Farmington drive 14 miles east on US 550 to the directional marker in the town of Aztec, then one-half mile north on Ruins Road to monument entrance. Mail address: P.O. Box 640, Aztec, NM 87410. Phone: 505/ 334-6174.

This site was once a large Anasazi settlement, consisting of several multistoried Great Houses, Great Kivas, plazas and other architectural features. The West Ruin, excavated by archeologist Earl Morris, is open to the public. The sandstone masonry walls of its 500 rooms rose two and three stories high in places. A number of kivas—small round rooms—were constructed within the building itself, and in the plaza stood the Great Kiva. This has been reconstructed to show what it may have been like 800 years ago.

The design of the settlement, its fine masonry work and the Great Kiva were of the kind that originated in Chaco Canyon (see below). Aztec has long been considered by archeologists to be part of the Chaco system, which consisted of over 150 outlying settlements throughout the San Juan River basin. The West Ruin, built about A.D. 1110, first reflected the Chaco influence in architecture and pottery styles. By the mid 1100s the population diminished as the Chaco system waned. Tree-ring dating indicates a drought that caused stress throughout the region. By 1225, the population had grown again and distinct changes in architecture and pottery styles occurred. Archeologists identify this as the Mesa Verde phase of occupation at Aztec. The settlement flourished again until abandonment around A.D. 1300.

Recently, National Park Service archeologists have taken a new look at the area in and around the monument. Newly mapped sites show evidence that Aztec was a large-scale, pre-planned settlement and archeologists are beginning to reinterpret the area as "Chaco moved north," a major trade, ceremonial and administrative site that became a new center for the Anasazi. The Park Service is now involved in acquiring 290 additional acres to include these newly identified sites.

The Museum. Here are exhibits of pottery, baskets, various utensils, and tools made and used in the pueblo. Displays explain architectural features and show how the people once lived.

The Name. Early pioneers, who were much impressed by what they had heard about the Aztec Indians in Mexico, called this ruin Aztec. There is, however, no known connection between the inhabitants of this pueblo and the Aztecs, who lived in the Valley of Mexico.

Special Feature. One of the great archeologists of the Southwest, Earl Morris, who was born near Aztec, excavated this site and reconstructed the Great Kiva. When he began his careful work, he found evidence that the once-important ceremonial chamber had been used as a garbage dump before the pueblo was abandoned. Finally the roof caught fire and collapsed. Nevertheless, Morris was able to figure out details of construction and rebuild the chamber.

This screen made of reeds slid up and down over a doorway at Aztec Ruins National Monument. National Park Service photo by George A. Grant.

Opposite: The circular Great Kiva at Aztec Ruins National Monument. Although it had burned at some time long ago, enough remained so that archeologist Earl Morris could restore its interior and its outer wall. National Park Service photo.

Archeologists found this old ladder when they were excavating Aztec Ruins. National Park Service photo.

Talus House in Frijoles Canyon,
partially reconstructed, in front of
caves dug in soft rock. National Park
Service photo by A.H. White.

Artist Paul Coze's conception of life in one of the human-made caves in Frijoles Canyon. Photo by Glen Haynes, used by permission of Paul Coze.

BANDELIER NATIONAL MONUMENT
(ban-duh-LEER)

From Santa Fe drive 18 miles north on US 285 to Pojoaque (po-WAH-kay), then 17 miles west on NM 502 to NM 4, then 11 miles to monument entrance. It is 3 miles farther to the Visitor Center. Mail address: HCR 1, Box 1, Los Alamos, NM 87544. Phone: 505/672-3861. Open daily, all year except December 25. Admission charged. Camping.

This beautiful and unusual site at the bottom of a deep gorge stretches out along a little stream called Rito de los Frijoles (REE-toh day lohs free-HO-lays), Spanish for "bean creek." Along a one-mile trail visitors can see ruins of dwellings built near the cliff walls, and behind them man-made caves. In a separate section of the monument, 11 miles north of Frijoles Canyon, is an unexcavated ruin called Tsankawi (SANK-ah-WEE). Here visitors may take a self-guided tour on a two-mile trail.

The Story. People have lived in the Bandelier area for thousands of years. In Anasazi times the population increased a great deal, then at the end of the thirteenth century there was a great drought in much of the Southwest. Many Anasazi people moved from their homes, seeking water. Some of them found it here in the deep canyons that cut into the Pajarito (PAH-hah-REE-toh) Plateau. (Pajarito is Spanish for "little bird.") In the bottom of Frijoles Canyon farmers planted fields of corn, beans, and squash and built a large pueblo called Tyuonyi (chew-OHN-yee), which means "a meeting place." At the same time, some inhabitants dug storage rooms and also living quarters in the walls of the canyon. This was not too difficult because the rock is very soft—actually welded volcanic ash.

People continued to live in the canyon until the late 1500s. Then for some reason they left, as did others from various parts of the Pajarito Plateau. Today people who are probably their descendants live at the Cochiti and San

In Bandelier National Monument, three-story dwellings once stood at the base of this cliff, which is a soft rock called tuff. Builders could easily hollow it out to make storage rooms at the rear of their masonry houses. The small holes held the ends of beams. National Park Service photo by A. H. White.

Ruins of a large village called Tyuonyi in Bandelier National Monument.

The ladder leads to a cave that was a kiva in Bandelier National Monument. National Park Service photo by Fred E. Mang, Jr.

Prehistoric people, walking from place to place in Bandelier National Monument, wore down trails in the soft rock. National Park Service photo by Natt Dodge.

Ildefonso pueblos along the Rio
Grande.

The Museum. A slide program at the
museum in the Visitor Center interprets life in the canyon in ancient times.
Exhibits show the arts and crafts of the
people who lived there.

The Name. The first anthropologist
who came west to make a study of sites
in New Mexico was Adolph Bandelier.
In the late nineteenth century he walked
thousands of miles over roadless areas
of the state, learning Indian languages, often sleeping on the ground
without a blanket, sometimes eating
only the parched corn that was a food
of the Indians among whom he lived.
One of Bandelier's discoveries was the
prehistoric settlement in Frijoles Canyon. To explain what he thought life
must have been like in this spot he
wrote a novel, *The Delight Makers,*
which is still very readable and informative. Because of his important
services to archeology and his particular connection with Frijoles Canyon,
the national monument was named in
his honor.

Special Feature. Ninety percent of
Bandelier National Monument is a
wilderness in which roads will never
be built. There are more than 70 miles
of trails. Backpacking, with a permit,
can be arranged at the visitor center.
A recent survey found that there may
be as many as 4,000 sites in the monument.

BLACKWATER DRAW, BLACKWATER DRAW MUSEUM

Midway betwen Clovis and Portales on
US 70. Mail address: ENMU Station
9, Portales, NM 88130. Phone: 505/
562-2254. The museum is open Mon-
day–Saturday, afternoon Sunday from
Memorial Day to Labor Day; Tuesday–
Saturday and afternoon Sunday the rest
of the year. The site is open Monday–
Saturday, Memorial Day–Labor Day;
Saturday and afternoon Sunday from
Labor Day–October, and March 1–
Memorial Day. Closed November–
February. Admission charged: admits
visitors to both the museum and the
site.

This alcove lies at the end of an arduous trail in Bandelier National
Monument. Across the back of the alcove are colored paintings, left there in
prehistoric times. National Park Service photo.

Indians used cooking pits like this in both prehistoric and historic times. Hundreds of these pits are scattered throughout Carlsbad Caverns National Park. National Park Service photo.

This site was discovered by C. W. Anderson and George Roberts, amateur archeologists, at the time when professional archeologists were just realizing that people had been in America for many thousands of years. On the surface, amid old sand dunes, Anderson and Roberts found some distinctive projectile points, together with mammoth bones. Then in August of 1932, Anderson met a professional archeologist, Edgar B. Howard, in Carlsbad, New Mexico. He showed Howard the points and told him about the bones. Howard immediately went to the site. He was much interested in what he saw, and scientific excavation soon began at Blackwater Draw. The distinctive points found there have been called Clovis points after the nearby town.

Hunters who used spear points of the Clovis type roamed widely about 11,000 years ago. Traces of their camps have been found in other parts of the United States as well as at the dig in Blackwater Draw.

Re-examination of a mammoth tusk found in an early excavation here produced evidence that the tusk had been cut off with the same technique used in working ivory in the Upper Paleolithic in Eurasia.

CAPULIN VOLCANO NATIONAL MONUMENT

From Capulin drive 3 miles north on New Mexico 325 to the Visitor Center which is open free, daily, all year. Closed certain holidays. Admission to the monument charged. Mail address: Capulin, NM 88414. Phone: 505/278-2201.

The archeological display in the Visitor Center relates to the Folsom culture. On exhibit are reproductions of Folsom points.

On the road up Capulin Mountain in the monument, there is a distant view of the country around the Folsom site, where artifacts of prehistoric people were first found associated with fossil bones of extinct animals. This site, preserved as Folsom Man State Monument, is unmarked and not accessible to the public.

Archeologists carefully record pictographs in Painted Grotto, in Carlsbad Caverns National Park. National Park Service photo.

CARLSBAD CAVERNS NATIONAL PARK

From Carlsbad drive 18 miles south on US 62, then 7 miles west on park road to the Visitor Center. Mail address: 3225 National Parks Highway, Carlsbad, NM 88220. Phone: 505/785-2232. Open daily, all year except December 25. Admission to the park is free; fees are charged for tours of the caverns. Camping outside park.

Prehistoric Indians apparently never ventured far into Carlsbad Caverns, although they did camp near the cave entrance. They made black and red paintings on the rock wall of the entrance, and they prepared some of their foods in rock-lined cooking pits. Many such pits have been found in the area. Some were constructed later by Apache Indians.

Along the park road in Walnut Canyon visitors may take a self-guided tour, which follows an ethnobotanical trail that identifies plants and the uses to which they were put by Indians of the area. There is also a primitive self-guided trail to Goat Cave.

In the Slaughter Canyon area of the park is Painted Grotto, a pictograph site. Permission to visit this site must be obtained from the superintendent at Park Headquarters.

CASAMERO RUINS

From Grants drive 20 miles west on Interstate 40 to Prewitt exit, then 1 mile east on US 66, then north on county road for about 4.5 miles toward a large electric generating plant. Mail address: Bureau of Land Management, 900 La Plata Highway, Caller Service 4104, Farmington, NM 87499-4104. Phone: 505/325-3581. Open free, at all times.

This site was excavated in the course of salvage archeology conducted at the time the generating plant was being planned. The beautifully made masonry walls and the remains of a great kiva identify it as one of the outlying townships that were connected with Chaco Canyon in the mid-eleventh century (see Chaco Canyon entry). The kiva—about 70 feet in diameter—is one of the largest known. A number of interpretive signs have been put up by the Bureau of Land Management, which administers the ruins.

Three examples of the beautiful and distinctive pottery made by the Anasazi people who once inhabited Chaco Canyon. National Park Service photo.

CHACO CULTURE NATIONAL HISTORICAL PARK
(CHAH-koh)
A World Heritage Site

From US 64 at Bloomfield drive south 28 miles on New Mexico 44, then at Blanco Trading Post take unpaved New Mexico 57, 30 miles to the Visitor Center. Or from Interstate 40 at Thoreau drive north 44 miles on paved New Mexico 57, past Crownpoint, then 20 miles on unpaved New Mexico 57 to the Historical Park. Before leaving Blanco Trading Post or Crownpoint check the condition of the unpaved road ahead. It is sometimes impassable after a rain. Mail address: Star Route 4, Box 6500, Bloomfield, NM 87413. Phone: 505/988-6727 or 6716. Open daily, all year. Admission charged. Camping: water is available but no other supplies.

Here, far from any present-day town, are a dozen large pueblos and over 3,500 smaller sites, the spectacular ruins of a major Anasazi culture center. Easy trails from the main road lead to a number of the most important sites,

and there are self-guided tours at those which have been named Pueblo Bonito, Chetro Ketl, Casa Rinconada and Pueblo Del Arroyo. In the summer, park rangers conduct guided tours through a number of sites, as staffing permits, and there are campfire programs from about Memorial Day to about Labor Day.

Any visit to Chaco Canyon should begin at the Visitor Center, where exhibits in the museum tell the story of human life here. Dioramas and displays help to explain the theories about how people could have prospered in a land that seems dry and desolate.

The Story. The 800 rooms of Pueblo Bonito, a planned, multistory village built in the form of a huge D around a courtyard, were constructed over the course of 300 years. In this pueblo, and in others in the canyon, the art of stonemasonry reached its highest development in the Southwest. Great stretches of wall made from precisely cut and shaped stone remain standing today.

In Chaco Canyon, as elsewhere in the Southwest, a long history of de-

Left:
In the Southwest archeologists find countless potsherds. These broken bits of pottery usually tell who lived at a certain place and even when they lived there. These sherds are all from Chaco Culture National Historical Park. National Park Service photo.

Right:
Stone tools left these marks at the base of a cliff in Chaco Canyon when they were sharpened on a slab of softer sandstone. National Park Service photo by George Grant.

The Great Kiva, Chetro Ketl, Chaco Canyon, after excavation and stabilization. This large ceremonial chamber, once roofed, served a whole community; small kivas were used by local groups. National Park Service photo by George A. Grant.

Different masons worked to build
this high building. The walls show
four types of stonework, ending with
the most painstaking and beautiful
in the top story. National Park
Service photo by George A. Grant.

After building these walls, masons
in Chaco Canyon covered their
elegant stonework with a coat of
plaster. National Park Service photo.

A wall and door with the ends of three original beams still in place, Chaco Canyon. National Park Service photo by Fred E. Mang, Jr.

velopment lay behind great achievements. It began in the canyon with the Basketmaker people, who by A.D. 400 were building dwellings of the kind called pithouses. They were farmers and craftsmen, quick to adopt new ideas from neighbors or strangers.

Apparently the villages in the canyon were hospitable to outsiders. Groups from other parts of the Southwest may have come in seasonally. By the eleventh century A.D. Chaco had become an important center of activities, the exact nature of which archeologists are still debating. It certainly excelled in producing for trade great quantities of elegant turquoise beads, ornaments and mosaics. Some of the many rooms in the big pueblos may have been for storage of grain, dried meat, and edible wild plant foods. Possibly an exchange system with other communities provided redistribution of all these supplies in times of drought or crop failure.

Traffic to and from the large settlements in the canyon flowed along 300 miles of roads that linked outlying villages with each other and with the center. Some led to distant sources of supply, even toward Mexico, a source of copper bells, macaws and other exotic things.

Although Chacoans had no burden-carrying animals or wheeled vehicles, they put enormous collective effort into building roads that ran in straight lines uphill and down, across ramps and on stairways where necessary. Many were almost 30 feet wide, excavated in places as deep as 4 or 5 feet to bedrock.

At intervals, adjoining their roads, the Chacoans put up buildings—some large, some small—for what purpose archeologists are not sure. Potsherds have been found scattered along the roads, but no tools used in construction or fires where people might have camped. The function of the roads is still a puzzle. (Elderly Navajos who lived in the area told archeologists that Anasazi people used the "trenches" for protection from giants.)

It was not only goods that Chaco exported over the roads. People from the canyon migrated to other places in the region, taking with them social customs and ceremonial practices and the idea of building preplanned pueblos. About 70 of these outlying town-

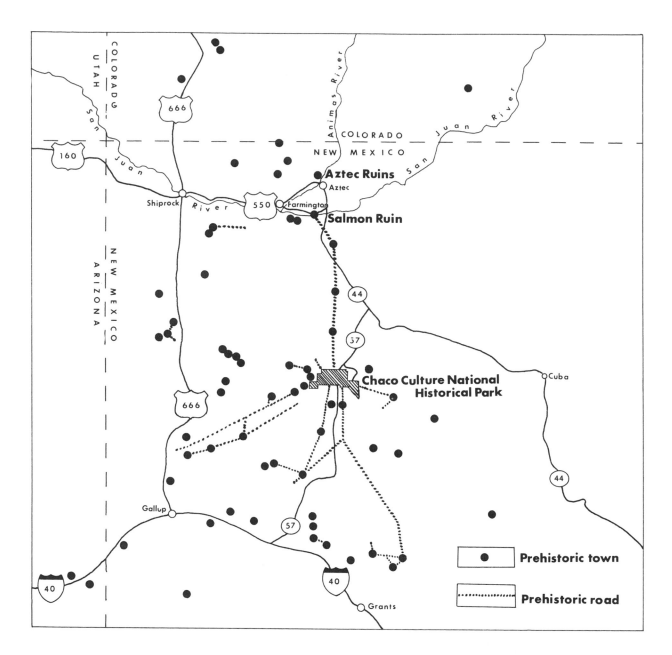

The Chaco Road System. The black dots indicate the main towns in the Arizona-Colorado-New Mexico area that were influenced by the Chaco culture. Archeologists have identified nearly 300 miles of straight roads (dotted lines) linking some of the towns with each other or with the great center in Chaco Canyon.

The dotted lines mark the edges of a 25-foot-wide road, part of the Chacoan communication system. In the background hand-hewn steps carry the road up a slope behind the late Dr. Robert H. Lister, former director of the Chaco Center. National Park Service photo by Thomas H. Wilson.

A group of kivas at Pueblo Bonito seen from the cliff which towers above the site. National Park Service photo by George A. Grant.

Two of the many examples of rock art that appear on cliff faces in Chaco Canyon and many other places in the Southwest. National Park Service photo.

ships have been located and studied. Some archeologists believe that the outliers were settled in order to produce food, which was then transported along the roads to the Chaco center. The settlements consisted of one or more groups of small dwellings and one great kiva, plus a large structure, built in the classic Chaco masonry style, which may have served as a public storehouse for food.

Other archeologists think that the main purpose of the migration to outlying villages was to relieve population pressure at the center. It is generally agreed that at some point the number of people in the canyon grew too large for the agricultural resources of the area. As R. Gwinn Vivian reported to the Society for American Archeology, "Redistribution of population was economically more feasible with primitive transport systems than large-scale redistribution of foodstuffs."

One of these Chacoan outliers may be visited at Salmon Ruins (see entry below), another at Dominguez and Escalante Ruin in Colorado (see entry above), a third at Chimney Rock (see above), and still another at Aztec (see entry above).

Besides their architectural and roadbuilding skills, the Chacoans had a talent for constructing irrigation systems and a technical knowledge that enabled them to establish a remarkable astronomical observatory (see above, next page).

In the late part of the twelfth century the greatness of Chaco Canyon came to an end. Archeologists are still debating exactly what pressures led to the abandonment of the canyon. It may well have been that the needs of the people exceeded the resources available, and what Vivian calls "redistribution of population" went on slowly over a number of years. Perhaps the Chacoan phenomenon did not just suddenly and mysteriously collapse. Instead it may have trickled away.

At any rate, the inhabitants of the canyon did eventually depart. After they left, their great buildings filled up gradually with windblown sand and dust, and many of them were only mounds when the first United States soldiers passed through the canyon on an exploring expedition in 1849.

Prehistoric Astronomers

Because it was important for prehistoric people to know when migrations of game would take place or when the time was at hand for planting crops, early hunters and farmers took a keen interest in the sun and moon and stars. Their recurring movements could be correlated with recurring events on earth, and people in widely separated parts of the world developed ways of noting major astronomical events.

In North America modern astronomers and archeologists working together have discovered ancient devices by which it was possible for prehistoric people to know exactly the days of the solstices and equinoxes and other regular occurrences. Sometimes these devices were alignments of stones, as at Bighorn Medicine Wheel in Wyoming. At Cahokia in Illinois circles of posts forming woodhenges were used. In the Southwest some astronomical observations were made by watching where beams of light fell through specially designed windows.

In the Chaco Canyon area of New Mexico ingenious ancient astronomers constructed a sophisticated calendrical device on top of a high butte. In this observatory large slabs of rock were arranged so that shafts of sunlight fell between them onto a group of spiral markings carved into a cliff wall. As the position of the sun changed with the seasons, the shafts of light traversed the face of the markings, indicating important dates to those who knew how to read them.

Skeptical archeologists at first found it hard to believe that accurate observations could be made using three rough-looking stone slabs and some seeming squiggles cut into a cliff. But after careful study they could find no reason to doubt that this was a true astronomical device invented by some Chacoan genius—or geniuses—700 or more years ago.

One geologist made a study of the slabs and concluded that there was no way in which they could have moved accidentally from their original position in the rock of the butte to their present location. In his opinion the slabs must have been moved and positioned by people. Other geologists disagree. They say the ancient Chacoans utilized rocks that had fallen naturally and created from them a marker for the seasons.

The existence and nature of this device, called the Sun Dagger Calendar, was made known to the world by Anna Sofaer, an artist and photographer, who found it while recording the rock art of Chaco Canyon. Whether the slabs were positioned by Chacoans or by nature, Sofaer says, their use indicates remarkable sophistication. Because of recent deterioration, the Park Service has closed Fajada Butte to all visitation.

Archeoastronomy is the name used for the growing new field of study concerned with the astronomical knowledge of prehistoric peoples. This study is making an important contribution to understanding the intellectual achievements of Native Americans.

At the right is a drawing of the shaft of light which has been called the Sun Dagger.

This is how Pueblo Bonito (in Chaco Canyon) looks when viewed from the top of the cliff. National Park Service photo by George A. Grant.

Pueblo Bonito (Spanish for "beautiful town") is by no means all there is to wonder at in Chaco Canyon, but it was the first to be thoroughly excavated and stabilized. Several other ruins have been explored and studied. Across the arroyo from Pueblo Bonito is Casa Rinconada, where a great kiva has been excavated and sufficiently restored to give an idea of the beauty and majesty of this ceremonial room. Behind the ruin called Kin Kletso an ancient trail leads up through a cleft in the cliff wall to a ruin called Pueblo Alto, on the mesa top.

Many sites in the canyon remain for future archeologists to study, including parts of a possible long-distance, line-of-site signaling network, and there are many aspects of the Chacoan phenomenon still to be understood, even after the completion of an ambitious, ten-year program, in which a number of "space-age" techniques were used.

The treasures of pottery and jewelry that archeologists found here have been removed to museums elsewhere.

CORONADO STATE MONUMENT

From Albuquerque drive north 20 miles on Interstate 25 to Cuba-Farmington Exit, then 3 miles west on New Mexico 44 to monument entrance. Mail address: P.O. Box 95, Bernalillo, NM 87004. Phone: 505/867-5351. Open free, Thursday–Monday. Closed certain holidays. Camping.

Here, on the west bank of the Rio Grande River a group of Anasazi people began to make their home about A.D. 1300. By the time the Spanish invaders arrived, in 1540, the pueblo, known as Kuaua (KWAH-wah) had grown tremendously. There were about 1200 ground-level rooms, and above them many other rooms, in places several stories high. The walls of the houses were made of adobe clay, which was moistened and built up in layers, each layer being allowed to dry before the next was added.

In the courtyards of the pueblo were a number of underground ceremonial chambers, or kivas. When archeologists excavated one of them they found murals painted on its plastered walls. Further investigation revealed 17 other layers of plaster underneath, and on each layer were more mural paintings of ceremonial activities. The archeologists worked out an ingenious method of removing the murals a layer at a time. An exhibit in the Visitor Center at the monument tells how they did it. Accurate reproductions of some of the paintings have been put on the wall of a reconstructed kiva at the site.

The people of Kuaua, which means "evergreen" in the Tiwa language, were farmers who grew corn, squash, tobacco, and cotton. They were good weavers and good potters, and they also made fine baskets. Many of their artifacts and religious objects can be seen in the museum at the Visitor Center.

The Name. The monument is named for the leader of the Spanish *conquistadores* who stayed somewhere in the vicinity of Kuaua for a while in the winter of 1540–41.

Atop the mesa in El Morro National Monument are these ruins of a pueblo built by ancient Zuni Indians. National Park Service photo.

DITTERT SITE

To visit this site, which is south of Grants, make arrangements through the Bureau of Land Management. El Malpais Information Center, 620 E. Santa Fe, Grants, NM 87020. Phone: 505/285-5406.

This site contains about 30 rooms and a kiva. Tree ring dates indicate that the latest construction took place during the thirteenth century. Nearby is a prehistoric roadway and a Great Kiva.

EL MORRO NATIONAL MONUMENT

From Grants drive 43 miles west on New Mexico 53; or from Gallup drive south 30 miles on New Mexico 602, then 24 miles east on New Mexico 53. Mail address: Ramah, NM 87321. Phone: 505/783-4226. Open free, daily, all year. User fee charged for hiking trails. Camping.

Although devoted primarily to preserving inscriptions made in historic times on a 200-foot-high sandstone promontory, this monument includes hundreds of petroglyphs—symbols and designs that Anasazi Indians pecked in the rock long before the first Spaniards arrived. On the mesa behind the cliff stand the ruins of two Pueblo villages, one of which has been partially excavated and stabilized. Visitors may take a self-guided tour of the site, which includes a huge pool that is fed by rains and melted snow, where inhabitants of the pueblos came for water. Handholds and footholds pecked in the rock show the route they followed up and down the cliff.

Exhibits in the Visitor Center interpret the history of the monument, both ancient and modern.

ERNEST THOMPSON SETON MUSEUM
(See Seton Museum)

Above: A Folsom point. *Right:* Two Clovis points. Clovis points vary in measurement. These (which are pictured here about half actual length) were found along with mammoth bones at the Lehner Site in Arizona. After Haury et al.

FLORENCE HAWLEY ELLIS MUSEUM OF ANTHROPOLOGY

At Espanola leave US 285 and follow US 84 northwest for 33 miles. At a sign marking "Ghost Ranch Road" (on which is a design of a cow's skull) drive right on a gravel road for 2 miles. *Note:* the museum is *not* at the Ghost Ranch Visitors' Center on US 84. Open free, Tuesday–Saturday; afternoon Sunday. Mail address: Ghost Ranch Conference Center, Abiquiu, NM 87510. Phone: 505/685-4333. Camping.

Exhibits here show the various local peoples and different types of land use from 14,000 B.P. to the end of the nineteenth century. Included are Paleo and Archaic materials and materials from nearby sites of the Gallina culture (eleventh to thirteenth centuries).

One exhibit is devoted to Sapawe Pueblo (A.D. 1350–1550), the largest clay-walled pueblo known in New Mexico. According to tradition, the people abandoned Sapawe because of drought and moved to the part of the still-existing San Juan Pueblo that lies on the west bank of the Rio Grande.

This museum is named in honor of a famous southwestern archeologist who died in 1991.

FOLSOM MUSEUM

In the town of Folsom. Mail address: Folsom, NM 88419. Phone: (summer) 505/278-2122; other times: 505/278-2477 or 3616. Open daily, Memorial weekend–Labor Day weekend; Saturday, Sunday, May and September; otherwise by appointment. Admission charged.

This small local history museum includes exhibits related to George McJunkin, the Black cowboy who discovered the nearby Folsom Site, which is of great importance to archeology but is not open to the public.

The full story of the discoverer of the Folsom Site is told for young readers by one of the authors of this book in *Black Cowboy: The Life and Legend of George McJunkin* which is available at this museum and at the nearby Capulin Volcano National Monument.

Fluted Points

When a projectile point has a channel, or depression, running lengthwise on one or both of its faces, it is said to be fluted. Clovis points, used by mammoth hunters about 11,000 years ago, and Folsom points, used by hunters of very large bison about 10,000 years ago, were fluted.

If fluting had any practical value, it was apparently that the thinned base could easily be inserted into the split end of a spear shaft. However, the labor involved in preparing these points was greater than the labor required to shape an unfluted point. In addition there was a great deal of breakage during manufacture. On the other hand, unfluted points seem to have been equally effective weapons, and they were more durable. This has led some archeologists to suggest that fluting may have had a ceremonial purpose.

How or when or where the practice of fluting began is not known. H. Müller-Beck, a Swiss archeologist, believes it may have started in Europe, possibly in southern Russia, at least 26,000 years ago. Other students of Early Man in America think fluting may have developed on the Bering Land Bridge, where men once hunted mammoths. The Land Bridge is now submerged, so all evidence of what went on there is lost. Still other archeologists believe that fluted points were first made in Alaska or on the southern Great Plains in the United States.

No matter where the custom began, it did not last long, as archeologists measure time. By about 9000 years ago point-makers had shifted from the fragile Folsom points to sturdier points, which were easier to manufacture and less likely to break.

The History of Prehistory

At one time antiquarians were content to say of an object, "This is a projectile point." Then excavators began to name points after the places where they found them. "This is a Clovis point," they said of a point like the ones first found near Clovis, New Mexico. Some museums still go no further with their exhibits.

"What was this point used for?" "What can it tell us about how it was made and about the people who made it?" Archeologists have gone on to try for answers to these questions, too.

"What can this dwelling, or this group of dwellings tell us about the people who made them and about their interaction with their environment? How did this interaction evolve through time?" As they tried to answer such questions archeologists called on men and women from other sciences to help them.

"How can we learn as much as possible and destroy sites as little as possible?" Archeologists had to deal with this question because the number of sites they can study is rapidly dwindling. They want sites and parts of sites to study in the future when they expect to have improved ways of getting information. To do as little damage as possible to evidence of the past, they came to use complex mathematics plus computer analyses and models as they squeezed maximum information from minimal samples.

They have learned how to learn a lot from a little in their race for knowledge against bulldozers making parking lots, against vandals who are interested only in making money from what objects they can sell, and against floods and the ordinary destructiveness of time.

GERONIMO SPRINGS MUSEUM

211 Main Street, Truth or Consequences, NM 87901. Phone: 505/894-6600. Open free, Monday–Saturday. Closed certain holidays.

This museum displays materials from many southwestern cultures including Mimbres, Tularosa, Socorro, Mogollon, Casas Grandes and Anasazi.

GHOST RANCH
(*See Florence Hawley Ellis Museum*)

GHOST RANCH LIVING MUSEUM, GATEWAY TO THE PAST

From Abiquiu drive 15 miles north to sign at entrance. Mail address: Ghost Ranch Living Museum, Abiquiu, NM 87501. Phone: 505/685-4312.

The visitor center and museum here have exhibits on the prehistory of the Chama Gateway Pueblos in the area.

GILA CLIFF DWELLINGS NATIONAL MONUMENT

From Silver City drive 44 miles north on New Mexico 15. Mail address: Rt. 11, Box 100, Silver City, NM 88061. Phone: 505/536-9461. Open free, daily, all year. Closed certain holidays. Camping.

From the trailhead a one-mile round-trip trail leads along a tree-shaded stream to ruins built in large caves, high above the canyon floor. In summer on Saturday nights, there are evening campfire talks explaining the archeology of the region. Visitors take self-guided tours. Displays in the Visitor Center interpret prehistoric life in the area.

The Story. Perhaps as early as A.D. 100, Mogollon people began to live within the borders of the present monument. They grew corn and beans, and for about 900 years they built dwellings that archeologists call pithouses because the floor was below ground level. About A.D. 1000, new ideas began to filter in from the Pueblo Indians

to the north. Square stone houses above ground took the place of pithouses. New kinds of white pottery, decorated with black designs, were also borrowed from the north, replacing the older red-on-brown ware.

The Mogollon built some of the new, square-roomed dwellings in caves in the cliffs, and some of these are the structures that have been stabilized and prepared for visitors to the monument.

About A.D. 1300 the houses were all abandoned. No one knows why the inhabitants left or where they went. After they moved away, Apache Indians settled in the area, but they did not become cliff dwellers.

Excavators at work at Gran Quivira, a unit of Salinas Pueblo Missions National Monument, where ruins of both Spanish and prehistoric Indian structures have been preserved. National Park Service photo by Fred E. Mang, Jr.

GRAN QUIVIRA
(gran kee-VEE-rah)
(Unit of Salinas Pueblo Missions National Monument)

From Mountainair on US 60 drive south 26 miles on New Mexico 55. Mail address: P.O. Box 498, Mountainair, NM 87036. Phone: 505/847-2770. Open free, daily. Closed December 25 and January 1.

Adjacent to the ruined Spanish mission at Gran Quivira is Las Humanas, largest of the Salinas pueblos. Las Humanas was an important trading center before and after the Spanish occupation.

The Story. People built pithouses of the Mogollon type in this area about A.D. 800. About A.D. 1100 they began to get ideas from the Anasazi who lived to the west. Soon black-on-white pottery became popular, and much the same lifeway came to be observed here as in the pueblos in the Rio Grande Valley. There was also trade with the Plains Indians.

One mound at the site contains more than 200 rooms built between A.D. 1300 and A.D. 1600. The remains of burned and filled kivas here mark the efforts of Spanish priests to abolish native religion. But the pueblo religious leaders simply turned an above-ground room into a ceremonial chamber in which to continue their traditional rituals.

The Museum. In the Visitor Center are display cases showing artifacts in their relation to the development of the culture of the people who lived here. An award-winning, forty-minute film of the excavation of one of the 21 house mounds at the site will be shown on request. A ten-minute video is also available. A self-guided tour leads through the site.

GUADALUPE RUIN

To visit this site, which is in a remote area northeast of Grants and cannot be reached in wet weather, contact: Bureau of Land Management, Rio Puerco Resource Area, 435 Montano Road NE, Albuquerque, NM 87107. Phone: 505/761-4504.

Here a 25 room pueblo with three kivas sits atop a sheer-sided butte above the Rio Puerco. It was built in the mid-900s, abandoned about A.D. 1130, then reoccupied and remodeled extensively during the thirteenth century.

HAWIKUH
(*See Zuni below*)

Ike Lovato, one of the Jemez Indian rangers who interpret Giusewa, which was built by their ancestors.

Ruins at Jemez State Monument. Museum of New Mexico photo.

HUPOBI RUIN

To make arrangements to see this site contact Bureau of Land Management, Taos Resource Area, Plaza Montevideo Building, Cruz Alta Road, P.O. Box 6168, Taos, NM 87571-6168. Phone: 505/758-8851.

This 1,000 room Anasazi adobe pueblo was occupied between A.D. 1300 and 1500. At the site are petroglyphs and extensive grid gardens.

JEMEZ STATE MONUMENT
(HEM-ess)

From Bernalillo drive 23 miles northwest on New Mexico 44, then northeast on New Mexico 4 to monument entrance on the northern edge of the town of Jemez Springs. Or from Los Alamos drive 38 miles west and south on New Mexico 4. Mail address: P.O. Box 143, Jemez Springs, NM 87025. Phone: 505/829-3530. Open daily. Closed certain holidays. Admission charged.

Here are the ruins of the pueblo of Giusewa (jee-SAY-wah), which dates from about A.D. 1300. It is known to have been very large, but how large is uncertain, because only part of it has been excavated. In places the buildings are three stories high.

The prehistoric inhabitants used the nearby hot springs as baths. Today their descendants live several miles down the canyon, in Jemez Pueblo. They are the only people who now speak the Towa language.

Rangers at the monument are members of Jemez Pueblo, and they have participated in preparing the museum exhibits at the Visitor Center. Displays interpret the life and history of Giusewa from the Indian point of view, with an audio accompaniment of traditional Jemez music. There are additional interpretive panels along the trail through the ruins.

The monument, a unit of the Museum of New Mexico, also preserves the seventeenth-century Franciscan mission of San José de los Jemez.

The Palace of the Governors, Santa Fe, is the oldest governmental building on the soil of the United States. Spanish colonial authorities established it about A.D. 1609. In the arcade along the front of the building Indians from various pueblos sell their craftwork. Inside is a small archeological exhibit. Photo by Russell D. Butcher.

KIT CARSON HISTORIC MUSEUM

On Old Kit Carson Rd., one-half block east of the plaza, Taos (TOWSS). Mail address: P.O. Drawer CCC, Taos, NM 87571. Phone: 505/758-0505. Open daily, all year. Closed certain holidays. Admission charged.

One room in this museum is devoted to Native American culture and includes exhibits of prehistoric material from the Taos area dating back as far as 3000 B.C. Most of the archeological material is Anasazi from after the year A.D. 1.

LOS ALAMOS HISTORICAL MUSEUM

On Central Avenue near 20th Street. Mail address: P.O. Box 43, Los Alamos, NM 87544. Phone: 505/662-6272. Open free, Monday–Saturday; afternoon Sunday. Closed certain holidays.

In the first room, in addition to displays about the geology of the area, are exhibits of artifacts that illuminate the lives of the hunters and farmers who lived on the Pajarito Plateau from A.D. 100 to 1500.

MAXWELL MUSEUM OF ANTHROPOLOGY
(*See University of New Mexico*)

MILLICENT ROGERS MUSEUM

From Taos drive 4 miles north to directional sign near the junction of US 64 and New Mexico 3. Phone: 505/758-2462. Open daily, all year. Admission charged.

In addition to modern Native American material, this museum exhibits some fine Mimbres and Anasazi pottery.

MUSEUM OF INDIAN ARTS AND CULTURE

710 Camino Lejo, Santa Fe, NM 87501. Phone: 505/827-8941. Open daily. Admission charged.

In addition to contemporary arts and crafts, exhibits here are taken from the extensive collections of prehistoric artifacts held by the Laboratory of Anthropology which is open only to scholars and researchers. Scheduled for

Virginia Pecos once served as a Ranger at the home of her ancestors in Pecos National Historic Park. National Park Service photo by Fred E. Mang, Jr.

the next few years are changing exhibits of prehistoric jewelry, stone work and Mimbres archeology.

NEW MEXICO STATE UNIVERSITY MUSEUM

On the campus of New Mexico State University, on University Ave., off US 80, Interstate 25, and Interstate 10, Las Cruces. Mail address: Box 3564, Las Cruces, NM 88003. Phone: 505/646-3739. Open free. Tuesday–Saturday, afternoon Sunday.

This general museum contains Mogollon pottery and stone tools from the period A.D. 800 to 1350, together with a considerable quantity of Casas Grandes pottery from northern Mexico. Exhibits also include local archeological finds and much ethnological material.

PALACE OF THE GOVERNORS

Palace Ave., on the Plaza, Santa Fe. Open free, daily, Tuesday–Sunday, mid-October–mid-March. Closed

certain holidays. Administered by the Museum of New Mexico, P.O. Box 2087, Santa Fe, NM 87504. Phone: 505/827-6344.

This handsome building was formerly the governor's residence under Spanish colonial, territorial and recent administrations. Erected in 1609, it has been in use continuously since then.

At one time the exhibits here included much prehistoric as well as historic material. Now only one room, the Nusbaum Room, recreates the museum's first archeological exhibit of material from the Pajarito Plateau. The Museum of Indian Arts and Culture (see above) has taken responsibility for displaying archeological material.

PECOS NATIONAL HISTORICAL PARK
(PAY-kohs)

From Santa Fe drive southeast 25 miles on Interstate 25 to Glorieta-Pecos exit, then 6 miles on State Road 50, turn right on State Road 63, 2 miles to the park. Or from Las Vegas drive west on Interstate 25 to Rowe exit, then 5 miles

on State Road 63 to the park. Mail address: P.O. Drawer 418, Pecos, NM 87552-0418. Phone: 505/757-6414. Open daily, all year. Closed certain holidays. Admission charged. Camping nearby.

Here, near the Pecos River, are the ruins of a pueblo that housed one of the largest town populations north of Mexico, when Coronado entered the area in 1541. Visitors may follow a trail on a self-guided tour of the ruins.

The Story. In the ninth century people began to settle in small groups along the upper reaches of the river. In time these small settlements grew together into larger settlements, and by 1540 Pecos was a huge, multistoried pueblo, constructed around an open plaza. At least 660 rooms provided living quarters for about 2,000 people.

The Pecos people were farmers, like the Anasazi, but their geographic location led them into special activities. Their pueblo stood at a crossroads, where Plains Indians met Pueblo Indians from the Rio Grande Valley, and where Indians from north and south along the Pecos River met. The pueblo

Pecos Indians built this wall not for defense but to outline the area of the town which was closed to visitors at night. National Park Service photo.

Pecos ruins, which were first investigated by Adolph Bandelier, who drove out in a buggy from Santa Fe, 25 miles away. National Park Service photo.

was a great center for trade. Many strangers came there.

Sometime in the 1620s a Franciscan priest built a huge church near Pecos and set about Christianizing the inhabitants. Apparently his success was incomplete. The pueblo continued to use ceremonial kivas.

In 1680 the Pecos people joined most of the other Pueblo Indians in a general revolt against the Spanish. They burned the church and drove the friars out. The church building which stands at Pecos today is much smaller than the original mission, signs of which were discovered only in 1967, during archeological excavations.

By 1838 the population of Pecos had dwindled from 2,000 to 17. Disease had killed many. Warfare killed others. The survivors moved to Jemez Pueblo, where their descendants live today.

Between 1915 and 1929 Dr. A. V. Kidder made very important excavations at the Pecos site. A vast number of interesting artifacts came from the dig. This collection is at Pecos and part of it is exhibited at the visitor

center which also has a 12-minute introductory film on Pecos history.

Dr. Kidder's discoveries made it possible to bring order into the chronology of a large area in the Southwest. In 1927 all archeologists who had been working in the area came to Pecos to exchange information and to adopt a terminology that all of them could use and understand. Honoring that first Southwestern conference, archeologists still meet every year for a Pecos Conference at some place in the Southwest.

PETROGLYPH NATIONAL MONUMENT

In Albuquerque, on Atrisco Drive NW, about one-half mile north of Taylor Ranch. Mail address: P.O. Box 1293, Albuquerque, NM 87103. Phone: 505/873-6620. Open daily. Admission charged.

From about A.D. 1300 to 1680 prehistoric Puebloan Indians carved a variety of realistic and symbolic drawings in the face of the basaltic escarpment created by a lava flow from a nearby

Grizzlier than Grizzlies

At the time when Paleo-Indians were hunting huge ice-age mammals 10,900 years ago, a giant short-faced bear went into a cave in what is now New Mexico. A hundred feet into the cave, in pitch blackness, the animal fell down a rock chimney. As it struggled to climb back out, it left claw marks on the cave wall. Probing around in the dark, it wandered farther and fell down another chimney, this time to its death.

In 1976 cave explorers found the animal's skeleton which was later identified as a bear that was bigger and faster and hence more dangerous than a Kodiak grizzly. That was one of the creatures with which the First Americans shared North America.

---

volcano. Several concentrated groups of petroglyphs are protected and interpreted within the monument, and self-guided tours to them may be taken along prepared trails. The National Park Service offers guided tours to other areas of the monument.

PICURIS PUEBLO
(pee-koo-REES)

From Taos drive southwest on New Mexico 68 to Embudo, then east about 16 miles on New Mexico 75. Mail address: P.O. Box 127, Penasco, NM 87553.

Archeological excavations at Picuris have established that the pueblo was founded between A.D. 1250 and 1300. Those who built their homes at the present site moved from another pueblo that once stood near Talpa (on New Mexico 3). The excavated features at Picuris are open to the public and may be photographed.

POSHU OINGE
(PO-shoe WIN-gay)

On US 84 about 2 miles east of Abiquiu. Mail address: Santa Fe National Forest, 1220 St. Francis Drive, Santa Fe, NM 87504. Phone: 505/988-6940. Open free, at all times.

Here are the remains of a pueblo from the fourteenth and fifteenth centuries that has about 500 rooms. A trail with interpretive signs leads to it.

Ancestors of the present-day inhabitants of Santa Clara Pueblo once lived in these rooms at Puyé Ruins. Photo by Ellen Conried Balch.

Reproduction of a painting of the Squash Blossom Girl, part of a mural found in a kiva in Awatovi, an ancient village on the Hopi Reservation.

A general view of Puyé Cliff, showing some of the masonry structures at the base together with holes leading into artificial caves in the cliff itself. Photo by Ellen Conried Balch.

Ruins of the old Quarai mission stand amid remains of a prehistoric pueblo in Salinas Pueblo Missions National Monument. Museum of New Mexico photo.

PUYÉ CLIFF RUINS, SANTA CLARA INDIAN RESERVATION (poo-YAY)

From Espanola on US 84 drive southwest on New Mexico 30 to directional sign, then 9 miles west on New Mexico 5 to entrance gate. Mail address: Tourism Dept., Santa Clara Pueblo, P.O. Box 580, Espanola, NM 87532. Phone: 505/753-7326. Open all year. Admission charged. Camping nearby.

Ancestors of the present-day Santa Clara Indians lived at Puyé Cliff. Some of their masonry dwellings were built along the base of the rock wall, other rooms were dug into the soft stone of the cliff itself, and on top of the cliff were several hundred additional rooms. Apparently the inhabitants moved away from Puyé Cliff seeking more fertile and better-watered lands, which they found near the site of the present Santa Clara Pueblo.

Parts of this very large ruin have been excavated and prepared for view by the public. The site is one of the few large prehistoric ruins administered by the descendants of the people who once lived there.

QUARAI
(car-EYE)
(Unit of Salinas Pueblo Missions National Monument)

From Mountainair on US 60 drive north on New Mexico 55, 8 miles to Punta de Agua, then 1 mile west from directional sign. Open free. Closed certain holidays. Camping nearby.

In addition to walls of a seventeenth-century Spanish mission that can be seen here, there are many unexcavated pueblo ruins. Archeological tests show that one part of the site was inhabited in the fourteenth and fifteenth centuries. Historical documents record that these people spoke the Tiwa language.

Before the Indians and Spaniards abandoned Quarai in the 1670s, it served occasionally as the center for the Inquisition in New Mexico. Although the Indians, considered inferiors, were not subject to the Inquisition, they still had to pay tithes to the state and did not escape punishment if they practiced ancient rituals.

The museum at Quarai has displays of prehistoric and historic artifacts that interpret life at Quarai. A self-guided trail leads .33 miles past unexcavated ruins and through the mission.

Part of the museum at Salmon Ruin, which was financed by a bond issue approved by citizens of San Juan County.

Archeologists excavating Salmon Ruin. Photo by Peter B. George.

RED ROCK STATE PARK MUSEUM

Five miles east of Gallup, just north of US 66. Mail address: P.O. Box 328, Church Rock, NM 87311. Phone: 505/863-1337. Open free, daily, Memorial Day–Labor Day. Remainder of the year, Monday–Friday.

Permanent, revolving, and temporary exhibits interpret the past and present Native American cultures of the Four Corners Region. The museum includes archeological displays.

Special Interest. The park is the home of the Inter-Tribal Indian Ceremonial held in August each year as well as Indian dances every evening during the summer months.

SALINAS PUEBLO MISSIONS NATIONAL MONUMENT
(sah-LEE-nus)

This monument consists of three separate units, located in three places: Abó (see above) and Quarai (see above), which were formerly New Mexico State Monuments, and Gran Quivira (see above), which was formerly a National Monument by itself. All three units were unified in 1981 to form the current Salinas Pueblo Missions National Monument. The Headquarters for the monument is located one block west of the intersection of US 60 and New Mexico 55 in Mountainair, New Mexico. Here, an informational audio-visual program introduces the visitor to the monument. Open free, daily, except certain holidays. For information write to: Salinas Pueblo Missions National Monument, P.O. Box 496, Mountainair, NM 87036. Phone: 505/847-2585.

SALMON RUIN
(SOL-mun)

From Bloomfield drive 2.5 miles west on US 64 to entrance and museum. Mail address: P.O. Box 125, Bloomfield, NM 87413. Phone: 505/632-2013. Open daily, all year. Closed certain holidays. Admission charged. Camping nearby.

The Salmon pueblo was one of several built by people who were influ-

Fanciful Archeology

The Swiss writer Erich von Daniken has started a fad that attracts people who are more interested in believing than in knowing. Without any evidence, often citing data inaccurately, and with disrespect for the abilities of Native Americans, he claims that many archeological features in the Americas were created by visitors from outer space. Although a carefully researched television program demonstrated to millions of viewers that there is no basis in fact for von Daniken's theories, believers persist.

Other theories, too, have been based on the racist notion that Indians had to get their ideas from somewhere else. At one time or another the Celts, the Welsh, the Irish, Phoenicians, Egyptians, and Africans were all put forward as originators of great achievements in the New World. The American Indians themselves were supposed by some to have been descended from the Ten Lost Tribes of Israel.

> That fancies flourish where facts are few
> Is true of Atlantis and also of Mu.

A tourist rests at the entrance to Sandia Cave, after climbing the spiral stairway from the path, far below.

---

enced by developments in the Chaco Canyon area, about 50 miles to the south. Tree-ring dates taken from roof beams show that the massive masonry structures were put up between A.D. 1088 and 1095. Built in the form of a squared C, the pueblo measured 430 feet along the back wall, 150 feet along the arms and was two stories high. In this preplanned, multiple dwelling were about 250 large, high-ceilinged rooms, arranged in groups for family units. Underground in the plaza was a ceremonial Great Kiva and, at the highest point in the structure, an unusual tower kiva.

After about 60 years of occupation, most of the first settlers left the pueblo. Only a few of the original inhabitants remained; then in the thirteenth century new people moved in, probably from the San Juan River valley. They made pottery in the style of Mesa Verde, and their culture seems to have been simpler than that of the Chacoans. They divided the large, orignal rooms into smaller units, by constructing poorly made masonry walls. By the beginning of the fourteenth century, these people, too, had abandoned the pueblo.

The ruin has been partially excavated and is undergoing stabilization. It can be visited on a self-guided tour. The San Juan County Archaeological Research Center and Museum at the site has exhibits of materials found there. The museum is the result of a cooperative endeavor by the citizens of San Juan County, who voted a $275,000 bond issue to finance construction of the Research Center and Library.

Excavation and interpretation of this important site were directed by the late Dr. Cynthia Irwin-Williams.

The Name. Salmon Ruin was named for George Salmon, who homesteaded in the area in the late 1800s and protected the site from vandals and pothunters.

Special Interest. In Heritage Park at the Salmon Ruin, reconstructions interpret Native American life of the past 10,000 years. Here are examples of many different artifacts and types of dwelling.

SANDIA CAVE
(san-DEE-ah)

Administered by the Forest Service of the U.S. Department of Agriculture. Mail address: 2113 Osuna Rd., Suite A, Albuquerque, NM 87113. Phone: 505/762-4650.

This cave is of interest because for many years archeologists believed that it had contained the oldest artifacts found in America. The remains of human occupation were originally dated at about 20,000 years B.P. (before present). Re-study of the material has cast doubt on this early date, but the cave does remain of interest as one of the two places in which Sandia points have been found. These points seem to be at least as old as the Clovis points that have been associated with the hunting of mammoths.

Material from the excavation is in the Museum of Anthropology, University of New Mexico, Albuquerque.

Prehistoric Firepower

The spear-thrower, also called a throwing-stick or atlatl, extended the distance a spear could travel and the force with which it could be hurled. After Indians discovered the greater accuracy and efficiency of the bow and arrow, they generally stopped using the atlatl and dart. Atlatls were still in use, however, when De Soto encountered Native Americans on the Louisiana coast in 1543.

Stone weapons changed a great deal in the millennia of their use. Very early in the Old World people learned to extend their grasp by jabbing a pointed stick into small creatures they could not easily reach with their bare hands. They also learned how to break certain kinds of stone to get sharp edges that were good for cutting or gouging. Then came a big innovation. Someone fastened a stick and a sharpened rock together—and made a spear.

At first this new tool was probably used only for poking, but it was effective. In America humans could apparently kill even mammoths with thrusting spears. They increased the range of their weapons when they found they could hurl a spear as well as thrust it. The spear had become a javelin—a projectile. Next its range was extended with the aid of a spear-thrower, also called a throwing stick or atlatl (AT-ul-AT-ul). People who used atlatls often made the shafts of their spears lighter than the shafts of thrusting spears, and these small spears, or javelins, are often called darts. Dart points, too, were likely to be smaller than the points on heavy thrusting spears.

For thousands of years American Indians got much of their protein food with the aid of darts and atlatls. Then came a device with which a person could put still more power behind projectiles—the bow. The bow acted as a spring: it stored up muscle power and then released a lot of it all at once.

As people increased the power behind the projectile, they were often able to decrease the size of the projectile shaft. For the sake of balance, the lighter shaft was equipped with a light point. Even reeds were used as the forepart of dart shafts and also for arrows, and some arrow points were very small.

Since arrows were easily transported in quantity, they made possible a great increase in firepower, and human destructiveness multiplied. Not only could they kill more animals and thus obtain more food; they could also kill more people. So, paradoxically, as soon as human beings were better able to provide for themselves, they also became less sure of surviving.

Archeologists may never know how it happened that some genius invented the bow. They do know that it appeared in the Old World and then in the New. Exactly how it got to the New World is not clear. Some archeologists speculate that it may have been re-invented here. It was in the Arctic about 4000 years ago. Its spread southward seems to have been slow. Apparently Southwestern people did not hunt with the bow and arrow until shortly after A.D. 200. The Plains people did not use the bow and arrow until even later.

The wood that went into making bows varied from place to place, depending on what was available. Some were made of several small pieces of wood ingeniously fitted together. Some were reinforced with sinews. Bows were long. Bows were short. Bows curved in different ways.

Some arrows may have been only sharpened wooden sticks. Some shafts were made of sturdy reeds. Very often a man identified his own arrows by painting some special mark or symbol on them.

Arrow points are abundant in areas where people depended heavily on hunting for food. In other areas, where most of the food came from agriculture, arrow points may be much less frequently found. In the largest ruins of the Southwest, for example, they are often far from numerous.

Taos Pueblo as it appears today.

SAN JUAN PUEBLO
(san-HWAN)

About 5 miles north of Española on New Mexico 68 and US 285. Mail address: Española, NM 87532. Phone: 505/852-4400. Open free, daylight hours. A visitor's permit must be obtained from the governor of the pueblo. Camping nearby.

This pueblo was in existence when the first Spaniards arrived. The name San Juan is a shortened form of San Juan de los Caballeros, the name given the pueblo by the Spanish conquerors.

SANTA CLARA PUEBLO

From Santa Fe drive north 30 miles on US 84-285 to Española; cross the Rio Grande and turn south on New Mexico 5, 2 miles to the pueblo. Mail address: P.O. Box 580, Española, NM 87532. Phone: 505/753-7326. Open free, daily, all year. Camping nearby.

This pueblo has apparently been on its present site about 800 years. Santa Clarans call themselves "Kha'p'ong" or "The People of the Singing Water." In earlier prehistoric times the Santa Clara people lived on the Pajarito Plateau, in the region of Puyé.

SETON MUSEUM

From Cimarron drive 5 miles south on New Mexico 21 to Philmont Camping Headquarters. Mail address: Philmont Scout Ranch, Cimarron, NM 87714. Open free, June 1–August 31, and Monday–Friday, September 1–May 31.

From its large collections of archeological and ethnological artifacts the museum offers exhibits that depict the life and culture of the Southwest.

TAOS PUEBLO
(TOWSS)

From Taos drive north 3 miles on New Mexico 3. Mail address: Taos, NM 87571. Phone: 505/758-4604. Open daily, all year. Parking fee required. Visitors may take photographs on payment of a fee. Camping nearby.

This pueblo has existed on its present site since prehistoric times, and the architecture of the buildings resembles the architecture of the pre-Spanish pueblo.

THREE RIVERS PETROGLYPH NATIONAL RECREATION SITE

Drive 28 miles south from Carrizozo (care-ee-SO-so) on US 54, then 5 miles east at Three Rivers, following signs on a gravel road. Phone: 505/525-8828. Open free, all year. Camping nearby.

A 1400-yard surfaced trail, with shaded rests along the way, leads through an area where people of the Jornada branch of the Mogollon culture made more than 500 rock carvings between the years A.D. 900 and 1400. Pictured on the jumbled boulders here are ceremonial figures, geometric figures, and animals—birds, frogs, lizards, mountain sheep, insects, and even an inchworm. Especially interesting are large, decorative pictures of fish in this very arid part of the country. Found here and almost nowhere else is a recurring design, made of a circle surrounded by dots.

TWIN ANGELS PUEBLO

Access to this site requires a four-wheel drive vehicle and a strenuous hike. Arrangements to visit should be made through the Bureau of Land Management, Farmington Resource Area, 1235 La Plata Highway, Farmington, NM 87401. Phone: 505/327-5344.

This 20-room pueblo with two kivas is perched on a sheer cliff overlooking Kutz Canyon. It was built between A.D. 1050 and 1150.

UNIVERSITY OF NEW MEXICO, MAXWELL MUSEUM OF ANTHROPOLOGY

On the campus, at University and Ash, N.E., Albuquerque 87131. Phone: 505/277-4404. Open free, Monday–Saturday, afternoon Sunday. Closed certain holidays.

This excellent museum emphasizes archeology of the Southwest and in addition contains exhibits of archeological and ethnological material from other parts of the world. Permanent exhibits include *People of the Southwest* and *Ancestors*. Rotating exhibits feature various subjects, including archeological material from the Gilbert and Dorothy Maxwell Collection.

VILLAGE VISTA SITE

About 15 miles northeast of Mimbres. Mail address: Forest Service, Mimbres Ranger District, P.O. Box 79, Mimbres, NM 88049. Phone: 505/536-2250. Open free, all year. As this book went to press, the site was being prepared for handicapped access.

Here is a site, with interpretive signs, once occupied by people of the Mimbres culture.

WESTERN NEW MEXICO UNIVERSITY MUSEUM

On the campus at 10th St. in Silver City. Mail address: P.O. Box 680, Silver City, NM 88062. Phone: 505/538-6386. Open Monday–Friday, afternoon Sunday. Closed Saturday and school holidays.

Here is the largest display of Mimbres pottery in the world. Its unique, idiosyncratic designs are often copied in commercial pottery. Also on display are some Casas Grandes and other prehistoric material.

ZIA PUEBLO
(TSEE-ah)

From Bernalillo drive northwest 18 miles on NM 44. Open free, during daylight hours. Visitors are not allowed to photograph, draw, or paint in the pueblo. Camping nearby.

This pueblo has been on its present site since about A.D. 1300. Excavations by the late Dr. Cynthia Irwin-Williams suggest that the ancestors of the Zia people, like the ancestors of some other Pueblo people, have lived in the same general area for nearly 8000 years.

The symbol for the sun that the ancient Zia used has been adopted as the design at the center of the New Mexico state flag. These are the words of the official salute to the flag: "I salute the flag of the State of New Mexico, the Zia symbol of perfect friendship among united cultures."

ZUNI PUEBLO
(ZOON-yee or ZOON-ee)

From Gallup drive south 30 miles on New Mexico 602, then 11 miles west on New Mexico 53. Open free, at any time. Arrangements for photographing must be made through the Zuni Tribal Office, Zuni, NM 87327, or phone: 505/782-2525. Camping nearby.

Zuni Indians have lived on or near the site of the present town since prehistoric times. About 50 miles south of the pueblo is the sacred Zuni Salt Lake, in the crater of an extinct volcano. Since ancient times the Zuni and other Indians have gathered salt there.

Other places of archeological interest on the Zuni Reservation are:

A:shiwi A:wan Museum and Heritage Center

In Zuni on the south side of State Highway 53. Mail address: Zuni Museum Project, P.O. Box 339, Zuni, NM 87237. Phone: 505/782-5559.

The mission of this new museum is to facilitate the interpretation of Zuni history and culture, to serve as a culture resource center for the Zuni community and to enhance cross-cultural awareness. Small exhibits are on display.

Hawikuh
(hah-wee-KOO)

About 12 miles south of Zuni Pueblo, Zuni Indian Reservation. For permission to visit the site, for the services of a guide, and information about fee, apply to Zuni Tribal office (see Village of the Great Kivas below).

Archeologists investigated this site in the early twentieth century, but did not do anything to stabilize the ruins they found here. As a result there remain for the most part only mounds of rubble, covered with potsherds and debris. However, a visit may be worthwhile in view of the history of the place.

The Story. Hawikuh was a town of perhaps 1500 people when Spanish explorers entered the Southwest in 1539, led by a Franciscan monk, Friar Marcos. With him came the famous Black slave, Estevan, who had accompanied Cabeza de Vaca on a seemingly impossible journey from the Gulf Coast north through Texas, then south to Mexico City.

While Marcos and Estevan were still in Mexico, they heard from Indians that there were seven fabulously rich cities of Cibola to the north. Marcos sent Estevan on ahead of his expedition, and at Hawikuh the Black explorer met his death.

Estevan had traveled far, had visited many people who lived as hunters and gatherers, and was skilled at getting along with them. A persuasive explanation of his death at Hawikuh seems to be that he arrived there in the company of wandering Indians who had joined Marcos and who belonged to groups that had given the sedentary Zunis a great deal of trouble. More important, Estevan looked different from any people the Zunis had ever seen—black skin, curly hair and beard—and he was dressed as if he might be a shaman or medicine man. The priests at Hawikuh, who were not shamans, were taking no chances with potential rivals in the field of religion, and Estevan's large following gave the impression that he might be regarded as having special powers. So the first Black explorer in North America, who happened also to be the first explorer from the Old World to enter New Mexico from Old Mexico, was killed by Zuni arrows.

Meanwhile Friar Marcos returned to Mexico City with tales of the Seven Cities of Cibola, one of which—Hawikuh—he claimed he had seen, although he had not been near the place. It was this hoax that sparked Coronado's expedition through the Southwest and changed the history of the people who lived there.

Village of the Great Kivas

On the Zuni Indian Reservation. For road directions and permission to visit the site, write: Zuni Tribal Office, Zuni, NM 87327, or phone: 505/782-2525.

This small, ruined settlement is notable for the two Great Kivas which identify it as one of the outliers, or colonies, established by people from Chaco Canyon (see entry above) in the eleventh century.

Tree-Ring Dating

Trees grow by adding layers of wood outside the layers that are already there. Some trees add a layer each year, and in years that are wet during the growing season, the layers are thick. In dry years they are thin. In an area where weather conditions are uniform, all trees that are weather-sensitive in this way tend to have the same pattern of thick and thin rings. By matching the ring pattern in a living tree with the ring pattern in a tree that was felled some time ago, it is often possible to tell the exact year in which the dead tree was cut.

Working backward from living trees, scientists have found a pattern of tree-ring growth in much of the Southwest that prevailed for many hundreds of years. They have made a master chart showing patterns of clusters of thick rings and thin rings. These patterns are called signatures, and each tree-ring signature differs from every other just as each handwritten signature differs from every other. By comparing the pattern of growth rings in a tree with the master chart it is possible to determine the exact years during which the tree was alive. In this way you can find out the exact year when the tree died or was cut down.

If the tree was used as a beam in a room, you can be sure it was not used before it was cut down. You have the beginning of a date for the room. If you find other beams in the same room all with the same date, you can be fairly sure when the roof was put on the building. If you find charcoal in the fireplace of the building that gives the same date as the roof beams, you can be reasonably sure that the building was finished and used in about the year given by the tree rings in the beams. This also means that you have some idea about the date of artifacts found in the room. The entire contents of the room were not likely to have been placed there before the room was built.

Tree-ring dating is also called dendrochronology.

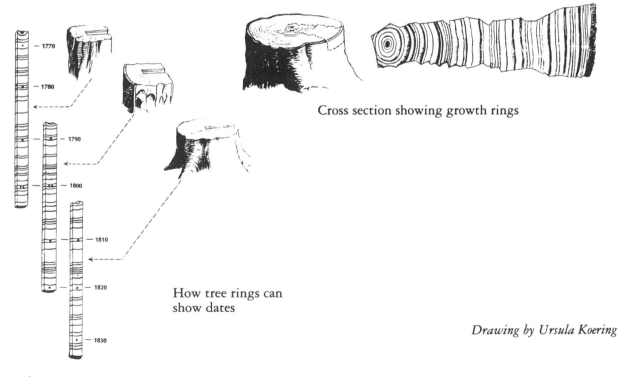

Cross section showing growth rings

How tree rings can show dates

Drawing by Ursula Koering

Are they dancers? These petroglyphs are near a site called Sand Island west of Bluff, Utah. Photo by Julia M. Johnson; copyright by Julia M. Johnson.

Utah

ALKALI RIDGE

From Monticello drive 13 miles south on US 191 to directional marker, then 8 miles to site. Or from Blanding drive 5 miles north on US 191 to directional marker, then 2 miles to site. Open free, at all times. Camping nearby.

Although no exhibits have been prepared for the public here, the site has long been of interest to archeologists. More than a thousand years ago a band of people settled in this land of cliffs and canyons. They hunted bighorn sheep, planted small fields of corn, and found it a good place in which to live. Their descendants continued to make their homes there for 500 years.

The firstcomers belonged to an early group of Anasazi people, called Basketmakers because they were very skilled at weaving baskets of many kinds. As time passed they developed new skills, following the general pattern of all the Anasazi in the region. Students of archeology are especially interested in this settlement at Alkali Ridge, because they can trace Anasazi life there, stage by stage, and also because the ceremonial kivas, which mark Anasazi culture in the Southwest, may have evolved in this particular area.

Alkali Ridge was excavated between 1931 and 1933 by J. O. Brew, of the Peabody Museum, at Harvard. Afterward, the site itself was covered over, and there is little for the casual visitor to see.

ANASAZI INDIAN VILLAGE STATE PARK

In Boulder on Utah 12. Mail address: P.O. Box 1329, Boulder, UT 84716. Phone: 801/335-7308. Open daily, all year. Admission charged. Camping nearby.

About 200 people occupied this village, also called the Coombs Site, from about A.D. 1050 to 1200. A self-guided tour leads through the site in which nearly 90 rooms have been excavated. A reconstructed six-room dwelling shows how the Anasazi lived. In the museum are a diorama of the original village, artifacts recovered from the site and exhibits relating to Anasazi culture.

ARCH CANYON RUIN

From Blanding drive south on US 191 to intersection with Utah 95, then about 20 miles west to the bottom of Comb Wash marked by a small sign, then north 3 miles on a graded road which ends at the head of a trail leading 1/4 mile to the site. Open free, at all times. Camping nearby.

This small ineresting Anasazi ruin has been partially stabilized and fenced to keep out cattle, but can be entered through a gate. For more information inquire at Bureau of Land Management, P.O. Box 7, Monticello, UT 84535. Phone: 801/587-2141.

Fremont Culture

In Utah about A.D. 900, many people began to live in somewhat the same way as the Anasazi farther south. Some archeologists call this Utah lifeway the Fremont culture and regard it as a subdivision of the Anasazi. Fremont people lived on the northern periphery of the Anasazi area and gathered wild foods, as their ancestors apparently had done for thousands of years, but they also raised corn. Unlike the Anasazi they wore moccasins rather than sandals. Much of their pottery was rather plain, and experts can easily distinguish it from Anasazi pottery, which was often more decorated. Like the Anasazi the Fremont people built dwellings of stone and adobe masonry.

In the eastern part of Utah the lifeway of the Fremont people differed somewhat from that of their neighbors in the western part, who are called Sevier (suh-VEER)-Fremont. Both the Fremont and the Sevier-Fremont left rock art on cliff walls throughout the area.

About A.D. 1100 the Fremont culture began to disappear. A recent theory suggests that Fremont people moved out of Utah, some to the south, where they merged with the ancestors of present-day Pueblos, some to the east, onto the Plains, probably through South Pass. According to this theory, which is based on cultural, skeletal, and linguistic evidence, the Shoshone Indians, whom the first white settlers found in Utah, were not descendants of the Fremont people but were fairly recent immigrants to the area.

One of many pictographs of figures without heads in Grand Gulch, Utah. Photo by Julia M. Johnson; copyright by Julia M. Johnson.

ARCHES NATIONAL PARK

From Moab drive 5 miles north on US 191 to Park Headquarters. Mail address: P.O. Box 907, Moab, UT 84532. Phone: 801/259-8161. Open daily, all year. Admission charged. Camping.

There are a number of pictograph and petroglyph sites in the park, the most accessible of which is the Courthouse Wash Panel. For directions to the site inquire at the Visitor Center. Some of the unusual paintings here are five feet or more tall, and are similar to paintings in Horseshoe Canyon (see entry below). On a portion of the same cliff are petroglyphs which have been carved into the sandstone. Unfortunately, because of its accessibility the site has been badly vandalized.

BARRIER CANYON
(See Horseshoe Canyon)

BEEF BASIN TOWERS

From the junction of US 191 and Utah 211, drive to Dugout Ranch on Utah 211, then 35 miles southwest on a gravel road that is open only during summer and fall. For detailed information apply at the Bureau of Land Management, San Juan Resource Area, 435 North Main St., P.O. Box 7, Monticello, UT 84535. Phone: 801/587-2141.

Here, in an area called Ruins Park, are numerous circular and square towers, some two stories high. There is also a small village site. Primitive trails lead to these structures that were built about the thirteenth century.

BRADFORD CANYON RUIN

For information about access, apply to Bureau of Land Management, San Juan Resource Area, 435 North Main St., P.O. Box 7, Monticello, UT 84535. Phone: 801/587-2141.

Here, on a series of terraces in a cliff, are granaries in caves and dwellings and surface ruins left by Anasazi peo-

Unlike most prehistoric structures in the Four Corners area, this one in Grand Gulch, Utah, was built, not of stone, but by the method called wattle and daub. The framework, made of woven branches, was then coated with mud. Photo by Julia M. Johnson; copyright by Julia M. Johnson.

ple in the eleventh century. Petroglyphs have been pecked in the nearby cliff face.

BRIGHAM YOUNG UNIVERSITY, MUSEUM OF PEOPLE AND CULTURE

710 N. 100 East, Provo, UT 84602 (off campus). Phone: 801/378-6112. Open free, Monday–Friday, September 1–May 1. Closed certain holidays.

This museum contains material of the Fremont culture in Utah, the Anasazi, the Hohokam, the Casas Grandes and the Mimbres cultures elesewhere in the Southwest.

BUTLER WASH OVERLOOK

From Blanding drive 15 miles west on Utah 95 to a turnout. Mail address: Bureau of Land Management, San Juan Resource Area, 435 North Main St., P.O. Box 7, Monticello, UT 84535. Phone: 801/587-2141.

From the turnout, a half-mile-long well-marked unpaved trail leads to 23 Anasazi structures from the mid-thir-

teenth century. At the site are restrooms, an interpretive sign and a nature guide brochure. Partially hidden nearby is a natural bridge.

BUTLER WASH PETROGLYPHS

Accessible by boat, 4 miles west of Bluff on the San Juan River. River travel permits for private boats are available from the Bureau of Land Management, Monticello, UT 84535. Phone: 801/672-2222.

Here are life-size rock carvings of human figures in a two-hundred-yard-long panel attributed to early Anasazi people. One-day commercial boat trips to the site are available, April 15–October 31. For information contact Wild Rivers Expeditions, P.O. Box 118, Bluff, UT 84512. Phone: 801/422-7654. Three- and four-day trips can also be arranged to visit this and other rock art sites along the San Juan River.

Prehistoric Indian rock art in Horse Canyon, Canyonlands National Park. National Park Service photo by N. Woodbridge Williams.

CALF CREEK RECREATION AREA

Along Utah 12, midway between Boulder and Escalante. Mail address: Bureau of Land Management, Escalante Resource Area, P.O. Box 225, Escalante, UT 84726. Phone: 801/826-4291. The office is on Utah 12 on the west edge of Escalante. Camping.

Several small Fremont-Anasazi ruins and pictographs are along 2.75 miles of the Lower Calf Creek Falls Foot Trail. At the trailhead are interpretive brochures. There are also small ruins along Utah 12, 1.5 miles south of Calf Creek Campground near the Escalante River Bridge.

CANYONLANDS NATIONAL PARK

To reach the Island in the Sky district of the park, turn west from US 191, 11 miles north of Moab. To reach the Needles district, drive west on Utah 211. Other districts require a four-wheel drive vehicle. Mail address: National Park Service, Moab, UT 84532-

2995. Phone: 801/259-7164. Open at all times. Admission charged. Primitive camping.

Throughout the park there are numerous small ruins of dwellings, granaries and kivas built by the Anasazi people between A.D. 900 and 1250. Visitors are invited to look at the ruins, but are forbidden to enter them.

The rock walls of the canyons offered innumerable flat surfaces for prehistoric artists, and a great deal of their work has been preserved. Visitors may see both pictographs, which are paintings on rock and petroglyphs, which are pictures pecked or scraped into rock.

CAPITOL REEF NATIONAL PARK

On Utah 24, 75 miles southeast of the junction of Utah 24 with Interstate 70. Mail address: Torrey, UT 84775. Phone: 801/425-3791. Open daily. Closed certain holidays. Admission charged. Camping.

The Fremont people once lived in this area, and a portion of the Visitor Center is devoted to them. Petro-

Handprints in Canyonlands National Park. National Park Service photo.

glyphs, probably made by Fremont people, may be seen near the highway.

CASTLE CREEK RUIN

From Utah 95 west of Blanding, drive 27 miles south on Utah 276. Mail address: Bureau of Land Management, San Juan Resource Area, 435 N. Main St., P.O. Box 7, Monticello, UT 84535. Phone: 801/587-2141.

Here against a cliff, between two springs, are several rooms connected by T-shaped doorways. A primitive trail from a turnout leads to the site.

CAVE CANYON TOWERS

Off Utah 95 in the Blanding area. For exact road directions contact the Bureau of Land Management, San Juan Resource Area, 435 N. Main St., P.O. Box 7, Monticello, UT 84535. Phone: 801/587-2141.

Here seven stone towers are clustered around a pool at the head of a canyon. Nearby are numerous rooms

built in various masonry styles that suggest occupation at different times. Not far away are other structures close to a group of petroglyphs, some of which may relate to solstice observation. Visitors are urged not to climb on or in the ruins.

CLEAR CREEK CANYON ROCK ART

Between Sevier and Cove Fort on Utah 44. Open free, at all times.

Many panels of petroglyphs may be seen along the walls of Clear Creek Canyon. The main concentration is between the mouths of Mill Creek and Dry Creek.

COLLEGE OF EASTERN UTAH PREHISTORIC MUSEUM

155 East Main, Price, UT 84501. Phone: 801/637-5060. Open Monday–Saturday. Closed certain holidays. Donations accepted.

The museum contains artifacts of the Fremont culture.

COTTONWOOD FALLS SITE

For information about access apply to Bureau of Land Management, San Juan Resource Area, 435 North Main St., P.O. Box 7, Monticello, UT 84535. Phone: 801/587-2141.

Here is a multistory Anasazi building with a nearby Great Kiva. A prehistoric roadway linked this site to others that are in present-day New Mexico.

Cliff dweller ruins on Westwater Creek near Blanding. Bureau of Land Management photo.

Anasazi people made their homes in areas such as this in Canyonlands National Park. National Park Service photo by George A. Grant.

Many small structures like this can be seen in protected areas in what is now Canyonlands National Park. National Park Service photo.

Prehistoric shields, made of buffalo hide, were found packed in juniper bark in a burial in the Capitol Reef National Park area. National Park Service photo by George A. Grant.

Petroglyphs in Capitol Reef National Park. National Park Service photo by Parker Hamilton.

COURTHOUSE WASH PANEL
(*See Arches National Park*)

DANGER CAVE STATE HISTORICAL SITE

One mile north of Wendover off US 40. For information write: Department of Natural Resources, Division of Parks and Recreation, 1636 W. North Temple, Salt Lake City, UT 84116. Phone: 801/533-4563.

This famous site, although so far undeveloped, has been opened to the public by the Utah Park system. For its significance see Introduction to Great Basin section.

Warning: Do not enter cave. The roof is unstable.

EDGE OF THE CEDARS STATE PARK

660 West 400 North, Blanding, UT 84511. Phone: 801/678-2238. Open daily. Closed certain holidays. Admission charged.

In the museum is a fine Anasazi pottery exhibit as well as exhibits of ma-

terial from prehistoric as well as historic Navajo and Ute cultures. Video presentations are available.

An Anasazi pueblo, dating from A.D. 800 to 1100, is located adjacent to the museum building.

FOUR CORNERS SCHOOL OF OUTDOOR EDUCATION

Mail address: East Route, Monticello, UT 84535. Phone: 1/800/525-4456 or 801/587-2859.

In addition to courses in the biology and history of the Colorado Plateau, the school offers numerous short courses in field archeology. A catalogue describes the courses that people may take at different times at important sites and excavations in all parts of the Four Corners region.

FREMONT INDIAN STATE PARK

Drive south from Richfield on Highway 89 to Clear Creek Junction. Go west on Interstate 70 for about five miles to the park. Mail address: 11550 Clear Creek Canyon Road, Sevier, UT

Edge of the Cedars Ruin, Blanding. Edge of the Cedars State Park.

84766. Phone: 801/527-4631. Open daily. Closed certain holidays. Admission charged. Camping.

In the Visitor Center a video program and exhibits introduce visitors to the Fremont people. Three trails lead to pictographs and petroglyphs. One trail is concrete and wheel chair accessible. There is also a self-guided auto trail. Possibly visitors may be able to observe archeologists at work in an excavation.

'GOULDINGS

At just about the point where US 191 crosses the border between Arizona and Utah, 24 miles north of Kayenta, drive west 3 miles on a local road. A small museum here exhibits some prehistoric artifacts.

Although its post office address is in Utah, this trading post and motel has long been associated with Navajoland in Arizona. Visitors who want to see prehistoric sites in Monument Valley can arrange for guided, four-wheel-drive day or half-day trips. For information, from April–November, write to Box 1, Monument Valley, Utah 84536. Phone: 801/727-3231.

GRAND GULCH

From Blanding drive south on US 191, then 35 miles southwest on Utah 95 to intersection with Utah 261, then 4 miles south on Utah 261 to Kane Gulch. A hiking trail leads down Kane Gulch to Grand Gulch, about a two-hour trip. Visitors who want to see a representative sample of Grand Gulch sites should plan to spend three days. The entire length of the Gulch is 52 miles. Open free, for day hikes. A fee is charged for overnight or longer. Visitors must register at the Kane Gulch Ranger Station and must carry drinking water.

This is a deep canyon, rich in archeological remains, with many large, well-preserved Anasazi dwellings. There are three major hiking trails into the Grand Gulch. Anyone interested in guide service should apply to the Bureau of Land Management, P.O. Box 7, Monticello, UT 84535. Phone: 801/587-2141.

Breech birth, a rare pictograph in Grand Gulch. It is part of a panel in an alcove with one called the Green Mask which intrigues archeologists because it depicts a face, also painted in green, on a mask made of human skin that was found elsewhere in the region. The original mask was not cared for properly and has disintegrated. Photo by Bob Powell; copyright, Bob Powell.

Pottery from Grand Gulch is now in the Field Museum of Natural History, Chicago; Smithsonian Institution, Washington, DC; University Museum, Philadelphia; and Hearst Museum, Berkeley. It was collected in part by Richard Wetherill, a member of a Quaker family who settled near Mancos, Colorado, in the 1880s. From the home ranch he and his brothers, John and Clayton, went out on many exploring expeditions and made many archeological discoveries.

In a cave in the Grand Gulch, Richard found, underneath layers of dust and debris containing things left by Pueblo people, artifacts made by Basketmaker people. This surely meant, said Wetherill, that the Basketmakers lived in the Southwest earlier than the Pueblos. Today the idea seems obvious, but at that time American archeologists had not made use of the principle of stratigraphy (the study of strata or layers in the earth), which had long been used in European archeology.

HOG SPRINGS PICNIC SITE

From Hanksville drive 37 miles south on Utah 95. Open at all times. Admission charged.

Near the picnic site is a rock shelter containing Indian pictographs, one of which is called the Moki Queen by local residents. Administered by the Bureau of Land Management.

HORSESHOE CANYON
(Barrier Canyon)

Accessible only by four-wheel drive vehicle and foot trail. From Green River drive 9 miles west on Interstate 70 to Utah 24, then south to sign for Goblin Valley State Park; continue to unimproved dirt road (next left), and follow Maze district signs to Hans Flat Ranger Station, where further directions to the canyon can be obtained. Mail address: National Park Service, Southeast Utah Group, Moab, UT 84532-2995. Phone: 801/259-7164.

Throughout Horseshoe Canyon are large paintings of human figures on sandstone cliff walls. These may have been made by Archaic hunter-gatherers who inhabited the area from 6000 B.C. to A.D. 1.

Part of a group of pictographs known as Big Man Panel in Grand Gulch, Utah. Photo by Julia M. Johnson; copyright by Julia M. Johnson.

An unusual tipi-shaped structure in an alcove in Grand Gulch, Utah. Photo by Julia M. Johnson; copyright by Julia M. Johnson.

SOUTHWEST: Utah   117

Detail showing masonry of round towers at Hovenweep National Monument.

HOVENWEEP NATIONAL MONUMENT

From Cortez, Colorado, drive north 18 miles on US 666 to Pleasant View; turn west at the Hovenweep directional sign and follow the graded road 27.2 miles to Square Tower Group, which is in Utah. Mail address: Mesa Verde National Park, CO 81330. Phone: 801/529-4465. Open free, all year. Camping.

In this extremely isolated spot are imposing and well-preserved towers and other structures built by people who followed about the same lifeway as the ancient farmers of Mesa Verde. Exact dates and many details about the Hovenweep people are not yet known, because there has been no excavation at this site. Visitors take self-guided tours on a number of trails leading to the most interesting of the ruins. A ranger on duty at the Visitor Center will answer questions.

The Name. On September 13, 1874, a party exploring for the United States government camped at this place. Ernest Ingersoll, a zoologist, and W. H. Jackson, a photographer, were members of the expedition. Ingersoll noted in his journal that the place was named by the explorers from two Indian words meaning "deserted canyon."

Special Feature. Hovenweep is a kind of bank in which archeological riches are being kept for future generations of scientists to excavate and study. Archeologists approve this policy, because new techniques are constantly being developed, which make it possible to learn more and more from the materials recovered at a site. When Hovenweep is excavated in the future, it will yield information that might be lost if digging went on today. Once a site is excavated it is destroyed as a source of scientific information.

LITTLE BLACK MOUNTAIN PETROGLYPH INTERPRETIVE SITE

Eight miles southeast of St. George. Four-wheel-drive vehicle recommended. For road direcitons inquire at Bureau of Land Management, Shivwits Resource Area, 225 N. Bluff, St. George, UT 84770. Phone: 801/628-4491.

About 500 designs or design elements appear here in an area 800 yards long on cliffs and boulders. Many different groups who traveled and traded through the area left this art work. Visitors are asked to stay on the trails and not to touch any of the petroglyphs.

Above and opposite: Many towers at Hovenweep National Monument are square. Others are circular or oval or D-shaped. Until scientific excavation is done, there can only be speculation about the meaning and use of the towers. However, it is known that one of the towers has an opening suitable for marking the summer and winter solstices. National Park Service photo by Fred E. Mang, Jr.

The symbols on this stone slab, called Newspaper Rock, may have had real meaning to the people who put them there, but experts agree that they do not constitute true writing. The symbols cover an area 25 feet long and 25 feet high in Indian Creek State Park. Photo by Norman Van Pelt.

MULE CANYON INDIAN RUINS

From Blanding drive south on US 191, then west 20 miles on Utah 95. Mail address: Bureau of Land Management, P.O. Box 7, Monticello, UT 84535. Phone: 801/587-2141. Open free, all year.

This site was discovered and excavated during a survey prior to the construction of the new Utah 95. After the ruins were stabilized, the Bureau of Land Management built trails, restrooms and a protective shelter over one structure.

Anasazi people lived here shortly before A.D. 1300. The small complex consists of rooms for dwelling and storage, a kiva and a tower that might have been used for defense or as a platform for sending signals with fire or smoke. A crawlway led from the kiva to one of the house rooms. The site was probably the home of an extended family of about eight adults and their children.

NAMPAWEAP

For road directions apply to Bureau of Land Management, Vermillion Resource Area, 225 N. Bluff, St. George, UT 85770. Phone: 801/628-4491.

At this site are hundreds of petroglyphs. Nampaweap means "foot canyon" in the Paiute language.

NATURAL BRIDGES NATIONAL MONUMENT

From Blanding drive 40 miles west on Utah 95. Mail address: Box 1, Natural Bridges, Lake Powell, UT 84533. Phone: 801/259-5174. Open all year. Trails may be closed during winter. Admission charged in summer. Camping.

Within the monument are 200 sites once occupied by Anasazi people. Hikers who follow the trails will pass a cliff dwelling with several rooms, granaries, and kivas, which may be viewed but not entered. Federal laws protecting antiquities are enforced.

NEWSPAPER ROCK STATE PARK

Drive 12 miles north of Monticello on US 191, then 12 miles west on Utah 211 to Indian Creek where one of the most easily accessible rock art panels is located. Phone: 801/678-2238. Open free, all year. Camping.

Here a large cliff wall is covered with Indian rock art that may have accumulated over a period of 1,500 years. It seems likely that the more recent petroglyphs were made by historic Ute Indians, but visible under them and around the edges are much older petroglyphs made by the Fremont and Anasazi people between A.D. 800 and 1300.

NINE MILE CANYON ROCK ART

Between Price and Myton on Utah 53. Open free, at all times.

Many rock-art panels are visible along the walls of this canyon. Occasional granaries and other structures, attributed to the Fremont culture, may also be seen. Before starting this trip be sure to have gasoline and drinking water.

PAROWAN GAP INDIAN DRAWINGS
(pair-oh-WAN)

From Cedar City drive north 18 miles on Interstate 15 to Parowan turnoff, then west on county road toward Utah 130. The site is next to the road. Open free, at all times. Phone: 801/586-2458. Camping nearby.

Drawings and designs seem to have been placed on the rock here by the Fremont people sometime between A.D. 900 and 1150. Administered by the Bureau of Land Management, Grand Resource Area, 885 S. Sand Flats Road, Moab, UT 84532. Phone: 801/259-8193.

POTASH ROAD PETROGLYPHS

From Moab drive 8 miles west on Utah 279. Mail address: Bureau of Land Management, Grand Resource Area, S. Sand Flats Road, P.O. Box M, Moab, UT 88532. Phone: 801/259-8193.

Rock art panels line the sheer cliffs on the north side of the highway for two miles. The panels include a variety of art styles and subjects. Artists made these panels from the Archaic period through the Pueblo to the days of the Ute.

RIVER HOUSE RUIN

For directions to this site near Bluff, apply to the Bureau of Land Management, San Juan Resource Area, 435 N. Main St., P.O. Box 7, Monticello, UT 84535. Phone: 801/587-2141.

This site, in a sandstone alcove, overlooks the San Juan River. In it are 14 rooms, some two stories tall, that date from the thirteenth century.

SAND ISLAND PETROGLYPHS

From Bluff drive 2 miles southwest on US 191 to directional marker. Open free, at all times. Camping.

A large panel of petroglyphs, protected by a wire fence, overlooks the San Juan River. The carvings of animals, human beings and abstract designs probably date back to Anasazi times. One of the figures is that of Kokopelli, the humpbacked flute player, who appeared frequently in Southwestern rock art. His exact significance is not known. Some interpret him as a trader, possibly with a pack on his back. Others believe he was a fertility figure.

SEGO CANYON PETROGLYPHS
(*See Thompson Wash Petroglyphs*)

SHAY CANYON PETROGLYPHS

From Monticello drive north on US 191, then 12 miles west on Utah 211 to a turnout. From here the site, 100 yards distant, is reached by a primitive trail. Mail address: Bureau of Land Management, San Juan Resource Area, 435 North Main St., P.O. Box 7, Monticello, UT 84535. Phone: 801/587-2141.

Here on towering sandstone cliffs is rock art in a great variety of styles and motifs. Prominent are Kokopelli figures.

SOUTH FORK INDIAN CANYON PICTOGRAPH SITE

Near Coral Pink Sand Dunes State Park, near Kanab. For exact road directions inquire at the Bureau of Land Management, Kanab Resource Area, P.O. Box 459, Kanab, UT 84741. Phone: 801/644-2672. For four-wheel drive vehicles only. At the end of the drive there is a twenty-minute walk. Open free, at all times. Camping nearby.

This site is a high-roofed, spacious rock shelter located well below the rim of a major tributary of scenic Cottonwood Canyon, one of the large, deeply cut drainages coming off the tablelands north and west of Kanab. On the sandstone shelter walls are numerous painted figures of people and animals, in addition to several more abstract elements. Some previously covered figures have been exposed by looters digging along the rear wall.

The badly vandalized deposits of the shelter contain large quantities of corn cobs and show some evidence of stone-lined storage cists with covers of small logs (a section of a log yielded a C-14 date of ca. A.D. 280). The site appears to be quite similar to a Basketmaker II site, Cave Du Pont, located just a few miles to the north. The pictographs are also taken to date from this early agricultural period.

Weather Prediction

Archeologists have developed many strategies for determining what the weather was like at various periods in the past—and how it affected the lives of Native Americans. Growth rings in trees, for example, reflect periods of drought and heavy rainfall which brought bad or good crops. The remains of various types of vegetation in layers of earth, which geologists can date, indicate whether plants that were tolerant of cool and dry or warm and wet weather were flourishing at one period or another.

Certain snails proliferate in wet climates, others in dry. By determining which type is found in a particular layer of earth associated with human remains, an archeologist can tell whether much or little rain fell on the people who lived there.

Most archeologists have theorized that from about 8000 B.C. to 4000 B.C. the weather in the Southwest was cool and dry. This notion has been challenged by an ingenious method of linking climate to the remains of the meat that people ate. Analysis of the faunal bones found in caves used by hunters in the Southwest indicate that many of these same animals now exist only in warmer, wetter environments to the north and east of the caves. Therefore, it is assumed, the Southwest in ancient times must have been warmer and wetter than it is now, and so was more attractive to hunters than archeologists previously thought.

THOMPSON WASH PETROGLYPHS

From Thompson drive 3.4 miles north on a local road. The site is marked on Utah highway maps as "Sego Canyon Petroglyphs." Mail address: Bureau of Land Management, Grand Resource Area, 885 S. Sand Flats Road, Moab, UT 84532. Phone: 801/259-8193. Open free, at all times.

There are extensive panels of both carving and painting on the rocks in this area. This rock art comes from three different cultures and three different time periods.

THREE KIVA PUEBLO

From Monticello drive south on US 191 about 4 miles to Montezuma Canyon Rd., then 3 miles into the canyon to an interpretive sign. Four-wheel-drive vehicle recommended because of deep sand in places. For information inquire at Monticello office of the Bureau of Land Management. Phone: 801/587-2141.

This village, the ruins of which have been stabilized, was occupied at least three different times from A.D. 900 to 1300. Close to the dwellings is an area that archeologists believe was a turkey pen.

UNIVERSITY OF UTAH, UTAH MUSEUM OF NATURAL HISTORY

On the campus, Wasatch Drive, Salt Lake City. Phone: 801/581-4303. Open daily. Admission charged.

Archeological exhibits in this museum include dioramas and materials from the important excavations at Hogup Cave and Danger Cave. For the story of Danger Cave, see Introduction to Great Basin section and entry above.

UTAH FIELD HOUSE OF NATURAL HISTORY STATE PARK

235 East Main St., Vernal, UT 84078. Phone: 801/789-3799. Open daily. Closed certain holidays. Admission charged.

Within this natural history mu-

Diorama showing what a prehistoric village, now in ruins, may have looked like when people lived in Zion National Park. National Park Service photo.

seum are displays of prehistoric artifacts. The cultures represented are primarily the Fremont, Basketmaker and Ute Indian.

UTAH MUSEUM OF NATURAL HISTORY
(*See University of Utah*)

WESTWATER FIVE KIVA RUIN

From the center of Blanding drive south on US Highway 191 2 miles, to the Scenic View 2 sign, turn right and follow to the end of the pavement, 2 miles. Mail address: Department of Natural Resources, P.O. Box 788, Blanding, UT 84511. Phone: 801/678-2238. Open free, daily, all year

Westwater Five Kiva ruin is an Anasazi cliff dwelling located across Westwater Canyon. It was occupied from about A.D. 1150 to 1275. It consists of several living rooms, five kivas, storage rooms and open area.

WHITE MESA INSTITUTE

College of Eastern Utah, San Juan Campus, Blanding, UT. Mail address: P.O. Box 211248, Salt Lake City, UT 84121-8248. Phone (at the college): 801/678-2201.

This Institute offers lectures on archeology and expeditions to a variety of archeological sites and areas. In addition there are opportunities to take part in excavation.

ZION NATIONAL PARK

From Kanab (kah-NAB) drive 17 miles north on US 89, then 24 miles west on Utah 9 to Park Headquarters. Mail address: Springdale, UT 84767. Phone: 801/772-3256. Open daily. Admission charged.

The deep canyons and towering cliffs of this area were known to ancient Basketmaker and Pueblo people. A number of sites have been excavated, but none have been prepared for the public. An archeological diorama in the Visitor Center museum depicts prehistoric settlements in the park.

The holes in this slab of rock were used by prehistoric California women as mortars for grinding seeds, particularly acorns, to prepare them for eating.

THE GREAT BASIN
AND CALIFORNIA

The peaks of the Rocky Mountains were a familiar sight to many a band of Big-Game Hunters 11,000 years ago. As they tracked mammoth and bison along the western edges of the Great Plains, they may have felt that the mountain range set a definite limit to their world. And indeed it usually did. At a few places, however, the Rockies presented no barrier to the hunters who wandered on foot. South Pass in Wyoming, for example, offered a route that rose like a broad gentle ramp, up and over the Continental Divide. Hunters could follow game across it without any sense that they were leaving the meat-rich Plains far behind, heading toward places where life would have to be lived in new way.

Slowly little groups of people filtered across the Divide and down into a land which scientists call the Great Basin, an enormous stretch of country lying between the Rockies and the Sierra Nevada. Today this is a desert region, broken by short chains of rugged mountains. From much of the desert land there is no outlet to the ocean. Any water that flows down from the mountains must remain landlocked in swamps or in lakes, only one of which—the Great Salt Lake in Utah—is now very large.

In the days of the Big-Game Hunters the landscape looked quite different. Each of several basins within the Great Basin was filled with a huge body of water. These basin lakes had been formed by the meltwater from Ice-Age glaciers and mountain snowfall. Following the Ice Age there was a rainy period for a while, at least in the mountains, and the runoff fed the lakes: One of them, called by geologists Lake Bonneville, which once reached a depth of about 900 feet, was still 90 feet deep by the time a small band of people began to visit its shore, more than 10,000 years ago.

By about 9,500 years ago the climate became arid. Vegetation became sparse. Game was less abundant than on the Plains. Mammoth hunting did not offer a way of life. Nor did bison roam in large herds. As a result human invaders had to look for other sources of food, and they had to try out new materials for some of their equipment.

Only two kinds of material existed in relative abundance— stone and fibrous plants—and people made the most of them. To the hunter's kit of stone tools, such as knives, scrapers, and projectile points, they added, in the course of time, flat stone implements for grinding small seeds. From plant fiber they fashioned a variety of things that Big-Game Hunters had never found necessary. To hold the seeds that had become essential foods in the new environment they made deep carrying baskets. Other baskets served for parching the seeds. Thin fibers could also be twisted into cord for nets, with which they caught small animals or birds. Other plant material went into sandals and aprons. Some who lived near the lakes fashioned reeds into the shapes of ducks, which they floated on the waters as decoys.

Those who came to the shores of Lake Bonneville sometimes took shelter in a cave now known as Danger Cave (so called because one of the archeologists who excavated it was almost buried beneath rock falling from its roof). There and in nearby caves people left signs of the extraordinary ways in which they managed to use whatever their harsh world offered. From layer after layer of debris archeologists reconstructed a picture of people constantly on the move, but not aimless wanderers. They had learned to take advantage of every edible thing in its own season, and they traveled from place to place according to a well-worked-out plan. Danger Cave, apparently, was a late-summer stopping place, where they harvested the tiny pickleweed seeds. Tons of dried stems from the plants accumulated over the years, after the seeds had been beaten out on the cave floor.

The Western Archaic
In other areas in the Great Basin groups of people adapted to the desert world in generally similar ways, although they may have come originally from different backgrounds. Some may have entered the far northern end of the Basin, then migrated southward, bringing with them a set of tools and a lifeway that has been called Old Cordilleran. Others, possibly descendants of the mammoth hunters, drifted across low passes in the Southwest. Wherever they came from, they developed a Desert or Western Archaic lifeway throughout the very large area that includes southwestern Wyoming, Utah, Nevada, and parts of California, Oregon, and Idaho.

After this desert way of life had taken shape, precarious though it was, it continued. The vast lakes, however, did not persist. As they dwindled, many groups of people moved on. Some of them migrated westward through passes into California, and in this new kind of country they found themselves forced to make adjustments in many different ways.

When Europeans first reached California, they found many distinct groups of people, speaking a great number of different languages or dialects. This probably meant that time after time a wandering band, each with its own language, moved into the area, found a niche for itself between the territories of other groups, and gradually took on some of the traits of its neighbors. (Some archeologists call this the "fish-trap" pattern of settlement, because the various bands seeking food entered California but never made their way out again).

Prehistoric Indians shaped this gigantic figure, which is 105 feet long, and outlined it in gravel on the desert near Blythe, California. Photo by Michael J. Harner.

Migration for Food

All up and down the coast, and inland, too, people found life attractive, and many of them continued an ancient pattern of local, seasonal migration in search of food. Wherever they stayed they left evidence of their habits. At various places on the coast they gathered oysters and clams, and great heaps of discarded shells remained for the archeologist to use in reconstructing the past. Some groups came to depend almost entirely on the sea for their living. They fished with spears and hooks, and hunted sea lions and dolphins.

Elsewhere the early Californians gouged out pits in the rock to use as mortars for grinding seeds and nuts, and hundreds of these food-processing places are still visible. Like many other prehistoric people, these early Californians decorated rock surfaces and cave walls with paintings and peckings which are intriguing but not very well understood.

For all the variety in their languages and in the details of their lives, the California people remained gatherers of seeds and sea foods and hunters of small animals. In other words, their lifeway up until historic times remained at the stage called Western Archaic. Unlike the people of the Southwestern pueblos, they never became farmers with solid, permanent dwellings and all the habits that go with the raising of crops. Some Californians did live in good-sized villages, where they had a year-round supply of food from the sea, but many continued their seasonal migrations, moving from one harvest to another. So, too, did the people who remained in the Great Basin. Like their ancestors thousands of years before, they journeyed from place to place, harvesting first one kind of food and then another, as it ripened.

For a brief time some groups in one part of Utah and at the southernmost edge of Nevada did try farming. But by A.D. 1200 they had given up. Apparently subsistence agriculture was not worth the struggle in this land of little rain. Those who had tried it seem to have departed, leaving the inhospitable region to newcomers who found it easier to forage for food than to grow it.

Baskets and Steatite Vessels

Because most of the Indians of California and the Great Basin were not farmers, the evidences of their lives are not easily seen today. They made lightweight, perishable baskets for gathering and storing their food, instead of manufacturing pottery, which was both cumbersome and fragile. And so the landscape is not littered with potsherds as it is in the Southwest. In a few places people did carve bowls and vessels from a soft rock called steatite, and a California people who lived near Santa Barbara, called Canaliño by the Spaniards, made elegant, large steatite jars for storing water and for cooking. The latter were not placed over the fire. Instead they were filled with water, which women kept at the boiling point by dropping in hot stones. It is interesting to note that on the East Coast of the United States some people also used steatite vessels before they made pottery.

Dwellings, like basketry, were made for the most part from perishable material, and people who stopped in caves did not build stone houses there as they did in the Southwest. The result has been that many archeological sites have not tempted park officials to restore them for visitors. Fortunately there are excellent museums to supplement the growing number of reconstructions.

The Great Basin and California are particularly rich in a special kind of artifact that intrigues and puzzles archeologists. In many places prehistoric artists used rock surfaces as backgrounds for paintings, called pictographs, and/or carvings in the stone, called petroglyphs.

For the most part this rock art cannot be accurately dated by the usual methods. It is almost always exposed, not buried together with other material that can be dated. Specialists who study it can sometimes associate it with datable habitation sites or with symbols that appear in connection with certain cultures. Occasionally ingenious techniques can be used. For example, dates have been found for petroglyphs which were pecked in rock around the Salton Sea in California.

The level of water in the sea has risen and fallen at various times in the past, and each time that a rock surface has been under water it has received a deposit of calcium carbonate. Because of the carbon content of these deposits, they can be dated by the C-14 method. During one dry period, some petroglyphs were scratched in a layer of deposit on a Salton Sea rock. Then the sea rose, and the petroglyphs were covered by a new deposit. Now, by dating the layer just above and the layer just below these petroglyphs, scientists estimate that they were made about 9000 years ago.

Many petroglyphs and pictographs are more recent. Some of those in the West show horses and men with rifles. Obviously these could not have been made before people from Europe introduced horses and guns. One recent example of rock art even shows a truck.

There has been much speculation about the meaning of petroglyphs and pictographs. One theory is that a great deal of rock art may reflect the visions of shamans. The elaborate, multicolored Chumash Indian paintings near Santa Barbara, California, may have been done by shamans under the influence of datura, which causes colorful hallucinations. Possibly the Blythe, California, intaglios also had their origin in the mystical beliefs and visions of shamans.

Although many rock-art sites have been opened to the public, archeologists and park officials have ambivalent feelings about encouraging visits to them. Since most are unguarded and unprotected, they are vulnerable to the peculiar kind of vandal who delights in defacing them. Wherever possible, barriers of some kind have been put up to discourage too close an approach, and visitors are urged to honor whatever means of protection have been installed.

Kokopelli, also known as the Humpbacked Flute Player, frequently appears in rock art in the Southwest. The figure is sometimes regarded as a fertility symbol and sometimes is interpreted as a wandering trader carrying on his back a pack containing his goods. Redrawn from Renaud.

Rock art in Fern Cave, a lava tube near Tule Lake, California.

At the Calico Early Man Archaeological Site, excavators dug in squares 5 feet on a side. As they proceeded, they left exposed a witness column which shows the kind of material through which they had dug. Photo by Fred Budinger.

California

ANTELOPE VALLEY INDIAN MUSEUM

Near Palmdale. From California 14 drive 17 miles east on Avenue M to between 150th and 170th streets East. Or from California 138 drive north on 165th Street East. Mail address: 4555 W. Ave. G, Lancaster, CA 93536. Phone: 805/942-0662. Open daily, October–second week of June, and certain other times by appointment. Admission charged.

The museum offers exhibits of artifacts, some of which are prehistoric, from California, the Great Basin and the Southwest. At times there are demonstrations by craft experts.

ANZA BORREGO DESERT STATE PARK PICTOGRAPH SITE

At State Park headquarters, 2 miles northwest of Borrego Springs inquire for exact directions to site. Mail address: P.O. Box 299, Borrego Springs,

CA 92004. Phone: 619/767-5311. The Visitor Center is open daily, October–May. Saturdays, Sundays, July 4 and Labor Day June–September.

Walks to the Pictograph Site are conducted by a rock art expert. The Visitor Center includes exhibits about the prehistoric Indians of the area, and by special arrangement visitors are allowed in the Daniel Laboratory to view materials from Cahuilla and Kumeyaay people who once lived in the area. On certain evenings lecturers talk about rock art and prehistoric people.

BLYTHE INTAGLIOS

From Blythe drive 17 miles north on US 95 to a roadside marker, "Giant Desert Figures," then west 1/2 mile on a dirt road to one fenced area; for a second area continue to the top of a rise and follow on foot a trail for 1/4 mile south.

An intaglio is a figure or design carved below the surface of the surrounding material. At this site Native Americans created gigantic intaglios on the desert floor by scraping the gravel away to reveal the lighter soil beneath

and piling the gravel so that it formed the outline for the figure or design. Some in the shape of a man measure as much as 175 feet from head to toe. Others represent animals with long tails.

The age and significance of the intaglios are not known. Possibly they represent visions of shamans. Or they may illustrate a religious story similar to that of Yuman people, who believed that if they dreamed of a certain god that had two forms—one of a man, the other of a panther—they would be lucky in hunting. In the intaglios these two forms often appear together.

Almost 300 of these rare forms of Native American art, sometimes called "geoglyphs," have been found on the desert floor near the Colorado River. Most of the sites are not visitable because they are on land reserved for military use. Many of those which can be seen have been vandalized by drivers of off-road vehicles who have almost obliterated some of them with wheel cuts. To protect those remaining, members of the Sierra Club and other organizations have put up fences.

Although it is possible to see the

Archeologists call the objects at the left, bifaces; those in the center, cutting and scraping tools; those at the right, blades and blade cores. All come from deep in the Calico Early Man Archaeological Site. Photo by Dan Griffin.

intaglios from the ground, a much better view can be had from the air. Addresses and phone numbers of chartered plane services can be found in the yellow pages for Lake Havasu City and Yuma, Arizona, and other nearby communities.

CALICO EARLY MAN ARCHAEOLOGICAL SITE

From Barstow on Interstate 15 drive east to Mineola Overpass, then follow the signs. Mail address: Bureau of Land Management, 150 Coolwater Ln., Barstow, CA 92311. Phone: 619/256-3591. Open free, Wednesday–Sunday with hourly guided tours. Closed certain holidays.

Beginning in 1964, excavation here was under the supervision of the late L. S. B. Leaky of Nairobi, Kenya, widely known for his discoveries of very early hominids in Africa. Later, Ruth Dee Simpson, San Bernardino County Museum Archaeologist, supervised excavation at the site.

The site was discovered during an archeological survey of Manix Basin where there had been a lake in the Ice Age. What appeared to be very old artifacts lay on the surface of the site above the basin. Were these objects made by human beings or by natural forces?

Some scientists have said they were made by nature and called them "geofacts." Other experts disagreed.

Excavation in a deposit at the site that was undisturbed has yielded large numbers of what Dr. Leaky and others insist are products of human craftsmanship. Uranium-thorium tests of specimens, conducted by the United States Geological Survey and the University of Southern California, have indicated the astonishing age of 200,000 plus or minus 20,000 years. The material tested was calcium carbonate which, it is claimed, had formed on the specimens *after* they were covered by a developing alluvial fan.

On the basis of these tests, archeologists connected with the site believe it is the oldest site in the Americas.

Obviously a date of 200,000 years for the presence of human beings in North America would have enormous implications for prehistory. Many archeologists regard this date with great

Dwarf Mammoths

On Santa Rosa Island off the California coast near Santa Barbara, excavators have found the remains of mammoths that apparently never attained a height of more than six feet. Elsewhere the crown of a mammoth's head was as much as 12 feet above the ground.

Some archeologists believe that men hunted the dwarf mammoths on Santa Rosa as far back as 29,000 years ago. Others think that the evidence for this date is shaky and that fires attributed to people were really brush fires. Perhaps more excavation on the island will remove all doubt.

Santa Rosa is part of the Channel Islands National Park (see entry).

---

skepticism. Their reasons include these: Human beings 200,000 years old would have been pre-Neanderthal. There is no evidence that humans of this period migrated across Asia and the Bering Land Bridge, as they would have had to do to reach America from their point of origin in Africa. In spite of an intensive search no evidence has been found that human beings evolved in the Americas from anthropoid ancestors. Some geologists claim that the objects said to be artifacts were really created by natural processes and not by human beings. They say burn marks that are claimed to be evidence of a hearth could have been the result of a brush fire caused by lightning. The configuration of rocks that is called a hearth, they believe, could easily have been caused by chance.

This site, the subject of great controversy, is open for anyone who wishes to make a personal evaluation of the evidence.

The operation and control of the Calico Man Site is a cooperative effort of the Friends of Calico Early Man Site, Inc., P.O. Box 535, Yermo, CA 92398, and the Bureau of Land Management.

CALIFORNIA STATE INDIAN MUSEUM

2618 K St., Sacramento, CA 95816. Phone: 916/324-0971. Open daily. Closed certain holidays. Admission charged.

This museum is devoted to the life of California Indians, past and recent. It has an excellent basket collection.

CALIFORNIA STATE UNIVERSITY, FULLERTON, MUSEUM OF ANTHROPOLOGY

West of the 57 Freeway (Orange Freeway) at Nutwood St. turnoff. The museum is in the Humanities Building, Room 313. Mail address: Fullerton, CA 92634. Phone: 714/773-3977. Open free, Monday–Friday. Closed during school vacations and certain holidays.

From time to time this museum has exhibits of prehistoric material from North America.

Painted Cave, San Marcos Pass, near Santa Barbara. A well-preserved example of prehistoric Indian rock art, probably painted by Chumash Indians. Santa Barbara Museum of Natural History photo.

CARPINTERIA VALLEY MUSEUM OF HISTORY

956 Maple Ave., Carpinteria, CA 93013. Phone: 805/684-3112. Open free, afternoons Tuesday–Sunday. Closed certain holidays.

This museum has a large number of artifacts, both prehistoric and historic, that reflect many aspects of Chumash life.

CATALINA ISLAND MUSEUM

In the Casino Building at Avalon, on Santa Catalina Island. Can be reached by boat from Los Angeles harbor or by plane from Long Beach airport. Mail address: P.O. Box 366, Avalon, CA 90704. Open free, daily. For detailed information about transportation, phone 213/510-2414.

In prehistoric times people who had mastered the use of boats lived on Santa Catalina and others of the eight Channel Islands which lie off the coast of southern California. When Spaniards first arrived, those who occupied the northern islands were Chumash Indians, and groups who spoke a Shosho-

nean language lived on the southern islands. However, archeologists often refer to the culture of all the islands at that time as Gabrielino or Pimugnan or Pimu.

Included in the Catalina Island Museum are materials covering a period of about 4000 years. Artifacts in the displays were excavated by archeologists from California universities and from the National Museum of the American Indian, in New York. The exhibits have been arranged to answer these questions: What did people use for dress and decoration? What did they use to make a living? What did they use in religious ceremonies?

CHANNEL ISLANDS NATIONAL PARK

For up-to-date information about transportation to the islands, contact Park Headquarters, 1901 Spinnaker Drive, Ventura, CA 93001. Phone: 805/644-8262. Commercial boat service is available from many southern California ports. Or visitors may use personally owned boats. Open free, daily, all year. No permit is needed for

Anacapa and Santa Barbara islands, but a permit to land on San Miguel must be obtained from park headquarters in advance of any trip. Primitive camping on East Anacapa and Santa Barbara islands. Campers must register in advance at Park Headquarters.

Included in this National Park are Santa Barbara Island, San Miguel Island, Santa Rosa Island, a portion of Santa Cruz Island, and three small islands that make up Anacapa. Archeologists believe that at least 5000 years ago, prehistoric hunters lived here and on three privately owned islands outside the park. Remains of their habitation, and of Chumash Indian occupation before and after the Spanish conquest, have been found at about 600 sites throughout the park. Self-guided and ranger-led walks take visitors past some of the sites. The Visitor Center, at Park Headquarters, in Ventura, has a variety of artifacts on display.

CHAW'SE INDIAN GRINDING ROCK
(See Indian Grinding Rock State Historic Park)

Sticks used in a game played by the Ohlone people, original inhabitants of the San Francisco area. From *People at the Edge of the World* by Betty Morrow (1991). Drawing by Linda Yamane, an Ohlone descendant.

Acorns

The prehistoric population was more dense in California than in many other parts of America north of Mexico. Some specialists believe that about 300,000 people were living in the present area of California when the Spanish began to settle there. Obviously these Indians had a food supply ample for maintaining such a population, and the most important single element in their diet was acorns.

Most varieties of oak tree produce acorns that contain tannic acid and are bitter tasting in their natural state. However, if acorns are soaked in water long enough, the tannic acid disappears, and the nut that is left is sweet and nourishing. Archeologists don't know when Indians discovered this source of food; they do know that the technique of preparing it spread along the West Coast wherever oak trees grew.

The process of leaching whole acorns was slow. It took months to get out the tannic acid. Finally someone made an invention to speed up the work. Using mortar and pestle of the kind that crushed hard-shelled

CHUMASH PAINTED CAVE

From Santa Barbara, drive on San Marcos Pass Road (California 154) to junction with Painted Cave Rd., then 4 miles to marker. Open free, at all times.

In a rock outcropping 20 feet above the road is a grotto about 15 feet deep. Here prehistoric artists painted on the stone many brilliant, colorful figures and designs that have given the cave its name. The cave itself is not open to the public but may be viewed from outside the grilled gate.

CLARKE MEMORIAL MUSEUM

3rd and E streets, Eureka, CA 95501. Phone: 707/443-1947. Open free, daily.

Among the ethnologic collections here are ten prehistoric zoomorphs (animal forms created in slate by grinding). These zoomorphs, unique to the area, were found on an island in Humboldt Bay. They have not been precisely dated but are believed to be at least 500 years old.

CLEAR LAKE STATE PARK

From Lakeport on California 29 drive south on local road to Kelseyville, then northeast 4 miles on Soda Bay Rd. to park entrance. Phone: 707/279-4293. Open at all times. Admission charged. Camping.

A group of prehistoric Indians, who lived in much the same way as the Pomo Indians, once had a settlement on this lake. From the few traces they left, archeologists can reconstruct something of their customs and daily activities.

Here, as in much of North America, a sweat house was important in prehistoric Indian life. In California it was usually a substantial, earth-covered structure, a little smaller than the dwellings people lived in. Men came to the sweat house, often at night, much as men of other cultures go to clubs. They took the baths together and often slept all night in the house. Apparently sweat baths were as much for pleasure as for reasons of health or because they had ceremonial significance. And men really sweated. They

seeds to make them edible, a woman ground the soft acorns into a flour. When this acorn flour was soaked in hot water, the tannic acid disappeared very quickly.

To do the leaching, a woman often made a small hollow in the sand beside a stream. In the hollow she placed a lining of leaves and poured in acorn flour. Then she filled a water-tight basket with water and dropped hot stones in it. When the water was hot, she poured it over the acorn flour. Several dousings completely carried the acid away. What remained was a moist cake that could be eaten without delay or dried and saved for future use. Dried acorn flour, mixed with water, was served as a kind of thick soup, or mush.

Acorn flour was not only tasty but nourishing. It contained about 21 percent fat, 5 percent protein, and 62 percent carbohydrate. Its fat content was much greater than that of either maize or wheat; its protein and carbohydrate content somewhat less.

The holes in this slab of rock were used by prehistoric California women as mortars for grinding seeds, particularly acorns, to prepare them for eating.

built a very hot fire, inside the house, and if the smoke got too thick they lay down on the floor, where they could breath fresh air. Often the houses were near streams or lakes or the ocean. After getting up a good sweat, the bathers plunged into the water. Then to dry themselves, some of them, in historic times at least, rolled in the sand.

Another structure that once existed at Clear Lake was a ceremonial house. It, like the sweat house, was earth-covered, but it was a great deal larger. People met here for dances and religious activities. California Indians never developed a priesthood. They had shamans, or medicine men, and they had at least two religious cults that survived into historic times. One, in north central California, is called the Kuksu. Men who belonged to the cult impersonated mythological characters, and initiations were very important. Another cult, in southern California, called the Toloache, also placed great emphasis on initiation rites and on the use of jimsonweed, which has hallucinogenic properties.

No one knows what cult was con-

nected with the ceremonial house at Clear Lake, but we can be sure that the religious beliefs and practices here did not differ greatly from those in neighboring areas. Although California Indians spoke many different languages, their ceremonial lives were patterned in similar ways.

A nature trail in the park, for which a folder has been prepared, identifies many plants in the area and tells how they were used by the Indians who lived here. Along the trail is the site of an Indian village. It is marked by a mortar hole and a grinding slab. When a woman wanted to grind acorns, she took a special basket that had a hole in the bottom and placed it in the mortar hole. Then she filled this receptacle with acorns, and used a stone pestle to crush them.

One of the plants identified along the nature trail is the California buckeye. This plant produces a fruit which is poisonous when eaten raw, but the Indians learned how to bake it and then soak it in a way that removed the poison. Roasted buckeyes were mashed or whipped, much as we mash or whip potatoes.

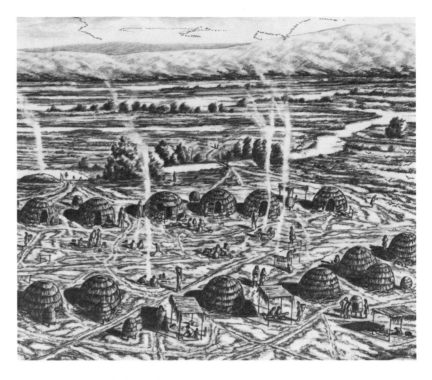

This is an artist's reconstruction of an Ohlone village, which once stood at the place now called Coyote Hills. Illustration by Michael Harney from *The Ohlone Way: Indian Life in the San Francisco–Monterey Bay Area,* by Malcolm Margolin. 1978.

COYOTE HILLS REGIONAL PARK

Drive west from Fremont or east from the Dumbarton Bridge on California 84 to Thornton Ave. exit, then north on the Paseo Padre Freeway, then left onto Patterson Ranch Road, which ends at the park. Mail address: East Bay Regional Park District, 11500 Skyline Blvd., Oakland, CA 94619. Phone 510/795-9385. Open daily, except certain holidays. Seasonal parking fee charged.

For more than 2,000 years Ohlone people lived here on the shoreline of the East Bay area near San Francisco. With plenty of sea and land animals and a variety of plant foods, these hunters and gatherers prospered, and they left behind four mounds of household debris and mollusc shells. Today one of the mounds is the site of a reconstructed reed house, a shade shelter, a dance circle, and a sweat house. A broadwalk leads across the marsh to another of the mounds. Park naturalists conduct tours and give group pro-

grams, usually on weekends. The schedule is available at the Visitor Center.

In the Center a large diorama presents the details of life in an Ohlone village. Also on exhibit is a full-size reed boat that the park staff reconstructed, using Ohlone methods, and then tried out on the waters of the bay. Books about the Ohlone available in the bookstore include the two from which drawings on pages 134, 136, and 144 were taken.

Examples of Indian rock art can be seen in many canyon areas in California. These drawings were cut into a soft tuff cliff at Emigrant Wash, in Death Valley National Monument. National Park Service photo.

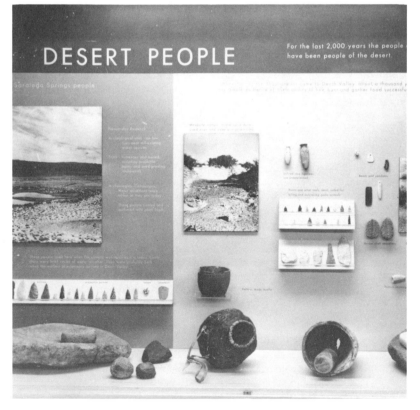

An exhibit in the museum at the headquarters of Death Valley National Monument sketches the life of Indians who lived in this desert area for 2000 years. National Park Service photo.

At an unknown date, possibly several thousand years ago, Native Americans in California carved mazes on the surface of boulders. This one, which came to light after a flood near Hemet, is one of the few that are accessible to the public. Photo courtesy of Daniel F. McCarthy.

CUYAMACA RANCHO STATE PARK
(KOO-yah-MA-ka)

From San Diego drive east on Interstate 8, then north on California 79 to the park and museum. Phone: 619/765-0755. Open free, daily, all year.

An Indian exhibit in the former Dyar residence in the park deals with the story of the Diegueño Indians of the area. The park has a short trail with interpretive signs that explain the way Indians used plants.

DEATH VALLEY NATIONAL MONUMENT

From Las Vegas, Nevada, drive northwest 87 miles on US 95 to Lathrop Wells, then south 23 miles on Nevada 373 to Death Valley Junction, then west 30 miles on California 190 to the Visitor Center and museum at Furnace Creek. Mail address: Death Valley, CA 92328. Phone: 619/786-2331. Open daily. Admission charged to Monument. Camping.

Exhibits in the museum tell briefly the story of human habitation of Death Valley from 6000 or 7000 B.C. to the present.

Petroglyphs may be seen at many places in the monument, notably at Klare Spring, in Titus Canyon, and along the ridges of Greenwater Canyon, near the Mesquite Springs campground, and in Emigrant Canyon.

EASTERN CALIFORNIA MUSEUM

Three blocks west of the Inyo County Courthouse, 155 N. Grant St., Independence. Mail address: P.O. Box 206, Independence, CA 93526. Phone: 619/878-2411; weekends 619/878-2010. Open free, Wednesday–Monday. Closed certain holidays.

This museum reports that it has about 6500 prehistoric artifacts that include a variety of archeological collections. A special display is devoted to Paiute-Shoshone basketry.

THE HAGGIN MUSEUM

Victory Park, 1201 North Pershing Avenue, Stockton, CA 95203-1699. Phone: 209/462-4116 or 1566. Open free, Tuesday–Sunday. Closed certain holidays.

Most of this museum's exhibits of Native American materials deal with the historic period, but there are some prehistoric exhibits among the North American displays.

HEMET MAZE STONE

From Hemet on California 74 (Florida Ave.) drive north on California Ave. about 3 miles. The road dead-ends in a small park administered by the Riverside County Parks Department, P.O. Box 3507, Riverside, CA 92519.

Here is one of the few petroglyphs in the form of a maze that is accessible to the public. It was discovered by hikers after heavy rain uncovered the boulder on which the maze had been pecked, perhaps as much as 3000 years ago. Archeologist Daniel McCarthy, who has studied this and other maze petroglyphs in the area, says "I know of no other similar aboriginal carvings anywhere else in America or in the world."

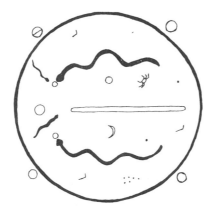

This design presents the world, the sun and moon, and snakes and animals with special powers. The Diegueño Indians used it in the puberty ceremony held for boys. After Waterman and Underhill.

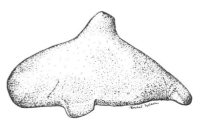

Whale effigy carved from stone, California.

INDIAN GRINDING ROCK STATE HISTORIC PARK

From Jackson drive northeast 10 miles on California 88 to Pine Grove, then 1.3 miles northwest on Pine Grove-Volcano Rd. Mail address: 14881 Pine Grove-Volcano Rd., Pine Grove, CA 95665. Phone: 209/296-7488. Open at all times except when closed by snow. Admission charged. Camping.

The Chaw'se Regional Indian Museum here has a collection of Sierra Nevada Indian artifacts. A Miwok village has been reconstructed nearby. The museum is closed certain holidays.

The Story. Miwok Indians once lived at this site, which they called Chaw'se (sha-tze). Here, on an outcrop of limestone 173 feet long and 82 feet wide, are 1,185 circular pits which have been worn in the rock. These pits are chaw'se—that is, stationary basins in which women used pestles to grind up seeds, particularly acorns, as one step in preparing them to be eaten.

On the same outcrop are 363 petroglyphs which have been pecked in the limestone.

The Indians who lived at Chaw'se no doubt had many of the customs of other Miwoks. They probably used money made of shell or of small polished and baked cylinders of a rock called magnesite. They built cone-shaped dwellings, some wholly above ground, others partly below ground. Often they dug large pits and then erected structures over them to serve as assembly places or dance houses. Men had special houses in which they took sweat baths.

Certainly the grinding of acorns was not all that went on at Chaw'se. For such large facilities there must also have been large storage arrangements. Wherever they lived the Miwoks seem to have erected granaries, which they built on posts, using a kind of basketry technique. Like other Indians of California, they had developed the art of basketmaking to a very high degree.

The baskets and other artifacts made by prehistoric Miwoks can be seen in various California museums. But nowhere is there a better example of the way these people turned bedrock into a tool essential to their livelihood.

There are several developed trails in the park, one leading to an exhibit that consists of reconstructions of eight bark dwelling houses, a ceremonial round-house, an acorn granary, a large shelter, and a hand-game house. Two display cases show where Miwok Indians lived in California and how they processed food.

INSCRIPTION CANYON

Northwest of Barstow, mostly on graded dirt roads. For detailed road directions consult the Bureau of Land Management, Barstow Resource Area, 150 Coolwater Lane, Barstow, CA 92311. Phone: 619/256-3591

Beautiful and unusual petroglyphs carved on basalt cliffs may be seen in the canyon, also called Black Canyon, and at other spots along the road.

Students from the University of Southern California excavating a site at Squaw Tank, in Joshua Tree National Monument. National Park Service photo.

JOSHUA TREE NATIONAL MONUMENT

74485 National Monument Drive, Twentynine Palms, CA 92277. Phone: 619/367-7511. Open year round. Entrance fee charged. Camping.

Joshua Tree National Monument is at the junction of two desert ecosystems—the low elevation (below 300 feet) Colorado Desert and the high elevation Mohave Desert. With the diversity of plant and animal life, humans have inhabited this area from post-Pleistocene times to the present.

One early prehistoric culture was first discovered in the Pinto Basin district of the monument. This assemblage, called the Pinto Basin Complex, was indicative of a big-game hunting and gathering society.

The Pinto Period lasted from approximately 5000 to 2000 B.C. It was a period of great climatic change. Moist environments turned to arid environments. Plants and animals changed. It was a period of human adaptation to a desert environment. This adaptation is a focal point of controversy in the California Desert chronologies.

In more recent times, the Joshua Tree region was known to be traditionally used by three Native American groups—the Serrano, the Chemehuevi, and the Cahuilla. These groups traveled through the area during the cooler months, utilizing natural rock overhangs for shelters and gathering local seeds and fruits for food. They documented their lifestyle with pictographs and petroglyphs.

Remnants of these past peoples still exist in the area. Archeological research continues in the monument and exhibits of material culture are in the Visitor Centers at Twentynine Palms and Black Rock Canyon. Inquire at the Visitor Centers for the easily accessible trail to the Barker Dam rock site or the Ryan Mountain Indian Cave.

KERN COUNTY MUSEUM

3801 Chester Ave., Bakersfield, CA 93304. Phone: 805/861-2132. Open daily. Closed certain holidays. Admission charged.

Random local archeological finds are included here with more recent arti-

San Dieguito and Diegueño

As you go through California museums or read about Indians, you may be puzzled by two names that look somewhat alike—San Dieguito and Diegueño. San Dieguito refers to a very early culture. Diegueño refers to a late culture, which extended into historic times.

The San Dieguito culture began perhaps 11,000 years ago in the southern part of the Great Basin. At that time the people apparently did not specialize in any one method of getting food. They hunted, did some fishing, and dug up edible roots. As the centuries passed, they became gatherers and grinders of small seeds. Later, about 7000 or 8000 years ago, when some of them moved to the coastal regions in southern California, they became adjusted to a diet of food from the sea, which supplemented their vegetable foods. Because our first knowledge of this culture comes from a site on the San Dieguito River north of San Diego, archeologists gave it the name San Dieguito. However, some important San Dieguito sites are a great distance from San Diego. One, for example, is at the lowest level of Ventana Cave, in southern Arizona.

The Kumeyaay Indians, called Diegueño by the Spanish, who have lived in the San Diego area for the last 1000 years or more, introduced pottery making and practiced cremation of their dead. During their ceremonials they made paintings on the ground, using fine powders for pigments. They used ground soapstone for white, iron oxide for red, charcoal for black and dried seeds for other colors.

---

facts, which are representative of Yokuts and other cultures in southern San Joaquin Valley. A diorama shows Yokuts basketweaving techniques.

KULE LOKLO

In Bear Valley, Point Reyes National Seashore, off California 1 at Olema. Phone: 415/663-1092. Open free, daily, all year. Hike-in camping nearby.

Kule Loklo is an authentic replica of a Coast Miwok Indian village. Such buildings as a ceremonial dance house, dwellings and a sweat house are based on archeological evidence and on the accounts of early European visitors to the area. Tours guided by Native Americans are available for school groups. Students are encouraged to learn how to do such things as weave mats, construct bird traps and make shell beads or ceremonial rattles.

For centuries before Europeans reached California, the peaceful Coast Miwok people lived along the shore, fishing, hunting and gathering acorns and wild plants. In 1579 the English pirate Francis Drake landed somewhere near Point Reyes, but it was almost 200 years before Spanish colonists and missionaries arrived. They made the Miwok people leave their homes to work at the missions, and the coastal Indian villages were abandoned. Archeologists have studied some of these village sites, but none are open to the public. Instead, Kule Loklo has been built to give a more vivid picture of Miwok life than would be offered by an actual site.

LAKE PERRIS REGIONAL INDIAN MUSEUM

From Highway 60 south of Riverside, take Moreno Beach Drive exit and proceed south to Lake Perris Recreation Area. Phone: 714/657-0676. Open daily. Admission charged.

Exhibits here emphasize the native people of the Mojave Desert and environs including both pre-contact and historic times.

LA PURISIMA MISSION STATE HISTORIC PARK

Three miles from Lompoc on California 246 and Purisima Road. Mail address: R. F. D. Box 102, Lompoc, CA 93436. Phone (at the mission): 805/733-3713. Open daily. Admission charged.

In the museum at the former mission are several displays that deal with Chumash prehistory and historic archeology.

LAS CRUCES ADOBE

From Santa Barbara, drive north on US 101 to junction with California 1, continue .5 mile to Gaviota State Park. Mail address: California Department of Parks and Recreation, Central Coast Region, 2211 Garden Road, Monterey, CA 93940. Phone: 805/567-5013. Open daily. Admission charged.

Here, where California's oldest surviving adobe building stands, the Chumash Indians lived from about A.D. 900 to 1500.

Children's class at the Marin Museum of the American Indian, which features hands-on exhibits. Photo by Joan Fray.

Prehistoric Indians pecked a great many animal figures and designs on the rocks in this canyon near China Lake, California. Maturango Museum photo.

LAVA BEDS NATIONAL MONUMENT

From Tulelake drive 9 miles south on California 139. Mail address: P.O. Box 867, Tulelake, CA 96134. Phone: 916/667-2282. Open daily. Admission charged.

At an unknown time Native Americans carved petroglyphs on a cliff face here. Off the road to Skull Cave, along a .75 mile trail, at Big Painted Cave and Symbol Bridge, are pictographs. Both the prehistoric petroglyphs and pictographs may have been related to religious activities. The pictographs can be viewed by appointment only. They are at a site that is holy to the Modoc Indians of today.

LOMPOC MUSEUM

200 South H St., Lompoc, CA 93436-7297. Phone: 805/736-3888. Open free, afternoons, Tuesday–Sunday. Closed certain holidays.

Exhibited here is material from 50 Chumash sites in northern Santa Barbara County. Among the displays are fine stone tools, sculptured steatite effigies, and Indian basketry collections. Material from southwestern, western and midwestern states, Alaska and Canada is also represented in the prehistoric artifact collections. Special exhibits change throughout the year. One gallery is devoted to the history of the Lompoc Valley.

MALIBU CREEK STATE PARK

From Malibu drive 3 miles north on Malibu Canyon Road. From US 101 at Las Virgines Road exit and drive south. Phone: 818/706-1310. Open daily, all year. Admission charged.

In the Visitor Center, open weekends, is a small exhibit on the Chumash and a painting of a large pictograph panel.

MARIN MUSEUM OF THE AMERICAN INDIAN

2200 Novato Blvd. Mail address: P.O. Box 864, Novato, CA 94948. Phone: 415/897-4064. Open Tuesday–Saturday, afternoon Sunday. Closed cer-

Rock art in Renegade Canyon.
Maturango Museum photo by R. T.
Sandberg.

tain holidays. Admission by donation.

In this primarily ethnographic museum hands-on activities give visitors a chance to learn how Native Americans lived before contact with people of European origin. Visitors may use a pump drill to make holes in shells, may grind acorns in stone mortars and play games. Surrounding the museum is a garden in which are plants once used by the original inhabitants of the area.

MIWOK PARK
(*See Marin Museum of the American Indian*)

MATURANGO MUSEUM OF THE INDIAN WELLS VALLEY

100 East Las Flores, Ridgecrest, CA 93556. Phone: 619/375-6900. Open Tuesday–Sunday, all year. Closed certain holidays. Admission charged.

This museum has exhibits of materials that span the period from Pinto Basin culture to recent Shoshonean culture in the Upper Mojave Desert. Displays include rock art from the area

and a photomural of petroglyphs from Renegade Canyon.

The museum also conducts spring and fall tours to Renegade Canyon on weekend days which do not interfere with the activities of the Naval Weapons Center (see Renegade Canyon entry below). A videotape on Coso style rock art is shown before each tour starts. The tapes are for sale.

MONTEREY STATE HISTORIC PARK

Park headquarters: 210 Oliver Street, Monterey, CA 93940. Phone: 408/373-2103. Available here is a walking-tour map and information about hours at various historic sites in the city. At two of them, the Pacific House and Cooper-Molera Adobe, are interpretive displays that feature prehistoric and historic archeology.

MUSEUM OF ANTHROPOLOGY

On the campus of California State University, Fullerton, CA 92634. Phone: 714/773-3977. Open free,

Monday–Friday. Closed during school vacations and certain holidays.

From time to time this museum has exhibits of prehistoric material from North America. Its basic collections are Egyptian.

NATURAL HISTORY MUSEUM OF LOS ANGELES COUNTY

In Exposition Park. 900 Exposition Blvd., Los Angeles, CA 90007. Phone: 213/744-3466. Open, Tuesday–Sunday. Closed Monday (except most Monday holidays) and certain holidays. Admission charged.

The Lando Hall of California and Southwest History includes prehistoric artifacts and reproductions of prehistoric dwellings. The museum also offers changing exhibits on aspects of archeology north of Mexico. Many permanent exhibits deal with pre-history south of the United States.

Dance regalia made of bird feathers were worn by the Ohlone people. From *People at the Edge of the World.* By Betty Morrow (1991). Drawing by Linda Yamane, who is an Ohlone descendant.

OAKLAND MUSEUM, HISTORY DIVISION

1000 Oak St., Oakland, CA 94607. Phone: 510/238-3842. Open free, Wednesday–Sunday. Closed certain holidays.

Archeological materials from several Bay area sites are part of a large exhibit devoted to the ethnography and cultural ecology of California Indians.

PALM SPRINGS DESERT MUSEUM

101 Museum Dr., Palm Springs, CA 92262. Phone: 619/325-7186. Open Tuesday–Saturday; afternoon Sunday, September 1–May 31. Admission charged.

This museum displays some local archeological material.

POINT REYES NATIONAL SEASHORE
(*See Kule Loklo*)

RENEGADE CANYON
(Also called Little Petroglyph Canyon)

China Lake Naval Weapons Center. It is necessary to make reservations two weeks in advance (to allow for security clearance) for tours that take place Saturdays and Sundays in spring and fall. Apply to Maturango Museum, P.O. Box 1776, Ridgecrest, CA 93556. Phone: 619/375-6900. Fee charged. Visitors caravan 42 miles in their own cars.

Here in a National Historic Landmark is one of the largest and best preserved concentrations of rock art anywhere in the United States. About 20,000 glyphs are known in the Coso Range as a whole. Abstract, anthropomorphic and zoomorphic designs were created by pecking or abrading away black desert varnish on basaltic boulders, cliff faces and canyon walls. The late Campbell Grant, an authority on rock art, suggested that many of the bighorn sheep designs were made by hunters who hoped by magic to improve their success in the chase. Some designs show the use of atlatls. Others show the later bow and arrow.

SAN BERNARDINO COUNTY MUSEUM

2024 Orange Tree Lane, Redlands, CA 92374. Phone: 714/798-8570 or 422-1610. Open free, Tuesday–Saturday; afternoon Sunday. Closed certain holidays.

This museum has displays covering the prehistoric and historic Indians of San Bernardino County. The Serrano, Luiseno, Gabrielino, Cahuilla, Chemehuevi, Panamint and Mohave are represented, as are ancient prehistoric cultures including Paleo-Indian and Archaic. The Calico Early Man assemblage represented by objects from excavation in the Calico Mountains (see entry above) near Yermo, California, has created widespread discussion in archeological circles. If the age of Calico material proves to be as great as some archeologists think it may be—200,000 years—then this museum will contain the oldest dated artifacts in the Americas.

SAN DIEGO MUSEUM OF MAN

1350 El Prado, Balboa Park, San Diego, CA 92101. Phone: 619/239-2001. Open daily. Admission charged, except on third Tuesday of each month.

This museum has rich resources of southern California and southwestern material. The exhibits change frequently.

SAN FRANCISCO STATE UNIVERSITY, ADÁN E. TREGANZA ANTHROPOLOGY MUSEUM

1600 Holloway Ave., San Francisco, CA 94132. Phone: 415/338-1642. Open free, Monday–Friday.

American archeological materials here represent many culture areas from the northern and central parts of the state, with examples of materials from the middle and later periods on through historic contact.

SAN JUAN BAUTISTA STATE HISTORIC PARK

On California 156, seven miles west of Hollister. Mail address: P.O. Box 1110, San Juan Bautista, CA 95045. Phone (at the park): 408/623-4881.

A diorama in the Santa Barbara Museum of Natural History shows prehistoric cave dwellers in Southern California. Santa Barbara Museum of Natural History photo.

At this former mission, which is now a parish church, is a small museum that includes informal displays of prehistoric archeological material.

SANTA BARBARA MUSEUM OF NATURAL HISTORY

2559 Puesta del Sol Rd., Santa Barbara, CA 93105. Phone: 805/682-4711. Open free, daily.

Archeological exhibits here are devoted largely to the Chumash Indians of southern California. Displays include culture history, tracing the ancestors of these people back to the Canaliño people (A.D. 1000–1769), Hunting People (2000 B.C.–A.D. 1000) and Oak Grove people (5000–2000 B.C.). Several displays show life on the eve of historic contact, focusing upon economy, food preparation, technology, arts in shell, stone and wood, as well as basketry, music, games, rituals and social organization. Dioramas show scenes of Canaliño, Oak Grove and Chumash life. A replica of a full-size Chumash plank canoe is on exhibit.

SANTA CRUZ CITY MUSEUM OF NATURAL HISTORY

1305 East Cliff Drive, Santa Cruz, CA 95062. Phone: 408/429-3773. Open free, Tuesday–Saturday, afternoon Sunday.

This museum includes some material on local prehistory.

SHELTER COVE

From Redway take Highway 101 to Shelter Cove Road. Mail address: Bureau of Land Management, Arcata Resource Area, 1125 16th St., Room 219, Arcata, CA 95521. Phone: 707/822-7648. Open free, daily. Camping nearby.

This is an information center that includes in its displays archeological materials from nearby excavations not open to the public. These materials are assumed to represent predecessors of the Sinkyone and Mattole, both Athabascan-speaking peoples.

SHERMAN MUSEUM

9010 Magnolia Ave., Riverside, CA 92503. Phone: 714/276-6327. From the Van Buren offramp of the Riverside Freeway, turn onto Magnolia Ave. Open weekday afternoons. Closed certain holidays. Voluntary contribution.

In this museum in the Sherman Indian High School, along with Indian material from the historic period, are prehistoric stone implements, potsherds from Arizona and southern California and Hohokam, Salado, Mimbres and Four Mile Polychrome bowls.

Sites for the Future

Archeological sites disappear as they are excavated, as parking lots spread, as workers dig trenches for gas lines and water mains. Development of all kinds threatens to eliminate sites that could be useful for study of the past. To save some of them, The Archeological Conservancy (415 Orchard Drive, Santa Fe, NM 87501; phone: 505/982-3278) buys or accepts as gifts land that has archeological significance. It then protects the sites for study in the future.

One that The Archeological Conservancy was seeking funds to buy as this book went to press was a walnut grove on the Borax Lake site in California. Here, more than half a century ago, Mark Harrington found Clovis points. This meant that people had lived in California much longer than anyone had known. What full excavation of the site will reveal about Clovis or possibly earlier people remains to be seen.

SOUTHWEST MUSEUM

234 Museum Dr., Highland Park, Los Angeles. Mail address: P.O. Box 41558, Los Angeles, CA 90041. Phone: 213/221-2163. Open afternoons, Tuesday–Sunday, year round. Admission charged.

Extensive exhibits are devoted to the Indians of all the Americas, with rich archeological materials from all areas of the New World.

There are particularly good exhibits of artifacts from California, the Plains and the Northwest Coast. Fine exhibits include Anasazi material and Hohokam and Mimbres pottery.

TREGANZA ANTHROPOLOGY MUSEUM
(See San Francisco State University)

TULARE COUNTY MUSEUM
(too-LAIR-ee)

27000 Mooney Blvd., Visalia, CA 93277. Phone: 209/733-6616. Open, summer, Wednesday–Monday; winter, Thursday–Monday. Closed certain holidays. Admission charged.

Exhibits here include many prehistoric baskets and weapons and a large display of shell money of various kinds.

UNIVERSITY OF CALIFORNIA, PHOEBE HEARST MUSEUM OF ANTHROPOLOGY
(Formerly the Lowie Museum)

103 Kroeber Hall, University of California, Berkeley, CA 94720. Phone: 510/642-3681. Open Tuesday–Friday; afternoons Saturday and Sunday. Closed certain holidays. Admission charged.

The former Lowie Museum has a vast collection of California and other American archeological material, parts of which are on display from time to time.

WILDER RANCH STATE PARK

From Santa Cruz drive north one mile on California 1 to the exit to Wilder Ranch State Park. The park entrance is .25 mile away. Mail address: California Department of Parks and Recreation, Central Coast Division, 2211 Garden Road, Monterey, CA 93940. Phone: 408/688-3241. Open daily. Admission charged.

In this park are several Native American sites, including Ohlone sites that were occupied from 1030 B.C. to A.D. 350.

YOSEMITE NATIONAL PARK

Mail address: National Park Service, P.O. Box 577, Yosemite National Park, CA 95389. Phone: 209/372-0282. Open daily, all year.

The Yosemite Museum, open free, has some prehistoric material in the Indian Cultural Exhibit room.

The Indian Village, also free, is a reconstruction of a Southern Miwok village on the site of a prehistoric village. During the summer demonstrators occasionally show how acorns were processed, how stone was worked, how baskets were made and how games were played.

Baskets, Bags, and Pots

Almost everywhere Indians sooner or later found that they could take grasses or shredded bark or other plant fibers and fashion them into implements that enriched life or—in very poor areas—made survival possible. Weaving and plaiting, they made baby carriers, nets to catch game or fowl or fish, containers for food, and baskets so fine they could be used as canteens or as pots for cooking.

The art of basketmaking seems to be older than the art of shaping and baking clay to form durable pots. Baskets were light and easily carried from place to place. On the other hand, pottery was heavy, and it broke easily. So people tended to cling to basketmaking as long as they were on the move, looking for sustenance. When they had a food supply from farming, they could settle down—indeed, they had to settle down—and then they could economically use heavy pots.

The art of pottery making had reached the Southwest by A.D. 300. Curiously, on the East Coast it appeared much earlier—about 2500 B.C.

In California and along the Northwest Coast, where food was relatively abundant without agriculture and where people lived together in large groups, they clung to basketry up to historic times. Apparently they felt satisfied with their old way of life and saw no great need for change. Pottery making did come into southern California in relatively recent times, when knowledge of the art spread from the Southwest and Mexico.

In the Great Basin basketry was the skill people used above all others. Strips of rabbit skin, woven basket fashion, formed their robes. Even their simple shelters were rather like big, crude baskets.

Baskets and baked clay pots were by no means the only kinds of container. In areas where steatite (soapstone) was available, some people carved vessels from this soft material. In other places they carved bowls of wood or shaped wood into boxes or used tough-skinned gourds as canteens for holding water. In the northern woodlands they often shaped tree bark into containers. Hunters on the Plains made pouches and bags and boxes from the stomachs and intestines and hides of buffalo. They even used hollow buffalo horns as containers for the live coals they carried from one campground to another.

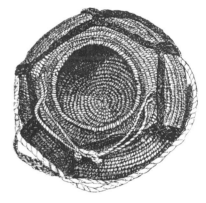

Two examples of basketry from the Mesa Verde area. *Above:* An intricately woven pillow. *Below:* A basket that contained charms used by a religious leader in performing healing ceremonies.

Prehistoric Indians mined steatite for cooking vessels. Smithsonian Institution photo.

Vast numbers of petroglyphs (drawings pecked in rock) show the elusive bighorn sheep, greatly prized by ancient hunters but hard to get. The petroglyphs may have been connected with the belief that a hunter could win magical power over an animal by drawing its likeness. Those shown here were found in the Lake Mead National Recreation Area. National Park Service photo.

NEVADA

CHURCHILL COUNTY MUSEUM

1050 South Maine Street, Fallon, NV 89406. Phone: 702/423-3677. Open free, daily.

This museum has displays of prehistoric Indian material discovered in nearby Hidden Cave (see entry below). On the second and fourth Saturdays of each month guided public tours to the cave begin here at 9:30 a.m.

GREAT BASIN NATIONAL PARK

From US 6-50 follow signs through Baker and on to the park. Mail address: Baker, Nevada 89311. Phone: 702/234-7331. Open free, daily, all year.

The entrance tunnel to one cave in this park passes through a room in which prehistoric Native Americans once lived, but there is no exhibit of material.

GRIMES POINT ARCHAEOLOGICAL AREA
National Register of Historic Places

From Fallon drive 10 miles east on US 50 to roadside marker. Open free, daily, all year. For information phone the Churchill County Museum (see Hidden Cave entry).

Grimes Point was first visited by Native Americans about 8000 years ago, when much of the now arid region was covered by ancient Lake Lahontan. Some of these early hunters and others who followed them left traces of camps—stone scrapers, bits of matting, scraps of bone. Many of them also spent time making petroglyphs in the boulders of the area. At one spot, which archeologists think may have been used 7000 years ago, numerous small pits have been carved in the rock, along with long grooves. At other places the rock engravings are abstract designs, or possibly markers for ancient game trails. No one is sure of their meaning or their exact age.

The boulders at Grimes Point are a deep, dark brown, but under the surface the color of the rock is much lighter. The dark color, called patina, or desert varnish, was caused by long-term chemical changes in the rock. Any scratch reveals the lighter surface beneath. In time scratches themselves acquire patina—the older they are, the darker. Thus students of rock art believe they can tell at least the relative ages of the engravings.

Visitors may see a good deal of rock art along the Grimes Point Petroglyph Trail, which was built by the Youth Conservation Corps and is administered by the Bureau of Land Management. An illustrated booklet is available, free, at the entrance to the site, and trail markers explain points of special interest.

HICKISON SUMMIT PETROGLYPHS

From Austin drive 24 miles east on US 50 to site entrance. Mail address: Bureau of Land Management, Battle Mountain District, 825 N. Second St., Battle Mountain, NV 89820. Phone:

Petroglyphs in Grapevine Wash, Lake Mead National Recreation Area. National Park Service photo.

702/635-4037. Open free, daily, all year. Camping.

A self-guided interpretive trail leads to the petroglyphs. They are of unknown age, are typical of the Great Basin curvilinear style and were produced by pecking, incising or scratching. Some archeologists believe they are connected with hunting or fertility magic.

HIDDEN CAVE

On the second and fourth Saturday of each month tours visit the site, starting from the Churchill County Museum, 1050 South Maine St., Fallon, NV 98406. Phone: 702/423-3677.

Hunter-gatherers apparently used this cave near ancient Lake Lahontan as a storage place for food and artifacts, beginning about 5365 B.C. and continuing up to about 800 B.C.

Archeologists have found a wealth of ancient implements, tools and ornaments buried under layers of dust and volcanic ash that was blown or washed into the deep cavern. One cache held obsidian projectile points, a neatly

folded fishing net and beads of shell that had probably come by trade from the West Coast. Some of this material is on exhibit at the Churchill County Museum. Over the years the cave was often vandalized but is now closed off except to the organized tours.

LAKE MEAD NATIONAL RECREATION AREA

Good highways lead into the area from Kingman, Arizona; Needles, California; Las Vegas and Glendale, Nevada. Mail address: Boulder City, NV 89005. Phone: 702/293-8906. Open free, all year. Camping.

People have lived in Nevada for at least 11,000 years, and the tools and weapons that indicate their presence at an early date have been found in many places in the Lake Mead National Recreation Area. The waters of Lake Mohave and Lake Mead have now covered nearly all the campsites or petroglyphs left by humans before the dawn of history.

The easiest place to see petroglyphs is in Grapevine Wash, on the Christ-

Lovelock Cave

In northwestern Nevada, Lovelock Cave once opened out on Lake Lahonton, an immense body of water that existed during and after the rainy period at the end of the Ice Age. About 4500 years ago, people began to visit this cave, and for a long time they used it as a place in which to store equipment. The implements they left there show how they exploited plant and animal life along the lakeshores. To attract ducks, for example, they used decoys fashioned from reeds that grew around the lake and sometimes made realistic with duck feathers woven along the sides. From reeds and a dozen other fibers, the cave's visitors made sandals, fishnets, mats, and baskets of various kinds. They used shredded fiber in clothing and wove blankets from animal fur and bird skins.

The concern these people felt for weaving and basketry appeared in another way. In the cave they left sickles made of bone and mountain-sheep horn that helped them harvest the grasses they used as fibers.

Few sites in the Great Basin area have yielded more information about the early people who lived there. Lovelock Cave itself has not been prepared for visitation by the public.

This duck decoy, made of reeds, was found in Lovelock Cave, Nevada. Some duck decoys were decorated with feathers. After Loud and Harrington.

mas Tree Pass Road, near Davis Dam, on Lake Mohave. Christmas Tree Pass can be reached from either Nevada 77, west of Bullhead City, Arizona, or from US 95 south of Searchlight, Nevada. It is not known when or by whom the petroglyphs in this area were made, but they may be very ancient.

Not far from the recreation area, near Las Vegas, archeologists have excavated Gypsum Cave. In it they found a fairly complete collection of the implements that Western Archaic people had developed in the desert area for use in gleaning an existence from so unpromising a terrain. Some of this material is in the Southwest Museum in Los Angeles.

The cave also yielded two quite unusual discoveries. One was a type of diamond-shaped projectile point that had not been seen before. The point seemed to be associated with the other novel feature—an unfamiliar kind of animal dung, apparently of great antiquity. Some very large animal had inhabited the cave and had left droppings on the floor; this happened after one group of people had been there and

before another group took up residence. But what animal?

M. R. Harrington, who was excavating the cave suspected the animal was a giant ground sloth, a creature that lived in the Americas at about the same time as mammoths. To make sure, he sent off samples of the dried dung to experts in natural history museums, and they agreed; a sloth had lived in the cave.

Since there were dates for sloths from other places, and since human use of the cave seemed to be contemporaneous with the existence of the sloth, the time for human use of Gypsum Cave appeared to have been more than 10,500 years ago. Long after the dung was discovered in Gypsum Cave, a radiocarbon date was obtained for it, and the date suggests that it may have been at least 10,500 years old.

Not all specialists are now convinced that the Gypsum Cave discovery proves that people hunted—or even lived—at the same time as sloths. But the discovery of sloth dung there does call attention to the importance of fossil fecal matter. Scientists are able

Plants for the World

Indians in the Americas domesticated more than a hundred kinds of plant. Some of these have become major sources of nourishment throughout much of the world. They include corn (maize), potatoes, peanuts, beans in many varieties, squash, pumpkins, manioc (cassava), chili peppers, sunflowers, sweet potatoes, avocados, pineapples, tomatoes, and cacao. Coca has given the world cocaine, for better or for worse, and tobacco has spread from the tropics to the Arctic to the benefit of no one. Much commercially grown cotton is derived from cotton domesticated by Native Americans.

All of these plants originated south of what is now the United States, but Indians north of Mexico adapted at least 58 imports to suit their needs. Another two dozen plants were independently cultivated either in the Southwest or in the East, among them pigweed, goosefoot, and marsh elder. Altogether, counting wild plants as well as cultivated plants, people north of Mexico used an astounding total of more than 1,100 different species. Many of these served as medicines, some for fiber or for smoking, and others as dyes, beverages, or seasonings.

Today, according to geographer William Denevan, three-fifths of the world's agricultural wealth comes from plants that Native Americans domesticated. They exceed in commercial value the cultigens of any of the other three places where agriculture was developed—Mesopotamia, Southeast Asia, and sub-Saharan Africa.

---

to discover an amazing amount about the lifeways of prehistoric people by studying their droppings, which are called coprolites.

LOST CITY MUSEUM OF ARCHEOLOGY

On Nevada 169 in Overton, near Lake Mead. Mail address: P.O. Box 807, Overton, NV 89040. Phone: 702/397-2193. Open daily, all year. Closed certain holidays. Admission charged.

This museum, operated by the Nevada State Museum, has extensive exhibits which begin with the artifacts made by Gypsum Cave people. Most of the materials come from ancient Basketmaker and Pueblo cultures. Of special interest are objects excavated in the Lost City area, along the nearby Muddy River. Several hundred sites, which have been dated between A.D. 500 and 1150, were once inhabited by people who built puebloan dwellings. Many of these sites were covered by water after the building of Boulder Dam (now named Hoover Dam).

The museum also contains materials from the culture of the Paiute people, who entered the area after A.D. 1100 and who still live in southern Nevada. The museum was built by the Civilian Conservation Corps during the Great Depression of the 1930s.

NEVADA HISTORICAL SOCIETY

1650 N. Virginia St., Reno, on the campus of the University of Nevada. Mail address: 1650 N. Virginia, Reno, NV 89503. Phone: 702/688-1190. Open free, Monday–Saturday, all year. Closed certain holidays.

In this museum are exhibits of artifacts from important Nevada archeological sites. Material from Lovelock Cave includes artifacts left there over a long period of time, beginning about 2500 B.C. Archeologists who have studied baskets, clothing, and weapons from the cave believe that its early visitors were probably ancestors of the Paiute Indians who were living in Nevada when Europeans first arrived.

The oldest artifacts from Fishbone Cave, also called Winnemucca Lake

Cave, seem to have been used by hunters and gatherers who entered this desert area about 11,000 years ago. Later people who used the cave as a storage place left fishing and hunting gear similar to that used near Lovelock Cave.

Pottery from Lost City, also called Pueblo Grande de Nevada, was made by farming people who built stone dwellings along the Muddy River, in southern Nevada, about A.D. 500. Their experiments with corn raising were apparently not successful on a long-term basis, and they abandoned the villages. Archeologists located several hundred sites in the area, many of which are now covered by water impounded by Hoover Dam. [The Lost City Museum (see entry above) near the dam, also has on exhibit a good deal of material left by these people when they moved away about a thousand years ago.]

Since neither Fishbone Cave, nor Lovelock Cave, nor the actual Lost City sites can be visited, the displays in both museums are of special importance.

Where Did the First Americans Get Their Ideas?

Archeologists agree that the first people to enter the Americas came from Asia. These folk no doubt brought with them ideas that had developed before they started to wander across the Bering Land Bridge. After they arrived in the Western Henmisphere, the early hunter-gatherers were largely on their own. And in the new environments of the two American continents, they invented ways of prospering. However, the question is often asked: Did they also get ideas from other parts of the world?

To this question archeologists have different answers. Some believe that an occasional boatload—or raft load—of people from Europe or Africa or Japan or China got washed up on American shores, bringing such things as knowledge of how to make pottery or how to cultivate gardens. Also, there have been claims that people from other continents brought certain plants and animals with them. Spaniards, of course, did bring horses.

About other aspects of Native American culture, agreement is by no means universal. Nevertheless, it seems clear that people the world over have had their lives enriched by borrowings from other cultures, and the invention of new ideas often consists of combining in new ways old ideas that come from a variety of sources.

So far, however, scholars have found only limited hints that specific ideas came to America from abroad.

NEVADA STATE MUSEUM

600 N. Carson St., Carson City, NV 89710. Phone: 702/687-4810. Open daily. Closed certain holidays. Admission charged.

This museum has exhibits of archeological materials from Nevada and ethnographic baskets from Nevada, the Northwest, the Southwest, California and the Great Plains. In addition to a life-size display of a Paiute camp scene, there are dioramas of a Paiute fishing camp, of salt mining, of pine-nut harvesting, of a mud hen drive and of an antelope hunt.

NEVADA STATE MUSEUM AND HISTORICAL SOCIETY

700 Twin Lakes Drive, Las Vegas, NV 89107. Phone: 702/486-5205. Open daily. Closed certain holidays. Admission charged.

This museum contains exhibits of prehistoric artifacts from major sites in southern Nevada.

ROCKY GAP SITE
(See *Willow Springs*)

UNIVERSITY OF NEVADA, LAS VEGAS, MARJORIE BARRICK MUSEUM OF NATURAL HISTORY

On the UNLV campus. Enter on Harmon at Swenson. Mail address: 4505 South Maryland Parkway, Las Vegas, NV 89154. Phone: 702/739-3381. Open free, Monday–Saturday. Closed certain holidays.

Archeology exhibits focus on the southern Nevada region and the Southwest.

VALLEY OF FIRE STATE PARK

From Las Vegas drive northeast on Interstate 15 to Valley of Fire exit, then on Nevada 169 to the park; total distance 55 miles. Or from Overton drive south on Nevada 169 to Valley of Fire turnoff; total distance 15 miles. Mail address: P.O. Box 515, Overton, NV 89040. Phone: 702/397-2088. Visitor Center open free, daily. Closed certain holidays. Camping.

The Story. Because of the very limited water supply, there was apparently never a large or continuous

Digging up Ancient Bacteria

In 1989 living bacteria came from the contents of the gut of a mastodon that had been butchered 11,500 years ago and stored under water in a swamp near Newark, Ohio. Commenting on the find, *Mammoth Trumpet* in August, 1991, noted that the bacteria were exactly the kind that live in the intestinal tracts of present-day mammals and were very different from bacteria in the swamp surrounding the mastodon remains. If the bacteria from the mastodon were present when the huge beast died, they would be the oldest living organisms ever found anywhere. If the bacteria were merely the descendants of organisms that lived 11,500 years ago, they had survived on vegetation that was growing at that time, and this is in itself astonishing. Also interesting is the fact that the mastodon's last meal was not what paleontologists thought it would be. It consisted of wetlands vegetation, not spruce forest vegetation which mastodons, being browsing animals, are usually thought to have fed on.

The presence of disarticulated mastodon remains in several separate clusters in the Newark swamp and in a number of other swamps suggests something else of interest about Paleo people. It appears that they may have stored meat under water to preserve it for future use.

---

occupation of the Valley of Fire. However, archeologists have found evidence that Anasazi people visited the area occasionally from about 300 B.C. to A.D. 1150. At various times, which cannot be exactly determined, the Indians left a large number of petroglyphs in the valley. Some of the designs are geometric. Others portray hands, feet, mountain sheep, birds, snakes, lizards, and atlatls—the throwing devices used by hunters before the introduction of bows and arrows.

Petroglyph Canyon may be visited on a half-mile, self-guided trail, which has markers to explain the examples of prehistoric rock art.

In the Visitor Center is a small display of material of archeological interest. A much larger archeological exhibit representing the area is in the Lost City Museum at Overton.

WILLOW SPRINGS
(Rocky Gap Site)

From Interstate 15 in Las Vegas, turn west on Charleston Blvd. and drive 15 miles to Red Rock Canyon Recreation Lands directional markers. Mail address: Bureau of Land Management, Stateline Resource Area, P.O. Box 7384, Las Vegas, NV 89125. Phone: 702/388-6627. Open free, daily, all year. Camping.

The Visitor Center offers brochures and interpretive exhibits. An interpretive trail takes visitors to agave-roasting pits used by prehistoric people and to the pictographs and petroglyphs they left on rocks in the area. The site is jointly administered by the Nevada Division of Parks and the Bureau of Land Management.

Animal symbols of ancient origin
were often the figures that
Northwest Coast Indians carved on
totem poles.

154

NORTHWEST COAST

At 4 o'clock in the afternoon, on March 28, 1778, the first white American to visit the Northwest Coast had his first glimpse of the Native Americans who lived in the place we now call Nootka Sound in British Columbia. He was John Ledyard, aboard the *Resolution,* one of two ships with which Captain Cook was exploring the Pacific.

Ledyard had a special interest in Indians. He had lived for several months among the Iroquois in the Northeast, after dropping out of Dartmouth College, which was primarily a college for Indians. Now he was keen to observe the Nootkas whose village he had reached at the end of a sea voyage more than halfway around the world from New England. In the journal that he kept with his own unique spelling, he had this to say:

"It was a matter of doubt with many of us whether we should find any inhabitants here, but we had scarcely entered the inlet before we saw that hardy, that intriped, that glorious creature man approaching us from the shore. . . . In the evening we were visited by several canoes full of the natives. . . . The country around this sound is generally high and mountainous . . . intirely covered with woods. . . . We saw no plantations or any appearance that exhibited any knowledge of the cultivation of the earth, all seemed to remain in a state of nature. . . . We purchased while here about 1500 beaver, beside other skins, but took none but the best . . . Neither did we purchas a quarter part of the beaver and other furr skins we might have done. . . ."

Top left: A stone club from British Columbia, that may have been used in battle or ceremonies. *Top right:* Ancient Northwest Coast Indians were expert carvers in bone, wood, and stone. This figure, made of steatite (soapstone) represents a guardian spirit. *Below:* British Columbian Indians used this ceremonial mask, which represents a bear. Originals are in the National Museum of the American Indian, Smithsonian Institution.

Of the Nootka canoes he saw, Ledyard wrote: "They are about 20 feet in length, contracted at each end, and about 3 feet broad in the middle . . . made from large . . . trees. . . . I had no sooner beheld these Americans than I set them down for the same kind of people that inhabited the opposite side of the continent. They are rather above the middle stature, copper-coloured, and of an athletic make. They have long black hair, which they generally wear in a club on the top of the head, they fill it when dressed with oil, paint and the downe of birds. They also paint their faces with red, blue and white colours . . . Their clothing generally consists of skins, but they have two other sorts of garments, the one is made of the inner rind of some sort of bark twisted and united together like the woof of our coarse cloaths, the other . . . is . . . principally made with the hair of their dogs, which are mostly white, and of the domestic kind: Upon this garment is displayed very naturally the manner of their catching the whale— we saw nothing so well done by a savage in our travels. . . . We saw them make use of no coverings to their feet or legs, and it was seldom they covered their heads: When they did it was with a kind of basket covering made after the manner of the Chinese . . . hats."

Cannibalism

Ledyard then went on to describe an event for which Europeans, for all their experience with killing in warfare, were not prepared: "[the Nootkas] are hospitable and the first boat that visited us . . . brought us what no doubt they thought the greatest possible regalia, and offered it to us to eat: This was a human arm roasted."

It is not clear what dark notion prompted the Nootkas to make this cannibalistic offering to strangers whose civilization would soon devour theirs. There is no doubt, however, that a form—or forms—of religious cannibalism existed on the Northwest Coast. Another coastal tribe, the Kwakiutl, had established a Cannibal Society. Members of this group in moments of religious frenzy took bites out of the arms of living people. They also ate the flesh of the dead, often of slaves killed for the purpose.

This cannibalism had nothing in common with the cannibalism practiced by some farming people who sacrificed things of great value—such as human life—in an effort to obtain good crops. Nor was the Kwakiutl custom like that of people who ate brave enemies, hoping thus to gain courage. Something different was involved. The Kwakiutls loathed the flesh they ate. Very often they spat it out, and the practice was regarded with revulsion by the community which also regarded it with awe. After eating flesh a man was isolated for a long time and then had to go through elaborate rituals before he could resume normal life.

It is difficult today to imagine what religious frenzy accompanied the Kwakiutl cannibal rite, or what prized result it was supposed to bring. But one thing is clear: The Kwakiutls, and probably the Nootkas, did not consider human flesh a delicacy. And they certainly did not consume it because they were hungry. No people in America ate so well as the Indians who lived on the Pacific coast from northern California to southern Alaska. These people had rich resources in shellfish and fish—salmon, halibut, cod, herrring, candlefish. They could get quantities of meat from seals, sea otters, porpoises, and whales. They also had a wide choice of land animals and birds, and they could vary their diet with berries of several different kinds.

The Northwest Coast Indians were indeed wealthy by prehistoric standards. Besides ample food they had the beautiful skins of a number of animals to make into clothing. They could weave garments from the shredded bark of certain plentiful trees, and they fashioned rainproof hats of fibers from cedar tree roots.

As Ledyard noted, they wove garments from the long hair of dogs, which they kept especially to be shorn. Women in certain coastal areas made expeditions inland to collect the mountain-goat wool that clung to bushes when it was shed. This they combined with dog hair to make fine blankets. Alone among North American Indians they wove with wool, and alone on the Northwest Coast the women around Puget Sound and in adjacent British Columbia used true looms. Where they got the idea no one knows. The nearest looms in America were in the distant Southwest, where the cloth was made from cotton, not wool, until the Spanish brought sheep to this continent.

Boards for Building

Another resource, one as important as food and just as available on the Northwest Coast, was a special kind of wood of exactly the right kind for making boats and houses. In the forests that grew down almost to the water's edge stood tall cedar trees with unique properties: the grain of the wood was straight, and men using wedges could split it into flat, even planks. These thick cedar boards made possible the huge buildings that impressed the artist who accompanied Captain Cook and Ledyard. Each dwelling—it might be 40 by 30 feet with a high, gabled roof—was large enough to house several families, and in some villages the massive structures stood row on row along the beach. Those who lived farther north than the Nootka—the Haida and Tlingit people—built the grandest houses of all. A dozen families could live in one of them.

The social relations between these villagers were unlike those in most parts of prehistoric North America. The differences were largely due to the fact that their easy food supply allowed them time to accumulate a wealth of possessions. One custom based on their economy of abundance was known as the potlatch, or gift-giving ceremony. This is how it went: suppose a chief's son was growing up and approaching the time when he was to be given a new name. Far in advance the chief would make preparations to celebrate the occasion by giving away property. When he had accumulated piles of blankets, furs, boxes of whale oil, containers filled with berries, and vast quantities of food, he sent out messengers in canoes to deliver invitations to people in other villages up and down the coast. At the appointed time the guests assembled, and the big plank house was taxed to capacity. Between great meals the chief ceremoniously gave away everything he had—and much that he had borrowed from relatives. The biggest gifts went to the most important guests, and everyone present remembered who got what.

Anthropologist Wayne Suttles says the potlatch was a way of "coping with abundance." If people in one village were short of supplies—because of bad luck in fishing or hunting, for example, or because too much rain spoiled salmon smoking—the giveaways evened things out.

"Gifts," Ruth Kirk and Richard Daugherty say in *Exploring Washington Archaeology,* "dealt with surplus in a way that brought honor far beyond that of selling or trading, yet in economic terms they amounted to a redistribution of food and goods. . . . Prestige lent momentum to the whole system." A man could assert his importance by gift giving. The more lavish his gifts, the higher his status, and nothing in Northwest Coast life was more essential than status. Those who had received the gifts, of course, had to proclaim their own importance by holding potlatches to which the giver was invited. And so in the end a man was likely to get back what his potlatch had cost him. Among the Kwakiutl this way of asserting superiority had a special quirk. The potlatch was often used to embarrass and humiliate a rival by giving him more costly gifts than he could possibly give in return. A man could not refuse a gift, even though he might have to sell himself into slavery to make a reciprocal gift.

Totem Poles

In historic times the rich men among the Haida often held potlatches to commemorate the raising of totem poles. A totem was an animal that was associated in some way with a man's family. Or it might be a monster or a supernatural being. Figures of these creatures were carved on masks or worn as crests on helmets. An important family might be entitled to a number of different crests. In prehistoric times people may have made small carvings to represent their totems, and later—in the eighteenth century— when they got steel tools, they began to carve the figures, one above the other, on huge wooden poles.

A totem pole could be rather like a coat of arms—advertising the ancestry of the man who raised it beside his house. Other totem poles were memorials to people who had died. Still another type, the ridicule or shame pole, might be set up to shame an important person who had failed to carry out some obligation, with a portrait of him carved upside down.

The property-conscious Northwest Coast Indians were aggressive and competitive in many ways. They were also creative. They had many ingenious implements for fishing, for hunting, for stor-

Indians made innumerable pictures and designs on rock surfaces, particularly in western North America. Archeologists differ about the meaning of this rock art but agree that it is not a form of writing. These designs were pecked into a rock in southeastern Oregon. Photo by Donald Martin, courtesy of Campbell Grant.

ing food, for killing whales, for keeping off rain, and their art was highly developed and unique in style.

Establishing the date at which their elaborate culture began is a problem that archeologists are not sure they have solved. Certainly it took time to develop, and certainly it was based on earlier lifeways. Much of American prehistory apparently began in Alaska during the latter part of the Ice Age, when Siberia was joined to North America by the Bering Land Bridge, a thousand miles wide. Some of those who wandered across the bridge continued eastward, following game.

It is possible that one or more of these small groups may have moved southward following the food-rich coast of the Pacific Ocean. This could have happened if some of the wanderers were skilled at using seaworthy canoes or if there were times when the great continental glacier met two seemingly contradictory conditions. The glacier had to be big enough, withholding enough water from the sea, to lower the ocean level and make the shoreline very different from the cliff-walled coast we know today. The coastline had to be one along which it was possible to walk. This required a second condition. The behavior of the glacier had to be such that extensions of it did not at all times block foot travel by flowing right down into the ocean, as happens in places today. Understandably no evidence has been found that people used this Pacific Coast route. If such evidence exists it lies covered by so much water that it is not likely to be retrieved until another great ice age again lowers the sea level.

However, people were not necessarily trapped in Alaska. Along the shore of the Arctic Ocean some groups could have found an easy travel route, and when they reached the mouth of the Mackenzie River good hunting led them south. After traveling the whole length of the river valley it would have been possible to cross where there was no natural barrier, from the headwaters of the Mackenzie into Alberta. There the open Plains spread out endlessly to the south.

Archeologists have found sites where these hunters camped and dropped their tools. One, known as Kogruk, is on the slope of the Brooks Mountains near the Arctic coast, in Alaska. Another, called Engigsciak, is at the mouth of the Firth river, in the Yukon. At the latter site, excavation indicates that hunters, when the local climate was warmer, killed bison of a kind that has long been extinct. Neither of these sites is open to the public. Indeed, visitors to Alaska and northwest Canada will find little evidence of prehistory on display. For one thing, travel is difficult in much of the area. For another, archeologists have only begun to examine this vast but little-inhabited portion of the continent.

Other southward-moving groups sifted into the high plateau region between the Continental Divide on the east and the coastal ranges on the west. In this Interior Plateau region those who began to live along rivers found an abundance of fish. As early as 11,000 years ago fishermen left tools at Five Mile Rapids on the Columbia River. Not far away, at a place called The Dalles, people also camped and caught salmon that ran in the river for nine months of the year. Farther up one of the river's tributaries, at the Marmes Site, archeologists have found the bones of people who arrived between 10,000 and 13,000 years ago. In Idaho a radiocarbon date suggests that stone and bone tools were left at Wilson Butte Cave about 14,000 years ago.

Very early, in other words, human beings found a way of living in the Interior Plateau by exploiting the food resources of the rivers that cut through it. They also gathered camas bulbs in spring and summer and ate them raw or cooked. Roots and tubers of other plants were another source of nourishment. Women ground some of them into a kind of flour, which they made into cakes and stored. They also harvested berries, sunflower seeds, and wild carrots.

As far as archeologists can now tell, these Riverine Plateau people eventually moved down the rivers to the coast. There they met other people who came more directly from the north. These two groups stimulated each other and became the ancestors of the Northwest Coast Indians. Once they reached the food-rich ocean they developed new tools, new food-gathering techniques, and social customs that were unique in all America. Their unusual lifeway spread throughout the long, narrow coastal region between northern California and southern Alaska.

Because steep mountains and thick woods came down to the edge of the water in the fjords which cut deeply into the land, travel had to be almost entirely by water. People paddled great distances in canoes, and in time they met others to the north who had their own way of managing life along the shore. From these northern people, who were Aleuts and Eskimos, the Northwest Coast tribes learned many things. The Aleuts and Eskimos, for their part, had ideas which had probably come from people who lived in the Amur River region of Siberia. Thus some of the ideas borrowed by the Northwest Coast Indians came indirectly from Asia. In addition, it is possible that some Asian traits reached them directly. Fishermen, possibly from Japan, may have been blown off course and drifted to America on the Japan current, which also brought the warmth and rain that distinguish the climate of the Northwest Coast from the cold and snowy inland climate in the same latitudes.

By combining the ways of living that they had developed along the rivers on the Interior Plateau with ideas that came from Asia, the Northwest Coast people produced a unique culture. Ideas even came from coastal dwellers in California, but there is no hint of Mexican influence. This absence of Mexican traits is one thing that sets the Northwestern lifeway apart from much of the rest of prehistoric Indian life in North America.

The stimuli coming from Alaska reflected an adjustment to coastal living that may have begun when the Bering Land Bridge still joined Siberia and Alaska. The coast of the Land Bridge curved around the North Pacific, with one end at a mountain which now appears on the map as Umnak Island, in the Aleutians. At the other end lay the Japanese island of Hokkaido. Along the intervening shore people may have spread out, exploiting bird and fish and sea-mammal resources. According to one theory before the end of the Ice Age, some of these wanderers from Asia had reached the vicinity of the Umnak Island mountain. Then the ocean rose, swollen by water from melting glaciers, and forced people onto higher ground. Some of them took refuge on the mountain, which the sea eventually surrounded and cut off from adjacent land.

Certain archeologists argue that among the descendants of these settlers on Umnak Island two separate traditions developed, beginning perhaps 4,500 years ago. Some of them, seeking new places to live, spread out along the other Aleutian islands, where the ocean remained open all year. There they developed a dialect, then a distinct language, Aleut. Other groups moved north from Umnak. Their language, too, changed, becoming Inuit, or Eskimo. (Native people who live in the Canadian Far North today generally call themselves Inuit, a name they prefer to Eskimo, which is a word from an Indian language meaning, "those who eat raw meat.")

Most of the Eskimo people lived on the edge of water that was covered over with ice for much of each year. Intense cold required

This mask, carved of wood, with abalone-shell eyes, was worn by a shaman on the Northwest Coast.

them to make adjustments quite unlike those of their relatives on the Aleutian islands.

The drift of Umnak people in two different directions, and along two different types of shore, resulted in two separate cultures—the Aleut and the Inuit or Eskimo, which in time developed subdivisions. Both Aleut and Eskimo were distinct from any Indian cultures, and both the Aleuts and Eskimos were physically different from Indians. They were more Mongoloid in appearance than any Indians, and they differed in blood type. No Indian has blood type B, but this type is not uncommon among Eskimo-Aleuts, and it is present in modern Mongoloid people in Asia. Differences in their teeth also distinguished the Aleut-Eskimos from neighboring Indians.

Physical anthropologists believe that the Mongoloid race appeared relatively recently and was still evolving when the earliest ancestors of the Indians entered North America. Mongoloids then continued to evolve in Asia and reached their characteristic present-day form less than 15,000 years ago. It was apparently from this modern Asian base that the ancestors of the Eskimos and Aleuts split off when they migrated to North America.

New Skills and Inventions

Later, when the Umnak people split and some of them took up residence on the Aleutians, they developed certain special skills. They made elegant baskets from the fine grasses that grew on the windswept islands. Since sea mammals were less abundant than they had been on Umnak Island, the Aleuts made increased use of fish and birds. Although Aleuts were largely dependent on driftwood for any wood they had, they developed a unique custom of carving wooden hats, and they were skilled carvers of masks for their ceremonies, some of which were very much like those of the Northwest Coast Indians farther south. Apparently the Aleuts borrowed ideas from their southern neighbors, who in turn borrowed from them.

The Umnak people who moved to the mainland—the Eskimos' ancestors—learned to protect themselves from the cold in a variety of ingenious ways. They invented clothes capable of retaining body heat, thus creating a microclimate in which they could survive. They developed sleds, and some Eskimos trained dogs to pull them. They learned how to harpoon seals in every season—in spring as the animals basked on shore, in summer on the open ocean, where hunters pursued them in light skin boats called kayaks. In winter they searched out the holes in the ice where seals came to breathe and drove their harpoons down from above. Many Eskimos also hunted caribou.

Wherever they were, at any time of year, Eskimos were able to build dwellings. In summer they used tents made of poles, possibly collected as driftwood, over which they stretched a cover made of skin. Some developed the dome-shaped winter igloos made of snow. Others made semisubterranean winter houses roofed with

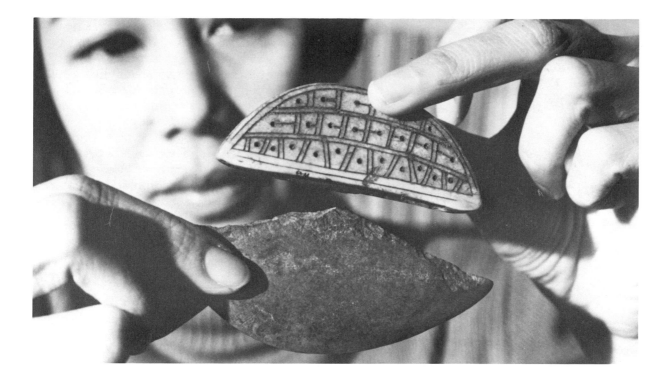

A prehistoric Eskimo woman's knife, called an ulu, from Cape Krusenstern in Alaska. National Park Service photo by Robert Belous.

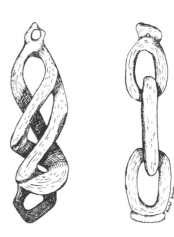

Left to right: An unusual stone bowl with a human effigy carved into the bottom, in which Eskimos burned oil for heat and light. For protection against the glare of sun on snow, prehistoric Eskimos carved these goggles from antler horn. Redrawn from Giddings. Two carvings of ivory from a burial at Ipiutak Site, Point Hope, Alaska. Redrawn from Larsen and Rainey.

driftwood covered with earth or sod. For light and heat they had lamps—shallow stone dishes filled with seal oil, in which a burning wick floated.

To judge from the discoveries archeologists have already made, a surprising amount of material left by Aleuts and Eskimos and their ancestors still lies in the earth waiting to be excavated. But there are great areas of Alaska and Canada that have not yet been studied, and for the most part visitors to this area of few roads will not be able to see archeological sites. There are, however, some excellent museum exhibits. The University of Alaska Museum displays artifacts from three particularly important sites—St. Lawrence Island, Ipiutak, and Cape Denbigh.

Included in this prehistory are Indians as well as Aleuts and Eskimos and their predecessors. In southwest Yukon, people who hunted in the subarctic forest made distinctive tools from tiny blades of flint, which they struck from larger chunks. No one knows with certainty who they were, but some archeologists suspect they may have been the ancestors of the Athabascan Indians who still live in the area. The Athabascan seem to have arrived long after the ancestors of the Paleo-Indians.

One other type of culture existed in part of the area included here with the Northwest Coast and Interior Plateau—that is, in southeastern Oregon and southern Idaho. This region is geologically part of the Great Basin, and the prehistoric Indians who lived there developed lifeways similar to those of Western Archaic culture people to the south. Indians who lived along the rivers of the Interior Plateau seem to have borrowed some traits from their Great Basin neighbors, but since they are described elsewhere in this book, there is no need to dwell on them here.

As long ago as 2500 B.C. Inuit hunters began making their camps close to the edge of the permanent ice cap in northern Canada. Because of the distinctive, tiny, sharp stone blades they used, their culture has become known as the Arctic Small Tool Tradition. Within the tradition, which lasted for nearly 3500 years, some archeologists like to distinguish two stages. The later one, which began about 600 B.C. is called the Dorset; the other, simply pre-Dorset. Around A.D. 1000 this ancient culture became what is known as the Thule.

Dorset sites on a Canadian island north of Greenland have yielded evidence that in summer the hunters lived in great longhouses (about 16 by 148 feet) roofed with skins anchored to stone foundations. Outside the communal dwelling, which may have housed 100 people, stood a row of cooking hearths.

Food was apparently abundant and the people "had eaten well, judging by our excavations," says Dr. Peter Schledermann of the University of Calgary, who has located more than 150 Inuit sites. "We unearthed an assortment of bones of birds and animals, geese, ducks, foxes, arctic hares, seals, walruses, belugas, and even narwhales." It was the bones, in fact, that led archeologists to the campsites. Even after several thousand years, the bones still nourished patches of lichens and mosses, marking the spots where leftovers from Dorset Inuit meals lay buried.

Archeologists believe the Dorset people may have spent the winters in snow houses out on the ice, where they hunted seals. Their successors, the Thule Inuit, had year-round settlements. Living in tents in summer, they built winter huts partially underground and dome-roofed with whale ribs covered with sod.

Excavation of Thule houses has yielded well-preserved bone, wood, and ivory tools—needle cases, ornaments, harpoon points. And surprisingly some Norse artifacts have also turned up. Iron boat rivets, some links from chain mail, pieces of an oak box (oak does not grow anywhere near the area), and a piece of woollen cloth all indicate that the Inuit had contact with Vikings, perhaps as early as the eleventh century. Did Norse artifacts reach the islands north of Greenland by gradual trade? Or did Viking sailors actually land there? Archeologists think either one or both may have happened.

Still to be fully understood also are small, sharp, iron knife blades discovered at ancient sites in north-central Canada. Fashioned from meteoritic iron and hafted to bone handles, the blades seem to have been used for carving and engraving bone. Some iron meteorites are found in Canada, but whether the Inuit who used the small tools got their material on the spot or by trade is a question.

Alaska

ALASKA STATE MUSEUM

395 Whittier Street, Juneau, AK 99801-1718. Phone: 907/465-2901. Open Tuesday–Saturday, winter; Monday–Sunday, summer. Closed certain holidays. Admission charged.

Ethnographic exhibits include archeological materials from each of Alaska's Native groups: Eskimo, Athabaskan, Aleut and Northwest Coast (Tlingit, Haida, and Tsimsian.) "Saving Alaska's Archaeological Heritage" is a traveling exhibit produced and circulated throughout Alaska by the Alaska State Museum.

ANCHORAGE MUSEUM OF HISTORY AND ART

121 West 7th Ave., Anchorage, AK 99501. Phone: 907/343-6173. Open free, Monday–Saturday, Memorial Day–Labor Day; Tuesday–Saturday, Labor Day–Memorial Day; afternoon Sunday, all year.

In addition to historical and con-temporary materials, archeological exhibits feature the art and culture of Eskimo, Aleut and Indian peoples.

The museum has lectures on prehistoric archeology during Alaska Archeology Week.

THE CAMPUS SITE

On the campus of the University of Alaska in Fairbanks.

There is nothing to be seen here today, but if you visit this campus you will be on the site of a 1933 discovery that was very important to archeology in Alaska. Here was found a group of artifacts that were unlike anything so far known in North America, including some very fine cores and blades. They formed the basis for the first serious attempt to link cultures in the New World with cultures in Asia. (See also University of Alaska entry below.)

DINJII ZHUUJ ENJIT MUSEUM

In Fort Yukon. Mail address: P.O. Box 276, Fort Yukon, AK 99740. Phone: 907/662-2487. Open afternoons, Monday–Friday, in summer; by ap-pointment in winter. Admission charged.

This museum has exhibits of the artifacts of prehistoric Athabascan Indians, who are related to the Navajo and Apache people of the Southwest.

KATMAI NATIONAL PARK AND PRESERVE
(KAT-my)

From the King Salmon Airport on Bristol Bay, scheduled commercial flights go to Brooks River Lodge in the Preserve. Mail address: P.O. Box 7, King Salmon, AK 99613. Phone: 907/246-3305. Open free, from about June–Sept. 15. Camping.

From Brooks River a nature trail, largely self-guided, leads to a partially reconstructed Eskimo dwelling. This large house was in use about 1000 years ago. The site has been excavated and roofed over. Some artifacts found in the excavation have been left in place and are open to view.

Left and opposite:
Archeologists digging in Katmai
National Monument, Alaska, look
up from their work to watch an
arctic fox, which has come to see
what is going on. National Park
Service photo.

Alaskans built this pithouse in
Katmai National Monument about
A.D. 120. A shelter now protects it,
and visitors can see artifacts in the
excavation just where they were
found. National Park Service photo.

A hat shaped like an eagle's head, used by Tlingit Indians in ceremonies.

An Eskimo hunting through the ice.

KODIAK ALUTIIQ CULTURE CENTER

214 W. Rezanoff. Mail address: 402 Center Ave., Kodiak, AK 99615. Phone: 907/486-1992. Open Monday–Friday, except certain holidays.

This museum has a small display of kayaks and other artifacts including masks, drums, baskets and dance fans.

PRATT MUSEUM

3779 Bartlett Street, Homer, AK 99603. Phone: 907/235-8635. Open daily, May–September; Tuesday–Sunday, October–April. Closed January and certain holidays. Admission charged.

Exhibits include "The First People: Eskimo and Dena'ina" and "Rock Paintings of Southcentral Alaska." The museum also houses an artifact collection from Kachemak Bay cultures.

SITKA NATIONAL HISTORICAL PARK

Visitor Center, Metlakahtla and Lincoln streets, Sitka. Mail address: P.O. Box 738, Sitka, AK 99835. Phone: 907/747-6281. Open free, daily.

Though not strictly devoted to a prehistoric site, this park preserves 14 Alaskan totem poles that were part of the Alaska exhibit at the St. Louis Exposition in 1904.

Tlingit Indians occupied the area around Sitka when whites—Russian fur traders—first arrived. Like other coastal people the Tlingits were great craftsmen. Woodcarvers even made into works of art the clubs that they used for killing the seals they harpooned, and they carved totem poles. Artifacts on display in the museum were chosen to illustrate major aspects of Tlingit culture—migration, settlement, subsistence, art, ceremony and societal relationships.

TANGLE LAKES NATIONAL REGISTER ARCHAEOLOGICAL DISTRICT

Enter from either the Richardson Highway, north from Valdez, or the Parks Highway, north from Anchorage. This 455,000-acre district begins at milepost 14 (east) or milepost 45 (west) on Denali Highway. It extends for approximately 30 miles. Ten trails are open to off-road vehicles. All trails are open to hikers who are warned that the ground is wet and marshy and rain boots and/or hip-waders are recommended for extended hikes. Mail address: Bureau of Land Management, Alaska State Office, 222 West 7th Ave., #13, Anchorage, AK 99513-7599. Phone: 907/271-5510. Open free, mid-May–early October. Camping.

In this area where people have lived for at least 10,000 years, there are more than 500 sites. Visitors are urged to look but not to disturb anything.

In Sitka National Historical Park, Alaska, are preserved several large totem poles, of which these are two. They are not actually prehistoric, but the carving tradition and the great interest in the animal symbols are of ancient origin. National Park Service photo by Harry G. Schmidt, Supt.

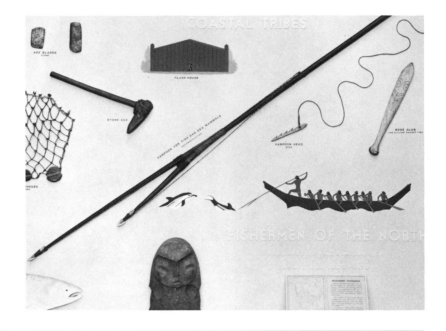

Prehistoric fishers of the Northwest Coast made tools and weapons like these. Field Museum of Natural History photo.

UNIVERSITY OF ALASKA MUSEUM

On the campus, four miles from Fairbanks. Mail address: University of Alaska, Fairbanks, AK 99701. Phone: 907/474-7505. Open free, daily, mid-May–mid-September; afternoons, mid-September–mid-May.

With a vast amount of material gathered in the course of an active archeological research program, this museum interprets pre-Eskimo and Eskimo lifeways.

Exhibits include a sample of artifacts from the Ipiutak site where many of the objects found are similar to those found in Siberia. The site itself is large and includes more than 600 houses.

Another important area represented in the museum is the Iyatayet site. Here

archeologists found for the first time very small, very delicate stone tools made by people who preceded the Eskimo. This site is a National Historic Landmark.

Other National Historic Landmarks are the sites at Gambel on the Northwest Cape of St. Lawrence Island. St. Lawrence, in the Bering Sea southwest of Nome, only 40 miles from Siberia, is large and treeless. The Eskimos who now live there are much like the Siberian Eskimos with whom they have active, friendly association.

In 1878 Russian traders obtained furs from the 1500 people who then lived on St. Lawrence, giving alcohol in exchange. Three years later the naturalist John Muir and an ethnographer visited the island and found the Eskimo dwellings filled with skeletons.

Most of the people on St. Lawrence had died in the winter of 1878–79, either of starvation or of an epidemic that accompanied it. Alcohol, brought by the traders, had caused the disaster. The Eskimo men had been drunk during the hunting season when they normally obtained their winter food supply.

None of the traders who visited the island, nor Muir himself, realized that St. Lawrence harbored a rich record of human life, stretching back several thousand years, which the University Museum's collections now reveal.

Some important recent additions to the museum's collections include material from excavations along the Trans-Alaskan Pipeline, sites along the Nenana River and cave sites along the Porcupine River.

Petroglyphs depicting marine creatures, Sproat Lake, Vancouver Island, British Columbia. Canadian Museum of Civilization photo. Courtesy of Campbell Grant.

British Columbia

CAMPBELL RIVER MUSEUM AND ARCHIVES

One hundred miles north of Nanaimo on Highway 19. Mail address: 1235 Island Highway, Campbell River, BC, V9W 2C7. Phone: 604/287-3103. Open daily, June–August; Monday–Saturday, September, April, May; afternoon Tuesday–Saturday, winter. Admission charged. Accessible by ferry from Vancouver, BC and Port Angeles, Washington. Camping nearby.

Exhibits feature prehistoric Kwakiutl, Salish and Nun-chah-nulth materials. Also on exhibit are ethnographic materials from the area.

As this book went to press, the museum was planning to move to a larger facility.

CHARLIE LAKE CAVE

Nine kilometers northwest of Fort St. John at the south end of Charlie Lake. Mail address: North Peace Historical Society, 9323 100th St., Fort St. John, BC V1J 4N4. Phone: 604/787-0430. Open free, when accessible.

Charlie Lake Cave is one of the oldest known sites of human habitation in Canada. Items found during a 1983 archeological excavation here have been dated from 10,500 years ago. Among the artifacts is a small stone bead that may be the oldest one known in North America and the earliest evidence of human adornment in Canada. The significant prehistoric discoveries support the theory that this area was once an ice-free corridor through which the Paleo-Indians, after crossing the Bering Strait from Asia, wandered and subsequently populated the continent. Archeologists from Simon Fraser University in Burnaby (see item below) have continued excavation. Visitors to the site are welcome. The cave is in the south-facing slope of a sandstone bedrock ridge. Unimproved footpaths from the bottom lead up to the cave, so visitors have to be able to do the climb to reach it. Note that the cave is on private property.

COURTENAY AND DISTRICT MUSEUM AND ARCHIVES

360 Cliffe Ave., Courtenay, BC V9N 2H9. Phone: 604/334-3611. Open daily, summer; Tuesday–Saturday, winter. Admission by donation. Camping nearby.

This museum displays a variety of prehistoric stone artifacts, a petroglyph and a replica of a Big House.

This 64-foot, ocean-going canoe, carved by Haida Indians from a single log, is now at the American Museum of Natural History, in New York.

GREATER VERNON MUSEUM AND ARCHIVES

3009 32nd Ave., Vernon, BC V1T 2L8. Phone: 604/542-3142. Open Monday–Saturday. Admission charged. Camping nearby.

This museum has a wide variety of Interior Salish material.

HOPE MUSEUM

In Hope follow signs to the Travel Info-Centre, 919 Water Ave., where the museum is housed. Mail address: P.O. Box 26, Hope, BC V0X 1L0. Phone: 604/869-7322. Open daily, May–September. The rest of the year tours may visit by appointment made in advance. Admission by donation. Camping nearby.

The exhibits include pre-Columbian rope, stone implements, beads and pieces for a betting game. There are numerous examples of basketry made by the Sto:lo people who still live in the area.

KAMLOOPS MUSEUM ASSOCIATION

207 Seymour St., Kamloops, BC V2C 2E7. Phone: 604/828-3576. Open free, daily, summer; Tuesday–Saturday, winter.

Here are displayed Interior Salish baskets, of both birch bark and the intricately patterned style made from cedar and other roots. Other exhibits include a cottonwood dugout canoe, a wide range of tools, weapons of stone and bone and a few items from burials in banks, exposed during roadway or building construction.

KELOWNA MUSEUM AND NATIONAL EXHIBITION CENTRE

470 Queensway Avenue, Kelowna, BC V1Y 6S7. Phone: 604/763-2417. Open Tuesday–Saturday, July–August. Upon request, Monday. Admission by donation.

Exhibits include Interior Salish archeological materials.

KITWANGA FORT NATIONAL HISTORIC SITE

In northwestern British Columbia, between New Hazelton and Terrace, near the junction of Highways 16 and 37. Mail address: Fort St. James Historical Park, Box 1148, Fort St. James, BC V0J 1P0. Phone: 604/996-7191. Open free, summer.

Seven interpretive panels along a trail to Ta'awdzep or Battle Hill, tell the story of this palisaded fort which was built by Gitwangak people to defend fishing rights, trade routes and clan prestige. The signs also tell the story of Nekt, the last great commander of the fort which had a system of logs designed to be rolled down the hill on approaching enemies.

Nearby are totem poles on native land which visitors are asked to respect.

'KSAN INDIAN VILLAGE AND MUSEUM

From New Hazelton on Highway 16, drive north to 'Ksan Museum. Mail

This engraving from the report of Captain Cook's third voyage, in 1778, shows a communal dwelling of the kind that Indians had long used on Nootka Sound in British Columbia.

address: P.O. Box 326, Hazelton, BC V0J 1Y0. Phone: 604/842-5723 or 5544. Open free, daily, May–October. Admission charged for guided tours. Camping.

This is a reconstruction of a Gitksan Indian village staffed by Indians, some of whom can be seen engaged in the practice of ancient crafts, including woodcarving. One of the buildings, called "Frog House of the Stone Age," is a replica of a large, prehistoric communal dwelling. In it visitors may see how Gitksans used bone, skins and especially cedar bark in making clothes, tools and utensils.

In the museum is a small collection of prehistoric artifacts.

Special Interest. During July, Gitksan Performing Dancers are featured.

KWAGIULTH MUSEUM AND CULTURAL CENTRE

At Cape Mudge Village, 2 miles south of Quathiaski Cove. Mail address: P.O. Box 8, Quathiaski Cove, Quadra Island, BC V0P 1N0. Phone: 604/285-3733. Open free, Monday–Saturday;

afternoon Sunday, July–August; afternoon Tuesday–Saturday, September–June. Wheelchair accessible.

Here along with children's programs and native cultural programs in summer are guided tours of the museum and petroglyphs.

MUSEUM OF NORTHERN BRITISH COLUMBIA

100 1st Avenue, East. Mail address: P.O. Box 669, Prince Rupert, BC V8J 3S1. Phone: 604/624-3207. Open daily, June–August; Monday–Saturday, September–May. Closed certain holidays. Admission by donation.

The museum preserves and exhibits artifacts relating to the 10,000 years of human habitation on the north coast of British Columbia. Although the collection is predominantly Tsimshian, some Haida, Tlingit, Kwakiutl and other Northwest Coast Native objects are included. Items exhibited include stone and bone tools, masks, ceremonial regalia related to the ceremony called potlatching, fishing and food gathering implements, baskets,

bentwood boxes, canoes and totem poles. Also on exhibit are miniature totem poles carved in argillite, a soft, black slate.

In June, July and August a harbor tour featuring Prince Rupert Harbour's rich archeological history is offered daily. Also, a Native carving shed, where Native artisans can be seen at work, is on the premises.

NANAIMO CENTENNIAL MUSEUM AND ARCHIVES

100 Cameron Road, Nanaimo, BC V9R 2X1. Phone: 604/753-1821. Open daily, summer. Closed Sunday and Monday, winter. Admission charged. Camping nearby.

Three dioramas here depict precontact life. Also shown are various tools. Outside the museum are an original petroglyph and several replicas.

South of Nanaimo is Petroglyph Provincial Park in which a good deal of ancient rock art may be seen. For information about the location of petroglyph sites, inquire at the museum.

NORTH PEACE MUSEUM

9323 100th Street, Fort St. John, BC V1J 4N4. Phone: 604/787-0430. Open daily, summer; afternoons Monday–Saturday, winter. Admission charged.

This museum exhibits archeological findings from 10,500 B.P. to historic times. (See Charlie Cave entry above.)

NORTHWESTERN NATIONAL EXHIBITION CENTRE

On High Level road, 'Ksan Grounds, Hazleton. Mail address: Box 333, Hazleton, BC V0J 1Y0. Phone: 604/842-5723. Open free, daily, summer; Thursday–Monday, winter.

The museum here displays the permanent collection of Gitskan artifacts from 'Ksan Indian Village (see entry above).

PENTICTON MUSEUM AND ARCHIVES
(pen-TICK-ton)

785 Main St., Penticton, BC V2A 5E3. Phone: 604/492-6025. Open free, Monday–Saturday. Closed certain holidays.

In addition to random local finds, some materials from organized excavations are on display here. Most of the artifacts were made by Salish Indians or their predecessors. Some materials were excavated by Washington State University archeologists.

PETROGLYPH PROVINCIAL PARK
(*See Nanaimo Centennial Museum and Archives*)

QUEEN CHARLOTTE ISLANDS MUSEUM

In Skidegate Landing. Mail address: Box 1, RR#1, Second Beach Skidegate, Queen Charlotte City, BC V0T 1S0. Phone: 604/559-4643. Open daily, May–October; afternoons Wednesday–Sunday, November–April. Admission charged.

The archeological exhibits here emphasize Haida art and artifacts.

ROYAL BRITISH COLUMBIA MUSEUM

675 Belleville Street, Victoria, BC V8V 1X4. Phone: 604/387-3701. Open daily, except certain holidays. Admission charged. Camping nearby.

The Archaeology Gallery uses a great many prehistoric artifacts to illustrate tool technology, types of sites, materials utilized and techniques employed by archeologists. An actual slice of an 8000 year old midden covers one wall, and a full-sized reproduction of a mudslide shows very ancient materials discovered by archeologists. On display are petroglyphs, pictographs, large stone bowls, woodworking tools, fishing and hunting equipment and objects for personal adornment. This gallery leads to the Ethnology Gallery in which are a full-sized totem pole and a longhouse.

Special Interest. The museum supervises Thunderbird Park in Victoria, where there are reproductions of totem poles from various parts of British Columbia and a full-scale Kwakiutl Indian house that is sometimes used for Indian ceremonies. Visitors to the park may watch several Native artists work on totem poles, masks, and other objects, some of which are for sale in the museum shop.

Heritage and Landmark Sites

In 1973 the United Nations Educational, Scientific and Cultural Organization (UNESCO), in order to strengthen the hand of those who are concerned with preserving the historic, cultural or environmental sites everywhere in the world, drafted an agreement called the World Heritage Convention. One hundred and nineteen countries have adhered to this agreement. Under it, emphasizing their great importance, two sites in Canada are listed: L'Anse aux Meadows National Historic Park, and Head-Smashed-in Buffalo Jump. In the United States the prehistoric World Heritage archeological sites are Mesa Verde, Cahokia Mounds, and Chaco Canyon.

On a national level certain sites in the United States and Canada are designated National Historic Landmarks.

Some of the symbols carved on basalt boulders by Native Americans at Wees Bar, Idaho. Archeologists think they may have been chiseled there with stone tools about 3000 years ago. From *Wees Bar Petroglyphs*, Information Series, No. 1, Boise District, Bureau of Land Management. After Nelle Tobias.

SECWEPEMC MUSEUM

Near the intersection of Highway 5 and Highway 1. Mail address: 345 Yellowhead Highway, Kamloops, BC V2H 1H1. Phone: 604/828-9801. Open, Monday–Friday, except holidays. Admission by donation. Camping nearby.

On display in this museum, which is on the edge of the Kamloops Indian Reserve, are archeological materials recovered from several Indian reserves.

SGAN GWAII
(skung-GWA-ee)

This is all that remains of a Haida settlement—some carved poles and the outlines of a longhouse. It can be reached only by boat from Queen Charlotte. For a list of boat-owners who will furnish transportation call or write to Gwaii Haanas South Moresby National Park Reserve, Box 37, Queen Charlotte, BC V0T 1S0. Phone: 604/559-8818. Permission to visit the site must be obtained in advance from the National Park Reserve.

SIMON FRASER UNIVERSITY MUSEUM OF ARCHAEOLOGY AND ETHNOLOGY

On the campus, Burnaby, BC V5A 1S6. Phone: 604/291-3325. Open by donation, Monday–Friday; afternoons Saturday and Sunday.

Displays here are devoted to archeology, physical anthropology and ethnology, particularly of the Pacific Northwest.

SURREY MUSEUM AND ARCHIVES

On the northeast corner of 60th Avenue and 176th St. Mail address: 6022 176th St., Surrey, BC V3S 4E7. Phone: 604/574-5744. Open free, Tuesday–Friday; afternoons Saturday and Sunday. Donations appreciated.

The prehistoric material here was excavated by archeologists in the 1970s mainly from the Crescent Beach site in south Surrey. It consists of stone woodworking and fishing tools, a small selection of hunting tools, some bone implements, a petroglyph and several significant zoomorphic bowls. The museum also displays Northwest Coast Indian basketry.

U'MISTA CULTURAL CENTRE

On Cormorant Island, reached by ferry from Vancouver Island. P.O. Box 253, Alert Bay, BC V0N 1A0. Phone: 604/974-5403. Open Monday–Friday, all year; also afternoon Saturday, May 1–September 20. Admission charged. Wheelchair accessible.

Along with ethnographic materials including a potlatch collection are examples of early art and artifacts from the area.

UNIVERSITY OF BRITISH COLUMBIA, MUSEUM OF ANTHROPOLOGY

On Point Grey overlooking the Strait of Georgia and English Bay. 2175 Westbrook Mall, UBC, Vancouver, BC V6J 3J9. Phone: 604/228-3825. Open afternoons, Tuesday–Sunday all year. Closed certain holidays. Wheelchair accessible. Admission charged, except Tuesday.

On exhibit here are Northwest Coast Indian artifacts from extensive ethnological and archeological holdings.

VANCOUVER MUSEUM

1100 Chestnut St., Vancouver, BC V6J 3J9. Phone: 604/736-4431. Open daily, all year. Closed certain holidays. Admission charged.

In the archeology section of this museum are random local finds and excavated materials representative of the lifeways in Fraser Canyon from 11,000 B.C. to 400 B.C. and of lifeways in the Fraser Delta from 1000 B.C. to A.D. 1808. One display shows how adze blades were manufactured from nephrite, sometimes called jade. Many artifacts are grouped by their function—for example, woodworking tools in one display, bone-shaping tools in another. Some exhibits show how artifacts were made.

An archeologist digs through 8000 years of debris accumulated in the Alpha Rock Shelter, near the Salmon River, in Idaho. Idaho State University photo.

Idaho

ALPHA ROCKSHELTER

From Salmon drive 20 miles north on US 93 to North Fork, then follow the Forest Service Road down the north side of Salmon River past Shoup, then cross the Salmon on the Pine Creek Bridge and continue along the south side of the river about 4 miles to a marker that indicates the site. Open free, at all times.

From a platform erected for the convenience of visitors it is possible to look into this rock shelter, which has been excavated. Paintings are visible on the roof of the overhang.

Occupation began here about 6000 B.C. and continued until 1000 B.C.. After that it was visited intermittently until about A.D. 1300. Broken animal bones and freshwater mussel shells show that the site was used by hunters and fishermen. Milling stones found among the debris indicate that women collected seeds and ground them to make them edible.

The people who lived in this and other rock shelters followed what is called the Bitterroot way of life. They may have been ancestors of the Northern Shoshone who inhabited the valley when Lewis and Clark visited it in 1805.

BIRDS OF PREY NATURAL AREA

South of Melba along the Snake River Mail address: Bureau of Land Management, Boise District, 3948 Development Ave., Boise, ID 83705. Phone: 208/334-1582. Open free, at all times. Primitive camping.

In this canyon there are about 200 uninterpreted sites, including petroglyphs. These are emphasized in Celebration Park at the north end of the canyon.

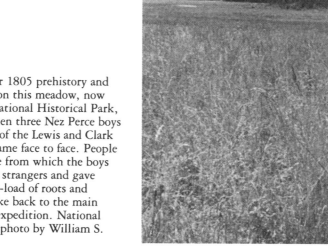

In September 1805 prehistory and history met on this meadow, now Nez Perce National Historical Park, in Idaho, when three Nez Perce boys and six men of the Lewis and Clark expedition came face to face. People in the village from which the boys came fed the strangers and gave them a horse-load of roots and salmon to take back to the main body of the expedition. National Park Service photo by William S. Keller.

BUREAU OF LAND MANAGEMENT

Each District Office of the Bureau of Land Management in Idaho usually has a small archeological display. In some offices publications about sites are available. The addresses of the district offices are:

Boise District Office
3948 Development Avenue
Boise, ID 83705
Phone: 208/384-3300

Burley District Office
Route 3, Box 1
Burley, ID 83318
Phone: 208/678-5514

Coeur d'Alene District Office
1808 N. Third Street
Coeur d'Alene, ID 83813
Phone: 208/769-5000

Idaho Falls District Office
940 Lincoln Road
Idaho Falls, ID 83401
Phone: 208/524-7500

Salmon District Office
P.O. Box 430
Salmon, ID 83467
Phone: 208/756-5400

Shoshone District Office
400 West "F" Street
P.O. Box 2-B
Shoshone, ID 83352
Phone: 208/886-2206

HELLS CANYON NATIONAL RECREATON AREA
(*See entry in Oregon section*)

HERRETT MUSEUM, COLLEGE OF SOUTHERN IDAHO

315 Falls Ave., P.O. Box 1238, Twin Falls, ID 83303-1238. Phone: 208/733-9554. Open free, Tuesday–Friday; afternoon Saturday.

This museum includes 3000 artifacts, mostly pre-Columbian, from North, Central and South America. One exhibit hall is designed for young visitors and the museum conducts programs for elementary school children.

IDAHO HISTORICAL MUSEUM

In Julia Davis Park. Mail address: 610 North Julia Davis Drive, Boise, ID 83702. Phone: 208/334-2120. Open free, Monday–Saturday; afternoon Sunday. Closed certain holidays.

This museum has a special display of projectile points and six cases of material on the prehistory of Idaho.

IDAHO STATE UNIVERSITY, IDAHO MUSEUM OF NATURAL HISTORY

On the campus in Pocatello. Mail address: P.O. Box 8096, Pocatello, ID 83209. Phone: 208/236-3366. Open free, Monday–Saturday; afternoon Sunday. Closed certain holidays.

Exhibits here are taken from the museum's large collection of prehistoric artifacts from the northern Great Basin and northern mountain regions.

Weis Rockshelter, in Idaho, was excavated between 1961 and 1964 by archeologists from Idaho State University, who discovered evidence of occupation going back 8000 years. Idaho State University photo.

INTERMOUNTAIN CULTURAL CENTER AND MUSEUM

In Weiser, drive north on US 95 to Indianhead Road, turn left and drive about 2 miles to stop sign by Weiser High School. Turn right toward five buildings. The Center is in a building with a clock tower. Mail address: P.O. Box 307, Weiser, ID 83672. Phone: 208/549-0205. Open Wednesday–Saturday, all year. Admission charged. Camping nearby.

Here is a collection of artifacts found near Weiser during the construction of an irrigation line in 1908. On exhibit are shell beads, projectile points, a hand axe, and other stone objects. The points are of the kind called "cache blades" because they were intended as burial gifts, not for use as weapons. Many of the artifacts were stained heavily with red ocher, a practice widely associated with ancient burial rites.

LENORE SITE

From Orofino drive 16 miles west on US 12 to the rest area. Open free, at all times.

Native Americans have lived in this area for 10,000 years. A sign at the rest area interprets the results of archeological excavations at the site.

LOLO TRAIL

From the Idaho–Montana line, this old trail parallels US 12 for 4 miles. Mail address: Bureau of Land Management, Idaho State Office, 3380 Americana Terrace, Boise, ID 83706. Phone: 208/384-3000. Open free, at all times.

This ancient Indian trail generally follows the ridge of the mountains north of the Lochsa River and extends for 150 miles through wilderness. It is not passable for ordinary tourist vehicles. In prehistoric and early historic times, Nez Perce Indians traveled along it to reach buffalo country in Montana. Lewis and Clark followed it in 1805 on their expedition to the West Coast.

McCAMMON PETROGLYPHS

From Pocatello drive about 18 miles southeast on Interstate 15 to a roadside rest between Inkom and McCammon. Open free, at all times. Camping nearby.

Here, protected by a fence, are several large boulders on which prehistoric Indians pecked designs and pictures. A state historical sign reads: "Over much of western North America, Indians made rough drawings like these, mainly in areas where they hunted and gathered food. Often called rock writing, these drawings are really not writing at all: their meaning—if any—could be interpreted only by the people who made them. Some probably are forms of magic, and some may have been made simply for fun. Many of them, including these, range in age from a few centuries to much older, but dating them precisely is difficult at best."

Other examples of rock art in Idaho have been found along the Snake River and in the south-central part of the state.

MAP ROCK PETROGLYPHS

From Nampa on Interstate 84 drive south on Highway 45. One mile north of the Snake River turn right on Map Rock Road, drive 7.8 miles to Map Rock which is on private property and is marked with an interpretive sign.

This petroglyph is on the National Register of Historic Places. A leaflet with information about Map Rock is available from Bureau of Land Management, Boise District, 3948 Development Ave., Boise, ID 83705. Phone: 208/384-3300.

MIDVALE QUARRY

On US 95 near Midvale.

Here a historical sign labeled "An Early Industry" indicates a nearby quarry that is of archeological interest but is not open to the public. The sign reads: "At the top of this hill 3 to 5000 years ago, prehistoric men had a rock quarry where they made a variety of stone tools. Projectiles, knives, and scrapers were among the tools made by these early people who camped at the foot of the hill. These nomads hunted deer and other game, collected plant foods, and fished in the river here. They had spears and spearthrowers for hunting and fishing, and mortars and pestles for grinding roots and berries. Archaeologists have not yet determined when this industry shut down."

NEZ PERCE NATIONAL HISTORICAL PARK (NEZ-PURS)

Park Headquarters is in Spalding, on US 95, 12 miles east of Lewiston. Mail address: P.O. Box 93, Spalding, ID 83551. Phone: 208/843-2261.

The park itself consists of 24 separate areas, two of which—the Weis Rockshelter and the Lenore Site—are archeological sites open to the public. Weippe Prairie, though not strictly an archeological site, has interest because it was here that Lewis and Clark first met Nez Perce Indians.

At the park's Visitor Center brochures and maps are available describing self-guided auto tours of site.

REDFISH ROCK SHELTER SITE
National Register of Historic Places

From Stanley drive south 4 miles on State Highway 75, turn right on Redfish Lake Road, drive .25 mile to a turnout on the right where there is an information board. From there a path leads across a footbridge to the rock shelter. Mail address: Sawtooth National Forest, Sawtooth National Recreation Area, Headquarters Office, Star Route, Ketchum, ID 83340. Phone: 208/726-7672.

Interpretive signs explain this site which was first occupied 10,000 years ago. Artifacts from the site are displayed at the Redfish Visitor Center 2 miles farther along Redfish Lake Road.

TREATY ROCK

Just west of the Burlington Railroad tracks where they intersect Interstate 90 in Post Falls. Open free, at all times.

In a small park here is a boulder with petroglyphs accompanied by an interpretive sign.

WEES BAR PETROGLYPHS

From Nampa on Interstate 84 drive east to the turnoff to Kuna, then drive south on local road 69 to Kuna, then from Kuna south to Swan Falls Dam. Walk across the dam to the primitive road on the south side of the Snake River. Walk on this road downriver 3.5 miles. By boat proceed from the ramp below Swan Falls Dam 3.5 miles downstream 1 mile below Priest Ranch to ruins of Wees House. The large terrace extending downriver from here is Wees Bar.

Here petroglyphs, which are collectively listed on the National Register of Historic Places, appear as designs pecked in the dark desert varnish that covers the basalt rocks. These designs, about which there has been much speculation, may date from between 1000 B.C. and A.D. 1500.

A leaflet with information about this petroglyph field is available from the Bureau of Land Management, Boise District, 3948 Development Ave., Boise, ID 83705. Phone: 208/384-3300.

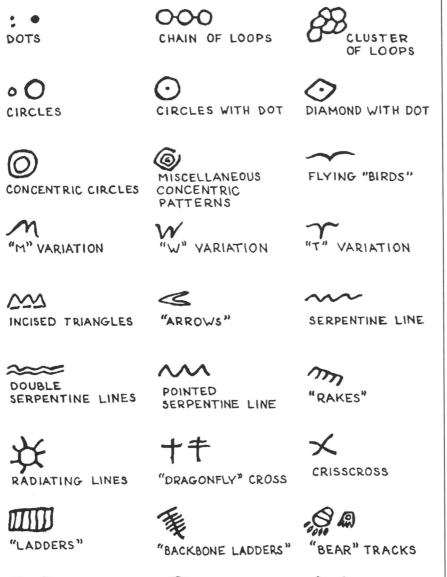

DOTS

CHAIN OF LOOPS

CLUSTER OF LOOPS

CIRCLES

CIRCLES WITH DOT

DIAMOND WITH DOT

CONCENTRIC CIRCLES

MISCELLANEOUS CONCENTRIC PATTERNS

FLYING "BIRDS"

"M" VARIATION

"W" VARIATION

"T" VARIATION

INCISED TRIANGLES

"ARROWS"

SERPENTINE LINE

DOUBLE SERPENTINE LINES

POINTED SERPENTINE LINE

"RAKES"

RADIATING LINES

"DRAGONFLY" CROSS

CRISSCROSS

"LADDERS"

"BACKBONE LADDERS"

"BEAR" TRACKS

"TIED" CIRCLES

HOLLOW FIGURES

STICK FIGURES

Some of the motifs in the Wees Bar petroglyphs and terms that have been used to describe them. After Nelle Tobias.

Do You Dig Digging?

Archeologists usually like to encourage people who want to learn about the science which they find so fascinating. But at an excavation everyone is usually too busy to explain what goes on. So, although they don't like to be rude, archeologists very often have to make an absolute rule that visitors may not come to their digs.

There are exceptions. If you want to watch the slow and painstaking work that goes into an excavation, you should ask the proper authorities if visitors are allowed. In national parks, ask park rangers. It may be possible for you to see a dig from a good vantage point. There may even be a ranger assigned to explain what is happening.

Here are some possibilities if you want to take part in archeological excavations. Every spring *Archeology Magazine* lists such opportunities throughout the world, including the United States and Canada.

The United States Forest Service participates in a Passport in Time Project in which volunteers are invited to take part (see page 36).

Crow Canyon Archaeological Center conducts a field school that offers a variety of ways in which people can take part in digs. Inquiries should go to the Center at 23390 County Road K, Cortez, CO 81321.

The Center for American Archeology offers a variety of programs in

---

Special Interest. A quarter mile downstream from the Wees Bar petroglyphs, high up in the cliffs, is a cave excavated in 1929 by the American Museum of Natural History. In it were found fishing tools and other indications that prehistoric people engaged in fishing at the nearby rapids.

WEIS ROCKSHELTER

Cottonwood, ID 83522. On US 95 a Nez Perce National Historical Park interpretive marker calls attention to the site. From this marker drive south 8 miles on the graveled Grave Creek Canyon Road. Camping nearby.

Weis Rockshelter is one of a series of niches in cliffs along the western slope of the Rocky Mountains in Idaho. People lived here for about 8,000 years, but their culture was somewhat different from that of the occupants of Alpha Rockshelter, near Shoup.

During excavation archeologists found many tools, including bone awls and needles for piercing and sewing skins, chipped stone projectile points

for hunting, and antler wedges for splitting wood. The hunters who made these tools may have been ancestors of the Nez Perce Indians of historic times

The Weis Rockshelter is one of many separate areas which make up the Nez Perce National Historical Park.

WILSON BUTTE CAVE

On Idaho 25 near Wilson Lake reservoir.

Here a historical sign labeled "Prehistoric Man" indicates a nearby cave which is of archeological interest, but which is not open to the public. The sign reads: "Archeological excavations show human occupation of the Snake River Plains for more than 10,000 years. Early men left weapons and other gear in a cave in a nearby butte. Bones show that they hunted game which is now extinct—camels, ancient horses, and ground sloths. In succeeding thousands of years, the climate grew extremely dry, much drier than it is today. Still later, it became less arid again. Through all these changes, man

succeeded in adapting and remained here."

A radiocarbon date indicates that the earliest visitors left their crude stone tools in the cave about 14,500 years ago.

Northwest Territories

PRINCE OF WALES NORTHERN HERITAGE CENTRE

In Yellowknife. Mail address: Box 1320, Yellowknife, NWT X1A 2L8. Phone: 403/873-7551. Open free, daily, summer; Tuesday–Friday; afternoons Saturday and Sunday, winter.

Permanent exhibits here include prehistoric artifacts from the Paleo period onward. There are also exhibits from the continuing field work conducted by the Centre.

which avocational archeologists can participate. For information apply to the Center at Kampsville, IL 62053. Phone: 618/653-4316.

Various museums conduct excavations on which volunteers are welcome. So too do many archeological societies.

A number of universities conduct field schools. Information about some of them appear with information about university museums in this book.

Earthwatch offers opportunities to participate in digs in many countries, including the United States. Apply to Earthwatch, 680 Mt. Auburn St., Box 403, Watertown, MA 02272. Phone: 617/926-8200.

Every summer, throughout Ontario, Canada, archeologists are usually conducting digs at which visitors are invited. For information write to Ontario Ministry of Culture & Communications, Archeology and Marine Heritage Unit, 77 Bloor Street West, Toronto, Canada M7A 2R9.

Every year a *Field School Guide* includes information about opportunities for participation in digs in the United States and Canada. For information about this publication write to American Anthropological Association, 1703 New Hampshire Ave., N.W., Washington, DC 20009. Phone: 202/232-8800.

Oregon

CAPE PERPETUA VISITOR CENTER

Three miles south of Yachats on US 101. Mail address: P.O. Box 274, Yachats, OR 97498. Open most days in summer; weekends only in winter.

The Visitor Center has exhibits and a video program that includes information on the prehistory of the Cape Perpetua area for the last 5000 years.

If excavation is in progress, visitors may be able to help in the process of exploring a midden.

CATLOW CAVE

About an hour's drive south of Frenchglen on Oregon 205, at a point where the paved road turns to the left, a directional sign points to a dirt road that continues straight on. The cave is about .5 mile along this dirt road. Mail address: Bureau of Land Management, Burns District Office, HC 74-12533 Highway 20 W, Hines, OR 97738.

Phone: 503/573-5241. Open free, at all times. Camping nearby.

When this cave was occupied about 8000 years ago it looked out over a large lake. There are no interpretive signs at the site which was one of the first to be excavated in Oregon.

In Catlow Cave archeologists found several objects that helped them to remember with a certain poignance that real people lived here. First they came upon two small sandals, about right for a child of five or six. Nearby were two tiny baskets and a small dart of the kind used in a well-known Indian game. For some reason a little girl one day left her sandals and her toys on the cave floor and never returned. Nor did anyone else disturb them for thousands of years.

CENTER FOR THE STUDY OF THE FIRST AMERICANS

Department of Anthropology, Oregon State University, Corvallis, OR 97331.

This active center on the campus of Oregon State University publishes a lively periodical, *The Mammoth Trumpet,* that carries news of what is going on in the field of research on the First Americans. In 1989 the Center organized "The First World Summit Conference on the Peopling of the Americas" at which archeologists from all over the world presented papers. Among the knotty problems considered were controversial dates for cultural material of 33,000 B.P. from Monte Verde in Chile, and 32,000 B.P. from Pedra Furada in Brazil.

CONFEDERATED TRIBES OF WARM SPRINGS MUSEUM

On Oregon 26 at Warm Springs. P.O. Box C, Warm Springs, OR 97761. Phone: 503/553-3331.

As this book went to press this museum was scheduled to open in the near future and planned to have some pre-contact material on display.

Archeologists at work on a site overlooking the ocean in the Cape Perpetua Scenic Area in Oregon. Photo courtesy of Carl Davis, Forest Archeologist, Siuslaw National Forest.

DESCHUTES COUNTY HISTORICAL SOCIETY

129 NW Idaho St., P.O. Box 5252, Bend, OR 97708. Phone: 503/389-1813. Open free, afternoons, Wednesday–Saturday. Closed December 25. Camping nearby.

Here are artifacts recovered from the Lava Island Rockshelter.

FAVELL MUSEUM OF WESTERN ART AND INDIAN ARTIFACTS

125 West Main St., Klamath Falls, OR 97601. Phone: 503/882-9996. Open Monday–Saturday. Admission charged.

In this museum devoted to western Americana are prehistoric materials among the thousands of Native American artifacts displayed. Included are Clovis and Folsom points, Mimbres ceramics and a variety of implements from the Columbia River region.

FORT ROCK CAVE HISTORICAL MARKER

On the east side of Oregon 31, about 18 miles north of Silver Lake.

This roadside marker indicates Fort Rock Cave at the foot of a butte, which can be seen about four miles away, although it is not open to the public. (The cave is named for a nearby volcanic formation called Fort Rock.)

No one knows exactly when Indians first took shelter at this spot. By 9,000 years ago they had already left in the cave some of the baskets and sandals which they wove with great skill from sagebrush fibers. Apparently they did not have a permanent camp there. At least they were all away from home one day when volcanic eruptions at Newberry Craters, north of Fort Rock, filled the air with glowing cinders and ash. The hot layer of ash that settled in the cave charred, but did not destroy, some of the 75 sandals scattered about on the floor. Later, people returned to the cave, and their household debris accumulated on top of the older layers.

This sign on Oregon 31, near the town of Fort Rock, calls attention to Fort Rock Cave: "Some of the earliest known inhabitants of this continent made their home in a cave in one of the low knolls dominated by Fort Rock, visible across this basin. Radio-carbon dating indicates that sandals found in the cave may be 9,000 years old. Fort Rock is the remnant of an ancient volcano rising 325 feet above the plain. A great lake covered this entire basin, spreading as far south as Picture Rock. It was in a cave facing that lake that the Fort Rock People lived." Oregon State Highway photo.

When archeologists excavated the cave they could establish a radiocarbon date not only for the charred sandals—and for the people who had made them—but also for the volcanic eruption. The sandals turned out to be the oldest woven artifacts so far discovered in this hemisphere. Moreover the sandals and basketry found here and at other Oregon caves were not the work of people who had recently taken up the art of weaving. A long period of experimentation, innovation, and practice obviously lay behind the fashioning of any artifacts so intricate.

In other Oregon caves, and at open campsites, there is evidence of even earlier visitors to the area. At one place archeologists found very primitive chopping tools. The signs of weathering on these tools indicated that they had been manufactured originally at some unknown date in the distant past. Then about 9,000 years ago they were picked up, sharpened, and reused.

The remains of daily life in caves known as Roaring Springs, Paisley, and Catlow indicate a scene quite unlike the present, semidesert landscape. These caves, like Fort Rock, were all formed by the action of waves at the edges of lakes that filled the valleys at the end of the Ice Age. Eventually the lakes dried up. Until then the people who lived on their shores had food resources different from those available today—and much richer.

HELLS CANYON NATIONAL RECREATION AREA

Along the Snake River in both Oregon and Idaho. Mail addresses: P.O. Box 490, Enterprise, OR 97828. Phone: 503/426-4978; P.O. Box 832, Riggins, ID 83549. Phone: 208/628-3916. Camping.

This large area administered by the Forest Service includes 200 pithouses, 350 rockshelters, and more than 200 rock art sites. People have occupied the canyon for at least 7000 years. The Forest Service has prepared an inter-

From the summit of Fort Rock, 300 feet above the prairie, visitors can see the butte in the distance where archeologists, digging in a cave, found sandals and basketry. Oregon State Highway photo.

pretive brochure about the prehistory of Hells Canyon and can provide information about numerous trails and sites along them. In addition to giving information about prehistoric occupation along the Snake River, which is rich in salmon and steelhead fish, the brochure includes this warning:

"The vandalism of archeological sites is prohibited by Federal law, and can result in fines of up to $20,000, imprisonment or both. Many archeological sites have already been looted or vandalized resulting in a tremendous loss of important information. This makes the remaining sites all the more valuable."

Three prehistoric sites in the area are readily accessible by auto. They are:

Buffalo Eddy

From Clarkson, WA, drive south on Washington 129 through Asotin. The road turns into Snake River Road. Ap-

proximately 18 miles upriver a rock outcrop runs alongside the road. On large boulders here and along the shoreline are very distinct pictographs. They are not indicated by signs.

Pittsburg Landing

From Whitebird, ID, on Idaho 95, turn west onto road 493. Follow this to Pittsburg Landing and Circle C Ranch. Continue on the Upper Landing Road about 1 mile to a petroglyph site where an interpretive sign is scheduled to be set up. There are evidences of pithouses in the vicinity.

Kirkwood Historic Ranch

The ranch, on the east bank of the Snake River, is best reached by boat from Hells Canyon Creek boat launch. National Recreation Trail Number 104 along the Snake River also provides access. Here beside Kirkwood Creek, which flows into the Snake, can be found a series of remnants of prehistoric pithouses.

HIGH DESERT MUSEUM

59800 South Highway 97, Bend, OR 97702. Phone: 503/382-4754. Open daily, except certain holidays. Admission charged.

This participation-oriented museum offers exhibits, demonstrations, slide shows and talks that include information about prehistoric Native Americans. One walk-through diorama depicts a Northern Paiute encampment ca. 1790. In 1994 the Museum plans to open a new wing entirely devoted to the region's Native American heritage.

HORNER MUSEUM
(See Oregon State University)

LAVA ISLAND ROCK SHELTER

From Bend follow Oregon 46 southwest for 7 miles, turn left onto Forest Road 41 and travel south for about .5 mile. Turn left onto Forest Road 1420 at the sign for Deschutes River Recreation Sites, then turn left about 1 mile at a small sign identifying "Rockshelter." From here it is a short drive to the parking lot at Lava Island Camp and the beginning of the trail to the rockshelter. Mail address: 1645 E. Highway 20, Bend, OR 97701. Phone: 503/388-2715. Open free, daily.

People used a shallow cave on the west bank of Deschutes River as a temporary camp 4000 years ago, and possibly as early as 7000 years ago. Interpretive signs along the half-mile trail describe the result of archeological excavations.

LAVA LANDS VISITOR CENTER

11 miles south of Bend on the west side of US 97. Mail address: 1645 E. Highway 20, Bend, OR 97701. Phone: 503/388-2715. Open free, daily.

Exhibits describe how prehistoric people made tools of obsidian. Included are tools recovered from the local area and drawings of early life. From time to time during the summer flint-knapping demonstrations take place outside the Visitor Center.

MACKS CANYON
ARCHAEOLOGICAL SITE
National Register of Historic Places

From Maupin drive north 2 miles on US 197, then west on Oregon 216. Access to the site is between Grass Valley and Tygh Valley. The site, on the terrace on the east side of the Deschutes River, is also accessible by boat. Mail address: Bureau of Land Management, Prineville, OR 97754. Phone: 503/447-4115. Open free, year round. Camping.

This village site contains 51 depressions where there were once dwellings. Seven of these have been excavated and are protected by a heavy-duty wire fence. Nearby, in summer only, is an interpretive sign explaining the site. Sagebrush and grass cover most of the depressions which are not readily recognized except by trained experts.

NURSERY SITE

From West Main Street in Medford drive about 3 miles toward Jacksonville, then turn right onto Hanley Road. The Nursery entrance is a few hundred yards beyond the intersection of Hanley Road and Ross Lane. Mail address: J. Herbert Stone Nursery,

Medford, OR 97501. Phone: 503/776-3600. Open free, Monday–Friday, except certain holidays. Camping nearby.

In the Visitor Center is an exhibit that deals with land-use patterns. About 15 prehistoric stone artifacts represent what was found in an excavation here.

OREGON HISTORICAL CENTER MUSEUM

1230 Southwest Park, Portland, OR 97205. Phone: 503/222-1741. Open free, Monday–Saturday; afternoon Sunday.

In its "Native American History of Oregon" exhibit the museum has displays of prehistoric artifacts, including the famous sandal from Fort Rock Cave dated at about 9000 B.P. Also on exhibit are canoes and a partial replica of a cedar house.

OREGON STATE UNIVERSITY, HORNER MUSEUM

Gill Coliseum, on the campus, Corvallis, OR 97331. Phone: 503/754-2951. Open September–May, Tuesday–Friday; afternoons Saturday and Sunday; June–August, Monday–Friday; afternoon Sunday. Closed certain holidays. Donation requested.

Exhibits here include woolly mammoth remains, basketry, pottery, stone pipes, flaked stone, and other artifacts, together with a map of Native American prehistoric culture areas and languages of Oregon.

SCHMINCK MEMORIAL MUSEUM

128 South "E" St., Lakeview, OR 97630. Phone: 503/947-3134. Open afternoons, Tuesday–Saturday. Closed certain holidays. Admission charged.

On display are artifacts from random local finds.

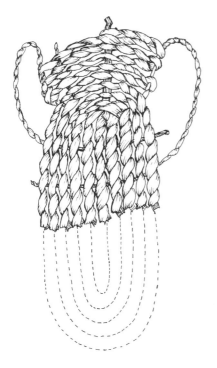

This remnant of a sandal from Roaring Springs Cave, in Oregon, shows a type of weaving mastered by early people in the Great Basin. After Cressman.

When water rises behind a new dam it often covers evidences of prehistoric life. People salvage what they can before the waters rise. Here, for instance, is a fragment of a larger stone that is now covered by the water behind the Dalles Dam in Washington. On this fragment is a pecked representation of a supernatural being. Photo, courtesy of Campbell Grant.

TAHKENITCH LANDING ARCHAEOLOGICAL SITE

Next to Tahkenitch Campground on the east side of US 101, 6.5 miles south of North Beach, 7 miles north of Reedsport. Mail address: Siuslaw National Forest, 545 SW Second Ave., Corvallis, OR 97333. Phone: 503/757-4480. Open free, daily.

This site on the west shore of Tahkenitch Lake provided evidence of hunting and fishing as early as 8000 years ago. People exploited shellfish and sea mammals beginning about 5000 years ago. Interpretive signs describe lifestyles of the early inhabitants.

TILLAMOOK COUNTY PIONEER MUSEUM (TILL-ah-mook)

2106 2nd St., Tillamook, OR 97141. Phone: 503/842-4553. Open Monday–Saturday; afternoon Sunday. Closed Monday, October–May 1 and certain holidays. Admission charged.

On display here are materials from Umnak Island in the Aleutian Islands, together with surface finds and material excavated from Oregon sites.

UNIVERSITY OF OREGON, MUSEUM OF NATURAL HISTORY

On the campus, Eugene, OR 97403. Phone: 503/686-3024. Open free, Monday–Friday, during the academic year.

The museum staff has conducted significant excavations, and archeological material from the Northwest Coast, Columbia Plateau and Great Basin is on display, along with material from other regions of North America. One exhibit contains material from Fort Rock Cave. Another deals with a large site now flooded by the dam pool at The Dalles.

WALLOWA COUNTY MUSEUM

Main St., Joseph, OR 97846. Phone: 503/432-1015. Open free, daily, mid-May–September 30. Donations accepted.

In the Nez Perce room here are Nez Perce artifacts which are not dated.

The lifeway of prehistoric people in a cave in the Grand Coulee area is recreated in a diorama at the Interpretive Center in Dry Falls, Washington. Washington State Parks photo.

Washington

ADAM EAST MUSEUM AND ART CENTER

122 West Third Ave., Moses Lake. Mail address: P.O. Drawer 1529, Moses Lake, WA 98837. Phone: 509/766-9395. Open free, Tuesday–Saturday, year round. Phone for hours.

The museum houses a large number of artifacts collected by Adam East along the Middle Columbia River. Detailed information about these finds is often lacking, but many of the objects were made by Salish Indians and their prehistoric predecessors.

BURKE MUSEUM
(*See University of Washington*)

CHELAN COUNTY MUSEUM

600 Cottage Ave., Cashmere, WA 98815. Phone: 509/782-3230. Open Monday–Saturday, April–October; afternoon Sunday. Admission by donation.

In two exhibit halls on the main level this museum displays prehistoric artifacts, some 9,000 years old, from dry caves in the region. Also displayed are photos and examples of rock art.

DRY FALLS INTERPRETIVE CENTER

From Coulee City on US 2 drive 2 miles west to junction with Washington 17, then follow directional markings. Mail address: HCR 1, Box 36, Coulee City, WA 99115. Phone: 509/632-5583. Open free, daily, May 15–September 15; at other times by appointment.

This building, with a spectacular view of the Grand Coulee area, has on exhibit some prehistoric artifacts. One display is devoted to the nearby Lake Lenore Caves which were inhabited in prehistoric times.

Drawn by Noelle Congdon for the Chelan County Museum, Washington, from fragments of a prehistoric bone carving found in the Columbia River area.

FORT SIMCOE MUSEUM (SIM-kwee)

Fort Simcoe State Park. From Toppenish drive 28 miles west on Washington 220. Mail address: Route 1, Box 39, White Swan, WA 98952. Phone: 509/874-2372. Open Wednesday–Sunday, April 1–October 30; Saturday and Sunday only remainder of year.

Some prehistoric but undated artifacts appear here among local ethnological materials.

GINKGO PETRIFIED FOREST STATE PARK INTERPRETIVE CENTER

From Ellensburg drive 27 miles east on Interstate 90 or on WA 10 to Vantage, then follow signs to park. Mail address: Vantage, WA 98950. Phone: 509/856-2700. Open free, daily, all year. Camping nearby.

At an unknown date early inhabitants of the Columbia Plateau region pecked many designs and pictures into basalt cliffs along the Columbia River. The rising water of Lake Wanapum, behind Wanapum Dam, would have covered all of these had not some been removed and placed where they are now, south of the balcony in the Interpretive Center. An exhibit in the center shows how the petroglyphs were made.

INDIAN PAINTED ROCKS

Northwest of Spokane near the Rutter Parkway Bridge over Little Spokane River. Open free, at all times.

Pictographs on the rocks here are similar to those found at Indian Painted Rocks near Yakima.

INDIAN PAINTED ROCKS

From Yakima city limits drive 3 miles northwest on US 12. Open free, at all times. Camping nearby.

Present-day Indians in the area have no idea who may have made paintings on the cliffs at this spot. They resemble others found in western North America and are sometimes interpreted as depicting religious experiences. They may also have been records of hunts or of meetings between people of different tribes. This particular display of rock art stands beside a modern highway that follows an old Indian trail leading to the Wemas Mountains.

KETTLE FALLS

In Coulee Dam National Recreation Area near junction of US 395 and Washington 25. Open free, May–October. Camping.

The present town of Kettle Falls was built some distance from the falls themselves, which are now submerged beneath Lake Roosevelt. Before the lake was formed by a dam across the Columbia River, the area was one of the largest Indian salmon fishing grounds, and had been since prehistoric times. Recent archeological work has revealed that people lived here for at least 9000 years, making this one of the oldest continuously occupied sites in the Northwest. In addition to permanent inhabitants, as many as a thousand others from many different tribes visited the falls in summer, when the salmon were migrating upstream

Prehistoric Indians on the Interior Plateau and the Northwest Coast often gave artificial shapes to the heads of their babies. This Chinook woman had her head flattened when she was very young, and now she is giving her own baby a fashionable head shape. Apparently this practice had no ill effects on the brain. Redrawn from Catlin.

to spawn. Using willow baskets, men caught the fish as they leaped up the falls. Women then smoked them or preserved the meat with fat and berries in a food called pemmican.

A hiking trail around the St. Paul's Mission site in the recreation area offers a view of the former fishing grounds.

The Name. The word "kettle" probably refers to the basins formed by the force of falling water in the rocky bed of the river.

LAKE LENORE CAVES

From Coulee City on US 2 drive 2 miles west, then 10 miles south on Washington 17 to directional sign, then .5 mile east to parking area. Mail address: Sun Lakes State Park, CR 1, Box 136, Coulee City, WA 99116. Phone: 509/632-5583. Open free, daylight hours. Camping nearby.

A trail leads to seven caves in Lower Grand Coulee that were inhabited by prehistoric Indians who apparently used them as temporary shelters while on hunting expeditions. Many small stone

scrapers have been found in the caves and these are taken as evidence that people who lived here prepared skins.

At Dry Falls Interpretive Center (see entry above), an exhibit is devoted to Lake Lenore Caves.

LAYSER CAVE

From Randle drive 7 miles south on Cispus Road (National Forest Road 23) to directional sign on left, then 2 miles on gravel road to parking. Long or wide vehicles may find the hairpin turns a problem. Mail address: Randle Ranger Station, US Highway 12, Randle, WA 98377. Phone: 206/497-7565. Open free, at all times.

An interpretive trail leads to a large rockshelter where hunters lived and worked about 7000 years ago. Discovered only in 1982 by Tim Layser, a Forest Service employee, the site had not been excavated. Artifacts recovered include projectile points, awls, scrapers and other material that suggested trade over a wide area. One especially interesting tool is a knife made by embedding tiny microblades in a

wooden handle. This material is on exhibit at the Cispus Learning Center on Cispus Road, two miles from the turnoff to the cave.

"Cave shelters such as found here were used by prehistoric man for temporary housing during hunting and gathering trips. The caves were formed by the plucking of basalt from the coulees by the rush of melt water during the Ice Age." An interpretive sign with this message has been placed near the Lake Lenore Cave Shelters, in Washington. Washington State Parks photo.

MAKAH CULTURAL AND RESEARCH CENTER
(mah-KAH)

Neah Bay, at the western end of Washington 112, the northwesternmost settlement in the contiguous 48 states. Open daily, June 1–September 15; Wednesday–Sunday, September 16–May 31. Mail address: P.O. Box 95, Neah Bay, WA 98357. Phone: 206/645-2711. Closed certain holidays. Admission charged. In Neah Bay, which is in the Reservation of the Makah Indian Nation, visitors should be careful not to invade the privacy of the residents.

The Makah Cultural and Research Center, built at a cost of $2 million, houses 55,000 artifacts recovered from the 2500-year-old Ozette archeological site.

Ozette was a village on the far tip of what is now called the Olympic Peninsula. Migrating whales passed by it every year, not far out at sea, and the men of Ozette became great whale hunters. In large canoes that held eight men each, they were able to kill and bring in whales that weighed as much as 30 tons.

At other times of the year Ozette people exploited the area's other rich resources, such as fish and plant roots and berries for food, and various kinds of wood for dishes, tools, and the large planks they used in house building. Each dwelling was big enough for several families, and it was constructed in such a way that it could be dismantled and moved to a new location for a seasonal harvest.

Much is known about the houses because the village stood at the foot of a bluff, and it was partially covered more than once by mud flows. The heavy, wet earth preserved entire dwellings, together with their contents.

Excavation of the site was done by a team of scientists led by Richard Daugherty, of Washington State University, working with a group from the Makah Indian Nation. Because perishable materials were found intact, much unusual information could be gathered about everyday life here. For example, a fragment of textile showed that a woman had woven it from threads made of cedarbark, plus dog wool mixed with cattail fluff. Other artifacts included harpoon blades of mussel shell, adzes and chisels for wood carving, beautifully carved clubs, combs, boxes, weaving equipment, spindle whorls, baskets, nets, and much more.

In addition to displays of objects from Ozette, the Makah Cultural and Research Center offers dioramas, a full-size longhouse, some hands-on exhibits, and an audio program. The Ozette excavations have stimulated a renaissance of traditional Makah craftsmanship, examples of which are on sale at the center.

MUSEUM OF NATIVE AMERICAN CULTURE
(Formerly Pacific Northwest Indian Center)

E. 200 Cataldo (reached by way of Boone St.), Spokane, WA 99202. Phone: 509/326-4550. Open daily, May–September; Tuesday–Sunday, October–April. Admission charged.

A projectile point from the Marmes Early Man Site. Marmes Rockshelter Project photo, Laboratory of Anthropology, Washington State University.

One of the most important Early Man sites was the Marmes Rockshelter, dated at more than 10,000 years ago, which was covered by water before excavation could be completed. This view shows the shelter after excavation had begun. Marmes Rockshelter Project photo, Laboratory of Anthropology, Washington State University.

This museum houses a collection of prehistoric artifacts from many Western areas. The building is located on the site of an early camping area of the Spokane Indians.

OLYMPIC NATIONAL PARK, PIONEER MEMORIAL VISITOR CENTER

2800 Hurricane Ridge Rd., Port Angeles, WA 98362. Open free, daily, except December 25. Camping in the park.

A large amount of ethnological and archeological material from Northwest Coast tribes is stored here and is available for scientific study. A small selection of this material is exhibited in the center.

OZETTE SITE

This site, on the Reservation of the Makah Indian Nation, was backfilled after excavation by Washington State University, and much of the extensive material recovered is now on exhibit at the Makah Cultural and Research Center (see entry above). The site can be reached by a 4.5-mile foot trail from the Olympic National Park Ranger Station on Hoko River Rd., which intersects US 112 just beyond Sekiu.

PACIFIC NORTHWEST INDIAN CENTER
(*See Museum of Native American Culture*)

ROCKY REACH DAM VISITOR CENTER

Seven miles north of Wenatchee on US 97. Phone: 509/663-8121. Open free, daily, all year.

Some exhibits here give information about prehistoric people in the now flooded river valley.

ROOSEVELT PETROGLYPHS

On Washington 14 about a mile east of Roosevelt. Mail address: Klicketat Historical Society, P.O. Box 86, Goldendale, WA. 98620. Phone: 509/773-4303. Open free, at all times.

Here, in a special park, the citizens of Roosevelt have installed and protected a group of petroglyphs collected from nearby sites along the Columbia River. These sites have been flooded by the reservoir behind John Day Dam.

SACAJAWEA STATE PARK AND INTERPRETIVE CENTER
(SOCK-ah-jah-WEE-ah)

From Pasco drive 6 miles southeast on US 395 to the Park directional sign. Mail address: 2503 Sacajawea Park Road, Pasco, WA 99301. Phone: 509/545-2361. Open free, Wednesday–Sunday, mid-April–mid-September.

One wing in the Interpretive Center features stone and bone tools of Sahaptin- and Cayuse-speaking peoples of the area from 9000 B.P. to A.D. 200. The other wing deals with the Lewis and Clark expedition and Sacajawea, the 16-year-old Native American interpreter for the expedition.

Large trenches were dug at right angles by bulldozer to remove sterile soil above the evidence of human occupation. Marmes Rockshelter Project photo, Laboratory of Anthropology, Washington State University.

SEATTLE ART MUSEUM

First Avenue and University, Seattle. Mail address: P.O. Box 22000, Seattle, WA 98122-9700. Phone: 206/625-8913. Open Tuesday–Sunday. Closed certain holidays. Admission charged.

In a large general collection are some archeological objects from the Northwest Coast and the Upper Mississippi valley.

SEQUIM-DUNGENES MUSEUM (SQUIM)

In Sequim turn north on 2nd Ave., go one block then turn right on Cedar. Museum is on the right at 175 West Cedar, Sequim, WA 98382. Phone: 206/683-8110. Open daily. Closed certain holidays. Donations accepted.

On display here are artifacts and many bones and the tusks of the mastodon excavated at the Manis Mastodon Site. Also there is a diorama of the site as it might have appeared 12,000 years ago.

This site is one of the few places where archeologists have discovered proof that prehistoric Americans hunted mastodons. In 1977 Clare and Emanuel Manis decided to build a duck pond in a low-lying spot in a field, and quite by chance chose the exact place where a partly butchered mastodon skeleton had been lying under layers of peat and earth for about 12,000 years. Digging with a backhoe, Manis turned up bones and tusks, realized they were something special, and immediately began searching for experts to take a look. Richard Daugherty, of Washington State University, and other scientists responded. Examination of a rib brought up by the hoe showed something very special indeed—a bone spear tip embedded in the rib. Apparently a hunter had thrust the spear through the mastodon's thick skin and muscle, and it had broken off in the rib without killing the animal. The wound had partly healed when hunters either drove the mastodon into a mud hole or found it mired there. Then, the scientists believe, the hunters dispatched it, possibly by breaking its skull with rocks. At any rate, excavation turned up the cracked head bones nearby, along with other bits of bone that had obviously been shaped into tools of some sort.

The kill may have been possible in part because the mastodon was old and feeble. Its bones showed signs of arthritis, and its teeth were worn down to the gumline—the result of much chewing on the woody plants on which mastodons browsed. (Unlike their cousins the mammoths, they were not usually grass eaters.) The body had lain on its side, and the uppermost bones showed butchering marks where the flesh had been stripped away. A stone chopping tool lay close by.

Excavation at the Manis Site continued for 8 years until 1985. At a 10,000-year level archeologists discovered a wooden tool and other evidence of human occupation. Visitors are offered a slide show of the dig.

SNOQUALMIE VALLEY HISTORICAL MUSEUM (sno-KWAL-mee)

222 North Bend Blvd., North Bend, WA 98045. Open free, afternoons, Saturday and Sunday, March–October. Tours by appointment.

Included here with historical exhibits are a display of undated Snoqualmie Indian artifacts.

UNIVERSITY OF WASHINGTON, THOMAS BURKE MEMORIAL STATE MUSEUM

On the campus, Seattle, WA 98195. Phone: 206/543-5590. Open daily. Closed certain holidays. Donations requested.

In addition to large displays on historic Native American cultures, this museum has some exhibits of prehistoric materials.

WAKEMAP MOUND (WAH-kem-up)

In Horsethief Lake State Park, east of Wishram, off Washington 14. Drive through the park to the river, then from the end of the road walk west on the path from which petroglyphs and pictographs are visible. Open free, at all times.

The mound here is actually an ancient village site, occupied at various times from the tenth century to the period of contact with Lewis and Clark. Each succeeding group of people built houses on top of former house sites, producing a mound of rubble. More interesting to the casual visitor now are examples of rock art, which may be seen on boulders along the river.

WANAPUM DAM AND HERITAGE CENTER

5 miles south of Interstate 90 on Highway 243. Phone: 509/754-3541. Open free, daily, April–November; Monday–Friday, December–March.

Exhibits depict life along the Columbia River from prehistoric to modern times, using a large collection of Native American artifacts. Video presentations and an interactive educational video are available.

WASHINGTON STATE HISTORICAL SOCIETY

315 North Stadium Way, Tacoma, WA 98403. Phone: 206/593-2830. Open Tuesday–Saturday; afternoon Sunday. Closed certain holidays. Admission charged.

This museum, which emphasizes Northwestern history, displays some prehistoric artifacts.

WASHINGTON STATE UNIVERSITY, MUSEUM OF ANTHROPOLOGY

In College hall, on the campus, Pullman. Mail address: Department of Anthropology, Washington State University, Pullman, WA 99164-4910. Phone: 509/335-3441. Open free, Monday–Friday, during the academic year.

As this book went to press this museum did not have on display material from the Marmes (MAR-muss) Rockshelter which it excavated and which is one of the most important early human sites in the United States. The site now lies under water in a reservoir in the southeastern corner of Washington.

The Story. For several years Washington State University conducted excavations in the Marmes Rockshelter, named for the owner of the property. Here, in the Palouse River Valley, near its junction with the valley of the Snake River, archeologists found layer after layer of debris that indicated people had first used the shelter 10,000 years ago, possibly even earlier. Digging revealed food-storage pits lined with matting, shell beads, grinding implements, projectile points, tools of various kinds, and more than a dozen burials.

One skeleton lay beneath a thick layer of volcanic ash, which geologists identified as having resulted from the eruption of Mount Mazama, at Crater Lake, in Oregon, about 6700 years ago. This was especially interesting in view of an Indian legend about Crater Lake. It was formed, according to the Indians, when a battle took place between the underworld chief who lived inside Mount Mazama and the chief of the world above. The underworld chief hurled out fiery rocks and great clouds of ash, and the earth shook, but in the end his rival succeeded in pushing him down into the mountain, forming the great hole, which then filled up with water, to create the lake. The discovery that a human being had lived in the rockshelter before the eruption suggested that Indian storytellers based their tale not on fantasy but on the 6700-year-old fact that an eruption really had happened.

One day a member of the Marmes expedition—a geologist—decided to have a trench dug in the terrace below the shelter. He called in a bulldozer to clear away the soil quickly, and as he walked behind the machine, he saw a fragment of bone. It turned out to be human bone. The bulldozer was replaced by trowels, and careful digging revealed portions of three skulls. Since they lay underneath material that was dated at 10,000 years B.P., the bones had to be older than that. Since they lay on top of soil known to have been deposited no more than 13,000 years ago, the bones were somewhere between 10,000 and 13,000 years old.

Near the skulls were found a spearpoint made of an animal bone and a tiny, delicately made bone needle with an eye in it. This was taken to mean that the people who lived here a hundred centuries ago sewed animal-skin clothing. Indeed the needle was so small that experts think it may have been used to sew watertight seams, as Eskimos are known to have done in much later times.

The Marmes discovery was very important, but those who made it were able to excavate only part of the site. A dam was under construction downriver, and when it was completed water rose rapidly behind it and approached the level of the rockshelter. People who were interested in the scientific importance of the site persuaded President Johnson to instruct the Army Corps of Engineers to protect it. A coffer dam was built around

the site, but someone had overlooked the nature of the soil under this barrier. It was gravel, through which the water from the reservoir seeped very readily. Nevertheless, optimistically, the archeologists lined the sides of their excavation with plastic and then had the hole filled with gravel, to prevent slumping. Someday, they hope, if several million dollars are forthcoming to pump out water and retrieve the site—or if the reservoir silts in so much that it has to be drained—scientists may return to finish their work.

WILLIS CAREY MUSEUM

Off US 2, Cashmere, WA 98815. Open free, Monday–Friday; afternoons Saturday and Sunday.

Both prehistoric and historic Native American artifacts are on exhibit here.

YAKIMA INDIAN NATION CULTURAL HERITAGE CENTER (YAK-ee-maw)

151 Fort Road, Toppenish, WA 98948. Phone: 509/865-2800. Open daily. Admission charged.

Part of the Heritage Center is a large Indian-owned museum. Among its exhibits are prehistoric tools and other artifacts from the Hurmiston, Oregon, site. The museum has in storage a large collection of petroglyphs that were rescued before they were flooded behind the dam on the Columbia River. Some of this rock art is on display, along with a replica of an earth lodge.

YAKIMA VALLEY MUSEUM

2105 Tieton Dr., Yakima, WA 98902. Phone: 509/248-0747. Open Wednesday–Friday; afternoons Saturday and Sunday. Admission charged. Closed certain holidays.

The principal Indian exhibits here are Yakima, Klickitat, and Sioux (Dakota). A small amount of undated prehistoric material is included.

A bone tool, called a flesher, for scraping hides of freshly killed animals, found at the Old Crow Site in Yukon, Canada. The left half of the artifact was cut off to be used in carbon-14 dating which indicated that the bone was 27,000 years old. A more recent linear accelerated radiocarbon date has given the figure of only about 1300 years B.P. This brings into serious question the surprisingly early date of the original test. Other studies of the site and finds made there have also raised questions about the 27,000 year date. Photo by Richard Garner. Canadian Museum of Civilization, Hull, Quebec.

Yukon

HERSCHEL ISLAND

Although no archeological sites in Yukon have been prepared for the public, excavation of thousand-year-old dwellings of the Thule culture is continuing on Herschel Island, and visitors may be able to see ongoing work. The Visitor Center has a few prehistoric artifacts on display. Open daily, May–October. For information call or write to Department of Renewable Resources, P.O. Box 2703, Whitehorse, YT Y1A 2C6. Phone: 403/667-5648.

KLUANE MUSEUM OF
NATURAL HISTORY
(clue-AH-neh)

At Haines Junction on Route 1 west of Whitehorse. Mail address: Kluane National Park Reserve, Haines Junction, YT Y0B 1L0. Phone: 403/634-2251. Open free, mid-May–September.

In the Visitor Reception Center are a few prehistoric artifacts, and along some trails in the park are markers indicating points of archeological interest.

MacBRIDE CENTENNIAL
MUSEUM

First Ave. and Wood St. Whitehorse, YT Y1A 3S9. Phone: 403/667-2709. Open daily, May 15–September; Sundays, October–April. Admission charged.

Some finds of prehistoric artifacts are exhibited in this museum, which also displays more recent Indian materials, along with relics of pioneer and Gold Rush times.

An aerial view of part of the Bannock Point Petroform Site, in Whiteshell
Provincial Park, Manitoba, where prehistoric people used rocks to create
designs on the ground.

198

GREAT PLAINS

"I observed the remains of an old village which had been fortified," Captain William Clark wrote in his journal on Oct. 19, 1804. He and other members of the Lewis and Clark Expedition noted several of these abandoned sites along the Missouri River before they stopped at a vigorous and hospitable settlement of Mandan Indians near present-day Bismarck, North Dakota. There for the next five months the exploring party camped on the very edge of prehistory.

The daily lives of the Mandans, their ceremonies and rituals, may well have resembled those of Indians whose villages and garden plots had been sprinkled along rivers in the flat heart of America for the preceding thousand years. Even before that, transient hunters left evidence of their wanderings over the Great Plains, just as they had in other parts of the country. The Plains environment, however, was unique. Accordingly human adjustments to it had special qualities.

This huge region extends from central Texas northward to southern Alberta, Saskatchewan, and Manitoba. On the west it begins at the foothills of the Rocky Mountains, and it stretches eastward through much of Oklahoma, all of Kansas and Nebraska, part of Iowa, and all of South and North Dakota. A feature common to most of the Plains is grass. In the east it grows tall, and the tall-grass country is often called prairie. The west, where the land is higher and rainfall less, is short-grass country.

When Europeans began to explore here they assumed, as have most people since then, that the prairies were very ancient. How-

A diorama showing how hunters drove buffalo over a cliff to make possible a large kill. Many such buffalo jumps have been studied on the Plains. Smithsonian Institution photo.

ever, this may not have been the case. In the not too distant past, trees grew in some places where whites found only grass. Forests covered large sections of the Plains at certain periods. Just when or why they disappeared is not altogether clear. Possibly a slight decrease in rainfall, together with forest fires, destroyed much of the tree cover. The grasses could survive, but perhaps the slower-growing trees then succumbed to the Indians' habit of setting grass fires to make hunting easy.

This change in vegetation had its effect on animal life. It gave bison a virtually limitless supply of food. Herds multiplied and roamed freely. Perhaps 30 million of the big animals were grazing on Plains grasses by the time Europeans first saw them. With such a resource people, too, could make the grasslands their home. Bison fed the Plains dwellers. Their hides gave them robes for warmth and material for shelter and for containers. Sinews were useful for sewing. Horns could be made into spoons, certain bones into scrapers. Dried bison dung (buffalo chips) made excellent fuel.

Even before the buffalo hunters, there were small groups on the Plains who followed the giant bison. These huge creatures—they were probably four times as heavy as modern buffalo—furnished an abundance of meat, as did mammoths, camels, and other game that is now extinct. Mammoth kill sites have been found in Oklahoma, Colorado, and Wyoming, and associated with the bones were projectile points of the kind first discovered at Clovis, New

Mexico. A whole series of other points were also used to kill large game animals on the plains. These too are identified in museums by the names of the sites where they were first found—Scottsbluff, Eden, Milnesand, Hell Gap, and others. Although they vary in shape, all are of beautifully worked stone. Perhaps it was the efficient use of these points that helped to bring extinction to several species of animal. At any rate the big game of Paleo-Indian times disappeared, and by about 6000 B.C. the lifeway of hunters on the Great Plains began to undergo change.

Archaic Period
Hunting continued in the next period, the Archaic, but in the absence of the large meat animals people ate more of the smaller ones, even squirrels, rats, and mice, which already had a place in their diet. They also accepted plants as food. Grinding stones to make seeds edible now appear in places where Archaic campsites come to light. Not many of these sites have been found. Perhaps no one has looked hard enough for them; or the climate may have been to blame. According to some weather experts a hot, dry period began about 5000 B.C., and vegetation declined in the western sections of the Plains. This could have meant that animal life was scarce, and people who depended on both plants and animals would have had little reason to stay in the area. Some dispute this idea, but archeologists have found only limited traces of human presence during the next 2500 years. Eastern sections of the Plains were not arid, and there the lifestyle resembled that of Archaic people who inhabited the heavily wooded areas from the Mississippi to the Atlantic coast. (Although archeological material from eastern Oklahoma is listed in this section of the book, it is culturally related to the Southeast.)

No mountain barrier separated the Plains from the woodlands. On the contrary, waterways linked the entire region from the Rocky Mountains to the Appalachians, and Woodland people could and did move freely along them. Ideas traveled too, but not always very fast. Pottery making, for example, had appeared as early as about 2400 B.C. in Florida, and in the Northeast by about 1000 B.C. It then took about a thousand years for the useful art of ceramics to reach the eastern Plains and even longer for it to spread into short-grass country.

Partly because pieces of broken pottery are numerous and easy to see, the human record on the Great Plains becomes clearer. The advent of gardening and corn raising makes the record clearer still, because farmers stay longer in one place and hence leave more debris in one place than hunters do.

How agriculture entered the Plains is a matter of discussion among the experts. Some believe it came from the south and west. Others think it may have been brought by people who moved westward out of the valleys of the Ohio and Illinois and Mississippi rivers. Apparently a migration did begin about A.D. 1, when a

Strange stone heads from the Southern Plains may be among the earliest works of art in the New World. *Left to right:* The Frederick Head was carved from sandstone. Original now in the Museum of the Great Plains, Lawton, Oklahoma. The Malakoff Heads (only the faces are shown here in reproduction). Originals in Texas Memorial Museum, Austin.

group settled on the Missouri River where Kansas City now stands. With them came customs typical of a lifeway known as Hopewellian, that centered in Ohio and Illinois. After that, settlements appeared farther and farther up the Missouri.

As the people moved northward the women, who did the planting, had a basic problem—the farther they went, the shorter was the dependable weather for crop growing. This meant that not all of their corn seeds would produce mature plants before frost. Nevertheless, along the Missouri River and elsewhere, they managed to save some hardy, early-ripened seeds each year, and gradually, by a process of selection, they developed strains suited to the climate of each area they settled.

Wherever corn became a successful crop, village life was possible for at least part of the year. Although these Plains settlements had much in common, they varied in many ways that intrigue the archeologist. Life in regions where farming developed early differed from life where it came late or not at all. And so, for convenience in reporting, archeologists who have been most concerned with the Great Plains area divide it into five subareas: Southern Plains, Central Plains, Middle Missouri, Northeastern Periphery, and Northwestern Plains.

There are several reasons why the Middle Missouri has yielded the most archeological "goodies." Along this stretch of the river, as it crosses South Dakota and North Dakota to its junction with the Yellowstone, the land was suited to the needs of village dwellers. It offered good soil for gardens. There was access to hunting grounds and plenty of timber for building the distinctive Plains Village houses. These are known as earth lodges because their framework of poles and upright logs was banked with earth or sod. A frequent house shape was a half dome, like those which Lewis and Clark saw among the Mandans, with roofs that sometimes covered a surprisingly big area. A hole in the center provided an escape for smoke and a source of light. In bad weather the smoke hole could be covered with an inverted bull boat—a circular craft made of bison skin stretched around a wooden frame.

In varying sizes and shapes—sometimes round, sometimes rectangular or square—the earth lodges housed Plains Village Indians along the Missouri from about A.D. 1000 to historic times. After they were abandoned the earth lodges attracted little attention until, at the end of World War II, dam building for flood control began along the Missouri. A program of salvage archeology in this rich area yielded much fascinating material.

Archeologists have done less excavating in the eastern Dakotas and southern Manitoba (the Northwestern Periphery subarea). As a result they are not altogether sure what happened there during the Plains Village period. They do know that at some time people built a good many burial mounds. Just when they began is not certain, but they may have continued into historic times. Perhaps the first mounds were the work of people who shared in the widespread Woodland lifeway. Almost certainly they were not farmers but hunters.

Woodland people did inhabit the long-grass part of the Central Plains subarea, which includes the westernmost part of Iowa, all of Kansas and Nebraska, eastern Colorado, and a little of southeastern Wyoming. Here were resources for men who hunted and for women who may have done a little gardening but who certainly had the knack of gathering seeds and roots. What happened to these groups after about A.D. 500 remains a mystery. All we know is that people with an entirely different life style moved in and stayed.

Changing Lifeways

These newcomers were village dwellers. Like their predecessors they hunted bison, but they were also gardeners, and they made new use of one particular part of the bison—they turned the shoulder blades into hoes for their cornfields. Along one river valley after another the Plains Village communities spread westward through the Central Plains. Proof that they were not transients appeared when archeologists dug into a site inhabited by people of the Mill Creek culture in Iowa. During the years they spent here—from perhaps A.D. 800 to 1400—they piled up a rich collection of trash 12 feet deep over a two-acre area.

Somewhat less wealthy were the earth-lodge builders who settled in the upper valley of the Republican River in Nebraska. However, they must have had large surpluses of corn, beans, squash, and sunflower, for they dug innumerable food storage pits both inside and outside their dwellings. The Upper Republican women were good potters; the men efficient hunters of deer, antelope, and bison. Why they disappeared shortly before the arrival of Europeans, archeologists cannot say. Possibly nomadic raiders from the west stole their surplus food and forced them to move toward safer places in the east. Or perhaps it was drought that robbed them of food.

A little farther to the west, where the prairie gives way to the short-grass country of the High Plains, lived the Dismal River people, who did little gardening but lived primarily by hunting. Instead of building earth lodges they made shelters of poles with roofs of skin or bundled grass. Probably they were the ancestors of the Plains Apaches who followed the buffalo herds on horseback in historic times.

Farther south in the Oklahoma and Texas panhandles, which are part of the Southern Plains subarea, people of the Antelope Creek culture had an interesting mixture of traits. Some of their patterns of living seem to have come from Upper Republican contacts; another custom—their way of building square houses of masonry and adobe mud—certainly reached them from the Pueblo people, across the mountains in New Mexico.

Close by these settlements lay the Llano Estacado—the Staked Plains—where, long before, Paleo-Indians hunted mammoths. Because the hard sod and the uncertain climate made farming almost impossible, this remained hunting country. Countless bison roamed there, and in late prehistoric times Comanche Indians made it their home.

Elsewhere in northern Texas and Oklahoma, village Indians resembled in many ways those of the Central Plains. The Washita River people, for example, built rectangular houses but daubed the outside with clay instead of banking the walls with earth. They gardened and hunted and also did some fishing. Similar villages dotted parts of north-central Texas.

Although south Texas is not strictly a part of the Great Plains, it is included here for convenience. This was not a hospitable or comfortable land. Along the coast plenty of rain fell in the course of a year, but it often did not fall at the right time for corn growing. Inland the climate was very dry. As a result, people who lived either on the coast or inland never took up agriculture, and so they did not gather in permanent farming villages. They simply subsisted on what was at hand—roots, nuts, seeds, and the fruit and stems of cactus. Along the coast they found fish and mollusks, and shell heaps accumulated as they did along the Pacific and Atlantic coasts. Their way of life, in short, was a continuation of the Western Archaic culture from which the farming cultures of the Southwest developed. Possibly these South Texans were immigrants who came to North America very early and were pushed into so harsh a land by later people. One basis for this theory is their language. It resembles the Hokan tongue which survived into historic times in California and which scholars believe is the oldest of all California languages.

Almost as difficult as south Texas are some parts of the Northwest Plains, which include Wyoming, Montana, the western Dakotas, and the southern end of Alberta and Saskatchewan. Corn did not prosper here, and people could not base their lives on farming. Instead they continued to live century after century much as their ancestors had in Archaic times. Some pottery did appear about A.D. 500, but it was never very useful to nomadic hunters because it was fragile and awkward to transport. More suitable containers could be made from hide and from the stomachs and intestines of bison.

Ways of hunting bison varied. The most spectacular was also the most productive—and wasteful. To secure a large quantity of meat with least trouble, men would drive a whole herd over a cliff. Indians used this technique, called the buffalo jump, both before and after they obtained horses.

Some of the buffalo hunters of historic times—the Blackfoot, Arapaho, and Assiniboine—were probably descendants of the prehistoric Northern Plains people. Others who hunted here after the arrival of horses had different origins. The Cheyenne and the Sioux were latecomers. Their ancestors had been Plains Village dwellers farther east—farmers who gave up farming and moved about living entirely by the chase, once horses were available.

From the colorful riders of historic times to the early makers of simple stone tools, the range of Plains life was wide and, like the Plains themselves, surprisingly varied. Our knowledge of it is far from complete but has accumulated very rapidly. As a result of decisions to build huge flood-control dams in the Missouri River Basin, the Smithsonian River Basin Survey and the National Park Service undertook a large and intensive salvage archeology program, especially in the Dakotas. The work done by the survey—and work done everywhere else on the Plains—has been well summarized and interpreted by Waldo R. Wedel in a very illuminating book, *Prehistoric Man on the Great Plains.*

Bison Bone Mining

Buffalo jumps, where hunters drove bison over cliffs to their death, resulted in thick deposits of the bones of the animals who died there. These bone beds were so extensive that they attracted commercial miners who carried away countless tons of bones which were used in fertilizer and as filter in the manufacture of sugar. One site alone produced more than 6,000 tons of processed fertilizer. Buffalo bones, ground up, were also mixed with prepared livestock feed. Unfortunately the miners also took away a great deal of information that might have helped archeologists understand the life of prehistoric people who lived on the Plains.

Alberta

HEAD-SMASHED-IN BUFFALO JUMP

From Fort Macleod, drive 12 miles west on Highway 2 and SR 785; follow signs. Mail address: Box 1977, Fort Macleod, AB TOL 0Z0. Phone: 403/553-2731. Open all year. Donations accepted.

This World Heritage Site is one of the oldest and largest buffalo jumps known. It was used for about 5500 years. Here, time after time, indigenous hunters drove herds of buffalo over the cliff, and layers of bones more than 30 feet deep now lie buried below the jump. Such a hunting method involved hundreds of people and a complex organization.

The Government of Alberta has built a $10 million interpretive center here which opened in 1987. In the first three months it attracted more than 100,000 visitors.

The *Bulletin* of the Society for American Archaeology reported, "The new visitor center is a dramatic structure carved into bedrock a few hundred meters south of the jump-off. Built like a staircase, the seven story building straddles the cliff face, allowing access to both the top and the bottom of the cliff through a series of stairs and elevators. Five of the seven floors are devoted to public displays, with one theme developed on each level. The major interpretive themes are the Plains environment, the culture of the Plains Indians, the operation of a buffalo jump, culture contact of the historic period and the science of archaeology."

LUXTON MUSEUM

One Birch Ave., Banff, AB TOL 0C0. Phone: 403/762-2388. Open daily, last week in June to September 7; Tuesday–Sunday in other seasons. Closed certain holidays. Admission charged.

Included with western Canadian ethnographic material in the museum are archeological specimens from the area. A diorama shows a buffalo jump.

PROVINCIAL MUSEUM OF ALBERTA

12845 102nd Ave., Edmonton, AB T5N 0M6. Phone: 403/453-9100. Open Monday–Friday. Closed certain holidays. Admission charged.

This museum has a small exhibit of prehistoric materials.

THE RIBSTONES

From Viking drive 6 miles east on Alberta 14. Open free, at all times.

Here on a farm is a provincial cairn that points out the ribstones—a kind of artifact found more in Alberta than in any other Plains province or state. A ribstone is a boulder on which prehistoric hunters pecked grooves that often resemble animal ribs. The Cree Indians in historic times thought that these petroglyphs represented buffalo ribs and that the boulders were dwelling places of the animals' guardian spirits. Sometimes a buffalo head was pecked near the grooves in a ribstone, along with circular depressions. These

Excavation at the Olsen-Chubbuck site in Colorado revealed this "river of bones," which remained after prehistoric bison were driven into an arroyo and butchered. Photo by Joe Ben Wheat, University of Colorado, Boulder.

holes, according to the Crees, allowed arrows (and bullets in historic times) to pass through without harming the guardian spirit within the stone.

UNIVERSITY OF ALBERTA, ANTHROPOLOGY EXHIBITS

Henry Marshall Tory Bldg., on the campus, Edmonton. Open free, Monday–Saturday, when the university is in session.

In the hallway on the main floor of the building are display cases of archeological material representing all stages of Alberta's prehistory, from Paleo times up to the period of contact with Europeans. There are also recent Eskimo artifacts. Displays are changed once or twice a year.

WRITING-ON-STONE PROVINCIAL PARK

Off Highway 501, about 22 miles east of Milk River town. Phone: 403/647-2364. Open free, daily, during summer months. Fee charged for camping.

In the archeological area of the park are large numbers of petroglyphs which may be seen on guided tours on weekday afternoons and twice daily on Saturday and Sunday. The park also offers an interpretive program with audiovisual shows.

Some of the petroglyphs show men on horseback. Although horses roamed the Plains in early Paleo-Indian times, they disappeared and were reintroduced by the Spanish in the sixteenth century. The pictures showing men on horseback must have been made sometime after A.D. 1730, which is thought to be the date when horses reached Alberta. Representations of men with bows and shields may have been made earlier.

Archeologists who have examined the site believe that much of this rock art is prehistoric. Possibly the figures of animals were made by young men as part of a religious rite called the guardian spirit quest. A youth in search of a guardian spirit went off alone to some remote spot, where he fasted and tried to dream of an animal which would become his protector and helper in later life.

Computerized studies of the petroglyphs seem to indicate that one or more cultures were continuously responsible for the rock art here.

Ginsburg and Margie and Paleo-Indians

One day in March 1978, archeologists learned a good deal about how stone and bone tools helped Paleo-Indians obtain food. They used replicas of such tools to butcher an elephant, named Ginsburg, that had died in the Boston Zoo. Ginsburg, except for her smaller size, closely resembled a mammoth, and all of her, except for certain parts kept for study in Boston, was trucked to Front Royal, Virginia. There Dr. Dennis Stanford of the Smithsonian Institution directed very precise studies of how projectile points penetrated the thick skin of the elephant and how stone and bone knives cut the hide and flesh. One finding made on the spot was that tools fashioned from elephant bone were very effective. "It might have been possible to kill and butcher a mammoth without using stone tools," Stanford said.

A similar opportunity to try out replicas of prehistoric tools on an elephant came in Denver in June 1979. Dr. Bruce Rippeteau, then Colorado State Archeologist, got a dead circus elephant named Margie on loan from a rendering plant, and with the aid of a hastily gathered group of experts proceeded to experiment with spears and other tools made of wood, stone, and bone. They proved that thin, fluted Clovis points could penetrate the animal's underbelly, provided their hafting was carefully tapered. Thin, slightly serrated blades were best for slicing meat, and a stone hand axe effectively peeled off the thick hide. The angles at which tools were held also affected their efficiency.

Colorado (eastern)

COLORADO HISTORY MUSEUM

1300 Broadway, Denver, CO 80203. Phone: 303/866-3682. Open daily. Closed certain holidays. Admission charged.

The Colorado History Museum, an institution of the Colorado Historical Society, has an extensive Mesa Verde collection from the prehistoric Anasazi Indians in southwestern Colorado, including bows and arrows, pottery, stone tools and weaving materials.

Accompanying these artifacts are two detailed dioramas: one represents an Anasazi cliff pueblo house and the other a crop irrigation system.

DENVER ART MUSEUM

100 West 14th Ave. Parkway, Denver, CO 80204. Phone: 303/575-2793. Open Tuesday–Saturday; afternoon Sunday. Closed certain holidays. Admission charged.

On exhibit in the Native Arts Department are examples of North American material, mostly ceramic, from both the Southwest and the Southeast. The collection includes a few examples of prehistoric basketry, stone sculpture, textiles and engraved shell.

DENVER MUSEUM OF NATURAL HISTORY

City Park in Denver. Mail address: 2001 Colorado Blvd., Denver, CO 80205. Phone: 303/322-7009. Open Monday–Saturday; afternoon Sunday and most holidays. Admission charged.

This museum first gained fame in the world of archeology for its excavation of the Folsom Site in New Mexico (see entry above), and it displays the original Folsom point, as it was found, between the ribs of an extinct bison.

A number of exhibits in the North American archeology section emphasize sites in Colorado and the South-west. Much of the material here resulted from H. M. Wormington's field work on Early Man which was sponsored by the museum.

One display contains materials from a site with an interesting history: A summer cloudburst in 1932 exposed some large bones along the South Platte River near the Dent railroad station 39 miles from Denver. Railroad workers reported the bones to Reverend Conrad Bilgery, S.J., a teacher at Regis College near Denver. Father Bilgery and members of the museum staff excavated and found under the pelvis of a mammoth a large spear point. This was the first evidence ever found in North America that human beings lived at the same time as mammoths and hunted them. The spear point had short indentations called flutes on each face near the base. It was a Clovis point— a type of projectile point found for the first time that same year in New Mexico near Clovis from which place it gets its name.

Dating of the Clovis-point finds revealed that hunters had been on the Plains at least 11,000 years ago, ear-

Margie's big leg bones provided a chance to see just how a twenty or thirty pound hammerstone, with or without a stone anvil, splintered the bone so that fragments could be shaped into tools. Dennis Stanford was on hand to join in experiments with bone. The archeologists also peered through microscopes at their tools after they had used them, to find out how wear had affected the implements.

Here scientists in Denver engage in experimental archeology as they butcher a 9,480 pound dead elephant using replicas of the prehistoric tools that Paleo hunters of mammoths used 13,000 years ago. This study became known as the Denver Elephant Project. Photo courtesy of Dr. Bruce Rippeteau.

lier than archeologists had previously thought. The Dent site is not open to the public.

FORT COLLINS MUSEUM

200 Mathews St., two blocks north of Mulberry St. (Colorado 14), Fort Collins, CO 80524. Phone: 303/221-6738. Open free, Tuesday–Saturday; afternoon Sunday.

On display is an extensive collection of Folsom artifacts collected in the 1920s and 1930s at the Lindenmeier Site in northern Colorado. This Paleo-Indian culture existed about 10,000 years ago.

KOSHARE INDIAN MUSEUM, INC.
(ko-SHAH-ray)

From US 50 in LaJunta drive south 18 blocks on Colorado Ave., then west 1 block. Mail address: P.O. Box 580, 115 W. 18th St., LaJunta, CO 81050. Phone: 719/384-4411. Open daily, summer; afternoons, winter. Admission charged.

This museum on the campus of Otero Junior College contains archeological materials and dioramas showing prehistoric Indian life. The collections have been assembled partly through the activities of an extraordinary troop of Boy Scouts who call themselves Koshares. The Koshares also perform Indian dances in authentic costumes on Saturday nights and at varying other dates in late June through early August and at the end of December. Inquire at the museum for a schedule of appearances.

LOUDEN-HENRITZE ARCHAEOLOGY MUSEUM

On the campus, Trinidad State Junior College. Mail address: Freudenthal Memorial Library, Trinidad State Junior College, Trinidad, CO 81082. Phone: 719/846-5508. Open free, daily, June–August.

The museum has a collection of artifacts pertaining to the culture, religion, food and tools of prehistoric people. The material was recovered during excavations in the Trinidad area.

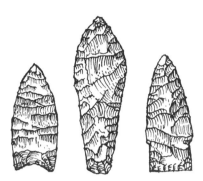

Paleo-Indian Big-Game Hunters of the Plains used these projectile points: Midland (left); Hell Gap (center); and Scottsbluff (right). Redrawn from Irwin and Wormington.

Outlines of Kokopelli, the humpbacked flute player, appear in many places throughout the Southwest, but never before 1981 had anyone discovered the mythological figure on the floor of a kiva. Here is what Joe Ben Wheat found in a dig at Yellow Jacket, Colorado. University of Colorado Museum photo by Joe Ben Wheat.

ROCKY MOUNTAIN NATIONAL PARK KAWUNEECHE VISITOR CENTER

Three miles north of Grand Lake and 48 miles west of Estes Park on US highway 34. Mail address: Estes Park, CO 80517. Phone: 303/586-3565. Open daily, all year. No admission is charged for the Visitor Center but admission is charged to proceed from Grand Lake into the park. Camping.

On display in the Visitor Center are some artifacts made by prehistoric people of the area, who may have been ancestral to the Utes and Arapahos of historic times.

UNIVERSITY OF COLORADO MUSEUM

On the campus, Henderson Bldg., Boulder, CO 80309. Phone: 303/492-6892. Open free, Monday–Friday. Closed certain holidays.

The McKenna room exhibits southwestern archeology in a combination of photographs, dioramas and objects. As this book went to press the main anthropology hall was scheduled to be reopened. It will contain exhibits on southwestern archeology.

VOGEL CANYON PETROGLYPHS

In the Comanche Grasslands. On Colorado 109 drive south from LaJunta 12 miles. At a sign turn right and drive 1.5 miles on David Canyon Road. At a sign turn left onto Grand Road and drive 2 miles. From the parking lot it is a .75 mile walk to the site. Mail address: Pike-San Isabel National Forest, 1920 Valley Drive, Pueblo, CO 81008. Phone: 719/545-8737. Open free, daily.

Here on the face of a cliff are 10 panels containing about 100 designs that were created in the late Archaic from about A.D. 1 to 1400. Visitors are warned not to disturb anything. As this book went to press a brochure on the site was in preparation.

The Paleo Palate

Paleo Indians dined on more than mammoth steak. The menu of 11,000 years ago was far more varied than that. Douglas Banforth of the University of Colorado confirmed this when he studied materials from a large excavation in Nebraska that had been stored, unlooked at, for many years.

Paleo people, he found, ate bear, beaver, bison, antelope, coyote, prairie dog, fox, rabbit, freshwater mussels, fish and many kinds of bird. To catch some of these creatures early dwellers on the Plains used bolas.

Evidence also emerged, from study of the long-forgotten Nebraska artifacts and refuse, that although some members of a Paleo community were specialists at doing the highly skilled work of making elegant projectile points, others did their hunting with points that were crude but effective.

The Nebraska materials also suggested that the Paleo lifeway was not uniform throughout North America. There were local variations as the early people adjusted to local environments.

WRAY MUSEUM

205 East Third St., Wray, CO 80758. Phone: 303/332-5063. Open Monday–Friday; afternoons, Saturday and Sunday. Admission charged.

Near this town in northeastern Colorado a heavy rainstorm in 1972 uncovered stone spear points and some bones that rancher Bob Jones could tell were extraordinarily big. He and a friend, Jack Miller, did a bit of digging and decided to call for expert archeological opinion. Dennis Stanford of the Smithsonian Institution responded. In several summers' work the Jones/Miller site proved to be an enormous killing field where hunters, 10,000 years ago, butchered bison that were indeed a third larger than modern bison. Altogether Stanford's crews excavated about 40,000 bones from 300 animals killed at two different times. Apparently the hunters had rigged a trap into which the bison were herded and dispatched with spears. Several hundred projectile points were recovered among the bones which were so thickly piled up that excavators had to devise a special way of digging to keep one fragile layer from being crushed while they were getting at another.

At the time of the dig there was no suitable museum in Wray, and the material from the site was taken to the Smithsonian in Washington, D.C. Then the local historical society bought a vacant building and raised money to convert it into a museum. In 1992 the Smithsonian provided photographs, artifacts and legends and set up a permanent exhibit explaining the dig and its importance.

In addition to the Jones/Miller exhibit the museum has displays from the nearby Selby-Dutton site which yielded large quantities of bones and stone and bone tools at least 10,000 years old. (There was some indication that this might have been a kill-site as much as 16,000 years ago.)

Another permanent exhibit, prepared by the Denver Museum of Natural History, gives a pictorial overview of archeology in the Southwest. There are also carefully prepared revolving exhibits of other archeological areas, worldwide.

The Pawnee Indian Village Museum in Republic County, Kansas, is constructed over and around the remains of a large Indian dwelling that was in use during historic times, but it closely resembled those of prehistoric times. Kansas State Historical Society photo.

Kansas

BARTON COUNTY HISTORICAL SOCIETY MUSEUM

85 South Highway 281, Great Bend. Mail address: P.O. Box 1091, Great Bend, KS 67530. Phone: 316/793-5125. Museum open free, afternoons, mid-April–mid-November. Special tours on request. Closed certain holidays.

On display here are dioramas and archeological material from Barton County, covering the period from Folsom times until contact with Europeans.

BENEDICTINE COLLEGE MUSEUM

Science Hall, on the north campus, Atchison. Open only by appointment.

Here are Hopewellian artifacts from Easton, Kansas, from Weston, Missouri, and from the important Renner Site in Kansas City, Missouri. Other materials come from a village site in Doniphan, Kansas, and from a Mimbres site in the Southwest.

CLINTON LAKE VISITOR CENTER

West of Lawrence. Mail address: Route 1, Box 120G, Lawrence, KS 66044. Phone: 913/843-7665. Open free, daily. Closed weekends in winter.

In the Visitor Center, at the north end of Clinton Lake Dam, is an exhibit on the archeology of the area. It consists of a montage of photos, artifacts and original art that interprets 9800 years of human occupation of the vicinity up to the time of the historic Kansa Indians.

CORONADO-QUIVIRA MUSEUM

105 West Lyon St., Lyons, KS 67554. Phone: 316/257-3941. Open Monday–Saturday, afternoon Sunday. Closed certain holidays. Admission charged.

Here on display are some artifacts made by the Quivira people before Coronado entered their territory. Exhibits include a reproduction of a Quiviran grass house. An education program for children includes hands-on artifacts.

EL CUARTELEJO RUINS
(See *Lake Scott State Park*)

ELLSWORTH COUNTY HISTORICAL SOCIETY HODGDEN HOUSE MUSEUM

Main St., Ellsworth, KS 67439. Phone: 913/472-3059. Open Tuesday–Saturday; afternoon Sunday. Donations appreciated.

One room here is devoted to about 20 replicas of petroglyphs that prehistoric Indians pecked in sandstone outcroppings in central Kansas. Some prehistoric artifacts are also on display.

A number of the figures in the petroglyphs represent animals. Although their exact meaning is not known, archeologists have speculated that they

may be of religious significance. Quite possibly the petroglyphs were symbols of the visions young men had or sought during their guardian spirit quests.

HILLSDALE LAKE PROJECT

From Paola drive 6 miles north on US 169 or from Olathe drive 14 miles south on US 169 to the Hillsdale exit, then drive west (through Hillsdale) 3 miles. Mail address: US Army Corps of Engineers, Hillsdale Lake Project Office, RR 3, Box 205, Paola, KS 66091. Phone: 913/783-4366. The Visitor Center is open free, daily, April–October. Closed certain holidays.

Excavation at this site, now covered by water, revealed occupation by people of the Nebo Hill Culture from 5000 to 4000 B.C. People also lived here through the Late Archaic and Plains Woodland periods up to A.D. 1300. Exhibits in the Visitor Center include graphic displays on the various peoples who have inhabited the area.

KANSAS HISTORICAL SOCIETY

Memorial Bldg., 120 S.W. 10th Ave., Topeka, KS 66612. Phone: 913/296-3251. Open free, Monday–Saturday; afternoon Sunday. Closed certain holidays.

In a gallery devoted to Kansas archeology are displays of material from Paleo, Archaic, Middle Woodland, and Central Plains cultures.

KANSAS MUSEUM OF HISTORY

6425 S.W. Sixth Street, Topeka, KS 66615-1099. Phone: 913/272-8681. Open free, Monday–Saturday; afternoon Sunday. Closed certain holidays.

Exhibits include dioramas of Kansas Indian life, displays of archeological material and dioramas of a Wichita grass lodge and Southern Cheyenne tipi.

This diorama in the Pawnee Indian Village Museum in Kansas depicts a moment of contact between white traders and a Pawnee village group. Kansas State Historical Society photo.

El Cuartelejo, the only known Indian pueblo in Kansas, as it may have looked when it was occupied at the time of contact with a Spanish expedition. Drawing courtesy Lake Scott State Park.

LAKE SCOTT STATE PARK

From Scott City drive north 12 miles on US 83, then 3 miles on Kansas 95. Mail address: Route 1, Box 50, Scott City, KS 67871. Phone: 316/872-2061. Open daily, all year. Admission charged to the park. Camping.

Here may be seen a reconstructed small pueblo, known as El Cuartelejo, built by Taos Indian refugees who in 1664 escaped from Spanish rule in New Mexico and joined a band of Plains Apache. There are interpretive markers at the site.

McPHERSON COUNTY OLD MILL MUSEUM

120 Mill St., Lindsborg. Mail address: P.O. Box 94, Lindsborg, KS 67456. Phone: 913/227-3595. Open Tuesday–Saturday; afternoon Sunday; April–October; afternoons Tuesday–Sunday, May–September. Closed certain holidays. Admission charged.

On display here is a limited number of prehistoric artifacts, some from the period when Coronado was exploring nearby, in search of Quivira.

PAWNEE INDIAN VILLAGE MUSEUM

From Belleville drive 15 miles west on US 36, then 7 miles north on Kansas 266. Mail address: Box 475, Route 1, Republic, KS 66964. Phone: 913/361-2255. Open free, Tuesday–Saturday; afternoon Sunday. Closed certain holidays.

Here on the carefully excavated site of a Pawnee village, is a museum that the Kansas Historical Society has constructed over and around the remains of a large dwelling. Although the village was inhabited after the arrival of European traders, it closely resembled those of prehistoric times.

Like many other people of the Central Plains, the Pawnees and their predecessors lived a divided life. Twice a year the entire community picked up and left for buffalo country, to the west. During the buffalo hunts they camped in tipis. Afterward they returned to their home base, a settlement of perhaps 40 huge, circular houses built near the fields where they raised corn, beans and squash. Each of these dwellings,

A Plains Indian Garden

A living garden can scarcely be prehistoric, but it can be a reasonable facsimile of an ancient Indian's vegetable patch—provided the modern gardener can find authentic seeds. Most varieties of vegetables grown today are very different from the ancestral plants which Indians cultivated. The new, improved types of corn, beans, and squash have become so widely used that the older types have almost disappeared. To save them from extinction became the hobby of Charles E. Hanson, Jr., an engineer in the U.S. Department of Agriculture. With the help of his wife and children, he collected and planted seeds of the old-time varieties, some of them rare or even the last in existence. Now a flourishing garden which resembles those of the Plains Indians is sponsored by the Nebraska Historical Society. It can be seen at the Museum of the Fur Trade, three miles east of Chadron, Nebraska, on US 20.

Figures and designs outlined on the ground with rocks were made by prehistoric people in Manitoba. Called petroforms, they are of unknown age.

called earth lodges because the framework of logs was covered with blocks of sod, sheltered as many as 40 people.

In the museum building, which somewhat resembles an earth lodge, display cases contain artifacts recovered in the course of excavating the site. Outside the museum a walk takes the visitor past underground storage pits and lodge floors.

RONIGER MEMORIAL MUSEUM

In Cottonwood Falls, on Courthouse Square, Union and Oak streets. Mail address: P.O. Box 70, Cottonwood Falls, KS 66845. Phone: 316/273-6310. Open free, afternoons, Tuesday–Sunday. Closed certain holidays.

Displayed here is a large number of artifacts from the surrounding area, some collected by two brothers excavating on their farm near Cottonwood Falls.

STERNBERG MEMORIAL MUSEUM

On the campus, Fort Hays State University, Hays. Mail address: 600 Park St., Fort Hays State University, Hays, KS 67601. Phone: 913/628-4286. Open free, Monday–Friday; afternoons, during vacations. Closed certain holidays.

Some exhibits here include prehistoric materials.

UNIVERSITY OF KANSAS, MUSEUM OF ANTHROPOLOGY

Spooner Hall, on the campus, Lawrence, KS 66045. Phone: 913/628-4286. Open free, Monday–Friday; afternoons Saturday and Sunday.

Official university expeditions on the Great Plains produced most of the archeological material on display here.

Manitoba

BANNOCK POINT PETROFORM SITE
(Formerly Ojibway Boulder Mosaics)

In Whiteshell Provincial Park. From Trans-Canada Highway 1 at the Manitoba-Ontario border, which is also the border of the park, drive about 20 miles west on Manitoba 44, then follow Manitoba 307 about 20 miles north to the site. Mail address: Historic Resources Branch, Manitoba Culture, Heritage and Citizenship, 3rd floor, 177 Lombard Avenue, Winnipeg, Manitoba R3B 0W5. Phone: 204/945-3844. Open from about the third weekend in May to about the last weekend in September. Admission to the park charged. Camping.

Exposed here are granite expanses which are interesting because the rock is perhaps the oldest in the world. It was scoured clear of soil by glaciers of the Ice Age. This bare granite serves as a background for large designs, called petroforms, which prehistoric people laid out, using both small rocks and huge boulders that had been pushed along by glaciers and left when the ice melted. Some of the designs are geometric; others are effigies, which include turtles and snakes. The snakes vary in length from a few feet to about 300 feet.

In addition to the visitable effigies, there are many others in Whiteshell Provincial Park that are not open to the public.

Who built the effigies and when is not known. Estimates, based on slight evidence, date them variously at a few hundred years ago or at as much as 3000 years ago.

Although many of the smaller sites would have been readily accessible from the numerous lakes and streams, larger more imposing sites are located far from prehistoric highways. Such sites might have been the scenes for secret rituals involving initiations and world renewal ceremonies.

The Museum. Near the petroforms at Nutimik, a log building houses exhibits of tools, weapons and ornaments made by prehistoric inhabitants of the area.

GRAND VALLEY INTERPRETIVE TRAIL

On Trans-Canada Highway (No. 1) 8 miles west of Brandon. Mail address: Historic Resources Branch, Manitoba Culture, Heritage and Citizenship, 3rd Floor, 177 Lombard Avenue, Winnipeg, Manitoba R3B 0W5. Phone: 204/945-3844. Open free, May–October.

The rich plant and animal resources of this portion of the Assiniboine River valley sustained many indigenous peoples long before Europeans settled the area. For at least 1200 years, hunters periodically stampeded bison down the valley slope onto the flood plain where the animals were trapped and killed with spears and arrows. Parts of the butchered carcasses were carried to camps on the slopes where meat was stripped from the bones and made into jerky and pemmican. The bones were fashioned into tools and ornaments, or smashed and boiled in clay pots to extract the "bone butter." The hides were made into shelters, clothing and containers. Freshwater clams, fish, beaver, muskrat and wild plants supple-

Above and opposite:
Figures and designs, outlined on the ground with rocks, were made by
prehistoric people in Manitoba. Called petroforms, they are of unknown age
and meaning. Manitoba government photo.

A close-up view of one of the petroforms in Whiteshell Provincial Park, Manitoba. Manitoba government photo.

mented the diet of bison meat. Stone tools were fashioned from local fine-grained stone and from Knife River Flint quarried in western North Dakota.

An interpretive trail leads the visitor from the highway down to the valley floor where a bison pound has been reconstructed.

KENOSEWUN CENTRE

In Lockport, 20 miles north of Winnipeg. Mail address: Historic Resources Branch, Manitoba Culture, Heritage and Citizenship, 3rd Floor, 177 Lombard Avenue, Winnipeg, Manitoba R3B 0W5. Phone: 204/945-3844. Open free, daily.

In the twelfth century A.D. hunters from the Red River Valley of the North began to trade with the settled farming peoples of what is now the American Midwest. Some traders married women from southern communities. These women are credited with bringing cultivation to the Canadian prairies centuries before the arrival of Europeans.

Archeological evidence confirms the local manufacture of milling stones and of hoes from the shoulder blades of bison. Crops were stored in bell-shaped pits up to two meters deep. The discovery of corn kernel remains gives further evidence of local cultivation during the period A.D. 1200 to 1500.

An on-site visitor and interpretive center contains displays of some of the artifacts found in the course of the excavations.

MANITOBA MUSEUM OF MAN AND NATURE

190 Rupert Avenue, Winnipeg. Phone: 204/943-3139. Open Monday–Saturday; afternoon Sunday and holidays. Admission charged.

Displays focus on the relationship between Native people and their environments in both prehistoric and historic times. These highlight the different ways of life characteristic of the northern plains, the parklands and the northern forests that cover most of northern Canada. Ethnographic material pertinent to the Inuit (Eskimo) who inhabit the Hudson Bay coast are also on display.

OJIBWAY BOULDER MOSAICS
(*See Bannock Point Petroform Site*)

WHITESHELL PARK
(*See Bannock Point Petroform Site*)

The hunting technique of driving buffalo herds over a cliff and then harvesting the meat began among the Indians about 4000 years ago. At Madison Buffalo Jump, a Montana State Archeological Site, there is much information about this ancient practice. Montana Fish and Game Department photo.

Montana

BIGHORN CANYON NATIONAL RECREATION AREA, VISITOR CENTER
(See entry of same name in Wyoming section)

CLACK MUSEUM
(See Wahkpa Chu'gn Site)

GALLATIN COUNTY COURT HOUSE
(GAL-ah-tun)

317 West Main St., Bozeman, MT 59715. Phone: 406/585-1311. Open free, Monday–Friday.

In the second floor lobby is a collection of artifacts from the Madison Buffalo Jump (see entry below) together with a display of projectile points from other sources.

MAC'S MUSEUM OF NATURAL HISTORY

At Powder River County High School, Broadus. This location may change.

Mail address: Powder River Historical Society, Broadus, MT 59317. Open free, on request at any hour, any day.

This private collection includes more than 4000 Indian items, some of which are prehistoric. A few are like artifacts that have been radiocarbon dated at about 2500 B.C. Others are more recent. Most of the Montana material has come from bison traps in Powder River country.

MADISON BUFFALO JUMP STATE PARK

West of Bozeman take the Logan exit from Interstate 90 and drive south six miles on a county dirt road. Mail address: Montana Department of Fish, Wildlife and Parks, 1400 South 19th St., Bozeman, MT 59715. Phone: 406/994-4042. Open daily, all year. Admission charged. Camping nearby.

Displays in the interpretive center at the park and along linking trails help to explain what went on here two thousand years ago.

On the eastern approaches to the Rocky Mountains, between central

An exhibit in the former Museum of the Rockies: bones of a mammoth from a kill site in Central Montana. Cut marks on the bones and the way some bones were broken indicate that the animal was butchered by people.

Wyoming and southern Alberta, several hundred places have been found where Indians killed bison by driving them over cliffs or bluffs. More than half of these sites are in Montana. The Madison Buffalo Jump is one of the first to be preserved and prepared for the public.

Whenever possible, Indians chose for the drive a gently rising stretch of prairie ending in a steep dropoff, which the bison could not see until it was too late to turn back. To guide the animals' approach, the hunters set up piles of rocks in two lines—far apart on the open prairie and funneling in toward the cliff. At some jumps the lines stretched out for as much as two miles. The rock piles were often large enough to conceal and protect the men who would spring up suddenly, wave blankets, and frighten the bison on toward the jump. Smaller rock piles would support a pole with something attached to flutter in the wind. Once started into the funnel, a herd ran faster and faster, then plunged over the brink. Any animals that were not killed by the fall could be dispatched with weapons.

In some places, where the jump was not very high, hunters might build a sort of corral, or pound, at the foot of the embankment. This would contain the bison until they could be killed with spears or shot with arrows.

At Madison Buffalo Jump, archeologists found evidence that Indians made their last drive about 200 years ago. They may have used it at intervals for about 2000 years before that.

Nearby stand dozens of tipi rings—stones arranged in circles, supposedly to hold down the edges of skin tipis. Here the hunters camped while they butchered and dried the buffalo meat, cured the skins, and made implements of bone and horn. As they worked they feasted. Some of the meat they roasted over fires, and some they stewed in skin containers. To make a stew a woman filled a skin pouch with water, then heated it and kept it boiling by dropping hot rocks into it. Many of these rocks have been found at the site.

At the top of the cliff are other tipi rings. Perhaps these mark shelters for lookouts who watched for bison or for enemies. Other small stone enclosures are something of a mystery here, as

These human figures were drawn on the wall of Pictograph Cave in Montana. Photo by Rick Pittsley.

they are elsewhere on the Plains. Some archeologists think they may have been eagle traps. Covered with brush they could conceal a man who waited for an eagle to dive for bait—perhaps a rabbit—fastened outside. When the bird struck, the man could seize its legs.

The stone enclosures may equally well have been shelters for young men who were fasting and seeking religious visions. Indians in historic times said they were fireplaces used in smoke signaling.

MISSOURI HEADWATERS STATE PARK

Six miles northwest of Three Forks. Mail address: 1400 South 19th St., Bozeman, MT 59115.

Here an interpretive center, signs and trails call attention to a prehistoric rock art panel.

MONTANA HISTORICAL SOCIETY

225 N. Roberts, Helena, MT 59620-9990. Phone: 406/444-2694. Open free, daily, Memorial Day–Labor Day; Monday–Saturday, Labor Day–Memorial Day. Closed certain holidays. Handicapped access provided. Camping nearby.

In the prehistoric section of the "Montana Homeland" exhibit are mammoth bones and replicas of Paleo artifacts, a Clovis point sequence illustrating steps in production, materials from a rich Clovis cache, a diorama of a buffalo jump, an explanation of the importance of the buffalo to Montana's early people, exhibits on plant harvesting, an explanation of rock art featuring replicated artifacts and pictographs from Pictograph Cave in Yellowstone County and photographs of prehistoric sites in the state.

One of the human figures drawn on the wall of Pictograph Cave in Montana. Photo by Rick Pittsley.

PARK COUNTY MUSEUM

118 W. Chinook, Livingston, MT 59047. Phone: 406/222-3506. Open June 1–Labor Day. Closed July 4. Other times by appointment. Admission charged.

Here are artifacts from many local collections, some dated as early as 11,500 B.P. There is a re-creation of the Stole Bison Butchering Site. The displays include explanations of the techniques of excavation, the chronology and tool types of the area and interpretation of a 9,500-year-old campsite.

PICTOGRAPH CAVE STATE PARK
National Historic Landmark

Seven miles southeast of Billings with access from Interstate 90 at the Lockwood exit #452. Mail address: Department of Fish, Wildlife and Parks, 2300 Lake Elmo Drive, Billings, MT 59105. Phone: 406/252-4654. Open daily April 15–October 15. Admission charged. Camping nearby.

When this large cave was discovered in 1937 its most obvious features were the pictographs on its walls—designs and figures of men and animals painted in red, white, and black. Interesting though these were, material that was even more valuable to archeologists lay in the cave floor. When they dug down through 23 feet of earth and debris that had accumulated there, they uncovered evidence of at least three different periods of occupation.

The first visitors were hunters who took shelter in the cave perhaps 10,000 years ago. Next came hunters who made baskets, ornaments and later the paintings on the cave walls. The upper layers of trash indicated the presence of still other hunters in late prehistoric times.

After Pictograph Cave had been excavated, a museum and a trail for visitors were prepared. Unfortunately the museum was vandalized, but the paintings, still in fair shape, are worth a visit. There are interpretive signs along the trail to the cave.

ULM PISHKUN BUFFALO JUMP STATE MONUMENT

Six miles north of Ulm off Interstate 15. Mail address: Department of Fish, Wildlife and Parks, P.O. Box 6609, Great Falls, MT 59406. Phone: 406/454-3441. Open free, April 15–October 15. Donations accepted.

Here, visible from the road, is one of the largest buffalo jumps in North America. Exact dating and other information about the site await further archeological investigation. Meanwhile there are interpretive signs along a semi-primitive trail along the base of the cliff.

Pishkun is the word for buffalo jump used by Indian hunters of the area.

WAHKPA CHU'GN SITE
(Listed in the National Historic Register as the "Too Close for Comfort Site")

Hill County Fairgrounds, Highway #2, west of Havre. Mail address: Box 1484, Havre, MT 59501. Phone: 406/265-9913. For tours phone: 406/265-5152. Open free, daily, mid-May–mid-September. For tours there is a charge.

This is a well-preserved bison kill and campsite. It was used on a number of occasions during the last 2000 years and there are evidences in the site of three different cultures, the Besant (2000 B.P.–1200 B.P.), the Avonlea (A.D. 150–250) and the Saddle Butte (A.D. 800–1200).

At the site is the H. Earl and Margaret Turner Clack Museum which houses and interprets artifacts from the site. Excavation here was first done by the Milk River Archaeological Society and later by professional archeologists.

The name "Wahkpa Chu'gn" is the Assiniboine Indian term meaning "little river."

The interior of a reconstructed Pawnee earth lodge. At the right are a paddle and a round bullboat made from a framework covered with buffalo hide. The kettle is from contact times. Nebraska State Historical Society photo.

Nebraska

ASH HOLLOW STATE HISTORIC PARK

From Ogalalla drive 22 miles northwest on US 26 to directional sign for park entrance. Phone: 308/778-5651. Open free, in daylight hours, all year. Visitor Center open daily, May 24–Labor Day. Camping.

Exhibits in the Visitor Center explain the use during Paleo times and by later prehistoric hunters of rockshelters in what is now the park.

HASTINGS MUSEUM

1330 N. Burlington Ave., Hastings, NE 68901. Phone: 402/461-2399. Open Monday–Saturday; afternoon Sunday and holidays. Admission charged.

Some prehistoric artifacts are exhibited here along with historic Indian material.

HUDSON-MENG SITE

17 miles NW of Crawford. Mail address: United States Forest Service, Nebraska National Forest, Chadron, NE 69337. Phone: 308/432-0300. Open free, at all times. Camping nearby.

Excavations here in the 1970s and again in 1991 have revealed bones of a 10,000-year-old species of extinct bison. Paleo-Indian Alberta points were found at the same location. When excavations are in progress they may be viewed by the public.

The Forest Service will build a $4.7 million 25,000 square foot interpretive center here that will cover the bone bed and permit year-round archeological research.

Like their prehistoric ancestors, Mandan Indians lived in round earth lodges along the Missouri River in North Dakota. When the artist George Catlin visited them in 1832 they allowed him to watch and sketch their ceremonies. From Catlin's *Eight Years,* Vol. 1.

MUSEUM OF NEBRASKA HISTORY

Fifteenth and P streets, Lincoln. Mail address: Nebraska State Historical Society, 1500 R Street, Lincoln, NE 68508. Phone: 402/471-4754. Open free, daily.

The museum, which is administered by the Nebraska State Historical Society, has large exhibits of prehistoric artifacts from Paleo to contact times. Of special interest are effigies etched on bone, pipes and pottery.

SCOTTSBLUFF NATIONAL MONUMENT

The monument is on the North Platte River, 3 miles west of Gering and 5 miles southwest of Scottsbluff. Mail address: P.O. Box 427, Gering, NE 69341. Phone: 308/436-4340. Open daily, except certain holidays and the off season.

In the Visitor Center is a case that contains archeological material, and information about ancient people in the area.

UNIVERSITY OF NEBRASKA STATE MUSEUM

Morrill Hall, on the city campus. Mail address: 307 Morrill Hall, 14th & U streets, Lincoln, NE 68508-0338. Phone: 402/472-6302. Open free, Monday–Saturday; afternoon Sunday and holidays.

A systematic collection of Nebraska artifacts, including stone tools, bone tools and pottery, is available for study at the Encounter Room. Visitors may bring to the museum specimens of their own to compare with the artifacts on exhibit or with other material in a "Discovery" box available from a staff member in the room.

An excavated block from the Lipscomb Site, a Folsom-period bison kill in the Texas Panhandle, is on exhibit on the second floor. The cast of a Fol-som point among the bones marks the spot where the real point was found.

In the Lipscomb Site dozens of bison skeletons lay in a very small area. Among the bones were projectile points, scrapers, stone knives and charcoal from fires. Apparently after the kill, the hunters made camp on the spot, built fires, took some of the meat, but left most of the carcasses as they had fallen.

In the Nomads of the Plains Gallery, artifacts of prehistoric inhabitants of Nebraska (A.D. 900–1200) are exhibited along with a painter's conception of the village site overlooking the Missouri River.

This circle, the significance of which is unknown, is outlined in boulders in Stutsman County, North Dakota. Redrawn from *American Anthropologist*.

Tipi Rings

One form of evidence of human presence on the Northern Plains is a large number of sites where Indians collected stones and laid them in circles. There are perhaps half a million of these circles in the Canadian province of Alberta alone. What were they for? Many archeologists think that the stones held down the edges of tents or tipis. Hence the name "tipi rings." Some rings, however, seem too small for tipis. Were they made to hold down children's play tents? Or were they small tipis in which medicine men held ceremonies? Other rings seem too big and elaborate for tipis. Did they have ritual significance? That was certainly true of other outlines made of rocks in the shape of animals, men, and women.

Aerial photography in the Central Plains has disclosed another type of ring made by digging a circular trench and heaping the earth into a mound inside the ring. Each such circle seems to have had a central position at a village site, and each one has signs of breaks in the circle at just the spots where the sun's rays would fall at sunrise at the time of the equinoxes. Were they calendar rings? Some archeologists think so.

North Dakota

DOUBLE DITCH INDIAN VILLAGE STATE HISTORIC SITE
National Register of Historic Places

From Bismarck drive north on US 83 to marker. Phone: 701/224-2666. Open free, at all times.

One of the largest Mandan villages in North Dakota once stood here, on the east bank of the Missouri River. Apparently the site had been abandoned by 1804, when Lewis and Clark visited the area. The outlines of earth lodges, refuse heaps and two dry fortification ditches are clearly visible. A shelter was constructed by the Works Progress Administration in the 1930s to protect maps, drawings and a description of the site.

FORT CLARK STATE HISTORIC SITE

From the intersection of North Dakota 48 and US 200A, drive 1 mile east, then 1 mile north to Fort Clark. The site is just north of the post office. Open free, at all times.

A Mandan village was standing here when Fort Clark was built, in 1829. The location of the village is clearly visible, and a small shelter constructed by the State Historical Society contains maps and a description of the area. The Mandans here all died in a smallpox epidemic in 1837. Arikara Indians occupied the site after that date.

HUFF INDIAN VILLAGE STATE HISTORIC SITE
National Register of Historic Places

From Interstate 94 at Mandan drive south on North Dakota 1806 to Huff, on the west bank of the Missouri River. The site is .5 mile south of Huff. Phone: 701/224-2666. Open free, at all times.

A marker describes the large Mandan village that once stood here. The rectangular outlines of individual house sites are clearly visible, as is a dry moat. At one time, in addition to the moat, there was a protective palisade, along which ten bastions were built.

KNIFE RIVER INDIAN VILLAGES NATIONAL HISTORIC SITE

From Stanton follow directional signs north on Highway 37 to the Visitor Center. Mail address: RR#1, Box 168, Stanton, ND 58571. Open free, all year. Camping nearby.

At three major sites in the area—Big Hidatsa, Lower Hidatsa, and Sakakawea—earth lodge rings of prehistoric villages are still visible, and one travois trail is well defined. The Visitor Center has exhibits, and a map of the sites is available.

Research here has revealed that Archaic people hunted in the area during the period 6,000 B.C. to A.D. 1, and there were signs of semisedentary occupation until about A.D. 1000.

By using a remote sensing device called a magnetometer, archeologists have been able to locate at one site a number of earth lodges that were buried, completely out of sight, underneath later earth lodges. The early villages were made up of small rectangular lodges, occupied by Hidatsa and

A Plains Indian tipi of this kind was easily put up and taken down. After Spanish horses became common on the Plains it was possible to have large tipis carried from place to place. Before that dogs were trained to carry smaller burdens. Canadian Museum of Civilization photo.

Mandan people. These were later replaced by circular lodges, of which there were more than 100 in the largest villages. Archeologists estimate that at the time Europeans arrived, there were probably more people living along the Missouri River in North Dakota than live there today. These villagers were successful farmers, with cultivated fields along terraces above streams. They also fished and hunted small and large game and engaged in a great deal of trade with Indians to the west.

With Europeans came diseases which killed as many as two-thirds of the population, and by 1862 the villages along the Knife River had been abandoned.

There seems to be no evidence for any major epidemics in the Americas before Europeans brought in measles, smallpox, and other diseases. One reason, archeologists think, may have been that New World villages had better sanitation than those in the Old World, because they lacked large numbers of penned-up, disease-carrying, domesticated animals.

MENOKEN INDIAN VILLAGE STATE HISTORIC SITE

From Menoken on Interstate 94 drive 1.25 miles north on county road. Mail address: State Historical Society of North Dakota, 612 E. Boulevard, Bismarck, ND 58505-0830. Phone: 701/ 224-2666. Open free, at all times.

A marker describes this former Mandan village which occupied 14 acres. House sites and a dry moat are clearly visible.

MOLANDER INDIAN VILLAGE STATE HISTORIC SITE

From Interstate 94 at Mandan drive north on North Dakota 1806 on the West Bank of the Missouri River to Price. The site is indicated by a marker 3 miles north of Price. Mail address: State Historical Society, 612 East Boulevard, Bismarck, ND 58505. Open free, at all times.

Here, clearly visible, are the remains of an earth-lodge village, which was once surrounded by a dry moat.

ON-A-SLANT INDIAN VILLAGE

In Lincoln State Park. From Mandan drive 4 miles south on North Dakota 1806. Mail address: Mandan, ND 58554. Phone: 701/663-9571. Open daily, all year. Camping nearby. Admission charged.

Mandan Indians, who were living at this site about A.D. 1750, chose an unusual location for their houses. Instead of building on level ground, they placed their dwellings on a slope. Hence the name On-A-Slant Indian Village. Four of the dwellings have been restored and are much like the circular earth lodges of late prehistoric times.

The Indian collection in the museum interprets the history of North Dakota tribes, with special attention to Mandan agriculture, hunting, home activities and social life.

The Story. At some unknown date, perhaps a thousand years ago, people began to cultivate gardens around little communities along the Missouri River in central North Dakota. They grew sunflowers, beans, squash and a remarkable variety of corn. Ordinary corn is a plant that needs warm temperatures and a long growing season. Certainly this was the kind the Indians first tried to raise in this cool, northern climate. They must have been disappointed and hungry very often before they managed to develop a new variety that ripened in only a little more than two months.

Perhaps it was the ancestors of the Mandans who became corn experts. At any rate, they were prosperous farmers when white traders first met them here and at other large, neighboring villages. By 1837, as the result of a devastating epidemic of smallpox that spread to the villages from a passenger on a river boat, only a few Mandans remained.

Special Interest. Fort Lincoln was the headquarters of Lt. Col. George Custer, whose campaign against the Plains Indians ended in his defeat at the battle of the Little Bighorn in Montana.

STATE HISTORICAL SOCIETY OF NORTH DAKOTA

In the North Dakota Heritage Center, on the Capitol grounds, 612 East Boulevard, Bismarck, ND 58505-0830. Phone: 701/224-2666. Open free, Monday–Saturday; afternoon Sunday. Closed certain holidays.

The Society has sponsored excavations since 1895 on sites ranging from Paleo-Indian flint quarries and earth-lodge villages through fur trade and Indian wars forts. Permanent exhibits cover the prehistory of the state, and temporary exhibits focus on specific events or portions of the collections. *The First People,* a permanent exhibit on prehistory was scheduled to open as this book went to press.

THREE AFFILIATED TRIBES MUSEUM

Two miles west of New Town on Route 23. Mail address: New Town, ND 58763. Phone: 701/627-4978. Open free, daily, May–October.

This museum, on the Fort Berthold Indian Reservation, has displays of prehistoric Plains Indian material.

WARD EARTH LODGE VILLAGE HISTORIC SITE

East of Pioneer Park on Burnt Boat Drive, Bismarck. Mail address: Bismarck Parks and Recreation District, 215 N. 6th St., Bismarck, ND 58501. Open daily.

A trail here leads through a site where 43 earth lodges were lived in by Mandan Indians from 1675–1780. The lodges seem to have been much like those used in prehistoric times. An interpretive guide book explains the site and the life of the people who lived there.

WRITING ROCK STATE HISTORIC SITE

From the junction of US 85 and North Dakota 5, drive west to Fortuna, then southwest on County Road to the site. Or from Grenora on North Dakota 50 drive north on County Road. Mail address: State Historical Society of North Dakota, 612 East Boulevard, Bismarck, ND 58505-0830. Phone: 701/224-2666. Open free, at all times.

Here the State Historical Society preserves two large glacial boulders, on which are carved petroglyphs probably representing the mythical thunderbird.

A mammoth kill site was excavated at Domebo, in Oklahoma, by the Museum of the Great Plains. This is an artist's conception of how the kill took place, displayed in a diorama at the museum. Museum of the Great Plains photo.

Oklahoma

A. D. BUCK MUSEUM OF SCIENCE AND HISTORY
(*See Northern Oklahoma College*)

CHEROKEE NATIONAL MUSEUM

On Willis Road, 3 miles south of Tahlequah off U.S. 62. Mail address: P.O. Box 515, Tahlequah, OK 74465. Phone: 918/456-6007. Open Monday–Friday, winter; Monday–Saturday, summer; afternoon Sunday. Closed certain holidays. Admission charged.

This museum is part of the Cherokee Heritage Center which is devoted mainly to the history of the Cherokee since the arrival of whites. A few exhibits display tools and pottery that were excavated in Tennessee just before Cherokee sites were covered by water behind the Tellico Dam. Most Tellico material is now at the Museum of the Cherokee Indian (see entry below) in North Carolina.

CHISHOLM TRAIL MUSEUM AND GOVERNOR SEAY MANSION

605 Zellers Ave., Kingfisher, OK 73750-4228. Phone: 405/375-5176. Open free, Tuesday–Saturday; afternoon Sunday. Closed certain holidays.

In this primarily historical museum are exhibits of prehistoric Indian material from the vicinity.

CREEK COUNCIL HOUSE MUSEUM

On the Town Square, Okmulgee, OK 74447. Phone: 918/756-2324.

As this book went to press this museum was undergoing renovation and its collection of prehistoric Caddoan material was being catalogued.

EAST CENTRAL UNIVERSITY MUSEUM

East Central University Library, Ada, OK 74820. Open free, Monday–Friday; by appointment, Saturday and Sunday. Closed certain holidays.

Exhibits in this museum are devoted to the Anasazi culture of the Southwest, the archeology of Texas and Arkansas and six sites in Oklahoma, all dated at about 1000 years ago. One display presents prehistoric carvings and a reproduction of a painted wall in a cave about 6 miles from Ada. Another identifies different types of projectile points from various parts of the United States and gives the time periods during which they were used. There is also an exhibit showing how prehistoric Indians made artifacts of stone.

GARDNER MANSION AND MUSEUM

Near Eagletown 6 miles East of Broken Bow on US 70. Mail address: Route 1, Box 576., Broken Bow, OK 74728. Phone: 405/584-6588. Open Monday–Saturday year round; afternoon Sunday. Admission charged.

The museum is in the home of former Choctaw Chief Jefferson Gardner. Prehistoric Native American artifacts are included in the exhibits.

Exhibit demonstrating the sequence of cultures that might be found in a dig in Oklahoma. Museum of the Great Plains photo.

GILCREASE MUSEUM

1400 Gilcrease Museum Road, Tulsa, OK 74127. Phone: 918/582-3122. Open free, Monday–Saturday; afternoons Sunday and holidays. Closed December 25.

The Thomas Gilcrease Institute of American History and Art has in three galleries extensive displays of American Indian artifacts from 12,000 years ago to the arrival of Europeans. The exhibits are arranged in chronological sequence, with one gallery containing Meso-American materials. One section illustrates techniques of manufacture; another, which is changed periodically, contains special exhibits of projectile points, pottery and engraved shell. Displays may also compare artifacts in time or in geographic relationships. Material from specific sites includes Spiro Mounds in Oklahoma and the Snyders Site in Illinois.

INDIAN CITY, U.S.A.

From Anadarko drive 2 miles south on Oklahoma 8. Mail address: P.O. Box 695, Anadarko, OK 73005. Phone: 405/247-5661. Open daily, all year. Closed certain holidays. Admission charged. Camping.

Here visitors may see reconstruction of various house types that were common in early historic and late prehistoric times. In a kind of large outdoor museum the living arrangements of the Navajo, Chiricahua Apache, Wichita, Kiowa, Caddo, Pawnee, and Pueblo Indians are brought to life. Many of the houses are furnished with typical tools, household equipment, toys, weapons, and musical instruments. A herd of buffalo grazes in a pasture adjoining the Indian City grounds.

An indoor museum contains material, some of it prehistoric, that supplements the outdoor exhibits.

All buildings here were constructed under the supervision of the Department of Anthropology, University of Oklahoma. Indians serve as guides through the outdoor area.

RISE AND DECLINE OF THE WICHITA INDIANS

From contact with Coronado in 1541, the Wichita slowly drifted south across Oklahoma to Spanish Fort on the Red River by 1750. In 1834, a small group lived at Devils Canyon.

Grass-thatched houses were constructed by Wichita Indians before and after contact with Europeans. Museum of the Great Plains photo.

KERR MUSEUM

From Poteau drive 6 miles southwest on US 271 to junction with US 59, then 4 miles southeast on US 59 and follow signs to Kerr Conference Center. Mail address: Eastern Oklahoma Historical Society, Rt. 1, Box 111, Poteau, OK 74953. Phone: 918/647-8221, ext. 116. Open Monday–Friday 9–5; afternoon weekends. Closed certain holidays. Admission charged.

Exhibits of prehistoric Native American artifacts include a collection of materials from the Spiro Mounds, located about 20 miles northeast of Poteau.

This museum exhibits the Heavener Runestone which archeologists generally do not accept as authentic.

MEMORIAL INDIAN MUSEUM

Allen and Second streets, Broken Bow, OK 74728. Open free, daily.

Exhibits include Native American artifacts from prehistoric times to the present. Especially interesting is the large collection of Caddoan pottery.

MUSEUM OF THE GREAT PLAINS

In Elmer Thomas Park, off US 62 West, in Lawton. Mail address: P.O. Box 68, Lawton, OK 73502. Phone: 405/581-3460. Open Monday–Saturday; afternoon Sunday. Closed certain holidays. Admission charged.

This museum offers exhibits of Paleo-Indian, Plains Archaic, and prehistoric Plains farmer materials. Some displays interpret the relationship between prehistoric peoples and the Plains environment. One diorama shows hunters who have trapped a mammoth. This is based on the museum's excavation of the Domebo (DUM-bo) Site, in Oklahoma, where a mammoth skeleton was recovered in association with artifacts. Dating of the bones indicated that hunters had killed the animal about 11,000 years ago. It was a female about 14 feet tall at the shoulder, and archeologists quipped that she may have had "a quarrelsome disposition," for the right shoulder had been previously broken, possibly in a fight with another mammoth.

Changing exhibits come from exchanges with other museums or from this museum's own large collection of prehistoric material.

A unique artifact on display is a naturally rounded ball of sandstone in which human features have been pecked. This crudely sculptured head was found near Frederick, Oklahoma; it may be very old. It was discovered more than 15 feet below the surface in a gravel bed, but unfortunately no datable material accompanied it, so archeologists can only speculate about its origin and age. Somewhat similar carvings, called the Malakoff Heads, are now in the Texas Memorial Museum, in Austin, Texas.

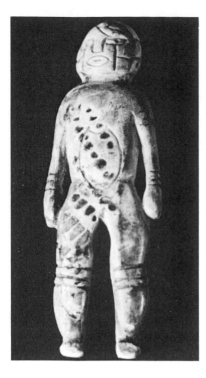

A shell figurine from Spiro Mounds. Department of Anthropology, University of Oklahoma photo.

MUSEUM OF THE RED RIVER

812 SE Lincoln, Idabel, OK 74745. Phone: 405/286-3616. Open Tuesday–Saturday; afternoon Sunday. Closed certain holidays. Admission free.

Exhibits here describe the Ice Age entry of people into the western hemisphere, then focus on the prehistory of southeast Oklahoma. Prehistoric cultures from other areas are also represented.

NO MAN'S LAND HISTORICAL MUSEUM

Panhandle State University Campus, Sewell St. Mail address: P.O. Box 278, Goodwell, OK 73939. Phone: 405/349-2670. Open free, Tuesday–Friday; afternoons Saturday and Sunday. Closed certain holidays.

"Dust Bowl" was a term used for part of the plains during a great drought during the thirties. The soil became so dry that it turned to dust and wind literally blew it away.

To work out plans for saving the soil, a county agricultural agent named William E. "Uncle Bill" Baker walked over much of the land in the Panhandle region of Oklahoma. As he did so he saw pieces of stone that were clearly not native to the area. They had been brought in from some other place, and moreover they had been shaped by skillful hands into projectile points, axes, drills and other tools.

"Uncle Bill" began a careful search of the ground over which he walked and he collected large numbers of artifacts. He also found artifacts in caves. Mr. Baker was not really an archeologist, but he developed a great interest in the prehistoric people who had lived where the "Okies" of the 1930s were being driven from the land. His finds, not yet scientifically studied and interpreted, are displayed in this museum, which was begun by the volunteer labor of students in the university.

NORTHERN OKLAHOMA COLLEGE, A. D. BUCK MUSEUM OF SCIENCE AND HISTORY

1220 East Grand, on the campus, Tonkawa, OK 74653. Phone: 405/628-3318. Open free, Sunday–Friday. Closed during winter.

In this general museum are exhibits of prehistoric artifacts.

OKLAHOMA HISTORICAL SOCIETY

Lincoln Blvd., Capitol Complex, Oklahoma City, OK 73105. Phone: 405/521-2491. Open free, Monday–Saturday.

In this historical museum are several archeological exhibits. One is devoted to materials excavated at the Spiro Mounds, in eastern Oklahoma.

PHILBROOK MUSEUM OF ART, INC.

2727 S. Rockford Rd., Tulsa, OK 74114. Phone: 918/749-7941. Open Tuesday–Saturday; afternoon Sunday. Closed certain holidays. Admission charged.

In this museum devoted to art there is Anasazi, Hohokam, Salado and Mimbres pottery.

PONCA CITY CULTURAL CENTER MUSEUM

1000 East Grand Ave., Ponca City, OK 74601. Phone: 405/767-0427. Open daily, except Tuesday. Closed certain holidays. Admission charged.

Housed in the municipally owned former mansion of an oil millionaire, the museum has exhibits of artifacts from prehistoric Native American cultures.

ROCK ART RESEARCH CENTER

Thunderbird Library, Rogers State College, Claremore, OK 74017-2099. Phone: 918/341-7510, ext. 330. Open free, when the college is in session.

Here on display or readily available are photographs of the rock art sites in the area. Tours of the sites can be arranged.

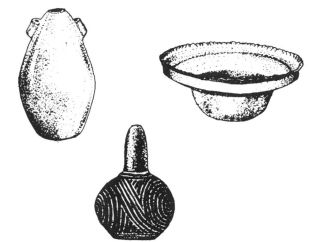

Above, left: Front and side views of a tobacco pipe made of clay, found at Spiro Mounds, in Oklahoma. The pipe represents a human sacrifice. After Hamilton. *Above, right:* Three of the many pots from Spiro Mounds. Originals in the Oklahoma Museum of Natural History, Norman, Oklahoma. *Below, left:* Prehistoric people often used masks in ceremonies. In the Southeast many were carved from wood. This one from Spiro Mounds is of red cedar, with shell inlays for eyes and mouth. Original in the National Museum of the American Indian. *Below, center:* Mississippian people made intricate carvings on pieces of conch shell. Found at Spiro Mounds, this is in the Oklahoma Museum of Natural History at the University of Oklahoma. *Below, right:* A gorget, a neck ornament, has the weeping-eye symbol which often appears in art of the Southeast. It was carved from conch shell and found at Spiro Mounds. Original in the National Museum of the American Indian.

Lucifer Pipe from Spiro Mounds,
University of Oklahoma Collection.
University of Oklahoma photo.

SOUTHERN PLAINS INDIAN MUSEUM

On Oklahoma 9 at east edge of Anadarko. Mail address: P.O. Box 749, Anadarko, OK 73005. Phone: 405/247-6221. Open free, Tuesday–Saturday, October–May; afternoon Sunday; Monday–Saturday, June–September; afternoon Sunday. Closed certain holidays.

This is primarily a museum of post-contact Indian artifacts and clothing, but a few exhibits include prehistoric artifacts.

SPIRO MOUNDS STATE ARCHAEOLOGICAL SITE (SPY-roh)

Six miles east and north of Spiro on the Spiro Mounds Rd. Mail address: Rt. 2, Box 339AA, Spiro, OK 74959. Phone: 918/962-2062. Open free, Tuesday–Sunday, May–October; Wednesday–Sunday, November–April. Closed certain holidays. Camping.

Here at the site are a reconstructed house, three reconstructed mounds and a walking trail with interpretive plaques. In the Interpretive Center are exhibits of artifacts, and some replicas of material in other museums. Slide shows at the center are a good introduction to the site.

The Story. On the bank of the Arkansas River near what is now the town of Spiro, a remarkable village stood in the late prehistoric times. Unlike the farming villages in the neighborhood, this one seems to have been inhabited by an elite group of priests and/or political leaders who somehow won the allegiance—and the labor—of large numbers of the farming people. Men and probably women from surrounding communities carried basketload after basketload of earth to build large mounds for their leaders. Some were topped with buildings—possibly temples or dwellings for priests. One was a burial mound. At the same time a group of excellent craftsworkers developed and became particularly adept at carving intricate designs on conch shells, which came all the way from the Gulf of Mexico. Women fashioned beautiful pottery in a great variety of styles, and much of it was buried with the dead, together with other grave

The Pocola Mining Company made a business of vandalism at the Spiro Mounds Site. Here miners are destroying evidence of a fascinating culture as they dig in Craig Mound looking for goodies to sell. Photo courtesy Dr. William E. Bell and the Oklahoma Museum of Natural History.

goods. The elaborately furnished Spiro burials were a rich storehouse of information about one way of living on this earth—until the day when a modern farmer's plough exposed the handiwork of an earlier farming people.

Soon a business operation began. The Pocola Mining Company was formed to extract artifacts from the mounds for commercial sale. Using explosives and road scoops the miners dug out great quantities of pottery, pearls, and other material which they transported by the wheelbarrow load to the roadside and sold. By 1935 about a third of the burial mound had been gutted, to the modest enrichment of the diggers and to the enormous impoverishment of science.

Later, two amateur archeologists, Mr. and Mrs. Henry W. Hamilton, set about undoing what little of the damage could be undone. For 16 years they traced artifacts to their buyers and recovered them whenever possible. The result of this patient endeavor was a surpisingly large amount of material

that revealed a culture akin to, but also distinct from, the cultures at Etowah in Georgia and Moundville in Alabama.

Thanks to the Hamiltons and to various scientific excavations that managed to glean data from part of the site not totally destroyed, it is now possible to get glimpses of Spiro culture.

Collections of Spiro artifacts may also be seen in the University of Oklahoma Museum of Natural History (see entry below) and the Oklahoma Historical Society Museum (see entry above).

UNIVERSITY OF OKLAHOMA, OKLAHOMA MUSEUM OF NATURAL HISTORY

On the campus, 1335 Asp Ave., Norman, OK 73019-0606. Phone: 405/325-4711. Open free, Tuesday–Friday; afternoons Saturday and Sunday. Closed certain holidays.

Permanent and changing exhibits drawn from the museum's extensive archeological collections focus on

Oklahoma's Indian past. Materials included are from the first mammoth hunters to early contact sites of the historic Caddo and Wichita. Of particular interest are artifacts from the Spiro Mounds Site, including engraved shell, carved stone effigy pipes and copper ornaments. Also displayed are artifacts from more recent American Indian people.

The Tales That Old Bones Tell

How old was this person when he died—and how do we know he was *he?* Specialists in the study of human bones can tell approximate age by the sawtooth-shaped edges of the various parts of the skull. At birth there are spaces between the skull bones. These spaces decrease at a known rate until, at about age 5, the parts are fused. A male skull usually has prominent eyebrow ridges and jaws; a female skull is usually more delicate. A female pelvic bone has a bigger opening (which facilitates childbirth) and a different shape. Children's arm and leg bones grow from the middle part outward toward the ends, and not until about age 15 in girls and later in boys are the center parts and the knobby ends completely fused. A child at birth has 270 bones, some of which fuse at a fairly regular rate until by adulthood the skeleton is made up of only 206 bones.

WASHITA VALLEY MUSEUM

In Wacker Park. 1100 North Ash St., Pauls Valley, OK 73075. Phone: 405/238-3048. Open free, afternoons Wednesday–Sunday. Donations accepted.

Prehistoric and historic Native American artifacts are on display here.

WESTERN TRAILS MUSEUM

Southwest of Clinton on US 66 and Interstate 40. Mail address: 2229 Gary Freeway, Clinton, OK 73601. Phone: 405/323-1020. Open free, Tuesday–Saturday; afternoon Sunday. Closed certain holidays.

Although the museum is devoted primarily to pioneer settler exhibits, it displays some prehistoric archeological material.

WOOLAROC MUSEUM
(WOOL-ah-rock)

From Bartlesville drive 14 miles southwest on Oklahoma 123 to entrance to the Frank Phillips Ranch, then 2 miles on ranch road to the museum. Mail address: Rt 3, Bartlesville,

OK 74003. Phone: 918/336-0307. Closed Monday, certain holidays. Admission charged.

In addition to historic displays this museum tells the story of prehistoric people in America, particularly in Oklahoma. Included in the archeological exhibits are materials 3000 years old representing the Oklahoma Basketmaker culture in the neighborhood of Kenton. Several cases contain artifacts from the Spiro Mounds, from Washita culture sites in western Oklahoma, and from Hopewell culture sites in northeastern Oklahoma. Other exhibits contain materials from Alaska and from the vicinity of Phoenix, Arizona.

The Name. Woolaroc comes from the first letters of *wo*ods, *la*kes, and *roc*ks—all common in the surrounding landscape.

Special Interest. In rugged woodland adjoining the museum, herds of bison, elk, and deer graze just as they did in prehistoric times.

Was a man a hunter or a farmer? Teeth can often give the clue. Eaters of tough meat wear down their teeth by middle adulthood. The teeth of those whose diets are chiefly bread or mush made from corn ground into meal on sandstone show different deterioration. They, too, are worn away, but before that happens they are likely to have many more cavities than do meat eaters' teeth.

Was this man a member of an upper or a lower class? Bone specialist Jane Buikstra studied the skeletons of men whose graves in burial mounds contained artifacts of many kinds. She discovered that those whose elaborate grave goods indicated high status often had signs of arthritis in the elbow bones. Those in lower-class burials were likely to have arthritis in the hands. This meant to her that upper-class men were hunters, whose elbows suffered from the use of spears or bows. Lower-class men were probably artisans, who used their hands for tool and weapon making.

Saskatchewan

BUFFALO POUND PROVINCIAL PARK

Northeast of Moose Jaw in the Qu'Appelle Valley. Phone: 306/693-2678 or 694-3659. Open year round.

In this area, used by early Indians as a corral for buffalo, a herd of the animals is now kept captive.

CAMP RAYNER SITE

Near Birsay on Highway 373. Mail address: c/o Saskatchewan Archaeological Society, #5-816 First Avenue North, Saskatoon, SK S7K 1Y3. Phone: 306/664-4124. Open free, at all times.

This site seems to have been occupied between 10,000 and 11,000 years ago. There may be ongoing excavation in summer.

CLEARWATER RIVER WILDERNESS PARK

In northwestern Saskatchewan about 500 kilometers from Prince Albert. For information apply to Director, Parks, Department of Parks, Recreation and Culture, 3211 Albert St., Regina, SK S4S 5W6.

On the upper portion of the Clearwater between Lloyd and Careen are three pictographs—reddish paintings on vertical rock surfaces.

GRASSLANDS NATIONAL PARK

From Val Marie, Provincial Highway 4 leads to this national park which preserves the mixed-grass prairie as it was in prehistoric times. Archeological evidence of human occupation of the area has been found. For information apply to Superintendent, South Grasslands National Park, Val Marie, SK S0N 2T0.

HERSCHEL PETROGLYPHS

On Grid road 2.5 kilometers west of Herschel. For information contact the Archaeological Society, #5, 186 1st Ave. North, Saskatoon, SK S7K 1Y3. Phone: 306/664-4124.

Here are rock carvings on two limestone boulders left by the last glaciation. Along the trail to these petroglyphs are eleven tipi rings. Visitors are urged to help protect the site which has been developed by the Rural Municipality of Mountain View and Saskatchewan Parks, Recreation and Culture.

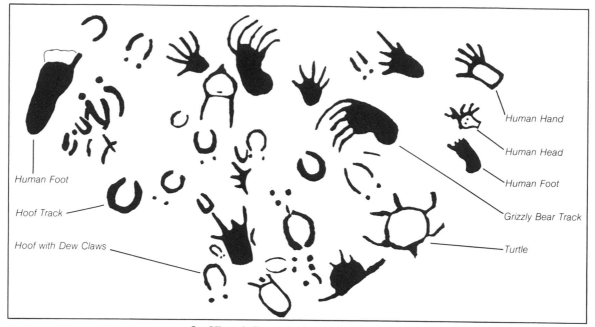

Human Hand

Human Head

Human Foot

Grizzly Bear Track

Turtle

Human Foot

Hoof Track

Hoof with Dew Claws

St. Victor's Petroglyphs, with tentative identification of some images. Source: St. Victor's Petroglyphs Historic Park, Saskatchewan.

INDIAN ROCK ART

Near Pelican Narrows at Medicine Rapids, Larocque Lake, and at 19 other sites in the Churchill River system. Phone: 306/787-2812. Open year round.

Here protected as heritage properties are pictographs done in red ochre of human and animal figures. The sites are accessible only by water.

MISTUSINNE STONE

From Elbow at the jucntion of Highway 19 and local road 749, drive 2 kilometers southwest. Open free, year round.

A plaque interprets a large stone that was relocated here when a dam was constructed on the South Saskatchewan River. The stone has been sacred to the Cree and other Plains Indians.

SASKATCHEWAN MUSEUM OF NATURAL HISTORY

College and Albert streets, Regina. Mail address: Regina, SK S4P 3V7.

Phone: 306/787-2815. Open free, daily, May–Labor Day; Monday–Friday, afternoons Saturday and Sunday, Labor Day–April 30. Closed December 25.

Here in the First Nations Gallery are exhibits devoted to prehistory in Saskatchewan. There is considerable material from excavations conducted by the museum staff. Exhibits include artifacts from various periods and cultures from Paleo-Indian to historic times.

ST. VICTOR'S PETROGLYPHS

In Petroglyphs Historic Park overlooking the community of St. Victor's. For information apply to Saskatchewan Parks and Renewable Resource, 3211 Albert St., Regina, SK S4S 5W6. Phone: 306/565-2700.

A long stairway leads up a stone outcropping or cliff to the top where carvings are in the horizontal surface of the rock. They are best seen on a clear day just before sunset when the shallow grooves are most visible.

WANUSKEWIN HERITAGE PARK
(Wah-nus-KAY-win)

For information about this park off Highway 11 on the north side of Saskatoon, which was not yet open as this book went to press, apply to Wanuskewin Heritage Park, R.R. #4, Saskatoon, SK S7K 3J7. Phone: 306/931-4522.

The word Wanuskewin is Cree for "seeking peace of mind" or "living in harmony." A 100 hectare park is being designed to interpret North American prehistory and Native American culture. In the park are 19 prehistoric sites including a medicine wheel, tipi rings, bison kills and habitation sites. Excavations so far completed show more than 6000 years of occupation of the area. An exhibition hall will include hands-on displays. A theater will offer a multi-projector slide presentation that will include archeology.

Size of Prehistoric Populations

Estimates of the total Native American population at the time Europeans arrived have varied widely. The documentary data for estimates—such as letters, diaries, official reports of explorers and colonial settlers—are not very reliable and are usually incomplete. We know that after 1492 the decrease in native population in certain areas was rapid and steep, but slower in other places, continuing until recent times. This variation in the amount and rate of depopulation makes it difficult to figure backward to an estimate of original population. However, sophisticated statistical methods have been applied convincingly to archeological, documentary, and ecological evidence. The numbers of villages and of house sites in villages give clues, as do skeletal remains and traces of fields and gardens. After considering all available figures, geographer William M. Denevan has concluded that in 1492 the population of North America was about 4,400,000 and that the total for North, South, and Central America was about 57,300,000.

South Dakota

BADLANDS NATIONAL PARK

From Kadoka drive 18 miles west on Interstate 90 to intersection with South Dakota 240, then 9 miles south on 240 to Ben Reifel Visitor Center. Or from Rapid City drive 43 miles southeast on South Dakota 44 to Scenic, then 21 miles south on South Dakota 27 to the White River Visitor Center. Mail address: P.O. Box 6, Interior, SD 57750. Phone: 605/433-5361. The Ben Reifel Center is open daily, all year. The White River Center is open daily, June–August. Admission charged. Camping.

Both Visitor Centers have exhibits that trace prehistoric and historic Indian life in the area, with emphasis on the Lakota. One display is devoted to the massacre at Wounded Knee.

The story of Wounded Knee began when, in the course of trying to stamp out a religious movement known as the Ghost Dance, which was spreading among Plains Indians, a unit of the U.S. Army arrested more than 250 Lakota three days after Christmas in 1890. All night these people, two-thirds of whom were women and children, camped at Wounded Knee Creek in South Dakota, surrounded by 500 soldiers. In the morning the soldiers disarmed the men and then proceeded to shoot indiscriminately, using rapid-fire guns. Almost all the unarmed captives were killed on the spot, but a few women escaped and ran for several miles before soldiers overtook and shot them. This was the massacre of Wounded Knee. In 1991 the U.S. Congress adopted a statement of regret for the army's action.

CROW CREEK INDIAN VILLAGE SITE
National Historic Landmark

On the Crow Creek Indian Reservation, south of Ft. Thompson, off South Dakota 34. Open free, at all times.

This is one of the few large, prehistoric sites in the region that has not been covered by water impounded behind dams on the Missouri River. Excavation in the 1950s revealed that some of the large, earth-lodge dwellings that once stood here had been burned. Probably they were destroyed at the time of abandonment of the village, which was surrounded by two ditches, presumably for defense. Later, erosion at one side of the site exposed human bones, and archeologists returned in 1978 for further investigation. What they discovered was a mass burial of 500 or more men, women, and children. From detailed examination of many bones they were able to piece together the following story.

The dry summer of the year 1325 followed a long period of droughts. Indian farmers along Crow Creek and other tributaries of the Missouri River began to suffer from malnutrition as crops failed year after year. Here, as elsewhere, bones show dietary deficiency in several ways. In adults they may become pitted with small holes. A well-nourished child's arm and leg bones grow at a regular rate from the center portion outward toward the ends, but in times of famine, growth stops, and this interruption results in a detectable line. Alternating periods of adequate and inadequate diet show up in alternating areas of growth and telltale lines. At Crow Creek one youth's bones showed 14 such periods of malnutrition, and those of almost all the other children indicated four or five hungry years.

It was not hunger, however, that killed about a third of the village's inhabitants. Probably they were raided by starving neighbors, who found that the Crow Creek people had not yet finished the new moat and fortification around their homes. Desperate to get at stored food, the raiders massacred all who could not or did not flee. Later the survivors must have returned and buried their dead in one huge grave, then left forever.

A regular pattern of feuds or warfare among these farming people seems not to have developed. Rather the Crow Creek raid was probably an act of extreme desperation. Among themselves, scientists think, these Indians were cooperative and compassionate. Evidence for this is the number of skeltons of handicapped and crippled people who survived in the community until the raid.

Excavation and study of the site was done by the Archeology Laboratory of the University of South Dakota. In 1981 all skeletal material was reburied at the site in response to insistence by Lakota people who believe that the excavation has desecrated a Native American cemetery. The Army Corps of Engineers, which administers the site, has stabilized the eroded bluff and has installed a memorial plaque on which is inscribed the Arikara song "Memorial to the Old Scout" in both the Caddoan and the English languages. The English reads: "Today we remember the ways of the old ones who were: The good ways that were ours." For further information call Rick Berg, Army Corps of Engineers, 402/221-4603.

CULTURAL HERITAGE CENTER

900 Governors Drive, Pierre, SD 57501. Phone: 605/773-3458. Open free, Monday–Friday; afternoon Saturday and Sunday.

A fairly extensive exhibit of Indian artifacts, some of them prehistoric, can be seen in this essentially pioneer-history museum.

MITCHELL PREHISTORIC INDIAN VILLAGE
National Historic Landmark

From South Dakota 37 at north edge of Mitchell, turn west on Cemetery Road. Proceed .25 mile and turn north on Indian Village Rd., .7 mile to the site. Mail address: P.O. Box 621, Mitchell, SD 57301. Phone: 605/996-5473. Open daily, May–October. Admission charged.

At this site of a mid-eleventh-century fortified farming community archeological research is going on. The project is funded jointly by the city and the federal government. At times in summer visitors may watch an archeological crew excavating. There are exhibits and video tapes in the museum. An earth lodge has been reconstructed on the grounds, and a garden of native plants may be visited in summer. Guides will explain the site and the research.

Mud Art

Prehistoric Native American artists worked in many media. Some painted on bison skins. Others carved on canyon walls. Still others decorated pots. Women wove grass into baskets and decorated them with porcupine quills. The list goes on and on, and in 1990 archeologists discovered art work done in mud that had stayed fresh for hundreds of years.

In a Tennessee cave, explorers came upon a mud-covered wall that had been kept moist by the high underground humidity. There they found designs pressed in the mud that were of the kind popular in the Mississippian period. Carbon-14 dating, from organic material associated with the mud glyphs (as the designs came to be called), revealed that the artists had done much of their work about A.D. 1248. Some designs were earlier, some later.

SHERMAN PARK INDIAN BURIAL MOUNDS

Sherman Park, West 22nd St. and Kiwanis Ave., Sioux Falls. Mail address: Park Department, 600 East 7th St., Sioux Falls, SD 57103. Open free, at all times. Camping.

In this municipal park are several mounds built by people who followed the Plains Woodland lifeway, 1600 years ago. One mound has been excavated by the W. H. Over State Museum of the University of South Dakota (see entry below). Artifacts recovered by the dig are in the university museum at Vermillion.

UNIVERSITY OF SOUTH DAKOTA, SHRINE TO MUSIC MUSEUM

Clark and Yale streets, Vermillion, SD 57069. Open free, Monday–Saturday; afternoon Sunday. Closed certain holidays.

In this museum's collection of North American musical instruments are some that are prehistoric.

W. H. OVER STATE MUSEUM

1110 Ratingen St., Vermillion. Mail address: 414 East Clark, Vermillion, SD 57069. Phone: 605/677-5228.

This museum, which has a large collection of Native American material, was undergoing complete renovation as this book went to press. For information apply at the mail address above.

WIND CAVE NATIONAL PARK

From Hot Springs drive 11 miles north on US 385. Or from Custer drive 19 miles south on US 385. Mail address: Hot Springs, SD 57747. Phone: 605/745-4600. Visitor Center open free, daily. Closed certain holidays. Camping May 15–Oct. 1.

One exhibit case here includes Arikara and Mandan pottery and projectile points. There are also a few random finds of points and other artifacts from earlier periods.

This diorama shows Archaic people in a rockshelter in Texas. Texas Memorial Museum photo.

Texas

ALABAMA-COUSHATTA INDIAN MUSEUM

From Livingston drive 17 miles east on US 190 to the Alabama-Coushatta Reservation. Mail address: Route 3, Box 640, Livingston, TX 77351. Phone: 409/563-4391 or 1/800/444-3507. Open free, Monday–Saturday; afternoon Sunday, Memorial Day–Labor Day; weekends, Labor Day–Memorial Day. Camping.

This museum, on the oldest Indian reservation in Texas, has exhibits relating to the history of the Alabama and Coushatta tribes and of other Texas tribes as well. There is a continuous slide show. There are also exhibits in the gift shop where a Native American woman makes fine traditional baskets that are for sale.

ALIBATES FLINT QUARRIES NATIONAL MONUMENT (AL-ah-bates)

From Amarillo, drive east 2 miles, then take Texas 136 to the monument. Admission free, daily, Memorial Day–Labor Day, only on tours led by a ranger at 10 AM and 2 PM. In other seasons, tours are by advance reservation. The tour is a walk of about one mile over moderately rough terrain. Write to Superintendent, Lake Meredith Recreation Area, P.O. Box 1460, Fritch, TX 79036, or phone 806/857-3151. Primitive camping is available nearby. Handicapped access is available on request in advance.

The Story. Here above the Canadian River, Paleo-Indians found a large outcrop of excellent stone—a varicolored flint that has an easily recognized marbled appearance. About 12,000 years ago people began to quarry it for use in making projectile points, knives, and the scrapers with which they removed hair and tissue from hides. Many

Clovis points used for hunting mammoths in New Mexico were made of Alibates flint. It remained popular with the Paleo-Indians who lived in the Texas Panhandle up to 7000 years ago. It was also sought by people who followed the Archaic lifeway at a later time. Hunters of the Woodland Period obtained flint at the quarries, and they left evidence of their presence nearby.

About A.D. 1200, Plains Village Indians settled near the flint outcrop. Their dwellings, made of mud and stone, resembled somewhat those of the Pueblo Indians of New Mexico. Like the Pueblos, these people were farmers who raised corn, beans, and squash. They also hunted buffalo, antelope, and other game, and they combined those two activities with exploiting the quarries. The flint they dug out was exchanged, sometimes over great distances, for such things as pottery, obsidian, catlinite, sea shells, and turquoise.

Evidence of the extent of mining of Alibates flint is impressive. Over the

Henry Hertner (at left), an amateur archeologist, led the campaign to have the Alibates Flint Quarry made into a National Monument. In this area prehistoric Indians made projectile points, knives, and scrapers from multicolored flint that they found there in large deposits. Texas Highway Department photo.

centuries, prehistoric Indians dug out hundreds of tons of the hard, beautiful stone. Several hundred quarry pits are still visible on the mile-long ridge in the national monument.

Alibates flint continued to be sought by Indians of the Plains. Even in historic times they made it into weapons whenever they could not get metal.

The Name. The word "Alibates" is derived from the name of Allie Bates, a cowboy who worked in this area in the early ranching days.

BAYLOR UNIVERSITY, STRECKER MUSEUM

West Basement, Sid Richardson Science Building, on the campus, Waco. Mail address: BU Box 7154, Baylor University, Waco, TX 76798-7154. Phone: 817/755-1110. Open free, daily. Closed certain holidays.

Exhibits emphasize the cultural heritage of central Texas from 12,500 B.C. to the arrival of the Spanish. There is an extensive research collection of prehistoric central Texas Indian artifacts.

BIG BEND NATIONAL PARK

From Marathon on US 90 drive south on Texas 385, 69 miles to Park Headquarters. Mail address: Big Bend National Park, TX 79834. Phone: 915/477-2291. Open daily, all year. Admission charged. Camping.

Along the Hot Springs Nature Trail in the park pictographs may be seen. On this trail and on two others are mortar holes in the rock used by prehistoric people for grinding seeds.

BRAZOSPORT MUSEUM OF NATURAL SCIENCE

400 College Drive, Brazosport, TX 77566. Phone: 713/265-7831. Open free, Tuesday–Saturday; afternoon Sunday.

In the Hall of Archaeology are artifacts representative of those found in south Texas.

Artifacts characteristic of the prehistoric Caddo Indians, and stages through which their culture passed, are shown in this exhibit. Texas Memorial Museum photo.

CADDOAN MOUNDS STATE HISTORICAL PARK

On Texas 21, 6 miles southwest of Alto. Mail address: Route 2, Box 85C, Alto, TX 75925. Phone: 409/858-3218. Open Wednesday–Sunday. Admission charged. Tours by reservation. Self-guided tours available. Camping.

This area, which encompasses three mounds and a village site, has been called "one of the major aboriginal sites in North America."

An exhibit room in the Visitor Center contains a short audio-visual program on the archeology of the site and a life-size diorama of domestic activities in front of a 28-foot-long mural depicting the village about A.D. 1100. A large number of original and replicated artifacts are displayed in cases and on panels describing the lives of the Early Caddo.

An illustrated trail guide leads visitors to three mounds and a village area

inhabited from about A.D. 780 to 1250 by Caddo Indians, perhaps the most prominent of the prehistoric inhabitants of Texas.

A confederation of Caddo groups occupied a large area between the Trinity River and the Red River and spread into what is now Arkansas and Louisiana. These groups referred to each other as Taychas, which meant "allies," or "friends." At first they mistakenly included Spaniards among their friends, and ironically the Spanish name for the whole of what is now the state of Texas was based on the Caddoan word.

The Caddo were farmers who hunted in winter, had a rich ceremonial life, and were famous for their pottery. At one stage they built large, earthen temple mounds, but by historic times had given up this practice. In many ways their culture resembled the Mississippian tradition, which flourished farther to the east. But whether Caddoan culture simply influenced—or was also influenced by—the Mississippian is still a matter of dispute.

CADDO INDIAN MUSEUM

In Longview, 701 Hardy Street, Longview, TX 75604. Phone: 903/759-5739. Open daily, on request. Admission by donation.

This is a small private museum in a building near the owner's home. The collection was started by Buddy Jones, a Cherokee, when he was 11½ years old. With the permission of ranch owners nearby, he excavated Caddo burials in order to save the material they contained from destruction by development. As he grew up he continued excavation and preservation of material from many burials, and he carefully catalogued everything. Much of the material is now on exhibit in the museum he built. He went on to college and became an archeologist and in 1991 was based in Florida. Transfer of the artifacts to a building in downtown Longview may take place at some future time.

Natural hollows in the rock in these semiarid hills formed reservoirs or tanks that provided a water supply for prehistoric hunters in Texas. Hueco Tanks State Historical Park photo, Texas Parks and Wildlife Department.

CAPROCK CANYONS STATE PARK

From Quitaque drive 3 miles north on Ranch Road 1065 to this park. Mail address: P.O. Box 204. Quitaque, TX 79255. Phone: 806/455-1492. Open daily. Admission charged. Camping.

In this park is a Folsom site more than 10,000 years old. The prairie here is preserved much as it must have been in Folsom times, and there is a herd of bison. The park includes an interpretive center. Altogether 641 archeological sites from various ages have been identified in the park. Most of them are undeveloped and visitors are asked to look but not to disturb anything.

CUEVAS AMARILLAS
(*See Las Cuevas*)

DEVIL'S RIVER NATURAL AREA

From Del Rio drive north 45 miles on Highway 277 to Dolan's Creek Road, then 22 miles to Park Headquarters. Mail address: HCR1, Box 13, Del Rio, TX 78840. Phone: 512/395-2133. Reservations are necessary in advance.

Each visitor must have a $25 passport, and there are charges (payable for a single person or for a group) of $60 a night for the use of a bunk house and $50 a day for the use of the dining hall. Visitors must bring their own food. There is no camping.

In this remote area there are pictographs.

EL PASO CENTENNIAL MUSEUM
(*See University of Texas*)

FORT WORTH MUSEUM OF SCIENCE AND HISTORY

1501 Montgomery St., Fort Worth, TX 76107. Phone: 817/732-1631. Open Monday–Saturday; afternoon Sunday. Closed certain holidays. Admission charged.

Both the Hall of Medicine and the Hall of Man in this museum contain archeological material, including a collection of pre-Columbian ceramics and stone implements.

Hueco Tanks, a complex of three massive granite outcrops rising several hundred feet above the desert floor, has numerous rock paintings. *Above:* A figure 23 inches tall that is an elaborate mask with abstract decoration and conical cap. *Below:* A horned serpent painted in red with decorated body. Illustrations by Wes Jernigan in Polly Schaafsma, *Indian Rock Art of the Southwest.*

HUECO TANKS STATE HISTORICAL PARK

From El Paso drive 32 miles northeast on US 62 to intersection with Ranch Road 2775, then to Park Headquarters. Mail address: Hueco Tanks Road, RR3, Box 1, El Paso, TX 79935. Phone: 915/857-1135. Open daily, all year. Admission charged. Camping.

The word *hueco* in Spanish means hollow. Throughout the park many huecos—natural hollows in hard rock—form reservoirs, or tanks, which provided a water supply for people as long ago as 8000 B.C. At that time Big-Game Hunters, using projectile points of the type called Folsom, camped near the tanks and left the bones of now extinct giant bison. Later, when there were no more big-game animals, people of the Western Archaic culture hunted small animals and gathered seeds and plants around the tanks. Still later, Mogollon people lived in villages and did farming in the area. Except at times when rains have filled the tanks, this semi-arid land seems too inhospitable for permanent settlement. However, in rats' nests dated at 13,000 years ago, scientists have found piñon nuts, which prove that there were once trees around the tanks, and until recent times there may have been enough moisture to support crops.

Many of the people who frequented the tanks painted pictures and designs on the walls of caves and shelters. Some of the paintings are lively and graphic, others are mainly designs. Archeologists who specialize in rock art believe that the various styles are characteristic of the different cultural groups that came to the area. A number of these pictograph sites are accessible to visitors.

INSTITUTE OF TEXAN CULTURES

801 S. Bowie St., southeast corner of Hemisfair Plaza, San Antonio. Mail address: P.O. Box 1226, San Antonio, TX 78294. Phone: 512/226-7651. Open free Tuesday–Sunday.

The Institute displays exhibits of Texas life, past and present, to tell the story of its ethnic and cultural heritage. Through a plan of borrowing artifacts or copying art from other mu-

Near Lubbock, Texas, the Texas Tech University Museum has excavated and opened for the public a stratified site at Lubbock Reservoir. Here Dr. W. C. Holden, former director of the museum, points to a layer deep in the canyon wall, indicating the great age of the site. Texas Tech University Museum photo.

seum or private collections, exhibits are changed frequently, and hands-on activities are encouraged. Some prehistoric Indian material is found in the newly renovated Native American area, in which visitors will find three murals on the life of the Lipan Apache, Caddo and El Paso Pueblo Indians and a genuine buffalo-hide tipi.

JOHN E. CONNER MUSEUM
(*See Texas A&I University*)

LAKE MEREDITH RECREATION AREA
(*See Alibates Flint Quarries*)

LAS CUEVAS
(Also called Cuevas Amarillas)

West of Big Bend National Park in the Big Bend Ranch State Natural Area which can be reached on Texas 170 from Presidio on the west or from Lajitas on the east. It is administered by the Texas Parks and Wildlife Department. Mail address (of the site): Barton Warnock Environmental Education Center, HCR 70, Box 375, Terlingua,

TX 79853. Phone: 915/424-3327. Open all year. Admission only by advance reservation on guided bus tours, fee $30. Buses leave from either Fort Leaton State Historical Park, Presidio, TX 79845, or the Barton Warnock Education Center.

This 61-acre site was inhabited for at least 5000 years. It contains several rock shelters with bedrock mortars used for grinding seeds and other plant materials. In addition there are many small shelters in the yellow tuff. Here hunter-gatherers lived near a year-round spring. By A.D. 1000 they began to trade with other people who practiced agriculture, made ceramics and used the bow and arrow.

At times the Barton Warnock Environmental Education Center offers lectures on the archeology of the area.

LUBBOCK LAKE LANDMARK STATE HISTORICAL PARK

On the northwest edge of Lubbock near the intersection of Loop 289 and Clovis Highway (US 84). P.O. Box 2212, Lubbock, TX 79408-2212. Phone:

806/741-0306. Open Tuesday–Saturday; Sunday afternoon. Admission charged.

This National Historic Landmark, located where there is a permanent water supply, has been visited by people from the Plains for about 12,000 years. Dr. Joe Ben Wheat conducted the first investigation and found fossil bones of extinct animals and projectile points under deep layers of earth. Excavation today continues under the direction of the museum of nearby Texas Tech University which has a small exhibit of artifacts from the site.

The Robert A. Nash Interpretive Center houses extensive exhibits and a children's educational center. It also maintains interpretive trails around the 20 acre site. In the summer, when excavations are conducted, visitors are invited to observe the work.

MONAHANS SANDHILL STATE PARK

Off Interstate 20, 6 miles east of Monahans. Phone: 915/943-2092. Open daily, all year. Admission charged.

At the Interpretive Center is a small exhibit of local finds relating to prehistoric Indian shelters, projectile points, and foodstuffs.

MUSEUM OF THE BIG BEND
(*See Sul Ross University*)

MUSEUM OF THE SOUTHWEST

1705 W. Missouri, Midland, TX 79701-6516. Phone: 915/683-2882.

As this book went to press this museum had no archeology exhibit, but it plans one for the future.

PANHANDLE-PLAINS HISTORICAL MUSEUM

2401 Fourth Ave., Canyon. Mail address: Box 967, W.T. Station, Canyon, TX 79016. Phone: 806/656-2244. Open free, Monday–Saturday; afternoon Sunday. Closed December 25.

In addition to a large collection of Comanche and Kiowa ethnological material, this museum displays random local finds and artifacts excavated by the Works Progress Administration in the 1930s. In the archeological exhibits are Clovis, Folsom and Plainview projectile points, used by hunters in Paleo times; also included are Archaic materials, artifacts from the Adobe Walls site and artifacts of the Panhandle culture from the South Canadian River, dated from A.D. 1300 to 1540.

PANTHER CAVE

In Amistad Recreation Area. From Comstock drive northwest on US 90 to Pecos River boat-ramp exit. Mail address: National Park Service, P.O. Box 420367, Del Rio, TX 78842. Phone: 512/775-7491. Open free, daily, all year. Camping nearby.

The Amistad Recreation Area was created after the construction of Amistad Dam on the Rio Grande River. Within the area Panther Cave is the only visitable prehistoric pictograph site. It is accessible only by private boat. Visitors must bring their own boats or make arrangements for use of private boats. From the Pecos River boat ramp the cave is approximately a 25-minute ride downstream, at the junction of the Rio Grande and Seminole Canyon. The National Park Service provides a courtesy dock at Panther Cave. The site is protected by a cyclone fence.

Remarkably rich and detailed pictures cover the whole wall and part of the ceiling of the cave. Archeologists believe the people who made the paintings relied on hunting for much of their food, because herds of deer appear frequently in the paintings here and in other, neighboring caves. The panthers, which give the cave its name, are large and realistically drawn—one is so big that it can be seen clearly from the top of the cliff on the opposite side of Seminole Canyon.

SEMINOLE CANYON STATE HISTORICAL PARK

From Del Rio drive 40 miles northwest on US 90 to directional sign between Comstock and Langtry. Mail address: P.O. Box 806, Comstock, TX 78837. Phone: 915/292-4464. Open daily, all year. Admission charged. Camping.

Very large rock shelters in the park contain unusual painted murals. The Visitor Center has a life-size diorama of Archaic domestic activities in a rock shelter, a half-scale reproduction of a rock art panel from Fate Bell Cave, numerous artifacts related to aboriginal and historic life in the Lower Pecos and a detailed discussion of Lower Pecos rock art styles and their chronology.

STRECKER MUSEUM
(*See Baylor University*)

Everyday prehistoric Caddoan life appears in this diorama. Texas Memorial Museum photo.

SUL ROSS UNIVERSITY, MUSEUM OF THE BIG BEND

On the campus, Alpine, entrance from US 90. Mail address: Sul Ross State University, Box C-210, Alpine, TX 79831. Phone: 915/837-8143. Open free, Tuesday–Sunday.

The archeological collections here relate to prehistoric Big Bend Basketmaker culture. There is also some Plains Indian material.

TEXARKANA HISTORICAL MUSEUM

219 State Line Ave., P.O. Box 2343, Texarkana, TX 75501. Phone: 214/793-4831. Open free, Tuesday–Friday; afternoons Saturday and Sunday.

This museum has a few Paleo and Archaic artifacts.

TEXAS A&I UNIVERSITY, JOHN E. CONNER MUSEUM

On the campus, on Santa Gertrudis, between Armstrong and University, Kingsville. Mail address: Campus Box 134, Kingsville, TX 78363. Phone: 512/595-2819. Open free, Tuesday–Saturday. Closed certain holidays.

Although this museum is not primarily concerned with archeology, it does display material from the La Paloma Mammoth site, and the exhibits here include prehistoric artifacts, among them materials found at a local Karankawa Indian site.

TEXAS MEMORIAL MUSEUM
(*See University of Texas*)

TEXAS TECH UNIVERSITY MUSEUM

Indiana Ave. and 4th St., Lubbock. Mail address: Box 43191, Lubbock, TX 79409-3191. Phone: 806/742-2442. Open free, Monday–Friday; afternon Saturday and Sunday. Closed certain holidays.

Some exhibits and dioramas here deal with Early Man, dating back to Clovis times, principally in Texas.

The U.P. Site

In 1960 Ivan Hayes was operating a dragline on the Union Pacific Railroad's right-of-way near Rawlins, Wyoming. In the muck, around the spring he was clearing, the dragline caught on some huge bones. Hayes reported this to Dr. George A. Agogino, at that time professor of anthropology at the University of Wyoming. Agogino quickly got money from the National Geographic Society. Then he persuaded Henry and Cynthia Irwin, a brother-sister team of archeologists, to bring their student crew from a dig elsewhere in Wyoming. Battling against mud and water, the excavators unearthed proof that hunters had butchered a mammoth at this spot. Its crushed skull indicated that they had probably killed it by hurling down rocks from the top of a bank above the stream where it had come to drink. Materials from the U.P. Mammoth Kill Site are in the Peabody Museum at Harvard University.

UNIVERSITY OF TEXAS AT AUSTIN, TEXAS MEMORIAL MUSEUM

2400 Trinity St., Austin, TX 78705. Phone: 512/471-1604. Open free, Monday–Saturday; afternoon Sunday. Closed certain holidays.

Archeological exhibits in this large museum introduce North American archeology as a whole, and also concentrate on the Paleo-Indian, Archaic and later periods of habitation. Dioramas show prehistoric lifeways of the Karankawas and Comanches. General exhibits include an Archaic rock shelter, Southwestern influences in Texas, Caddoan cultural stages and material culture. An exhibit featuring the Blackwater Draw Site in New Mexico illustrates how archeologists can determine the sequence of cultures in the layers of excavated earth. Artifacts from this site date to Llano (10,000+ B.C.), Folsom (8000 B.C.) and Portales cultures (5000 B.C.).

As this book went to press the exhibits throughout the museum were undergoing extensive renovation. Included in the renovation plans was a new area to be devoted to exhibits of sites, some well known, some still being excavated.

UNIVERSITY OF TEXAS, EL PASO CENTENNIAL MUSEUM

On the campus at University Ave. and Wiggins Road, El Paso, TX 79968. Phone: 915/747-5565. Open free, Monday–Saturday. Closed certain holidays.

Exhibits emphasize prehistoric cultures of the El Paso area, including material from caves in the nearby Hueco Mountains. Other displays are devoted to the Mogollon culture and to pottery and ornaments from the Casas Grandes area of northwestern Mexico. A diorama shows prehistoric Pueblo life near El Paso.

WASHINGTON SQUARE MOUND SITE

In Washington Square, Nacogdoches, TX 75961, near the old high school. Open free, daily, all year.

In this well-preserved Caddoan ceremonial complex there may be on-going excavation.

WILDERNESS PARK MUSEUM

2000 Transmountain Rd., El Paso, TX 79999. Phone: 915/755-4332. Open free, Tuesday–Saturday; afternoon Sunday.

In this museum, administered by the city, are dioramas showing a Folsom hunt, a pithouse scene and a scene from the Hueco Tanks area (see entry above). Other displays feature pottery, tool making, food plants, basketry and a reconstructed pithouse.

WITTE MEMORIAL MUSEUM

3801 Broadway, Brackenridge Park, San Antonio, TX 78209. Open daily. Closed certain holidays. Admission by donation.

This museum, which has an active archeological program, grew up around materials from the Pecos River area and now displays material from many parts of Texas and the Southwest.

A Note about Sacred Sites

In an effort to find out which archeological sites Native Americans regard as sacred, we asked people at the Native American Rights Fund which places they thought visitors ought to stay away from. Beyond approving of our decision not to give road directions to Big Horn Medicine Wheel, the staff at the Fund did not provide us with the information we sought. We hope we have not inadvertently sent visitors to places where their presence would be offensive to worshippers.

Wyoming

BIGHORN CANYON NATIONAL RECREATION AREA, VISITOR CENTER

Off US Alternate 14, near Lovell, on Wyoming 37. Mail address: Ft. Smith, MT 59035. Phone: 406/666-2412. Open free, daily, all year. Closed certain holidays.

In the Bighorn Visitor Center is an archeological display.

BIGHORN MEDICINE WHEEL

This archeological site is sacred to Native Americans who worship there. They request that visitors stay away and do not invade their privacy.

BUFFALO BILL HISTORICAL CENTER

720 Sheridan Ave., Cody, WY 82414. Phone: 307/587-4771. Open daily, May–October; afternoons, Tuesday–

Sunday, March, April and November. Closed December–February. Closed certain holidays. Admission charged.

This is a four-part complex of which the Plains Indian Museum is one part. One wing contains prehistoric artifacts found in the Cody area.

GREYBULL MUSEUM

325 Greybull Ave., Box 348, Greybull, WY 82426. Phone: 307/765-2444. Open free, seasonally. Call for hours.

This museum has a few prehistoric artifacts.

HOT SPRINGS STATE PARK

In Thermopolis, WY off Highway 20. Mail address: 220 Park St., Thermopolis, WY 82443. Phone: 307/864-2176. Open daily. Admission charged.

Guided tours of Legend Rock State Petroglyph Site may be scheduled at the park office.

Special Features. Visitors can see a buffalo herd here. They can also soak

free in the Big Spring (called Bah Guewana by the Shoshone Indians) thanks to the terms of a treaty between the Shoshone and the state of Wyoming.

JOHNSON COUNTY, JIM GATCHELL MEMORIAL MUSEUM

10 Fort St., Buffalo. Mail address: P.O. Box 596, Buffalo, WY 82834. Phone: 307/684-9331. Open free, daily, June 1–Labor Day. Closed July 4.

In addition to random local finds, the Jim Gatchell Museum displays prehistoric artifacts recovered in a dig conducted by the University of Wyoming at a buffalo jump in the area.

MAMMOTH VISITOR CENTER, YELLOWSTONE NATIONAL PARK

The North Enrance to the park is always open. The other four entrances are open to wheeled vehicles from early May through October and to tracked over-snow vehicles mid-December to mid-March. They are closed to all vehicle traffic the rest of the year. Mail address: P.O. Box 168, Yellowstone National Park, WY 82190. Phone: 307/344-7381. Admission charged. Camping.

The Mammoth Visitor Center is on US 89, 5 miles south of the North Entrance and is open daily. Five exhibits in the Visitor Center contain material about Indians in the park. One exhibit concentrates on prehistoric artwork and artifacts collected in the park.

MEDICINE LODGE STATE ARCHAEOLOGICAL SITE

From Hyattville, follow signs on an asphalt county road 6 miles north to site. Mail address: P.O. Box 62, Hyattville, WY 82428. Phone: 307/ 469-2234. Open free, May 1–November 4.

The University of Wyoming excavated this site then filled it to be reopened at some future time. There are exhibits in the Visitor Center, and signs along the red sandstone cliffs interpret the petroglyphs there.

NATURAL HISTORY MUSEUM, WESTERN WYOMING COMMUNITY COLLEGE

On the campus which is accessible from Interstate 80, College Drive, Exit 103. Mail address: P.O. Box 428, 2500 College Drive, Rock Springs, WY 82902-0428. Phone: 307/382-1666. Open free, afternoons Monday–Friday, September–May; all day Monday–Friday, summer months. Camping nearby.

Changing exhibits dealing primarily with the prehistory of southwestern Wyoming are drawn from extensive holdings in the museum's possession. It is one of two federal depositories for archeological material in Wyoming.

The museum conducts at least one summer field school every year.

OBSIDIAN CLIFF

In Yellowstone National Park. The North Entrance to the park is always open. The other four entrances are open to wheeled vehicles from early May–October and to tracked over-snow vehicles mid-December–mid-March. They are closed to all vehicle traffic the rest of the year. Mail address: P.O. Box 168, Yellowstone National Park, WY 82190. Phone: 307/344-7381. Admission charged. Camping.

From the North Entrance drive 5 miles south on US 89 to Mammoth Hot Springs, then about 12 miles south toward Norris to the cliff.

East of the road may be seen a dark mass of stone known to pioneer explorers as Glass Mountain. It is quite literally that—a mountain of volcanic glass, or obsidian.

Prehistoric hunters made projectile points and knives of obsidian, which are sharper than steel. However, sources of the material are rather rare, and early archeologists were puzzled when many obsidian artifacts turned up in the burial mounds of Ohio and Illinois. Was it possible that people had brought the volcanic glass all the way from Yellowstone? It was. One of the trails they followed to the quarry at Obsidian Cliff was worn so deep into the earth that it could still be seen in historic times.

Few present-day archeologists have doubted that Indians carried on trade and traveled great distances for things they wanted. Nevertheless, James B. Griffin, of the University of Michigan, decided to test various obsidian samples by a process called neutron activation. Working with members of the university's chemistry department, he proved that Obsidian Cliff and two other places in Yellowstone are the sources of obsidian used in many artifacts found at midwestern sites.

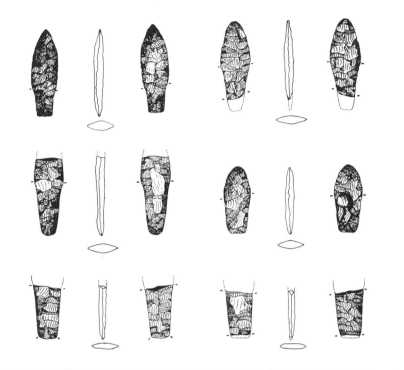

Drawings of various projectile points found at the Hell Gap Site, in Wyoming. Photo courtesy of George Agogino.

PLAINS INDIAN MUSEUM
(See Buffalo Bill Historical Center)

ROCKPILE MUSEUM

In Gillette on West 2nd St. or Highway 14-16 West. Mail address: Box 922, Gillette, WY 82716. Phone: 307/682-5723. Open free, Tuesday–Friday, October 16–May 15; Tuesday–Sunday. May 16–October 15. Donations welcome. Camping nearby.

This museum has a few cases of miscellaneous prehistoric artifacts.

SWEETWATER COUNTY HISTORICAL MUSEUM

80 West Flaming Gorge Way, Sweetwater County Courthouse, Green-River, WY 82935. Phone: 307/875-2611, ext. 263 or 307/362-7870, ext. 263. Open free, Monday–Friday; afternoon Saturday, July and August. Camping nearby.

This museum has three dioramas protraying the life of prehistoric Indians of the area. It also has a few prehistoric stone artifacts.

UNIVERSITY OF WYOMING ANTHROPOLOGY MUSEUM

On the campus, Anthropology Building, Laramie. Mail address: P.O. Box 3431, Laramie, WY 82071. Phone: 307/766-5136. Open free, Monday–Friday. Closed certin holidays.

Exhibits contain material from the university's extensive collection of Paleo-Indian artifacts and of material from later prehistoric sites.

WYOMING STATE MUSEUM

Barrett Building, 24th and Central avenues, Cheyenne. Mail address: A.M.H. Dept., Barrett Building, Cheyenne, WY 82002. Phone: 307/777-7024. Open free, daily, summer; closed Sunday, winter. Closed certain holidays.

Interpretive displays in this primarily historical museum include archeological material dating from early prehistoric times.

The debris in Russell Cave, Alabama, contained so many nutshells that archeologists think the cave was not a year-round shelter but was visited mainly in fall, when nuts would be ripe.

254

THE SOUTHEAST

At the end of the Ice Age people wandered eastward as well as westward from the Plains, following the trails of big game. By 10,000 B.C. (possibly earlier) these Paleo hunters had appeared east of the Mississippi River and south of the Ohio. Perhaps they crossed the great water barriers on the ice in winter, or perhaps they had watercraft made of logs or of skins stretched around a framework of branches. No one knows how they reached the Southeast, but there is evidence that early Americans were not limited to land in their travels. Paleo-Indian artifacts 7000 years old have been found on islands in the Caribbean Sea, obviously left there by people who had watercraft, although no vestiges of their boats or rafts have been found.

Paleo-Indian Period
No glaciers ever reached into the Southeast, but there was heavy rainfall, which nourished a dense forest cover. In the shady woods mastodons could find enough to eat, for they were browsers, living mostly on twigs and leaves. In open, unshaded areas there was grass for mammoths. Both animals must have been game for Paleo-Indians in the Southeast, and collectors have picked up innumerable projectile points of the kind that the Big-Game Hunters alone used. Indeed, the concentration of fluted points of the Clovis type is greater at certain places in the Southeast than it is anywhere in the Southwest.

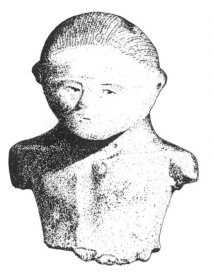

Prehistoric people in the Macon, Georgia, area modeled this head as part of a pottery vessel. Original in the museum, Ocmulgee National Monument, Macon.

Archaic Period

After the big game disappeared, descendants of Paleo-Indians gradually had to make adjustments to a changing climate and to many new environments. At first hunters of the next—the Archaic—period faced their changing world with no better equipment than that of their ancestors. In time, however, they elaborated new tools and new ways of getting nourishment in a land no longer rich in the huge animals that had brought such great rewards for a single kill. Sometime between 6000 B.C. and 4000 B.C. knowledge became widespread that mollusks could be harvested. People who camped often or long on the same site near rivers began to eat freshwater clams and mussels, and here the change in climate played a special role. Rainfall was decreasing. As a result, rivers dwindled and grew sluggish, and in the shallow, slow-moving waters, shellfish were easy to gather. Since it took a great many mollusks to feed a family, the piles of discarded shells grew higher and higher as long as the weather remained warm and dry. But when rainfall increased again, streams grew deeper and their currents sped up. It was more difficult now to pick shellfish off the bottom. People turned to other food sources, and the inland shell mounds ceased to grow.

Along the coasts of the Atlantic Ocean and the Gulf of Mexico the harvest of saltwater mollusks continued uninterrupted. There the shell mounds kept increasing in size right into historic times. Their extent in some places is monumental. Even though centuries of habitation contributed to their growth, it is hard to believe that so many oysters and clams could have been consumed.

This is not to say that all Archaic people concentrated on shellfish. They didn't. Many were meateaters, hunters of deer and smaller game, who supplemented their diet with nuts, roots, and seeds. They, too, left debris where they camped, and many a hummock in a modern farmer's field has turned out to be a mound of Archaic garbage, partially converted into soil.

The Eastern Archaic hunters differed from Paleo-Indians in their social relationships. Big-Game Hunters probably worked together in groups as they pursued large animals. But people who lived in wooded areas found it more efficient to search as individuals for their smaller quarry. For them hunting was a solitary, not a collective, enterprise. So, too, was a good deal of the foraging that went on. Large-scale cooperation was not required for harvesting nuts, seeds, and roots. Moreover, these were usually not abundant enough to support a large band that remained long in one place.

An exception was the shellfish eaters. During at least part of each year, they could live in larger groups than had ever been possible in the past. But at certain seasons many of them seem to have dispersed, as they turned away from mollusks and sought other food.

Life changed in many ways in the Archaic period. There was a general, very intensive search for new things to eat. At the same time there was an increase in the number and variety of implements used to gather and process the new foods. For example, Archaic people harvested hard-shelled seeds, for which they needed crushing tools. To make nutcrackers they first pecked several small depressions in a stone. Nuts fixed in these depressions could then be easily cracked by a blow from a hammerstone. Grinding stones and mortars and pestles came into use for pulverizing small seeds. In pots carved from steatite (soapstone) tough seeds could be cooked to a soft mush.

Still further specialization marked the end of this stage. The old, simple and rather fluid ways of the hunter began to disappear. Instead of depending entirely on what grew naturally, people created a new source of food by planting gardens. Larger groups could now live together, for part of the year at least, in semi-permanent villages. In some places women began to make a crude sort of pottery from clay that was mixed with grass or moss and then baked in a fire. (This is called fiber-tempered pottery.)

With the arrival of squash, beans, and corn from Mexico, there was a large jump in available calories. Population increased. So did the activities and responsibilities that men and women invented for themselves. As settled communities developed, some individuals could now spend a good deal of time in pursuits other than foodgetting, and many of the activities they chose centered around burials and burial ceremonies.

The winged serpent appears in a variety of forms in many prehistoric Indian cultures. A follower of the Mississippian lifeway made this design. After Clarence B. Moore.

At the same time, women had more leisure for making pottery in better and more beautiful forms than before. Good pottery vessels, in turn, increased the available food by providing better means of storing it. They also made cooking easier and so brought a more varied diet. The quality of life changed.

Woodland Period

With the appearance of agriculture, there began what is known as the Woodland period. Within this widespread general cultural pattern, some interesting developments came to many parts of the Southeast. One was the custom of building earthen mounds over the bodies, the bones, or the remains from cremations of the dead.

At first, during Early Woodland times, burial mounds in the Southeast were small and conical in shape. They were heaped up by the thousand, often a little way outside villages, wherever people dwelt along rivers, large streams, or the ridges of hills. As time passed, mound construction grew more complex. First a low platform was built, in preparation for a mass funeral. After bodies were placed on it, they were covered with earth. Later burials might be made in the mound and more layers added, until the structure rose as much as 20 feet.

The burial-mound idea seems to have spread to the Southeast from Illinois and Ohio, where it had already become very important in the lives of people who followed a lifeway called Hopewellian. For mortuary offerings, which they placed in graves, these

These figurines, each two feet high and carved from marble, were found at Etowah Mounds, Cartersville, Georgia. They may be portraits of the man and woman with whom they were buried.

people required a great deal of material obtainable only in distant places—shells from the seacoast, for example. Perhaps the Hopewellians made long journeys for the shells, or they may have got them by trade. In either event, information about their religious customs traveled along the routes that led to the source of the shells. And where the burial-mound idea spread, so, too, did its trappings—elaborate ornaments, tobacco pipes, tools and weapons of polished stone, ornaments of mica, and specially made mortuary vessels.

The intense activity of burial-mound rituals finally began to wear out in one place, then in another. But as this stage was ending another had already begun.

The Mississippian Period

Religious and ceremonial practices in much of the Southeast now centered around a new kind of mound. People constructed large, flat-topped, earthen pyramids which served as platforms for temples—buildings with thatched roofs, on which effigies of birds were sometimes perched. Because the temple-mound idea took form and then spread out vigorously from places along the Mississippi River, the cultural developments that went with it have been called Mississippian.

Those who followed the Mississippian lifeway became expert farmers and organizers. Populations grew tremendously around ceremonial centers, and huge pyramids were built by people who moved vast quantities of earth in baskets. Sometimes 20 or more large mounds marked a great ceremonial site. Arts and crafts flourished as the Mississippian cultures reached a climax.

In some areas temple-mound building became associated with a complex of human activities that archeologists used to call the Southern Cult. This final development in ceremonial and religious practices has also been called the Southern Death Cult, or the Buzzard Cult, and with good reason. Those who practiced it were preoccupied with death.

Recent studies have cast doubt on the idea that there really was a religious movement that could be called a cult of death. Nevertheless there was a great proliferation of grave goods, and many of the new artifacts were both elaborate and most skillfully made. Native copper was hammered into ornate headdresses, plaques, ear spools, and celts (a kind of axe). Craftsmen engraved intricate symbolic designs on shell, which was imported from the Gulf Coast. Sculptors shaped stone into excellent likenesses of people and animals. They also carved and polished stone axes, complete with stone handles. Such monolithic axes were useless for real work, but were obviously important for some ceremonial purpose. Symbols abounded—among them skulls, bones, and an eye in the palm of a hand. An eye that wept appeared everywhere in engravings and on pottery. So, too, did spiders and warriors with wings.

Workers in flint created graceful fantasies in this intractable material—ceremonial knives adorned with crescents and curlicues.

Human sacrifice was illustrated in various ways on artifacts, and it obviously was practiced in this death-centered culture. Pottery appeared in a great variety of nonutilitarian forms, made only for burial with the dead. Exuberant life was expressed in many ways—all celebrating the negation of life. If there was a Death Cult, it seemed to be imaginative about preparing for its own death, and die it did.

With a dramatic suddenness that still baffles investigators, the building of earthen pyramids ceased, and the lifeway associated with them vanished. Various theories have been put forward to explain what happened. Perhaps some great prehistoric epidemic sapped the vitality of the people. (This disease theory still lacks supporting evidence.) Perhaps the shock of the European invasion spread panic and sealed the fate of the culture, which was already in decline. Certainly the presence of Spanish troops under De Soto was disastrous to large numbers of Indian people in the Southeast. When De Soto arrived in 1539, some mound building was still going on, but little if any was done after his men withdrew at the end of their vain search for loot—a search that led them from Florida to Georgia, then all the way west into Arkansas. Not only did the Europeans disrupt Indian life by killing and enslaving great numbers of people, they were also an enormous drain on food resources. Wherever the Spanish army went, the Indian economy had to provide food for 700 soldiers, for a large number of slaves, for 200 horses, and for hogs that ate corn and multipled much faster than the Spanish butchered them.

The invaders also brought with them diseases to which the Indians had not developed any immunity, and as a result the population suddenly began to dwindle. If there was still vitality in the customs and beliefs that encouraged people to build temple mounds, that vitality soon disappeared.

Historic Indian tribes lived on in the vicinity of the mounds, which soon became as ancient and mysterious to them as to the Europeans who were overwhelming the land. It is these huge, earthen structures that make up many of the archeological sites now open to the public in the Southeast.

Some of the historic Indian tribes in the Southeast were surely descendants of the people who once engaged in the prodigious labor of piling up mounds. However, proof is usually lacking that a particular tribe is related to the builders of mounds near which it lived. On the other hand, scientific excavation has been able to disprove one myth: There was no mysterious vanished race of Mound Builders.

Indians who followed the Mississippian lifeway pecked these designs on a rock in Alabama. Frank Jones and Spencer Waters photo, courtesy Campbell Grant.

This pottery bottle is from Moundville Archaeological Park, Alabama. Original in the National Museum of the American Indian, Smithsonian Institution.

Alabama

ALABAMA DEPARTMENT OF ARCHIVES AND HISTORY

624 Washington Avenue, Montgomery, AL 36130. Phone: 205/242-4363. Open free, daily. Closed certain holidays.

Archeological exhibits emphasize the central Alabama region and interpret the history of Native Americans from prehistory to the Indian removal (1837).

ALABAMA MUSEUM OF NATURAL HISTORY
(*See University of Alabama and Moundville Archaeological Park*)

BIRMINGHAM MUSEUM OF ART

2000 Eighth Ave. N., Birmingham, AL 35203-2278. Phone: 205/254-2565. Open free, Tuesday–Saturday; afternoon Sunday. Closed certain holidays. Closed for renovations during 1992, to re-open 1993.

Permanent exhibits here are scheduled to include North American Indian art, along with pre-Columbian art from Central and South America. There are changing exhibitions each year.

FORT TOULOUSE/JACKSON PARK

Off US 231, 12 miles northeast of Montgomery. Phone: 205/567-3002. Open daily, except certain holidays. Admission charged. Camping.

On the grounds near the site of two eighteenth-century French forts, early hunting people once camped. Indians inhabited this area for 5000 years and built several large temple mounds, one of which remains today. Prehistoric and historic artifacts are exhibited in the Visitor Center.

HORSESHOE BEND NATIONAL MILITARY PARK

From Dadeville drive 12 miles north on Alabama 49. Open free, at all times. Closed December 25. Camping nearby.

Although not concerned with prehistoric archeology, this park is of interest because here, in March 1814, a thousand Red Stick Creek warriors faced a three-thousand-man army, led by Andrew Jackson. Jackson's superior forces won and decisively broke the power of the Creeks, which extended far back into prehistoric times.

INDIAN MOUND

South end of Court St., Florence, AL 35630. Phone: 205/760-6427. Open Tuesday–Saturday. Closed certain holidays. Admission charged.

This is one of the largest Mississippian mounds in the Tennessee Valley, built about A.D. 1200. It is 43 feet high and originally had steps on one side. A museum near the base contains artifacts collected in the area.

MOUNDVILLE ARCHAEOLOGICAL PARK
(Part of Mound State Monument)

From Tuscaloosa drive 13 miles south on Alabama 69 to the park at Mound-

This black pottery vessel from Moundville Archaeological Park has incised designs, shown here in white to make them more visible.

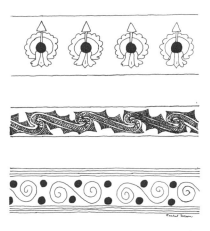

Three designs used on pottery made by Mississippian Indians. Pots are on display in the museum at Moundville Archaeological Park.

ville. Mail address: P.O. Box 66, Moundville, AL 35474. Phone: 205/ 371-2572. Open daily, except certain holidays. Admission charged. Camping.

This combination archeological site and museum is a division of the Alabama Museum of Natural History. Artifacts from the site and others in the area illustrate the cultural traits and physical characteristics of the prehistoric people who lived here. On top of the principal mound in the monument is a restoration of a temple, which includes a life-size exhibit of a ceremony of the kind that once went on there. A reconstructed village of five huts shows people performing the everyday tasks of Moundville Indians in prehistoric times.

The Story. Between the years A.D. 1200 and A.D. 1400 a large settlement prospered in peace at this site. People in the village were good-looking, muscular, and of medium height. Though naturally handsome, they often allowed a custom which they probably thought improved their appearance: they altered the shapes of

babies' heads by strapping them to wooden cradleboards. The soft baby bones were readily and permanently flattened.

Men and women wore clothing made of woven fabrics and cured animal skins. For warmth in cold weather they had robes made of feathers. They adorned themselves with delicate shell necklaces and pendants, copper bracelets and armbands, and ear decorations called earplugs. Hairdos received a good deal of attention, and women used long bone hairpins.

The houses in this community consisted of frames made of logs, over which there was a covering of reeds and canes woven into mats and then plastered with mixed clay and sand.

Food was plentiful. Men hunted in the nearby forest and fished in Black Warrior River, on the banks of which their village stood. They shaped barbless fishhooks of bone, wove fishnets, and made traps, snares, bows, and arrows. Corn, beans, and pumpkins grew readily in soil that was exceedingly fertile. To harvest their various crops they

made tools much like those used by Indians elsewhere in eastern America. They also had woodworking tools and grinding implements for making cornmeal. Eating utensils were cut from shell.

Women apparently had time and energy for making pots that were often very lovely. Everyone seems to have had the time necessary for ceremonies and rituals and for the labor of building the 40 mounds on which they placed temples and other important structures. Although they did not build any burial mounds, these people devoted a great deal of effort to mortuary customs. As in many other Indian societies, precious belongings were buried with the dead. These grave goods give us much of our information about the lifeway of the people who made and used them.

Examples of the material culture and technology of these people are on display in the museum.

A Park Ranger at Russell Cave National Monument, Alabama, indicates the layers of debris accumulated in more than 8000 years of human occupation of the cave. National Park Service photo.

This diorama shows how archeologists at Moundville Archaeological Park think the village may have looked 500 years ago. The structure on top of the mound at right was a religious and political center of the community. University of Alabama, Museum of Natural History photo.

OLD CAHAWBA

In Selma turn off State Highway 22 (Broad St.) onto Dallas Ave. and drive 8 miles to the Cahawba River Bridge, go on .75 mile, turn left on a county road marked "To Cahawba." After 3.5 miles where the road dead-ends, turn left and proceed 3 miles to Cahawba. Mail address: 719 Tremont St., Selma, AL 36701. Phone: 205/875-2529.

As this book went to press a history park was being prepared. The Visitor Center will interpret a 16th century Indian village here and exhibit Archaic materials from the site.

RUSSELL CAVE NATIONAL MONUMENT

From Bridgeport on US 72 drive west on County Road 91 to Mt. Carmel, then turn north onto County Road 75, which leads to the monument entrance. Total distance from Bridgeport about 8 miles. Mail address: Russell Cave National Monument, Bridgeport, AL 35740. Phone: 205/495-2672. Open free, daily. Closed December 25.

A record of more than 8000 years of human life is preserved in this monument. In Russell Cave itself an exhibit shows how archeologists did the excavation. There is also an audiovisual presentation and, nearby, a self-guided ethnobotanical trail. The museum near the cave contains interpretive exhibits.

The Story. Long ago hunters found that the gaping hole now called Russell Cave provided shelter, and they camped on its rock-strewn floor. Bits of charcoal, dated by the carbon-14 method, show that men, women, and children warmed themselves at fires here sometime between 8000 and 9000 years ago. Usually their visits were in fall and winter, when quantities of nuts could be harvested in the neighboring forest. Hunting at that time of year was good, too, and fish and shellfish were easy to harvest in the nearby Tennessee River.

Year after year families kept visiting the cave, cooking over fires, dropping trash, losing tools. After a while the floor on which they camped was so littered that tidying-up seemed necessary. Loads of dirt were brought in to

Busk

For many eastern Indians in historic times the most important ceremony of the year was the summer corn festival. Among the Creeks, who may be directly descended from one group of temple-mound builders, the ceremony was called the "pushkita." English-speaking people shortened this word to "busk."

The ceremony, a kind of New Year celebration, took place when corn first ripened. People put out all fires and engaged in various rites which were supposed to purify. They drank the Black Drink, took ceremonial baths, and then, as a sign that they had rid themselves of evil, they started new fires. Boys who had reached puberty took new names during the busk and were thenceforth regarded as men. The ceremonies lasted for eight days and ended with dancing.

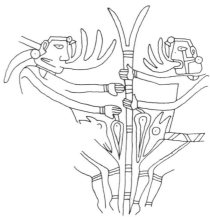

One element of the busk ceremony is shown in this design, which was engraved on a conch shell found at Spiro Mounds, Oklahoma. The symbols coming from the men's mouths may represent speech. Original in the National Museum of the American Indian, Smithsonian Institution.

---

cover the debris, and the cave floors slowly rose high above its original level.

At last, about 500 B.C., the lifeway of the cave's visitors changed a great deal. They began to make pottery, and many sherds littered the floor. The favorite weapon was now the bow and arrow instead of the spear and spear-thrower, which had been used until then. Tools became more varied as people learned to garden as well as hunt.

Farming increased in importance, and beginning about A.D. 1000, people stopped at Russell Cave less and less often. This was a time when many communities in the Southeast were building temple mounds. Some evidence of the temple-mound lifeway was left in the cave, but not a great deal.

Some historic Native Americans used the cave shelter from 1540 to 1650.

During all these centuries of occupation, debris piled up on the floor until it reached a depth of 43 feet. In 1953 four members of the Tennessee Archaeological Society begn to dig into the litter. A little excavating was enough to tell them that the job was too big for such a small crew and too important to be left undone. The am-

ateurs called in the Smithsonian Institution, which, together with the National Geographic Society, excavated the cave and by so doing added greatly to our knowledge of the early inhabitants of the Southeast. In all of North America no excavation before this had provided such a detailed record of human life over such a long period. No excavation in the Southeast had provided an earlier date. The National Geographic Society later bought the cave property and donated it to the public. In 1961 it was made a national monument.

UNIVERSITY OF ALABAMA, ALABAMA MUSEUM OF NATURAL HISTORY

University of Alabama, on the campus, Tuscaloosa. Mail address: P.O. Box 870340, Tuscaloosa, AL 35487-0340. Phone: 205/348-2040. Open free, daily, when the university is in session.

Exhibits here emphasize worldwide ethnology and geology.

Special Interest. A traveling exhibit traces Indian life in Alabama from Pa-

leo times, before 8000 B.C., through all the major cultural developments, including the historic period. Information about the schedule of the exhibit may be obtained from the museum.

The museum also conducts a field school in archeology at the Moundville Archaeological Park (see entry above) and an expedition and other scientific endeavors for high school and younger students. Enquiries should be directed to the address above.

Left to right: An effigy vessel in the shape of a frog, found in a burial mound in Arkansas. Original in the National Museum of the American Indian, Smithsonian Institution. This unusual-shaped water jar was found in Arkansas. Original in the National Museum of the American Indian, Smithsonian Institution. The winged-serpent design was engraved on a conch shell found at Spiro Mounds. Original in the University of Arkansas Museum, Fayetteville.

Arkansas

ARKANSAS MUSEUM OF SCIENCE AND HISTORY

MacArthur Park, Little Rock, AR 72202. Phone: 501/324-9231. Open Monday–Saturday; afternoon Sunday. Admission charged, except Monday for self-guided tours.

Here in a Native American gallery is a pottery collection that came more than a century ago from the Thibault site which may have been a ceremonial mound. The pottery tells the story of the occupation of the site on the Arkansas River from 500 B.C. through the Woodland and Mississippian periods to A.D. 1541 and later.

ARKANSAS STATE UNIVERSITY MUSEUM

On the campus, Jonesboro. Mail address: Box 490, State University, Jonesboro, AR 72467. Phone: 501/972-2074. Open free, Monday–Friday; afternoons Saturday and Sunday. Closed certain holidays.

The archeological exhibits in this general museum are devoted to prehistory in northeastern Arkansas. The eight exhibits of the Paleo through the Archaic, Woodland, and Mississippian mound-building stages contain time lines and labels telling the story revealed by the artifacts. Another exhibit contains a collection of effigy pots and explains the five steps in making pottery. Seven pedestal exhibits show a collection of restructured pots and projectile points from the surface collection of one amateur archeologist. A three-panel exhibit concludes the story with photographic displays showing correct archeological methods with labels that implore the public to help prevent the destruction of sites.

HAMPSON MUSEUM STATE PARK

US 61 at Lake Drive, Wilson. Mail address: P.O. Box 156, Wilson, AR 72395-0156. Phone: 501/655-8622. Open Tuesday–Saturday; afternoon, Sunday. Closed certain holidays. Admission charged.

Material from the Nodena site, which

Model Archeology Program

Anyone who wants to watch a dig—or to do volunteer work in one—may be able to do so in Arkansas. The Arkansas Archeological Survey employs a staff of full-time archeologists, with one of them attached to each state-supported college and university. This network is salvaging a great deal of valuable information that would otherwise be lost, as grading machines turn scores of thousands of acres of land into absolutely level fields. Any farmer or amateur archeologist who finds material that may be of scientific interest can phone the nearest college, and an expert will normally be out to investigate within two hours. In addition, of course, the Archeological Survey team gathers information from places where roads are being made or foundations dug or artifacts discovered by amateurs. The Survey also sponsors a training program each June for members of the Arkansas Archeological Society.

If a dig is visitable, the State Archeologist can send you to it. Write to Arkansas Archeological Survey, P.O. Box 1249, Fayetteville, AR 72601, or phone 505/575-3556.

---

has been declared a National Historic Landmark, is on display here. The museum, 7 miles from the site, is owned by the state of Arkansas and operated by the Department of Parks and Tourism.

Dr. J. K. Hampson, who excavated the material, began collecting artifacts when he was 9 years old and continued in this avocation for 70 years. His greatest activity centered at the Nodena site, which covered more than two acres of the Hampson family plantation. In the course of his excavation he uncovered many burials, and because he was a physician he was particularly interested in what the study of bones could tell him about prehistoric people and their customs and diseases. He found, for one thing, that they were apparently peaceful. In all the burials he discovered only two evidences of death by violence.

Numerous pots, including many effigy jars, are on display in the museum, along with chunkey stones (used in a game), ornaments and other artifacts that represent the Mississippian lifeway at Nodena site and elsewhere.

HENDERSON STATE UNIVERSITY MUSEUM

On the campus, Arkadelphia. Mail address: HSU Box H-7657, Arkadelphia, AR 71923. Phone: 501/246-7311. Open free, during college semesters and by appointment.

This museum has over 600 pieces of Caddoan pottery. About 100 are on display, along with Caddoan stone, bone, and shell tools and ornaments.

The Caddoan archeological area is named after the Indians of historic times who spoke a Caddoan language and who apparently were descendants of prehistoric groups in Texas, Arkansas, Louisiana, and Oklahoma. The Caddoans shared religious and political ideas with their neighbors to the east, built mounds, and buried their honored dead with a wealth of grave goods. Caddoan pottery vessels are elaborately made, engraved with intricate designs, and are among the most beautiful in the prehistoric southeastern tradition.

HOT SPRINGS NATIONAL PARK MUSEUM

In the Visitor Center, Central and Reserve avenues, Hot Springs National Park, AR 71902. Open free, daily. Closed December 25.

In the Visitor Center a few Caddoan artifacts are on display, together with explanations of the prehistoric human use of the water from the hot springs. Drawings show how Indians made implements from a very hard local stone called novaculite.

MUSEUM OF SCIENCE AND NATURAL HISTORY

MacArthur Park, 500 E. 9th St., Little Rock, AR 72202. Phone: 501/371-3521. Open free, Tuesday–Saturday; afternoon, Sunday.

One hall in this museum is devoted to material found in prehistoric sites in Arkansas.

PARKIN ARCHEOLOGICAL STATE PARK
National Historic Landmark

On the north edge of the city of Parkin at the junction of US 64 and Arkansas 184. For information about when it is open inquire at Arkansas State Parks, One Capital Mall, 4A-900, Little Rock, AR 72201. Phone: 501/682-1191.

An interpretive center at this site was scheduled to open as this book went to press. The center planned to offer tours and audiovisual programs and to give visitors a chance to watch ongoing archeological research.

The very large and well preserved site was occupied from about A.D. 1350 to 1550. It may have been the town of Casqui that De Soto visited in the summer of 1541. Relations between Indians and Spaniards seem to have been friendly, but the latter may have brought diseases that wiped out the settlement, as happened in other places.

TOLTEC MOUNDS ARCHEOLOGICAL STATE PARK
(Knapp Mounds)

From North Little Rock drive 9 miles southeast on US 165, then .5 mile west on Arkansas 386. Mail address: Toltec Mounds Rd., Scott, AR 72142-9502. Phone: 501/961-9442. Open daily, except Monday and certain holidays. Admission charged for guided tours.

Various groups of people occupied this site for over 1000 years, beginning about A.D. 600.Some of them built large, earthen mounds, probably for ceremonial purposes—18 altogether, of which nine are still visible. An earthen embankment six feet high and a mile long once surrounded the site.

In the Visitor Center are archeological exhibits, audiovisual programs, and an archeological laboratory. Full-time research goes on here, and when excavation is in progress visitors may watch. Guided tours are available.

The Name. Former owners of the site thought the mounds had been built by Toltec Indians from Mexico. Although this was discovered not to be so, the name persisted.

THE UNIVERSITY MUSEUM

At N. Barland Avenue, on the campus, University of Arkansas, Fayetteville, AR 72701. Phone: 501/575-3555. Open Monday–Saturday; afternoon, Sunday. Closed University holidays. Admission by donation.

The prehistory of Arkansas is featured in this museum. A sequence of exhibit panels chronicles Indian development in the state. Included are baskets, sandals, and other perishable items preserved in the dry bluff shelters of the Ozarks. These shelters are areas at the bases of overhanging rock ledges under bluffs or cliffs. Many are quite dry—completely protected from rain and snow—and for that reason they attracted prehistoric people. The absence of moisture also meant that baskets, sandals, clothing, garbage—any organic material left there—did not decay. Things which ordinarily would have been lost to the archeologist have survived, and they tell a story of the life of non-farming people who inhabited the shelters from about 8000 B.C. to about A.D. 950.

Ozark Bluff hunters used spears and darts tipped with large stone points. Women gathered nuts and wild plants, made excellent baskets and mats, and wove blankets of feather and hemp. Some of their textiles, cordage, and baskets are on display in the museum. The Ozark Bluff people did not bury grave goods with the dead. A blanket, a mat, and a basketry pillow are about the only offerings found in the graves, and so less is known about this culture than about some others. Perhaps a little more could have been found out if collectors had not looted the shelters before archeologists got there.

One display in the museum contains material from the famous Spiro Mounds Site in Oklahoma, which yielded much fascinating material even after extensive vandalizing. Featured are pearl and shell beads, engraved shell cups and gorgets, a stone earspool and monolithic axe. In another exhibit is spectacular pottery from the late prehistoric cultures of the eastern and southwestern parts of the state. Separate exhibits feature effigy pottery vessels, projectile points, and how archeologists excavate sites.

What Was the Food of Archaic People in the Southeast?

Here is an answer provided by Frank Schambach and Leslie Newell in *Crossroads of the Past: 12,000 Years of Indian Life in Arkansas* (Arkansas Archeological Survey and Arkansas Humanities Council).

"Biologically people require two basic things from food: protein to build and maintain their muscles and energy from fats or carbohydrates to make them work. The protein in nuts is highly digestible, as good as meat protein, while their high fat content makes them superior to most meats as a source of energy. Hickory nuts, the favorite of the Southeastern Indians, yield up to 693 calories of energy per 100-gram serving, which contains 13.2 grams of protein and 68.7 grams of fat. Black walnuts, another favorite, yield 628 calories per 100 grams and contain an impressive 20.5 grams of protein and 59.3 grams of fat. By comparison modern prime beef (54% lean and 46% fat) yields only 428 calories per 100 grams, 13.6 grams of protein, and 41 grams of fat.

"The high fat content in nuts made them the ideal staple in the Southeastern Indian diet because the available meats and fish were (except bear) all exceedingly lean. Venison is a good source of protein (21 grams per 100-gram serving) but dangerously low in fat (4 grams per 100-gram serving). Hunters who tried to live on venison alone would feel the terrible fatigue of 'fat starvation' within days and die within weeks. Rabbits and most fresh water fish are also 'fat starvation' foods. Raccoon, opossum, squirrel, and turkey are lean, but adequate."

Florida

CANAVERAL NATIONAL SEASHORE

In New Smyrna Beach. Leave US 1 or Interstate 95 at Exit 84 and follow A1A to the park. Mail address: 2532 Garden St., Titusville, FL 32796. Phone: 407/267-1110. Open free, daily. Camping.

In this 60,000 acre park are more than sixty prehistoric middens and burial mounds. Turtle Mound and Castle Windy Midden, both prepared for visitation, are in the north end of the park. The Castle Windy Midden has a self-guided trail as does Turtle Mound which is on the National Historic Register. It is 35 feet high and is one of the largest middens on the east coast of Florida. It grew up as Indians harvested oysters and discarded the shells over a period of several thousand years.

The site is largely unexcavated and doubtless contains much material that can throw light on prehistoric Florida. It would now be lost to science had it not been for a campaign by local citizens when an attempt was made to quarry its shells for road construction. Their efforts brought state protection to the site, but other mounds have disappeared as road builders hauled their contents away. Acquired by the federal government, Turtle Mound in 1975 became a part of Canaveral National Seashore and is now administered by the National Park Service.

Special Feature. A self-guided nature trail, complete with a booklet and a boardwalk, leads to the top of Turtle Mound, providing a good view of the Atlantic Ocean and the lagoon behind. Yaupon plants, which belong to the holly family, grow near the trail. It was from the leaves of this plant, or its close relative the cassina holly, that Indians in the Southeast made the Black Drink, which played an important part in certain ceremonies. First the leaves were parched, then steeped in a large jar of water. The result was a liquid containing a great deal of caffeine.

Before performing certain ceremonies, Indians drank some of this Black Drink from conch shell cups. Sometimes other herbs were added to make it an emetic. The vomiting it induced was supposed to have a purifying effect. Without the emetic herbs, people often used the Black Drink just as we use coffee or tea today.

Florida Key Dwellers

Visitors to the keys and glades of southern Florida in the late nineteenth century were often amazed at the vast deposits of shells which had been left there by prehistoric people. In some places these refuse heaps had been turned into built-up living and ceremonial areas. On one key, for example, early inhabitants had constructed a monumental sea wall more than ten feet high, mostly of conch shells. It was "as level and broad on top as a turnpike," said the archeologist Frank Cushing, who explored it. Beyond the wall were terraces, with a graded way leading to five large mounds and an especially big pyramidal mound, which probably supported a temple.

Cushing speculated that at first people built up the keys with shells, then extended the sea walls to make enclosures that served as fish traps, into which they paddled their canoes, driving the fish ahead of them. As mud and debris accumulated in canals between shell heaps, they dug it out and formed little garden patches. They also built platforms for dwellings and cisterns to catch rain for drinking water. As time passed the settlements grew more and more elaborate, and so did the lives of the people who occupied them. At Key Marco, where Cushing did a famous job of excavating, he uncovered a wealth of beautiful and fascinating material. Much of it looked as if it had just been finished. Even perishable things such as cordage, mats, and objects made of wood had been preserved in the salty bogs.

CRYSTAL RIVER STATE ARCHAEOLOGICAL SITE

From the town of Crystal River drive northwest a short distance on US 19 to directional sign, then turn west on a paved road which leads directly to the museum. Mail address: Route 3, Box 610, Crystal River, FL 32629. Phone: 904/795-3817. Open daily, all year. Admission charged.

In addition to housing interpretive exhibits and artifacts excavated in the vicinity, the museum in this Florida state park offers a view through its windows of three different types of mound—refuse mounds, burial mounds, and a temple mound. Trails lead from the museum to the mounds.

The Story. Beginning about 2100 years ago, Indians developed a settlement here on the banks of the Crystal River. In time this became a very important ceremonial center, and activities continued here for about 1600 years.

In the course of excavations, which began in 1903, more than 450 burials have been found. Some of the grave goods have proved that there was trade between Crystal River Indians and Indians who lived in distant places—as far north as Ohio. Two stone slabs may indicate that these people were also affected by ideas from Mexico. Carvings on one of the slabs resemble those on stones called steles, which were erected in ancient Mexico to commemorate special events.

FLORIDA MUSEUM OF NATURAL HISTORY, FLORIDA STATE UNIVERSITY

On the campus, Gainesville, FL 32611. Phone: 904/392-1721. Open free, Monday–Saturday; afternoons, Sunday and certain holidays.

In this museum, which emphasizes hands-on exhibits and calls attention to concepts spanning different cultures, visitors can walk through life-size reconstructions—for example, a Florida cave or a Mayan palace. Of particular interest to those concerned with prehistory north of Mexico is a reconstruction of a 500-year-old Timucuan village.

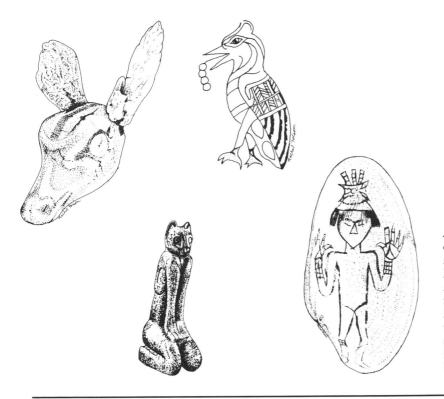

Above, left: The Key Marco artist who carved this deer's head made the ears movable. Original in the University Museum, Philadelphia. *Above, right:* A woodpecker painted on wood, from Key Marco. After Cushing. *Below, left:* This panther-like figure was carved by a Key dweller. *Below, right:* A humorous shell painting from Key Marco. Original in the University Museum, Philadelphia.

FORT CAROLINE NATIONAL MEMORIAL

12713 Fort Caroline Rd., Jacksonville, FL 32225. Phone: 904/641-7155. Open free, all year. Closed certain holidays.

In the museum at the Visitor Center are exhibits of Timucuan Indian artifacts from excavations at the fort and elsewhere in Florida.

FORT MATANZAS NATIONAL MONUMENT

From St. Augustine drive 14 miles south on Florida A1A. Mail address: Castillo de San Marcos National Monument, 1 Castillo Drive, East, St. Augustine, FL 32084. Phone: (field office) 904/471-0116, (headquarters) 904/829-6506. Open free, all year. Closed December 25. Camping nearby.

Within the park are several large prehistoric middens.

GULF ISLANDS NATIONAL SEASHORE

From Interstate 10 in Pensacola take spur 110 and follow signs. Mail address: 1801 Gulf Breeze Parkway, Gulf Breeze, FL 32561. Phone: 904/934-2604. Open free, daily.

Here are both prehistoric and historic sites and small museum exhibits related to people who have lived on the Gulf Coast.

HISTORICAL MUSEUM OF SOUTHERN FLORIDA

101 W. Flagler St., Miami, FL 33130. Phone: 305/375-1492. Open Monday–Saturday; afternoon, Sunday. Closed December 25. Admission charged.

Random local finds and materials professionally excavated throw light on the lifeways of the Calusa and Te-questa Indians from about 600 B.C. to the historic period. The Calusa lived on the west coast of Florida, south of Tampa Bay; the Tequestas on the east coast, from the upper Florida keys to what is now Martin County. The exhibits show how people adjusted to an environment that lacked metal and hard stone by substituting seashells and wood for materials that would have been used in other areas.

Underwater Sites in Florida

Near Charlotte Harbor in southwest Florida are two small bodies of water, one called Little Salt Spring, the other called Warm Mineral Springs. Though they are rather shallow at the edges, they fall away toward the center, where a kind of chimney in the limestone, called a sinkhole, leads down to a water-filled cavern far below (Little Salt Spring is about 200 feet deep). These were ideal spots for scuba divers, who some years ago began bringing up stone projectile points and the bones of animals and human beings. By the time scientists were called on to identify and date the finds, Warm Mineral Springs had been greatly disturbed, and the material from it was not as useful to archeologists as it might have been. However, human bones and the bones of a saber-toothed tiger from the site proved to be about 10,000 years old. Whether one killed the other could not be determined.

Fortunately a foundation grant and cooperation from the University of Miami gave archeologists a chance to work at the much less disturbed Little Salt Spring site, which turned out to be very rich and exciting. There were actually two phases to the work, one under water and one on land. Deep in the spring itself divers found a ledge which was dry land 12,000 years ago, when sea level and the water-table level in Florida were much lower than today. On the ledge lay the shell of a giant extinct tortoise, obviously killed by a sharp wooden spear that was still stuck in its body. The wood, by C-14 dating, is 12,030 years old.

People who lived on Weeden Island, Florida, about 1000 years ago, modeled this clay bottle in the shape of a dove. Original in the National Museum of the American Indian, Smithsonian Institution.

HISTORIC SPANISH POINT
National Historic Register

500 North Tamiami Trail, Osprey. Mail address: P.O. Box 846, Osprey, FL 34229. Phone: 813/966-5214. Open Monday–Saturday; afternoon, Sunday. Closed certain holidays. Phone for schedule of guided tours. Tram tours available for those unable to walk. Admission charged.

Amid historic exhibits is a large Archaic shell midden and burial mound. As this book went to press plans were under way to open a cutaway of the midden to inspection by visitors. In addition there is an interactive exhibit in which young people can experience some of the excitement of archeology. An audiovisual program is based on discoveries made in the midden.

INDIAN TEMPLE MOUND MUSEUM
(*See Temple Mound Museum*)

LAKE JACKSON MOUNDS
STATE ARCHAEOLOGICAL SITE

Six miles north of Tallahassee off US 27. Phone: 904/562-0042. Open free, daily.

Excavations at this ceremonial mound site have revealed that people lived in the area from about A.D. 1300 to historic times. A nature trail leads to one visitable mound.

MADIRA BICKEL MOUND
STATE ARCHAEOLOGICAL SITE

From Bradenton drive 5 miles north on US 41 and US 19, following US 19 to the left and state park directional signs to the mound site, which is on Terra Ceia Island. Phone: 813/722-1017. Open free, all year.

Some Indians occupied this site, which is near present-day St. Petersburg, apparently from about A.D. 1 to about 1600. The earliest inhabitants lived as shellfish harvesters. Abundant food from the sea nourished them, and they left only a few tools behind in their piles of discarded shells. Slowly

Also on the ledge were human bones. Archeologists speculate that both the tortoise and its hunter had tumbled over the edge of the sinkhole. Unable to climb out, the luckless hunter eventually starved to death. His remains and those of his prey were submerged when the water table rose and lay undisturbed until divers came upon them.

Nearby on the ledge lay a wooden weapon, shaped much like a boomerang. This killing stick is unique because it is the oldest one ever found anywhere in the world, and the only one so far discovered in the Americas. When archeologists tested a model of the boomerang, it proved capable of bringing down game at a hundred yards.

Divers also found Paleo campgrounds from about the same period, now under water but on dry land before the water level rose, about 8000 years ago, and covered all the remains of human occupancy. Water in the spring is both high in mineral content and low in oxygen, and that accounts for the excellent preservation of wood and of the bones of both people and extinct animals—mammoth, mastodon, and ground sloth.

Excavation in now boggy earth around the sinkhole has revealed that people camped there about 6000 years ago and buried their dead nearby. The burials led archeologists to think there may be as many as a thousand graves at the site. From one of them came the remarkably well preserved body of a woman wrapped in a shroud made of a kind of bark cloth and covered with a net woven from grapevines.

This clay vessel was created in the form of a kneeling figure. Original in the National Museum of the American Indian, Smithsonian Institution.

---

their lifeway changed, and they began to adopt customs that made existence a good deal more complicated. Like many others in the Southeast, they became greatly occupied with burying the dead.

After about A.D. 700 their rituals and their pottery closely resembled those of the Weeden Island people, who also lived close to St. Petersburg. Sometimes single bodies of the dead were placed within low mounds of sand. Often the bones from a number of skeletons would be bundled together for burial in a mound. Artifacts associated with these burials included specially made pottery, polished stone celts, shell beads, and shell cups. Pottery of the Weeden Island type is unusually attractive, and it was found here in abundance.

Sometime after A.D. 1400 this area came under the influence of dynamic new ideas associated with the building of temple mounds. The people became much more proficient farmers, adopted a new style of pottery making, and spent a great deal of time and energy heaping up an earthen pyramid on which they placed a ceremonial structure. At the time the Spaniards first visited Florida, temple-mound builders still lived here.

MUSEUM OF ARCHAEOLOGY

203 Southwest First Ave., Ft. Lauderdale, FL 33301. Phone: 305/525-8778. Open Tuesday–Saturday; afternoon, Sunday. Closed June 30–October 1, and certain holidays.

Here is an unusual exhibit of Tequesta artifacts from A.D. 500 to 1780. The Tequesta people lived in the southernmost part of Florida.

MUSEUM OF FLORIDA
HISTORY

500 South Bronough St., Tallahassee, FL 32399. Phone: 904/488-1673. Open free, Monday–Saturday; afternoon, Sunday. Closed certain holidays.

Here are two exhibits that deal with prehistoric Florida themes. One is on Early Man, the other on the prehistoric environment.

A clay figure on display in Temple Mound Museum, Fort Walton Beach. Florida News Bureau, Dept. of Commerce photo by Eric Tournay.

MUSEUM OF SCIENCE AND HISTORY

1025 Museum Circle, Jacksonville, FL 32207-9854. Phone: 904/296-7062. Open Monday–Saturday; afternoon, Sunday. Admission charged. Closed certain holidays.

This museum exhibits a scale model of Dent Mound, a Jacksonville archeological site.

SAFETY HARBOR SITE

In Philippe Park, 1 mile northeast of Safety Harbor on County Road 30. Open free, daily.

Here, on a point of land that extends into Tampa Bay, Timucua Indians built a temple mound in late prehistoric times. The mound, which is 150 feet in diameter and 25 feet high, is protected by the Pinellas County Park Department.

Part of the area has been excavated, and a large amount of material recovered. Some of it is on display in the county courthouse in Clearwater.

ST. PETERSBURG HISTORICAL MUSEUM

On the approach to the Pier, 335 2nd Avenue NE, St. Petersburg, FL 33701. Phone: 813/894-1052. Open Monday–Saturday; afternoon, Sunday. Admission charged.

Included in this historical museum are some prehistoric materials collected in Pinellas County that reflect the important Weeden Island and Safety Harbor cultures which developed nearby. Most are from the early 1500s. Exhibits change, so call for more information on exhibit openings.

SAN LUIS ARCHAEOLOGICAL AND HISTORIC SITE

2020 West Mission Road, Tallahassee, FL 32304. Phone: 904/487-3711. Open free, Monday–Saturday; afternoon, Sunday and holidays, except Christmas and Thanksgiving.

At this site, which is primarily concerned with interpreting Spanish colonial history, archeologists have found

Turtle Mound, south of New Smyrna Beach, Florida, grew to its present height of 50 feet as prehistoric Indians of the area harvested oysters and discarded the shells. Several years ago it was threatened with destruction, but a campaign on the part of local citizens led to state protection of the site. Canaveral National Seashore photo.

evidence of Native American activity from the Paleo, Middle Archaic, Late Archaic, Middle Woodland, and Late Mississippian periods. The earliest artifact found is a 12,000-year-old projectile point. Excavations have revealed a great deal of information not only about the 17th century Spanish mission but about a very large Apalachee Council House.

SILVER GLEN SPRINGS SITE

East of Ocala. Mail address: U.S. Forest Service, Lake George Ranger District, Route 2, Box 701, Silver Springs, FL 32688. Phone: 904/625-2520. Open to day use. Admission charged. No facilities.

At this site, which was in the process of being developed as this book went to press, there was a pre-ceramic Archaic shell midden beside a large spring. One feature of the developed site will be an exhibit of prehistoric material.

SOUTH FLORIDA MUSEUM AND PLANETARIUM

201 Tenth St. West, Bradenton, FL 34205. Phone: 813/746-4131. Open Tuesday–Friday; afternoons, Saturday, Sunday. Closed certain holidays. Admission charged.

Prehistoric artifacts are on display here, together with information about the different types of mound found in Florida before the arrival of Europeans. Dioramas give an artist's interpretation of a Calusa village scene and of a wedding among the Timucua people in Florida in prehistoric times.

TEMPLE MOUND MUSEUM

139 Miracle Strip Parkway, Fort Walton Beach, FL 32548. Phone: 904/243-6521. Open Monday–Saturday. Admission charged.

This museum, which is operated by the city of Fort Walton Beach, introduces the visitor to 10,000 years of Native American life on the Gulf Coast. Beginning with artifacts from Paleo-Indian times, the exhibits carry prehistory forward chronologically to historic time. Of particular interest are the Weeden Island culture ceramic artifacts. There is also a large exhibit of Fort Walton pottery.

The mound, on top of which a temple once stood, has been restored. Archeologists have estimated that Indians constructed the mound by moving 500,000 basketloads of earth.

Indians pecked these circular designs on a granite boulder near Etowah Mounds, in Georgia. The boulder is now on the campus of Reinhardt College, Waleska, Georgia. Margaret Perryman Smith photo, courtesy Campbell Grant.

Georgia

COLUMBUS MUSEUM OF ARTS AND SCIENCES

1251 Wynnton Rd., Columbus, GA 31906. Phone: 404/322-0400. Open free, Tuesday–Saturday; afternoon, Sunday. Closed certain holidays.

Here are displays of artifacts from Paleo through Mississippian cultures. Dioramas show how a site is excavated and how Archaic and Mississippian people lived.

ETOWAH MOUNDS STATE HISTORIC SITE
(ET-oh-wah)
National Historic Landmark

From US 41 at Cartersville, drive 1 mile west on the Georgia 61 Spur, then continue 2 miles following directional signs to museum and headquarters. Mail address: Route 2, Cartersville, GA 30120. Phone: 404/382-2704. Open Tuesday–Saturday; afternoon, Sunday. Closed certain holidays. Admission charged. Camping nearby.

The museum at this site gives an excellent general view of prehistoric life in the area, beginning about 5000 B.C., and at the same time it provides real insight into what archeologists do as they search for information about the past. Of special interest is the period beginning about A.D. 1000, when Etowah was occupied by people who built temple mounds.

During excavation archeologists were astonished at the richness of the grave goods they found buried in tombs, particularly those discovered at the foot of one of the mounds. Exhibits in the museum show something of the society that produced this wealth and the gorgeous costumes worn by some of the inhabitants of Etowah. This relatively small group must have had high status in the community, though exactly what it was is not entirely clear. Members of the group certainly had special privileges, including the right to be buried with ritual objects.

Ornaments and ceremonial paraphernalia found in the graves were often made of materials from distant places, and one exhibit in the museum traces the amazing extent of trade—obsidian and grizzly bear teeth from the Rocky Mountains, for example, and turtle shell and shark's teeth from the seacoast. Very similar grave goods have been found in burials at other Southeastern sites, indicating that finished objects may have been traded among various communities. Beautifully worked stone axes, engraved copper headdresses, and large stone knives unsuited for work of any kind indicate that skilled craftsworkers created the objects for ceremonial purposes, and perhaps they themselves were among the elite group.

Exhibits in the museum include explanations of the ceremonial paraphernalia. The grounds outside are worth a walk, and a superb view of the entire area rewards the visitor who makes the steep climb to the top of the large mound in the Etowah complex.

Present-day visitors at Etowah Mounds State Historic Site, in Georgia, can climb steps on the same ramp used by prehistoric Indians when they went to the building which stood on the flat top of the large mound, at right in this aerial photograph. Georgia Historical Commission photo.

As archeologists dug at Etowah Mounds State Historic Site, they came across evidence of an ancient structure. The rows of holes show where upright wall posts once stood. Georgia Historical Commission photo.

FORT KING GEORGE HISTORIC SITE

From Darien take exit 10 off Interstate 95. Mail address: P.O. Box 711, Darien, GA 31305. Phone: 912/437-4770. Open Tuesday–Saturday; afternoon, Sunday. Admission charged.

Here is a Native American village site. Included with historic material in the museum are prehistoric artifacts some of which are dated to about 3000 B.C. One of the exhibits is a dugout canoe.

FORT MOUNTAIN STATE PARK

From Chatsworth drive 7 miles southeast on US 76 and Georgia 52. Mail address: Route 3, Box 1K, Chatsworth, GA 30705. Phone: 404/695-2621. Open free, during daylight hours. Camping nearby.

In this park at the southern end of the Blue Ridge Mountains at an elevation of 2800 feet is a wall 855 feet long. It zigzags serpent-like between two cliffs. Some archeologists think this structure was built for ceremonial purposes by Woodland Indians at least 1000 years ago.

KOLOMOKI MOUNDS STATE PARK
(koh-loh-MOH-kee)

From Blakely drive 2 miles north on US 27, then follow directional signs 4 miles to the Visitor Center Museum and mounds. Mail address: Blakely, GA 31723. Phone: 912/723-5296. Open Tuesday–Saturday; afternoon, Sunday. Closed certain holidays. Admission charged. Camping. This site includes the largest mound group in the Gulf Coast area and is also noteworthy because of the very careful detective work done by the archeologists who have excavated and interpreted it.

The Story. Hunters probably camped here several thousand years ago, beside an artesian spring near Little Kolomoki Creek, but the earliest visitors left only the scantiest of traces. Then a succession of peoples visited the area, at least briefly, during a period of several thousand years. By about A.D. 700 a small village had been established, and women were making pottery that resembled the kind made at Weeden Island, farther south. From then on the populations grew, and a distinct Kolomoki lifeway developed.

The daily existence of the ordinary people must have differed greatly from that of the leaders. Commoners did the work of farming, doubtless following patterns of behavior that were widespread throughout the Southeast. The leaders, on the other hand, probably did no farm work. Rather they acted as executives who directed public projects and supervised and organized ceremonies and rituals in the temple on top of the platform mound or in the plaza at the foot of the mound.

One of the complex operations connected with ritual activity was the manufacture of grave goods. First the raw material had to be obtained—shell from the Gulf of Mexico, copper, galena, and mica from much more distant places. These materials were transformed by craftsworkers into ornaments and other artifacts buried with the bodies of important people.

All of this activity was coordinated by members of the ruling group. They supervised at least a thousand men, women, and children, who must have been involved in the final construction of the pyramid. At that time the work

This ceremonial earth lodge at Ocmulgee National Monument has been reconstructed over the original clay floor. National Park Service photo.

force dug, carried, and dumped the heavy clay necessary to create a cap six feet thick, covering the top of the pyramid, which measured 325 feet by 200 feet at its base.

An almost equally large crew of workers had to be directed when it came time to raise a mound for the burial of an important personage at Kolomoki. For such a burial laborers first dug a large pit, about seven feet deep. Then the cremated bones were laid in the bottom, together with ornaments, beads, and precious possessions. Next, large rocks were brought in (one measured 6 × 3 × 2 feet) to fill the hole about halfway. When this had been covered with a large, rounded heap of clay and more stones, graves at the side were made for wives and other members of the household, who were sacrificed. Quantities of specially made mortuary pottery accompanied these burials. Continuous processions of workers added layers of earth and clay, some of which they had to bring from a spot half a mile away, in the side of a steep bluff.

The finished burial mounds were as much as 50 feet in diameter and from 6 to 20 feet high. To complete the mortuary ceremonies more people were sacrificed. Why do archeologists suspect there were sacrifices? Excavation shows that numerous heads with no bodies attached had been buried in the mounds. Many of the heads bore decorations in just the positions they would have had if held there by skin and hair. Where copper ornaments were present, there were even bits of skin and hair left on the bone as a result of the preservative action of the copper. In other words, recently severed heads had been buried, not fleshless skulls. A likely explanation was that the heads were cut off in the course of human sacrifice.

The Museum. Exhibits illustrate Kolomoki life—hunting, cooking, fishing, planting, house building, pottery making, working with copper, and making decorations of shell. Dioramas and paintings show construction of mounds, and there are fine displays of pottery, especially the kind used only as mortuary ware. Exhibits also give an idea of life in several earlier periods, when people with quite different cultural patterns lived here.

OCMULGEE NATIONAL MONUMENT
(ohk-MULL-ghee)

At the southeast edge of Macon on US 80. Mail address: 1207 Emery Highway, Macon, GA 31201. Phone: 912/752-8257. Open free, daily. Closed December 25 and January 1.

Ocmulgee was the first large site in the Southeast to be scientifically investigated. Temple mounds, a reconstructed ceremonial building, and exhibits in the museum at the Visitor Center recreate the whole history of Indian life in central Georgia.

The Story. The first people to enter Georgia seem to have arrived about 8000 B.C. They were Paleo-Indians, hunters of mammoths and other Ice-Age game. A very small, wandering population remained in the area for about 3000 years. Some who camped near Ocmulgee left behind a projectile point, many scrapers, and a few other tools.

Interior view of the earth lodge at Ocmulgee National Monument. The raised platform, shaped like a bird of prey, has three places where dignitaries sat during ceremonies or councils. National Park Service photo.

When the big game disappeared, hunters turned to new ways of getting food. In some parts of the Southeast they discovered they could lead an easier life by harvesting freshwater clams and mussels. However, those who camped at Ocmulgee did not become shellfish eaters. The equipment they left behind shows that they continued hunting, although the game now consisted of smaller animals. When game was scarce in one place the hunters moved on to another, following a route that brought them back repeatedly to their old campsite at Ocmulgee.

Not long after 1000 B.C. a whole new way of life began in this part of Georgia. People had learned to grow food in gardens. They cultivated pumpkins, beans, and sunflowers, and this food supply made it possible to live in villages. Settlement allowed women to adopt an invention that had been in use much earlier in other parts of the Southeast—crude pottery. These early Woodland farmers gradually expanded their gardens, and now they had more free time. Arts and crafts developed. Their pottery improved.

About A.D. 900 some aggressive people of the Early Mississippian culture invaded the area. Just where they came from no one knows for sure, possibly from the Mississippi Valley near the mouth of the Missouri River, possibly from Tennessee. Whatever their origin, they drove out the earlier inhabitants and began intensive and very successful corn farming.

The newcomers also brought along elaborate political and religious customs and the habit of building very large ceremonial lodges entirely covered with earth. Here at Ocmulgee one of these earth lodges, constructed rather like a huge Eskimo igloo, has been restored. The roof is new, but it was possible to keep the original floor intact. This was made of a special clay which packs down very hard when walked on.

Meticulous work in excavating the earth lodge revealed that it was used and then burned—perhaps accidentally, but more probably as part of a ritual or as a safety measure. The earthen roof was heavy and often damp, and the supporting beams must have rotted quickly. Fortunately for archeologists, the burned wood collapsed and

Mound building took many forms in the Southeast. Rock Eagle Effigy Mound near Eatonton, Georgia, can be seen in its entirety from the top of a tower which has been built for the convenience of visitors. The effigy is made up of thousands of white quartz rocks.

preserved the circular floor with its molded seats for 47 people around the edge. At one end is a platform in the shape of a raptor, designed in a way that was popular all over the Southeast in late prehistoric times. Apparently important people sat on the platform, where there are seats for three.

The lodge was a place for religious ceremonies and civic gatherings, particularly those held in winter. Because of its thousand-year-old floor, it has been called the oldest public building site in the United States.

Across an open space opposite the earth lodge stands a large, flat-topped mound nearly 50 feet tall. Like many other great mounds in the Southeast, this one served as the foundation for a temple. The original temple stood on a low platform. After a time this building was burned, perhaps when a leader died, and the site was entirely covered with earth, which served as the foundation for a new temple. This pattern of destruction and rebuilding went on, again and again.

Over a period of 200 years other, smaller mounds supported additional temples, and at one end of the village is a mound which apparently served as a cemetery. All of this building took a vast amount of time. More work, too, went into digging moats or ditches, which may have served for protection. What happened in the end at Ocmulgee is something of a mystery.

Possibly descendants of the earlier people mingled with newcomers and settled nearby. Certainly people who shared traits with both the Woodland and Mississippian people developed what is known as the Lamar culture and built mounds nearby. Some of their descendants became Creek Indians of historic times.

The Museum. All of this story—and much more—is told in the museum. Models and dioramas illuminate various aspects of the lives of those who inhabited the area for 10,000 years. Exhibits display many artifacts, including a large collection of pipes.

Among the special exhibits of pottery is one showing how women at Ocmulgee made and decorated their vessels. Visitors who are familiar with

Diorama of an Indian ceremony at Ocmulgee National Monument. National Park Service photo by Jack E. Boucher.

pottery making in other parts of the country will find interesting differences here.

The Name. Ocmulgee comes from a Creek Indian word meaning "bubbling, boiling water."

After the Creeks were forced to leave the Southeast in the 1800s, they made new homes for themselves in Oklahoma, where they called one of their towns Okmulgee—the old name, spelled differently.

ROCK EAGLE EFFIGY MOUND

From Eatonton drive 7 miles north on US 441 to the Rock Eagle 4-H Center. Mail address: 350 Rock Eagle Road, N.W., Eatonton, GA 31024. Phone: 404/485-2831. Open free, at all times. Camping.

Prehistoric Indians carried great numbers of white, quartz rocks a considerable distance to use in building this effigy which is in the shape of a huge bird, called an eagle by some archeologists, a buzzard by others. The wings stretch out across a flat hilltop for 120 feet, tip to tip, and the depth

of the original rockpile is thought to have been about 10 feet. At the foot of the bird a modern tower has been constructed so that visitors can see the whole of it, looking down from above. Another bird effigy of this sort is in the vicinity and is scheduled to be open to the public by 1994.

The date when the effigy was built and its purpose are not known, but archeologists believe it must have marked a ceremonial gathering place. Excavation revealed a small pointed quartz tool and some fragments of calcined and unburned human, bird, and animal bones.

ROOD CREEK MOUNDS

From Columbus drive south on Georgia 27. About 11 miles south of Cusseta turn west on Georgia 39 and follow signs to Florence Marina Visitor Center. This site is managed by the U.S. Army Corps of Engineers. Phone: 912/838-4706. Open Saturdays, all year. Admission charged.

Here are eight mounds that served as a center for political and ceremonial

Women who once lived at Swift Creek, Georgia, used implements like these to press designs into their pottery while the clay was still moist.

activities in the Mississippian period. Visits to the mounds may be made only with a tour conducted every Saturday morning, lasting about 1.5 hours. At the Visitor Center are exhibits of prehistoric artifacts.

THRONATEESKA HERITAGE FOUNDATION MUSEUM

100 Roosevelt Ave., Albany, GA 31701. Phone: 912/432-6955. Open free, Tuesday–Saturday. Closed certain holidays.

In this general museum are some prehistoric projectile points from the Paleo period together with tools and pottery from the Archaic, Woodland and Mississippian periods. Most of the material comes from sites in Georgia.

TRACK ROCK ARCHAEOLOGICAL AREA, CHATTAHOOCHEE NATIONAL FOREST

From Blairsville drive 8 miles south on US 19, then east 5 miles on Forest Service Road 95 to marker. Mail address: Georgia Department of Natural Resources, 205 Butler St. SE, Atlanta, GA 30334. Phone (at the site): 404/536-0541. Open free, at all times. Camping nearby.

Here, in a 52-acre area are preserved rock carvings of ancient Indian origin; they resemble animal and bird tracks, crosses, circles, and human footprints.

Pebble Tools

Knowing the trick, a person can pick up a certain kind of water-worn pebble or cobble, strike it a few times with a hammerstone, and make it into a useful tool for chopping. Pebble tools of this kind were among the earliest created by humans, and they have been found by the ton on the surface of the ground in certain parts of Alabama.

Did recent Indian hunters knock out these artifacts for one-time or emergency use? Or were the choppers made a very long time ago by people whose tool kit was very, very simple? These questions occurred to archeologists, both amateur and professional, as they encountered thousands of rounded stones that had distinct chopping or cutting edges. Often the stones looked very old because they had weathered deeply. Always they resembled tools found in the Old World, which were known to be very ancient. However, there seemed to be no way to discover the exact age of the Alabama artifacts. Even when the tools were found buried in the earth, luck has not been with the diggers. So far dating has been uncertain.

As a result, a fascinating mystery remains unsolved. Some archeologists suspect that the pebble tools are evidence that people who did not know how to make stone projectile points lived in America before the days of the big-game-hunting Paleo-Indians. Other archeologists think the pebble tools may have been made in a hurry by much later people, who regarded them as expendable.

Louisiana

LOUISIANA STATE EXHIBIT MUSEUM

3015 Greenwood Rd., P.O. Box 9067, Shreveport, LA 71139. Phone: 318/226-7123. Open free, Monday–Saturday; afternoon, Sunday. Closed December 25 and January 1.

Displays of Paleo-Indian and other projectile points can be seen in the Capitol Historical Gallery of this museum. Exhibits from mounds, including the Gahagan Mound in Red River Parish, show examples of ornaments, pottery, and other artifacts. Among the exhibits is a 1000-year-old dugout canoe.

Special Feature. A large diorama, built under the guidance of an archeologist, shows the Poverty Point Site in northern Louisiana when it was a flourishing village. (See entry below.)

Although no one can be sure exactly what the Poverty Point dwellings looked like, those in the diorama show the probable shape of huts thatched with grass, palmetto leaves, or bark.

The appearance of the women is based on figurines made of baked clay found at the site. (No male figurines seem to have been made.) The women wore short, belted skirts in summer and probably heavier deerskin clothing in cold weather. One of the figurines shows a woman carrying a baby on a cradleboard.

LOUISIANA STATE UNIVERSITY, MUSEUM OF GEOSCIENCE

On the campus, Baton Rouge, LA 70803. Phone: 504/388-2934. Open during university sessions Saturday, afternoon Sunday. Phone for summer hours and weekday group tours. Closed certain holidays. Admission charged.

In this museum devoted chiefly to earth sciences is an Indian room that contains artifacts and dioramas representing prehistoric Native American life.

Special Feature. Jack E. Anglim, who later became chief exhibits specialist for the Smithsonian Institution in Washington, created the dioramas that show prehistoric scenes. He based his work on information collected from digs

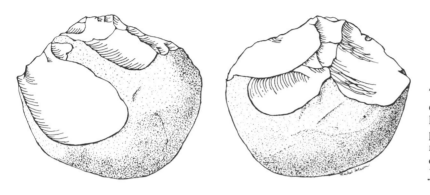

The pebble tool was one of the earliest implements developed by humans. These two views are of a pebble tool from Alabama, where many such artifacts have been discovered. After Lively and Josselyn.

conducted by the Works Progress Administration in the 1930s. One diorama represents a Troyville-Coles Creek temple mound. Another presents a Marksville burial mound. The third shows a Tchufuncte camp site.

Anglim miniaturized a dig by such devices as using mousebones to represent human bones. He made skulls from beeswax, used chemically treated parsley to create trees and bushes, and converted steel wool into Spanish moss and oatmeal into shells.

MARKSVILLE STATE COMMEMORATIVE AREA

Adjacent to Marksville on Louisiana 5. Mail address: 700 Martin Luther King Drive, Marksville, LA 71351. Phone: 318/253-8954. Open daily. Closed certain holidays. Admission charged.

In a 40-acre tract at this site are several burial and temple mounds and a museum, which offers an audiovisual program.

The Story. As early as 1500 B.C. people seem to have used this site, which was then close to the Mississippi River.

Eventually the river shifted course, and its banks are now 30 miles away. Today Old River Lake is all that remains of the ancient channel. About A.D. 300 a permanent village began to grow here along the riverbank, and in unbroken sequence, until about the time Europeans arrived, the Marksville people increased their food supply and the range and variety of their implements, art forms, and religious customs.

Three types of mound were build at different times over a period of two millenia. Some are refuse heaps or middens, some conical burial mounds, some temple mounds. One, no longer in its original shape, was a conical mound atop a truncated pyramid.

Archeologists have found this site of great interest. Excavation was done by the Smithsonian Institution, and Louisiana State University, in cooperation with the Works Progress Administration.

Exhibits in the museum installed under the supervision of Dr. James A. Ford, of the American Museum of Natural History, and Robert S. Neitzel of the Louisiana State Parks and Rec-

reation Commission, display material recovered in the course of the excavations and illustrate the many changes in the lives of those who lived here for such a long time.

During the period of occupation when people were building burial mounds, they were greatly influenced by the Hopewell lifeway, which centered far to the north. A special variant of Hopewell has been called Marksville, after this site, where it was first identified.

Aerial photographs in the museum show the large number of mounds in and near the area and the relation of these mounds to the former bed of the Mississippi River.

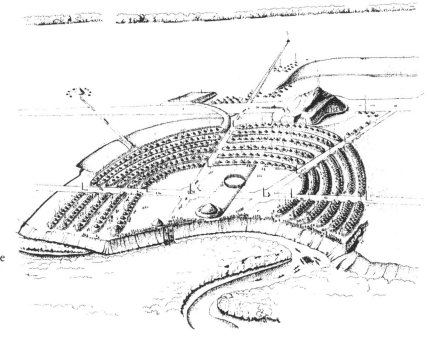

The Poverty Point Site as it may have looked 2500 years ago. From *Poverty Point*, by J.C. Gibson, Louisiana Archaeological Survey and Antiquities Commission, Anthropological Study No. 7.

POVERTY POINT STATE COMMEMORATIVE AREA

From Interstate 20 drive north on Louisiana 17 to Epps, then northeast on Louisiana 577. Mail address: Box 208A, Epps, LA 71237. Phone: 318/926-5492. Open daily. Admission charged.

This site went almost unnoticed until 1953, when Dr. James A. Ford examined an aerial photograph taken by an Army mapmaker. The photograph revealed a mound and long, low hummocks of earth, which had been laid out in a very definite geometric pattern. These proved to be a series of artificial terraces, built in the form of six concentric arcs. The whole configuration measured more than .75 mile across, and its very size concealed its real nature.

Archeological work at the site soon told an amazing story. Apparently several thousand people at a time lived in this settlement for more than a thousand years, beginning perhaps about 1500 B.C., and the construction they did was remarkable.

To form the terraces, on which they placed their dwellings, people carried earth and heaped it to a height of 6 feet or more. Each terrace was about 80 feet wide at the base, and there were six of them, one inside the other. The total linear measurement of these concentric ridges added up to 7.4 miles.

On the west side of the village these same people built a ceremonial mound, 700 feet by 800 feet at the base and 72 feet high. About a mile due north they put up another large mound, also used for ceremonies. One other was cone-shaped and contained evidence of cremation. Archeologists have estimated that workers transported 20 million basketloads of earth, 50 pounds at a time to build the earthwork.

The bow and arrow were not known at Poverty Point. Like other Archaic people, the men used spear-throwers. Hunters may also have captured large birds with bolas. These were weights, either oval or pear-shaped, tied at the ends of strings in groups of three or more. The hunter whirled the weighted strings around and released them at just the right moment to make them wrap themselves around the birds.

The special hematite used for the bola weights had to be imported from Southwestern Arkansas or southern Missouri, some distance away. Other material that Poverty Point people wanted came from even more remote places. They got flint from Ohio, slate from the vicinity of Lake Michigan, and copper from Lake Superior. Soapstone for making pots may have come by dugout canoe or raft as much as 500 miles, from a quarry in North Carolina.

The Macon (pronounced: mason) Ridge close by has no stone—a fact that led to a curious invention called the Poverty Point object. Each of these objects was molded from a small handful of top soil, then baked as hard as rock. Some were roughly spherical. Others were carefully made in other geometric shapes. The balls were then used in cooking. First the women dug a pit in the ground. Next they fashioned some of the balls from soil, laid them in the pit, and built a fire over them. Presently they raked out the coals and the hard-baked balls, lined the hot pit with grass, laid food on the grass, covered it with the heated balls and left it to cook, clam-bake style. Women made, according to estimates, 24 million of the balls during the period the village was occupied.

Another unusual trait of Poverty Point people was their use of very small, sharp stone tools called microflints. These may have been drills or punches.

Some archeologists have speculated that the Poverty Point mounds were inspired by pyramid building in Mexico. Recent research, however, seems to indicate that the mounds do not really resemble Mexican structures and that they were a local phenomenon.

Agriculture played little part in life at Poverty Point. Its inhabitants gathered food from the fertile land and river and did some hunting, but they had some customs characteristic of farmers everywhere. For example, they made female figurines, probably thinking thus to encourage fertility. They had grinding implements as did people who raised corn in Mexico. The very fact that they built geometric earthworks suggests agriculture. Their mounds were so constructed that the equinox could be recognized when the sun rose directly in line with certain features of the earthworks. Such information about the seasons was always of importance to farmers or to people who wanted to keep track of the seasons when wild food would be ready to harvest.

Much about this unusual site remains a mystery. What kind of social organization made possible the immense labor people put into the earthworks? How did they carry on extensive trade? What was the significance of the mound in the shape of a bird?

Details of the Poverty Point lifestyle may be seen in exhibits in the Visitor Center museum which include an exquisitely carved tiny crystal owl and other bird effigies. There are also sightseeing trails and an observation tower where visitors may view the overall design of the site.

TUNICA-BILOXI REGIONAL INDIAN CENTER AND MUSEUM

On the Tunica-Biloxi Reservation, Louisiana Highway 1, in Marksville. Mail address: P.O. Box 231, Marksville, LA 71351. Phone: 318/253-8174. Open Tuesday–Sunday. Admission charged.

This museum, staffed by members of the Tunica-Biloxi Tribe, is built to resemble a prehistoric temple mound. It houses an assemblage of artifacts, largely historic, that is called the "Tunica Treasure."

The prehistoric part of this "treasure" is included among artifacts that Leonard Chartier dug out of graves of ancestors of the Tunica-Biloxi people. Chartier, a guard at the Louisiana State Prison, expected to make a fortune from the sale of the results of his pot hunting. The Peabody Museum of Harvard University obtained the material, but never paid Chartier for the stolen goods. In time the material came into the possession of the state of Louisiana. Finally the 20th Judicial District Court decided that the Tunica-Biloxi Tribe, not Chartier or the state of Louisiana, was the rightful owner of the grave offerings.

Although only a small part of the "treasure" is prehistoric, the museum which now protects it, interprets the past lifeway of the once powerful Tunica Tribe. The surviving members of the tribe have been greatly encouraged by the recovery of things that belonged to their ancestors, and they are building a Tunica Historical Village, scheduled to open as this book went to press. The Tunica-Biloxi Tribe has also acquired and operates the Marksville State Commemorative Area Museum (see above).

WILLIAMSON MUSEUM

Two miles east of Interstate 49 on Highway 6 at 210 Kyser Hall, Northwestern State University, Natchitoches, LA 71497. Phone: 318/357-4364. Open free, Monday–Friday when university is in session.

In an extensive Southeastern Indian collection are prehistoric materials, particularly Caddoan. The museum curates collections for several important Louisiana sites.

The National Museum of the American Indian, Smithsonian Institution, has this water jar from Louisiana in its collection. The prehistoric potter incised the intricate design on the moist clay before firing the vessel.

Pottery bowl made in the Mississippian Period. Original at Mississippi State University.

Mississippi

COBB INSTITUTE OF ARCHAEOLOGY
(*See Mississippi State University*)

GRAND VILLAGE OF THE NATCHEZ INDIANS
National Historic Landmark

In Natchez from US 61 (Seargent S. Prentiss Drive) turn onto Jefferson Davis Boulevard which leads to the Grand Village. Mail address: 400 Jefferson Davis Boulevard, Natchez, MS 39120. Phone: 601/446-6502. Open free, daily, all year.

At this site, which reached its greatest importance about A.D. 1500, are plaza areas and platform mounds, three of which have been restored. Museum exhibits and educational programs interpret the life of the people who built the mounds. The Natchez disappeared as a people after their defeat by the French at this site in 1730.

MISSISSIPPI STATE HISTORICAL MUSEUM

Capitol and North State Streets, Jackson. Mail address: P.O. Box 571, Jackson, MS 39205. Phone: 601/359-6920. Open free, Monday–Saturday; afternoon, Sunday. Closed major holidays.

Archeological artifacts on exhibit represent the Archaic, Woodland, and Mississippian eras in the state. Plans are under way to install new interpretive exhibits on the prehistoric and protohistoric eras.

MISSISSIPPI STATE UNIVERSITY, COBB INSTITUTE OF ARCHAEOLOGY

On the campus, Mississippi State. Mail address: P.O. Drawer AR, Mississippi State, MS 39762. Phone: 601/325-3826. Open free, Monday–Friday. Closed certain holidays.

Some exhibits contain material of the Mississippian culture.

NANIH WAIYA HISTORIC SITE

From Louisville drive 12 miles south on Mississippi 397, then right 2 miles on Mississippi 490, then left 5 miles on Mississippi 393 to Nanih Waiyah State Park. Open free, daily.

There is a mound at this site where Native Americans lived for about 1500 years before contact with Europeans.

NATCHEZ TRACE PARKWAY

In the late 1930s the National Park Service began constructing a parkway that closely follows ancient Indian trails, now called the Natchez Trace, that went between Natchez in Mississippi to Nashville in Tennessee. As this book went to press 410 miles of the 450 miles between the two cities had been completed. For up-to-date information write to Natchez Trace Parkway, RR1, NT-143, Tupelo, MS 38801. Phone: 601/842-1572.

Within the boundaries of the Mississippi portion of the parkway are groups of prehistoric mounds that the Park Service has prepared for visitation. They are listed here in the order

Emerald Mound, a ceremonial site near Natchez Trace Parkway. National Park Service photo by Don Black.

of their location beginning at the Natchez end of the parkway. All are open free.

Emerald Mound
(Parkway milepost 10.3)

Emerald Mound is the second largest temple mound in the United States. Its base measures 770 by 435 feet and covers nearly eight acres. Only Monks Mound, in Cahokia Mounds Historic Site in Illinois is larger. Two interpretive panels at the site tell how Indians constructed this immense earthwork.

The Story. People who followed the Mississippian lifeway began to build Emerald Mound about A.D. 1250, and they continued to live here until about A.D. 1600. After finishing the huge, flat-topped platform, they went on to add at one end of it a second mound, itself as large as many of those in the Southeast that rest directly on the ground. On the principal mound there may once have been many ceremonial structures, and on top of the second one there was certainly a temple.

The whole Emerald Mound complex served as a ceremonial center for farmers who lived nearby in thatch-covered houses, which had walls plastered with clay. These people made fine pottery and were skilled at fabricating a variety of tools and ornaments. As did the earlier farmers at Bynum Mounds (see entry below), they obtained some of their materials from the Gulf Coast, and their copper came from far away to the north, near Lake Superior. What happened to them in the end is something of a mystery, but Emerald Mound, like many others, was still in use when De Soto's marauding expedition passed through the Southeast in A.D. 1540–1541. Many other mounds, including the important Anna Mound group, dot this vicinity, but since none of them have been prepared for the public they cannot be visited.

Archeological excavations here reveal a close connection between these mound builders and the Natchez Indians whom De Soto met.

Mangum Mound
(Parkway milepost 45.7)

Copper ornaments and other artifacts found in burials here have revealed much to archeologists about the people who built the mound. Interpretive signs, a map, four exhibits, and an audio station provide explanations of the site.

Boyd Mounds
(Parkway milepost 106.9)

This village site with several burial mounds is marked with an interpretive sign, and an audio station tells the story of the Indians who lived here. These mounds were built up gradually as a cemetery between A.D. 1300 and A.D. 1500.

Bynum Mounds
(Parkway milepost 232.4)

Here is a group of burial mounds, two of which can easily be seen from a hard surfaced path. An interpretive panel and short audio program give information about the far-flung trading activities of the Indians who once lived at the site.

The Story. The site was first occupied from around 100 B.C. for about 300 years. About A.D. 700, people who followed the Middle Woodland way of life settled here and built circular houses thatched with grass. They hunted, fished, gathered wild fruits and nuts, and they may also have maintained small gardens. After a time they adopted the custom, popular elsewhere during this period, of building earthen mounds over the remains of the dead. Altogether six of these burial mounds were constructed in the vicinity of their village.

Gradually life became richer and more complex for the Bynum people. They obtained materials for weapons, ornaments, and tools by trading with other Indians who lived in distant places. Flint came from Ohio, marine shells from the Gulf Coast, and greenstone for their grooved and polished axes from Alabama. Like the people at Emerald Mound, they imported copper from Lake Superior. Why they abandoned this site about A.D. 800 no one knows. In the early 1800s Chickasaws, who may have been descendants of the builders of these mounds, settled here.

Chickasaw Village Site
(Parkway milepost 261.8)

In exhibits at the site of an ancient village the daily life of Chickasaw Indians is described. A short nature trail with interpretive signs describes Indian uses of plants and an audio program tells of Chickasaw Village life before their removal to Oklahoma in the 1830s.

Tupelo Visitor Center
Natchez Trace Parkway
(Parkway milepost 266.0)

On Natchez Trace Parkway, 2 miles north of the Tupelo entrance (from US 78). Open free, daily, all year. Closed December 25.

On display here are some of the artifacts and other objects found in the excavation of prehistoric Indian mounds and villages along the parkway. A free film program introduces both the prehistory and the history of the trace. A library contains all the research reports on the excavations along the parkway.

Pharr Mounds
(Parkway milepost 286.7)

This site was first occupied about 2500 B.C. Here are eight large, dome-shaped burial mounds, scattered over an area of 90 acres, built and used from about A.D. 1 to 200 by nomadic hunters and gatherers, who returned to the site at times to bury the dead with their possessions. Archeological investigations also revealed on the same site a Woodland period palisaded village that was occupied about A.D. 1000 to 1200.

An interpretive shelter houses three exhibits that explain how the mounds were constructed and used.

Bear Creek Mound
(Parkway milepost 308.8)

Here is a ceremonial mound and an adjacent village. The site was occupied intermittently beginning as early as 7000 B.C. by hunters.

OWL CREEK INDIAN MOUNDS, TOMBIGBEE NATIONAL FOREST

From Houston on Mississippi 8 drive 10 miles north on Mississippi 15 to Old Houlka, then east on Forest Service Rd. 903 for 4.5 miles to the parking area near the mounds. Open free, at all times. Camping at Davis Lake, 1.5 miles from the mounds.

Here, near the place where De Soto made his winter camp, are two reconstructed ceremonial mounds. These, together with three other mounds, once surrounded a village plaza.

WINTERVILLE MOUNDS STATE PARK

From Greenville drive north 10 miles on Mississippi 1. Open Wednesday–Saturday; afternoon, Sunday. Closed certain holidays. Admission charged.

A large, Mississippian-period ceremonial center was built here about A.D. 1200–1400. The great main mound is about 55 feet high. A museum in the Visitor Center contains an outstanding collection of artifacts, some of which were excavated from the site by Jeffrey Brain of the Peabody Museum.

A section of the ancient trail used by Native Americans walking between Tennessee and Mississippi. The modern Natchez Trace Parkway follows the same general route. Along the way are the remains of a number of mounds near which the National Park Service has placed interpretive markers. National Park Service photo.

At Oconaluftee Indian Village a Cherokee Indian demonstrates how his ancestors made a dugout canoe by hollowing out a log with the help of fire and a stone axe.

North Carolina

CATAWBA COLLEGE, MUSEUM OF ANTHROPOLOGY

At the north edge of Salisbury off US 601 on Brenner Ave., Heath Hill Forest, South Campus of Catawba College, Salisbury, NC 28144. Open free, most afternoons. For confirmation write, or phone 704/637-4111.

Archeological exhibits in this museum emphasize the South Atlantic Piedmont. They include lithic technology.

Visitors who have special interests are given free guided tours that include the Research Laboratory of Archaeology.

GREENSBORO HISTORICAL MUSEUM

130 Summit Ave., Greensboro, NC 27401. Phone: 919/373-2043. Open free, Tuesday–Saturday; afternoon, Sunday. Closed certain holidays.

Exhibits of artifacts collected in the Piedmont area represent 16 cultures from Paleo-Indian times to about A.D. 1700.

MORROW MOUNTAIN STATE PARK NATURAL HISTORY MUSEUM

From Albemarle on US 52 or North Carolina 24 and 27, drive to junction with North Carolina 740 and follow directional signs to park entrance. Mail address: Route 5, Box 430, Albemarle, NC 28001. Phone: 704/982-4402. Open free, daily, summer; weekends the rest of the year.

In this small natural history museum an archeological display contains artifacts from each of the local cultures along with explanations of their use.

In the reconstructed Council House, Oconaluftee Indian Village, a Cherokee woman describes the social and cultural life of the Cherokees, 250 years ago.

MUSEUM OF THE CHEROKEE

On US 441 at Drama Rd., Cherokee, NC 28719. Phone: 704/497-3481. Open daily, all year. Closed certain holidays. Admission charged.

Exhibits and audiovisual programs tell the story of Cherokee life from prehistoric times to the present.

OCONALUFTEE INDIAN VILLAGE

From Cherokee drive north on US 441 to intersection with North Carolina 19; turn at directional sign and drive .5 mile to village entrance. Mail address: P.O. Box 398, Cherokee, NC 28719. Phone: 704/497-2315. Open daily, mid-May–October. Admission charged. Camping nearby.

In this reconstructed Cherokee Indian village an ancient way of life is recreated in authentic detail. Well-informed Cherokee guides escort the visitor through the village, where live demonstrations of Cherokee skills, crafts, and art as practiced over 200 years ago are demonstrated. In the council house and on the square-ground, lecturers explain important points of Cherokee culture. Plants used by the Indians are identified in an herb garden and along a nature trail.

SCHIELE MUSEUM OF NATURAL HISTORY

1500 E. Garrison Blvd., Gastonia, NC 28053. Phone: 704/866-6900. Open free, Tuesday–Friday; afternoons, Saturday and Sunday.

Materials from sites in North Carolina illustrate Paleo, Archaic, and Woodland cultures. Dioramas show the domestic activities of Mesa Verde, pre-Columbian Cherokee, and other peoples.

SCIENCE MUSEUMS OF CHARLOTTE, INC.

Discovery Place, 301 N. Tryon Street, Charlotte, NC 28202. Phone: 704/372-6261. Open daily, all year. Closed certain holidays. Admission charged.

In this museum exhibits rotate. The collection includes pre-Columbian artifacts from North America.

At Town Creek Indian Mound is a reconstructed palisade, surrounding a temple that looks the same as it did 400 years ago. North Carolina Department of Agriculture photo.

TOWN CREEK INDIAN MOUND STATE HISTORIC SITE

From Mount Gilead drive east on North Carolina 73, then north on State Rd. 1160 toward North Carolina 731 to directional sign; total distance, about 5.5 miles from Mount Gilead. Mail address: Route 3, Box 50, Mt. Gilead, NC 27306. Phone: 919/439-6802. Open free, April 1–October 31, Monday–Saturday; afternoon, Sunday; November–March 31, Tuesday–Saturday; afternoon, Sunday. Closed certain holidays. Phone: 919/439-6802. Guided tours on weekdays by reservation. Camping nearby.

The Story. Midway in the fifteenth century a group of energetic, aggressive people entered this area, driving out the earlier inhabitants. These newcomers, like the invaders who took over Ocmulgee in Georgia, had been influenced by the Mississippian culture. They were farmers who had extraordinary ability to make the land productive. They also had some very distinctive customs. Along with their practical skill they brought a whole constellation of religious ideas, building habits, ceremonial practices, and even a game called chunkey.

On a high bluff, near the place where a stream now called Town Creek joins the Little River, the newcomers made a clearing and surrounded it with a high palisade of logs interwoven with cane. Two openings in the palisade served as entrances, but there was also a third, half underground, along the bluff. Inside the palisade they leveled off a plaza and around it, as time passed, they built ceremonial structures. The main one was a mound, constructed in one layer after another, starting with a low platform on which a religious building or temple stood. Later the mound was enlarged and made higher, as a base for another temple. At the center of the plaza stood a group of ceremonial buildings arranged in a square. Across the plaza from the major temple is a reconstruction of a minor temple which probably served as the home of the high priest.

The newcomers occupied their village at Town Creek for only about 200 years. During that time they seem to

A restored painting in the temple, also restored, at Town Creek Indian Mound State Historical Site. North Carolina Department of Agriculture photo.

have been at war often with their neighbors. But whether they gave up in defeat or left for some other reason no one knows. After their departure in the early seventeenth century, bands of people who had very different customs moved in. They spoke a language related to the language of the Sioux Indians of the West, and they were living there when Europeans first came.

The Museum. In the museum in the Visitor Center are an audiovisual program and displays of material discovered during excavation of the site. Archeologists have investigated most of the ceremonial area, and based on their data and on historical records, reconstructions have been built of the major temple, the earthen mound, a minor temple, a mortuary, a game pole, and a palisade surrounding the ceremonial area.

UNIVERSITY OF NORTH CAROLINA, RESEARCH LABORATORIES OF ANTHROPOLOGY

Alumni Building, on the campus, Chapel Hill. Mail address: CB #3120, Alumni Building, University of North Carolina, Chapel Hill, NC 27599-3120. Phone: 919/962-6574. Open free, Monday–Friday.

Displays here include pottery and artifacts found in North Carolina.

WAKE FOREST UNIVERSITY, MUSEUM OF ANTHROPOLOGY

Take Silas Creek exit from Interstate 40; go north to Wake Forest University. Mail address: P.O. Box 7267, Winston Salem, NC 27109. Phone: 919/759-5282. Open free Tuesday–Friday, afternoons, Saturday and Sunday. Inquire about special hours June, July, August. Donations accepted.

Here is a large collection of artifacts primarily from the Piedmont and western North Carolina ranging from the Paleo to the Mississippian period.

Part of the reconstructed village area at Chucalissa Indian Town and Museum, Memphis, Tennessee. Memphis State University photo.

South Carolina

CHARLES TOWNE LANDING SITE

From Interstate 26 in Charleston, drive south on South Carolina 7 to South Carolina 171, then southeast on 171 to the Charles Towne Landing sign. Mail address: 1500 Old Town Rd., Charleston, SC 29407. Phone: 803/556-4450. Open daily, all year. Admission charged.

In addition to a reconstruction of an English colonial settlement and fortification, there are exhibits and pictorial displays here, together with artifacts, of a sixteenth-century Indian settlement that once occupied the area. The site was excavated and interpreted by the Institute of Archeology and Anthropology of the University of South Carolina.

SANTEE INDIAN MOUND

From the town of Santee take Interstate 95 north to turnoff just beyond the Lake Marion Bridge; turn left on dirt road at the sign to Fort Watson and Santee Indian Mound; continue through the U.S. Fish and Wildlife Refuge, about 1 mile, to the site. Open free, at all times.

A large temple mound was built here in prehistoric times by people who followed the Mississippian lifeway. Long after the site was abandoned it was reoccupied by the British, during the American Revolution. The British camped near the foot of the mound and fortified its top. An interpretive sign tells something of the history of the site.

SEWEE MOUND ARCHAEOLOGICAL AREA, FRANCIS MARION NATIONAL FOREST

From Summerville drive 21 miles north on US 17, then turn right and drive southeast 4 miles on South Carolina 402. Open free, at all times. Camping.

The U.S. Forest Service has opened this well-preserved shell mound to the public. Visitors are reminded that the Antiquities Act provides severe penalties for collecting any artifacts from the area.

Tennessee

C.H. NASH MUSEUM
(*See Chucalissa Indian Town and Museum*)

CHATTANOOGA REGIONAL HISTORY MUSEUM

400 Chestnut St., Chattanooga, TN 37402. Phone: 615-265-3247. Open Monday–Friday; afternoons, Saturday and Sunday. Closed certain holidays. Admission charged.

"The Early Land and Early People" exhibit here includes material from the Paleo, Archaic, Woodland, and Mississippian periods. There is also an exhibit that shows what an archeological dig is like. Another exhibit demonstrates how people made stone tools.

CHUCALISSA INDIAN TOWN AND MUSEUM
(CHOO-kah-LEE-sah)

From US 61 at the southern edge of Memphis, drive 4.5 miles west on Mitchell Rd. and follow directional signs to museum entrance. Mail address: C.H. Nash Museum, Memphis State University, 1987 Indian Village Drive, Memphis, TN 38109. Phone: 901/785-3160. Open Tuesday–Saturday; afternoon, Sunday. Closed certain holidays. Admission charged. Camping nearby.

The Story. People settled here about A.D. 1000 and occupied the site repeatedly for more than 500 years. Their village developed in two parts—one for ordinary folk, the other for religious and political leaders. The houses of the leaders bordered a large plaza in front of a platform mound and were made of poles or posts, finished outside with mud-and-straw plaster, and roofed with overlapping bundles of long, heavy grass.

The principal chief's house and another structure, possibly a temple, stood on the large platform mound made of earth, which at first was low. As years went by, one set of buildings after another was purposely burned, perhaps when a leader died, and the whole platform was then covered with a mantle of new earth. Each mantle

This life-size exhibit in the reconstructed village area at Chucalissa Indian Town and Museum shows the town chief receiving messengers from another town. He is accompanied by his secondary chiefs and advisors. C.H. Nash Museum photo, Memphis State University.

Stratigraphy

Above: Small objects of this sort are often called plummets. They may have been used as sinkers on fishlines or fishnets. *Right:* A pipe, carved in stone, from about A.D. 1600. Found in a mound at Shiloh National Military Park.

If a river floods every year and deposits silt on the land, the top layer of silt is the most recent. The bottom layer is the oldest. This fact has been important to geologists in determining the age of rocks and soil.

When people live in the same place a long time and keep throwing rubbish in the same garbage pile, the newest rubbish will be on top. The oldest will be on the bottom. To archeologists this can be very important in determining dates.

When people change their fashions, or adopt new foods, or take up the use of new implements, there is a change in what they throw away. Layers may form in a trash pile, easily distinguished from each other by the difference in objects they contain. Layers may form, too, when some material such as dust or silt or volcanic ash covers a trash heap and clearly separates an old deposit of rubbish from a new deposit later added above it.

By comparing what lies in the layers, which are called strata, it is possible to say that one type of artifact is older or younger in relation to another. You have a relative date. Relative dates are not perfect, by any means, but they do help to arrange events in some kind of order.

In certain places the layers in archeological sites are very clear and offer excellent clues. In many dry caves, for example, the strata are very helpful, unless pack rats have done a lot of burrowing in the debris. Pack rats and other rodents can dig holes into which material from top layers

added height and breadth to the foundation for the next buildings that were constructed, until at last a sizable mound dominated the village.

The women of Chucalissa did cooking and wove baskets, mats, and textiles. They also made quantities of pottery, some of it very lovely, some very plain, for use as kitchenware.

The men did some hunting, made tools of bone and stone and wood, and cared for crops in their fields. Like other people who built temple mounds at this time, they must have been expert farmers. They may even have raised a variety of corn that was unusually productive. At any rate, they had adequate food to support a community of about a thousand common people, as well as a large number of religious and political leaders, who spent much time and energy on ceremonies.

Probably a fire was kept burning in the temple day and night, and people in relays had to tend it carefully. For rituals and festivals crowds gathered in the plaza and shared in such events as the busk, or ripe corn ceremony.

For some reason not known, these people left their homes and temples before the arrival of the first French explorers in 1673, and so we cannot be certain which, if any, modern Indians are their descendants. Today Choctaw Indians, originally from central Mississippi, act as guides and conduct tours around the site.

The Name. Chucalissa is a word from modern Choctaw which means "house abandoned."

The Museum. A large part of the Chucalissa site has been made into an outdoor museum. Eight of the prehistoric houses and a corncrib have been reconstructed. Three of these have life-size exhibits showing a variety of daily activities of the prehistoric villagers. A long archeological trench, showing a cross section of the village deposits, has been roofed over and serves as an entryway to the village reconstruction area.

An indoor museum displays material recovered from the site and also from other sites in the Southeast. Some of the most informative exhibits to be found anywhere show the "how's" of archeology: how potsherds tell a story of the people who made the pots; how cane was split and woven into baskets;

in the deposit can fall. When this happens recent things can end up under things that are much older. Also, burrowers often bring old things to the surface, where they are found above objects that are much more recent. It is because animals and worms and people keep stirring things up that archeologists have to be very careful as they dig and as they draw conclusions from what they find.

Although it is not always true that new things lie above old things in digs, it is true often enough to be a real help. In looking for clues about time, archeologists don't depend solely on stratigraphy—the study of strata. They use many other ways of dating what they find, and when they find that several different dating methods all produce the same result, they feel fairly confident they have a date on which they can depend.

The first stratigraphic excavation in the United States was begun in 1902 by Dr. Max Uhle, a German, who had worked in Peru. At Emeryville, on the shore of San Francisco Bay, Uhle excavated a mound made up of a vast accumulation of oyster and clam shells. Periodically, over a very long time, prehistoric people had visited this spot, collected oysters and clams, and thrown the shells away. The shells eventually piled up into an immense heap, along with other remnants of living. The contents

(*Continued on page 298*)

and how blowguns were made. In one room of the museum visitors may hear a lecture, illustrated with slides, about the archeology of the site and the life of its former inhabitants.

The museum, a part of the Memphis State University Department of Anthropology, sponsors each August a Midsouth Indian Heritage Festival with local Native American groups. Events include traditional dancing, stickball games, and blowgun marksmanship.

Special Interest. The first excavation here began with the support of the Tennessee Division of State Parks and with the help of prisoners from the Penal Farm. According to an article in the *Tennessee Historical Quarterly,* "Undoubtedly it was, for many, the most creative work they had ever undertaken, and they dug carefully, painstakingly, taking enormous and justifiable pride in their digs. . . . One particular prisoner—Driver by name—found the archeologist's conventional tools totally unacceptable and so devised and made his own, instruments which now form the backbone of our tool kit!"

CUMBERLAND GAP NATIONAL HISTORICAL PARK

From the west take the Corbin exit from Interstate 75 and travel about 45 miles on US 25E. From the south take Tennessee 33 from Knoxville, through Tazewell and Harrogate, Tennessee. From the north take the 11 west exit from Interstate 81, connecting with Virginia 58 at Kingsport. Virginia 58 intersects US 25 E about 3 miles from the park Visitor Center. Mail address: P.O. Box 1848, Middlesboro, KY 40965. Phone: 606/248-2817. Open free, daily, all year. Closed December 25. Camping.

A prehistoric trail ran from Cumberland Gap to the Ohio River. This trail and others in Kentucky are the subject of an exhibit in the Visitor Center. Other exhibits relate to the entry of whites into what had hitherto been Indian land.

CUMBERLAND SCIENCE MUSEUM

800 Ridley Blvd., Nashville, TN 37203. Phone: 615/259-6099. Open Tuesday–Saturday; afternoon, Sunday. Admission charged. Closed certain holidays.

Displays devoted to Native American life from prehistoric times include an exhibit on mound builders.

McCLUNG MUSEUM
(*See University of Tennessee*)

OLD STONE FORT STATE ARCHAEOLOGICAL AREA

Just west of the city limits of Manchester, on US 41. Mail address: Route 7, Box 7400, Manchester, TN 37355. Phone: 615/723-5073. Open free, during daylight hours.

The Story. On a high bluff that rises where the Little Duck River flows into the Duck River, early pioneers found sections of a wall that had obviously been built by humans. Legends grew up about the site. Some said it was built by Vikings to protect themselves

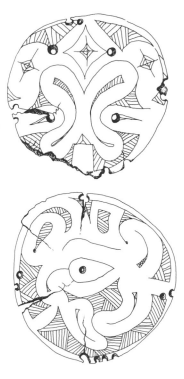

These engraved rattles, made of bone, were attached to the knees of a dancer. Redrawn from *Midcontinental Journal of Archaeology*. Originals found at Pinson Mounds State Archaeological Area.

(*Continued from page 297*)

of the mound varied from bottom to top, showing that cultural changes had taken place through time.

After Uhle had completed his work another archeologist, Nels Nelson, a Dane, also studied shell mounds in the San Francisco area. Nelson maintained that he could not see any significance to the admittedly small differences he found from one stratum to another in the mounds. Later, however, when he excavated in the Galisteo region, south of Santa Fe in New Mexico, Nelson remembered what Uhle had said about stratigraphy. For the first time in the Southwest Nelson used the stratigraphic method to study layers in a trash pile and thereby laid the basis for the first relative chronology in the area.

A. V. Kidder, digging at nearby Pecos, seized on the method and worked out in detail a relative dating for pottery in the Rio Grande Valley and for the cultures that had produced the pottery. Kidder's work brought order on a large scale into Southwestern archeology.

from Indians. Others said it was constructed by a Welshman named Madoc who they believed discovered America about A.D. 1170.

In 1966 archeologists from the University of Tennessee settled the question. They excavated the site, which includes more than 2000 feet of wall on just one of its sides, and found that the wall had been built over a long period of time, beginning about A.D. 1 and ending sometime before A.D. 400. The people who did all this vast labor seem to have been influenced by the Hopewell lifeway centered in the Ohio River valley.

Apparently the builders of the Old Stone Fort did not live at the site, which resembled Hopewell ceremonial sites.

Excavations since 1966 in the Normandy and Tims Ford Reservoir Sites have revealed where the users of this ceremonial site may have lived.

PINSON MOUNDS STATE ARCHAEOLOGICAL AREA

From Jackson drive 8 miles south on Tennessee 45 to Pinson, then left on Ozier Rd., 2.5 miles to the park. Mail address: 460 Ozier Rd., Pinson, TN 38366. Phone: 901/988-5614. Open free, daily.

This site was preserved thanks to the concern of local citizens who convinced the state of Tennessee to buy the land and make it into a park. There are more than twelve mounds in the group, along with village sites and earthworks. Most of the mounds seem to have been used for burial, although those with flat tops may have been for ceremonial purposes. Archeologists still hope to determine more about the people who probably lived here and constructed the mounds betwen A.D. 1 and 500.

The Museum. Built to resemble a mound, the museum houses interpretive exhibits and a small theater where archeology programs and films are scheduled from time to time. Several miles of nature trails take the visitor

The game of chunkey was popular in prehistoric times in Tennessee and at many other places east of the Rocky Mountains. In 1832 George Catlin made this drawing of Mandan Indians enjoying the sport. Participants threw spears, each one hoping to land his just where the rolling, doughnut-shaped chunkey stone stopped. The man who came closest won. From Smithsonian Report, 1885.

Delicately flaked flint artifacts, apparently for ceremonial purposes, were found in Tennessee. Originals in the McClung Museum, Knoxville.

past the most interesting spots in the park.

SEQUOYAH BIRTHPLACE MUSEUM

From Vonore drive 1 mile east on US 41 to Tennessee 360, then south on 360 to museum near Tellico Lake. Mail address: P.O. Box 69, Vonore, TN 37885. Phone: 615/884-6246. Open daily, all year. Admission charged.

This museum is notable on two counts. It commemorates the birth of Sequoyah, the Native American who invented a form of writing and spelling called a syllabary that made his people, the Cherokee, fully literate in a very short time.

The museum is also near the Tellico reservoir which flooded a large area rich in archeological sites. Beginning in 1967 excavation rescued the cultural remains at many of the sites, and some of the artifacts are on display here.

Another collection of Tellico material is on exhibit at the Cherokee National Museum in Tahlequah, Oklahoma (see entry above).

SHILOH MOUNDS, SHILOH NATIONAL MILITARY PARK (SHY-low)

From Savannah drive 4 miles west on US 64, then 6 miles south on Tennessee 22. Mail address: Shiloh, TN 38376. Phone: 901/689-5275. Open free, daily. Closed December 25.

About three-quarters of a mile from Park Headquarters is a cluster of mounds on a bluff above the Tennessee River. As early as 1899 a fine effigy pipe was found there, but most of the digging was done in 1934 by Works Progress Administration labor under the direction of Dr. Frank H. H. Roberts, of the Smithsonian Institution.

In all, there are more than 30 mounds in the Shiloh group. Six large ones have flat tops, and temples once stood on them. The seventh large mound, in the shape of an oval dome, was used for burial of the dead. Many smaller mounds were dwelling sites.

The Story. The people who began to live here (perhaps 600 to 800 years ago) followed cultural patterns resembling those of many other mound-

building Indians in the Southeast. They constructed platforms for temples then periodically burned the buildings and added a new layer to the whole outside of the mound. They buried important leaders in graves stocked with pottery, ornaments, and ceremonial objects. Like the inhabitants of Etowah in Georgia they seem to have held great feasts in the plaza between the mounds, and afterward they threw the refuse into deep pits. As a result of studying the remains of the feasts archeologists know that these people must have been corn farmers, that they also fished, gathered clams, and hunted for wild game.

The dwellings near the large mounds were made of upright posts, with saplings and split cane woven in between. This latticework was then daubed over with clay. For roofs, the builders made a close wickerwork of canes and branches, which they covered with leaves and grass, and then over this they plastered clay.

People here, as at many other Southeastern towns, played a game called chunkey, using a discoidal

The Meaning of a Mound

What does a mound show about the people who built it?

A mound has a definite shape. It is planned. It is not spontaneous or haphazard. This means that there was a social mechanism for planning and for getting plans carried out.

A mound means division of labor. There were planners, or leaders, involved in its construction, and there were those who carried out the plans—who were led. In other words, there were social classes, at least in rudimentary form. There were rulers and ruled.

Rulers had to have time in which to do their ruling. They had to be able to eat without spending all of their days obtaining food. This meant either that leaders were very successful part-time food getters or that they were fed out of the stores grown or collected by others. Moreover the food supply had to be large enough to sustain the common people while they expended an immense amount of energy in piling up huge quantities of earth.

Mounds also mean that their builders had religious beliefs. They had adopted or invented ways to feel comfortable amid the baffling complexities of life and the painfully recurrent fact of death. To judge from what we know has happened among similar groups of people who have been directly observed, the leisure-time activities of some members of the mound-builder community must have gone into developing reas-

---

(wheel-shaped) stone. According to Europeans who witnessed the game in historic times, contestants holding greased spears gathered at one end of a long, flat field. A signal was given, and a man rolled the chunkey stone down the field. A moment later the players hurled their spears, each one hoping to estimate the distance the stone would roll before it stopped. The winner—the man who landed his spear closest to the spot where the stone came to a halt—then collected the bets he had made with the other contestants. A number of chunkey stones turned up in the excavations at Shiloh, as did evidence of another gambling game played with marked counters that resembled dice.

By the time Europeans arrived in Tennessee the inhabitants of this site had left. Investigators have not yet been able to say for sure which of the historic Indian tribes may have been descendants of the builders of Shiloh Mounds.

The Name. After driving the Indians from Tennessee, whites settled in the neighborhood of this group of ancient mounds and built Shiloh Church, named for the biblical Shiloh which, perhaps coincidentally, was the site of a temple on a mountain. In 1862 a bloody Civil War battle was fought here at Shiloh, and to commemorate it the site was made a National Military Park. Visitors to the park can get a glimpse of history and of prehistory as well.

TENNESSEE STATE MUSEUM

Polk Cultural Center, 505 Deaderick Street, Nashville, TN 37219. Phone: 615/741-2692. Open free, Monday–Saturday; afternoon, Sunday. Closed certain holidays. Donations appreciated.

Here more than 500 prehistoric artifacts are used in exhibits to explain aspects of Paleo, Archaic, Woodland, and Mississippian cultures in Tennessee. Of special interest are Mississippian effigies and utilitarian pottery, ceremonial implements and pipes, and items of personal adornment made from shell, copper and stone.

suring myths and shamanistic procedures. As time went by, these may have led to ceremonies and rituals supervised by full-time specialists, whom we would call priests.

The religious beliefs which mound builders held provided motivation for the great trouble they took in burying their dead, often amid riches and almost always under great heaps of earth. By such activity people must have sought either to influence events in some magic way or to do something that seemed to fit the living satisfactorily into the immutable flow of events.

Mound builders also had thoughts for the welfare of loved ones—or feared ones—who had died. They were solicitous for the continuing comfort of those whom they regarded as in some way important. In imagination they created circumstances that lay ahead for those who had ceased to live in the flesh, and then they laid palpable conveniences—garments, meals, weapons, implements, amulets—close to the bodies or bones of the deceased. Here were real objects that could be taken as testimony to the reality of some kind of ongoing existence.

Mounds tell us all this about people who lived within nature and at the same time erected a world outside it—a world of the supernatural. Mounds say that their builders elaborated life in ways that were different from those worked out by earlier people. The simplicity of the shape of the mound belies the intricacy of the society that produced it.

UNIVERSITY OF TENNESSEE, McCLUNG MUSEUM

On campus, 1327 Circle Park Dr., Knoxville, TN 37996. Phone: 615/974-2144. Open free, Monday–Saturday; afternoon, Sunday. Closed certain holidays.

Materials in the Frank H. McClung Museum, gathered by careful scientific excavation, throw light on Paleo, Archaic, Woodland, and Mississippian cultures in the Southeast. Many important finds came to the museum at the time when the Tennessee Valley Authority was building flood-control dams. In a crash program of salvage archeology, thousands of relief workers dug at many sites in the river basins, saving what could be excavated before the water rose.

For the exhibit, "The American Indian in Tennessee: An Archaeological Perspective," the museum has prepared a detailed teacher's guide to the 26 exhibits, 22 of which deal with prehistory.

Special Feature. The museum houses the collections of Thomas M. N. Lewis and Madeline Kneberg Lewis, archeologists who contributed greatly to knowledge of southeastern cultures. Their work at the famous Eva Site in Benton County disclosed a long period of development of lifeways in that part of Tennessee, beginning about 5200 B.C. Some of the Eva people who settled along riverbanks harvested tremendous quantities of clams and mussels, and their heaps of discarded shells offered a convenient place for burials. In some of those which the Lewises excavated were found an amazing number of skeletons of adults who lived to be 60 or 70 years old. (Usually prehistoric people died at a much earlier age.) Skeletal remains also indicated a rather inbred population. Apparently people lived here almost undisturbed for generations. However, the different levels of occupation did show changes in food habits from time to time. During some periods a great amount of deer and other meat was eaten, but almost no shellfish.

Serpent Mound in Ohio. It is nearly one-quarter of a mile long, 20 feet wide, and 4 to 5 feet high. The date of construction is not known. Ohio Historical Society photo.

NORTH CENTRAL

A young newspaperman named Ephraim George Squier moved from Connecticut to the small Ohio town of Chillicothe in 1845 and began to edit the newspaper there. Near his new home he saw a number of large earthen mounds—artificial, he was told—and he immediately grew curious about them. A physician, Dr. E. H. Davis, also of Chillicothe, shared Squier's interest.

Working as a team, these two amateurs started to investigate. Inside the mounds they discovered human bones and artifacts. Surveys in Ohio and other states revealed more and more sites where vast quantities of earth had been piled up by human hands. Before long Squier and Davis had dug into more than 200 of the mounds, and these were only a sampling of what existed in the Midwest.

Obviously a sizable and well-organized population had carried out these tremendous projects. Innumerable craftsworkers must have been engaged in making the grave goods lavished on burials. Why did an apparent obsession with funeral ceremonies move these people? And what mysterious fate overtook them in the end? Neither pioneer settlers nor the Native Americans they encountered in the area had any clues to offer.

Squier and Davis needed financial help for their investigations, and they got it from the young American Ethnological Society. Within a year Squier had a report ready. Soon it had expanded into a big book, and in 1848 the newly established Smithsonian Institution brought it out under the title *Ancient Monuments of the Mississippi Valley.*

A Hopewell man wearing copper earspools, necklace of copper and pearls, and headdress of deer antlers. The reconstructed figurine is in the Field Museum of Natural History, Chicago.

The Squier and Davis report was the Smithsonian's first publication. It also marked the beginning of widespread interest in the earthworks that were a very prominent feature in America's nineteenth-century landscape. The two men visited, dug into, and surveyed mound after mound in the central part of the United States. Then Squier drafted beautiful maps of the sites and wrote careful descriptions. In addition, a good many theories came from his facile pen, and here he shared the views of those who were at that time busy driving the original Americans off the land. Indians, in Squier's opinion, were such inferior creatures that they could never have built the great earthen structures in the Mississippi and Ohio valleys. Nor could they have made the sculptured pipes, the pottery, and the handsome ornaments he and Davis were finding in ancient graves. Another people—a separate race of Mound Builders—must have been the creators of such works.

More than a hundred years later archeologists were still plagued with the myth of the Mound Builders, which Squier and Davis and the Smithsonian Institution had done much to circulate. So persistent was the notion of a mysterious, extinct race that Robert Silverberg has found ample material for tracing its history in a fascinating book, *The Mound Builders of Ancient America*.

The fact, of course, is that Indians were quite capable of the esthetic and social achievements that Squier and Davis and a host of other investigators observed. It was also true that by the nineteenth century all mound building had ceased. The art forms associated with mounds were no longer remembered in the central United States, and Indians knew as little as whites about what had happened to earlier dwellers on the land.

Interpretation of the Mounds

There are still a great many unanswered questions. Archeologists do not all agree in their interpretations of material that continuing excavation turns up. However, what has so far emerged as a result of recent scientific study is roughly this:

Toward the end of the Archaic period, about 3000 years ago, groups of people in parts of the northeastern and north-central United States seem to have developed special burial practices. They covered the dead with mounds of earth. Other customs later came to be linked with mound burial. People began to place offerings in graves—such things as food and weapons and ornaments. Ceremonial activities were added to the making and burying of grave goods. Fire took on importance in these rituals. Bodies were sometimes cremated, and mortuary offerings were broken and burned. In many places bodies were first exposed until the flesh had decayed or had been removed by scavengers. Then the bones were covered with a kind of paint made from the mineral known as red ocher, which is an oxide of iron. Sometimes red ocher powder was sprinkled in quantity over both the remains and the grave goods.

No one knows why this mineral was considered important for burials. One suggestion is that red blood is associated with life, and therefore blood-colored ocher in a burial may have been a wordless way of trying to summon continued life for the person who was being buried.

The Red Ocher people in Illinois made pottery, which they often placed in their small, low, burial mounds, along with projectile points and beads of copper and shell. Pottery, of course, is hard to transport. Those who make it do not usually travel much. This means that Red Ocher people must have been able to get all the food they needed within a small area. They were good hunters and skilled in the use of every kind of wild food. Eventually some of their descendants, whose lifeway is known as the Morton culture, learned to grow food in gardens. They built bigger mounds, and their grave goods became more elaborate.

Meanwhile, in the Ohio Valley, to the east, groups of hunters had been developing lifeways that were similar to those in Illinois. They started with simple graves in small mounds. Later they placed the dead in log tombs, over which they heaped earth. On top of the first burial they added others, gradually building up a high structure shaped like a cone. Groups of these conical mounds covered whole mortuary areas near villages. Here, too, ceremonies and the creation of grave goods—including pottery—occupied large numbers of people and led to the distinctive culture now called Adena.

The Woodland Lifeway

Adena people began to make pottery about 1000 B.C., as did many other groups in the eastern two-thirds of North America. For archeologists, pottery marks the beginning of a new period. They call it Woodland, and they agree that it is distinguished also by the development of agriculture. Woodland is perhaps an unfortunate term for a lifeway that extended from the eastern forest lands onto the treeless plains, but since the name appears in most books and museums, it is hard to avoid.

About 100 B.C. another lifeway, called Hopewell, appeared in Ohio. Hopewell was named for a farmer, M. C. Hopewell, on whose land near Chillicothe archeologists excavated one of the richest of all burial mounds. Hopewell grave goods were beautiful, lavish, and sophisticated. Experts have found them baffling, as well. Suddenly, in many places, large Hopewell burial mounds were being constructed in groups, often surrounded by earthen walls built in the form of immense circles, octagons, and squares.

These astonishing earthworks required millions of cubic feet of soil to be transported in baskets and piled up to form the mounds and miles of embankments, some as much as 20 feet high. An engineer, James A. Marshall, has studied these ancient engineering projects and has come to the conclusion that they are the product of much mathematical knowledge. A standard unit of measurement was used, and separate earthworks were sometimes precisely lined up, although miles apart.

In each Hopewellian center there must have been an elite group with power and status enough to command enormous labor for building the earthworks and mounds. In the upper ranks of this society, in addition to the ruling group, the priests, and the engineers, were professional artisans who created all of the beautiful objects that went into the burial mounds. Funerary offerings included daggers and knives chipped from huge pieces of obsidian, smoking pipes carved from stone in the shapes of animals and birds, and sheets of mica precisely cut in the outlines of birds or serpents or human hands, possibly for use as stencils. In one mound group alone archeologists found 100,000 freshwater pearls.

A great deal of the raw material for grave goods came from distant places. Mica and quartz crystal were brought from the Appalachian Mountains. The obsidian had to be transported all the way from the Southwest or from the Yellowstone area, in Wyoming. Silver for beads came from Ontario, copper for beads and other ornaments from around Lake Superior. Florida provided shells and the teeth of shark and alligator, while sources closer to home furnished bear teeth for necklaces, feathers for gorgeous feather-cloth robes, and pearls by the hundreds of thousands. And all this was then buried in tombs under earth and stone laboriously heaped up to form the large mounds.

Ceremonies and Trade

Funerals of those who belonged to the highest classes were held with pomp and grandeur. At the same time Hopewell ceremonialism stimulated a very intricate economy, as people from one center engaged in trade with others over a wide area. A relentless search for raw material had to go on because the need could never be satisfied while a steady stream of manufactured objects was disappearing underground.

The dynamic Hopewellian ideas eventually dominated areas from Weeden Island, in Florida, all the way to the Canadian border, and from Kansas City to New York State. But wherever the Hopewell influence went, the local people seem to have kept their own basic patterns of existence while they adopted—or perhaps submitted to—the new system. Villages continued much as they had been before Hopewellian times, and powerful central cities did not form around the mounds themselves.

What exactly was the Hopewell phenomenon? It cannot be called a culture, because people in various regions kept their own ways, rather than being united in a homogeneous set of practices. Nor was it a unified political system, although in various areas large numbers of ordinary folk did participate in the special engineering projects. Although there were certainly religious elements in Hopewell, it was too complex a mixture to be called simply a cult. The economic, the political and the religious were intertwined, and some sort of socioreligious stimulation seemed to motivate the system.

In the Ohio Valley, Hopewell and Adena existed side by side and probably borrowed notions from each other, although their

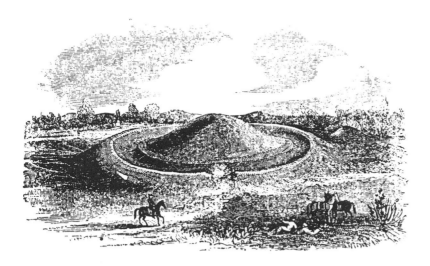

Some conical mounds were surrounded by circular earthworks. This remarkably symmetrical one, in Greenup County, Kentucky, had a narrow gateway through the embankment and a causeway across the ditch. From *Ancient Monuments of the Mississippi Valley* by E. G. Squier, A.M., and E. H. Davis, M.D., *Smithsonian Contribution to Knowledge, Volume* I, 1847.

relationship may not always have been completely friendly. In the end large numbers of Adena seem to have given in to pressure of some sort. Groups of them migrated southward into Kentucky; others went eastward all the way to Chesapeake Bay.

For more than 600 years the Hopewellian elite lived intricate lives that centered around death. Then for reasons no one yet understands, their influence declined and finally disappeared, not only in Ohio but also in all their other centers. What could have happened?

One suggestion is that a slight change of climate may have brought a long period of crop failure. Without a stable food base people could no longer afford to provide the luxuries demanded by the elite. And so the system died, although its practitioners lived on.

Another suggestion is that greatly increased population brought about greatly increased competition for food. This meant raids or warfare. There is evidence of burning and massacre and the building of defenses at several Hopewell centers. Conflict might also have stopped the trading for raw materials that were essential to the manufacture of elaborate grave goods. Without these necessary exotic materials the system itself ground to a halt.

Or it may be simply that everyone got tired of the whole business. Perhaps a kind of disillusionment set in: Why squander life to celebrate death? People may well have found unendurable the contradiction between creating wealth and destroying it for the glory in death of the powerful, who probably weren't very lovable taskmasters when they were alive. Whatever the reason, Hopewell mound building ceased about A.D. 500, and before long the system had vanished, leaving no trace except the great structures that were soon covered with forest or sod.

The period from about A.D. 600 to 800 in Illinois has been called a kind of "Dark Age." People apparently built no mounds, wore no rich ceremonial dress, made no elegant grave goods. Villages housed only small groups, and people who had once been skilled farmers raised only small field crops to supplement their hunting. In other words, they lived much as their ancestors had done 2000 years before.

The Mississippian Culture

Then change began again along the Mississippi River, near the mouth of the Missouri, in the area where several important, age-old travel routes came together. This was also a region where the soil was particularly good for growing corn. Here, about A.D. 800, a new way of life appeared. Before long there was new mound building. Separate social classes developed once more, along with intense ceremonialism, including once again an emphasis on death. However, the new religiosity had many very distinct features. Rituals were aimed at ensuring the productivity of crops. The new, flat-topped, pyramidal mounds served chiefly as platforms for religious structures, although priests or leaders were sometimes buried in them. The prosperity of communities often led to a wealth of beautiful artifacts, but they were not all intended primarily to be grave goods.

The origin of this lifeway, which archeologists call Mississippian, has not been established to everyone's satisfaction. It may have evolved out of existing cultures. At any rate, Mississippian habits of farming, of temple-mound building, of pottery making, and of religious rituals spread widely throughout much of the Mississippi drainage system and spilled over into other areas of the Southeast as well.

Between A.D. 1200 and 1500 these people flourished. Then their society, like that of the Hopewell, began to decline. Although temple mounds in some places were still built and used in historic times, by the late seventeenth century all the great centers were abandoned, and Mississippian ceremonialism had withered and died.

In the nineteenth century all these giant earthworks—and the spectacular quantities of loot that came from them—were bound to intrigue both professional and amateur investigators. They also attracted mound-miners, who were animated by the spirit of free enterprise. These men dug up objects not for what they could learn by studying them but for what they could earn by selling them. There was a market for archeological goodies, and much that scientists would like to have in museums has now disappeared. The

DAILY LIFE
SOUTHERN FARMERS

INDIANS OF THE CENTRAL MISSISSIPPI VALLEY
TEMPLE MOUND STAGE
A.D. 1400-1700

The life of farmers who built temple mounds in the central valley of the Mississippi River is suggested in this exhibit. Field Museum of Natural History photo.

amazing thing is that unrifled burials do still exist, and very often professional people are called in to excavate them.

Other Lifeways
Mound builders, however, were not the only prehistoric inhabitants of the North Central area. Near the town of Modoc, in southern Illinois, for example, ancient hunters 10,000 years ago discovered a shelter under overhanging rock in the bluffs along the Mississippi River. Off and on, until about 3000 B.C., families slept, ate, and made tools and weapons in this dry, protected spot. Later, small bands of hunters used it in spring and fall. All of them left the trash of daily living, and by the time archeologists discovered the Modoc shelter, 27 feet of refuse had piled up on the floor.

South of Modoc, along the Ohio River, hunters now known as Baumer people settled in semipermanent villages about 3000 years ago. Men continued to search for game, but they came home to solid dwellings made of upright logs, where women and children lived the year round. This kind of existence was possible because the Baumer people and some of their neighbors had learned to store large supplies of acorns and hickory nuts in pits underground. In winter, when the earth was frozen, empty pits were sometimes used as graves.

Farther up the Ohio, particularly in Kentucky, hunting-and-gathering people harvested great quantities of freshwater shellfish and established seasonal camps on riverbanks. As the piles of discarded shells grew higher, they were often used as burial places. Very few of these shell mounds can now be seen, but some have been studied by scientists.

More than a thousand burials are known to have been made at Indian Knoll, on the Green River, in Kentucky, and the site has been examined with a view to finding out what the mortuary practices could reveal about the social organization of the people who occupied the area between five and six thousand years ago. Artifacts buried with the dead offered clues—shell beads, projectile points, awls, and other implements. The fact that tools customarily used by women were often found in men's and children's graves, and that hunting equipment was buried with women and children, indicated to archeologists that this society was more or less egalitarian. In societies known to have definite classes, mortuary goods are much more likely to be differentiated according to sex and/or status in the community.

Everywhere, as people exploited their environment, they sought not only new foods but also new materials for tools and weapons. Near the Great Lakes, about 3000 B.C., they found one material little known elsewhere—deposits of pure copper, that could be mined with stone tools. By a process of heating and hammering the metal, they fashioned it into knives, projectile points, drills, and adzes. Later they used it—and traded it to others for use—in beads and ornaments and ceremonial objects.

Toward the end of Hopewellian times there appeared in Wisconsin, Iowa, and Illinois mounds of a new kind, less spectacular than the great burial mounds and very different in appearance. Some were simply long, low rod-shaped piles of earth. Others were built in the shapes of lizards, panthers, bears, geese, deer, beaver, birds and other animals, and so they have been called effigy mounds. (In Michigan and Minnesota long, straight plain mounds were also built at this same time.) Burials in effigy mounds were seldom accompanied by elaborate offerings. A little pottery, some shell beads and a tool or two were about all the grave goods usually found in association with an effigy mound. Sometimes the grave was placed at a vital spot of the effigy animal—the heart or head. Often a group of mounds stretched out along a high ridge overlooking a valley. As for the significance of the effigy forms, archeologists can only guess that they may have been connected in some way with clan totems or with some other mythological belief.

Between A.D. 1100 and A.D. 1400, Woodland Indians of the Great Lakes region used tools and weapons like these. Field Museum of Natural History photo.

Illinois

BURPEE NATURAL HISTORY MUSEUM

737 N. Main, Rockford, IL 61103. Phone: 815/965-3433. Open Tuesday–Friday; Saturday by appointment. Admission charged.

Random finds, identified by county of origin are on exhibit. These include Paleo, Archaic, and Woodland artifacts from local collections, from surface finds, and from limited excavations. In its Indian exhibit the museum has on display tools and pottery shards from this area. There is also a hands-on archeology display with information about local mounds and pottery making.

CAHOKIA MOUNDS STATE HISTORIC SITE
A World Heritage Site

From St. Louis, MO, drive 5 miles east on Interstate 55-70 to Illinois 111 exit; then south to Collinsville Rd.; then left 1.5 miles to site entrance.

Mail address: Cahokia Mounds, P.O. Box 681, Collinsville, IL 62234. Phone: 618/346-5160. Open free, daily, May 1–October 31; Tuesday–Saturday; afternoon, Sunday, Nov. 1–April 30. Closed certain holidays. Free guided tours of excavations, mid-June to Sept. 1.

This extensive park contains the central section of the largest archeological site north of Mexico. It includes the largest mound in the United States (Monks Mound)—an artificial pyramid of earth 100 feet high at its summit—and 68 smaller mounds.

Some archeologists believe that at one time as many as 30,000 people may have lived in and around Cahokia—a population more dense than at any other place in America north of the Valley of Mexico. Others believe it is necessary to rethink the population figure. They suggest that Cahokia might have been a great trading and ceremonial center, or a defense fortress, where large numbers of people came and went but did not have permanent homes. The dwelling areas may

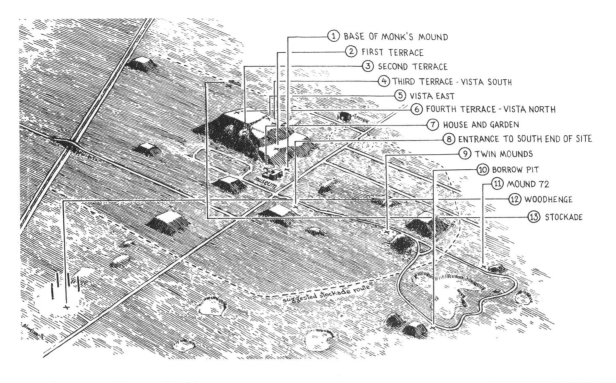

1. BASE OF MONK'S MOUND
2. FIRST TERRACE
3. SECOND TERRACE
4. THIRD TERRACE - VISTA SOUTH
5. VISTA EAST
6. FOURTH TERRACE - VISTA NORTH
7. HOUSE AND GARDEN
8. ENTRANCE TO SOUTH END OF SITE
9. TWIN MOUNDS
10. BORROW PIT
11. MOUND 72
12. WOODHENGE
13. STOCKADE

Map of the Central City, at Cahokia Mounds State Historic Site.

have been used chiefly by caretakers, civic leaders, and members of the military and the priesthood. At any rate, wealth and vigor made Cahokia a center from which the Mississippian culture spread over a vast area.

The Story. About A.D. 700 Late Woodland people built small villages and planted corn in a fertile area called the American Bottom along the east side of the Mississippi River, opposite St. Louis. Later, around A.D. 850, another people arrived, bringing with them Mississippian lifeways. Eventually they became dominant. Their corn was an extraordinarily productive variety, and they increased their yields by using an efficient flint hoe to dig deeply and to kill weeds that competed with corn plants.

Raw material for the hoes came from the area near the present town of Mill Creek, in southern Illinois. There, in a deposit of soft clay, people discovered flint nodules that were somewhat flat. This shape easily lent itself to the making of large, oval hoe blades, which could be attached to wooden handles. To get at the nodules, they dug shafts,

some almost 30 feet deep, often with side corridors at the bottom.

Convinced that the hoe blade had been an important tool, archeologists did an experiment. They attached blades to long handles and tried to dig up the tough bottomland soil at Cahokia. To their surprise, this turned out to be backbreaking work. The hoes did not seem nearly so efficient as had been expected. Later this minor mystery may have been solved when excavators near Cahokia discovered a beautifully carved figurine of a woman with a hoe in her hand. The blade was bound to a short stick handle that bent at a right angle, and the woman was kneeling to use it. Perhaps the archeologists would not have found it so hard to dig if they had knelt and used a short-handled hoe.

With good tools to use and good seed to plant, farmers produced large crops on the rich land near Cahokia. There was enough corn, together with abundant resources of fish, game, nuts, and berries, to feed many families. As the population grew, increasing complexities marked the ways in which

The Interpretive Center (*bottom of photo*) and Monks Mound (*top*) in Cahokia Mounds State Historic Site. Photo courtesy Cahokia Mounds State Historic Site.

people related to each other and to their environment. In the larger community certain important structures were used for civic and religious affairs. To emphasize their importance, leaders had these public buildings placed on earthen mounds, which elevated them above the flat landscape. Large open plazas in front of the buildings gave them further distinction. Inspiration for this pattern of construction was once thought to have come from Mexico, where similar towns existed at the time. However, it now seems that the mound and plaza idea was a slow, indigenous development rather than a sudden intrusion from Mexico.

From this busy and growing settlement it was possible for traders to take long canoe trips on the Mississippi and its tributaries—the Missouri, Ohio, Illinois, Tennessee, and Arkansas rivers. Raw material reached Cahokia from the Gulf of Mexico, the Appalachian Mountains, the Great Lakes, and the Rockies. With trade came an exchange of ideas. Cahokians exported art forms, even attitudes toward life, along the routes they used, and they in turn re-

ceived stimulation from many places, some very distant.

As time passed, the number of mounds at Cahokia increased to about 120 within an area of about 4000 acres. Possibly the region became overpopulated, and resources were depleted. For that reason or some other, groups of Cahokians began to move away. In the new communities they set up they continued to follow the Mississippian way of life.

Some of these new settlements were established in regions where people were still living in Late Woodland ways. One such place was Aztalan, Wisconsin (see entry below).

Cahokia itself prospered, though not entirely at ease. The center of the community was encircled by a defensive log wall, with bastions at regular intervals, which was reconstructed at least four times between A.D. 1100 and 1300. What enemy was feared is not clear, but the threat of attack apparently existed for 200 years or more. By A.D. 1500 Cahokia was abandoned.

Nineteenth-century settlers found good farmland in the American Bot-

MOUND OF EARTH BUILT OVER SACRED ENCLOSURE

CREMATION AND BURIAL IN A SACRED ENCLOSURE LATER COVERED BY A MOUND OF EARTH

Two stages in mound building. First, Indians cremated and buried a body within a sacred enclosure. Then they heaped up basketloads of earth over the burial, forming a mound. Field Museum of Natural History photo.

tom, and they leveled some of the mounds with their plows. For a while Trappist monks made gardens on top of the big, main temple mound, now called Monks Mound. At one time there was danger that it might be torn apart to make fill for a railroad bed. Highway builders and industrial developers destroyed many of the other earthworks. Those which remain are now protected by the State Historic Preservation Agency.

For years both amateur and professional archeologists worked at the site, and since 1960 intensive scientific work has been going on there. Excavations have established much good information about daily life during the Mississippian occupation. People built their house walls of posts set upright in trenches in the earth, then wove branches in between, basketfashion. Over this they spread a layer of mud plaster. To protect the plaster from rain, they added an outer covering of woven reed mats. Roofs thatched with dried grass were supported by large center poles.

This kind of dwelling didn't last

long. The roof caught fire easily, and the whole building might burn. When that happened, or when a house weakened with age or rot, a new one was often put up on the same site. Houses rebuilt on one spot for hundreds of years left a series of understandable hints about household affairs.

Other hints need further study. For example, there seems to be evidence that Cahokians sought good crops by conducting ceremonies that included sacrifice of the most valuable of all things—human life. This practice was known in Mexico, where maize agriculture originated. However, the full extent and meaning of human sacrifice in the Mississippian culture is not yet understood.

Possibly associated with agriculture was another discovery, reported in 1964 by Warren L. Wittry and further studied in 1978–79. Five very large circles once defined by upright posts, were revealed in the course of excavation. They resemble the Stonehenge circles in England and are called woodhenges. Wittry's interpretation was that the circles formed a sort of calendar

Reconstructed house of a type built by people of the Woodland culture a thousand years ago. Illinois State Museum photo by Marlin Rees.

that indicated the seasons and kept track of important dates—for feast days, ceremonies, and the right times for planting and harvesting. When Wittry checked the alignment of post holes in relation to the rising sun, he found that alignments did mark the solstices and equinoxes.

The Name. When French explorers entered Illinois in 1673 they met several Algonquian-speaking tribes that had formed a confederacy. These Indians called themselves the Illini (ILL-in-ee) or Illiniwek. One tribe, known as the Cahokia, lived in the American Bottom near the mounds—which by association became known as the Cahokia Mounds. But the Cahokia Indians were latecomers to this area. The true descendants of the people who built the mounds are not known.

The Interpretive Center. This building, which opened in 1989, cost $8.2 million and uses many techniques to interpret Cahokia Mounds and Native American culture generally. A model gives an overview of the 2200 acre Historic Site. Murals, one of which is 30 feet long, show Cahokia during its peak period. Every half-hour a 15-minute show introduces visitors to the history of the site. Five sunken displays show visitors what archeologists saw as they dug into the earth. A walk-through diorama gives a visitor a chance to feel what it was like to be in the ancient community. Throughout the Center are panels that show how archeologists have learned about Cahokia. Self-guided tour tapes are available at the museum shop.

Special Feature. Excavations and a field school often take place in summer months. Every September a three-day festival, "Heritage America," draws Native American dancers, musicians and craft workers from all over the country.

Working from various archeological clues, an artist painted this version of an Oneota harvest ceremony. Field Museum of Natural History photo.

FIELD MUSEUM OF NATURAL HISTORY

Roosevelt Rd. at Lake Shore Dr., Chicago, IL 60605. Phone: 312/322-8859. Open daily, except December 25 and January 1. Admission charged.

Exhibits and dioramas in Halls 4 through 10 on the main floor are devoted to the Indians of the Americas. Hall 4 tells the story of people in the New World from the time of their arrival from Asia to the time of the arrival of Europeans. In one section are exhibits showing techniques for manufacturing stone tools and the methods used by archeologists in excavating and interpreting prehistoric material.

Other halls also throw some light on prehistory. Hall 5 contains exhibits on Indians of the prairies and woodlands. One feature is a full-size (55' × 40' × 18') reconstruction of a Pawnee earth lodge. Here there are daily programs about Pawnee life.

Separate halls are devoted to the Southwest, the West, and the Northwest. In addition there are halls for Indians of Middle and South America.

Visitors may join scheduled guided tours through parts of the Indian exhibits. Those who are seriously interested in archeology may use the museum's excellent library.

Special Interest. Anyone who comes here after visiting sites open to visitors in other parts of the country will find certain things that could not be seen at the sites themselves. For example, the museum has in its collection material from the original Hopewell Site, and its Hopewell exhibit gives a good idea of how these people built their burial mounds, how they dressed, and what their ornaments were like.

FORD COUNTY HISTORICAL SOCIETY

In the Heritage Room in the Court House, Paxton, IL. Mail address: P.O. Box 213, Paxton, IL 60957. Open free, Monday–Friday.

An exhibit here includes artifacts found in Ford County representing the Paleo, Archaic, Early, Middle, and Late Woodland and Mississippian periods.

ILLINOIS STATE MUSEUM

Spring and Edward streets, Springfield. Mail address: State Museum Building, Springfield, IL 62706. Phone: 217/782-7386. Open free, Monday–Saturday; afternoon, Sunday. Closed certain holidays.

Archeological exhibits in this general museum cover the whole range from Paleo-Indian times to the historic period. A series of dioramas shows the major steps in human cultural development.

Archeologists connected with the museum have excavated many important sites in Illinois and elsewhere, and some of the material they have found is included in exhibits. Of special importance is their work at the Modoc Rock Shelter, where they helped to uncover one of the longest records of human existence in North America.

Modoc Rock Shelter is at the base of a high sandstone bluff on the Illinois side of the Mississippi River, south of St. Louis. The shelter protects an area 25 feet deep and about 300 feet long. Nine thousand years ago Archaic

A deposit of fresh-water mussel shells found in an Archaic midden at the Quasar Site in Illinois. Photo courtesy of the Center for American Archeology.

hunters and gatherers began to live under this overhang, which is named for the nearby village of Modoc.

For 500 years the shelter served groups of people, at first as a short-term campsite, then as a permanent base, later as a hunting camp. Then for some reason it was not used for a while, until Woodland Indians began to stop there on occasion and to leave broken pottery and other signs of their visits.

Sheltered from the rain, layer on layer of human history piled up to a depth of 27 feet. Archeologists now read the story with special attention because it reveals that Archaic Indians in the East followed the same general pattern of existence as that of Archaic people in the West. Clear evidence of this had not appeared before the Modoc Rock Shelter was excavated.

Here also was evidence of steadily changing adjustments to a changing environment. The people who lived on the bank of the great waterway could interact with travelers. Theirs was a relatively rich world, and they learned how to get the most out of it.

Modoc Rock Shelter is a National Historic Landmark. Its location is marked by a plaque. There are no exhibits at the site.

KAMPSVILLE ARCHEOLOGICAL CENTER

In Kampsville, 75 miles northeast of St. Louis, MO on Illinois 100. Administered by the Center for American Archeology, P.O. Box 366, Kampsville, IL 62053. Phone: 618/653-4316.

The Kampsville Archeological Museum, one of 20 buildings in the Center complex, is open May–October, Tuesday–Sunday. Closed certain holidays. Admission charged. An annual public event, called Archeology Day, is held first Saturday in August; site tours, laboratory displays, prehistoric technology demonstrations, lectures, and artifact identification are part of the program.

From mid-June through mid-August, visitors to Kampsville are able to view an archeological excavation in progress. The site changes every few years, but the dig is always located

Red Paint people in Archaic times hunted moose using spears and spear-throwers (atlatls). Field Museum of Natural History photo.

within several miles of Kampsville. Special tours of varying lengths to suit various interests can be arranged for a fee any time during May–October.

At the center are sophisticated research facilities for professional archeologists. The Education Program also provides a varied curriculum for all ages and backgrounds. One-week archeological field schools are held June–August for high school students and for non-college adults; and there is a five-week high school student option that allows students to design and conduct their own research project under the supervision of the Center's professional staff.

A college-level field school run by the University of Chicago, teaches field archeology as well as courses in bioarcheology. Archeology and prehistoric technology workshops for teachers are offered in the fall.

Junior high school students participate in week-long prehistoric technology sessions held in May, September, and October, during which they make tools, gather native materials, and build houses based on prehistoric models. A catalog providing detailed informa-

tion about the entire curriculum is available.

The Kampsville Archeological Museum is dedicated to the exhibition and interpretation of material culture and lifeways spanning the entire 12,000 years of lower Illinois Valley prehistory. On display are artifacts, reproductions of ceremonies and daily life, and aspects of subsistence and economy, environment, and aboriginal technologies.

Of particular interest to young people are the interactive exhibits. One brings the visitor inside a reconstruction of the main excavation block at the world-famous Koster Site (see below). Another provides activity stations where children—and adults—can actually use different kinds of prehistoric tools to saw and drill wood, punch leather, grind an axe head, and crack a nut. Still another consists of stone and ceramic debris which can be leisurely handled while questions about prehistoric technology are asked and answered by other exhibits.

The final exhibit allows children to play the role of an archeologist. They are living in the 27th century and try-

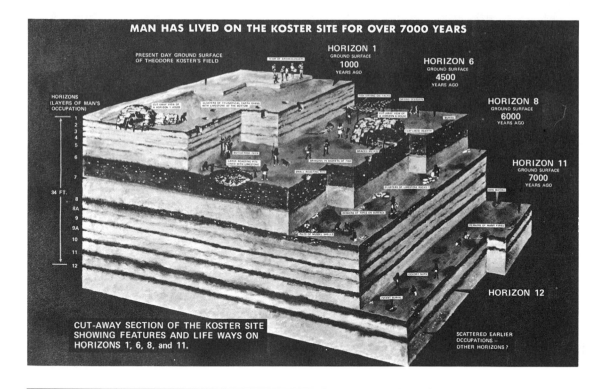

MAN HAS LIVED ON THE KOSTER SITE FOR OVER 7000 YEARS

CUT-AWAY SECTION OF THE KOSTER SITE
SHOWING FEATURES AND LIFE WAYS ON
HORIZONS 1, 6, 8, and 11.

ing to reconstruct 20th century life from just the trash and debris that has not degraded during the last 700 years. In addition to teaching archeology, this exhibit also makes a powerful conservation statement.

Artifacts on display in the museum have all been recovered from sites investigated by the Center. In all, over 3500 sites have been recorded in the lower Illinois and adjacent Mississippi River valleys by Center projects during more than 30 years of continuous investigation in this region. Ten of these years were spent excavating the Koster Site, and the centerpiece of the museum is a reconstruction of its main excavation block.

The Koster Site. This unusual site was named for Theodore Koster, a farmer who for a long time turned up potsherds whenever he plowed his cornfield near the Illinois River. His neighbor, Harlin Helton, thought that archeologists ought to do some serious digging on the Koster farm. Helton persuaded Dr. Stuart Struever, of Northwestern University, to make test excavations in 1969, and that started a most important and rewarding project.

Subsequent digging astonished and delighted both Mr. Koster and Dr. Struever—and crews of helpers. (Workers at the site ranged from junior high-school, college, and graduate-school students to senior citizens in nonacademic work groups.) Excavation revealed that time after time between 6500 B.C. and A.D. 1000, people lived in this protected spot near the foot of a limestone bluff. Each time its inhabitants abandoned the site, all the debris they left was gradually covered by earth washed down from the bluff. Thus was formed what Dr. Struever called a "fossilized layer cake"—first a layer of sterile soil untouched by people, then an icing rich in the lost, broken, or buried remains of human activity. Another sterile layer followed, then came another filling of archeological goodies, and so on.

By the time the Koster Site was closed to the public in 1979, 13 layers of habitation had been excavated and studied. (The levels are called horizons.) Computer analysis of material recovered at the site later indicated that there were probably more than 20 occupation levels. Digs elsewhere in the

University of Chicago students excavating at the 7000-year-old Bullseye Site. Photo courtesy of the Center for American Archeology.

United States have also revealed multiple horizons, but this is the first where archeologists have found such extensive Archaic village areas, one above another, so clearly separated and so readily dated.

With the help of men and women skilled in nearly a dozen branches of science, archeologists have been able to elaborate the story of the early inhabitants of Illinois. Geologists studied the sterile soil, which was fortunately the kind that best preserves bone, seeds, fish scales, shells. An expert on moisture-loving snails used them as clues to the climate at different times. Botanists found that for a long period the staple food was hickory nuts. Later a variety of other nuts and plants was harvested. Bones of deer, small animals, and enormous numbers of fish, analyzed by specialists, helped to reveal the seasons when people lived at the site. Other specialists studied what Koster Site people looked like, what diseases they suffered, and how they related to their environment.

All these and many other scientific findings added up to some surprises.

For example, there seems to have been a stable society here as early as 6500 B.C., almost 4,000 years earlier than scientists had thought more or less sedentary people could efficiently exploit plant and animal food. Moreover, the early Koster inhabitants apparently chose plants that yielded the most for the least labor and that provided the most nutritious diet.

Horizon 8 at the site disclosed the earliest permanent dwellings in North America, dated at about 5000 B.C. At about this same time there is evidence that squash was being intentionally grown, and by 2000 B.C. a number of wild plants were being cultivated throughout the lower Illinois River valley. Corn does not appear until after A.D. 500, but it soon becomes the major subsistence item in the prehistoric diet.

Perhaps the change to reliance on corn was not entirely to the farmers' advantage. Their bones often give evidence that they were not so well nourished as their hunting-and-gathering forebears.

Center scientists who studied Koster and other lower Illinois Valley sites are now convinced that people there did not always live chiefly by the hunt. They depended on a well-balanced diet from plant, animal, and aquatic resources, and they began cultivating wild plants thousands of years earlier than was suspected only a few decades ago.

Twin Ditch Site. The Education Program of the Kampsville Archeological Center has discovered artifacts at this site that predate the lowest levels of the Koster site. Here were undisturbed points left where they had been made 10,000 years ago.

Quasar Site. The Field School of the Kampsville Archeological Center has conducted excavations at this Archaic site which dates at 5000 B.C. to 3000 B.C. This site was apparently occupied for a long time because of the rich river and floodplain resources.

Special Interest. An annual contribution to the Center for American Archeology entitles the donor to take part in certain membership activities, receive complimentary admission to Archeology Day, receive the Center's semiannual newsletter and qualify for discounts in the museum store.

Junior high school students, taking part in the Kampsville Archeological Center's prehistoric technology program, learn how to make chipped stone tools. Center for American Archeology photo.

Junior high school students participate in the Kampsville Archeological Center's prehistoric technology program. Here they are constructing a Native American house. Center for American Archeology photo.

Work at the famous Koster site was begun in 1972. Work at the site was completed and it was backfilled in 1979. Photo courtesy of Center for American Archeology.

Portrait of a Leader

In 1952 archeologists digging at a site on the Illinois River uncovered the skeleton of an Indian who had been buried there at some time between A.D. 900 and A.D. 1200. With only his bones and few artifacts to study, the scientists have put together an amazingly complete picture of the man.

Evidence that he was a leader is in the articles placed beside him in the grave: two necklaces with a total of 468 beads, each laboriously shaped of shell brought from the Gulf of Mexico; bracelets and anklets of shell beads; four projectile points; a stone of use in grinding red pigment; a pottery jar. Other objects are the sort of thing that might be given to someone who held office—a large stone ceremonial blade, a piece of galena ore imported from the north, a tobacco pipe, an animal rib that had been carved for some purpose, and a long rod made of horn. Negative evidence that the man was important lay in the other burials nearby. They contained much less wealth in the form of grave goods.

After examining the skull, Bartlett Frost, of the Detroit Historical Museum, modeled the bust shown here, basing his work on information that physical anthropologists have put together. Size of facial muscles, for example, is indicated by bony structure where the muscles are attached. Skin thickness and nose shape are determined by other measurements. The result is this portrait of an Indian leader in Illinois a thousand years ago.

Illinois Archeological Survey photo.

LAKEVIEW CENTER FOR THE ARTS AND SCIENCES

1125 Lake Ave., Peoria, IL 61614. Phone: 309/686-7000. Open free, Tuesday–Saturday; afternoon, Sunday; evening, Wednesday. Closed certain holidays.

In the gallery of this institution there is a section devoted to Illinois archeology. Exhibits change from time to time.

MADISON COUNTY HISTORICAL MUSEUM

715 N. Main St., Edwardsville, IL 62025. Phone: 618/656-7562. Open free, Wednesday–Friday; afternoon, Sunday. Closed certain holidays.

Nearly 3000 artifacts in the Indian collection of the museum are grouped by types—axes together, bannerstones together, and so on. Although some of the material seems to be at least 4000 years old, it is not arranged chronologically or by cultures. A number of artifacts are from Cahokia Mounds. In addition to Illinois material, mostly from Madison County, there are some artifacts from the prehistoric Southwest.

MISSISSIPPI PALISADES STATE PARK

From Savanna drive 2 miles north on Illinois 84 to directional sign on the right. Open free, all year. Roads may be closed during periods of freezing and thawing. Camping.

Within the park are old Indian trails and numerous mounds in which archeologists have done little excavating.

PERE MARQUETTE STATE PARK (PEER mar-KET)

From Alton drive 19 miles northwest via Great River Rd. to Grafton, then 5 miles west on Illinois 100 to the park entrance. Open free, all year, except when roads are closed during freezing and thawing. Camping.

Beginning around A.D. 1. Native

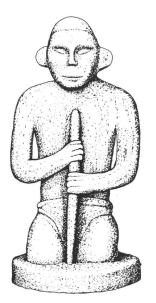

Figurines like this one, which was found at Knight Mounds in Illinois, have provided archeologists with information about the appearance of Indians who followed the Hopewell lifeway. After a reproduction in the Field Museum of Natural History, Chicago.

Americans left evidence of their presence at 18 different sites in this park, which is named for the seventeenth-century French explorer, Father Jacques Marquette.

When Marquette traveled the Illinois and Mississippi rivers, two distinct mound-builder cultures had developed, flourished, and died along their banks. A group known as the Jersey Bluff people once made their homes in the rocky palisades near the park, and they may have been the forerunners of the great mound builders at Cahokia, a little way to the south. In adjacent Calhoun County a much earlier people, who followed the Hopewell lifeway, buried their dead in less prominent earthworks. But the gifts they put into the graves were spectacular. At one of the sites—the Knight Mound, which is not visitable—they buried small, baked-clay figurines. These portrait statues were purposely broken at the time of burial, but they have been reconstructed and are one of the chief sources of information about Hopewell appearance and dress.

SOUTHERN ILLINOIS UNIVERSITY, UNIVERSITY MUSEUM

Faner Hall, on the campus, Carbondale, IL 62901. Open free, Monday–Friday; afternoon, Sunday. Closed holidays and when the university is not in session.

Here the Center for Archeological Investigations has extensive archeological collections from the Midwest.

STARVED ROCK STATE PARK

From Ottawa drive 6 miles west on Illinois 71 to the east entrance of the park. Or from La Salle drive 6 miles east on Illinois 71, then .75 mile north on Illinois 178 to west entrance. Mail address: P.O. Box 116, Utica, IL 61373. Phone: 815/667-4726 or 4906. Open free, all year. Camping.

In this beautiful place on the bank of the Illinois River are old Indian trails through the woods, shelter caves and open sites where prehistoric people camped, and the remains of several burial mounds.

The Story. When the first wandering hunters entered Illinois, perhaps 10,000 years ago, a band of them discovered Starved Rock and camped there. The Rock is a section of the Illinois River bluff which rises 125 feet straight up from the water. It can be approached only from one side, and so its flat circular top made it an ideal lookout spot.

During the Archaic Period, people sometimes camped on the Rock. At other times men probably camped below, brought chunks of stone to the top of the bluff, and sat about making projectile points and tools. The remains of their workshops have turned up in archeological excavations. One such group also left behind a copper spearpoint, one of the earliest known. Others, over a period of two or three thousand years, lost or discarded their hammerstones, scrapers, drills, and grinding tools around their campsites on the Rock.

Later, when people began to follow the Woodland way of life, women cooked here and threw away their broken pots. On the flatlands nearby, the dead were buried in mounds. Still later, other groups visited the Rock, at least occasionally, up until historic times.

The Name. According to legend, the Illini Indians who lived along the river were attacked by Ottawa and Potawatomi warriors. The Illini fled to the top of the Rock, which they were able to defend until their food gave out. In the end many died of hunger. Hence the name Starved Rock.

UNIVERSITY OF ILLINOIS, MUSEUM OF NATURAL HISTORY

438 Natural History Building, 1301 West Green Street, Urbana, IL 61801. Phone: 217/333-2517. Open free, Monday–Saturday; afternoon, Sunday. Closed certain holidays.

In the museum's fourth floor galleries, the exhibit "Ancient Midwestern Lifeways" depicts pre-Columbian Native American ways of life in Illinois and surrounding areas from periods beginning 10,000 B.C. and ending A.D. 1600.

Indiana

ANGEL MOUNDS STATE HISTORIC SITE

From downtown Evansville drive 7 miles east on Indiana 662 to a point 2.5 miles west of Newburgh, then south .75 mile on Fuquay Rd. to Pollack Ave., then east .5 mile to the entrance. Mail address: 8215 Pollack Ave., Evansville, IN 47715. Phone: 812/853-3956. Open free, Tuesday–Saturday; afternoon, Sunday. Closed January 1–March 15.

People who followed the lifeway that archeologists called Mississippian lived here on the bank of the Ohio River from about A.D. 1300 to 1500. Like others in their day, they were farmers, traders, and builders of temple mounds. What makes this site unusual and important is its fate in modern times. It lies in a spot that industry has not invaded. It escaped extreme depredation by relic hunters, and in 1938 was purchased by the Indiana Historical Society, which deeded it to the state of Indiana. For more than 20 years the

site was made available, with adequate financing, to archeologist Glenn A. Black to excavate. Foot by foot he studied the village, which probably marks the most northeasterly extension of the Mississippian culture.

Black dug into the mounds. He stripped away soil from the living areas and unearthed more than $2^{1}/_{2}$ million pieces of material.

The people who built the mounds were immigrants, probably from Illinois. They may not have been entirely welcome, for they chose to build in a spot that was easy to defend. In front of their village an island in the river shielded them from approach across open water. A stream, now dry, protected the site from the rear. For extra safety the settlers surrounded the village with a palisade. This wall, about a mile in length, was made of stout posts placed upright in the ground. Branches were woven between the posts and then plastered over with mud. At intervals in the palisade were bastions, or lookout towers.

In times of peace the river channel between shore and the island offered an easy place to fish. The surrounding

This drawing of a prehistoric burial mound in Ohio was published in *Ancient Monuments of the Mississippi Valley,* by E. G. Squier and E. H. Davis. National Park Service photo.

A few of the many artifacts recovered at Angel Mounds State Historic Site, Indiana. In twenty years of excavation at this site more than two million pieces of material were found and examined. Indiana Department of Natural Resources photo.

land, which lay above the water level of most spring floods, was good for farming. In the woods not far away there was game.

Inside the palisade these hard-working people built 11 mounds, the largest with three distinct terraces. A religious structure may have stood on the lowest terrace. Possibly the house of the principal chief occupied the terrace above that. Higher still, on the northeast corner, was a conical mound. Perhaps the chief made ceremonial use of this prominence, the top of which was 44 feet above the surrounding land. Some experts think he may have mounted it daily to greet the rising sun.

A second large mound is believed to be the location of the main religious structure in the town. Between this temple mound and the chief's mound was the town square, where important ceremonies took place. On ordinary days people gambled in the square and young men played games. Members of the upper class probably lived close to

the square; common people, farther away.

The town as a whole seems to have served as the religious center for an area that extended outward for 50 or 60 miles. What happened to it in the end is not known. Like other Mississippian settlements it was deserted when Europeans reached the Ohio Valley.

The Museum. In the Interpretive Center are exhibits, both permanent and changing, of jewelry, effigies, and other artifacts from the wealth of archeological material found here. An audiovisual program offers orientation and the story of the mounds.

Reconstructions on the site show a part of the high defensive stockade, the temple with a museum inside, thatched winter and summer houses and a round house.

The Name. Angel was the family name of the people who once owned the mounds.

This partly reconstructed defensive wall shows how people at Angel Mounds State Historic Site, Indiana, built palisades and house walls, using poles, branches, and mud. Indiana Department of Natural Resources photo.

CHILDREN'S MUSEUM OF INDIANAPOLIS

3000 N. Meridian St. Mail address: P.O. Box 3000, Indianapolis, IN 46206. Phone: 317/924-5431. Open Tuesday–Saturday, afternoon, Sunday. Closed Labor Day, Memorial Day and certain other holidays. Admission charged except Thursday 4–8 p.m., Martin Luther King Day, and President's Day.

Among the museum's many exhibits are Indian artifacts, prehistoric and historic. Exhibits and dioramas have been designed to show grade-school children how tools, weapons, and utensils were made and how they were related to the everyday life of the people who used them. There is also a display showing an archeological dig. Mini-exhibits from the museum's large collection change from time to time.

EITELJORG MUSEUM OF AMERICAN INDIAN AND WESTERN ART

500 West Washington St., Indianapolis, IN 46204-2707. Phone: 317/636-WEST. Open Tuesday–Saturday; afternoon, Sunday. Closed Monday, except June through August. Closed certain holidays. Admission charged.

Included in this important museum's collection of Native American artifacts are a few prehistoric pots from the Southwest.

GLENN A. BLACK LABORATORY OF ARCHAEOLOGY

Ninth and Fess Streets, Bloomington, IN 47405. Phone: 812/855-9544. Open free, Monday–Friday. Weekend access is through Mathers Museum. Equipped for disabled.

Exhibits emphasize the archeology of the Great Lakes and Ohio Valley areas, and depict prehistoric Indian life through artifacts. These are arranged in chronological order from the Paleo-Indian period at end of the Ice Age to the beginning of the historic period when trading posts were established around A.D. 1750. Collections on exhibit include objects found during excavations at Fort Ouiatenon and at Angel Mounds (see entry above). There are exhibits with Ice Age animal remains and an exhibit of prehistoric artifact types compared to modern examples. One exhibit shows an archeological dig with some of the tools used in an actual excavation.

INDIANA STATE MUSEUM

202 N. Alabama St., Indianapolis, IN 46204. Phone: 317/232-1637. Open free, daily, all year. Closed certain holidays.

In the prehistoric gallery of this museum, exhibits tell the story of the first inhabitants up to contact with Europeans and before they were influenced by white traders.

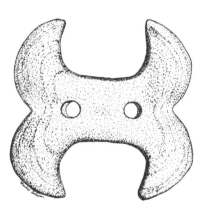

Birdstones have been found throughout the North Central area, and their exact use and function are still disputed. This birdstone may have been used as a weight on an atlatl. Original in the Milwaukee Public Museum.

The bannerstone, also, is an artifact that has thus far defied exact identification. This one was cut from slate and finely polished. It is of the type called "winged"; others were shaped like butterflies. Original in the National Museum of the American Indian, Smithsonian Institution.

MATHERS MUSEUM, INDIANA UNIVERSITY

416 North Indiana Ave., Bloomington, IN 47405. Phone: 812/855-MUSE. Open free, Tuesday–Friday; afternoons, Saturday and Sunday.

This is a museum of world cultures and occasionally exhibits North American archeological materials.

MIAMI COUNTY MUSEUM

51 North Broadway, Peru, IN 46970. Phone: 317/473-9183. Open Tuesday–Saturday. Closed certain holidays. Handicapped accessible. Admission charged.

The prehistoric artifacts on display represent a time frame in Miami County history from 10,000 B.C. to A.D. 1500 and are representative of the Paleo-Indian, Archaic, and Woodland (Adena, Hopewell, and Mississippian) cultures.

MOUNDS STATE PARK

From Anderson drive 4 miles east on Indiana 232. Mail address: 4306 Mounds Road, Anderson, IN 46017. Phone: 317/642-6627. Open year round. Admission charged. Camping.

Nine of the ten prehistoric earthworks in the park are attributed to the Adena culture. The largest, the Great Mound, seems to have been designed for use as a ceremonial enclosure. Nearly 16,300 cubic yards of earth were moved to create a circular structure 1200 feet around and almost 15 feet high. Recent archeological work seems to indicate the mound was used for astronomical alignments and recording the sunsets at the spring/fall equinoxes and summer/winter solstices. Artifacts found on the Great Mound's central platform point to Hopewell as well as Adena use of the mound complex.

WYANDOTTE CAVE

From Interstate 64 turn south onto Indiana 66 to intersection with Indiana 62, then east through Leavenworth on Indiana 62 to the cave. Mail address: Leavenworth, IN 47137. Phone: 812/738-2782. Open daily, all year. Closed December 25. Admission charged. Camping nearby.

Although people usually visit this state-owned cave to see the cave itself, it is of archeological interest on more than one count. Apparently two different groups of people came here at two different times to do two different types of mining. One group hammered out and carried away large quantities of a soft mineral called calcite. What they used it for is not known, possibly because calcite turns to dust under certain conditions. The other group dug out nodules of flint embedded in the walls in a different section of the cave. The flint was, of course, raw material for projectile points, scrapers, and other tools.

At still another place, in the dried mud on the floor of a corridor that had long been blocked off by a calcite formation, Indian moccasin footprints were found going farther into the cave but not returning. One possible explanation is that the footprints led to a cave exit, which was later closed by a rockfall.

Some scientists believe the cave was also used from time to time as a shelter by Indians from 7000 B.C. to A.D. 1500.

Birdstones, Boatstones, Bannerstones

In 1840 some theological students from Connecticut found in an Indian burial a highly polished stone that somewhat resembled a bird. In 1848 Squier and Davis included illustrations of similar stones in their *Ancient Monuments of the Mississippi Valley.* From that time on farmers and others began to collect these strange objects. Birdstones turned up all over Ohio and Indiana and in western New York, western Pennsylvania, eastern Illinois, southeastern Wisconsin, southern Michigan, and lower Canada.

The carefully shaped images sometimes resembled creatures other than birds. Some looked a little like boats (these were called boatstones). Others, less representational in form, got the name bannerstone, possibly because they were thought to resemble the small banners that in some societies were attached to ceremonial staffs. The kind of stone used in these objects was very often attractive. Banded slate was a favorite material. So was porphyry, which has a mottled, varicolored appearance. The range of shades in these artifacts was wide and so was the range of shapes.

But what was their origin, their use, their meaning? Answers to these questions were as numerous as facts about them were scarce. They were called handles for knives, emblems of maternity designed to be worn in women's hair, stone bayonets, totemic emblems, cornhuskers, necklace ornaments, fetishes, decorations for the tops of staffs used by medicine men. One man argued that the birdstones were somehow connected with the widespread thunderbird myth.

Arthur Parker, an archeologist and himself a Native American, speculated that at least one type of bannerstone was attached to the shaft of a spear. Its purpose was to give weight to the spear, and also to keep it on course, as feathers do for an arrow. Parker experimented with this arrangement and discovered that the spear went much straighter, faster, and about 25 percent farther than one with an unweighted shaft.

Another theory is that a good many bird/bannerstones were used as weights on atlatls (and not on spears themselves), to give added momentum for launching the weapon. Some evidence does suggest that some bannerstones were so used. It also seems possible that some birdstones had no such mechanical value but were for magical or ceremonial purposes.

Archeologist Thorne Deuel believes that bannerstones developed from atlatl weights but were either decorations or ceremonial objects carried by men to show they were good hunters. Later, he thinks, they evolved still further into flat forms that had bannerstone outlines but were worn as gorgets.

Cailup B. Curren, Jr., of the University of Alabama, has speculated that some at least of the "gorgets" may have served as tools that potters used for smoothing and shaping clay vessels. The idea occurred to him when he noticed that a kind of modern ceramic tool called a rib was remarkably like certain of the two-holed, polished stone prehistoric objects. Inquiry revealed that in some places the first appearance of these "gorgets" coincided with the first appearance of ceramics.

Whatever future researchers discover about these problematical objects, one thing is certain: Many forgers have gone into the business of making birdstones and have found it very profitable.

Caveat emptor!

These rounded heaps of earth are part of nine mounds built by Native Americans nearly 2000 years ago in an area used for ceremonies and funeral rites. The site is now part of Mounds State Park, Indiana. Indiana Natural Resources photo.

At Effigy Mounds National Monument, in Iowa, one young worker digs carefully with trowel and whisk broom. Another shovels loosened earth into a screen that fits over a wheel barrow. The screen catches any small objects missed by the boys in the pit. National Park Service photo.

Iowa

BLOOD RUN NATIONAL HISTORIC LANDMARK

Mail address: Lyon County Conservation Board, 311 First Ave. East, Rock Rapids, IA 51246. Phone: 712/472-2217. Visits by appointment only.

This is probably the largest Oneota village and burial site in the United States. Occupation began about A.D. 900 and reached its most active period at the end of the 1600s and beginning of the 1700s. Originally there were more than 200 mounds here but only about 100 remain. In the village site are boulder circles that may have served as fortifications or may have been related to shelters. There are also pitted boulders, the significance of which is unknown. The site covers approximately 1000 acres of which only 200 are owned and protected by the state. The rest are in private hands.

DAVENPORT MUSEUM
(*See Putnam Museum*)

EFFIGY MOUNDS NATIONAL MONUMENT

From Marquette drive 3 miles north on Iowa 76 to monument entrance. Mail address: RR1, Box 25A, Harper's Ferry, IA 52146. Open daily, all year except December 25. Admission charged. Camping nearby.

Here on high land, which was by-passed instead of being scoured down by glaciers of the Ice Age, people built nearly 200 mounds during a period of at least 1500 years. Some of these mounds are likenesses—effigies—of birds or bears. Others are cone-shaped and were built by people whose customs differed from those of the effigy-mound builders. It is possible to see a good sample of both types by walking along a trail that starts at the monument's Visitor Center.

The Story. Twelve thousand years ago in Iowa, Paleo-Indians hunted mammoths and giant bison, which grazed on prairie grasses. But changes in climate brought changes in vegetation, and forest slowly covered much of the land along the banks of the Yellow

Two students in archeology, working at Effigy Mounds National Monument, in Iowa, prepare to remove a column of earth intact, so that it may be studied in a laboratory. Examining different pollen grains in each layer of the soil discloses what plants grew there at a given time in the past. National Park Service photo.

River, where it flows into the Mississippi. The big game of earlier times disappeared and people turned to hunting smaller animals.

The earliest tools that have been discovered near Effigy Mounds are woodworking implements—axes, adzes, gouges. Obviously the people who made this kind of tool lived in wooded country. Other evidence shows that they hunted forest mammals, fished, and gathered freshwater mussels. Plants, too, made up part of their diet—wild rice, nuts, fruits, berries. They sewed clothing and wove baskets, using awls that were made of bone or copper. Their religious leaders conducted ceremonies aimed at curing illness and warding off bad luck, but if they had any special burial customs few signs of them have survived.

Their successors, however, began to take a deep interest in death ceremonials. By 2000 years ago they were following the pattern of many other groups of the North Central area. First they allowed the flesh of their dead to disintegrate. Then they gathered up the bones in bundles, which they buried

along with spearpoints and large, knifelike artifacts. Often they covered the bones with red ocher.

Later, knowledge of how to make pottery came into this area, and over the years potters improved their techniques and changed the styles of the vessels they made. Gradually people adopted other new customs and accepted new beliefs. Between 100 B.C. and A.D. 300 they participated in a phenomenon known as Hopewell.

Hopewell ideas about death and burial included the belief that a wealth of beautiful objects should be placed in graves. To get the material for their grave goods, Hopewellians in Iowa, like those in other places, engaged in trade. Mica for their decorations came from the distant Appalachian Mountains. They used obsidian from Yellowstone Park, conch shells from the Gulf of Mexico, and copper from the Great Lakes area. As in other Hopewellian settlements, mounds were built over the dead. Three such burial mounds can be seen near the Visitor Center in the monument.

A new fashion in mound building

Outlined in white in this photo is the Great Bear Group of mounds in Effigy Mounds National Monument. National Park Service photo by James E. Mount.

began here about A.D. 500. The new style dictated that burial mounds should be in the form of effigies—huge earthen likenesses of birds or bears. Twenty-seven such effigy mounds are in the monument.

The Effigy Mound people apparently lived in ways that resembled those of the Hopewellians, but they differed in some ways too, and not only in the kind of mound they built. They did not bury grave goods with their dead. They put copper to practical use in tools instead of merely shaping it into decorations.

By A.D. 1400, Indians who lived here were following the Oneota lifeway. Now they spent more time farming than earlier people had, and they lived in larger communities. Apparently, among the descendants of the Oneota were the Iowa Indians, whom Europeans later encountered in the region and from whom the state of Iowa gets its name.

The Museum. Exhibits in the Visitor Center throw light on the prehistory of the monument area, and an audio-visual presentation interprets the ar-

cheological findings. Two paintings show what people may have looked like, what they wore, and how they built mounds.

FISH FARM MOUNDS

From New Albin drive 4 miles south on Iowa 26. Mail address: Iowa State Preserves Board, Wallace State Office Building, Des Moines, IA 50319. Open free, daily, all year. Camping.

At this site, which overlooks the Mississippi River, reached by a short walk up stairs, are about 30 prehistoric Indian mounds representative of the Hopewellian phenomenon.

GROUT MUSEUM OF HISTORY AND SCIENCE

Park Ave. at South St., Waterloo. Open free, Tuesday–Friday; afternoon, Saturday, in summer; afternoons, Tuesday–Saturday, during the rest of the year. Closed certain holidays.

Four exhibit cases here are devoted to early Big-Game Hunters, bison hunters, Iowa's first farmers, and later Indians of Iowa.

LITTLE MAQUOKETA RIVER MOUNDS

One half mile south of Sageville in Dubuque County. Mail address: Iowa State Preserves Board, Wallace State Office Building, Des Moines, IA 50319.

Here, reached by a stairway up a fairly steep hill, are 24 conical and linear mounds that range in height from 10 to 50 inches and are from 10 to 40 feet in diameter. The mounds are attributed to Woodland Indians and date from about A.D. 700 to A.D. 1300. The Iowa State Preserves Board's plans for developing the area are in accordance with the desire of Native Americans that the burial mounds not be disturbed. A fence will surround the mounds, but a trail will lead up a 200 foot bluff which gives an overview of the preserve.

MALCHOW MOUNDS

One mile north of Kingston in Des Moines County. Mail address: Iowa State Preserves Board, Wallace State Office Building, Des Moines IA 50319. Open free, daily.

This group of 56 Hopewell Mounds, is reached by a short walk up a gentle incline, dates from 250 B.C. to A.D. 350.

MILLS COUNTY HISTORICAL MUSEUM

East of Square in Glenwood Lake Park. Mail address: P.O. Box 190, Glenwood, IA 51534. Phone: 712/527-5038. Open Sundays, Memorial Day–Labor Day and by appointment.

This museum displays 15,000 Native American artifacts, including some that date back 10,000 years or more.

PIKES PEAK STATE PARK

From McGregor drive 1.5 miles south on Iowa 340. Mail address: R#1, McGregor, IA 52157. Phone: 319/873-2341. Open free, daily, all year. Camping.

Here, overlooking the Mississippi River, are several mounds, including an impressive effigy mound in the form of a bear.

PUTNAM MUSEUM
(Formerly Davenport Museum)

1717 W. 12th St., Davenport, IA 52804. Phone: 319/324-1933. Open Tuesday–Saturday; afternoon, Sunday. Closed certain holidays. Admission charged.

Examples of Middle Mississippian pottery of several kinds from Tennessee and Arkansas, together with Hopewell artifacts from Iowa and Illinois, are in the Putnam collection.

Special Interest. Over a hundred years ago, Jacob Gass, a Lutheran minister and passionate amateur archeologist, managed to get under the skin of some colleagues in the Davenport, Iowa, Academy of Natural Science. To even the score, they concocted an elaborate hoax. On one piece of slate from an old building they drew the signs of the zodiac; on another they scratched let-

ters from various alphabets that they found in a Webster dictionary. Then they buried the slates in a mound and encouraged Gass to excavate there. He did not suspect his find was not genuine, and word spread that he had dug up proof that the mounds were built by people whose written language resembled those of ancient Mediterranean countries. The Davenport tablets became a sensation. Some experts suspected a hoax, but the perpetrators themselves were now ashamed to reveal their plot. Years later some of them confessed, and the records of the affair, together with the tablets, are in the Putnam Museum.

SANFORD MUSEUM AND PLANETARIUM

117 East Willow, Cherokee, IA 51012. Phone: 712/225-3922. Open free, Monday–Friday; afternoons, Saturday and Sunday.

This museum includes exhibits on Pleistocene fauna and Archaic, Woodland, Great Oasis, Mill Pond, and Oneota peoples. It also offers classes in Iowa pre-history, primitive technology, and projectile points. The collections include materials from the Plains, the Southwest, and Northwest coast.

SIOUX CITY PUBLIC MUSEUM

2901 Jackson St., Sioux City, IA 51104. Phone: 712/279-6174. Open free, Monday–Saturday; afternoon, Sunday. Closed certain holidays.

In addition to ethnological exhibits from the Plains and North Central areas, this museum has some archeological material from northwest Iowa.

SLINDE MOUNDS

About six miles northwest of Waukon in Allamakee County. Mail address: Iowa State Preserves Board, Wallace State Office Building, Des Moines, IA 50319. Open free, daily.

Here, overlooking the Upper Iowa River, are 15 mounds from the Middle and Late Woodland cultures, dated at about A.D. 300 to 1400. It is necessary to walk .5 mile to visit this site. The walk is not recommended except for those who are physically fit.

Glacial Kame Culture

When the great ice sheet of the Pleistocene retreated, it left ridges of gravel in many places. Sometimes these ridges are known as glacial kames. *Kame* is a Scottish word for ridge and is pronounced like "came."

Some time after one group of hunting people entered and established themselves in an area that had been glaciated, they began to bury their dead in the gravel ridges. Because they left a distinctive set of grave goods with these burials, archeologists have named them Glacial Kame people. Many of their burials have been found in northern parts of Ohio and Indiana, southern parts of Michigan and Ontario, and also in eastern Illinois and southeastern Wisconsin.

As far as is now known, the people who followed the Glacial Kame lifeway lived at some time betwen 2000 B.C. and 1000 B.C. Their rather elaborate burials included many ornaments but very few tools, a fact which leads some archeologists to think they may have been forerunners of the Adena and Hopewell people, who placed great emphasis on funerary practices. It is also possible, though not proved, that the whole later tradition of placing burials in artifical mounds derived from the Glacial Kame practice of using natural mounds.

No Glacial Kame sites have been prepared for the public.

STATE HISTORICAL SOCIETY OF IOWA MUSEUM

600 E. Locust, Des Moines, IA 50319. Phone: 515/281-5111. Open free, Tuesday–Saturday; afternoon, Sunday. Closed certain holidays.

Permanent exhibits show human utilization of natural resources from prehistoric times to the present. There are also temporary exhibits on a variety of topics that are changed several times a year.

TOOLESBORO MOUNDS
National Historic Landmark

From Wapello drive 6 miles east on Iowa 99. Mail address: State Historical Society, Capitol Complex, Des Moines, IA 50319. Phone: 515/281-5111. Open free, afternoon, Friday–Monday. Special appointments any time.

A group of Hopewell burial mounds here dates from the Middle Woodland period (200 B.C. to A.D. 400) Nearby is the Demonstration Prairie Plot in which grow the plants that flourished in the vicinity when the Hopewell people lived here. The Visitor Center contains displays and photographs that illuminate the Hopewell phenomenon and the vegetation in the prairie plot.

TURKEY RIVER MOUNDS

From Guttenberg on US 52, drive 4.5 miles southeast. Mail address: Iowa State Preserves Board, Wallace State Office Building, Des Moines, IA 50319. Open free, daily.

Here 45 conical and linear burial mounds are on a 200 foot high ridge at the confluence of the Turkey River and the Mississippi. This site, atop nearly perpendicular cliffs, overlooks part of the Upper Mississippi River Wildlife and Fish Refuge. The mounds were built about 2000 years ago. The walk to the site is very steep.

UNIVERSITY OF IOWA MUSEUM OF NATURAL HISTORY

Macbride Hall, on the campus, Iowa City, IA 52242. Phone: 319/335-0481. Open free, Monday–Saturday; afternoon, Sunday. Closed certain holidays.

In the "Native Cultures of Iowa" exhibit in the Iowa Hall Gallery, a Paleo-Indian diorama begins the story of human life in Iowa at about 12,000 years ago. Other exhibits interpret the hunters and foragers of the Archaic period from 8500 B.P. to 3500 B.P. another exhibit is devoted to the Woodland period from about 2500 B.P. to A.D. 1300. Still others show life in the villages of the Great Oasis (A.D. 900–1200), the life of the Mill Creek people (A.D. 900–1300), and of the Glenwood people (A.D. 900–1250). Another exhibit is devoted to the Oneota people (A.D. 900–1650), and there is information about Native Americans of the area from 1650 to the present.

Archeologists believe that one type of Adena house looked like this. Often mud plaster was added to the walls. No original dwelling now exists, but some were destroyed by fire, which baked the mud and preserved the imprint of posts and interwoven branches. After Webb.

This stone pipe is from the original Adena Mound, in Ohio. Ohio Historical Society photo.

Kentucky

ADENA PARK

From Lexington drive 8 miles north on US 27, then turn off onto Old Ironworks Rd., and from this turn onto Mount Horeb Pike. The park is on the south side of North Elkhorn Creek. Open free, by appointment arranged through the Department of Campus Recreation of the University of Kentucky in Lexington. Mail address: Room 135, Seaton Center, University of Kentucky, Lexington, KY 40506-0219. Phone: 606/257-2898.

In the park is a circular earthwork, of the kind known as a "sacred circle," which surrounds a flat area where a structure once stood. A ditch and an embankment crossed by a causeway form part of the site, which was built and used as a ceremonial center by Adena people. The park is owned by the University of Kentucky.

ASHLAND CENTRAL PARK

Two blocks south of US 60 in Ashland. Open free, daily, all year.

In the playground area in this city park, markers indicate five burial mounds. These are a small fraction of the total number that once existed where the city of Ashland now stands, on the bank of the Ohio River. Professional archeologists have not investigated the mounds in Central Park, and it is not known who built them or when.

BEHRINGER-CRAWFORD MUSEUM

In Covington's Devou Park. Mail address: P.O. Box 67, Covington, KY 41012. Phone: 606/491-4003. Open Tuesday–Saturday, February–November; afternoon, Sunday. Closed certain holidays. Admission charged.

Included in the archeological exhibits are collections of Paleo, Archaic, Woodland, and Fort Ancient materials.

BIG BONE LICK STATE PARK

From Covington drive southwest on Interstate 75, then west on Kentucky 338, a total distance of 22 miles. Mail address: 3380 Beaver Road, Union, KY 41091. Phone: 606/384-3522. Open daily, February–January. Admission charged. Camping.

In prehistoric times mastodons, mammoths, sloths, and horses came to a swampy area here, attracted by the abundant salt in it. Prehistoric hunters followed the animals and left some of their weapons. A few of these are in the park museum along with bones of some of the animals that became mired in the swamp and died.

BLUE LICKS MUSEUM

Blue Licks Battlefield State Park. From Lexington drive 40 miles northeast on US 68 to Blue Licks Spring, then follow directional markers. Mail address: P.O. Box 66, Mt. Olivet, KY 41064. Phone: 606/289-5507. Open daily, April–October. Admission charged. Camping.

Adena

One of the nineteenth-century governors of Ohio lived near Chillicothe on a large estate, which he called Adena. Like other property nearby, his grounds had been occupied in prehistoric times by people who built large, cone-shaped earthen mounds, in which they buried their dead. But unlike most mounds, the one at Adena remained more or less undisturbed until 1901, when an archeologist was allowed to excavate it. The material he uncovered seemed to be the work of a people with very definite and identifiable traits.

When artifacts and burials from other mounds were compared to those at Adena, a general pattern emerged. People with similar traits had lived in prehistoric times throughout most of Ohio, eastern Indiana, northern Kentucky, western Pennsylvania, and parts of West Virginia.

Much of Adena life centered around rituals in honor of the dead. Few people ever had more ways of handling burials. Sometimes they placed an individual in a bark-lined pit on the floor of a house, which was then covered with a mound of earth. They cremated other bodies then buried the remains. Sometimes part of a body was cremated and part buried. Often bodies were left to decay, perhaps lying on raised platforms, and then the cleaned bones were buried. Ritual bowls were made from some skulls, and bone from the skullcap might be shaped and engraved to make gorgets.

Toward the end of their history, which lasted from about 1000 B.C. to about A.D. 200, the Adena seem to have paid honor mainly to a few important people, who were buried in stout, log tombs, surrounded by their possessions. These grave goods included copper bracelets and rings, beads of shell and copper, smoking pipes, and ornaments of mica, polished stone, and other materials.

Archeologists have found the skeletons in log tombs especially interesting. Many were tall—men and women both over six feet. Almost all the skulls were flattened at the back, as a result of binding to a cradleboard in infancy. Some also had a groove at the sides, which seems to indicate further binding to give the skull a rounded shape.

Smoking played a part in ceremonies, and the Adena made innumerable pipes, some of clay and some of stone. Often a man's pipe was buried with him, but occasionally archeologists have found large numbers of them associated with a single burial, perhaps because the dead man was a pipe maker.

In some of their ceremonies, possibly designed to bring good hunting, men wore headdresses imitating deer antlers and masks imitating wolf or puma heads. The jaws of bears and other animals were also carefully cut and ground to make ornaments or charms of some sort.

The Adena culture was similar in many ways to the richer, more elaborate Hopewell phenomenon which coexisted with it for centuries and shared some of the same territory. The original Adena mound cannot be visited, but the house on the estate for which is was named is open to the public.

Ten thousand years ago a spring of saltwater flowed in the park. Attracted by the salt, mastodons, mammoths, bison, and other animals visited the spring. Big-Game Hunters followed the animals, which sometimes got stuck in the mud and died there.

After the animals of the Ice Age disappeared, hunters continued to camp near the spring from time to time. Finally, about A.D. 1400, people who followed the Fort Ancient lifeway made their homes nearby. Their village, known as the Fox Field Site, has been excavated, and artifacts from it are on exhibit at the museum in the park. Other exhibits contain projectile points used by the early hunters, fishhooks, and stone tools made by later people. Bones of some of the extinct animals are also on display.

Gigantic herds of buffalo in ancient times made a regular path, called a trace, to various salt licks in Kentucky. Near the Falls of the Ohio, at Louisville, they had a crossing, as did the mammoths and mastodons. Prehistoric peoples also followed trade routes to the crossing. At least one trading expedition may have made its way to the Falls from the neighborhood of Poverty Point, far down the Mississippi, in Louisiana (see entry above). Evidence suggesting such a visit was a cache of small, baked clay balls of the kind that Poverty Point people used in cooking. Possibly visitors from Louisiana brought the balls along or they or someone else may have made them on the spot.

On the Indiana side of the river there was once a settlement of shellfish eaters, who left piles of discarded mussel shells ten feet deep for almost a mile along the riverbank. Their tools and those of other groups who lived in the area turn up often near the Falls, but no visitable sites remain.

MAMMOTH CAVE NATIONAL PARK

From Bowling Green drive 22 miles north on Intestate 65 to Park City, then north on Kentucky 255 to park entrance; from here it is 5 miles to park headquarters. From points north and east, take Interstate 65 to Cave City, then Kentucky 70, 10 miles to park headquarters. Mail address: Mammoth Cave, KY 42259. Phone: 502/758-2251. Open daily, all year. Admission charged. Camping.

Indians knew about and sometimes ventured into Mammoth Cave in Archaic times, 3000 years ago, before they made pottery or did any farming. During one such visit a young girl died. Before moving on, her people buried her in a grass-lined grave at the cave's mouth.

By at least 400 B.C., people had grown bold enough to enter the dark, underground passages. There they found various minerals such as gypsum and epsomite, which they used in some way. No one knows which minerals they valued or why, but they sought them far underground. Two and a half miles of cave walls show evidence of their mining activity. As tools they used stone hammers and scrapers made of mussel shells. For light they carried torches made from bundles of reeds.

When modern visitors entered, remnants of ancient torches still lay on the cave floor, as did worn-out sandals woven from strips of the inner bark of the pawpaw tree. Here and at nearby Salts Cave, collectors began to find and carry away feather blankets, cloth woven in black and white stripes, dishes made of dried squash rind, string bags, and basket coffins made of cane. Much of this material disappeared into private collections before the caves were put under government protection. A few articles are on exhibit in the museum at Mammoth Cave Park Headquarters.

In 1935 an explorer came upon the body of an ancient miner who had been killed by a falling rock. Instead of decaying, his flesh had simply dried in the cool, pure cave air.

Explorers in nearby Salts Cave in 1875 also came upon the desiccated body of a nine-year-old boy. Scientists determined that the boy lived at least 2000 years ago, during the Woodland period, and was possibly a member of an Adena population. Other signs of human activities in Salts Cave have been dated back to about 1500 B.C.

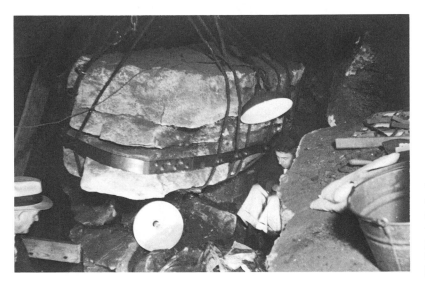

Two thousand years ago an Indian was mining gypsum $2^1/_2$ miles from the entrance to Mammoth Cave when a huge rock fell on him. The photo shows archeologists removing the rock. National Park Service photo.

NORTHERN KENTUCKY UNIVERSITY, MUSEUM AND LABORATORIES OF ANTHROPOLOGY

On the campus, 200 Charles O. Landrum Academic Center, Nunn Drive, Highland Heights. Mail address: Museum and Labs of Anthropology, Northern Kentucky University, Highland Heights, KY 41099-6210. Phone: 606/572-5959. Open free, Monday–Friday and by appointment. Closed June–July, except by appointment, and certain holidays. Tours and special programs for groups by appointment.

Exhibits on a variety of themes and topics include archeological materials from Northern Kentucky and the Central Ohio Valley.

SPEED ART MUSEUM

2035 S. Third St., Louisville, KY 40208. Phone: 502/636-2893. Open Tuesday–Saturday; afternoon, Sunday. Closed certain holidays. Admission charged.

Prehistoric material on display in the J. B. Speed Art Museum consists mainly of artifacts made by the Adena people in Kentucky and southern Indiana. There are also some Paleo-Indian artifacts.

UNIVERSITY OF KENTUCKY

211 Lafferty hall, on the main campus, Lexington, KY 40506. Phone: 606/257-7112. Open free, Monday–Friday. Closed certain holidays.

Exhibits here illustrate the culture history of Kentucky from Paleo-Indian times to the present. Since this was the heartland of the Adena culture, items from Adena tombs are on display.

WICKLIFFE MOUNDS

From Cairo, Ill., drive across the Ohio River Bridge, then 5 miles southeast on US 51 to directional sign near Wickliffe. The site is administered by the Wickliffe Mounds Research Center, Murray State University, P.O. Box 155, Wickliffe, KY 42087. Phone:

502/335-3681. Open March 1–November 30, except Thanksgiving Day. At other times open by appointment only. Admission charged.

Here, close to the place where the Ohio River flows into the Mississippi, was once a large community that followed the Mississippian lifeway. Several of the temple and platform mounds and one burial mound built by these people are protected by buildings in which they may be viewed in a partially excavated state. Only about 10 percent of the site has been excavated. From early June to the middle of September, volunteers are welcome if they make advance arrangements.

Prehistoric copper miners at work.
Smithsonian Institution photo.

Michigan

CHIPPEWA NATURE CENTER

400 South Badour Rd., Midland, MI
48640. Phone: 517/631-0830. Open
Monday–Saturday; afternoon, Sunday. Closed certain holidays. Admission charged.

Dioramas and exhibits of prehistoric Native American material include artifacts found at nearby sites in
an area called the Oxbow Archaeological District.

CRANBROOK INSTITUTE OF SCIENCE

500 Long Pine Rd., Bloomfield Hills,
MI 48303. Phone: 313/645-3230.
Open Monday–Friday; afternoons,
Saturday and Sunday. Admission
charged.

This very active, general science
museum is interested in archeology and
has good exhibits on prehistoric Indian life and culture, including one on
Starved Rock (Illinois) stratigraphy and
another on the sequence of cultures in
Michigan.

GREAT LAKES INDIAN MUSEUM

6325 West Jefferson Ave., Detroit, MI
48209. Phone: 313/833-7900. Open
Wednesday–Sunday, May–October.
Admission charged.

Interpretive exhibits here trace Native American history from prehistoric
times to the present. Of special interest is material from a burial mound on
the bank of the Detroit River, which
is on the grounds of the museum.
Originally a group of mounds built
more than 1200 years ago stood on the
site. All had been destroyed except this
one when Fort Wayne was constructed. Fortunately the command-
ing officer forbade unauthorized
digging. Then in 1944 the Aboriginal
Research Club and the University of
Michigan were given permission to
excavate.

HISTORICAL MUSEUM OF BAY COUNTY

321 Washington Ave., Bay City, MI
48708. Phone: 517/893-5733. Open
free, Monday–Friday; afternoon, Sunday.

In this general museum, devoted to
the history of the Great Lakes area, are
small exhibits of projectile points and
stone tools used by prehistoric inhabitants of Michigan.

HISTORIC FORT WAYNE
(*See Great Lakes Indian Museum*)

ISLE ROYALE NATIONAL PARK

For information on how to reach the
park by boat or plane, apply to: Isle
Royale National Park, Houghton, MI
49931. Phone: 906/482-0986.
Camping.

Prehistoric copper mines can be seen
on Isle Royale, an island in an archi-
pelago in Lake Superior. Beginning
4500 years ago, Indians dug pits to
expose copper-bearing rock. Using
cobbles as hammerstones, they probably broke up the chunks to get at the
lumps and veins of pure copper.

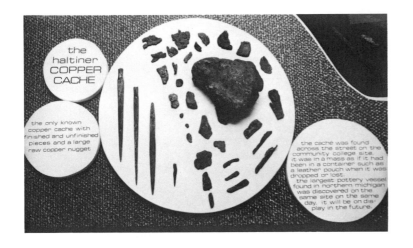

An exhibit in the Jesse Besser Museum, Alpena, Michigan.

Some of the lumps were small. Others were very large. In 1874 one solid mass of copper was found on Isle Royale that weighed 5720 pounds. On it were clear marks that showed where prehistoric hammerstones had battered off small chunks of the malleable metal. Obviously it had once been even larger. After this immense nugget was exhibited to the public for a while, it was melted down for commercial use.

There are about 1000 of the old mining pits in the park. In or near them has been found evidence that they were worked until historic times. Some of the prehistoric miners were ancestors of modern Algonquian, Iroquoian, and Siouan groups.

JESSE BESSER MUSEUM

491 Johnson St., Alpena, MI 49707. Phone: 517/356-2202. Open Monday–Friday; afternoons, Saturday and Sunday. Closed certain holidays. Admission charged.

A collection of 20,000 artifacts traces the story of prehistoric people in the Great Lakes area. The Gallery of Early Man contains many Old Copper Culture artifacts found near the museum, including a cache composed of a large, raw copper nugget, 31 partially worked pieces, and 3 finished artifacts. Loan exhibits from other museums are regularly featured.

KALAMAZOO PUBLIC MUSEUM

315 S. Rose St., Kalamazoo, MI 49007. Phone: 616/345-7092. Open Monday–Saturday; afternoon, Sunday, September–May. Admission charged.

Some prehistoric archeological material from the Southwest and from Eastern Woodland cultures in the United States is exhibited in this museum, which emphasizes history.

MICHIGAN HISTORICAL MUSEUM

717 W. Allegan St., Lansing, MI 48915. Phone: 517/373-3559. Open free, Monday–Saturday; afternoon, Sunday.

Exhibits and dioramas introduce prehistoric materials and objects relating to the fur trade.

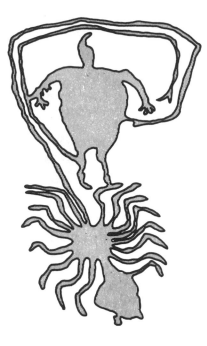

This figure, painted in shades of violet in a Michigan cave, is known as the Spider Man. However, some archeologists believe the lower part of the picture represents not a spider but a campfire. From *Great Lakes Informant,* Michigan Department of State.

MICHIGAN STATE UNIVERSITY MUSEUM

Circle Dr., East Lansing, MI 48823. Phone: 517/355-2370. Open free, Monday–Friday; afternoons, Saturday and Sunday. Closed certain holidays.

Some of the North American prehistoric exhibits in this museum are devoted to Michigan archeology. Others show the culture areas of the continent and techniques used in archeological excavation.

NORTON MOUNDS
National Historic Landmark

From Campau Square in Grand Rapids drive 4 miles south along Grand River on Market St. to the railroad crossing, where Market St. becomes Indian Mound Rd. This is the mound area. It is undeveloped and not open to the public. Mail address: Public Museum of Grand Rapids, 54 Jefferson St., Grand Rapids, MI 49503. Phone: 616/456-3977.

Here are 13 mounds, clearly visible, which are all that remain of about 17 once standing on the property. Although the site lies outside Grand Rapids, it is owned by the city museum which is seeking to have it developed and interpreted in the future.

The Story. People who practiced the Hopewell lifeway moved from the Illinois River valley to this place about A.D. 200. Here, as elsewhere, they began to pile up earth over the bodies of their dead. Around the mounds they built low, earthen enclosures. When a leading member of the community died, lavish funeral ceremonies were held, and gifts were placed in the grave. To get material for their burials, the Hopewell traded with other people in distant places. Copper for beads and tools came from northern Michigan; conch shells for ornaments from the Gulf of Mexico. Decorations and silhouette designs were cut from sheets of mica, which had to be brought from the far-off Appalachian Mountains. Sources close to home provided material for polished stone tools, chipped projectile points, headdresses of deer antlers, and beads of beaver teeth.

For 200 years people continued to

Hopewell funeral ceremony is depicted in this diorama. University of Michigan Museum of Anthropology photo.

build their burial mounds here and at a site, now destroyed, in the center of Grand Rapids. Then for some unknown reason mound building stopped.

Archeologists from the University of Michigan have excavated Norton Mounds, and some of the materials they recovered are on exhibit nearby in the Public Museum of Grand Rapids. A leaflet about the mounds may be obtained at the museum from its director.

PUBLIC MUSEUM OF GRAND RAPIDS

54 Jefferson St. S.E., Grand Rapids, MI 49503. Phone: 616/456-3977. Open free, Monday–Friday; afternoons, Saturday, Sunday, and holidays. Closed December 25.

This museum contains a major exhibit entitled "The People of the Grand," which tells the story of the habitation of the Grand River valley, in the Grand Rapids vicinity, from Paleo-Indian times through the establishment of the first permanent European settlement. The exhibit in-

cludes four life-size, three-dimensional scenes: Paleo-Indians hunting mastodons; a Hopewell burial ceremony at the Norton Indian Mounds; a contact-period scene of an Indian village and fur traders; and a log cabin mission of 1825. Artifacts of the various Indian cultures, with audiovisual accompaniment, provide a picture of what life was like during the past 10,000 years.

Special Interest. A new $32 million exhibition facility, scheduled to open in 1994, will contain a major exhibit, "The Anishinabek: The People of This Place" which will explore the past and present of the People of the Three Fires—the Odawa, Chippewa, and Potawatomi of West Michigan.

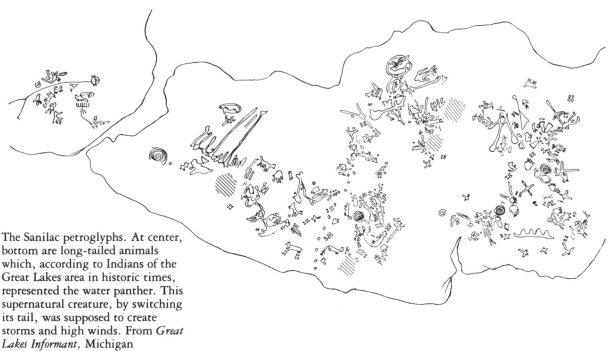

The Sanilac petroglyphs. At center, bottom are long-tailed animals which, according to Indians of the Great Lakes area in historic times, represented the water panther. This supernatural creature, by switching its tail, was supposed to create storms and high winds. From *Great Lakes Informant*, Michigan Department of State.

SANILAC PETROGLYPHS STATE PARK

In Sanilac County's Greenleaf Township, approximately 4 miles east of Michigan 53 and .25 mile south of the junction of the Bay City-Forestville Road and Germainia Road. Open during summer on regular schedule and by appointment only during spring and fall. Closed, winter. Tours available with a guide. Call Port Crescent State Park for information 517/738-8663.

This park, created through the efforts of the Michigan Archaeological Society, protects a flat sandstone outcrop, where at some unknown time in the past people carved abstract designs and the figures of animals and human beings. One image depicts a hunter with bow and arrow. Some of the carvings have been almost destroyed by weather and by the shoes of people who walked over them. A shelter now helps to keep them from further damage.

UNIVERSITY OF MICHIGAN EXHIBIT MUSEUM

Geddes St. and North University Ave., Ann Arbor. Mail address: 1109 Geddes Ave., Ann Arbor, MI 48109-1079. Phone: 313/764-0478. Open free, Tuesday–Saturday; afternoon, Sunday. Closed certain holidays.

In this general natural science museum are exhibits on early Indian sites in Michigan. There are also exhibits of Eskimo, Northwest Coast, and Woodland material. Several displays show the manufacture, evolution, and use of Old World tools, some of which were ancestral to prehistoric American tools. Fourteen small dioramas, six of which are devoted to Michigan, show aspects of various Native American cultures before the arrival of Europeans.

The Museum of Anthropology in this same building conducts archeological research. Its collections are for scientific study and are not open to the public.

The Visitor Center at Jeffers Petroglyph State Park. Minnesota Historical Society photo.

Minnesota

GRAND MOUND CENTER

From International Falls, drive 17 miles west on Minnesota 11. Mail address: Route 7, Box 453, International Falls, MN 56649. Phone: 218/279-3332. Open free, daily, May 1–Labor Day; Saturday and Sunday, September–April.

The Grand Mound is the lagest prehistoric burial mound in the northern Midwest, one of the few to survive in Minnesota, where there were once 10,000 or more. Together with four smaller mounds, this immense earthen structure was built by people of the Laurel culture, who occupied the area along the Rainy River from about 200 B.C. to A.D. 800. They were Woodland people, who fished and hunted and made an unusual smoothly finished pottery. Two distinctive types of Laurel tool were a detachable, togglehead harpoon point and a chisel made from a beaver incisor tooth.

For many years steamboats from Ontario made special trips, bringing people to dig for artifacts in the Grand Mound. The site is now protected by the Minnesota Historical Society and has been investigated by archeologists.

The Interpretive Center at the site offers extensive exhibits, which relate the Rainy River peoples to the larger North American Indian scene. One display, called "How We Know," introduces the visitor to the methods and tools that archeologists use in reconstructing the past. The exhibits surround an indoor forest scene, recreating the environment in which Laurel people lived and adapted to the harsh, northern climate.

An audiovisual program tells the story of fanciful nineteenth-century attempts to explain mound building, which was once supposed to have been done by the Lost Tribes of Israel or other mysterious predecessors of the Indians. Films and lectures are also offered from time to time.

A self-guided natural trail leads from the Interpretive Center to the Grand Mound.

Many Native Americans liked a certain soft, red stone for making the bowls of pipes. The stone, called catlinite because the artist George Catlin was the first to write about it, occurs in a very large deposit in Pipestone National Monument, Minnesota. This diorama at the monument shows people at work quarrying catlinite. National Park Service photo.

HELMER MYRE STATE PARK

The park is several miles east of Albert Lea, near the intersection of Interstate 90 and Interstate 35. Mail address: Route 3, Box 33, Albert Lea, MN 56007. Phone: 507/373-5084. Open May–October. Admission charged. Camping.

The Interpretive Center here exhibits a large collection of prehistoric artifacts, including some early Paleo points.

ITASCA STATE PARK
Itasca Headwaters National Register Historic District

Near intersection of Minnesota 200 and US 71, 21 miles north of Park Rapids. Mail address: Lake Itasca, MN 56460. Phone: 218/266-3634. Open daily, May–October. Admission charged. Camping.

Here, on the shores of Lake Itasca, at the source of the Mississippi River, are numerous ancient burial mounds, a Dakota Indian village site, and a bison kill site. At the latter site, aborig-

inal hunters camped sometime between 8000 and 7000 years ago and waited in ambush to kill bison fording a stream during fall migration. Investigators of the site found many stone tools and animal bones, including the skeleton of a dog—the earliest evidence of that animal to be discovered in Minnesota.

Exhibits at the museum on the north shore of Lake Itasca interpret the archeological finds.

JEFFERS PETROGLYPHS STATE PARK

At junction of US 71 and County Rd. 10, drive 3 miles east on 10, then 1 mile south on County Rd. 2. Mail address: Rural Route 1, Box 118, Bingham Lake, MN 56118. Phone 507/877-3647. Open free, daily, May 1–Labor Day.

This site contains the largest known concentration of aboriginal rock art in Minnesota, consisting of more than 2000 figures, carved on a sloping outcrop of red quartzite about 700 feet long and 150 feet wide at its widest point. Studies indicate that the carv-

ings were made by several groups, over a long period of time. The representations of atlatls—devices used by hunters for throwing darts or spears—indicate that a large number of the carvings may have been made as early as 3000 B.C. Others include characteristic symbols of the Siouan peoples and probably were made between A.D. 900 and 1700.

An interpretive building contains information about the site, which is surrounded by a virgin prairie area, one of the few that remain much as they were before the arrival of Europeans.

MILLE LACS KATHIO STATE PARK
National Historic Landmark

On Minnesota 169 near Onamia. Mail address: Star Route Box 85, Onamia, MN 56359. Phone: 612/532-3523. Open May–October. Admission charged. Camping.

The Interpretive Center explains the archeology of the park where village sites and mound groups are marked

A pipe maker at work, using the soft stone called catlinite, quarried in Pipestone National Monument. Only Native Americans are now allowed to dig the stone. National Park Service photo.

with signs. Some sites are Archaic, dated at about 3000 B.C. At other sites archeologists have found direct evidence of ties between Late Woodland and Early Historic Dakota peoples.

MOUNDS PARK

Mounds Blvd. and East St., St. Paul. Open free, at all times.

This park preserves 6 burial mounds, all that remain out of 18 or more that once stood in the area. Visitors are asked not to climb or picnic on the mounds. This is a cemetery.

PIPESTONE NATIONAL MONUMENT

From Pipestone, Minnesota, at the junction of US 75 and MN 23, drive .5 mile north on US 75 and .5 mile west. Mail address: P.O. Box 727, Pipestone, MN 56164. Phone: 507/ 825-5464. Open all year. Admission charged. Camping nearby.

[We are indebted for the following information about pipes to Timothy L. Blue, a Dakota, teacher of mathe-matics and art history who has written scholarly papers on pipes and given demonstrations on carving them from the soft stone found at the monument.]

Among almost all Native North Americans pipe-smoking has religious significance. The smoking of the pipe, before and after negotiations, consummated an agreement. So important was the pipe to Native North Americans that pilgrimages were often made to the Minnesota quarry area to obtain the much-preferred red-pipestone called catlinite. The quarry was apparently known to a large part of the North American continent and was widely regarded as a sacred area.

Pipestone is a sedimentary claystone which has been altered by chemical and physical action after having been laid down by flooding deposits. It is soft and easily carved.

Archeologists do not know exactly when Native North Americans began quarrying the Minnesota catlinite, but some think it may have been about 2300 years ago. There was quarrying at the site when the first white people appeared in the area. At that time the Dakotas, commonly referred to as Sioux, controlled the quarry and traded the stone to other tribes. Today, only Native North Americans are allowed to quarry the stone, and they continue to do so.

Pipes, now almost always associated with tobacco smoking, were long used for smoking other herbal blends. In the Southeast pipes have been dated at 1590 B.C. But no one knows exactly when tobacco, originally a Mexican plant, reached northern areas of the continent. The earliest identifiable traces of tobacco have been dated at A.D. 1000, although it probably reached the United States area before that. Pipes seem to have been a northern invention that spread south into Mexico.

The stem of the pipe was elaborately decorated with symbolic ornaments and played an important role in ceremonies. The pipe, when smoked, was passed from one person to another clockwise, establishing strong relationships between individuals and groups. Because of the pipe's use in

Timothy Blue, a Dakota, quarrying stone in Pipestone National Monument. Photo by Karen Savage-Blue.

forging close bonds, Europeans often called a calumet a "peace pipe." The word *calumet* itself is of French origin and appropriately refers to a reed which was used as the stem of one style of pipe. The pipe was actually given to travelers to ensure their safe passage across territories claimed by different Native North Americans. The traveler would, upon approaching a group, hold the pipe in sight. Those seeing it would then be aware of the traveler's peaceful intentions. Hence the term "peace pipe."

From the Plains cultures the pipe spread to the West, North, South, and East. In the eastern woodlands the pipe became much elaborated, especially the stem. As the usage of the pipe became widespread, it served to increase bonds between groups of people who traded with each other. It also played a role in the formation of military alliances, and some archeologists have argued that it had an important part in developing the Iroquois Confederacy.

One of the earliest white men to visit the Minnesota quarry was artist George Catlin who came here in 1836. Catlin made drawings and paintings that show the quarry and people at work. In his notes, later expanded into a detailed description, he writes that behind the quarry line rises a natural wall "two miles in length and thirty feet high, with a beautiful cascade leaping from its top into a basin. On the prairie, at the base of the wall, the pipe clay is dug up at two and three feet depth. There are seen five immense granite boulders, under which there are 'Three Maidens,' according to their tradition, who eternally dwell there—the guardian spirits of the place—and must be consulted before the pipestone can be dug up."

Catlin sent samples of the stone east to Washington where a scientist friend analyzed it, proclaimed it a new mineral, and called it "catlinite" in honor of George Catlin.

Beginning at the Visitor Center, where there is an interpretive slideshow, museum, and small store, a circle trail leads to the quarry pits and other points of interest in the monument area. Also at the monument, pipemaking, quillwork, and beading demonstrations are done for the benefit of visitors.

In 1932 George Catlin saw this very old Minitaree chief smoking a pipe, the bowl of which was carved from the kind of stone geologists now call catlinite. From George Catlin's *Illustrations of the Manners, Customs, and Condition of North American Indians*.

Missouri

ATKINS MUSEUM OF FINE ARTS
(*See William Rockhill Nelson Gallery*)

CLAY COUNTY HISTORICAL MUSEUM

14 North Main St., Liberty, MO 64068. Phone: 816/781-8062. Open free, afternoons, Tuesday–Sunday. Closed certain holidays.

In this museum are some materials representative of the Nebo Hill culture, which the museum dates at 5000 B.C.

COLLEGE OF THE OZARKS, RALPH FOSTER MUSEUM

From Springfield drive 40 miles south on US 65. The school is 2 miles south of Branson at Point Lookout. Phone: 417/334-6411. Open Monday–Saturday; afternoon, Sunday, April–December. Admission charged.

This museum has on display 625 pieces of pottery from the Mississippian culture. There are also exhibits of artifacts made by Ozark Bluff Dwellers and materials from other, later cultures.

GRAHAM CAVE STATE PARK

Take the Danville-Montgomery City exit from Interstate 70, then drive 2 miles west on County TT to park entrance. Mail address: Missouri Department of Natural Resources, P.O. Box 176, Jefferson City, MO 65102. Phone: 314/751-2479. Open free, daily, Memorial Day–Labor Day. Camping.

Graham Cave is a natural rockshelter 20 feet high and 120 feet wide, in which people camped at intervals for 10,000 years. During that time the cave floor was littered with the waste they left, with chunks of rock that fell from the ceiling, and with quantities of fine dust blown in by wind. All this material piled up to a depth of six or seven feet, forming a series of layers, in which archeologists could read the story of Missouri's early inhabitants.

Graham Cave in Missouri, formed by an overhanging rock, attracted hunters from the time of the Ice Age on, and for more than 10,000 years debris and remains of human life accumulated there. Graham Cave State Park photo.

Hunters first took shelter here after the end of the Ice Age, when prairie vegetation extended from the present Great Plains to the vicinity of the cave and farther east. Groups of later people who followed the Archaic lifeway camped at the cave. Still later, people of the Woodland culture stopped here from time to time.

One interesting find in the cave is a large, flat rock around which smaller rocks are arranged. Quite clearly, ancient campers built fires on the big rock, then sat around it on the small ones, perhaps engaging in some kind of ceremony.

Because the cave contains evidence of human life over such a long span of time and because it lies on the western fringe of the Woodland culture area, this site is of great importance to archeologists.

The cave itself may be seen but cannot be entered. Interpretive signs and leaflets give a good idea of what was discovered here and how.

Near the cave are a museum and Interpretive Center.

KIMMSWICK MUSEUM

About 15 miles south of St. Louis off Interstate 55 on US 61–69 in Kimmswick, MO 63052. Phone: 314/464-2976. Open free, Monday–Saturday; afternoon, Sunday.

Here is a small exhibit of material from the Kimmswick site in nearby Mastodon State Park (see entry below).

KIMMSWICK SITE
(*See Mastodon State Park*)

LINE CREEK
ARCHAEOLOGICAL MUSEUM

5940 NW Waukomis, Kansas City, MO 64151. Phone: 816/587-8822. Open afternoons, Saturday–Sunday. Closed certain holidays. Open weekdays by reservation for organized groups. Fee varies according to program.

This small museum, dealing with prehistoric Native Americans, is located on a Hopewell site. It features a lifesize diorama and artifacts from the Hopewell lifeway as well as material from other prehistoric periods. The theater room offers a slide show presentation. Various hands-on activities are available throughout the museum.

LONG BRANCH LAKE
VISITOR CENTER

On the east side of the dam, just outside Macon, MO 63552. Open free, daily, May–November; weekdays, except holidays, December–April.

Before construction of the dam by the Army Corps of Engineers, archeologists recovered artifacts indicating that the area had been occupied from Paleo times to the period of contact with Europeans. Archeological exhibits in the Visitor Center tell the story of the site, which is now covered by water.

MASTODON STATE PARK
(Kimmswick Site)

Twenty miles south of St. Louis at the Imperial Exit on Interstate 55, signs give directions to the park. Mail address: 1551 Seckman Road, Imperial, MO 63052. Phone: 314/464-2976.

Open free, Monday–Saturday; afternoon, Sunday.

Here an Interpretive Center has been created by the Mastodon Park Committee, which one of its founders proudly says was sparked by housewives.

Archeologists have long suspected that early hunters who killed mammoths also found mastodons a source of meat. Proof of mammoth hunting has appeared at many sites, particularly in plains areas, where spearpoints and other stone tools have been found in association with the animals' bones. Although mastodon remains had come to light in several bone beds in formerly forested places, clear proof of a kill eluded searchers until 1977, when the Manis Site was discovered in the state of Washington. Then, in 1979, excavation in Mastodon State Park turned up a Clovis point of the kind used by mammoth hunters 11,000 or more years ago. The point lay on top of some mastodon bones and beneath others—unmistakable evidence that a human being had been involved in the animals' death. Further digging resulted in the discovery of more Clovis spearheads, as well as stone flakes of the kind made by sharpening stone tools, which suggest that this might also have been a hunters' campsite.

The park and the Kimmswick Museum are the work of a group of devoted citizens, who managed to raise enough money to buy the site and save it from commercial development. The area contains much still unstudied material and fragile specimens, preserved from decomposition by minerals in the water.

MISSOURI HISTORICAL SOCIETY

Jefferson Memorial Building, Forest Park, St. Louis, MO 63112. Phone: 314/361-1424. Open free, Tuesday–Sunday. Closed certain holidays.

Artifacts on display here came primarily from digs in Missouri or the middle Mississippi Valley. Paleo, Archaic, Woodland, and Mississippian periods are represented.

MISSOURI STATE MUSEUM

Room B-2, State Capitol Building, 201 W. Capitol Ave., Jefferson City, MO 65101. Phone: 314/751-2854. Open free, daily. Closed certain holidays.

The History Hall contains exhibits depicting Missouri's Native American cultures. Archeological and historical exhibits are integrated into a chronological sequence illustrating Missouri's development since prehistoric times.

OSAGE VILLAGE STATE HISTORIC SITE

From Nevada on US 54 drive east 5.5 miles to County Road C, then north through Walker, following signs to the site. Mail address: Missouri Department of Natural Resources, Division of Parks, Recreation, and Historic Preservation, P.O. Box 176, Jefferson City, MO 65102. Phone: 314/751-8458. Open free, daily.

The Osage people probably settled here about 50 years before they first came into contact with whites. They soon built about 100 rectangular lodges that varied in length from 30 feet to 50 feet and in width from 15 to 20 feet.

A walking tour takes visitors past an archeological excavation, a burial mound and various historic features. From a hilltop at the site visitors can get an excellent view of the entire village area. An intrepretive kiosk tells about Osage history and includes some archeological interpretation.

RALPH FOSTER MUSEUM
(See College of the Ozarks)

SAINT JOSEPH MUSEUM

Eleventh and Charles streets, St. Joseph, MO 64501-2874. Phone: 816/232-8471. Open Monday–Saturday; afternoon, Sunday. Closed certain holidays. Admission charged except Sunday and holidays.

The Native American collections in this museum are national in scope and include some archeological material.

A bird bowl, found at the Campbell Site, in Missouri.

Left:
This pottery vessel, modeled in the shape of a head, was incised before firing. Found at the Campbell Site, in Missouri.

SAINT LOUIS ART MUSEUM

1 Fine Arts Drive, Forest Park, St. Louis, MO 63110. Phone: 314/721-0072. Open free, Wednesday–Sunday; afternoon and evening, Tuesday. Closed certain holidays.

Some prehistoric artifacts are on exhibit here. They include copper plaques from southeast Missouri.

SAINT LOUIS SCIENCE CENTER
(Formerly Museum of Science and Natural History)

5050 Oakland, Ave., St. Louis, MO 63110. Phone: 314/289-4400. Open free, daily. Closed certain holidays.

In an exhibit called "Ecology and Environment" are displays of artifacts of the Mississippian culture. Other exhibits, called interactive, allow the visitor to press buttons and find comparisons of such aspects of prehistoric and modern life as energy sources, weather, and food production.

SOUTHEAST MISSOURI STATE UNIVERSITY MUSEUM

One University Plaza, Cape Girardeau, MO 63701. Phone: 314/651-2260. Open free, Monday–Friday, all year.

On display here is a collection of Early Middle Mississippian artifacts. Exhibits consist of pottery with small rim effigies, water vessels, ornaments, axes, farming tools, celts, and other implements.

THOUSAND HILLS STATE PARK

From Kirksville drive 3 miles west on Missouri 6, then 2 miles south on Missouri 157 to park. Mail address: Route 3, Kirksville, MO 63501. Phone: 816/665-6995. Open free, daily, all year. Camping.

Here a cluster of petroglyphs (rock carvings), protected by a building are interpreted for the public. The carvings depict footprints, crosses, sunbursts, arrows, animals, thunderbirds, and other designs. The people who made them are believed to be associated with the Woodland or Mississippian lifeways. Interpretations of the petroglyphs vary, but it is generally believed that they served a ceremonial purpose. The building covering the petroglyphs is open by advance appointment.

TOWOSAHGY STATE PARK
(toe-wah-SOG-ee)

From East Prairie drive 6 miles east on Missouri 80, then 2 miles south on County Rd. AA, then 3 miles south on County Rd. FF; turn east and go 1 mile on gravel road, then south 1 mile on gravel. Mail address: Department of Natural Resources, Division of Parks, Recreation, and Historic Preservation, P.O. Box 176, Jefferson City, MO 65102. Phone: 314/751-2479.

Between A.D. 1000 and 1400 people of the Mississippian culture were living in a 30-acre village and civic-ceremonial center at this site. They built mounds around a large central plaza, and on at least two they placed structures that were probably temples or other important community buildings. A portion of the center was fortified by a system of vertical-log

Salvaging what they can of the past, archeologists race against rising water in a new reservoir. National Park Service photo.

stockade walls and a bastion, or defensive projection of the wall line. A large borrow pit and several smaller ones furnished the earth from which the mounds were built. The people of the village farmed nearby and they made pottery in styles that were popular in other villages in southeastern Missouri.

As this book went to press an Interpretive Center was scheduled to open in the near future.

TRUMAN DAM VISITOR CENTER

In Warsaw. Mail address: U.S. Army Corps of Engineers, Harry S. Truman Visitor Center, Warsaw, MO 65355. Phone: 816/438-2216 or -7317. Open free, daily, except December, January, and February.

Before construction of the dam by the Army Corps of Engineers, excavation at the site, which is now covered by water, yielded evidence that mastodons were hunted here in Paleo times. The exhibits in the Visitor Center show replicas of artifacts and bones recovered by archeologists.

UNIVERSITY OF MISSOURI– COLUMBIA, MUSEUM OF ANTHROPOLOGY

On the campus, 104 Swallow Hall, Columbia, MO 65211. Phone: 314/882-3764. Handicapped accessible. Open free, Monday–Friday. Closed certain holidays.

The museum's archeological collections include many artifacts dating from 9000 B.C. to modern times. The focus of the exhibits is on the prehistory of Missouri and the Midwest. In addition, ethnographic materials from Alaska, the Northwest, the Southwest, and the Plains chronicle the richness and diversity of Native American cultures throughout the United States.

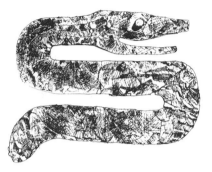

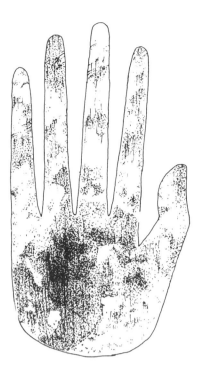

An ornament in the shape of a snake, cut from a sheet of mica. The original, found at Turner Mound, Ohio, is now in the Peabody Museum, Harvard University.

This mica grave offering, in the form of a hand, was made by the Hopewellian people of Ohio. Original in the Ohio Historical Center collection.

VAN METER STATE PARK

From Marshall drive 8 miles north on Missouri 41 to junction with Missouri 122, then 4 miles west to park. Mail address: Department of Natural Resources, Division of Parks, Recreation, and Historic Preservation, P.O. Box 176, Jefferson City, MO 65102. Phone at Visitor Center: 816/886-7537. Open free, daily, all year. Camping.

In this park are several visible and interpreted archeological sites. Research indicates that people inhabited the area as early as 10,000 B.C. and the Missouri Indians, for whom the state is named, were the last major tribe to live here. A large earthwork in the park, called the Old Fort, is associated with the Oneota culture and possibly with the Missouri Indians. Just north of the Old Fort site is a cluster of burial mounds.

At one stage perhaps 5000 people lived in the village on the high land here known as the Pinnacles.

A Visitor Center interprets the history of the Missouri Indians.

WASHINGTON STATE PARK

From DeSoto drive 15 miles south on Missouri 21. Mail address: Department of Natural Resources, P.O. Box 176, Jefferson City, MO 65102. Phone: 314/751-2479. Open daily, all year. Camping fee charged.

In this park are petroglyphs (rock carvings) and a museum which includes archeological exhibits. A folder available at the park gives directions to the petroglyph sites, which are viewable year-round.

At Site 1 several hundred symbols were carved in the rock, presumably between A.D. 1000 and 1600. The designs include birds, arrows, squares, ovals, circles, footprints, claws, and human figures. The birds may represent the eagle, buzzard, or hawk, which were important in many Indian cultures over a wide area. Speech scrolls issue from the mouths of several human figures and one bird. Like the balloons in modern day comic strips, they seem to indicate that talking is going on.

Site 2 has symbols that were connected with the mound builders—maces, bilobed arrows, crosses.

Some archeologists believe that ancient trails crossed in this area and that people came together here for special rites or ceremonies. Possibly the symbols were associated with such ceremonies. Or they may have been devices to help people memorize certain songs or rituals.

WILLIAM ROCKHILL NELSON GALLERY AND ATKINS MUSEUM OF FINE ARTS

4525 Oak St., Kansas City, MO 64111. Open Tuesday–Saturday; afternoon, Sunday. Closed certain holidays. Admission charged except on Saturday.

Some prehistoric material is included in exhibits devoted to Indian pottery and jewelry.

Top to bottom: The bird of prey often appeared as an element in mound builders' designs. This ornament was cut from a sheet of hammered copper. Original on exhibit at Mound City National Monument. The bird motif, sometimes very stylized, was also carved by Adena mound builders on small pieces of stone. These engraved Adena tablets, found in burials, were probably used somehow in funeral ceremonies. After Webb and Baby.

Ohio

ALLEN COUNTY MUSEUM

620 W. Market St., Lima, OH 45801. Phone: 419/222-9426. Open free, afternoons, Tuesday–Sunday. Closed certain holidays.

A feature of this museum is a diorama showing how Glacial Kame people buried their dead, together with material from a Glacial Kame grave found near Lima. Other displays contain materials from Paleo-Indian, Archaic, Adena, Hopewell, Cole Creek, Fort Ancient, and Erie cultures.

CAMPBELL MOUND
(*See Shrum Mound*)

CINCINNATI ART MUSEUM

Eden Park, Cincinnati, OH 45202. Phone: 513/721-5204. Open free Saturday; afternoon, Sunday. Closed certain holidays.

The archeological materials on display here are representative of the Adena, Hopewell, and Fort Ancient cultures of Ohio. Ethnographic materials from the Plains, Southwest, and the Northwest Coast are also on exhibit.

Special Feature. A small engraved piece of stone in the museum is the Waverly tablet, one of 12 similar objects called Adena tablets found in ancient Adena burial mounds. The others are now in the collection at the Museum Center listed below.

Some Adena tablets appear to have been coated with a red pigment. This may indicate that they were used as stamps to print red-colored designs on clothing or on the bodies either of the dead or of those taking part in funeral ceremonies. Some connection with burial practices seems likely because Adena people sprinkled red ocher over the remains of the dead and even over the grave goods placed in tombs. Adena people may also have used tablets to identify members of social or religious groups.

Careful study of the designs on tablets indicates that many if not all of them represent birds of prey, such as the vulture, duck hawk, and carrion

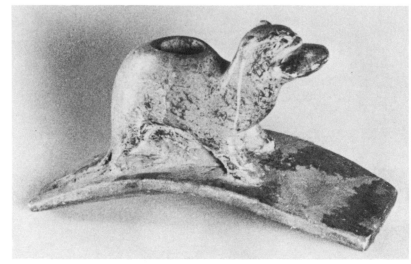

Styles in smoking pipes varied from one place to another and changed as time went on. This one, in the form of a fish and a bird, was carved by Hopewellian people in Ohio. Original in the Field Museum of Natural History, Chicago.

On this platform pipe found in Tremper Mound, Ohio, an artist carved the effigy of an otter. Ohio Historical Society photo.

crow. On some tablets the figures are quite realistic. On others, such as the Cincinnati tablet, the design seems to contain very stylized elements of wings, beaks, and eyes. Flesh-eating birds seem to have been important in all the burial mound cultures, possibly because they acted as scavengers and helped to clean the bones of bodies which were exposed and allowed to decompose before burial or cremation.

CLEVELAND MUSEUM OF ART

11150 East Blvd. at University Circle, Cleveland, OH 44106. Phone: 216/421-7340. Open free, Tuesday–Saturday; afternoon, Sunday; evening, Wednesday. Closed certain holidays.

A number of prehistoric art objects are on display. They include Mimbres and other southwestern pottery, a Copena stone bird effigy pipe, and an Adena sandstone pipe from Ohio.

CLEVELAND MUSEUM OF NATURAL HISTORY

Wade Oval, University Circle, Cleveland, OH 44106. Phone: 216/231-4600. Open Monday–Saturday; after-

noon, Sunday. Closed certain holidays. Admission charged.

On display here are materials on prehistoric peoples in Ohio and other North American areas. Dioramas show reconstructions of ancient life. Exhibits of current fieldwork change from time to time.

CLINTON COUNTY HISTORICAL SOCIETY AND MUSEUM

149 East Locust St. Mail address: P.O. Box 529, Wilmington, OH 45177. Phone: 513/382-4684. Open afternoons, Tuesday–Sunday, March–December. Closed certain holidays. Admission charged.

A small collection of archeological material includes an exhibit of projectile points.

DAYTON MUSEUM OF NATURAL HISTORY

2629 Ridge Ave., Dayton, OH 45414. Phone: 513/275-7431. Open Monday–Saturday; afternoons, Sunday and all holidays. Admission charged.

A conventionalized bird of prey engraved on a stone tablet. Ohio Historical Society photo.

This imaginary creature, carved in stone, came from Turner Mounds, Madisonville, Ohio. Original in the Peabody Museum, Harvard University.

Exhibits include Ohio material from Paleo times (14,000 B.C.) to Fort Ancient (A.D. 1500). Expansion of the museum will be ongoing for several years.

FIRELANDS MUSEUM

4 Case Ave. (at the rear of the Public Library). Mail address: P.O. Box 572, Norwalk, OH 44857. Phone: 419/668-6038. Open afternoons, Saturday and Sunday, April, May, October, November; afternoons, Tuesday–Sunday, June–September. Admission charged.

One room here includes archeological materials from the Archaic, Early Woodland, and Hopewell periods.

FLINT RIDGE STATE MEMORIAL

From Brownsville drive 3 miles north on County 668. Phone: 614/787-2476. Open Wednesday–Sunday, April 1–October 31. Admission charged. Administered by the Ohio Historical Society.

In hilly country between Newark and Zanesville, Native Americans once mined the fine translucent, varicolored flint that covered an area of five square miles in deposits from one to ten feet thick. To break off chunks of the flint, they first drove wooden or bone wedges into natural cracks in the rock, using hammerstones, some of which weighed as much as 25 pounds. Then with smaller hammerstones they shaped what are called blanks. Some blanks were chipped to make finished artifacts on the spot. People carried other blanks back to their villages, where they did the painstaking work of chipping them into projectile points or knives or drills or scrapers.

Miners also shaped flint into blocks called cores, which were sometimes carried for considerable distances. When a man wanted a new knife, he struck a flake off one of these cores and had a cutting tool almost as sharp as a steel blade.

In prehistoric times the flint from this huge quarry was so prized that it was traded over great distances—as far east as the Atlantic Coast, as far west as the present site of Kansas City, and as far south as Louisiana.

The Museum. At the quarry the Ohio Historical Society maintains a museum that tells the geological story of the formation of the flint and the archeological story of the use that people made of it over a very long period of time. Exhibits show how flint was mined and then made into artifacts.

A model in the museum at Fort Hill State Memorial, in Ohio, shows what a building in a large Hopewell ceremonial area once looked like. Ohio Historical Society photo.

FORT ANCIENT STATE MEMORIAL

From Lebanon drive 7 miles southeast on Ohio 350. The earthworks are open April 1–May 17 and September 8–October 31; (park and museum) Saturday, afternoon, Sunday; May 23–September 7 (museum) Wednesday–Saturday; afternoons, Sunday and holidays; (park) Wednesday–Sunday and holidays. Admission charged. Administered by the Ohio Historical Society.

The Story. Here a bluff rises 275 feet above the Little Miami River. On this natural eminence two different Indian peoples lived at two different times.

The first settlers arrived about 200 B.C. From that time until about A.D. 500 they followed the Hopewell way of life. All around the top of the bluff they built a wall of limestone slabs and earth that varies in height from 4 to 23 feet. Apparently the wall was designed to have some significance in relation to social and religious activities. The Hopewell people here, as elsewhere, enclosed the areas where they

performed rituals and conducted elaborate funeral ceremonies.

The Hopewell people may have raised some corn, were skilled artisans, and traded widely. The grizzly bear teeth they used in ornaments came from the Rocky Mountains, as did obsidian. They got shark teeth from the Atlantic Coast, shells from the Gulf of Mexico, copper from the Lake Superior region, and mica from the southern Appalachians. But here, as elsewhere in the Ohio Valley, they eventually gave up building large earthworks and trading over great distances for exotic materials.

After the Hopewell settlement was abandoned, apparently no one lived on the hilltop for a long time. Then about A.D. 1000 a group of Indians who followed what is called the Fort Ancient lifeway settled on part of the site—the South Fort. They also built homes in the valley below the bluff. These Fort Ancient people grew more corn than had the earlier people, and they hunted and fished and made a variety of artifacts, but none of them were so skillfully fashioned as the earlier Hopewell tools and ornaments.

About A.D. 1600 Fort Ancient people left the site, for what reason no one knows. It was uninhabited when the first Europeans entered the area.

The Museum. Here are exhibits that give a good deal of information about the two distinct cultures connected with the site. One display deals with the chronology of this area over a span of 10,000 years.

FORT HILL STATE MEMORIAL

From Hillsboro drive 16 miles southeast on Ohio 124, then 2 miles north on Ohio 41. Or from Chillicothe (chil-ee-KOTH-ee) drive 20 miles southwest on US 50, to Bainbridge, then 12 miles south on Ohio 41. The grounds are open daily during daylight hours. Admission charged. Camping nearby. Administered by Ohio Historical Society.

At a date not yet known, Fort Hill became an important center for people who practiced Hopewell rituals. Around the flat top of the hill, which stands out from the surrounding land, people built a wall of earth and rock.

Rock art attracted the attention of E. G. Squier and E. H. Davis who made the first serious investigation of the prehistory of the Mississippi River drainage. They found petroglyphs, which they called "sculptured rocks," on the banks of the Guyandotte River in West Virginia (left), and they copied one of these (above). From *Ancient Monuments of the Mississippi Valley*.

At its base the wall is about 40 feet thick, and in places it is 15 feet high. Earthworks of this kind were common at Hopewell sites. Many of them seem to have had only ritual use.

On the flat land below the hill two structures were built. One was circular, possibly used as temporary housing for visitors who came for ceremonies. No other such circular building is known in Ohio. The second was exceedingly large—120 feet long and 80 feet wide. It may have been a craft workshop.

The Museum. Archeological exhibits here illuminate the Hopewell lifeway. Models show the site and its structures as they may have looked when it was occupied. One display includes material on older cultures in Ohio.

INDIAN RIDGE MUSEUM

8714 West Ridge Rd., Elyria, OH 44035. Phone: 216/323-2167. Open afternoons, Tuesday–Sunday. Admission charged.

Exhibits include a large private collection of Erie, Hopewell, and Adena artifacts.

INSCRIPTION ROCK

Kelleys Island, in Lake Erie, north of Sandusky. Open free, at all times. Administered by the Ohio Historical Society. Camping nearby.

Inscription Rock is a large boulder on which prehistoric people carved symbols and figures of animals, birds, and humans. No one knows exactly what the inscriptions mean or who made them, but they probably date from A.D. 1000 to 1650. There is an interpretive sign at the site.

KNOB PRAIRIE MOUND
(Enon Mound)

One mile south of Interstate 70 in Enon. Open free, at all times.

This large, remarkably well preserved mound was probably built by Adena people.

Prehistoric features are clearly visible at Mound City Group National Monument, in Ohio. Here in the foreground is an enclosure wall. In the background are mounds. National Park Service photo.

LEO PETROGLYPH

From Jackson on US 35 drive 5 miles north on Ohio 93 to Coalton, then northwest on Ohio 337 to Leo. The site is on an unpaved road northwest of Leo. Open free, during daylight hours, all year. Administered by the Ohio Historical Society.

This site is similar to Inscription Rock. Here prehistoric Indians carved symbols and figures on a stone slab, but their date and meaning are not known.

MARIETTA MOUND

In the cemetery, Marietta, OH.

The large mound, originally part of a complex of mounds and earthworks, was set aside to be the center of the town cemetery when Marietta was first settled, in 1788. Two of the earthwork squares were also fenced. These unusual precautions saved the site from the total destruction that went on when many other Ohio towns were built. Some artifacts from the Marietta complex are in the Peabody Museum, at Harvard.

MIAMISBURG MOUND STATE MEMORIAL

On Mound Ave., 3 miles west of Interstate 75, 1 mile south of junction Interstate 75 and Ohio 725. Open free, during daylight hours, all year. Administered by the Ohio Historical Society. Camping nearby.

This cone-shaped Adena mound, 68 feet high, is the largest of its kind in Ohio.

MIAMI COUNTY ARCHAEOLOGICAL MUSEUM

From Pleasant Hill drive one mile west on Lauver Rd. to directional sign just west of the Stillwater River bridge. Mail address: 8212 W. Lauver Rd., Pleasant Hill, OH 45359. Phone: 513/676-5103. Open free, any time, by appointment.

Some of the materials on display here are random local finds from each of five prehistoric Indian cultures of the area, beginning with Paleo-Indian and ending with Fort Ancient.

Archeologists excavating at Mound City Group National Monument, in Ohio, found holes in which posts once stood. This was evidence that a structure had occupied the spot where a burial mound was later raised. National Park Service photo.

MIAMI FORT

In Shawnee Lookout Park, Cincinnati. Mail address: Hamilton County Park District, 10245 Winton Road, Cincinnati, OH 45231. Phone: 513/521-7275. Open daily, all year. Admission charged for vehicles.

In this park, which is part of an area on the National Historic Register, are 40 sites including burial mounds, a village, and a walled enclosure. A trail goes around the earthworks and several mounds. A museum provides information about the site.

MOUNDBUILDERS
STATE MEMORIAL
(Newark Earthworks)

Administered by the Ohio Historical Society, Newark Earthworks is the collective name for three separate sections of a huge prehistoric site on which the modern city of Newark has been built. The three areas are now preserved as public parks. Their names, with road directions, are given below. All are open daily.

An amazing group of people settled near Newark about 1800 years ago. They followed the Hopewell lifeway, but apparently with more than usual energy and a taste for grandiose public works. Like other Hopewellians, they buried their dead under mounds of earth in special ceremonial areas. Here they conducted death rituals and other social and economic activities inside tremendous enclosures made by heaping up earth into walls or embankments 8 to 14 feet high. One of the enclosures was a square, another an octagon, several were circular. All were linked together by long corridors between high, parallel earthen walls. A separate corridor extended from the site to the bank of the Licking River in an almost straight avenue, two and a half miles long.

For many years, a civil engineer, named James A. Marshall, studied and surveyed Hopewell earthworks, which he believed were the achievement of people with a real knowledge of geometry. Hopewellians, he says, used a consistent unit of measurement, equal to 187 feet. Before starting work, they apparently drew up plans, as engineers

do today, and made grids 187 feet on a side that guided them in construction. (This same unit of measurement seems to have been used by builders of the great religious ceremonial center at Teotihuacan, in Mexico.)

A few important individuals seem to have lived at the Newark religious center itself. Possibly they were leaders of the groups that regarded the area as a focal point in their elaborate ceremonial life. The dwellings of ordinary people were built in outlying areas.

Like Hopewell people in other places, those at Newark were superb craftsworkers. They made personal ornaments of many kinds—earrings, combs, necklaces, headdresses. They were skilled weavers, using thread they made from various plant fibers, including the bark of certain trees. Many if not most of the splendid things they created were made only to be buried with the dead.

When an important personage died, the body was dressed in rich clothing and covered with decorations. It might then be placed in a tomb. More likely it was cremated. At first small mounds

An aerial view of the Newark Earthworks (right); (opposite) a map of the Earthworks made by E. G. Squier and E. H. Davis before 1847. An engineer, James A. Marshall, studied various Ohio earthworks and reported that a unit of measurement 187 feet long was commonly used in their construction. The inset at lower left of the map shows how this unit of measurement fits the rectangular area at the center right of the map. Ohio Historical Society photo; map from *Ancient Monuments of the Mississippi Valley;* inset redrawn from *Early Man.*

of earth were heaped over the remains of the dead. Later, much more earth was added to cover a group of the small heaps, creating one sizable mound.

Archeologists believe that the ceremonies, which required such great expenditure of effort and great destruction of wealth, were reserved for members of an upper class. Funerals for common people were certainly more simple.

Much of the original complex of structures at Newark has been destroyed by the expansion of the city. The three portions that survive are:

Moundbuilders State Memorial

Enter from the junction of S. 21st St. and Cooper. Park open April 1–October 21, Wednesday–Sunday. Museum open May 23–September 7, Wednesday–Saturday; afternoons, Sunday and holidays; September 12–October 25, Monday–Saturday; afternoon, Sunday. Admission charged.

This is the area known as the Great Circle Earthworks. The circular embankment enclosed ceremonial grounds 1200 feet in diameter, covering about 26 acres. Within the enclosure are four mounds. High earthen walls once lined a corridor that led from the Great Circle to a smaller, square enclosure now called Wright Earthworks. The museum displays artifacts, chosen for their artistic interest, mainly made by the Adena and Hopewell people.

Octagon Mound State Memorial

N. 23rd Street and Parkview. Open free, daylight hours, all year.

Here an eight-sided enclosure of 50 acres adjoins another which is circular in form and covers about 20 acres. Several small mounds stand inside the octagon. This well-preserved area is now the municipal golf course.

Wright Earthworks

James and Waldo Streets. Open free, daylight hours, all year.

Only part of the original square enclosure survives here. Before modern settlement began, it was possible to see that the square was linked by corridors to another area, of unknown shape, and by a very long passageway to still another, built in the shape of an octagon.

MOUND CITY GROUP
NATIONAL MONUMENT

From Chillicothe drive 4 miles north on Ohio 104. Mail address: Chillicothe, OH 45601. Phone: 614/774-1125. Open daily. Closed certain holidays. Admission charged.

A large part of the enclosure at Mound City has been allowed to grow tall grasses to help the area appear as it did in prehistoric times.

At an undetermined date in the future the Mound City Group will be enlarged by the addition of Hopeton, a typical Hopewell complex about a mile away.

Visitor Center. Exhibits here are designed to help visitors understand the Hopewell story. Outdoor audio programs provide explanations of mound

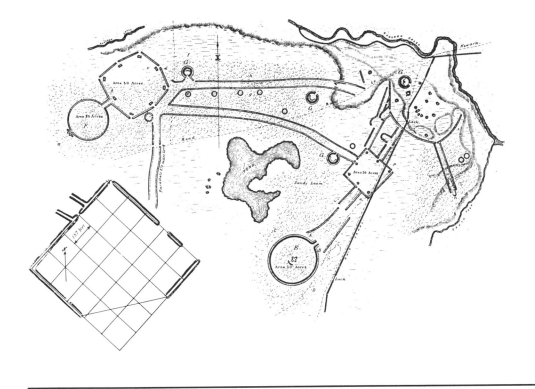

construction and a glimpse into the lives of these prehistoric people. An eight-minute videotape program in the museum provides a look at the life and customs of Hopewell times.

The Story. By about 200 B.C. some Native Americans here in the Scioto River Valley had begun to follow the Hopewell way of life. They paid great attention to personal decoration and became very skillful at fashioning beautiful ornaments. They also devoted themselves to performing elaborate ceremonials and to building earthen mounds over the remains of the dead. Many burials were accompanied by fine pottery, carvings, jewelry, and other objects made by sophisticated craftsworkers with a variety of materials, some of which are foreign to the Ohio area.

The location of the Mound City Group on the bank of the Scioto River was no accident, for the river provided easy transportation and was a dependable source of food in the form of fish and clams. But for some reason the Hopewell lifeway declined, and by about A.D. 500 it had vanished.

The Mound City site was mapped and partially excavated by the pioneer archeologists E. G. Squier and E. H. Davis. Their work produced spectacular artifacts, which were ultimately acquired by the British Museum, in London, where they remain today. In 1920–21 the Ohio Historical Society did further excavation, and much of the material discovered at that time is on exhibit at the Mound City Group Visitor Center. Excavation, started in 1963 as a National Park Service program and continuing until 1975, revealed further information about the mounds and their ancient builders. This work made possible an improved restoration of the site.

A rectangular earthen embankment encloses the 13-acre mound area. Within this enclosure visitors may start a tour. Several of the 23 mounds are given specific interpretation. One contained a burial site, in which the cremated remains of four bodies were elaborately buried with sheets of mica.

In another, excavators found many beautifully carved pipes, replicas of which are on display in the Visitor Center. Offerings to the dead varied from one mound to another. At one point archeologists, instead of restoring an excavated mound, have created a post pattern outlining the charnel house structure in relation to the mound that later covered it.

MUSEUM CENTER

Union Terminal, 1301 Western Ave., Cincinnati, OH 45203. Phone: 513/287-7020. Open daily. Closed December 25. Admission charged.

The Center is being developed to house the Cincinnati Historical Society and the Cincinnati Museum of Natural History. As this book went to press there was no permanent exhibit of North American archeological material on display. When the Center is completed an archeology hall will have permanent exhibits. Traveling exhibits regularly appear at the Museum of Natural History.

Serpent Mound, Ohio, as it appears in an aerial photograph (right) and (opposite) as it was mapped in 1846. Ohio Historical Society photo; engraving from *Ancient Monuments of the Mississippi Valley.*

OHIO HISTORICAL CENTER (OHIO HISTORICAL SOCIETY)

1985 Velma Ave., Columbus, OH 43211. Phone: 614/297-2300. Open free, daily, all year. Closed certain holidays.

One exhibit here, "The First Ohioans," presents cultures of the Ohio area from the late Pleistocene to the present day. In addition to displaying much of the Society's important archeological collection, the exhibits include scale models and dioramas with life-size mannequins. Computer programs introduce visitors to the display and its themes.

PIKETON MOUNDS

In the cemetery in Piketon. Open free, daily.

This site was once part of an extensive system of ceremonial and burial mounds, three of which remain.

SEIP MOUND (SIPE)

From Bainbridge drive 3 miles east on US 50. Open free, daily, all year. Administered by the Ohio Historical Society.

This site is part of a Hopewell burial complex that was once extensive. Several mounds are still visible, the largest an oval 150 feet wide, 250 feet long, and 32 feet high. An earthwork in the form of a circle 2000 feet in diameter surrounds the mound. In addition there is a smaller earthen circle and a partly preserved earthen square.

From the Seip mounds came much of the early information about the Hopewell lifeway. One grave yielded a great collection of ornaments made of mica, copper, and silver and so many thousands of pearls that it was called "the great pearl burial."

An exhibit pavilion is located at the site. Material from the mounds can also be seen in the Ohio Historical Center, in Columbus.

SERPENT MOUND STATE MEMORIAL

On Ohio 73, 4 miles northwest of Locust Grove. Phone: 513/587-2796. Open May 23–September 7, Wednesday–Saturday; afternoons, Sunday and holidays. September 12–October 25, Saturday; afternoon, Sunday. Admission charged.

At this place long ago (the exact date it not known), Indians used small stones and lumps of clay to trace on the ground an outline of a huge snake. Then they covered these markers with great quantities of yellow clay, which they dug up nearby. The result was a modeled form that resembled a writhing snake with open mouth.

Many Indian groups attached great significance to snakes. Many built snake effigies, but none is larger than this one. It is nearly one-quarter of a mile long, 20 feet wide, and 4 or 5 feet high. The people who labored to pile up so much earth did not leave in the mound itself any clues to their identity or to the time when they did their work. However, archeologists think it is likely

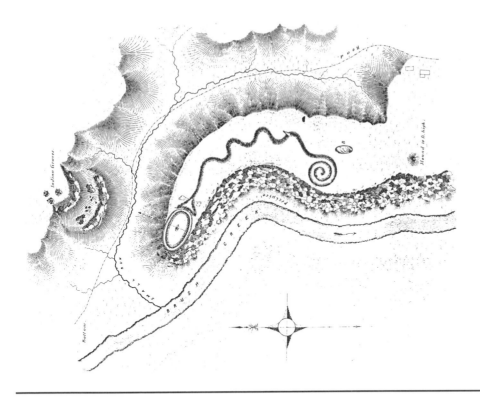

that whoever shaped the serpent also built the burial mound found nearby, and that mound did offer clues.

Among the things in the mound were some leaf-shaped knife blades, some points that had stems, chunks of sandstone in which there were deep grooves, bone tubes and awls, and a pigment called red ocher. All these were objects that usually are associated with the Adena people, who are known to have lived in this part of Ohio from about 800 B.C. to A.D. 100. The evidence uncovered so far does not prove that people who built the burial mound also constructed Serpent Mound, but archeologists believe they did.

The Museum. Exhibits include an interpretation of the site, models of the steps taken in reconstruction of the effigy and nearby burial mound, some Adena artifacts and their use, and chronology. A diorama shows a conical burial mound with an Adena grave to which another burial was later added by Fort Ancient people.

Special Interest. The preservation of Serpent Mound was one of the first American archeological conservation projects. When white men first learned about the mound, it lay in the midst of a forest and seemed to be in no danger. Then, just before the Civil War, a tornado mowed down the big trees along its whole length. Farmers completed the job and began to cultivate the area. Some years later F. W. Putnam, an archeologist from Harvard University, visited the mound and then went home to talk about the need for protecting it. As he tells it, "Several of Boston's noble and earnest women issued a private circular." They soon collected enough money to buy the mound, which was given in trust to the Peabody Museum, at Harvard. Later the museum turned it over to the Ohio Historical Society, which now administers it.

SHRUM MOUND
(Also called Campbell Mound)

On McKinley Ave., .5 mile south of Trabue Rd., Columbus. Open free, all year, daylight hours.

This example of an Adena mound is administered by the Ohio Historical Society.

STORY MOUND

Delano Ave., one block south of Allen Ave., Chillicothe. Open free, during daylight hours, year-round. Administered by the Ohio Historical Society.

Here, easily visible through a fence, is an Adena burial mound. In size and shape it is similar to the original Adena mound, which has been destroyed by excavation.

A pottery head from Seip Mound, in Ohio, shows how skulls were artifically shaped by binding in infancy. Ohio Historical Society photo.

SUNWATCH
ARCHAEOLOGICAL PARK
National Historic Landmark

In Dayton from exit 51 on Interstate 75 go west on Edwin C. Moses Boulevard which becomes Nicholas Road. Cross South Broadway and turn left and drive on West River Road one mile. Mail address: 2301 West River Road, Dayton, OH 45418-2815. Phone: 513/268-8199. The Dayton Society of Natural History operates Sunwatch. Open year-round, Monday–Saturday; afternoons, Sunday and holidays. Admission charged. Handicapped access.

At this site a walk of one to two hours introduces visitors to a twelfth-century Fort Ancient village. Here it is possible to see restored lodges and excavations in progress and observe how people developed a complex system for keeping track of time with observations of the sun.

In the Visitor Center are artifacts recovered during 17 years of excavation, an audiovisual program, educational programs, and demonstrations.

WARREN COUNTY
HISTORICAL SOCIETY

105 S. Broadway, Lebanon. Mail address: P.O. Box 223, Lebanon, OH 45036. Phone: 513/932-1817. Open Tuesday–Saturday; afternoon, Sunday. Closed certain holidays. Admission charged.

Prehistoric material exhibited here is from Hopewell and Fort Ancient cultures.

WESTERN RESERVE
HISTORICAL SOCIETY

10825 East Boulevard, Cleveland, OH 44106. Phone: 216/721-5722. Open Tuesday–Sunday. Admission charged.

A feature of this historical museum is an introduction to Native American cultures which has been arranged for children. It includes eight small dioramas, presenting scenes of life from a wide variety of geographic areas. In addition there is special emphasis on life in northern Ohio, both at the time of contact with Europeans and earlier. Guided tours only.

WYANDOT COUNTY
HISTORICAL SOCIETY

130 South Seventh St., Upper Sandusky, OH 43351. Phone: 419/294-3857. Open afternoons, Tuesday–Sunday, March 1–November 1; weekends only in winter. Admission charged.

Here are some random local archeological finds, including some material from mounds.

Delf Norona Museum, Moundsville, West Virginia. Grave Creek Mound in background. Delf Norona Museum photo.

West Virginia

BLENNERHASSETT ISLAND

Excursion boats from Point Park in Parkersburg take visitors to Blennerhassett Island Wednesday–Sunday, June–August; Saturday and Sunday, May, September, and October.

Excavation is usually going on at one of the numerous archeological sites on the island, where materials range in age from 9000 B.C. to eighteenth century A.D. Selected artifacts are displayed in the Visitor Center, Blennerhassett Museum Building in Parkersburg. For information write to Blennerhassett Historical Park Commission, Parkersburg, WV 26102, or phone: 304/428-3000.

CEMETERY MOUND

City Cemetery, Romney.
Here in the municipal cemetery is a prehistoric Indian mound.

DELF NORONA MUSEUM AND CULTURAL CENTRE

801 Jefferson Ave., Moundsville, WV 26041. Open Monday–Saturday; afternoon, Sunday. Closed certain holidays. Admission charged.

The museum is adjacent to Grave Creek Mound State Park and provides access to the grounds on which the mound stands. Grave Creek is the largest of all the mounds known to have been built by Adena people. When first measured in 1838, it stood 69 feet high and had a flat top 60 feet in diameter. Around its summit ran a low wall, or parapet. A circular ditch surrounded the base.

In 1838 some enthusiastic citizens began to excavate the mound, hoping to find archeological treasure that would lure tourists and, as one newspaper story put it, produce admission fees "in copious torrents." Two tunnels and a shaft did reveal graves near the center of the mound. One of these burial vaults was soon turned into a candle-lit museum, with skeletons and artifacts on display.

One object, supposed to have been found in the excavation, was an engraved stone tablet with markings widely believed to be letters in some undeciphered language. The "writing" stirred up a great controversy before scholars came to agree that the tablet was a fake, planted in the mound by some hoaxer.

Neither the tablet nor the exhibit in the tomb brought commercial success to the venture. The original museum was soon abandoned; the tunnels and shaft caved in, and most of the excavated material disappeared. So did the famous tablet.

Fortunately a careful account of the interior of the mound was written by a doctor, in 1839. This and other accounts and records were discovered and collected by Delf Norona, former director of the present museum, who put the story together in an interesting booklet, *Moundsville's Mammoth Mound*, published by the West Virginia Archeological Society.

Grave Creek Mound, also known as Mammoth Mound, is one of about 100 that once stood on the present site of the city of Moundsville. Its builders probably began it in late Archaic times, then in several distinct stages made

The prehistoric village of Aztalan in Wisconsin was the most northerly outpost of the Mississippian way of life. This diorama by Arminta Neal shows an everyday scene at Aztalan. Photo by Daryl Cornick.

additions, which they used as burial places for important people. Almost all the other mounds in the area have been destroyed by modern industrial construction. A somewhat similar one, Cresap Mound, ten miles away, was excavated by Don W. Dragoo, of the Carnegie Museum. Another, Natrium Mound, was excavated by Ralph Solecki, of the Smithsonian Institution.

The Museum. A series of exhibits portrays and interprets what is known about the life of the prehistoric Adena people associated with the construction of Grave Creek Mound. The museum's permanent collection includes material from about 1000 B.C. to A.D. 700.

GRAVE CREEK MOUND STATE PARK
(Mammoth Mound)
(*See Delf Norona Museum and Cultural Centre*)

SOUTH CHARLESTON
(Criel Mound)

In downtown South Charleston, on US 60. Open free, daily, all year.

This prehistoric mound has been greatly altered by modern use. A hundred years ago its top was taken off to make room for a judges' stand at horse races held on the site. Later a bandstand was built into its side.

WEST VIRGINIA STATE MUSEUM

Capitol Complex, Charleston, WV 25305. Phone: 304/348-0220. Open free, daily. Closed certain holidays.

Major displays here are devoted to prehistoric cultures of West Virginia and to contact period Indians. One exhibit features what was once called the Kanawah (can-NOAH) Madonna, an almost life-size, badly eroded, carved wooden figure holding a buffalo in its arms. Discovered in a cave near Malden, NJ, it has been radiocarbon dated at early sixteenth century.

Wisconsin

AZTALAN MUSEUM
(AZ-ta-lan)

Adjacent to Aztalan State Park. From Lake Mills drive 3 miles east on County Road B to the center of Aztalan, then south to park entrance. Mail address: N 6264 Highway Q, Jefferson, WI 53549. Phone: 414/648-8845. Open Monday–Saturday; afternoon, Sunday, May 15–September 30. Admission charged.

Materials found at the Aztalan site (see below) are on exhibit here. Artifacts include a section of the wood and clay palisade around the original settlement at the site. This piece of wall was baked as hard as brick when the town was burned.

AZTALAN STATE PARK

From Lake Mills drive 3 miles east on County Trunk B to the center of Aztalan, then south to park entrance. Mail address: N 6264 Highway Q, Jefferson, WI 53549. Open free, daily. Closed to vehicles October 15–April 15.

This is one of the most important sites in Wisconsin. Seven hundred years ago a busy town stood here, completely protected by a palisade built of upright poles 12 to 19 feet high, placed close together. Branches were woven between the poles, then the entire structure was covered with a thick plaster of clay. Watchtowers built at frequent intervals reinforced this stockade, which surrounded not only the dwellings but also fields and ceremonial mounds and burial areas.

Portions of the stockade have now been restored, as have two large, pyramidal mounds. One of these rises in a series of terraces, the other in an unbroken slope. Ten conical mounds also remain, although 74 once stood in a double line within the palisade.

Working with information supplied by archeologists, an artist painted this view of Aztalan as it may have looked during the period from A.D. 1100 to A.D. 1300. Milwaukee Public Museum photo.

Archeologists at Aztalan State Park uncovered post holes indicating that a square dwelling once stood here.

An exhibit case in the park interprets Aztalan culture for summer visitors, but is removed in winter. There is no official museum. However, random local finds of material from the Aztalan area are exhibited in the Aztalan Museum adjoining the park.

The Story. Sometime after A.D. 1100 a group of people, probably from Cahokia in Illinois, started out in search of a new home. Possibly the emigrants left because there was too large a population at Cahokia to be supported by the surrounding farmlands, rich though they were. Or perhaps some kind of feud had developed in the community.

Nobody is sure why some people moved away, but move they did—up the Mississippi River, then up the Rock River, then up the Crawfish River. Finally, on the banks of the Crawfish, the wanderers found a site to their liking. It offered good farmland, good fishing, and good hunting in the nearby woods. All around, however, were people who followed the Woodland lifeway, which was very different from the Mississippian.

The Woodland people were less advanced than the newcomers. Their arts were less developed. Their ceremonial life was much more simple. The two groups did not get along. This explains the strong outer palisades and watchtowers and the additional inner palisades that divided up the settlement into smaller areas that were easy to defend.

For nearly 200 years the Mississippian farmers, who with their families never numbered more than 500, managed to live on, surrounded by a hostile community. They kept to their own ways and continued to conduct their own kinds of ceremony, including one that may have been religious in nature but was certainly not reassuring to their neighbors. The Mississippians practiced cannibalism, and since the victims in cannibalistic rites were very likely captured Woodland Indians, the latter may have had good reason for taking a dim view of the alien culture in their midst. In the end they seem to have destroyed it completely. The entire town of Aztalan, including the log palisades, was burned to the ground, and no one knows what became of those who once lived there.

The Name. In the early part of the nineteenth century readers of books and magazines in the United States were excited by reports of mysterious pyramids supposedly built by the ancient Aztecs of Mexico. Two men in Wisconsin had these stories in mind when they discovered the flat-topped pyramidal mounds on the banks of the Crawfish. With very little trouble the two enthusiastic pioneers developed the theory that their site was the original homeland of the Aztecs, and they called the place Aztalan.

Special Feature. You may wonder how archeologists can be sure that the log palisade around Aztalan was 12 to 19 feet high and plastered over with clay. After all, the wood should have decayed in 600 years, and clay would long ago have been washed away by rain.

The fact is that the fire which burned Aztalan was so intense that it baked the clay brick-hard. Chunks of this "Aztalan brick" still show the marks of the wooden posts, and when pieced

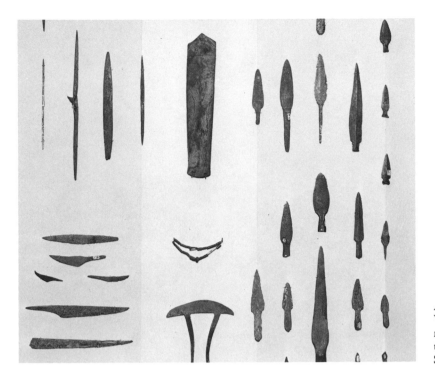

At one time Archaic people in Wisconsin and other northern areas made tools of the pure copper that they found in deposits near Lake Superior. Photo by Daryl Cornick.

together, they tell exactly how high the palisade was.

BELOIT COLLEGE, LOGAN MUSEUM OF ANTHROPOLOGY

Prospect at Bushnell, Beloit, WI 53511. Phone: 608/363-2677. Open free, Tuesday–Sunday. Closed school holidays.

Along with extensive archeological displays of materials from many parts of the world, this museum has these Wisconsin exhibits: Paleo-Indian, Effigy Mound culture, Archaic Period, Middle Woodland Period, Middle Mississippian, and Oneota culture. Dioramas of archeological subjects include one showing an effigy mound on the Beloit campus. On the second floor of the museum are southwestern exhibits. Among these is a full-scale Pueblo house.

BURNETT COUNTY HISTORICAL SOCIETY MUSEUM

In Siren. Mail address: P.O. Box 31, Siren, WI 54872. Phone: 715/349-2219. Open daily, all year. Admission charged.

Exhibits here cover prehistoric periods from Paleo through late Woodland. There are dioramas and numerous displays of artifacts.

The Historical Society is also responsible for the Fort Folle Avoine Historical Park (see entry below).

COPPER CULTURE STATE PARK

From junction of US 41 and Wisconsin 22 in Oconto, drive .2 mile west on Wisconsin 22 (Main Street), then follow directional signs. Open free, daily, all year. Camping nearby.

This small park contains the undeveloped site of an important archeological discovery.

The Story. For a great many years Midwestern farmers found strange green objects in their fields when they

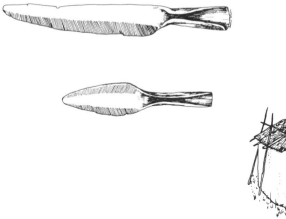

A knife and projectile point of copper, typical artifacts of the Old Copper culture. Note sockets for hafting.

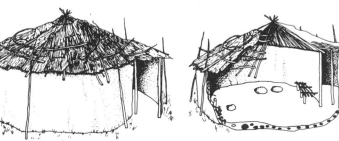

Reconstructed exterior and cutaway of a house at Aztalan. After R. R. Burke.

plowed. Nobody was sure what these objects were. Then in 1945 the Mississippi River washed away part of its bank near Potosi, Wisconsin, and exposed what is called the Osceola Site. Excavation revealed chipped stone tools and human burials. With them were some objects that proved to be copper tools turned green by corrosion.

A few years later a boy at Oconto found some bones in a gravel pit. His first thought was that he had stumbled upon evidence of a murder, and he reported his discovery to the sheriff. It was an archeologist, however, who solved the mystery. The bones belonged to a Native American who had been buried for a very long time. In the same gravel pit were other burials, many of them, and made in three different ways. Some of the bodies had been cremated. Some had been buried only after the flesh was removed from the bones. About half had been buried while the flesh was still intact. This was all interesting, but most exciting to archeologists was the discovery of copper tools with many of the burials.

Archeologists now began to talk about an Old Copper culture, because the tools were much more ancient than others made of copper by such people as the Hopewell. Carbon-14 dates show that the Old Copper people lived perhaps 5000 years ago.

This date suggested that Indians in Wisconsin were using metal almost as early as people in the Old World, but the Indians never learned to smelt it. Nor did they harden it by adding another metal to form an alloy. Perhaps the softness of copper led them to abandon it in favor of stone. Perhaps a hostile group got control of the mines and kept the Old Copper people away from their source of supply until they forgot about the metal. For whatever reason, Indians in Wisconsin had stopped making much use of copper long before the arrival of Europeans in the area.

DEVILS LAKE STATE PARK

From Baraboo drive 3 miles south on Wisconsin 123 to park entrance. Mail address: Box 426, Campbellsport, WI 53010. Phone: 608/356-8301. Open daily, all year. Admission charged to park. Visitor Center open free, Monday–Sunday, summer; weekends in fall. Camping.

Effigy mounds in the park are indicated by explanatory signs. One in the shape of a bear and another that resembles a lynx are at the north end of the lake. A bird-shaped mound is at the south end.

In the Visitor Center a diorama shows Indians building the bear effigy mound.

The park is one unit of the Ice Age National Scientific Reserve (see below).

FORTS FOLLE AVOINE HISTORICAL PARK (FALL-ah-VON)

Drive 4 miles north of Webster on Highway 35, then left on County Road U, 2.6 miles to entrance. Mail address: Burnett County Historical Society, P.O. Box 31, Siren, WI 54872. Phone: 715/349-2219. Open daily, May 1–October 15. Admission charged.

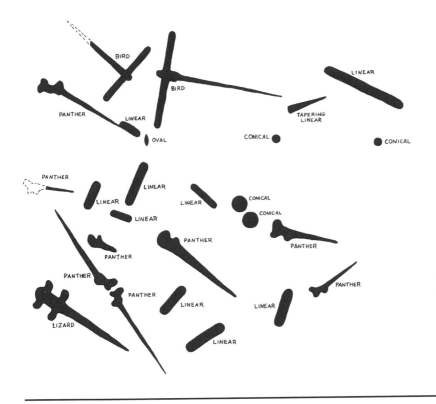

Prehistoric people in Wisconsin built mounds as monuments to the dead. Some were simply linear shapes. The smallest one here is about 100 feet long. Others were effigies in the shapes of animals. This group, in Lizard Mound State Park, takes its name from the unusual lizard effigy, lower left.

In the museum are numerous exhibits of prehistoric cultural material including projectile points, celts, axes, and pottery. A special feature of the park is a reconstructed Ojibway village.

HIGH CLIFF STATE PARK

From Menasha (man-ASH-a) drive about ten miles east on Wisconsin 114 to park entrance, or from Stockbridge drive north on Wisconsin 55 to park entrance. Mail address: Parks and Recreation, 140 Main St., Menasha, WI 54952. Phone: 414/751-5106. Open daily, all year. Admission charged. Camping April 1–November 30.

On top of the bluff in the park, 200 feet above Lake Winnebago, prehistoric people built 13 effigy mounds. Some are in the shape of lizards and others represent birds. All are about two feet high, but they vary in length from 25 to 285 feet.

HOARD HISTORICAL MUSEUM

407 Merchants Avenue, Fort Atkinson, WI 53538. Phone: 414/563-7769. Open free, Tuesday–Saturday; afternoon, first Sunday of each month.

Displays contain artifacts from the Paleo through the Woodland and Mississippian cultures. Of special interest is material that came from excavation of nearby village sites and of effigy and burial mounds.

About a mile from the museum, in Fort Atkinson, is Panther Intaglio (see entry below) which is open at all times.

ICE AGE NATIONAL SCIENTIFIC RESERVE

There are visitable archeological sites in some of the nine separate units of the Reserve which is affiliated with the National Park system. For information about road directions, dates, fees, and camping write to the Wisconsin Department of Natural Resources, Bureau of Parks and Recreation, DNR, Box 7921, Madison, WI 53707.

LIZARD MOUND COUNTY PARK

From West Bend drive 4 miles northeast on Wisconsin 144, then 1 mile east on County Trunk A to directional marker. Mail address: Land Use and Park Department, 432 East Washington St., West Bend, WI 53095. Phone: 414/335-4445. Open free, April 1–November 15.

In this park there are 31 good examples of effigy mounds, three to four feet high, which represent birds, panthers, and lizards. A number are geometrical—either linear or conical in form.

About 5000 effigy mounds have been found in southern Wisconsin—approximately 98 percent of all that are known in North America. Some of them are so large that it was presumably from the vantage point of treetops that their builders were able to view them as a whole—if they ever did. In any event, they seem to have had clear patterns in mind as they worked.

The creators of effigy mounds usually buried the dead in them, but often

Prehistoric Indians belonging to a group called Old Copper people hunted deer with spears and spear-throwers, as shown in this diorama by Arminta Neal. Photo by Daryl Cornick.

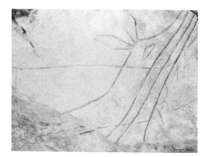

At some time in the distant past this deer head was incised in stone at a rockshelter near Disco, Wisconsin. Photo by Warren Wittry, courtesy Campbell Grant.

they did not leave offerings in the graves. As a result, archeologists know less about the Effigy Mound people than they do about people who left abundant gifts with burials. One important question is when the building of effigy mounds began. At least one specialist believes the custom may have started in Archaic times. Others say that a more likely date is between A.D. 600 and 1000.

Generally speaking, the people who built effigy mounds were part of the widespread Woodland culture. They had pottery, engaged in hunting and fishing, and also did some farming. In winter and in summer they scattered and lived in small bands. At planting time in the spring, and again at harvest time in the fall, the bands seem to have come together, forming temporary communities. At such times there was a good deal of manpower and womanpower available—enough to do the considerble work involved in building mounds.

No one knows for sure why effigy mounds take the shapes they do. Perhaps they represented creatures sacred

to the person buried in them. The burials, incidentally, were often made at spots in the effigies that were possibly considered vital to the creatures whose shapes had been modeled in earth. Skeletons have been found where effigy wings or legs joined bodies, or in the areas of the head, heart, or groin.

LOGAN MUSEUM OF
ANTHROPOLOGY
(*See Beloit College*)

MAN MOUND PARK

From Baraboo drive east on Eighth Ave. (Wisconsin 33), then north on County Trunk T to the first intersection, then east to the mound. Phone: 608/356-1001. Open free, at all times. Camping nearby.

This large effigy mound in a county park is unusual because it resembles a human figure. Most other effigy mounds are likenesses of birds, serpents, or four-legged mammals.

MENASHA MOUNDS

Smith Park, Menasha. Mail address: Parks and Recreation Dept., 140 Main St., Menasha, WI 54952. Phone: 414/751-5106. Open free, at all times.

In municipally owned Smith Park are three effigy mounds said to resemble panthers. The largest is 180 feet long. A marker in the park indicates that they were built about A.D. 900.

MENDOTA MENTAL HEALTH
INSTITUTE MOUND

On the grounds of Mendota Mental Health Institute, Madison. Open free, at all times.

Here, on the hospital grounds, is a 6-foot-high effigy mound in the form of a bird that has a wingspread of 624 feet.

MILWAUKEE PUBLIC MUSEUM

800 West Wells St., Milwaukee WI 53233. Phone: 414/278-2702. Open daily, all year. Closed certain holidays. Admission charged.

In addition to a major exhibit of

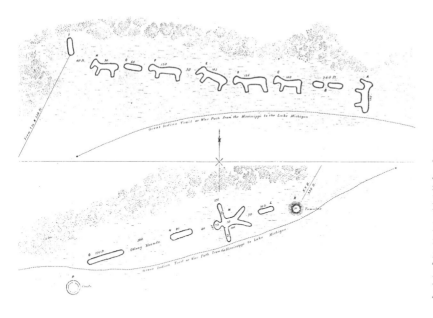

Here, shown in two sections and drawn from an actual survey, is a group of effigy mounds that stretched for nearly half a mile on high prairie ground along a trail in Wisconsin between the Mississippi River and Lake Michigan. Six of the figures may represent bears and vary in length from 90 feet to 120 feet. The human figure is 125 feet long. From *Ancient Monuments of the Mississippi Valley.*

prehistoric material from Mexico and Central and South America, the museum has on exhibit some artifacts from the Southwest and one small display of southeastern material.

MUSCODA MOUNDS
(MUSS-koh-dah)

From Muscoda drive one mile west on Wisconsin 60 across the Wisconsin River to directional sign. Open free, at all times. Camping nearby.

This group of effigy mounds, on private land, has not been developed but is open to the public. The mounds can be seen from an unsurfaced road that passes them.

NATURAL BRIDGE STATE PARK

From Devils Lake State Park drive south on US 12 to County Rd. C, then west to Natural Bridge entrance. Open spring to fall. Admission to the park charged.

A self-guided trail in the park is devoted to explaining how Native Americans used plants.

NELSON DEWEY STATE PARK

From Cassville drive 2 miles northwest on County Trunk VV to the park. Open daily, except when there is snow on the ground. Admission charged. Camping.

In this park overlooking the Mississippi River are a number of prehistoric effigy mounds.

NEVILLE PUBLIC MUSEUM

210 Museum Place, Green Bay, WI 54303. Phone: 414/448-4460. Open free, Tuesday–Saturday; afternoons, Sunday–Monday. Closed certain holidays.

A permanent exhibit, "On the Edge of the Inland Sea," covers 12,000 years of northeastern Wisconsin prehistory from the end of the Pleistocene epoch through the arrival of Jean Nicolet in 1634. The Paleo-Indian, Archaic, Woodland, and Oneota cultures are covered as well as the glacial and postglacial environments of the area.

OCONTO COUNTY HISTORICAL SOCIETY MUSEUM
(oh-KAHN-toh)

917 Park Ave., Oconto, WI 54153. Phone: 414/834-2260. Open daily, June–September. Admission charged.

In the annex of this museum are examples of Old Copper culture material found at the Oconto Site, on the western edge of the town. This site is now part of Copper Culture State Park.

OSHKOSH PUBLIC MUSEUM

1331 Algoma Blvd., Oshkosh, WI 54901. Phone: 414/236-5150. Open free, Tuesday–Saturday; afternoon, Sunday.

Various members of the staff of this museum have gathered material from several excavations in the area. This material, plus some collected by early Wisconsin archeologists and supplemented by random local finds, illustrates cultures from Paleo-Indian times through Archaic, Woodland, and Mississippian, up to the present.

PANTHER INTAGLIO

From Fort Atkinson drive west on Wisconsin 106 to the site. Open free, at all times. Camping nearby.

Here is a large effigy dug into the earth instead of raised above it. The intaglio effect is created by a depression about a foot deep. No burials have been found at the site. In the vicinity are effigies of the usual kind, modeled in the form of a mound.

PERROT STATE PARK
(pair-OH)

From Trempealeau drive 2 miles west along the Mississippi River. Mail address: Route 1, P.O. Box 407, Trempealeau, WI 54661. Open daily, all year. Admission charged. Camping.

In this park are a few conical, effigy, and Hopewell mounds.

ROCHE-A-CRI STATE PARK
(ROWSH-ah-CREE)

From Friendship, drive 1 mile north on Wisconsin 13. Phone: 608/339-3385. Open daily, last week of May–October. Admission charged. Camping.

In the side of a mound in the park are petroglyphs now almost completely obliterated by superimposed modern graffiti. There is an interpretive marker at the site.

The Name. Early French explorers gave the area its name, which means "crevice in the rock," because of a wide crack in the cliff that was visible from a distance.

SHEBOYGAN COUNTY MUSEUM

3110 Erie Ave., Sheboygan, WI 53081. Phone: 414/458-6144. Open Tuesday–Saturday; afternoon, Sunday, April 1–September 30. Admission charged.

In this museum are random local finds from Old Copper, Hopewellian, and Upper Mississippian cultures.

SHEBOYGAN MOUND PARK

From Sheboygan drive south on US Business 141, then east on County Trunk EE, then south on S. 12th St. to Riverdale Country Club. Here turn east on Panther Ave., then south on S. Ninth St. to the park entrance. Open free, at all times. Camping nearby.

In this city park are 33 effigy mounds, called the Kletzien Group. Some resemble deer and panthers. Others are conical and linear in shape. As with many effigy mound burials elsewhere, there were very few artifacts found in the graves here. Therefore, little is known about the people who built these earthen structures. From carbon-14 dates obtained at other sites, it is supposed that the Sheboygan Mounds were built between A.D. 500 and 1000.

STATE HISTORICAL MUSEUM

30 North Carroll Street, Madison, WI 53706. Phone: 608/262-7700. Open free. Tuesday–Sunday. Closed certain holidays.

On the second floor is the exhibit "People of the Woodlands: Wisconsin Indian Ways." The exhibit covers the lifestyles of Wisconsin Indians from prehistoric times into the twentieth century. All prehistoric periods are included and there is an activity area with a full-size reproduction of an Aztalan house.

Turtle Mound as it appeared in 1919 on the University of Wisconsin campus at Madison. State Historical Society of Wisconsin photo by George R. Fox.

STATE HISTORICAL SOCIETY OF WISCONSIN

816 State Street, Madison, WI 53706. Phone: 608/264-6400. Open free, Monday–Saturday. Closed certain holidays.

Prehistoric Wisconsin copper and stone implements are on exhibit in the lower level.

STEVENS POINT MUSEUM OF NATURAL HISTORY
(*See University of Wisconsin*)

UNIVERSITY OF WISCONSIN ARBORETUM

On the shore of Lake Winagra, 1207 Seminole Highway, Madison. Open free, at all times.

There are three groups of mounds in the University Arboretum, all of which can be visited. No effort has been made to interpret them.

UNIVERSITY OF WISCONSIN CAMPUS

Madison. Open free, at all times.

At four places on the campus there are prehistoric mounds, several of them near the Lake Shore dormitories.

Two are on Observatory Hill, on Picnic Point, and one group near Eagle Heights, the student housing units. Some, but not all, are marked by plaques.

UNIVERSITY OF WISCONSIN, STEVENS POINT

Learning Resources Bldg., on the campus, Stevens Point, WI 54481. Phone: 715/346-2858. Open free, Monday–Saturday; afternoon, Sunday.

On display in this museum are local Indian artifacts and an exhibit of Eskimo material.

WYALUSING STATE PARK
(WYE-uh-LOOSE-ing)

From Prairie du Chien (du-SHEEN) drive 6 miles southeast on US 18, then 5 miles west on County Trunk C, then south .75 mile on County Trunk X, to junction with State Park Road, which is the park entrance. Mail address: Department of Natural Resources, 13342 County Highway C, Bagley, WI 53801. Phone: 608/996-2261. Open daily, all year. Admission charged. Camping.

Sentinel Ridge, a high divide in the park, was used by prehistoric people as a burial spot. Here they built mounds over the bodies of the dead. One large group, known as "a procession of mounds," stretches out in a line along the ridge and can be reached by auto and an easy trail from the parking lot.

Health was of great interest to prehistoric Native Americans, who died young as a rule. This diorama shows people of the Eastern Woodlands culture attempting to drive out disease with a curing ceremony in which some of the participants wear masks called false faces. Canadian Museum of Civilization photo.

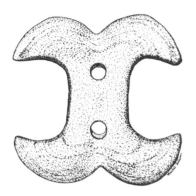

NORTHEAST

After the last Ice-Age glacier disappeared from northern North America, one feature was common to all the land from Labrador south to Virginia. The area became forested. Everyone who lived in the region during the next 10,000 years had to adjust in one way or another to that fact. As a result, there were similarities in the prehistoric cultures of the Northeast, but there were also marked differences in lifeways. These arose in part from necessarily different responses to climate and food resources. They also arose from the influences of diverse cultures in neighboring areas.

People arrived in the northern part of the Northeast even before trees began to grow on land recently laid bare by retreating ice. The first to come were Paleo hunters, who sometimes tracked their quarry very close indeed to the edge of the ice. For example, the Debert (deh-BURT) Site in Nova Scotia yielded evidence that people camped there 11,000 years ago, when snowfields were just five miles away, and it was only 65 miles to the ice itself. Even in such a chilly world tundra vegetation fed herds of grazing animals, which in turn provided food for hunters.

Other groups of Paleo-Indians stayed behind, in the region farther south. After the glaciers contracted, this area was the first to be covered by trees, which eventually spread northward into Canada. What we know about the Big-Game Hunters in the Northeast comes from a small number of sites, including the Williamson Site in Virginia, the Shoop Site in Pennsylvania, Bull Brook and Wapanucket No. 8 in Massachusetts, Reagan in Vermont, and the Vail Site in Maine. The latter is probably unique in the eastern United States because unbroken projectile points were found at a caribou kill very close to the associated campsite. None of these Paleo sites are prepared for the public, but artifacts from some of them can be seen in major northeastern museums.

Archaic Period

As they did elsewhere, Paleo-Indians in all of the Northeast slowly developed new lifeways in the forest environment, and during the next period, known as the Archaic, they learned to exploit new resources. Along some rivers and seashores they harvested quantities of mollusks, and the shells they discarded piled up in heaps. Many of these heaps, all the way from Virginia to the Maritime Provinces of Canada, have now disappeared under water because sea level has risen in relation to the land, but where they survived archeologists have studied them—along the banks of the Hudson River, for example, and on Cape Cod and the coast of Maine.

At one place, unfortunately not open to the public, the shell middens tell a story of considerable social change. At Ellsworth Falls, Maine, excavation has revealed four distinct stages of social development. In the oldest, known as the Kelley Phase and dated before 3000 B.C., people made heavy, chipped tools. The implements they used for scraping hides or wood were large and crude. Their hammerstones were essentially large pebbles, or cobbles. Flakes struck from the cobbles seem to have served as knives.

By about 2000 B.C. a much more elaborate tool kit had developed at this site. There were adzes and gouges—woodworking tools useful in making dugout canoes, among other things. Six hundred years later they had refined their tools still further—they used plummets, possibly as weights on fishing nets or as bolas. They made weights to improve the balance and efficiency of their atlatls, and in time they began to use pottery. Finally hunters at Ellsworth Falls began to use smaller projectile points. This suggests that they had bows and arrows. They may even have done some gardening. They had entered what is called the Woodland cultural period.

Fish Trapping

In broad outline this one site tells what happened in varying ways at various times all over the Northeast. Where Boston now stands, Archaic people who depended on the sea for food made an elaborate adjustment to their environment and reached a high level of social organization earlier than did those at Ellsworth Falls. At Boston—and elsewhere—they trapped fish in devices called weirs. These were arrangements of various kinds built so that fish could more easily swin into them than out of them.

The Boston Site, known as the Boylston Street Fish Weir, was covered by the New England Mutual Life Insurance Company building. When construction workers were digging the foundation for this building they encountered evidence of earlier construction. Archeologists studied the site, dug further, and found that 65,000 wooden stakes had been driven into clay, above which shallow tidal waters once rose and fell. Between the upright stakes branches had been woven basket-fashion, permitting water to pass through but creating an obstacle for fish. Later 12 feet of silt had been deposited above the tops of the stakes. This meant that the water had risen in relation to the land. Then, as Boston expanded in historic times, landfill had been dumped on top of the silt, driving the water away from the area.

Estimates by geologists and dates obtained by the radiocarbon method place the time of construction of the Boylston Street Fish Weir between 4000 B.C. and 2000 B.C. The Archaic people who used the trap had obviously achieved a rather highly organized society; otherwise they could not have built and maintained such a large and complicated device for obtaining food.

Snowshoes

A quite different invention—snowshoes—helped those who lived inland to get food in the dead of winter. Some experts think snowshoes may have come into the Northeast from northern Eurasia. Others believe they may have been an independent invention made by northeastern Indians during early Archaic times. Whichever it was, hunters could now walk and even run on top of soft snow. They could actually travel faster than the game they hunted.

At the time when people were harvesting fish in Boston and mollusks at Ellsworth Falls, other groups had begun to develop a lifeway known as Laurentian in northern New York, Ontario, Quebec, and parts of New England and Pennsylvania. Hunters used broad, heavy projectile points, and their meat diet was supplemented with fish, nuts, berries, and seeds. At many Laurentian campsites evidence points to short stays by small groups. Here and there, however, where they found an abundance of fish or waterfowl or acorns, several groups gathered in large settlements for part of the year.

In central New York and northern Pennsylvania a quite distinct lifeway, known as the Lamoka, developed in a few places, paralleling in time and in some of its traits the Laurentian culture. Lamoka people mainly hunted and fished. At one time or another they consumed more than 30 different kinds of animal and left the bones in trash heaps. They were also great eaters of acorns and other nuts and seeds, which they parched and ground into meal. Some of their grinding stones were very large, and they seem to have pounded some of their food with big stone pestles, using hollow stumps for mortars.

Toward the end of the Archaic Period, about 1000 B.C., hunters in some areas began to travel more and more in canoes. In Pennsylvania, New York, and New Jersey, for example, they tended to camp along riverbanks and to make short expeditions into the forests for food.

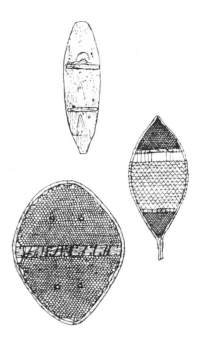

Various types of snowshoe: a bearpaw snowshoe, used by Naskapi Indians, with four eyelets through which lashings were placed to hold it firmly on the foot (bottom); a woven snowshoe made by Onondaga Indians (center); and a wooden snowshoe from Manitoba (top). After Birket-Smith, Turner, Beauchamp.

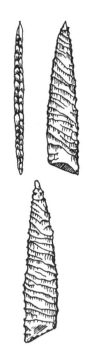

Three views of a flint point, 1⅝ inches long. This delicate artifact was made by craftsmen at Cape Denbigh, in Alaska, more than 4000 years ago. Similar small tools were made by pre-Dorset people in Canada. After Giddings.

At about this same time women acquired a new kind of cooking vessel. For centuries in the past they had been preparing stews and soups in watertight kettles of skin or wood or bark, into which they dropped hot stones to make the liquid boil. Now they began to use large, heavy vessels carved from a soft stone called steatite or soapstone. The old-fashioned method of stone boiling continued, but it was easier to do in the large steatite pots, which also held heat much better than vessels of wood or skin. Canoes made it possible to take the heavy vessels along when it was necessary to move camp. If a pot broke, it was cut up to make beads, gorgets, ladles, and spoons.

Woodland Period

This time of change, called by some archeologists the Transitional Period, merged into another period known as the Woodland. If any one thing sets off the Early Woodland lifeway it is the acquisition of pottery. Vessels of baked clay replaced the cumbersome steatite pots, and since they could be set directly over the fire they gave new freedom to the women who made and used them.

Another new concern of Early Woodland women was gardening. Just how or when they came by the idea is not known, but between about 1000 B.C. and 500 B.C. they were caring for little patches of sunflowers, Jerusalem artichokes and several other plants that we customarily think of as weeds.

With a more stable food supply came further changes in life. People could settle down near garden patches, although men made constant trips into the forests for game. Before long the gardening areas increased. Trees were cleared along stream banks to make larger fields. Eventually squash, and later, corn and beans began to supplement older food plants. During these Middle Woodland times, which lasted from about 500 B.C. to about A.D. 700, agriculture became important from Virginia as far north as the St. Lawrence River. Abbott Farm, in New Jersey, which archeologists studied for a hundred years, was inhabited during this time. In New York, Ontario, and New England, the lifeway known as Point Peninsula began to develop from a hunting culture into one that accepted the idea of farming.

Development of Villages

From now on, with a few exceptions, lifeways all over the Northeast developed slowly but steadily in much the same directions. Villages, some of them quite large, took the place of single farms. Many of these settlements were fortified by log stockades. Corn and beans became more and more important in the diet. In western Pennsylvania one Late Woodland culture is known as the Monnongahela. In New York and around the lower Great Lakes the Owasco culture evolved from earlier lifeways.

It was from the Owasco that the prehistoric Iroquois developed. By the time Europeans came to New York and the St. Lawrence River area, some of their great towns had a thousand inhabitants, with fields covering several hundred acres of cleared and cultivated ground.

From Paleo times until the day when Europeans arrived on the Atlantic coast, the numbers of northeastern Indians increased a great deal. This does not seem to have been the result of large migration from other areas. Rather it was a steady growth of resident populations as they improved their methods of obtaining food.

Although people may not have moved into the Northeast, ideas and customs and inventions did. From the south in Early Woodland times knowledge of pottery making entered Virginia and moved up the coast. Possibly the pottery idea also entered the northern part of the region from some place far to the west, in Canada. Corn and beans—and perhaps some of the notions and social behavior connected with agriculture—came ultimately from Mexico. Cultures, such as the Adena, which were stimulated by agriculture in the Ohio Valley, affected people in part of the Northeast. There were also minor influences from the Hopewell of Ohio. The custom of burying the dead in mounds appeared in a number of places; Virginia was one. There in a burial mound Thomas Jefferson conducted the first scientific excavation in the United States.

Possibly there were influences in pottery styles or implement design that came somehow from northwestern or northeastern Eurasia. Immigration did take place at more than one time across the Bering Strait, and immigrants who followed that route certainly brought their cultures with them. It is not so easy to see how ideas could have crossed westward from northern Europe, but the use of small craft for island-hopping has been suggested as a possibility. Also scholars have suggested that people may have crossed the water barrier in the north when it was covered with ice floes, following the edge of the ice and subsisting, as the Eskimo (Inuit) did, on the sea mammals and fish available there.

The Northeast never attained the population density of the Mississippi Valley. Nor did arts and crafts and social organization reach such levels of development as in the major centers of Native American life. But much more happened in 12,000 years in the Northeast than one would guess from the number of visitable archeological sites. These are few indeed, and an important reason is that a humid climate and generally acid soil in the region have conspired to destroy most organic matter left by prehistoric peoples.

But even though site areas are minimal, some good museums are in the Northeast. They serve as excellent introductions to the area and to Indian life elsewhere as well.

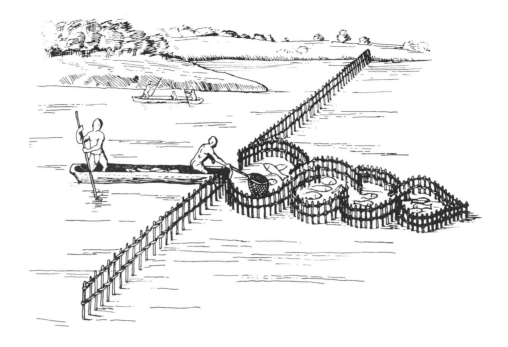

Fish traps of several kinds were used in rivers and estuaries along the Atlantic Coast. This one, built by Indians in Virginia, was sketched by Hariot, one of the first French artists to visit America. Fishermen drove stakes into the river bottom and then wove branches between the stakes, basket-fashion, allowing the water to pass through but creating an obstacle for the fish. After Hariot.

Connecticut

AMERICAN INDIAN ARCHAEOLOGICAL INSTITUTE

Take Route 47 through Washington Depot to intersection with Connecticut 199, then 1.5 miles on Connecticut 199 to Curtis Road. Mail address: P.O. Box 1260, Curtis Road, Washington, CT 06793-0260. Phone: 203/868-0518. Open daily. Closed major holidays. Admission by donation.

A permanent exhibit, "As We Tell Our Stories: Living Traditions and the Algonkian Peoples of Indian New England," explores native history and culture through voices of the region's indigenous peoples. Other exhibits include a furnished longhouse, a simulated archeological site, native plant trails, a seventeenth-century Indian village and garden, and a prehistoric shelter.

Special Feature. By appointment the museum conducts group tours and holds crafts demonstrations.

BRUCE MUSEUM

1 Museum Drive, Greenwich, CT. Phone: 203/869-0376. Open Tuesday–Saturday; afternoon, Sunday. Admission by donation.

The museum's Native American displays include such diverse materials as pre-Columbian spindle whorls and Cherokee lacrosse racquets. New archeological materials are frequently added.

CONNECTICUT STATE LIBRARY MUSEUM
(*See Museum of Connecticut History*)

CONNECTICUT STATE MUSEUM OF NATURAL HISTORY

At the University of Connecticut, U-23, Storrs, CT 06269-3023. Phone: 203/486-4460. Open free, afternoons daily. Closed certain holidays.

Included in the exhibits here is some information about prehistoric Indians.

Dr. Roger Moeller of the American Indian Archaeological Institute directed excavation of this Paleo-Indian site. From it came evidence that people have been living in Connecticut for $10,190 \pm 300$ years. American Indian Archaeological Institute photo.

DAY-LEWIS MUSEUM OF INDIAN ARTIFACTS

158 Main St., Farmington, CT 06032. Phone: 203/677-2140 or 203/678-1645. Open afternoon, Wednesday. Closed August, December, January, February. Admission by donation.

In a field adjoining this museum farmers plowed up many artifacts and in 1967 Yale University, which owns the museum, began excavation. What has been found is displayed in the museum. There is only small evidence of Paleo or Early Archaic use of the site, but beginning about 6000 B.C. hunter-gatherers made repeated brief visits over a period of 2000 years. There is also evidence of later occupation, but much of this has been disturbed by repeated plowing.

The Farmington Historical Society supervises the museum, and volunteers who work there have been trained by professional archeologists.

MATTATUCK MUSEUM OF THE MATTATUCK HISTORICAL SOCIETY
(MATT-a-tuck)

144 West Main St., Waterbury, CT. Open free, afternoons, Tuesday–Sunday. Closed, Sunday, July and August, and certain holidays.

One display of Indian artifacts, mostly from the Northeast, may be seen here.

MUSEUM OF CONNECTICUT HISTORY

231 Capitol Ave., Hartford, CT 06106. Phone: 203/566-3056. Open free, Monday–Friday; morning, Saturday. Closed certain holidays.

Some prehistoric artifacts are displayed here.

NEW BRITAIN YOUTH MUSEUM

30 High St., New Britain, CT. Open free, Saturday; afternoons, Monday–Friday. Closed certain holidays.

This small but active museum has changing exhibits, which include dioramas and prehistoric Indian material.

Special Interest. The museum prepares display kits on prehistoric Native American life which schools, churches, or other institutions may borrow for educational use. The staff conducts a training program for teenagers in museum work and encourages those interested in archeology.

Detail from a diorama in the Hagley Museum in Wilmington, Delaware, that shows Indian life in a rockshelter. The woman is making cornmeal by breaking up kernels of corn in a hollow tree stump. Hagley Museum photo.

PEABODY MUSEUM
OF NATURAL HISTORY
(*See Yale University*)

ROARING BROOK
NATURE CENTER

70 Gracey Road, Canton, CT 06019. Phone: 203/693-0263. Open Tuesday–Saturday; afternoons, Sunday and Monday in July and August. Admission charged.

This center devoted primarily to local flora and fauna includes an Eastern Woodland longhouse of the type used in this area before contact with Europeans.

STAMFORD MUSEUM AND
NATURE CENTER

39 Scofieldtown Road, Stamford, CT 06903. Phone: 203/322-1646. Open Monday–Saturday; afternoon, Sunday and certain holidays. Admission charged.

A permanent exhibit, "People of the Dawn," shows the influence of the environment on the cultures of four groups—the Northeast Woodland, Central Plains, Southwest Desert, and Northwest Coast. The stories are told through artifacts, dioramas, crafts, and photographs.

TANTAQUIDGEON
INDIAN MUSEUM

Route 32, Norwich–New London Road, Uncasville, CT 06382. Phone: 203/848-9145. Open Tuesday–Sunday, May–October. Admission by donation.

This museum, run by Mohegans and devoted to Mohegan and other Northeastern Indians of the historic period, has a few random finds of prehistoric artifacts.

YALE UNIVERSITY,
PEABODY MUSEUM
OF NATURAL HISTORY

170 Whitney Ave. Mail address: P.O. Box 6666, New Haven, CT 06511-8161. Phone: 203/432-5050. Open Monday–Saturday; afternoon, Sunday. Closed certain holidays. Admission charged except Monday–Friday 3–5 p.m.

Money contributed by George Peabody, in the nineteenth century, financed this museum, which bears his name. It houses an extensive archeological collection, from which is taken the material for exhibits both permanent and changing. A hall is devoted to Plains Indians.

This diorama shows a prehistoric Indian settlement in what is now Washington, D.C. Smithsonian Institution photo.

Delaware

HAGLEY MUSEUM

Barley Mill Rd., Greenville, DE 19807. Open free, Tuesday–Saturday and Monday holidays; afternoon, Sunday.

This museum has a diorama that shows an Indian habitation in a rockshelter.

IRON HILL MUSEUM

From Newark drive south on Delaware 896, past the intersection with Interstate 95, then west on the Old Baltimore Pike. The museum is between Cooch's Bridge, Delaware, and Elkton, Maryland. Open free, by appointment. Phone: 302/368-5703.

In 1964 an all-Black school ceased to operate in this building, and a group of volunteers sponsored by the Delaware Academy of Science turned it into a museum. Since then exhibits designed primarily for school children have been developed, showing the lives of Woodland Indians of the vicinity.

One exhibit centers around the Harland Mill Steatite Quarry, where prehistoric Indians obtained soapstone from which they made vessels for cooking. A general exhibit traces the history of Indians from Paleo times to the historic period. Indian foods are displayed, and there are dioramas, on Delaware (Lenni Lenape) village life and trapping methods.

MEETING HOUSE GALLERIES
A Delaware State Museums Site

316 S. Governors Ave., Dover, DE 19901. Open Tuesday–Saturday. Closed certain holidays. Admission by donation. For information about tours phone: 302/739-4266.

An exhibit "Discover Archaeology" interprets archeology, its methods and its relations to other sciences. It displays artifacts representing 12,000 years of Delaware cultural history.

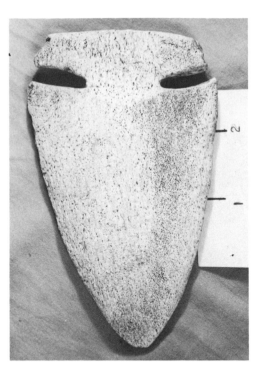

Left: In the eastern woodlands, as well as on the Plains, Indians worked porcupine quills, often dyed, into intricate designs. Here Micmac Indians in Maine have pressed quills into a birch bark box. Robert Abbe Museum of Stone Age Antiquities photo. *Right:* This projectile point from Maine was made of whale bone. Robert Abbe Museum of Stone Age Antiquities photo.

District of Columbia

NATIONAL GALLERY OF ART

4th St. and Constitution Ave. NW, Washington, DC 20565. Phone: 202/737-4215. Open free, daily. Closed certain holidays.

In the past this museum has had important exhibitions of prehistoric North American material. It would be wise to check to see what is currently on display.

NATIONAL MUSEUM OF THE AMERICAN INDIAN, SMITHSONIAN INSTITUTION

This great $106,000,000 museum is scheduled to open at a future date on the Mall in the nation's capital. Native Americans are involved in the planning of exhibits which will cover both prehistoric and historic periods. Pending completion of the new facility, most of the Smithsonian's prehistoric ar-

cheological resources are not on display. Some, however, are included in the large "Seeds of Change" exhibition that was running in the National Museum of Natural History as this book went to press.

The new facility will be the first federally funded museum devoted exclusively to the First Americans. In addition to preserving and interpreting the Indian past, it will have a stage for dance and theatrical performances and for ceremonies. Also it will display contemporary arts and crafts.

The future National Museum of the American Indian will consist of two sections. In addition to the new building in Washington, there is already a major section in New York (see entry below). For information about the Washington section write to Smithsonian Institution, SI Building, Room 153, Stop 010, Washington, DC 20560. Phone: 202/357-2700.

NATIONAL MUSEUM OF NATURAL HISTORY, SMITHSONIAN INSTITUTION

10th St. and Constitution Ave. NW, Washington, DC 20560. Phone: 202/357-2020. Open free, daily, except December 25.

In the "Seeds of Change" exhibition, the largest ever produced by the National Museum of Natural History, are displays demonstrating the contribution Native Americans made to people everywhere with two plants they domesticated in prehistoric times—corn and the potato. The plants have spread around the globe and play a very important role in the world's diet.

One diorama shows a Hopi tending corn plants. In the diorama are many corn-related artifacts.

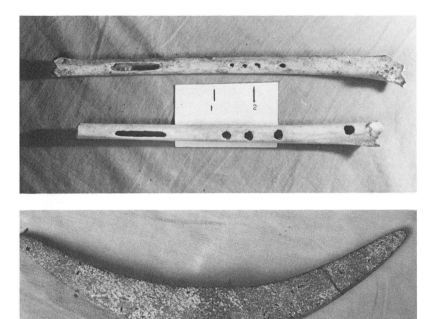

Above: Flutes were popular musical instruments among prehistoric Indians in many places. These, made of bone, come from Maine. Robert Abbe Museum of Stone Age Antiquities photo. *Below:* Weights that Archaic Indians used to increase the efficiency of atlatls were made in different shapes in different places. In Maine, where many people were familiar with whales, some craftsperson made this weight to resemble the tail of one kind of whale. Robert Abbe Museum of Stone Age Antiquities photo.

Maine

ABBE MUSEUM

Acadia National Park. From Bar Harbor drive south on Maine 3 to Sieur de Monts Spring. Mail address: P.O. Box 177, Bar Harbor, ME 04609. Open daily, Memorial Day–Labor Day. Admission charged. Camping in Acadia National Park.

The Robert Abbe Museum of Stone Age Antiquities contains materials from Woodland sites, both coastal and interior. One diorama shows summer activity in prehistoric times; another shows an autumn camp and chores associated with salmon fishing.

ANCIENT PEMAQUID RESTORATION
(See Colonial Pemaquid State Historic Site

AROOSTOOK HISTORICAL AND ART MUSEUM

109 Main St., Houlton, ME 04730. Phone: 207/532-4216. Open afternoons, Monday–Friday, May 29–September 28. Admission charged.

Stone tools on exhibit here were made by people of the Red Paint culture.

COLONIAL PEMAQUID STATE HISTORIC SITE

Pemaquid Beach, off State 130 next to New Harbor, on the same site as Fort William Henry. Open daily, Memorial Day–Labor Day; Saturday and Sunday remainder of year. Admission charged. Camping nearby.

The Abnakis once lived at this site and left refuse heaped up in a midden. A few artifacts recovered from the midden are on display in the museum, which is devoted primarily to the English occupation of the area in the seventeenth and eighteenth centuries.

Mimbres women often decorated their pottery with pictures of animals. *Top to bottom:* Duck; Turkey; Deer. Redrawn from Gladwin.

Animals for Food

As they explored their different environments on this continent, Indians seem to have tried just about every likely source of nourishment. The food resources in a desert area were of course quite different from those near a large river in the Southeast. Plains dwellers had foods quite unlike those available to inhabitants of the Northwest Coast.

Archeologists study all the animal bones they find in an excavation in an effort to discover the diet of the people who lived there, and also to find out about prehistoric ecology.

Here is a list of animal remains found at one site in Massachusetts, which was inhabited between A.D. 900 and 1500: beaver, dog, red fox, grey fox, black bear, mink, harbor seal, white-tailed deer, red-throated loon, great blue heron, mallard, black duck, red-tailed hawk, bald eagle, great auk, snapping turtle, Plymouth turtle, roughtail sting ray, Atlantic sturgeon, black sea bass, sculpin, sea robin, scup, wolffish, bay scallop, blue mussel, quahog, surf clam, long clam, lobed moon shell, moon shell, boat shell, thick-lipped drill, conch, and channeled conch.

DAMARISCOTTA RIVER SHELL MOUNDS
(Oyster Shell Banks)
(dam-uh-riss-COTT-uh)

For road directions inquire at Information Booth, US Business 1. Mail address: Box 217, Damariscotta, ME 04543. Phone: 207/563-5318. Open free.

Mounds, which consist mostly of oyster shells, were left here by prehistoric people, probably some time after 2000 B.C. The mounds can be seen from across the Damariscotta River. Artifacts from the site are in the Peabody Museum, Harvard University.

MAINE STATE MUSEUM

In the State Capitol Complex, Augusta. Mail address: State House Station 83, Augusta, ME 04333-0083. Phone: 207/289-2301. Open free, Monday–Saturday; afternoon, Sunday. Closed certain holidays.

Here an exhibit, "12,000 Years in Maine," features more than 2000 artifacts dating from the end of the last Ice Age up to the nineteenth century.

Special Feature. One display is devoted to the Red Paint people, who lived along the Penobscot River in Maine about 4000 years ago. They are so called because they used the mineral red ocher in burial ceremonies, sprinkling quantities of it on the dead and over all the gifts they placed in graves. Among the gifts were familiar objects, such as knives, projectile points, and woodworking tools. Less common were net sinkers, polished slate objects that resemble bayonets, implements of flint and iron pyrite for making fire, and mysterious little perfectly rounded pebbles. Since there are no visitable Red Paint sites in the United States, the display here is of special interest. The Port au Choix Site in Newfoundland (see entry below) was occupied by people who had many of the same cultural patterns.

WILSON MUSEUM

Perkins St., Castine (kas-TEEN), ME. Mail address: P.O. Box 196, Castine, ME 04421. Phone: 207/326-8753. Open free, afternoons, Tuesday–Sunday, May 27–October 1.

Exhibits of prehistoric artifacts represent some of the major Indian cultures in North America. They include material from the Northeast, Ohio mounds, southwestern pueblos, the Great Plains, and Eskimo areas in Canada.

Special Feature. One display of material found in a Red Paint grave contains fire lighters. These were pieces of iron pyrite, which were struck with flint to make sparks.

In addition to the study of plant and animal remains found at sites, analysis of ancient desiccated human feces, called coprolites, can tell archeologists not only what people ate but also something about their environment. The presence of corn indicates farming. Predominance of wild plants may mean that gardening was secondary to gathering.

Researchers at Chaco Canyon were somewhat surprised by what coprolites revealed there. As had been expected, Chacoans ate deer meat, but they also consumed an enormous number of smaller animals—chipmunks, voles and prairie dogs. The chunks of bone that people chewed, apparently not very well, were quite large enough for identification by specialists in animal anatomy.

The corn in the Chacoan diet seems mostly to have been cooked with either the flowers or seeds of the bee plant. Possibly the plant added flavor to a corn dish, though this was not necessarily the reason for its use.

Maryland

ACCOKEEK CREEK SITE COMPLEX

In Piscataway Park. Mail address: National Park Service, 1100 Ohio Drive SW, Washington, DC 20242.

Here on the Potomac River in southern Maryland are four sites: a Late Archaic through Middle Woodland site, an early Late Woodland village, a sixteenth-century village, and a 1675 Susquehannock Indian Fort. There are no on-site exhibits of the park's prehistory, but the Park Service offers occasional tours.

DORCHESTER HERITAGE MUSEUM

From Cambridge, drive 3 miles east on Maryland 343 to Horn Point Rd., .5 mile west of entrance to Maryland Center for Environmental and Estuarine Studies. Mail address: 1904 Horn Point Rd., Cambridge, MD 21613. Phone: 301/228-5530 or 1899. Open afternoons, Saturday and Sunday. Groups by appointment. Admission by donation.

Interpretive exhibits here feature prehistoric Indian artifacts.

HISTORIC ST. MARY'S CITY

From Washington, DC drive 60 miles south on Maryland Route 5. Mail address: Box 39, St. Mary's City, MD 20686. Phone: 301/862-0990. Open Wednesday–Sunday, except certain holidays. Admission charged.

In addition to historic exhibits some prehistoric Woodlands material is displayed.

JEFFERSON PATTERSON PARK AND MUSEUM

From the Washington, DC Beltway drive south on Maryland 4 to 3 miles south of Prince Frederick, turn right onto Route 264. Go about 2 miles, turn left onto Route 265, go 6 miles to the Park entrance. Mail address: SR 2, Box 50A, St. Leonard, MD 20685. Phone: 301/586-0050 or 0055. Open Wednesday–Sunday, April 15–October 15.

In the Visitor Center, which concentrates on historic archeology, is a permanent exhibit, "12,000 Years of the Chesapeake: An Archaeological Story." It tells how archeologists have interpreted the evolution of human societies in the Chesapeake Bay region, using artifacts from on-site excavations. The Park and Museum are listed on the National Register of Historic Places.

Ross McCurdy (left) and Dr. Maurice Robbins (right) of the Massachusetts Archaeological Society.
Massachusetts Archaeological Society photo.

Massachusetts

CAPE COD NATIONAL SEASHORE

Follow US 6 on Cape Cod to Eastham, where the Salt Pond Visitor Center is located. Mail address: South Wellfleet, MA 02663. Phone: 508/349-3785. Visitor Center open free, daily. Closed December 25.

The Native Americans first encountered by the Pilgrims were Wampanoags. These people may have lived on Cape Cod for 8000 years or more before a boatload of the *Mayflower's* passengers disembarked and helped themselves to corn which the Indians had stored underground in a large basket. The Wampanoags hunted and fished as well as farmed. Their arrowheads, fishline sinkers, and other implements are still to be found at sites on Cape Cod, even after more than 300 years of European occupation. A large display in the museum shows how some of the implements were used.

From the Visitor Center it is a short drive to Indian Rock, at Skiff Hill. The rock, a 20-ton glacial granite boulder, has deep grooves where Indians sharpened bone harpoon heads, fishhooks, and stone axes. Originally the giant whetstone stood a hundred feet down the hill at the edge of Nauset Marsh. It was moved when it seemed in danger of being lost in the marsh. Indian Rock is only one of several such sharpening stones in the neighborhood.

Along the beaches and ponds of the National Seashore there are heaps of discarded shells, where prehistoric people camped and ate seafood. These have not been excavated. Visitors are earnestly requested not to disturb them.

CHILDREN'S MUSEUM, INC.

Russells Mills Rd., Dartmouth, MA. Open free, Tuesday–Friday; afternoons, Saturday and Sunday. Closed certain holidays and from late December to early February.

In addition to historic Indian materials from the Plains and the Southwest, this museum has a few prehistoric Wampanoag Indian artifacts from the immediate vicinity.

COHASSET HISTORICAL SOCIETY, MARITIME MUSEUM

Elm St., Cohasset, MA 02025. Open free, afternoons, Tuesday–Sunday, mid-June–September.

This museum devoted to local history includes a case of Indian artifacts found in the area. These are primarily Algonquian and include early stone tools.

DIGHTON ROCK STATE PARK (DIE-ton)

Go north from Fall River on Massachusetts 24, take Main St. exit at Assonet, and follow directional signs to the park. Mail address: Department of Environmental Management, 100 Cambridge St., Boston, MA 02202. Phone: 617/727-3160. Open free, daily, during daylight hours.

Tools made of flint were used by Paleo-Indians for preparing animal hides. These scrapers, 9000 years old, came from the Wapanucket Site at Assawompsett Lake in Massachusetts. Massachusetts Archaeological Society photo.

Dighton Rock is a 40-ton boulder on which inscriptions have been carved. Ever since the seventeenth century, the rock has inspired study and controversy. Among the theories advanced to explain the inscriptions is the assumption made by Cotton Mather and others that the carvings were made by Native Americans. Another theory, suggested in the book *Dighton Rock* by E. B. Delabarre, of Brown University, is that a Portuguese explorer, Miguel Corereal, visited the spot in A.D. 1511.

These, along with two other theories, are presented on panels in the Dighton Rock Museum, at the site. In 1963 the rock was raised out of the Taunton River and is now housed within the same museum.

Special Interest. At one time certain markings on the rock were supposed to have been made by Vikings. This prompted the nineteenth-century violinist Ole Bull to buy it for the Royal Society of Copenhagen. When scholars disproved the idea of Norse origin, the society gave the rock to the Old Colony Historical Society, of Taunton, which then presented it to the Commonwealth of Massachusetts.

FRUITLANDS MUSEUMS

Prospect Hill Road, Harvard, MA 01451. Phone: 508/456-3924. Open Tuesday–Sunday, mid-May–mid-October, and holiday Mondays. Admission charged.

The American Indian Museum in this complex contains dioramas and a selection of prehistoric implements, arts, and industries, including stone tools collected by Henry David Thoreau.

MEMORIAL HALL MUSEUM

Deerfield, MA 01342. Phone: 413-774-7476. Open May 1–October 31, Monday–Friday; afternoons, Saturday and Sunday. Admission charged.

In this building Native American artifacts have been on exhibit since 1799. An Indian Room has a display "Introducing a Native American Perspective" that includes prehistoric atlatl weights, bifacial blades, steatite vessels from the ancestral homeland of the Pocumtuck people and other Indians of the Northeast, including the historic Iroquois, Abnaki, and Micmac.

PEABODY MUSEUM OF ARCHAEOLOGY AND ETHNOLOGY, HARVARD UNIVERSITY

11 Divinity Ave., Cambridge MA 02138. Phone: 617/495-2248. Open Monday–Saturday; afternoon, Sunday. Admission charged except Monday when admission is free.

This large museum with a great deal of material from Central and South America has about half a million archeological objects from North America. North American Indian Hall was opened in 1990. In addition, there is a gallery with materials from the Southwest.

PLIMOTH PLANTATION, INC.

Warren Avenue, Plymouth. Mail address: Box 1620, Plymouth, MA 02360. Phone: 508/746-1622. Open daily, April–November. Admission charged.

To show how Native Americans lived at the time of the arrival of Europeans, this museum has an outdoor exhibit based on the customs of an extended Wampanoag family, its longhouse and planted fields.

ROBBINS MUSEUM OF ARCHAEOLOGY

17 Jackson St., Middleborough. Mail address: P.O. Box 700, Middleborough, MA 02346-0700. Phone: 508/947-9005.

This was formerly the Bronson Museum in Attleboro. As this book went to press this new museum was open on Wednesday and Saturday with a few exhibits. By the mid-1990s it is scheduled to be fully open and its theme will be: "People and the Land: 10,000 Years in New England."

ROBERT S. PEABODY MUSEUM OF ARCHAEOLOGY, PHILLIPS ACADEMY

Main St., Andover, MA 01810. Phone: 508/749-4490. Open free, Tuesday–Friday; morning, Saturday. Closed certain holidays.

Materials drawn from the extensive collections of the museum are arranged in displays that illustrate the daily lives of people of various cultures, the techniques of archeologists who dig up and study prehistoric cultures, and the theories that finally emerge.

Exhibits from sites that cannot be visited include the Boylston Street Fish Weir in Boston, Bull Brook Site, Massachusetts, which yielded much important information about Paleo people in New England, and Labrador Eskimo sites.

Material on the Boreal Archaic people shows how they differed from southern Archaic people because of their heavy reliance on hunting and fishing rather than on plant foods, while at the same time they used many of the same tools.

Exhibits showing cultural influences on New England indicate the spread of burial-cult ideas from the Adena in Ohio, of copper artifacts from the Great Lakes, and of agriculture from areas to the south.

A diorama of Pecos Pueblo is based on information gathered during excavations conducted by the museum. Among other major sites in other areas represented is the important site at Tehuacan, Mexico.

New Brunswick

ARCHAEOLOGICAL SERVICES NEW BRUNSWICK

Old Soldiers Barracks, Queen Street, Fredericton, New Brunswick E3B 5C3. Phone: 506/453-2792. Open daily.

Although this is only a storage, research and management center, the personnel at this government agency are pleased to arrange a tour of the facility when called upon to do so.

NEWS BRUNSWICK MUSEUM

277 Douglas Ave., St. John, New Brunswick, E2K 1E5. Phone: 506/658-1842. Open daily, May 1–August 31; Tuesday–Sunday, September 1–April 30. Closed certain holidays. Admission charged.

Exhibits in this museum are changed frequently, but there are always some archeological materials on display.

A Wampanoag one-family summer house, shown under construction at Plimoth Plantation. Fish are drying on the rack in the foreground. Plimoth Plantation photo.

An Icelandic map, made nearly 600 years after the Vikings are said to have visited America, shows a peninsula called Promontorium Winlandiae. This tongue of land some archeologists interpret as the tip of Newfoundland Island, the traditional Vinland where old sagas say the Vikings lived. L'Anse aux Meadows is at the northern end of Newfoundland. The map shown here is redrawn from a 1670 copy.

Newfoundland

L'ANSE AUX MEADOWS NATIONAL HISTORIC PARK (LANSS-oh-meadows) A World Heritage Site

The park is 400 kilometers north of Corner Brook. Take highway 430 north to Highway 436, near St. Anthony. Follow highway 436 to the park on the northern tip of the Great Northern Peninsula. Open free, daily, in summer.

In 1960 the Norwegian explorer Helge Ingstad found a group of mounds here. Ingstad theorized that this might be the site of an ancient Viking settlement—perhaps even Leif Ericksson's Vinland. Beginning the next year, he and his archeologist wife, Anne, together with archeologists from other countries, spent seven summers excavating the mounds. One appeared to be ruins of a turf house nearly 80 feet long, with slightly curving walls resembling those of Norse buildings. In it they found a stone lamp and other things of the kind used by Norsemen.

Besides other houses, they excavated what appeared to be a sauna and the remains of a blacksmith shop, where iron from a nearby bog had been smelted and made into tools.

The Ingstads reported that carbon-14 tests of charcoal revealed a date of about A.D. 1000 for the site—which would make it contemporary with Leif Ericksson.

Two Canadian archeologists, Thomas E. Lee and Robert E. Lee interpreted the carbon-14 dates as evidence that the site was originally inhabited, long before the Norse period by aboriginal people and, in post-Viking times, occasionally visited by whalers from Europe.

Later excavation in the park did, indeed, reveal that during 6,000 years a series of different indigenous peoples used this site and left tools in their campgrounds. The latest of these were Dorset people who were here at about A.D. 800.

Among the new areas excavated was a peat bog in which were found pieces of wood worked with metal tools. These, the archeologists believed, indicated the presence of Norse carpenters. Metal rivets of the kind used in Norse shipbuilding also turned up.

Whether or not L'Anse aux Meadows was Leif Ericksson's settlement, it is an interesting site developed for visitors by the Canadian government.

The Name. Contrary to popular belief, L'Anse aux Meadows does not mean "Bay of Meadows." Instead, *Meadows* is a corruption of the French word *méduses,* meaning "jellyfish." Many of the first settlers in the area were French; hence the name.

MARY MARCH REGIONAL MUSEUM

In the Provincial Building, Grand Falls-Windsor, A2A 1W9. Phone: 709/489-9331. Open free, daily.

Exhibits here emphasize Newfoundland prehistory, with artifacts from Paleo to modern times. There is Dorset, pre-Dorset and Beothuk material in the displays.

NEWFOUNDLAND MUSEUM

285 Duckworth St., St. John's. Phone: 709/576-2460. Open free, Monday–Friday; afternoons, Saturday and Sunday.

Collections of artifacts made by the Beothuk (bee-AWTH-uk) Indians, whose last survivor died in 1829, are being augmented by archeological materials which this museum is excavating in cooperation with the Canadian Museum of Civilization. Also on exhibit are Nascapi Indian artifacts from Labrador, a selection of Dorset and Thule Eskimo artifacts, and a large display of the cultural effects of the Maritime Archaic peoples who lived along the shores of Newfoundland and Labrador.

The Beothuk, primarily coastal people, moved inland for a month or so in autumn. There they hunted caribou, by building a fence, or barrier, of fallen trees, that extended along the Exploits River for 40 miles. In spring and fall the hunters waited at gaps which had been purposely created in this fence for the migrating caribou herds to pass through. As the animals crowded into the narrow openings, hunters found it easy to kill as many as they wanted. The meat was smoked and cached for use later.

PORT AU CHOIX
NATIONAL HISTORIC SITE
(PORT-oh-shwah)

In Port au Choix on the Great Northern Peninsula. At Deer Lake, take highway 430 north to the Port Saunders–Port au Choix turnoff. The Visitor Centre is 15 kilometers from this intersection. Open free, daily, in summer; at other seasons on request.

In 1967 excavation of the basement for a new theater in this small fishing village turned up so many bones and artifacts that building operations were stopped and archeologists continued the digging. This, they found, was one of several spots along the shore where graves had been dug in beach sand. The crushed seashell in the sand had helped to preserve the remains of people who lived and died here from about 1900 B.C. to 1280 B.C.

Somewhat as did the Red Paint people, who lived farther south in New England, these Archaic hunters and fishermen deposited a pigment called red ocher in graves. They also left gifts for the dead. Their choice of gifts, however, was sometimes unusual. Instead of placing a woman's tools with her body, supposedly for use in an afterlife, and a man's tools with his body, they occasionally did just the opposite. They put men's axes and hunting charms and amulets in women's graves. And some needles for sewing were recovered from men's graves. Some of the burials of children were accompanied by lavish gifts of all kinds. Apparently an article's supposed usefulness in afterlife was not the only criterion for grave goods. These people also gave things they treasured when they buried those they loved.

Among the artifacts recovered at the site were beautifully carved stone effigies of whales, small images of birds, and other hunting charms; a wealth of harpoons, points, and daggers made from bone and ivory; and animal teeth, especially beaver incisors, which seem to have been made into woodworking tools.

To judge from the type of material found in the graves, these people may have lived inland in the winter, existing mainly on caribou meat. In summer they lived here on the coast, where they fished and caught marine mammals. The fact that they were able to venture out to sea in boats of some sort is obvious, for Newfoundland is an island, and at its nearest point the mainland is ten miles away.

The culture of these seacoast dwellers resembled that of other Archaic people, and they may have come originally from the New England region. However, they also had distinctive traits of their own. For that reason some archeologists are inclined to put them in a special category, called Maritime Archaic.

Many of the Maritime Archaic artifacts resembled those of Dorset people who lived in the area at a later time. However, there is no evidence that the Dorsets borrowed these implements from their predecessors. Apparently the two peoples, living in the same environment, developed the same kinds of tool for dealing with it.

The Museum. Most of the exhibits here deal with the archeology of the Port au Choix area, which is now a National Historic Site, maintained by the Canadian Department of Northern Affairs.

The First—and Future—Museums of the American Indian

When the American colonists were breaking away from England, many of the rebellious colonials formed themselves into societies that followed Indian models. Some of these societies took the name of a Lenni Lenape chief who had taught early white settlers how to manage life in the unfamiliar American environment. The chief's name was Tammany, and the Tammany Society in New York City established the first museum for Indian artifacts, many of which were no doubt identical to artifacts that had been made before the arrival of people from Europe. The museum was at Tammany headquarters in Manhattan from 1790 to 1798.

Also in Manhattan, for much of the Twentieth Century, was the world's largest museum devoted to the American Indian. Started by George Heye, who had inherited a huge fortune, its exhibits from North and South America filled a big building, and an immense overflow of artifacts was stored in a warehouse in the Bronx.

Heye often visited Indian reservations in a chauffeur-driven limousine, and there he sometimes bought everything in sight. Only a small portion of the 400,000 objects in his collection could be exhibited at one time in what was known as the Museum of the American Indian, Heye Foundation, and has now become part of the Smithsonian Institution. In 1993 it is scheduled to open in new quarters in the Custom House at the Battery in Manhattan. There its title will be the George Gustav Heye Center of the National Museum of the American Indian, Smithsonian Institution.

New Hampshire

LACONIA PUBLIC LIBRARY

695 Main Street, Laconia, NH 03246. Phone: 603/524-4775. Open free, by appointment.

On the third floor of the library are displayed prehistoric artifacts from Lake Winnipesaukee and the Laconia area.

LIBBY MUSEUM

From Wolfeboro drive 4 miles north on New Hampshire 109. P.O. Box 629, Wolfeboro, NH 03894. Phone: 603/569-1035. Open Tuesday–Sunday, June 1–September 27. Admission by donation.

In addition to Abnaki artifacts, this museum has on display a map of Indian trails and campsites in the area.

MANCHESTER HISTORIC ASSOCIATION

129 Amherst St., Manchester, NH 03101. Phone: 603/622-7531. Open free, Tuesday–Friday; afternoon, Saturday. Closed state and national holidays and Tuesdays following Monday holidays.

In addition to random local finds, this museum displays materials from controlled excavations near the Amoskeag Falls at Manchester. The falls apparently provided a good fishing spot and attracted prehistoric Indians from as far away as Maine and New York. Visits to the region obviously began a very long time ago, for a Clovis point was found in the excavation at the falls. Projectile points of this type found elsewhere were associated with hunters of big game which had long been extinct. Later materials, which resembled artifacts made by the Iroquois, were also recovered at the site.

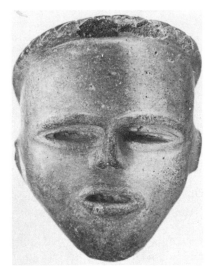

This ceramic likeness of a human face appears to have been part of a smoking pipe. It was found in 1975 in New Jersey at the Minisink Site on the Benna Kill, which flows into the Delaware River. Seton Hall University Archaeological Research Center photo by Herbert Kraft.

PHILLIPS EXETER ACADEMY, PHILLIPS MUSEUM OF ANTHROPOLOGY

On the Campus, Exeter, NH 03833. Open free, mornings, Monday–Friday, during school year; by appointment in summer. Phone: 603/772-4311, ext. 253.

The Dr. P. Phillips Museum of Anthropology houses an extensive North American basket collection and a large mask collection, as well as limited ceramics collections from the American Southwest and several collections of North American prehistoric artifacts. The museum acts as a repository for the New Hampshire Archeological Society.

UNIVERSITY OF NEW HAMPSHIRE, ANTHROPOLOGY LABORATORY

Parsons Hall, College Rd., Durham, NH 03824. Phone: 603/862-1547. Open free, by appointment.

Archaeological Research Services of the Department of Sociology and Anthropology maintains an active program of field research in central New England. Visitors may arrange a guided tour of the laboratory facility on campus and view various stages of artifact processing and analysis, as well as small, changing exhibits of cultural materials from sites in the Lakes Region and Coastal Zone of New Hampshire.

WOODMAN INSTITUTE

182–192 Central Ave., Dover, NH 03820. Phone: 603/742-1038. Open free, Tuesday–Saturday. Closed certain holidays.

Artifacts of the Red Paint people of Maine and other prehistoric New England materials are on display here in the Annie E. Woodman Institute.

Chalk lines have been added to make clearly visible the pecked figures in this petroglyph, which is the first to be found in New Jersey. It is on display in the Seton Hall University Museum. Seton Hall University Archaeological Research Center photo by Herbert Kraft.

New Jersey

THE MORRIS MUSEUM

6 Normandy Heights Road, Morristown, NJ 07960. Phone: 201/538-0454. Open Monday–Saturday; afternoon, Sunday. Closed certain holidays. Admission charged.

This general museum has on exhibit Native American material from the Plains area, the Southwest, and the Northwest Coast, as well as a gallery on Woodland Indians. One display shows a Lenape village as it might have looked before Europeans arrived. There is also material from earlier periods.

NEWARK MUSEUM

49 Washington St., Newark, NJ 07102. Phone: 201/596-6550. Open free, afternoons, Wednesday–Sunday. Closed certain holidays.

Included in this general museum is a gallery devoted to Native American material, some of it from the prehistoric period. Of special interest is a diorama showing a central New Jersey Indian village, the work of Dwight Franklin, who pioneered in developing this form of museum exhibit.

NEW JERSEY STATE MUSEUM

205 West State St., Trenton, NJ 08625. Phone: 609/292-6464. Open free, Tuesday–Saturday. Closed certain holidays.

In the permanent exhibit here are displays that illustrate and interpret Native American life. There is material from the Paleo, Archaic, and Woodland periods, with an emphasis on the Lenni Lenape Indians of New Jersey. Also included in some of the displays is material excavated at the Abbott Farm Site near Trenton (see Watson House below).

A video show and an interactive program, changed from time to time, are devoted to the Indians of eastern North America. For young people, preschool to college age, there are classes that offer an interpretation of prehistoric New Jersey life.

SETON HALL UNIVERSITY, ARCHAEOLOGICAL RESEARCH CENTER AND MUSEUM

Fahy Hall, South Orange Avenue, South Orange, NJ 07079. Phone: 201/761-9543. Open free, Monday–Saturday when university is in session.

The museum has a comprehensive exhibit on the pre-history and the early Indian/European contact period of New Jersey, ca. 10,000 B.C.–A.D. 1750, together with selected ethnographic material made by later Lenape or Delaware Indians. The exhibit includes two petroglyphs found in New Jersey. Many of the exhibited artifacts were obtained from excavations in the Delaware River Valley.

Other permanent displays include archeological and ethnographic material from the Northeast, Great Plains, Southwest, West Coast, British Columbia, and Alaska.

Albany to Buffalo

The Mohawk Trail, another name for US 20 and New York 5, provides an easy, gently graded route from Albany to Buffalo. As the name implies, it follows a prehistoric Indian trail that once linked the villages of all the tribes belonging to what white men called the Iroquois Confederacy.

Many other modern travel routes in the United States follow old Indian trails. A usual sequence was this: First, animals made paths to and from watering places or feeding grounds or salt licks. Indian hunters followed the animals, widening the trails, some of which later proved useful as means of communication between Indian settlements. Pioneers of European origin then used the Indian paths—on foot at first, later on horseback. Next wagons went along the same trails. Still later, when railroads were built, civil engineers often found that the best routes had been followed by the drivers of the horse-drawn wagons. Finally, when automobile roads were needed, highways often took the same easy grades that the Indians discovered long ago.

SPACE FARMS ZOOLOGICAL PARK AND MUSEUM

Midway between Sussex and Branchville on County 519. Mail address: 218 Route 519, Sussex, NJ 07461. Phone: 201/875-5800 or 3223. Museum open daily. Closed December 25. Admission charged.

The museum includes materials collected by the owner, Ralph Space, during 60 years of amateur archeological activity in New Jersey and New York.

THUNDERBIRD MUSEUM

Mt. Laurel Road, east of Moorestown. Open afternoons, Saturday and Sunday; at other times by appointment. Admission charged.

A wide variety of prehistoric artifacts from New Jersey and also from other areas is on display in this privately owned museum.

WATSON HOUSE
(Abbott Farm Site)

151 Westcott Ave., Trenton, NJ 08610. Open free, by appointment. Write, or phone: 609/888-2062.

This house, which was built in 1708, now serves as a headquarters and museum for the Daughters of the American Revolution. Its grounds overlap an extensive archeological area known as the Abbott Farm Site. Prehistoric artifacts on display in the museum were recovered in 1966 by the Unami Chapter of the Archeological Society of New Jersey, from the area immediately surrounding the house.

Excavation at the site has gone on at intervals for the last 100 years and has attracted wide attention. Much of the early material recovered is in the Peabody Museum, at Harvard.

In 1872 a physician, Dr. Charles Conrad Abbott, owner of a farm which included part of the site, published a book, *The Stone Age in New Jersey,* about the artifacts he was finding in the area. Thereafter he gave up the practice of medicine and devoted the rest of his life to archeology. Dr. Abbott put forth several theories to explain the material, some of which seemed spectacularly old. More recent researches have not supported his ideas.

In 1936, with funds provided by the Works Progress Administration, Dr. Dorothy Cross began extensive excavation of the site, which extends for 3.5 miles along a bluff above the Delaware River. She recovered materials that showed that somewhere between 8000 B.C. and 3000 B.C. Indians walked along the bluff and dropped projectile points in one small area. At about A.D. 100, Woodland people carved steatite (soapstone) bowls at the site and adorned themselves with steatite beads and gorgets and pendants. Somewhat later the knowledge of clay pottery making came to them from other Indians, who lived to the south. Soon after A.D. 350, they began to garden. Their pottery became more varied in form and style.

Although they were far from the centers of the most active Indian life, in the Ohio and Mississippi valleys, the people at Abbott Farm were not entirely isolated. They traveled and traded, and travelers came to them.

One visitor from central New York State brought with him a variety of personal belongings that showed he was a man of importance. While he was there, he died and was buried with his exotic finery.

THE VILLAGE OF WATERLOO
National Historic Site

In New Jersey, drive west on US 80 to Exit 25, then 2.5 miles south to entrance. Mail address: Stanhope, NJ 07874. Phone: 201/347-0900. Open Tuesday–Sunday. Closed certain holidays. Admission charged. Camping nearby.

The Indian Museum here has exhibits that trace the history of New Jersey's prehistoric peoples from Paleo times through European contact. Display panels are divided into major chronological periods, each showing a variety of archeological materials from excavated sites in the state. There are also panels on the spiritual and religious beliefs of the Lenape people and a small replica of the last historic Big House from Dewey, Oklahoma.

In another part of Waterloo Village is a reconstructed Lenape settlement (see Winakung below).

WINAKUNG

In the Village of Waterloo (see entry above).

Here on an island is a Lenape (Delaware) village reconstructed as of A.D. 1625. Included are a completely furnished bark longhouse, dugout canoes, a fish weir, a sweat lodge, and even carvings of "little people"—spirit pranksters who caused the unwary to trip on roots or have other minor mishaps. Also there are hunting trails equipped with snares for catching game. The longhouses are based on information obtained in excavations in the upper Delaware Valley, and there is a simulated archeological site.

Inside a Lenape dwelling recreated on an island called Winakung ("place of sassafras") in Historic Waterloo Village, New Jersey. Waterloo Foundation for the Arts, Inc., photo.

In the sixteenth century the English artist John White painted this scene showing how Indians had made dugout canoes for centuries, using fire and stone tools. From the engraving of White's watercolor by Theodore De Bry published in Frankfurt, Germany, 1590.

New York

AMERICAN MUSEUM OF NATURAL HISTORY

Central Park West at 79th St., New York, NY 10024. Phone: 212/769-5100. Open daily. Admission by donation.

On display in the Hall of Eastern Woodland Indians are fluted stone spearpoints made by Paleo-Indians and other hunting tools, such as the atlatl (spearthrower), developed by the Archaic Indians. Richly carved ornaments and pottery are among the examples of artifacts from the Burial Mound people and the Temple Mound Builders.

The pre-contact artifacts in the Hall of Plains Indians were used mostly for buffalo hunting. Examples include dart points, skin scrapers, awls, knife blades, and arrow and spearshaft straighteners.

The Hall of Northwest Coast Indians presents extraordinary totem poles, grave posts, house poles and masks.

One exhibit shows how the Kwakiutl Indians felled trees and split huge planks from them for house building before the introduction of metal tools by Europeans.

The 64-foot Haida canoe on display in the museum's 77th Street lobby is the largest Northwest canoe in any museum.

BEAR MOUNTAIN TRAILSIDE HISTORICAL MUSEUM

In Bear Mountain State Park, 45 miles north of New York City, off Palisades Parkway. Parking at the main Bear Mountain parking lot. Daily Red and Tan Bus Line service from New York City. Open free, daily. A charge for parking.

Native American artifacts, mainly from Orange, Rockland, and Ulster counties, are used in exhibits that show prehistoric shelter, food, weapons, and art in New York State. The Paleo, Archaic, and Woodland periods, from about 7000 B.C. to the seventeenth century, are represented.

BROOKLYN MUSEUM

200 Eastern Pkwy., Brooklyn, NY 11238. Phone: 718/638-5000. Open Wednesday–Sunday. Closed certain holidays. Admission charged.

In this large general museum are many exhibits of North American archeological materials, including stone images from the Mimbres culture.

BUFFALO MUSEUM OF SCIENCE

1020 Humboldt Parkway, Buffalo, NY 14211-1293. Phone: 716/896-5200. Open Tuesday–Sunday. Admission charged.

This natural science museum includes extensive collections of prehistoric material from western New York, northwestern Pennsylvania, southeast Ontario, Florida, and Tennessee.

CASTILE HISTORICAL HOUSE
(kass-TILE)

17 East Park Rd., Castile, NY 14427. Phone: 716/493-5370 or 2894. Open free, afternoons, Tuesday–Sunday. Others times by appointment.

Although most of the material in this museum is from the historic period, some of it throws light on Seneca Indian prehistory. Three miles away, in Letchworth State Park, is a Seneca council house dating from the time of the American Revolution.

CAYUGA MUSEUM
(kay-YOO-gah)

203 Genesee St., Auburn, NY 13021. Phone: 315/253-8051. Open free, afternoons, Tuesday–Sunday.

Materials from the Point Peninsula to the Owasco culture (A.D. 100 to 1500) and from the later Iroquoian culture are displayed here.

CHAUTAUQUA COUNTY HISTORICAL SOCIETY
(shuh-TAW-quah)

Main and Portage streets, Westfield. Mail address: P.O. Box 7, Westfield, NY 14787. Open Monday, Tuesday, and Thursday; afternoon, Saturday. Admission charged.

Displays include prehistoric and historic Algonquian and Iroquoian baskets, lithics, and reconstructed Iroquoian pottery.

CHEMUNG COUNTY HISTORICAL SOCIETY, INC.
(shuh-MUNG)

Historical Center, 415 East Water St., Elmira, NY 14901. Phone: 607/734-4167. Open free, afternoons, Tuesday–Saturday. Closed certain holidays.

Material from the society's extensive archeological collections are displayed in exhibits on Paleo-Indian occupation of the Northeast, Archaic period cultures, including the Lamoka Lake Site, and Woodland peoples. Contact period and contemporary Iroquois cultures are also featured.

CHENANGO MUSEUM

45 Rexford St., Norwich, NY 13815. Phone: 607/334-9227 or 9184. Open by appointment.

This museum has projectile points from Paleo-Indian, Archaic, Transitional, and Woodland periods in the Chenango and Oneida area.

FORT STANWIX MUSEUM

207 North James St., Rome, NY 13440. Open Monday–Saturday; afternoon, Sunday. Closed certain holidays. Admission charged.

With paintings, dioramas, and displays of random local finds of artifacts, this museum sketches the life of prehistoric Indians in the area from Paleo times, about 7000 years ago, to the Iroquois occupation of the historic period.

Special Interest. The museum, operated by the Rome Historical Society, is located adjacent to Fort Stanwix National Monument, the site of a fort built in colonial times. The area was important in the Indian period because it was what Indians called the "Great Carry"—the land route over which they portaged canoes between two water routes, one going south and east to the Hudson and Atlantic, the other going northwest to the Great Lakes.

This fragment of a pot rim shows how Iroquois women decorated their pottery by pressing designs in the wet clay before firing. Université du Québec à Trois-Rivières photo.

FORT WILLIAM HENRY RESTORATION AND MUSEUM

Canada St., Lake George, NY 12845. Open daily, May–October; evenings, daily, July, August. Admission charged.

Included with historic exhibits are displays of archeological material relating to the aboriginal occupation of northern New York and the Lake George–Lake Champlain area in particular. A diorama shows how small animals were caught in a deadfall trap.

The Indian village surrounded by a wooden stockade is a reconstruction of an eighteenth-century Iroquois settlement, which closely resembled villages of late prehistoric times.

GARVIES POINT MUSEUM

Barry Drive, Glen Cove, NY 11542. Phone: 516/671-0300. Open daily, all year. Closed holidays, November–March. Admission charged.

Some of the exhibits here are devoted to the archeology of the area, with displays of prehistoric artifacts. Dioramas illustrate the daily life of Native Americans.

HARTWICK COLLEGE, YAGER MUSEUM

On the campus, Oneonta, NY 13820. Phone: 607/431-4480. Open free, Monday–Saturday; afternoon, Sunday.

The Yager Museum has a comprehensive collection of prehistorc and contact period archeological materials from the Upper Susquehanna valley. It also has both ethnographic and archeological collections from the Southwest.

HOWE PUBLIC LIBRARY

155 N. Main St., Wellsville, NY 14895. Open free, Monday, Tuesday, Thursday, Friday, Saturday, winter; Monday–Friday, summer. Closed certain holidays.

Here is a small display of identified local artifacts from the Paleo period to the historic Iroquois.

IROQUOIS INDIAN MUSEUM

From Interstate 88 at the Cobbleskill-Middleburgh exit take Route 7 east 1 mile to Caverns Road. Drive 1 mile right on Caverns Road. Mail address: P.O. Box 158, Schoharie, NY 12157. Phone: 518/295-8553 or 234-2276. Open Tuesday–Sunday. Closed certain holidays. Admission charged.

This museum, devoted to the history and culture of the Iroquois in New York and Canada, displays prehistoric material, including some from the Owasco culture.

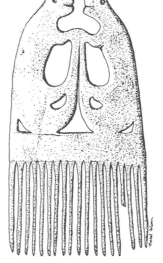

The custom of making bear effigies on combs fashioned from antler or bone was popular among the Iroquois and their predecessors in New York State. On the right is a Seneca antler comb of about A.D. 1550–1575 from a site in Livingston County. Rochester Museum & Science Center photo by James Osen. On the left is a prehistoric bone comb. Original in the National Museum of the American Indian, Smithsonian Institution.

MOHAWK-CAUGHNAWAGA MUSEUM
(cog-nah-WAH-gah)

In Fonda on New York 5. Mail address: Box 627, Fonda, NY 12068. Phone: 518/853-3646. Open daily, May 15–October 15. Admission charged.

In addition to an outdoor exhibit area, Iroquois artifacts are on display inside the museum, which is on the site of an excavated Iroquois settlement.

NATIONAL MUSEUM OF THE AMERICAN INDIAN, SMITHSONIAN INSTITUTION

In New York City at Broadway and 155th St. By bus numbers M4 or M5. By subway, IRT local uptown (No. 1) to 157th St. Mail address: 3753 Broadway, New York, NY 10032-1596. Phone: 212/283-2420. Open Tuesday–Saturday; afternoon, Sunday. Closed major holidays. Admission charged.

This museum, now a part of the Smithsonian Institution, is one of two sections of the National Museum of the American Indian. The other section is scheduled to open in Washington, D.C. in 1998. As this book went to press, the New York section was scheduled to move in 1994 to the Old Custom House at the Battery at the southern end of Manhattan.

No museum has richer archeological resources than this one, but because it is moving to new quarters, no attempt will be made here to describe the exhibits.

NATIONAL SHRINE OF KATERI TEKAKWITHA

One-quarter mile west of Fonda, off New York Thruway at exit 28, on Route 5. Mail address: Box 627, Fonda, NY 12068. Phone: 518/853-3646.

The Native American exhibit here includes archeological material, but the Shrine does not consider itself a museum.

NEW YORK STATE MUSEUM

Empire State Plaza, Albany, NY 12230. Phone: 518/474-5877. Open free, daily. Closed certain holidays. Donations suggested.

Life-sized dioramas combine artifacts and scientific specimens to tell the story of people in the Northeast from Paleo times to the contact period. Films, lectures, and learning programs are offered for adults and children.

A prehistoric village once stood at Nichols Pond, between Canastota and Morrisville, N.Y. It may have been this village that Samuel de Champlain attacked in A.D. 1615, as shown in this picture, reprinted from his *Voyages*. Smithsonian Institution National Anthropological Archives.

NIAGARA COUNTY HISTORICAL CENTER

Pioneer Building, 215 Niagara St., Lockport, NY 14094. Open afternoons, Thursday–Sunday. Donations accepted. Closed certain holidays.

Artifacts from local prehistoric Native American sites are on exhibit here, together with a diorama showing an Iroquois Indian village.

NICHOLS POND

From Morrisville on US 20 drive north on county road toward Canastota to directional sign, then west to the Champlain-Oneida Battleground and Nichols Pond. Open free, at all times, weather permitting. Camping.

An Oneida, or Mohawk, Indian village stood at this place in late prehistoric times, and there is some reason to think that it was attacked by·the French explorer Samuel de Champlain in A.D. 1615. Champlain was accompanied by about 500 Huron and Algonquian Indians from Canada, in addition to a dozen men of his own,

who were armed with arquebuses. Since the village seemed very well protected by a high palisade, Champlain tried a special stratagem. He ordered a tower built close to the palisade. Standing on the tower, his gunners could fire down into the village. More than this was needed, however, to overcome the inhabitants. They withstood the seige, and the French adventurer was forced to return to Canada. The illustration of the palisaded village which appears in Champlain's *Voyages* is probably a fairly accurate picture of the village which once stood here and which dates from prehistoric times.

ONTARIO COUNTY HISTORICAL SOCIETY

55 Main St., Canandaigua (can-an-DAY-gwah), NY 14424. Phone: 716/394-4975. Open free, Tuesday–Saturday. Closed certain holidays.

Permanent and temporary exhibits include artifacts from local Seneca Indian village sites.

OSSINING HISTORICAL SOCIETY MUSEUM

196 Croton Ave., Ossining, NY 10562. Open free, afternoon, Monday, September–June, or by appointment.

This museum has locally collected artifacts, some of which have been dated to 5000 B.C., and some of which were made in contact times by the Sint Sinck tribe of the Wappinger Confederacy.

OWASCO MUSEUM

In Emerson Park, 3 miles south of Route 20, near Auburn. Mail address: Cayuga Museum, 203 Genesee St., Auburn, NY 13021. Phone: 315/253-8051. Open free, daily, Memorial Day–Labor Day.

Exhibits here tell the story of Native American culture in the region from Paleo times to 1760. Nearby, roughly on the site of a prehistoric settlement, an ongoing project is the construction of an authentic Owasco village. Visitors are encouraged to participate in the project.

This diorama in the Rochester Museum & Science Center shows an Iroquois village scene about A.D. 1600. Rochester Museum & Science Center photo by William G. Frank.

Arthur C. Parker, Seneca Indian, directed the Rochester Museum for many years. Rochester Museum & Science Center photo.

OYSTERPONDS HISTORICAL SOCIETY, INC.

Village Lane, Orient, L.I., NY 11957. Open, afternoons, Tuesday, Thursday, Saturday, Sunday, and holidays. Admission charged.

Local Indian artifacts on display here include a Clovis point, stone pots and tools dated at about 4000 B.C., and some material dating from 1000 B.C. to A.D. 1600.

POWELL HOUSE

434 Park Ave., Huntington, L.I., NY 11743. Office open, Monday–Friday; tours Sunday afternoon or by appointment. Admission charged.

On exhibit here are materials recovered from excavations in the vicinity. The museum, which stands at the intersection of old Indian trails, is operated by the Huntington Historical Society.

ROBERSON MUSEUM AND SCIENCE CENTER

30 Front Street, Binghamton, NY 13905. Phone: 607/772-0660. Open Tuesday–Saturday; afternoon, Sunday. Admission charged.

The archeological collection includes local and regional artifacts from the Paleo-Indian to the historic period.

ROCHESTER MUSEUM & SCIENCE CENTER

657 East Avenue, Rochester, NY 14603. Phone: 716/271-4320. Accessible from the New York State Thruway via the Interstate 490 Expressway, Monroe Avenue, Culver Road, and Goodman Street exits. Open Monday–Saturday; afternoon, Sunday. Closed December 25. Admission charged.

Numerous displays cover all New York State Indian cultures from the Archaic to the historic period, including Adena, Hopewell, Point Peninsula, Owasco, and prehistoric Iroquois.

Exhibits are arranged to show how people adapted to their environment and how their tools are clues to the way they managed life. Of particular interest are cases that show the sequence of New York projectile points. One entire alcove is devoted to the life of hunters during the Archaic period, before the use of the bow and arrow. Other exhibits are devoted to the Arctic, Northwest Coast, Southwest, Plains, and Southeast culture areas.

In addition to prehistoric material, many exhibits show Indian life at the time of first contact with Europeans and later.

"At the Western Door," a permanent exhibit, using more than 2,000 items, traces Seneca culture as it changed after contact with the Dutch, the French, and the English. "Face to Face" is an exhibit that organizes objects from different cultures that have similar functions or meanings.

Dioramas show the construction of a prehistoric Iroquois longhouse, the life-size interior of a prehistoric longhouse, a Haida Indian village, the Zuni pueblo, and how an archeological site is excavated.

Special Interest. The museum has fostered a long relationship with the Western New York Senecas and achieved national prominence under the directorship of Dr. Arthur C. Parker, a Seneca.

Designs scratched on slate by prehistoric Indians near Lake Kidgemakooge, in Nova Scotia. Photo by Arthur Kelsall, courtesy of Campbell Grant.

SENECA-IROQUOIS NATIONAL MUSEUM

In Salamanca on the Allegany Indian Reservation. Take New York 17 to exit 20. Mail address: P.O. Box 442, Broad St. Ext., Salamanca, NY 14779. Phone: 716/945-1738. Open daily, April 1–September 30, Monday–Friday, October–March 31. Closed January and certain holidays.

The collections exhibited here cover the period 9000 B.P. to the present and were all gathered in Iroquois territory. The museum places particular emphasis on the heritage of the Seneca who were known as the Keeper of the Western Door of the Iroquois Confederacy. Guided tours can be arranged for groups.

SIX NATIONS INDIAN MUSEUM

Off New York 3, 1 mile east of Onchiota. Mail address: HCR 1, Box 10, Onchiota, NY 12968. Phone: 518/891-2299. Open daily, summer. Admission charged.

This museum, dedicated to preserving all aspects of Iroquois culture, has exhibits of prehistoric Iroquois pottery and other artifacts, as well as some pre-Iroquois material, largely from the St. Lawrence River valley and the Lake Champlain regions. Displays show how various articles were made and used.

SOUTHOLD INDIAN MUSEUM

Bayview Road, Southold, NY 11971. Phone: 516/765-5577. Open free, Sunday afternoons. At other times by appointment.

Sponsored by the Long Island Chapter of the New York State Archaeological Association, the museum has a large collection of Algonquin pottery and tools as well as Eskimo (Inuit) and western Indian material. Exhibits and murals show how the Algonquins hunted, fished, farmed, made cloth from bark, played, and even gambled. Other displays illustrate the evolution of Indian culture from Paleo times to contact with Europeans. Of special interest is a display of stone tools with their present-day counterparts.

TIOGA COUNTY HISTORICAL SOCIETY MUSEUM
(tie-OH-gah)

110–112 Front St., Owego, NY 13827. Phone: 607/687-2460. Open free, Tuesday–Saturday; evening, Wednesday. Closed certain holidays.

Artifacts collected in the immediate area represent cultures from about 2500 B.C. to historic times. A special display is devoted to the Engelbert Site, which is about ten miles from Owego. In this display are materials representing Lamoka, Late Owasco, prehistoric Iroquois, and Susquehannock cultures.

YAGER MUSEUM
(See Hartwick College)

Nova Scotia

NOVA SCOTIA MUSEUM

1747 Summer Street, Halifax, NS, B3H 3A6. Phone: 902/424-7353. Open free, May 15–October 15, Monday–Saturday; afternoon, Sunday. October 16–May 14, Tuesday–Saturday; afternoon, Sunday.

Permanent exhibits here present the archeology of Nova Scotia. In addition there are occasional short-term exhibits that deal with prehistory.

The museum is the headquarters of the Nova Scotia Museum Complex.

Ontario

AGAWA ROCK PICTOGRAPHS

In Lake Superior Park near Agawa Bay Campground. A sign on Highway 17 directs to a parking area near the site, which is reached by a trail. Mail address: Ontario Provincial Park Service, Ministry of Natural Resources, P.O. Box 1160, Wawa, Ontario P0S 1K0. Phone: 705-856-2396.

Here on a cliff face on the shore of Lake Superior are strongly colored rock paintings of various kinds that appear to have been made over a long period of time.

ASSIGINACK MUSEUM AND MILL COMPLEX
(ass-SIG-in-ack)

Nelson and Queen streets, Manitowaning (MAN-it-toh-WAH-ning). Open Monday–Saturday; afternoon, Sunday, June–September. Admission charged.

Here may be seen artifacts from the nearby Sheguiandah Site (see below), on loan from the Royal Ontario Museum.

In 1934 the Seine River band of Ojibwa Indians, in Ontario, were still building longhouses much like those used in prehistoric times. Here the pole framework of a ceremonial longhouse has been completed. Canadian Museum of Civilization photo.

A diorama of an Iroquois village of longhouses surrounded by a palisade. Canadian Museum of Civilization photo.

BRUCE COUNTY MUSEUM

33 Victoria St. North, Southampton, Ontario, N0H 2L0. Phone; 519/797-3644. Open Monday–Friday; afternoon, Sunday; Saturday (summer only). Admission by donation.

Artifacts on display here are Archaic, Middle Woodland, and Iroquoian.

CANADIAN MUSEUM OF CIVILIZATION

Formerly the National Museum of Man in Ottawa, this important museum has changed its name and moved into new quarters across the river in Hull, Quebec. As *America's Ancient Treasures* went to press, new archeological exhibits of material from all periods of Canadian prehistory were in the process of construction. For information about displays from the museum's large collections that are now completed, write to Canadian Museum of Civilization, 100 Laurier Street, P.O. Box 3100, Station B, Hull, Quebec J8X 4H2. Or phone: 819/994-0840.

CRAWFORD LAKE CONSERVATION AREA

Near Milton, off Highway 401. Open daily, July–August; weekends and holidays, remainder of year. Admission charged.

This is the site of an important prehistoric Iroquoian village. The Interpretive Centre focuses on both the natural history of the lake and the archeology of the area. Several longhouses have been reconstructed.

HURONIA MUSEUM

Little Lake Park, P.O. Box 638, Midland, Ontario L4R 4P4. Phone: 705/526-2844 or 8757. Open daily, May–October; Monday–Friday, November–March. Admission charged, covering both the museum and Huron Indian Village (see entry below).

The museum contains both Native and Euro-Canadian material from 42 archeological excavations in south-central Ontario. The material dates from Paleo times to the present.

HURON INDIAN VILLAGE

Also in Little Lake Park (see above) is a recreated two-acre village that portrays Huron life prior to the arrival of Europeans. Buildings, tools—even wood smoke and music—give visitors a sense of what a dynamic Native society was like prior to A.D. 1600.

JOSEPH BRANT MUSEUM

426 Brant St., Burlington. Open Monday–Saturday; afternoon, Sunday. Admission charged.

This museum, named for Joseph Brant, an Iroquois leader on the English side during the American Revolution, features Brant memorabilia and has other material, some of it prehistoric, representative of Iroquois culture.

This exhibit shows how the Eskimo hunted seal. Canadian Museum of Civilization photo.

LITTLE CURRENT-HOWLAND MUSEUM

Sheguiandah, Ontario P0P 1W0. Phone: 705/368-2367. Open daily, only in summer. Donations welcome.

Here is a display of artifacts from the Sheguiandah Site (see entry below) including bifaces and cores. There is also an exhibit on flint knapping.

MUSEUM OF INDIAN ARCHAEOLOGY AND LAWSON PREHISTORIC INDIAN VILLAGE

Off Wonderland Road North, just south of Highway 22. Mail address: 1600 Attawandaron Road, London, Ontario N6G 3M6. Phone: 519/473-1360. Museum open daily, April–November; afternoons, Wednesday–Sunday, December–March. Village closed, winter. Admission charged.

Here at the Lawson Prehistoric Indian Village Site is a partial reconstruction of a fifteenth-century Neutral Village. A large display gallery in the museum portrays the 11,000-year history of Native Americans in south-western Ontario. There are audiovisual and hands-on programs. On site excavations take place May to September.

PERTH MUSEUM
(The Archibald M. Campbell Memorial Museum)

5 Gore St. East, Perth. Open Monday–Saturday; afternoon, Sunday, April 1–December 23; afternoons, Saturday and Sunday, January 1–March 31. Admission charged.

In addition to random local finds this museum houses some archeological material from the southwestern part of the United States.

PETROGLYPHS PROVINCIAL PARK

Northeast of Peterborough, 55 kilometers off Northey's Bay Road, about 11 kilometers from Highway 28. Mail address: Ministry of Natural Resources, P.O. Box 500, Bancroft, Ontario K0L 1C0. Phone: 613/332-3940, 705/877-2552 (park office). Open second Friday in May–Thanksgiving Day. Admission charged.

In this park are 900 petroglyphs carved in marble. A specially designed building has been placed over the main body of these rock carvings which seem to have been made between 500 and 1000 years ago by Algonkian-speaking people. The Ojibwa Anishinabe Nation today regards this as a sacred site. The Ministry of Natural Resources opened it to the general public after mining prospectors found it in 1954.

(Left) In Petroglyphs Provincial Park, Ontario, Native Americans carved these symbols—not in the usual perpendicular rocks but in soft marble bedrock that sloped gently inward. Hammerstones used in pecking the glyphs were found in crevices in the rock. An underground stream gurgles beneath the site, perhaps a reason for people's choice of the site. (Right) A shelter built over the site protects it from weather and vandals. Petroglyphs Provincial Park photo.

ROYAL ONTARIO MUSEUM

100 Queen's Park Crescent, Toronto M5S 2C6. Phone: 416/586-5549. Open daily, June–August. Closed Monday, September–May, and certain holidays. Admission charged.

In this, Canada's largest museum, exhibits span natural and human history throughout the ages and around the world.

In a series of galleries devoted to the cultures, past and present, of the native peoples of the Americas, the first is "The Ontario Prehistory Gallery." It relates the story of the prehistoric peoples of the province from the first arrival of humans in North America— "a much-debated date amongst archeologists, with estimates ranging from 150,000 to 12,000 years ago"— to the Iroquoian culture of 400 years ago. The gallery comprises four dioramas and 13 cases containing over 1000 maps, drawings, paintings, and artifacts. Among the objects on display are stone tools, copper knives, spear points, pottery and stone pipes, a rattle pipe, and a unique turtle effigy, carved from a conch shell by Woodland Indians 3000 to 2500 years ago. The dioramas, which illustrate different periods of human development in Ontario, include a display of the earliest humans butchering a young woolly mammoth. The exit from the gallery features a granite wall showing prehistoric red ochre paintings, based on two actual sites in Ontario.

SAINTE-MARIE-AMONG-THE-HURONS

Midland, Ontario. Phone: 705/526-7838. Open daily, mid-May–Thanksgiving. Admission charged.

The museum here contains a large display of archeological material pertaining to the life of prehistoric people of the area.

SERPENT MOUND
PROVINCIAL PARK

From Peterboro drive southeast to the north shore of Rice Lake. Open mid-May–mid-October. Admission charged.

Here about 80 feet above the lake is a mound that depicts a snake. It is 189 feet in length and averages 5 feet in height, 24 feet in width. Near the head is an oval mound that contained four burials.

Serpent Mound seems not to be the work of Effigy Mound people who were active in Wisconsin. It is instead a rare example of a mound built by people who followed a lifeway called Point Peninsula. A cremation in the mound has a radiocarbon date of A.D. 130.

SHEGUIANDAH SITE
(SHEG-wee-AN-duh)

From Sudbury drive 41 miles west on Trans-Canada 17, then 43 miles south on Provincial Road 68 through Little Current to the Little Current–Howland Centennial Museum at the edge of the town of Sheguiandah. The museum is open daily, June–August; afternoons, May, September, October. Admission charged.

At this site, near the museum, an excavation conducted for several years has produced considerable controversy in archeological circles. Dr. Thomas E. Lee, who was in charge of the dig, reported that he had found crude choppers and scapers made of quartzite *underneath* several levels of deposits in which there were signs of human occupation. These crude tools had been tumbled about and mixed in what appeared to be glacial till—that is, an aggregation of clay, sand, and rock deposited by a glacier. It looked to Dr. Lee—and to some eminent geologists—as if the front edge of a glacier had pushed a very ancient campsite for a short distance, thus disturbing the artifacts which had been left there. If this is what happened, the people who made these quartzite tools lived in Canada *before* the last great glacial advance.

The archeologists who believed that Dr. Lee had found very old artifacts estimated their age at 30,000 years, at the very least. According to some responsible estimates, they were much older than that. Not all archeologists, however, agreed that the Sheguiandah materials were of such antiquity.

In 1991 a multi-disciplinary team from Laurentian University, Royal Ontario Museum, York University, Waterloo University, and the Canadian Geological Survey re-excavated the site. These investigators concluded that what Dr. Lee had called glacial till was really colluvium deposited by a flood about 9600 years ago. The team also excavated two small swamps at the site and found artifacts carbon dated to 9200 to 9500 years ago. In addition, they found evidence of much disturbance of the strata at the site. Two parts of one artifact were separated by more than two vertical feet. Charcoal found at a depth of three feet was less than 100 years old. The team of investigators came to the conclusion Sheguiandan was a large, interesting stratified site probably no more than 9500 years old.

A

B

Excavation in progress, in 1953, at the Sheguiandah Site. All the rocks visible in the photograph had been quarried by human beings, and in the rubble many broken and unfinished stone tools were found. Among them, shown in the drawings were (a) gravers and (b) a knife. Photo and drawings by Thomas E. Lee.

SIMCOE COUNTY MUSEUM AND ARCHIVES (SIM-coe)

From Barrie drive 4 miles north on Ontario 27 to West Hwy. 26, then .5 mile west to museum, adjacent to Springwater Park. Mail address: RR 2, Minesing, Ontario, L0L 1Y0. Phone: 705/728-3721. Open Monday–Saturday; afternoon, Sunday. Admission charged.

Materials from a number of systematically excavated sites may be seen here. The cultures represented are the Laurentian, Middleport, Lalonde, and Huron. The earliest materials have been dated at sometime between 3000 and 2000 B.C. An electrified map shows the location of the sites and clearly indicates what culture and period are represented at each site.

SOUTHWOLD EARTHWORKS

Iona, Ontario. Phone: 519/322-2365. Open free, all year.

Here are the remains of a prehistoric Neutral Indian village enclosed by earthworks and a ditch.

THUNDER BAY MUSEUM

219 May St. South, Thunder Bay, Ontario P7E 1B5. Phone: 807/623-0801. Open daily, June 15–September 15. Admission charged.

Artifacts of the Paleo and the Copper Culture periods found at a site in the vicinity are on display, together with Woodland material.

UNITED COUNTIES MUSEUM

731 Second St. W., Cornwall. Open Monday–Saturday; afternoon, Sunday, May 1–October 31.

On display here are some Point Peninsula artifacts.

UNIVERSITY OF WESTERN ONTARIO, MUSEUM OF INDIAN ARCHAEOLOGY AND PIONEER LIFE

On the campus, London. Phone: 519/473-1360. Open free, Monday–Friday.

Here are exhibits illustrative of the archeology of the surrounding area.

WOODLAND CULTURAL CENTRE

184 Mohawk St., Brantford. Open daily. Admission charged.

Along with a wide variety of material illustrating the historic culture of Woodland First Nations is a section devoted to prehistoric artifacts. The museum has resource persons and a mobile resource unit that travels widely, explaining Woodland Indian life, past and present. Also housed here is an Indian Hall of Fame.

Two students in the 1982 Carnegie Museum field school work on a wall profile in a multi-component site the earliest level of which was C-14 dated to 5350 B.C. Carnegie Museum of Natural History photo.

Pennsylvania

CARNEGIE MUSEUM OF NATURAL HISTORY

4400 Forbes Ave., Pittsburgh, PA 15213. Phone: 412/665-2602. Open Tuesday–Saturday; afternoons, Sunday and Monday, July 4–Labor Day. Closed certain holidays. Admission charged.

Archeological exhibits are under development. The Hall of Native Americans and the Western Pennsylvania Archaeology Hall are scheduled to open as this book goes to press.

FORT LIGONIER

50 miles east of Pittsburgh, on US 30 in Ligonier. Open daily, April–October. Admission charged.

In this reconstruction of a fort of the period of the French and Indian War numerous archeological objects are on exhibit.

FRANKLIN AND MARSHALL COLLEGE, NORTH MUSEUM

College and Buchanan Avenues, Lancaster, PA. Mail address: P.O. Box 3003, Lancaster, PA 17604-3003. Phone: 717/291-3941. Open free, Tuesday–Saturday; afternoon, Sunday. Donations accepted.

Included in this museum, which has a strong emphasis on programs for children, are exhibits on Native American culture and archeology.

INDIAN STEPS MUSEUM

From Airville (east of York), where Pennsylvania 74 and Pennsylvania 425 intersect, take a local road east to the museum, which is on the west bank of the Susquehanna River. Phone: 717/862-3948. Open free, Tuesday–Sunday, April 1–October 31. Donations accepted.

In seven rooms containing American Indian material are exhibits devoted to the Susquehannock and Cherokee Indians. All periods from Paleo through Late Woodland are represented. Exhibits include plaster casts of petroglyphs which are now submerged under water impounded behind a dam on the Susquehanna River.

The Name. Before the dam was built it was possible to reach the river's edge by steps which prehistoric people cut in the rock. Hence the name Indian Steps Museum.

Special Interest. This museum was constructed on the site where the Susquehannock tribe, decimated by smallpox, ceased to exist, after it lost a battle with the Massowomeke Indians.

Archeologists at work in Meadowcroft Rock Shelter, near Avella, Pennsylvania, where 14,500-year-old evidence of Paleo-Indian occupation was found. University of Pittsburgh photo.

MATSON MUSEUM OF ANTHROPOLOGY

Pennsylvania State University, 409 Carpenter Building, University Park, PA 16802. Phone: 814/865-3853. Open free, Monday–Friday; morning, Saturday; afternoon, Sunday when the university is in session. Phone for summer hours.

The North American Room here includes exhibits on Pennsylvanian archeology. The Sheep Rock Shelter display features rare examples of usually perishable textiles, cordage and botanic specimens up to 9000 years old. Two exhibits emphasize prehistoric jasper quarrying and the use of pyrotechnology in tool-making. In addition to the permanent exhibits, the museum offers changing exhibits based on current research being done by faculty and students and on selections from permanent collections.

MERCER MUSEUM

Pine and Ashland streets, Doylestown, PA. Mail address: 84 South Pine Street, Doylestown, PA 18901. Phone: 215/345-0210. Open Monday–Saturday; afternoon, Sunday. Closed certain holidays. Admission charged.

Here, along with tools and implements which European settlers used in the United States before the Industrial Revolution, are tools of the prehistoric Lenni Lenape Indians.

MONROE COUNTY HISTORICAL ASSOCIATION

537 Ann St., Stroudsburg, PA 18360. Phone: 717/421-7703. Open free, afternoon, Tuesday.

On exhibit are local finds, mostly of Lenni Lenape origin.

NORTH MUSEUM
(See Franklin and Marshall College)

Woodland Indians made a great variety of containers from birch bark. Some were cooking vessels, some were used for storage, others for hauling water. The practice of making such containers continued into historic time. Passamaquody Indians decorated this small round box with pictographs. Robert Abbe Museum of Stone Age Antiquities photo.

SOMMERHEIM

In Scott County Park, 3 miles west of Erie on Pennsylvania 5. Open free, mornings, Monday–Friday, in summer.

This was the site of a Native American settlement between 1000 B.C. and A.D. 1.

STATE MUSEUM
OF PENNSYLVANIA
(Formerly the William Penn Memorial Museum)

Third and North streets, adjacent to the State Capitol. Mail address: P.O. Box 1026, Harrisburg, PA 17108-1026. Phone: 717/787-4978. Open free, Tuesday–Saturday; afternoon, Sunday. Closed certain holidays.

In the Hall of Anthropology are exhibits of prehistoric cultures beginning 10,000 years ago. Various displays show archeological methods and the results they achieve. Of special interest is a full size diorama that depicts the life cycle of a Lenape (Delaware) boy during late Woodland times.

TIOGA POINT MUSEUM
(tie-OH-gah)

724 S. Main St., Athens. Open free, afternoons, Monday, Wednesday, Saturday; evening, Monday.

The prehistoric Indian collection here consists mainly of random local finds, but there are materials from three systematically excavated sites—Murray Garden, Spanish Hill, and Abbe-Brennan—which provided data about several cultures. One exhibit shows the chronologic sequence of different local pottery types.

UNIVERSITY MUSEUM
OF ARCHAEOLOGY AND
ANTHROPOLOGY

University of Pennsylvania, 33rd and Spruce Streets, Philadelphia, PA 19104. Phone: 215/898-4045.

As this book went to press the museum had no prehistoric North American exhibit on display, but exhibits in this very important museum change from time to time.

VENANGO COUNTY
COURTHOUSE

Liberty and 12th streets, Franklin, PA 16323. Open free, Monday–Friday.

Display cases here are devoted to material from 18 Pennsylvania sites.

WYOMING HISTORICAL AND
GEOLOGICAL SOCIETY

69 South Franklin St., Wilkes Barre, PA. Mail address: 49 South Franklin St., Wilkes Barre, PA. Phone: 717/822-1727. Open free, afternoons, Tuesday–Friday; 10 a.m.–4 p.m., Saturday.

Archeological exhibits here illuminate the prehistory of the Susquehanna River valley from the Archaic to the historic period. Included are displays of Owasco and prehistoric Huron material.

At the Micmac Indian Village, on Prince Edward Island, this prehistoric Indian dwelling has been reconstructed as part of an exhibit. Artifacts found in the area are also on display in a museum there. Micmac Indian Village photo.

Prince Edward Island

MICMAC INDIAN VILLAGE (MICK-mack)

Rocky Point, Prince Edward Island. From Charlottetown travel west on Route 1 to Cornwall, then follow Route 19 to Rocky Point. Mail address: Director of Archives & Heritage, Public Archives, P.O. Box 1000, Charlottetown, PEI, C2A 7M4. Phone: 902/ 675-3800. Open daily, June 1–October 1. Admission charged.

Here, in an outdoor setting, the proprietors have reconstructed a sixteenth-century Micmac village. Indoors is a museum with random local finds of prehistoric artifacts.

Québec

AMERINDIAN MUSEUM, POINTE-BLEUE

407 Amisht, Pointe-Bleue, Québec G0W 2H0. Phone: 418/275-4842. Open Monday–Friday, all year. Admission charged.

Exhibits here display North American artifacts from archeological excavation of sites near Lac Saint-Jean.

CANADIAN MUSEUM OF CIVILIZATION (MUSÉE CANADIEN DES CIVILISATIONS)

100 Laurier St., P.O. Box 3100, Station B, Hull, Québec J8X 4H2.

As this book went to press, this museum was reorganizing its exhibits in a new building. For information about hours, fees, and exhibits available apply to the address above. The museum plans to have at least some temporary archeological exhibits.

CENTRE D'INTERPRÉTATION DE LA RIVIÈRE MÉTABETCHOUANE

243 rue Hébert, Desbiens, Lac Saint-Jean, Québec G0W 1N0. Phone: 418/ 346-5341. Open May–October. Admission charged.

This center includes the prehistory of the Lac Saint-Jean region and has exhibits of prehistoric artifacts.

LA GALLITHÈQUE

Saint-Laurent-de-Gallichan, Abitibi, Québec. Open June–September. Admission charged.

Artifact collections from prehistoric sites from the Lake Abitibi region are included.

Fishnet sinker from Red Mill, Québec. Université du Québec à Trois Rivières photo.

Eskimos engraved this mask in steatite on Qajartalik Island near Wakeham Bay, Québec. Bernard Saladin d'Anglure photo, courtesy Campbell Grant.

Two axes (left) and gouge (right) with polished cutting edges used by Archaic people in Canada. Université du Québec à Trois Rivières photo.

One type of structure which the Inuit (Eskimos) apparently never built was this kind of beaconlike column, 13 feet high. Many like it have been found on the Ungava shoreline. If they were beacons, they could have been very useful as landmarks to seagoing Norsemen. Photo by Thomas E. Lee.

McCORD MUSEUM OF CANADIAN HISTORY

690 Sherbrooke Street West, Montreal, Québec H3A 1E9. Phone: 514/398-7100.

As this book went to press this museum was undergoing major renovation and expansion. When it reopens it will have a permanent gallery devoted to ethnological and archeological exhibits on the First Nations of Canada.

MÉTABECHOUANE INTERPRETIVE CENTER
(*See Centre d'Interprétation de la rivière Métabechaouane*)

MUSÉE DES SEPT-ÎLES, REGIONAL MUSEUM OF THE QUÉBEC NORTH SHORE

500 boulevard Laure, Sept-Îles, Québec G4R 1X7. Phone: 418/968-2070. Open daily, June 24–Labor Day. Admission charged. Open free, daily the rest of the year.

The museum includes exhibits on the prehistory of the Québec North Shore (Côte du Nord).

PARC ARCHÉOLOGIQUE DE LA POINTE DU BUISSON

30 kilometers from Montreal on route 132 ouest, Port Mercier. Mail address: 333 rue Émond, Melocheville, Québec J0S 1J0. Phone: 514/429-7857. Open mid-May–Labor Day. Admission charged. Groups by appointment all year.

Archeologists have found abundant evidence that people hunted, fished, and camped here beginning about 5000 years ago. Their life is explained in an Interpretive Center.

UNIVERSITÉ DU QUÉBEC À TROIS RIVIÈRES, MUSÉE D'ARCHÉOLOGIE

Pavillon Robert-Lionel Séguin, 2750 boulevard des Forges, Trois Rivières, Québec G9A 5H7. Phone: 819/376-5032. Open free, Tuesday–Friday; afternoons, Saturday and Sunday.

The main section of the museum presents artifacts from the Early Archaic through the Woodland period in Québec. Material from the Trois Rivières region is included as are exhibits on everyday native life.

UNIVERSITÉ LAVAL, CENTRE D'ÉTUDES NORDIQUES

On the campus, Siège Social, Québec. Open free, Monday through Saturday; afternoon, Sunday, when the university is in session.

This small but well-planned museum features material from Arctic Québec, in culture sequences as it was excavated, especially Norse remains, but also Dorset, Thule, Paleo, and Archaic.

Expecting to find remains of the Dorset culture on Ungava Peninsula in Northern Québec, Dr. Thomas E. Lee began investigations there in 1964 for the Centre d'Études Nordiques. What he found led him to suspect that the Norse had been in the area. In subsequent years he found increasing evidence that convinced him and many—but not all—archeologists that there had indeed been Norse settlements along the coast of Ungava Bay and even inland at Payne Lake.

What the Ungava site called Longhouse #2 looked like when discovered. The same site, after excavation and partial restoration, turned out to be an 83-foot-long structure of the kind that the Norse built. A fourth room at the right was left unexcavated. None of the Ungava sites are open to the public. Photos by Thomas E. Lee and Robert E. Lee.

Rhode Island

BROWN UNIVERSITY, HAFFENREFFER MUSEUM

Mount Hope Grant, off Rhode Island 136. Mail address: Bristol, RI 02819. Phone: 401/253-8388. Open weekdays, in summer; closed January, February, March; open Saturday and Sunday during the rest of the year. Admission charged.

Only about two percent of this museum's vast collection is on display at any one time. Exhibits are changed every year or two. As this book went to press a retrospective on the collections of the founder, Jacob Haffenreffer, was about to open. The exhibit—and probably others to come—emphasize the artifacts, lifeways, and traditions of the Native peoples of New England. A new exhibit on the Plains Indians is projected.

FORT NINIGRET

In Charlestown, off US 1A. Mail address: Division of Planning and Development, Department of Environmental Management, 83 Park St., Providence, RI 02903. Phone: 401/277-2776. Open free, daily, all year.

Interpretive signs explain that excavation revealed at least two periods when Native Americans inhabited this site, high on a bluff overlooking a tidal lagoon. The first, between A.D. 700 and 1300, is known only from bits of pottery. The second occupation, in the seventeenth century, overlapped the period of contact with Europeans. At that time Niantic Indians built a fortified trading post on the bluff. One possible reason for the fort may have been the fact that a great deal of wampum, a form of currency, was manufactured here from shell, and its makers may have felt the need to protect it.

There are interpretive signs but no buildings or exhibits at the site.

HAFFENREFFER MUSEUM
(*See Brown University*)

MUSEUM OF NATURAL HISTORY AND CORMACK PLANETARIUM

Roger Williams Park, Providence, RI 02905. Phone: 401/785-9451. Open free, Tuesday–Sunday. Closed Mondays, holidays.

The archeological portion of "The Narragansett Bay Worlds" exhibit reconstructs the prehistory of the region and includes a timeline, several cases of artifacts, and a replica of an actual shell midden from a site in North Kingstown, RI. Cultural and archeological material are periodically shown in other areas of the museum. On occasion there are exhibits of materials excavated by Warren K. Moorehead at the Fort Ancient site in Ohio.

A grid over an area where knappers manufactured stone tools, at a site in Virginia, made it possible to map the exact position of each object found. Thunderbird Research Corporation photo.

MUSEUM OF PRIMITIVE ART AND CULTURE

1058 Kingstown Road, Peace Dale, RI 02883. Phone: 401/783-5711. Open Tuesday–Thursday 11 a.m.–2 p.m. or by appointment. Donations accepted.

In its collection of North American cultural material are artifacts from New England and from other parts of the United States. The University of Rhode Island is responsible for curating the collections here.

ROGER WILLIAMS PARK MUSEUM OF NATURAL HISTORY

Roger Williams Park, Providence, RI. Open free, daily. Closed certain holidays.

Although most of the material in this museum is post-contact, there are some items and some whole exhibits that throw light on prehistory. One case shows hypothesized routes by which Indians entered America. Another presents a chronological chart for North American archeology, with appropriate tools and weapons for each period. A third shows the differences in physical appearance among Indians of different regions. There is also an exhibit on the plants domesticated by Indians and a summary of their accomplishments in prehistoric times.

TOMAQUAG INDIAN MEMORIAL MUSEUM

325 Summit Road, Arcadia, RI 02826. Phone: 401/539-7213. Open free, Saturday and Sunday, April 1–the week before Thanksgiving.

Here may be seen archeological displays from various sites in both New England and other areas of the United States. From time to time there are special activities for children.

Vermont

CHIMNEY POINT STATE HISTORIC SITE MUSEUM OF NATIVE AMERICAN HERITAGE

Fifteen miles south of Vergennes, on Highway 125. Mail address: RD 3, Box 3546, Vergennes, VT 05491. Phone: 802/759-2412. Open Wednesday–Sunday, all year. Admission charged.

Here, on the remains of an Archaic site on the shore of Lake Champlain, the Visitor Center houses a collection of artifacts from the Archaic and Woodland cultures of Vermont.

A Dalton spearpoint (late Paleo-Indian) just as excavators found it in the ground at a site in Virginia. Thunderbird Research Corporation photo.

Virginia

DIVISION OF ARCHAEOLOGY, VIRGINIA DEPARTMENT OF HISTORIC RESOURCES

221 Governor Street, Richmond, VA 23219. Phone: 804/786-3141.

This agency coordinates Virginia Archaeology Week which places exhibits in local museums across the state.

FLOWERDEW HUNDRED

From Richmond drive south on Interstate 95, then east on Virginia 10, then north on local road 639; or from Williamsburg drive west on Virginia 5, then south on local road 639. The site is on the south side of the James River about 5 miles east of the Benjamin Harrison Bridge. Mail address: 1617 Flowerdew Hundred Road, Hopewell, VA 23860. Phone: 804/541-8897. Open daily, Tuesday–Sunday, April 1–November 30. Admission charged.

The plantation, which was named after the Flowerdew family from England, was one of the earliest English settlements in North America. Excavation has revealed Native American occupation of the same area as early as 9000 B.C. Artifacts from the period before 1618, when the English took over, are on display in a museum here, along with materials that range from the Colonial period up through the Civil War.

HISTORIC CRAB ORCHARD MUSEUM AND PIONEER PARK, INC.

At intersection of Virginia 19 and Virginia 460, Tazewell. Mail address: P.O. Box 12 (Route 19/460), Tazewell, VA 24651. Phone: 703/988-6755. Open Tuesday–Saturday; afternoon, Sunday, April–October. Admission charged.

The museum interprets the prehistoric and historic life of Tazewell County and southwest Virginia, with special emphasis on artifacts of the Archaic and late Woodland periods.

Excavators at a site in Virginia found an area they call a chipping floor where a great many chunks of stone revealed that it had been used as a place for the manufacture of stone implements. Thunderbird Research Corporation photo.

JAMESTOWN SETTLEMENT

From Williamsburg drive south 6 miles on Virginia 31 to entrance. Mail address: P.O. Box JF, Williamsburg, VA 23187. Phone: 804/229-1607. Open daily, all year. Closed December 25 and January 1. Admission charged.

Artifacts representing all chronological periods of Indian occupation in coastal Virginia are exhibited in the museum's Powhatan Indian Gallery. The earliest date to about 8000 B.C. Included are stone projectile points, axes, knives, tools, grinding stones, and pottery vessels.

PAMUNKEY INDIAN MUSEUM

From Interstate 95, Kings Dominion exit, drive east on Virginia 30, then south on Virginia 632 or 633 to Pamunkey Indian Reservation. Mail address: Route 1, Box 2050, King William, VA 23086. Phone: 804/843-4792. Open Monday–Saturday; afternoon, Sunday. Admission charged.

Exhibits here depict Pamunkey history from Paleo times to the present.

Tools and other materials are shown as they would have been seen and used by Native Americans of various periods. Original artifacts are supplemented with replicas.

The Pamunkey Indians were part of the great Powhatan Confederacy—more than 30 tribes that lived on the coastal plain from the border of what is now North Carolina north to Washington, D.C. At the time Europeans arrived Chief Powhatan and his daughter, Pocohontas, lived among the Pamunkey.

PEAKS OF OTTER
VISITOR CENTER

At Mile Post 86 on the Blue Ridge Pkwy. Mail address: Route 2, Box 163, Bedford, VA 24523. Phone: 703/586-4357. Open free, daily, June–October.

In addition to wildlife exhibits, this museum displays materials that archeologists recovered from a prehistoric campsite nearby. The site, which was discovered in the course of building a lake, had been occupied by wandering hunters 5100 to 5600 years ago,

according to a radiocarbon date obtained from charcoal from a firepit. Below this was another occupation, which has not been exactly dated, although it is thought to have been 1000 years earlier. The site has now been flooded by Lake Abbott.

VALENTINE MUSEUM

1015 East Clay St., Richmond, VA 23219. Phone: 804/649-0711. Open Monday–Saturday; afternoon, Sunday. Admission charged.

Although this museum focuses on the "Life and History of Richmond," it maintains some Native American material.

The museum has a school program covering the culture of the original population of the area, the Algonquian-speaking Powhatan Indians.

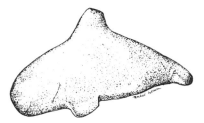

ARCHEOLOGICAL ORGANIZATIONS

Anyone who wants to get in touch with others who are interested in archeology would do well to ask the state archeologist for the address of the nearest local organization. Also museums can usually direct people to archeological societies. In addition here is a list of those organizations that are part of the Council of Affiliated Societies. The Council can be reached through David Jeanne, Newsletter Editor, 305 Hickory, Springfield, LA 71075-2633.

Arizona Archaeological & Historical Society
William D. Hohmann
3255 Camino Campestre
Tucson, AZ 85716
602/795-4581

Arizona Archaeological Society.
John W. Hohmann
725 W. Brown #18
Tempe, AZ 85281
602/968-1683

Arkansas Archaeological Society
100 Unity Lane
Crossett, AR 71635
501/364-9561

Arkansas Archaeological Society
Hester Davis
P.O. Box 1249
Fayetteville, AR 72702
501/575-3556

Northwest Arkansas Archaeological Society
James Cherry
P.O. Box 1154
Fayetteville, AR 72702

Sacramento Archaeological Society
Eloise R. Barter
2601 Sierra Blvd.
Sacramento, CA 95864
916/485-5976

Fort Guijarros Museum Foundation
Ron May/Carolyn Kyle
P.O. Box 231500
San Diego, CA 92123

San Diego Archaeological Society
Michael Sampson
4640 E. Talmadge Dr.
San Diego, CA 92116
619/283-5960

Colorado Archaeological Society
Susan M. Collins
1300 Broadway
Denver, CO 80203
303/440-8572

Kansas Anthropological Association
William B. Lees
Kansas State Historical Society
120 W. 10th St.
Topeka, KS 66612
913/296-2625

Kansas City Archaeological Society
Mary J. Adair
Museum of Anthropology
University of Kansas
Lawrence, KS 66045
913/864-4245

Louisiana Archeological Society
Richard A. Weinstein
7628 N. Coventry Circle
Baton Rouge, LA 70808
504/766-7142

Louisiana Archaeological Society
David R. Jeane
305 Hickory
Springhill, LA 71075-2633
318/539-5944

Maine Archaeological Society
Richard A. Doyle
P.O. Box 9715-253
Portland, ME 04104
207/657-4574

Massachusetts Archaeological Society
Jane A. McGahan
74 Congress St., Apt. 1
Greenfield, MA 01301
413/774-2300

Massachusetts Archaeological Society
Janice M. Weeks
12 Long Ave.
Greenfield, MA 01013
413/773-7870

Mississippi Archaeological Association
Janet Rafferty
P.O. Drawer AR
Mississippi State, MS 39762
601/325-3826

Mississippi Archaeological Association
Choctaw Branch
Kenneth H. Carleton
P.O. Box 6005
Philadelphia, MS 39350
601/656-5251

Missouri Archaeological Society
Earl H. Lubensky
1408 Bradford Dr.
Columbia, MO 65203
314/443-5576

Archaeological Society of North Carolina
Vin Steponaitis
Research Labs of Anthropology
University of North Carolina
Chapel Hill, NC 27599
919/933-2041

Nova Scotia Archaeology Society
Robert Ferguson
Canadian Parks Service
Historic Properties
Halifax, NS
Canada B3J 159
902/426-9509

Texas Archaeological Society
Pat Mercado-Allinger
14804 Great Willow Dr.
Austin, TX 78728
512/251-2639

Houston Archaeological Society
Leland W. Patterson
418 Wycliffe
Houston, TX 77079
713/468-4464

Utah Statewide Archaeological Society
Leon Chamberlain
441 S. 400 W.
Vernal, UT 84078

Wisconsin Archaeological Society
Elizabeth D. Benchley
4600 N. Morris Blvd.
Milwaukee, WI 53211
414/963-1072

STATE AND PROVINCIAL ARCHEOLOGISTS

Alabama

Gregory C. Rhinehart
  Chief
  Planning and Protection Division
  Alabama Historical Commission
  725 Monroe St.
  Montgomery, AL 36130
  205/242-3184

Alaska

Bob Shaw
  Senior Archaeologist
  Office of History and Archaeology
  P.O. Box 107001
  Anchorage, AK 99501-7001
  907/762-2622   907/762-2630

Arizona

Paul Fish
  Curator of Archaeology
  Arizona State Museum
  University of Arizona
  Tucson, AZ 85721
  602/621-2556   602/323-0080

Arkansas

Hester Davis
  State Archaeologist
  Arkansas Archaeological Survey
  P.O. Box 1249
  Fayetteville, AR 72702-1249
  501/575-3556

California

William Seidel
  Office of Historic Preservation
  P.O. Box 942896
  Sacramento, CA 94296-0001
  916/322-9623

Colorado

Susan M. Collins
  State Archaeologist
  Colorado Historical Society
  1300 Broadway
  Denver, CO 80203
  303/866-2736

Connecticut

Nicholas F. Bellantoni
  State Archaeologist
  State Museum of Natural History
  U-23 University of Connecticut
  Storrs, CT 06268-3023
  203/486-5248   203/486-4460

Delaware

Daniel Griffith
  State Historic Preservation Officer
  Bureau of Archaeology & Historic
    Preservation
  15 The Green
  P.O. Box 1401
  Dover, DE 19903
  302/739-5313

District of Columbia

Nancy Kassner
  Archaeologist
  Historic Preservation Office
  614 H Street, NW—Rm. 305
  Washington, DC 20001
  202/727-7360

Florida

James J. Miller
  State Archaeologist
  Division of Historical Resources
  500 S. Bronough St.
  Tallahassee, FL 32399-0250
  904/487-2299

Georgia

Lewis H. Larson, Jr.
  State Archaeologist
  Martha Munro, Rm. 208
  West Georgia College
  Carrollton, GA 30118
  404/836-6455   404/836-6454

Idaho

Thomas J. Green
  State Archaeologist
  210 Main St.
  Boise, ID 83702
  208/334-3847

Illinois

Thomas E. Emerson
  Chief Archaeologist
  Preservation Services Division
  Illinois Historic Preservation Agency
  Old State Capitol Building
  Springfield, IL 62701
  217/732-1334

Indiana

Chris Peebles
  Dept. of Anthropology
  Indiana University
  Bloomington, IN 47405
  812/855-1203

Iowa

William Green
  State Archaeologist
  University of Iowa
  305 Eastlawn
  Iowa City, IA 52242
  319/335-2389

Kansas

Thomas A. Witty, Jr.
  State Archaeologist
  120 W. Tenth
  Topeka, KS 66612
  913/296-4781

Kentucky

R. Berle Clay
  State Archaeologist
  Dept. of Anthropology
  University of Kentucky
  Lexington, KY 40506-0024
  606/257-5735

Louisiana

Kathleen Byrd
  State Archaeologist
  Div. of Archaeology
  Capitol Annex Building
  P.O. Box 44247
  Baton Rouge, LA 70804
  504/342-8170

Maine

Bruce Bourque
  State Archaeologist
  Main State Museum
  Augusta, ME 04333
  207/289-2301

Maryland

Maryland Historic Trust
  Attn: M. L. deSarran, Librarian
  21 State Circle
  Annapolis, MD 21401

Massachusetts

Brona Simon
  State Archaeologist, D-SHPO
  Massachusetts Historical
    Commission
  80 Boylston St.
  Boston, MA 02116
  617/727-8470

Michigan

John R. Halsey
  State Archaeologist
  Michigan Historical Center
  Dept. of State
  Lansing, MI 48918-1847
  517/373-6358   FAX: 517/373-0851

Minnesota

Christy Hohman-Caine
  204 Research Lab Bldg.
  Univ. of Minnesota-Duluth
  Duluth, MN 55812
  218/726-7154

Mississippi

Samuel McGahey
  Staff Archaeologist
  Dept. of Archives & History
  P.O. Box 571
  Jackson, MS 39205
  601/359-6940

Missouri

Michael S. Weichman
  Sr. Archaeologist
  Dept. of Natural Resources
  Historic Preservation Program
  P.O. Box 176
  Jefferson City, MO 65102
  314/751-7958

Montana

David Schwab
  State Archaeologist
  Montana Historical Society
  225 N. Roberts
  Helena, MT 59620
  406/444-7715

Nebraska

Gayle Carlson
  Curator of Anthropology
  State Historical Society
  1500 R. St.
  P.O. Box 82554
  Lincoln, NE 68501
  402/471-4787

Nevada

Alice Becker
  Staff Archaeologist
  State Historic Preservation Office
  201 S. Fall St., Rm. 106
  Carson City, NV 89710
  702/885-5138

New Hampshire

Gary W. Hume
  State Archaeologist
  Div. of Historical Resources
  Walker Building
  P.O. Box 2043
  Concord, NH 03302-2043
  603/271-3483   603/271-3558

New Jersey

Dr. Lorraine E. Williams
State Archaeologist
New Jersey State Museum
205 W. State St.
Trenton, NJ 08625-0530
609/292-8594

New Mexico

Dr. Lynn Sebastian
State Archaeologist
Historic Preservation Div.
Villa Rivera Bldg.
228 E. Palace Ave.
Santa Fe, NM 87503
505/827-6320

New York

Dr. Robert E. Funk
State Archaeologist
New York State Museum
3122 Cultural Education Center
Empire State Plaza
Albany, NY 12230
518/474-5813

North Carolina

Stephen R. Claggett
State Archaeologist
Office of State Archaeology
State Historic Preservation Office
Div. of Archives & History
Dept. of Cultural Resources
109 E. Jones St.
Raleigh, NC 27611-2807
919/733-7342

North Dakota

State Historical Society of North Dakota
Archeology &
Historic Preservation Div.
North Dakota Heritage Center
612 E. Boulevard
Bismarck, ND 58505-0830
701/224-2672

Ohio

Franco Ruffini
Deputy SHPO
Ohio Historic Preservation Office
Ohio Historical Society
1982 Velma Ave.
Columbus, OH 43211
614/297-2470

Oklahoma

Robert L. Brooks
State Archaeologist
Oklahoma Archeological Survey
University of Oklahoma
1808 Newton Dr., Rm. 116
Norman, OK 73019
405/325-7211

Oregon

Dr. Leland Gilsen
Archaeologist
State Parks & Recreation Div.
Historic Preservation Office
525 Trade St. SE
Salem, OR 97310
503/378-5001

Pennsylvania

Kurt Carr
Chief
Div. of Archaeology & Protection
P.O. Box 1026
Harrisburg, PA 17120
717/783-8947

Rhode Island

Paul Robinson
Principal/State Archaeologist
Historic Preservation Commission
Old State House
150 Benefit St.
Providence, RI 02903
401/277-2678

South Carolina

Dr. Bruce Rippeteau
State Archaeologist, Director
S.C. Institute of Archaeology &
Anthropology
University of South Carolina
1321 Pendleton St.
Columbia, SC 29208
803/799-1963   803/777-8170

South Dakota

James K. Haug
State Archaeologist
State Archaeological Research Center
2425 E. St. Charles St.
P.O. Box 1257
Rapid City, SD 57701-5005
605/394-1936

Tennessee

Nick Fielder
State Archaeologist
Dept. of Environment &
Conservation
Div. of Archaeology
5103 Edmonson Pike
Nashville, TN 37211
615/741-1588

Texas

Robert J. Mallouf
State Archaeologist
Box 12276, Capitol Station
Austin, TX 78711
512/463-6090

Utah

David B. Madsen
State Archaeologist
Division of State History
300 Rio Grande
Salt Lake City, UT 84101
801/533-4563

Vermont

Giovanna Peebles
State Archaeologist
Division for Historic Preservation
58 E. State St.
Montpelier, VT 05602
802/828-3226

Virginia

M. Catherine Slusser
State Archaeologist
Dept. of Historic Resources
221 Governors St.
Richmond, VA 23219
804/225-3556

Washington

Dr. Robert G. Whitlam
State Archaeologist
111 W. 21st Ave., MS KL-11
Olympia, WA 98504-5411
206/753-4405

West Virginia

Jeffrey R. Graybill
  Archaeologist
  Division of Tourism & Parks
  P.O. Box 283
  Parkersburg, WV 26102
  304/428-3000

Wisconsin

Robert A. Birmingham
  State Historical Society of Wisconsin
  816 State St.
  Madison, WI 53706
  608/262-0991

Wyoming

Mark E. Miller
  State Archaeologist
  Dept. of Anthropology
  Box 3431—University Station
  Laramie, WY 82071
  307/766-5301

PROVINCIAL ARCHEOLOGISTS IN CANADA

Alberta

Dr. Jack Brink, Head
  Resource Management Section
  Archaeological Survey of Alberta
  8820–112 Street
  Edmonton, Alberta T6G 2P8
  403/427-2355

British Columbia

Art Charlton, Chief
  Resource Management Division
  Heritage Conservation Branch
  1016 Langley Street
  Victoria, B.C. V8W 1V8
  604/387-5038

Manitoba

Leo Pettipas
  Historic Resources Branch
  Department of Culture, Heritage
    and Recreation
  177 Lombard Avenue, 3rd floor
  Winnipeg, Manitoba R3B 0W5
  204/945-4392

New Brunswick

Provincial Archaeologist
  Department of Culture and
    Historical Resources
  Centennial Building
  Fredericton, New Brunswick
    E3B 5H1
  506/453-2792

Newfoundland

David Mills
  Curator of Archaeology/Ethnology
  Historic Resources Division
  Department of Tourism, Recreation
    and Culture
  Government of Newfoundland and
    Labrador
  Newfoundland Museum
  285 Duckworth Street
  St. John's, Newfoundland A1C 1G9
  709/576-2460

Northwest Territories

Director
  Prince of Wales Northern Heritage
    Centre
  Department of Justice and Public
    Services
  Government of the Northwest
    Territories
  Yellowknife, N.W.T. X1A 2L9
  403/873-7685

Nova Scotia

Bob Ogilvy
  Curator of Special Places
  Nova Scotia Museum
  1747 Summer Street
  Halifax, Nova Scotia B3H 3A6
  902/429-4610

Brian Cuthbertson
  Head, Heritage
  Department of Culture, Recreation
    and Fitness
  Government of Nova Scotia
  P.O. Box 864
  Halifax, Nova Scotia B3J 2V2

Ontario

Roberta O'Brien, Supervisor
  Archaeological Unit
  Heritage Branch
  Ministry of Citizenship and Culture
  77 Bloor Street, West, 2nd floor
  Toronto, Ontario M7A 2R9
  416/965-8258

Prince Edward Island

Harry Holman
  Director of Archives and Heritage
  Provincial Archivist, Public Archives
  P.O. Box 1000
  Charlottetown, P.E.I. C1A 7M4
  902/368-4290

Québec

Charles A. Martijn
  Direction generale du patrimoine
  Ministère des affaires culturelles
  225 Grande Allée, est
  Québec (Québec) G1R 5G5
  418/643-7544

Saskatchewan

Brian Spurling, Supervisor
  Archaeological Resource
    Management Section
  Heritage Conservation Division
  Saskatchewan Culture and Recreation
  2002 Victoria Avenue
  Regina, Saskatchewan S4P 3V7
  306/787-5774

Yukon

Dale Perry, Director
  Heritage Branch
  Department of Tourism, Heritage and
    Cultural Resources
  P.O. Box 2703
  Whitehorse, Yukon Y1A 2C6
  403/667-5363

Federal Level

Dr. Ian Dyck, Chief
  Archaeological Survey of Canada
  National Museum of Man
  Ottawa, Ontario K1A 0M8
  819/994-6110

FOR FURTHER READING

A good place to inquire about archeological publications for a given area is the office of the nearest state archeologist. The addresses and phone numbers of the state archeologists are listed on pages 429–33. These experts can also direct interested persons to local archeological societies, some of which are listed on pages 427–28. The societies, and also museums, can often provide valuable reading lists.

A good bibliography for all of the United States and Canada can be found in Brian M. Fagan, *Ancient North America: The Archaeology of a Continent* (Thames and Hudson, New York, 1991).

Because these sources of information are readily available, this edition of *America's Ancient Treasures,* does not repeat the list of suggested readings that appeared in earlier editions. However, we cannot leave the subject without calling attention to the fact that without the labors and writings of countless archeologists, none of us would have any idea of the fascinating elaboration of human life that took place in America before 1492.

GLOSSARY

Here are some words and terms that may be encountered at archeological sites and exhibits and in readily available literature about archeology. Words defined in the text of this book are not included in the glossary, but may be found by referring to the index.

abrader; abradingstone. A stone tool used in grinding or shaping tools or other articles.

absolute dates. When archeologists know how many years ago a dwelling was built or between what calendar years a pot was made, they say they have an absolute date. Absolute dates can be obtained in various ways—for example, from certain kinds of *tree rings* (see feature in text) in certain places. Dates obtained from the analysis of the carbon-14 (see feature in text) content of organic matter are considered absolute dates, although they cannot be pinpointed at an exact calendar year.

acculturation. The process by which one group of people takes on the lifeways, institutions, technology of another group with which it has close association. Usually the less advanced group is influenced by the more advanced group, but the acculturation process may also be reciprocal. Individuals as well as groups may become acculturated.

adobe. A gritty, clay-like buff or brown material used in the prehistoric Southwest as mortar, plaster, amorphous building material for walls, and occasionally as hand-molded, sun-dried bricks, called *adobes*. This type of construction is still used in the Southwest. The word comes from Spanish.

altithermal. A period also called the Great Drought, or Long Drought, which lasted from about 5000 B.C. to 2000 B.C.

amateur. One who is actively interested in archeology but has not had advanced academic training in the subject or who does not make his living in some pursuit connected with the study of prehistory. Amateurs have made important contributions to archeology, and many professionals welcome their help.

Amateurs can be useful in various ways. They can provide extra eyes to look for sites, extra hands for digging and record keeping and sorting, and extra brains, too. It does not take a college education to be intelligent, but it does take intelligence to be an archeologist, whether amateur or professional.

Amerind; Amerindian. A shortcut word meaning American Indian, sometimes used as a convenient way to distinguish American aborigines from the inhabitants of India. Some scholars have objected to the word, which was already in use at the time of a Congress of Americanists in New York in 1902. The menu for the Congress banquet included "Amerind Siouxp." When it came time for Frederic Ward Putnam to speak at the banquet, he remarked, "Amerind seems to have been placed where it belongs—in the soup."

The Amerind Foundation of Dragoon, Arizona, an important archeological research organization, obviously does not agree with Putnam.

amino acid racemization. Certain substances in living organisms are called L-amino acids. When an organism dies, L-amino acids slowly change into D-amino acids (the technical word for this change is racemization). The longer an organism has been dead, the more D-amino acids it contains in relation to L-amino acids. A comparison of the two forms of amino acid tells how long an organism has been dead. However, the history of the temperature of the soil in which the dead organism was buried must be taken into account. The rate of change of L into D-amino acid can vary widely from one place to another, depending on temperature.

 Amino acid racemization dates for some skeletal material in Southern California are older than many archeologists are willing to accept, but some researchers claim the method gives dates that check well with C-14 dates on the same material. The method is supposed to work with reasonable accuracy up to 100,000 years ago.

anathermal. A period, a little cooler than the present, which lasted from 7000 B.C. to 5000 B.C.

archeomagnetism. See paleomagnetism.

articulated. Archeologists say a skeleton is articulated when the bones in it are in the same relationship to each other as they were when the person (or other creature) was alive.

assemblage. A collection of artifacts, features, and non-human-made remains that are clearly associated with each other. An assemblage may be in a dig, or may come from a dig or from the surface.

associated; association. When archeologists say an artifact was found associated with certain other material, they mean that it is necessary to assume that the artifact and the material belong together; they were probably made and/or used by the same people at about the same time

 Artifacts may be found next to each other in the earth and still not be associated. For example, in the Southwest a modern pipeline may lie within inches of the wall of an ancient kiva. The two are not in association as archeologists use the term. The pipeline is *intrusive*. Indians often dug into trash heaps left by earlier people, making holes in which to bury the dead. The burials are intrusive.

 An archeologist constantly questions and evaluates the association of material in a site. Have all the artifacts been lying together in a certain layer of earth for the same length of time? Or did a tool, for example, drop through a rodent hole to a lower level? The reverse may also be true. Did a rodent carry an object upward from somewhere deep underground, and can the object therefore belong to an earlier culture than its position indicates?

Atlantis. A mythical prehistoric continent, which was supposed to have existed between Africa and the New World before sinking beneath the surface of the Atlantic Ocean. Some people persist in believing in it, although scientists have failed to find evidence that it existed, and oceanographers who have studied the sea floor say it did not.

backfill. As an archeological crew digs a site it often piles the excavated earth to one side. Later it puts the earth back to fill in the excavation. The purpose of backfilling may be simply to prevent erosion. It also helps to prevent vandalizing of unexcavated portions of a site which scientists hope to study at some later time.

biface; bifacial. A stone artifact from which flakes have been removed from both of two opposite sides.

biomass. The total plant and animal life, calculated by weight, existing at a given time on a given land area.

blade. An early kind of tool was made by knocking off chips from a stone in order to shape it into usable form. Later, people made a great technological advance when they found that they could strike some kinds of stone in a certain way and knock off a chip that had two sharp edges. Each edge could serve as a knife, and such a chip was often called a blade, if it was large, or a micro-blade, if small. A blade could also be reshaped to form a projectile point or any one of several other kinds of tool. Instead of making only one tool out of a chunk of stone, a knapper (see below) could now make many tools. The amount of cutting edge that could be obtained from one piece of stone was greatly increased. One present-day experimenter found that he could get up to 75 inches of working edge from a two-pound nodule of flint. Prehistoric people saved a great deal of energy when they adopted the practice of making blades. They did not have to mine or transport nearly as much stone as had been necessary before. Also the invention of blades led to still another invention—handles. A handle made it easier—and much safer—to manipulate a sharp, two-edged blade.

blank. A partly finished stone artifact, given rough shape at a quarry or workshop and often taken elsewhere for completion. Blanks were presumably made in quantity because they were easier to carry from place to place than heavy, unshaped lumps of flint or other stone. Caches of blanks have turned up in burials, on habitation sites, and also in places where no other artifacts are found. Some rough tools found at quarries, although they have been called blanks, may instead have been made on the spot, used, and then discarded. Close examination of the edges of these "blanks" reveals the kind of dulling that comes from use on wood. Presumably the toolmakers brought wood to the quarry and shaped it there, where they had readily available sharp flakes of stone. Laborious resharpening of a worn edge was not necessary, since a new flake could be struck off and shaped with a few quick blows.

blowout. When wind blows away topsoil in an arid region it creates a blowout. Sometimes when earth is removed in this way archeological sites are revealed.

bola. A weight, usually globular or pear-shaped, made of stone, bone, ivory, or ceramic, and grooved or pierced so it could be fastened to a thong. Bolas, tied together usually three to a group, were used for hunting. The hunter threw the bolas so as to entangle the legs and/or wings of the prey.

buck. A male deer. People who have the illusion that they are members of a superior race sometimes use this word to refer to young Indian males. The term is offensive to Native Americans.

burial. Archeologists can learn a great deal about prehistoric societies by studying skeletons and the way they were buried. In some cultures bodies were buried stretched out in an extended position; in others they were placed in the ground in a fetal, or flexed, position with knees drawn up to chest. In still other societies the dead were exposed on platforms or in charnel houses. When the flesh had been removed by decay or scavengers, the disarticulated bones were made into a bundle and buried. Sometimes bodies were cremated and the remains buried. Careful study of bones can reveal sex, age, and often something about nutrition and disease. Goods interred with a burial give many clues to the social position of the person buried and the kind of culture from which he or she came.

burin. A piece of stone with a sharp point, used like a one-tooth saw for shaping or engraving bone or shell or wood. A blade (see above) or a flake could be formed into any one of about twenty varieties of the tool.

cache. When archeologists find a group of identical artifacts buried together they call the collection a cache — from the French word meaning to hide. Sometimes the artifacts are finished; sometimes they are not. Often it is difficult to know whether the objects in a cache were hidden for safe keeping, for ceremonial purposes, or for some other reason.

calibrated dates. This term usually refers to radiocarbon dates that have been checked against tree ring dates. Accurate calibration of radiocarbon dates is not possible before 6285 B.C.

cesium magnetometer. An operator walks across a field carrying this device, which detects large structures underground and is more efficient than a proton magnetometer (see below), which does the same thing.

chiefdom. When a group of people had an ample food supply in one place, they often developed a social structure based on wealth. On the Northwest Coast of the United States, for example, a social pyramid evolved, with the most prestigious man at the top. He was a chief, and the sedentary people over whom he ruled formed a chiefdom. Many less affluent, more mobile groups also had chiefs, but these individuals had less power and their societies are not called chiefdoms.

chopper; chopping tool. This stone tool had a single cutting edge and could be held in one hand and used for chopping. Some archeologists say a chopper is made by knocking off flakes from only one side of a piece of stone, and that a chopping tool is made by knock-

ing flakes off both sides. But the use of this distinction is not universal.

coiling. A term used in both pottery and basketry. When a potter shapes moist clay into a long, ropelike form, then builds up a pot by winding this clay round and round on itself, the method is called coiling.

A basket is said to be coiled when a long bundle of fibrous material is laid up, spiral fashion. Each coil is sewed by a slender splint to the coil below it. The basketmaker pierces the fiber bundle with a bone awl and passes the splint through the hole thus made.

collagen dating. Collagen is a protein abundant in living bone. Like all protein it contains nitrogen, which makes up about 4 percent of its weight. After death the collagen remains in bone, but it decays at a measurable rate. The amount of decay can be determined by measuring the percentage of nitrogen that remains in the collagen. However, the length of time it takes nitrogen to disappear from bone varies with temperature and other aspects of the environment. Therefore the nitrogen test cannot give an absolute date. It can tell only whether two pieces of bone in the same deposit are of the same age. If, for example, the nitrogen test shows that a leg bone in one part of a dig is older than a skull found in another part, then the archeologist must conclude that the person to whom the skull belonged was buried there at a date later than another person, whose leg bone was found. In other words, by itself collagen dating can only give relative dates for different bone samples from a particular site.

core. The part of a stone that is left after chips or blades have been removed. A core may be waste material or it may itself be a tool.

cross dating. When a date for a certain type of pottery, for example, is known at one site, an archeologist attributes a similar date to another site in which the same kind of pottery appears. This is cross dating. It is not precise, but it is helpful.

cultural evolution. The progressive development of a culture.

culture. All that a group of people makes, does, thinks, believes.

culture area. A geographic area in which one culture prevailed at a given time.

culture trait. Any phenomenon that is an element in the total culture of a group of people.

dating methods. See absolute dating, amino acid racemization, collagen dating, cross dating, deep sea core dating, fission track dating, glottochronology, magnetic dating, nitrogen dating, paleomagnetic dating, potassium-argon dating, relative dating, tephrachronology, thermoluminiscent dating, varve dating.

debitage. When material is struck off a stone in order to make an artifact, the waste material is called debitage. Study of debitage can reveal a good deal about techniques used by knappers (see below).

deduction. A process of thinking sometimes used in archeology, which involves reasoning from the general to the specific, or, as one archeologist put it, "from a lucky guess" about what prehistoric people were doing "to a provable fact."

deep sea core dating. Changes in climate produce changes in the life forms in the ocean, and as sea creatures die their shells or skeletons accumulate in sediment on the ocean floor. When drilling equipment recovers sediment cores, the sequence of life forms can be studied and equated to changes in climate on land. This broad method of dating gives information about the Pleistocene, or Ice Age, during which human beings lived. So in a very general way deep sea cores can give some information about the conditions in which people have existed for the last 1,500,000 years.

desert pavement. Because some Southwestern archeological finds have been made in what is called desert pavement, the words appear in archeological literature. They refer to terrain that is thickly covered—or paved—with small rocks. Vegetation is scarce, and for this reason soil, sand, and gravel have not been held in place and have been blown away by wind or washed away by infrequent but violent rainstorms, leaving only rocks too large for wind or water to move.

desert varnish. See patination.

diagnostic trait. A cultural trait that helps to distinguish one group of people from another. A diagnostic trait appears in one group but not in another with which it might be confused.

diffusion. The movement of human ideas or customs— even domesticated plants and animals—from one place to another. When people migrate they take their habits with them. This is primary diffusion. When ideas or customs, but not the people who have them, move from one place to another, the phenomenon is called secondary diffusion. The spread of agriculture across much of North America was secondary diffusion.

disarticulated. Bones out of their natural arrangement. *See also articulated.*

ecotone. The dividing line between two different ecological communities.

fission track dating. Spontaneous fission of minute amounts of uranium leaves tracks in obsidian, human-made glass, or other crystals. These tracks can be observed by special techniques, and the number of tracks is proportional to the time that has elapsed since the material was formed.

flake. A chip that has been forced off a larger piece of stone. Tools are shaped and sharpened by flaking. A tool can also be made from a flake itself.

flaking tool. An implement, often a piece of antler, used in tool making to press flakes off a piece of stone.

flotation. Minute bits of vegetation, tiny mollusks, and insects in the soil of a dig can tell archeologists much about the environment in which people once lived at a site which is being excavated. In order to recover these very small, often very light, bits of evidence, archeologists put soil into water which may be mixed with any one of several chemicals. The heavy particles sink to the bottom and the sought-after, light-weight material rises to the surface, where it can be removed and studied.

fluorine dating. Bones and teeth absorb fluorine when they are in the soil. The longer they are buried, the more they absorb, so it is possible to obtain relative dates (see below) for bones buried at different times in the same area.

glottochronology. A way of arriving at a date of separation between two languages that have a common origin by studying the extent to which they have diverged from each other.

graver. A tool for engraving. *See also burin.*

grid system. A way of dividing a site into quadrangles to make it easy to describe exactly where in the site a find is made.

hearth. A place where a fire has been built, sometimes identified by charcoal, sometimes by baked earth. Hearths often appear in one layer of soil after another as an archeologist digs down through a site, and they are an indication of a succession of camps or habitations. Charcoal from a hearth can be dated by the radiocarbon method. Baked clay in a hearth can be dated by the paleomagnetic method. Either method tells when human activity went on at the spot.

Holocene. The period after the Pleistocene (see below).

hydration rate. See obsidian hydration.

hypothesis. An unproved theory. Scientists find hypotheses useful as they search for new knowledge. In a science such as archeology, which is developing rapidly, new hypotheses are constantly appearing, and hypotheses that are not very old are constantly being discarded. These discarded hypotheses are signs of growth and advance. When investigators have tried a theory and found it wanting, they have eliminated one wrong solution to a problem. They know one direction in which they do not have to go in order to find an answer. So to a good scientist it is not frustrating to have to give up a hypothesis. Indeed this act can be a source of satifaction and pleasure. In a very real sense it turns the searcher away from illusion.

indirect dating. When object A is found clearly associated with object B, whose date is known, the date of B is given to A. This is called indirect dating.

induction. A process of thinking much used in archeology, which involves reasoning from the specific to the general. *See also deduction.*

industry. When similar sets of particular kinds of artifact appear again and again, archeologists refer to these similar groups of artifacts as an industry. They are presumed to have been made by people who had a common culture.

in situ. An archeologist uses these Latin words (meaning "in place") to say that an object is in exactly the place where it was found.

knapper. One who makes stone implements by chipping.

law of superposition. In undisturbed desposits of soil the top layer is the most recent, the bottom layer the oldest.

lexico-statistical dating. See glottochronology.

lithic. Having to do with stone.

magnetic dating. Clay contains iron that is slightly magnetic. When clay is baked—in pottery or beneath a fire—the magnetic fields of the molecules of this iron are aligned in relation to the position of the earth's magnetic pole at the time when the clay was very hot. If the clay has not been moved since it was last heated, it is possible to determine where the pole was when the clay was hot. The magnetic pole of the earth is known to have wandered, and its wanderings have been charted in a general way for hundreds of thousands of years. The exact position of the pole has been traced throughout the last 2000 years. Accordingly it is possible, by determining the orientation of the iron molecules in unmoved baked clay, to determine the date at which it was last heated. This fact makes it possible to determine when a campfire baked the clay beneath it or when a kiln was last used for firing pottery. If pottery was left in the kiln after the last firing, it is possible to date the pottery. This method is also called paleomagnetic dating.

magnetic surveying. See proton magnetometer.

model. A theory that is to be tested to see if it is valid. *See also hypothesis.*

Mongoloid. A major race of humankind to which American Indians, Eskimos, and Aleuts belong.

Mu. A mythical, sunken continent supposed to have been in the Pacific Ocean. *See also Atlantis.*

neutron activization analysis. Each natural deposit of obsidian, flint, clay, and of some other lithic materials, contains a unique pattern of trace elements. Neutron activization makes it possible to determine from what source an obsidian blade or a flint arrowhead or the clay in a pot comes. In a laboratory the artifact is subject to a bombardment of neutrons. These neutrons, interacting with the nuclei of trace elements in the material, form radioactive isotopes. Each isotope gives off gamma rays with a characteristic energy. By measuring the energy of each ray, it is possible to identify the isotope from which it comes. Then, by discovering the pattern of trace elements in an object and comparing it with the patterns of trace elements in natural deposits of the material, it is possible to determine from which quarry the material comes.

For example, neutron activation analysis of certain Hopewell artifacts made of obsidian has proved that the source of the obsidian was in what is now Yellowstone National Park. This fact in turn throws light on the trade routes used by Hopewellians.

nitrogen dating. See collagen dating.

obsidian hydration dating. In each specific environment, the surface of an obsidian artifact absorbs water at a steady rate, forming what is called a hydration layer. The thicker the layer, the older the artifact.

osteodontokeratic. When there is no sign that a people used wood or stone for tools, and when it is supposed that this people did make tools of bones, teeth, and horns, their culture is said to be osteodontokeratic. It is difficult to see why this jaw-breaker, which is not found in most large dictionaries, serves any purpose except to make its user seem learned. It would be just as accurate and a lot easier to understand if scientists referred to "bone-tooth-horn" cultures.

paleo-. A prefix meaning ancient, or prehistoric. The name Paleo-Indians is applied to the earliest people who are known to have lived in the Americas. Special sciences are devoted to paleoastronomy, paleobotany, paleoecology, paleoethnobotany, paleopathology, paleopedology, paleoserology, paleozoology, etc.

paleomagnetic dating. See magnetic dating.

palynology. The study of pollen. Each kind of flowering plant produces pollen that is unique, and an expert can tell by looking at a pollen grain exactly what plant produced it. Pollen grains have tough coverings that can last a long time. By studying pollen grains found in ancient soils it is possible to tell what kinds of plants were growing nearby when the soil was formed. Palynology helps archeologists find out what plant resources were available to ancient peoples at different times and what the climate was at those times.

paradigm. Archeologists make increasing use of this word, borrowed from other sciences. It means pattern, or type.

patination. The surface of metal or rock may change color and texture as a result of the action of chemicals in the soil or atmosphere. This new film on a surface is called patina, and the amount of patination is sometimes used as a very rough indicator of age. Because chemical environments vary greatly from place to place and even from time to time, the method is far from precise. The patina on rocks in the southwestern part of the United States is often called desert varnish.

pedology. See soil analysis.

pilaster. Pillar-like structures in the inside walls of Anasazi kivas. Pilasters supported roof beams.

Pleistocene. The million and a half years of the history of the earth that preceded the Holocene period, which began about 11,000 years ago and includes the present. The Pleistocene is sometimes called the Ice Age.

pollen analysis. See palynology.

post mould. When one end of a pole or post is buried in the earth, it leaves an outline clearly visible in the soil, long after the post itself has decayed and disappeared. This outline is known as a post mould. By noting carefully the pattern of post moulds at a site, it is often possible to determine the size and shape and method of construction of dwellings or other buildings. Post moulds can reveal that a settlement was surrounded by a palisade and thus presumably had enemies. Post moulds can even reveal the plan used by ancient astronomers to observe the solstices or equinoxes or other phenomena.

potassium-argon dating. In potassium-bearing minerals potassium decays at a known rate, forming the gas argon. The proportion of argon to potassium can tell the age of a specimen from 50,000 years back to 50,000,000 years ago. Because potassium-argon analysis only yields dates so remote from the present, it has had little application in American archeology, although it has been useful in determining the age of ancient human remains found in deep layers of the earth in Africa.

problematical. Any object that presents a problem that an archeologist admits he or she can't solve.

proton magnetometer. A device for measuring variations in the intensity of magnetic fields in the soil. By detecting such variations it is often possible to locate buried walls, ditches, an artifacts without digging. The proton magnetometer is one of the instruments used in remote sensing (see below. *See also cesium magnetometer.*

quantitative archeology. By counting, by measuring, by using statistical methods and computers, archeologists are learning much about prehistoric people that they have not been able to learn by other means. For example, they think they can tell the number of people who lived in certain places at any one time merely by measuring the number of square feet in the area that was inhabited.

Archeologists can find what people ate, and in what proportions, by counting the various kinds of bones and shells and seeds found in refuse heaps. From a tabulation of bones it is possible to go on to making an estimate of the weight of the edible meat that was once supported by those bones. Together with other data this figure may indicate how much protein, on an average, each person in a community probably consumed in relation to other elements in the diet.

racemization. See amino acid racemization.

relative dates. When archeologists say that event A occurred before or after event B, they have a relative date for A.

remote sensing. Any one of several techniques for obtaining information from a distance is called remote sensing. Aerial photography, imagery from satellites, detection of buried structures, by radar or by proton magnetometer, are forms of remote sensing.

retouch. When a cutting tool made of stone is retouched, it is sharpened. Retouching is done in one of two ways—either by blows that knock small flakes off an edge (percussion retouch), or by pressure to force flakes off (pressure retouch).

salvage archeology. The saving of as much archeological information as possible before a site is destroyed by construction, possibly of a skyscraper or parking lot or pipeline or dam. In the United States the first major program of salvage archeology was undertaken in the 1930s, ahead of the construction and dam building done by the Tennessee Valley Authority.

scraper. A piece of stone so sharpened in one portion that it could serve as a chisel or for cleaning hides or for smoothing wood or bone. This kind of tool was made in various forms and was sometimes hafted.

secondary burial. The burial of disarticulated (see above) bones after flesh has been removed from them by decay, predators, or cleaning.

seriation. Archeologists sometimes arrange artifacts, such as pottery, in a progressive series to obtain relative dates (see above). This process is called seriation.

shaman. A person who is regarded as having healing powers derived from supernatural sources. A holy person; a religious leader; a "medicine man."

sipapu (see-pah-pooh). A small hole in the floor of a kiva (ceremonial chamber). Today in a Pueblo kiva the hole represents the opening to the underworld through which the ancestors of the Pueblo people are supposed to have emerged. Such openings in the floors of prehistoric kivas are believed to have had the same symbolic significance.

soil analysis (pedology). By analyzing the soil at a site it is possible to learn a great deal about the environment at the time when people lived there. It is even possible to learn how densely a site was populated: the more phosphate in the soil, the denser the population.

sterile soil. An archeologist calls soil sterile if it contains no evidence of human activity.

striking platform. The flat surface on a piece of stone which a knapper strikes in order to detach a flake or a blade (see above).

surface find. An artifact found on the surface of the ground.

tephrachronology. Volcanic ash, which is called tephra, is often deposited around volcanoes—even at some distance from them—following eruptions. The chemical content of tephra is unique for each eruption. If artifacts lie below tephra known to have come from a certain eruption, the artifacts predate the eruption. If the calendar date for the eruption is known, as is sometimes the case, a date is known, before which the artifacts must have been made.

thermoluminescence dating. Radioactive materials in pottery decay and produce electrons and other carriers of electric charges which, when heated, produce light. The older a piece of pottery, the more light is produced. Measurement of the light by a complicated process yields the age of a piece of pottery with a margin of error of not more than 10 percent.

uniface. A stone tool on which an edge is created by chipping from one side only. *See also biface.*

varve dating. A moving glacier grinds some rocks into fine powder, which is carried along by the ice. When melt water from a glacier accumulates in a lake, the powder settles to the bottom. Each melting season leaves a distinct layer of powder, called a varve. When artifacts are associated with varves, relative dates (see above) can be obtained. When one varve in a series can be connected with a dated event, exact years can be assigned to every varve in the series, giving absolute dates (see above).

zoomorphs. Pottery or stone carvings in the shape of animals.

ACKNOWLEDGMENTS

First we wish to thank Abby Fountain without whose long labors this revision would not have been possible. She assisted in many ways to see the work through to completion.

We are very grateful to Carrie Jenkins who helped to solve a difficult problem, and to Betty Bacon who gave valuable help with research.

In addition to thanking all those who helped with the first three editions of this work we must acknowledge our indebtedness to the following who generously provided information:

Margaret Adelph, Patricia Allen, David Alloway, Gary C. Anderson, David Anthony, Nancy Jo Arthur, Rich Athearr, Victoria Atkins, Joan M. Azelmo.

Jim Badolph, Jenny Baird, Henry A. Baker, Leo R. Barker, Tyler Bastian, Larry Beame, Alice M. Becker, Dorothy Beckham, Barbara Bell, Lila E. Belt, Rick Berg, Kathleen M. Bird, Robert A. Birmingham, Timothy L. Blue, A. J. Bock, Alexandra Bonney, Bruce J. Bourque, Rebecca L. Bowen, Doug Bowman, R. B. Bradbury, Bruce Bradley, James W. Bradley, Melinda Brazzale, Robert L. Brooks, Mack Brooms, David S. Brose, Colin Bruce, Dan Bruce, A. P. Buchner, Bishop T. Buckle, Nellie White Bundy.

Linda O. Cain, Marsha A. Chance, Jefferson Chapman, LuAnn Cheek, Timothy J. Chester, Carol Chilton, Elinor R. Clack, Wayne E. Clark, Linda Clark, Ray L. Claycomb, Andy Cloud, Patricia E. Coats, Edward G. Cole, Susan M. Collins, Jack Cooper, Wesley Cowan, Verna L. Cowin, Stephen D. Cox, Marilou Creary, Paula R. Cressy, Gary Cummins, James D. Currivan, Rhonda Curtis.

Walter D. Dabney, Karen J. Dalman, Carl Davis, Hester Davis, Bill Day, Sharon Dean, Evan De Bloois, Mary Jo Dennis, Jane des Granges, Pierre Desrosiers, Mary Devine, C. L. Dill, E. James Dixon, John Douglas, Margie Douthit, Melissa L. Dunlap.

Richard N. Ellis, Sally Erickson, Connie Escobar, Deborah Ethier, Dori Eubank, Genevieve Eustache.

Robert P. Fay, Kenneth Feder, Eric Finkelstein, Susan E. Finn, Paul Fish, Mary L. Fitt, Donald W. Foster, Joan E. Freeman, Mary Theresa Bonhage Freund, Robert E. Funk.

Leland Gilsen, Jerry W. Goodman, Richard Gould, Campbell Grant, Larry Grantham, Jeffrey R. Graybill, Thomas J. Green, William Green, Marleen Greenway, H. F. Gregory, David W. Griggs. Alice Gromski, Ann Grube, Andrew Gulliford, E. Guno.

John W. Hall, Greg Hare, Robert E. Haltiner, Richard C. Hanes, Buddy Haney, Mary Harrington, Billy R. Harrison, James N. Haskett, Nancy W. Hawkins, Ann Hayes, Charles F. Hayes III, Joe Samuel Hays, Ava Herron, Mary Herron, John A. Hesse, Robert C. Heyder, Ray Hillman, Berard Hofman, Linda Hogarth, Christy Hohman-Caine, John W. Hohmann, David M. Hollingsworth, Nigel Holman, Ross R. Hopkins, Julie Howard, Dana Howlett, Bonnie C. Hughes, James Hunter.

William R. Iseminger.

Mrs. James L. Jones, Mary L. James, Julia M. Johnson, Lynda Johnson, Mark Johnson, Bridget Jones, Charlott Jones, Chris Judson, Noel D. Justice.

Joan Kachel, Jay Kaplan, Paul Katz, Renee Keller, Susan Kennelly, Glenda King, Laird and Ruth King, Gay

Kinkade, Judy Kirk, Ann Kosky, Herbert C. Kraft, Barb Kubik, Marge Kuhlman, Bryan W. Kwapil, Gaither Galleher Kyhos, JoAnn M. Kyral.

James D. LaBatt, Micheline Lachance, Dulane M. Laird, John Laird, Jeff LaLande, Frederick Lange, Janet Larsen, Alan Lawless, Sam Lawson, Dorman Lehman, Stephen H. Lekson, Ginny Leslie, Rich Lewis, Robin M. Lillie, Robert D. Lindy, Ike Lovato, Richard P. Lucas.

James A. Mack, R. S. Manuel, Jackie Marin, Clare and Emanuel Marmes, Roger Marois, Debbie Martin, A. J. Martinez, Dan Mather, Barbara Mead, Michael D. Metcalf, Elaine Moore, Norma Morris, Lee Mortenson, Denise Mowchan, Mary Murphy, Daniel F. McCarthy, Rick McClure, Mark A. McConaughy, Maureen McHale, Yvonne McMillan, John McMurdo.

Toni I. Nagel, Tessie Naranjo, Lori Naughton, Gary Nellis, Dean E. Nelson, Mark Nelson, Gerrie Noble, Donna North, Myrl Nyren.

Erin O'Donnell, Steve Ohrn, Stephen J. Olsen, Maureen O'Neill, Jill Osborn, Kay Oster, Stacey Otte, Margaret Potter Otto.

Debby Padgett, Wanda Palma, David A. Pape, Edgar Perry, Robert Petersen, Peter J. Pilles, Rich Pittsley, Jack Pollock, JoAnne Popham, Stephen R. Potter, Mary Lucas Powell, Robert Powell, Dale C. Price, Robert C. Price.

Richard C. Quick.

David Radford, Ann Rasor, Pat Reagan-Woodward, Carol Rector, William Reddy, J. Jefferson Reid, David L. Rhoades, Sally Richards, Barbara Rigutto, Laurie Risch, Lisa Roach, Jerry Rogers, Nancy Romaine, Lester Ross.

Roy A. Salls, Michael Sampson, Sherwin N. Sandberg, W. W. Sauer, George Schrimper, Art Selin, Beth Sennett, Robert D. Shaw, M. Catherine Slusser, Helen Simons, Wendell Simpson, K. C. Smith, Mimi Smith, Patricia F. Smith, Signe Snortland, Lore Solo, Karin B. Stanford, Brenda Stephens, James A. Stewart, Frances Stiles, Charles Stout, Jerry M. Sullivan, Anna Symanski, Lloyd A. Swanger.

Gladys Tantaquidgeon, Chris Turnbow, Barbara B. Taylor, Billy R. Templeton, Bruce Thomsen, Gary A. Thorson, Peter B. Tirrell, Gordon Topham, Debbie Trueman, William G. Truesdell, Elizabeth C. Tyne.

Charon F. Urban.

Donna-marie Viene.

Henry Walker, David H. Wadsworth, Ruth Warfield, Barbara L. Waskowich, Bruce Weber, Kathy Weber, Michael Weichman, Ann Welborn, McMillan West, Robert G. Whitlam, B. Wiley, Lorraine Williams, Ruth Williams, Nancy R. Wizner, Bruce Womak, J. Woods, Jim Woodward, Margaret Wyatt.

Jack Young.

Debby Zieglowsky.

Index

A. D. Buck Museum of Science and History, 229
Abbe-Brennan Site, 419
Abbe Museum, 389
Abbott, Charles Conrad, 402
Abbott Farm Site, 382, 401, 402
Abitibi Lake sites, 420
Abnaki Indians, 389, 393, 399
Abo, 67, 100
Acadia National Park, Abbe Museum, 389
Accokeek Creek Site, 391
Acknowledgments, 41
Acoma Pueblo, 67
"Acorns," 134–35
Adam East Museum and Art Center, 189
Adan E. Treganza Anthropology Museum, 144
"Adena," 337
Adena culture: characteristics, 305–7, 336, 337; mentioned, 328, 339, 355, 356, 359, 360, 362, 365, 367, 368, 383, 394, 409
Adena Mound, 365
Adena Park, 336
Adobe Walls Site, 248
aerial photographs, 198, 226, 275, 283, 284, 362, 364
Agate House, 34
Agawa Rock Pictographs, 411
Agogino, George A., 250
agriculture: acorns, 134–35; bee plant, 391; buckeyes, 135; corn, 3–5, 151, 202, 218,

228, 257, 263, 312, 320, 382, 388; cotton, 27, 63; domestication of plants, xxvi, 3, 4, 26, 151, 215, 382, 391, 424; gardens to visit, 240, 291, 335, 375, 384, 394; general development, 26, 391; grid gardens, 93; irrigation, 5, 9, 18, 27, 35, 55, 60, 84, 208, and salt damage, 35; native plant gardens, 143, 151, 240, 288, 291, 384; pickleweed, 126; pollen analysis, 332; tobacco, 347; yaupon, 267; Great Plains, 201–4, 218; Nevada, 151; North Central, 305, 309, 312, 320; Northeast, 382, 388, 394, 424; Southeast, 257, 261, 263, 278, 287, 291; Southwest, xxvi, 3–4, 42–43
Alabama, 235, 260–63, 282, 283
Alabama-Coushatta Indian Museum, 242
Alabama Department of Archives and History, 260
Alabama Indians, 242
Alabama Museum of Natural History, 260, 263
Alaska, 142, 166–70, 236, 353, 401
Alaska State Museum, 166
"Albany to Buffalo," 402
Alberta, Canada, 206–7
Aleuts, 15, 161, 162, 166
Algonquin (Algonkian) peoples, 315, 341, 384, 392, 405, 408, 410, 413, 426
Alibates Flint Quarries National Monument, 242–43

Alkali Ridge, 107
Allen County Museum, 355
Alpha Rockshelter, 177
amateurs, 44. *See also* field schools; visiting excavations; volunteering
American Anthropological Association, 183
American Indian Archaeological Institute, 384, 385
American Museum of Natural History, 404
Amerind Foundation, Inc., 15
Amerindian Museum, Pointe-Bleue, 420
Amistad Recreation Area, 248
Amoskeag Falls, 399
Anasazi culture: classified, 46; described, 4, 7–10, 30; discussed, 55–61, 78–86; mentioned, 7, 16–17, 21, 25, 28, 30, 37, 43, 46, 47, 51, 55, 64, 71, 78, 87, 93, 94, 107–11 passim, 114, 120, 121, 123, 146, 153, 208, 229, 232; settlements at Aztec Ruins, 68, Bandelier, 71–74, Chimney Rock, 47, Dominguez and Escalante, 51–52, Glen Canyon, 21, Grand Canyon, 21, Kinlichee, 25, Petrified Forest, 34
Anasazi Heritage Center, 46, 50
Anasazi Indian Village State Park, 107
Anasazi National Park, 46
Anchorage Museum of History and Art, 166
Ancient Monuments of the Mississippi Valley, 303, 325, 329, 359, 362
Ancient Pemaquid Restoration, 389

Blennerhassett Island, 367
Blood Run National Historic Landmark, 331
blood types, 162
Blue Licks Museum, 336, 338
Blue Ridge Mountains, 276
Blue, Timothy L., 347, 348
Blythe Intaglios, 127, 129, 130
bone artifacts, 182, 190, 193, 196, 197, 203, 216, 298, 337, 389, 398, 407
bones, animal, study of, 122, 320, 390
bones, human, study of, 236–37, 301
Borax Lake, 146
Boreal Archaic culture, 394
Boulder Dam, 151
Boy Scouts, 209
Boyd Mounds, 287
Boylston Street Fish Weir, 380–81, 394
Bradford Canyon Ruin, 108
Brain, Jeffrey, 288
Brant, Joseph, 412
Brazosport Museum of Natural Science, 243
Brew, J. O., 107
Brigham Young University, Museum of People and Culture, 109
Bright Angel Pueblo, 22
British Columbia, Canada, 171–76, 401
Bronson Museum, 394
Brooklyn Museum, 405
Brown University, 423
Browns Park, 51
Bruce County Museum, 412
Bruce Museum, 384
Buffalo Bill Historical Center, 251
Buffalo Eddy, 186
buffalo jumps, 200, 205, 206, 219–21, 251
Buffalo Museum of Science, 405
Buffalo Pound Provincial Park, 237
Buikstra, Jane, 237
Bull Brook Site, 379, 394
Bullseye Site, 320
Bureau of Land Management, 46, 47, 53, 61, 64, 77, 115, 116, 178
Burnett County Historical Society Museum, 371
Burpee Natural History Museum, 311
"Busk," 263
Butler Wash Overlook, 109
Butler Wash Petroglyphs, 109
Bynum Mounds, 287

C-14 dating: described, 12–13; mentioned, 22, 51, 121, 128, 150, 160, 182, 197, 219, 231, 241, 246, 262, 368, 372, 376, 381, 396, 415, 417, 426
C. H. Nash Museum, 295
Cabeza de Vaca, 105
Caddo Indian Museum, 244
Caddo Indians, 230, 235, 244
Caddoan culture, 231, 244, 245, 247, 249, 250, 265, 285

Caddoan Mounds State Historical Park, 244
Cahokia Indians, 315
Cahokia Mounds, 287
Cahokia Mounds State Historic Site, 311–15, 323, 324, 370
Cahuilla Indians, 130, 140, 144
Calf Creek Recreation Area, 110
Calico Mountains, 144
Calico Early Man Archaeological Site, 130, 132, 144
California, 127, 130–46, 205
California State Indian Museum, 132
California State University, Fullerton, Museum, 132
Calusa Indians, 269, 273
Camp Rayner Site, 237
Campbell Mound, 355, 365
Campbell River Museum and Archives, 171
Campbell Site, 351, 352
Campus Site, 166
Canada, 142, 183
Canadian Museum of Civilization, 397, 412, 420
Canadian River, 242, 248
Canaliño Indians, 128, 145
canals, 18, 27, 33, 35
Canaveral National Seashore, 267
cannibalism, 156, 370
canoes, 145, 155, 172, 187, 192, 276, 282, 290, 380, 381, 404; portage, 405
Canyon de Chelly National Monument, 8, 14, 16–17, 24
Canyon Pintado Historic District, 46, 61
Canyonlands National Park, 110, 111, 113
Cape Cod National Seashore, 392
Cape Denbigh, 164, 382
Cape Krusenstern, 163
Cape Perpetua Visitor Center, 183, 184
Cape Royal Ruin, 22
Capitol Reef National Park, 110, 114
Caprock Canyons State Park, 245
Capulin Volcano, 76
"Carbon-14 Dating," 12–13. See also C-14 dating
caribou hunting, 380, 397
Carling Reservoir Site, 17
Carlsbad Caverns National Park, 76, 77
Carnegie Museum, 368, 417
Carpinteria Valley Museum of History, 133
Carson, Christopher "Kit," 17, 94
Casa Grande Ruins National Monument, 17, 18, 19
Casa Malpais, 18
Casa Rinconada, 66, 78, 86
Casamero Ruins, 77
Casas Grandes, Mexico, 5, 95, 104, 109, 250
Castile Historical House, 405
Castle Creek Ruin, 111
Castle Windy Midden, 267
Catalina Island Museum, 133

Catawba College, Museum of Anthropology, 290
Catlin, George, 225, 299, 346, 348, 349
catlinite, 25, 346, 347, 348
Catlow Cave, 183
Cave Du Pont, 121
cave dwellers, 8, 145, 189; and caves, 21, 29, 71, 73, 74, 75, 77, 90, 91, 98, 117, 170, 171, 185, 262. See also caves by name
cave paintings, 17, 74, 75, 77, 133, 248, 342
Cave Towers, 111
caves by name: Catlow, 183; Charlie Lake, 171; Chumash, 134; Danger Cave, 114, 122, 126; Fate Bell, 248; Fishbone, 151; Fort Rock, 184, 185; Goat, 77; Graham, 349, 350; Gypsum, 150, 151; Hidden, 149; Lovelock, 150, 151; Mammoth, 338; Painted Grotto, 77; Pictograph, 221, 222, 223, 250; Panther, 248; Russell, 254, 262, 263; Salts, 338; Sandia, 101; Ventana, 41; Winnemucca, 151; Wyandotte, 328
Cayuga Museum, 405
Cayuse-speaking peoples, 193
Cedar Tree Tower, 59–60
Cemetery Mound, 367
Center for American Archeology, 182, 317, 320
Center for Archeological Investigations, 324
Center for the Study of the First Americans, 183
Center of Southwest Studies, 46
Centre D'interprétation de la Rivière Métabetchouane, 420
ceremonial centers, 18, 26, 48, 58, 68, 86, 250, 292, 352, 362
ceremonial lodge, 277
ceremonial practices: Anasazi, 65; ball game, 6; Basketmaker, 9; Black Drink, 263, 267; burial, 9, 179, 257, 271, 274, 276, 304, 305, 314, 337, 343, 355, 398, 407; busk, 296; Cahokian, 314; calumet, 348; dance platform, 23, 67; Death Cult, 258, 259; dreams, 130; false faces, 378, and masks, 156, 161, 233, 246, 421; Ghost Dance, 239; Guardian Spirit Quest, 207, 213; harvest, 4, 316; healing/curing, 60, 147, 353, 378; kachina, 33; kivas, 57–58, 68, 86, 96; Kuksu cult, 135; Mississippian, 258, 259; North Central, 332; potlatch, 157, 158, 176; puberty, 139, 263; shamans, 105, 129, 130; Snake Dance, 42; Southern Cult, 258, 261, 354; sweat house, 134, 141; Toloache cult, 135; others, 280, 295, 306, 308, 326, 332
Chaco Canyon: discussed, 78–86; mentioned, 10, 30, 47, 48, 391; outliers listed, 84
Chaco Culture National Historical Park, 78–86

Makah Cultural Research Center, 192, 193
Makah Indians, 192
Malakoff Heads, 202, 231
Malchow Mounds, 334
Malibu Creek State Park, 142
malnutrition, 240, 267
Mammoth Cave National Park, 338
mammoth exhbit, 187. *See also* hunting:
    mammoth
Mammoth Mound, 367
Mammoth Trumpet, The, 183
Mammoth Visitor Center, Yellowstone
    National Park, 252
Man Mound Park, 374
Manchester Historic Association, 399
Mandan Indians, 199, 203, 225, 226, 227,
    228, 241, 299
Mangum Mound, 287
Manis, Emanuel, and Clare Manis, 194
Manis Mastodon Site, 194, 351
Manitoba, 198, 216–18, 381
Manitoba Museum of Man and Nature, 218
Manix Basin, 131
Many Cherries Canyon, 24
Map Rock Petroglyphs, 180
Marana Mound, 26
Maricopa Indians, 7
Marietta Mound, 360
Marin Museum of the American Indian, 142
Maritime Archaic, 397, 398
Maritime Museum, Cohasset Historical
    Society, 392
Marksville lifeway, 283
Marksville State Commemorative Area, 283,
    285
Marmes Early Man Site, 160, 193, 195, 196
Marmes Rockshelter, 193, 194, 195, 196
Marquette, Jacques, 324
Marshall, James A., 305, 361
Maryland, 391
Mary March Regional Museum, 397
masks. *See* personal adornment: masks
Mason, Charles, 59, 60
Massachusetts, 392–94
Massowomeke Indians, 417
mastodons. *See* hunting: mastodon
Mastodon State Park, 350–51
Mather, Cotton, 393
Mathers Museum, Indiana University, 328
Matson Museum of Anthropology, 418
Mattale Indians, 145
Mattatuck Museum, 385
Maturango Museum of Indian Wells Valley,
    143, 144
Maxwell, Dorothy, and Gilbert Maxwell, 104
Maxwell Museum of Anthropology, 94
Mayflower, the, 392
maze stone, 138
McBride Centennial Museum, 197
McCammon Petroglyphs, 179

McCarthy, Daniel, 138
McClung Museum, 297, 301
McCord Museum, 422
McCurdy, Ross, 392
McJunkin, George, 88
McPhee Reservoir, 46
McPherson County Old Mill Museum, 214
Meadowcroft Rock Shelter, xviii, 418
"Meaning of a Mound, The," 300–301
Medicine Lodge State Archaeological Site, 252
medicine wheel, 238, 251
Meeting House Gallery, 387
Memorial Hall Museum, 393
Memorial Indian Museum, 231
Menasha Mounds, 374
Mendota Mental Health Institute Mound, 374
Menoken Indian Village State Historic Site,
    227
Mercer Museum, 418
Mesa Southwest Museum, 26
Mesa Verde National Park: discussed, 54, 55–
    61, 62, 63; mentioned, xxv, 8, 10, 30, 37,
    51–52, 64, 68, 101, 118, 147, 208, 291
Meso-american culture, 230
Métabechouane Interpretive Centre, 422
meteorites, 165
Mexico, xxvi, 3, 4, 5, 6, 22, 35, 143, 147,
    161, 257, 268, 285, 313, 314, 347, 361,
    375, 383; Tehuacan site, 394
Miami County, Indiana, Museum, 328
Miami County, Ohio, Archaeological
    Museum, 360
Miami Fort, 361
Miamisburg Mound State Memorial, 360
mica, 306, 332, 342, 354, 363
Michigan, 340–44
Michigan Historical Museum, 341
Michigan State University Museum, 342
Micmac Indian Village, 420
Micmac Indians, 388, 393
middens. *See* shell mounds
Middleport culture, 416
Midsouth Indian Heritage Festival, 297
Midvale Quarry, 180
migrations, xxii, 15, 17, 22, 27, 30, 37–38,
    40, 41, 53, 56, 68, 81, 84, 99, 101, 127,
    160–62, 164, 166, 171, 201, 204, 278,
    292, 307, 313, 316, 370, 424
Mill Creek, 111
Mill Creek culture, 203
Mill Pond peoples, 334, 335
Mille Lacs Kathio State Park, 346
Millicent Rogers Museum, 94
Mills County Historical Museum, 334
Milwaukee Public Museum, 374–75
Mimbres culture (pottery), 5, 39, 61, 94,
    104, 109, 145, 146, 184, 212, 232, 356,
    390, 405
Mimbres River, 5
Minataree Indian Chief, 349

mining, 20, 147, 152, 242, 312, 328, 338,
    339, 340, 341, 357, 372
Minisink Site, 400
Minnesota, 345–48
Missions, Spanish, 67, 92, 93, 99
Mississippi, 286–88
Mississippi Palisades State Park, 323
Mississippi River (Valley), 201, 258, 278,
    283, 308, 309, 312, 316, 319, 332–35
    passim, 246, 351, 372, 375, 402; Upper
    Valley, 194
Mississippi State Historical Museum, 286
Mississippi State University, Cobb Museum,
    286
Mississippian culture: described, 258–59;
    mentioned, 25, 233, 240, 244, 257, 260,
    261, 264, 265, 273, 274, 278, 281, 286,
    288, 292, 293, 295, 300, 308, 312, 325,
    326, 334, 339, 349, 351, 352, 368, 370,
    371, 376
Missouri, 349–54
Missouri Headwaters State Park, 221
Missouri Historical Society, 351
Missouri Indians, 354
Missouri River, 199, 202, 203, 205, 226,
    227, 228, 230, 240, 278, 313; Headwaters
    park, 221
Missouri State Museum, 351
Mistusinne Stone, 238
Mitchell Prehistoric Village, 240
Miwok Indians, 139, 141, 146
Miwok Park, 143
moats, 226, 227, 240, 279
"Model Archeology Program," 265
Modoc Indians, 142
Modoc Rock Shelter, 309, 316
Moeller, Roger, 385
Mogollon-Anasazi pueblo, 25
Mogollon culture, 4–5, 18, 25, 41, 43, 45,
    90, 91, 92, 94, 104, 246, 250
Mohave Indians, 144
Mohawk-Caughnawaga Museum, 407
Mohawk Indians, 408
Mohawk Trail, 402
Mohegan Indians, 386
Mojave Desert, 141
Mojave Indians, 39
Moki Queen, 116
Molander Indian Village State Historic Site,
    227
Monahans Sandhills, 248
Monks Mound, 287, 311, 313, 314
Monongahela culture, 382
Monroe County Historical Association, 418
Montana, 219–23
Montana Historical Society, 221
Montana State Archaeological Site, 219
Monterey State Historic Park, 143
Montezuma Castle National Monument, 2,
    26–27, 40, 65

Nelson Dewey State Park, 375
Nelson, Nels, 298
Neutral Indians, 413, 416
neutron activation analysis, 252
Nevada, 148–53
Nevada Historical Society, 151
Nevada State Museum, 152
Nevada State Museum and Historical Society, 152
Nevada Division of Parks, 153
Neville Public Museum, 375
New Archeology, xx
New Britain Youth Museum, 385
New Brunswick, 395
New Brunswick Museum, 395
New Hampshire, 399–400
New Jersey, 401–3
New Jersey State Museum, 401
New Mexico, 67–105
New Mexico State University Museum, 94
New York, 404–10
New York State Museum, 407
Newark Earthworks, 361, 362
Newark Museum, 401
Newell, Leslie, 267
Newfoundland, 296–98
Newfoundland Museum, 397
Newspaper Rock, Arizona, 34
Newspaper Rock Petroglyphs, 33
Newspaper Rock State Park, 120
Newspaper Rock, Utah, 120
Nez Perce Indians, 178, 179, 180, 182, 188
Nez Perce National Historical Park, 178, 180, 182
Niagara County Historical Center, 408
Niantic Indians, 423
Nichols Pond, 408
Nicolet, Jean, 375
Nine Mile Canyon Rock Art, 120
No Man's Land Museum, 232
Nodena site, 264–65
Nokachok Kachina doll, 33
Nootka Indians, 155, 156
Nootka Sound, 173
Norona, Delf, 367
Norse explorers, 165, 396, 422, 423
North Carolina, 290–93
North Central Area, 302–77
North Dakota, 226–28
North Dakota Heritage Center, 228
North Dakota State Historical Society, 226, 227, 228
North Museum, Franklin and Marshall College, 417
North Peace Museum, 174
North Platte River, 225
Northeast, 379–426
Northern Kentucky University, 339
Northern Oklahoma College, A. D. Buck Museum, 232

Northwest Coast, 146, 155–97, 316, 334, 344, 353, 355, 386, 401, 404, 409
Northwest Coast Indians, 155–61, 401, 404
Northwest Territories, 182
Northwestern National Exhibition Centre, 174
Northwestern State University, Williamson Museum, 285
Northwestern University, 319
Norton Mounds, 342–43
"Note About Sacred Sites, A," 251
Nova Scotia, 411
Nova Scotia Museum, 411
Nun-chah-nulth culture, 171
Nursery Site, 187

Oak Grove people, 145
Oakland Museum, History Division, 144
Obelisk Cave, 56
obsidian, 187, 252, 306, 332; source tested, 252
Obsidian Cliff, 252
Ocmulgee National Monument, 256, 277–80
Oconaluftee Indian Village, 290, 291
Oconto County Historical Society Museum, 375
Oconto Site, 375
Octagon Mound State Memorial, 362
Odawa people, 343
Ohio, 252, 268, 302, 354, 355–66, 390
Ohio Historical Center, 364
Ohio Historical Society, 357, 358, 361, 362, 363
Ohio River, 201, 297, 305, 306, 309, 313, 325, 327, 336, 338, 339, 383, 402
Ohlone Indians, 134, 136, 144, 146
Okmulgee, 280
Ojibway Boulder Mosaics, 216, 218
Ojibway Indians, 411, 413
Ojibway Village, 373
Oklahoma, 204, 229–36, 263, 288, 403
Oklahoma Basketmaker Culture, 236
Oklahoma Historical Society, 232
Old Cahawba, 262
Old Copper Culture, 341, 372, 374, 375, 376, 416
Old Cordilleran lifeway, 126
Old Crow Site, 197
Old Fort Site, 354
Old Oraibi, 33
Old River Lake, 283
Old Stone Fort State Park, 297
Olsen-Chubbuck Site, 207
Olympic National Park, Pioneer Memorial, 193
On-A-Slant Indian Village, 228
Oneida Indians, 405, 408
Oneota culture and people, 316, 331, 333, 334, 335, 354, 371, 375
Onondaga Indians, 381

Ontario, Canada, 405, 411–16
Ontario County Historical Society, 408
Oraibi Pueblo, 33
Oregon, 183–88
Oregon Historical Center Museum, 187
Oregon State University, 183
Oregon State University, Horner Museum, 183, 187
Osage Indians, 351
Osage Village State Historic Site, 351
Osceola Site, 372
Oshara Tradition, xxvi, 8
Oshkosh Public Museum, 376
Ossining Historical Society Museum, 408
Otero Junior College, 209
Ottawa Indians, 324
Over State Museum, 241
overpopulation, 48, 52, 68, 84, 307
Owasco culture, 382, 405, 406, 408, 409, 410, 419
Owasco Museum, 408
Owl Creek Indian Mounds, 288
Oxbow Archaeology District, 340
Oyster Ponds Historical Society, 409
Oyster Shell Banks, 390
Ozark Bluff culture, 266
Ozark Bluff Dwellers, 349
Ozette Site, 192, 193

Pacific Northwest Indian Center, 193
painted caves, 17, 74, 75, 77, 133, 134, 248
Painted Desert Visitor Center, 34
Painted Grotto, 77
Painted Hand Pueblo, 61
painted kiva, 53, 98
Painted Rocks State Park, 33
Paiute Indians, 151, 152; Northern, 186
Paiute language, 120
Paiute-Shoshone basketry, 138
Pajarito Plateau, 71, 94, 95, 103
Palace of the Governors, 94–95
"Paleo and Archaic," 26
Paleo-Indians: dates for, xxiii–xxiv; habitat for, xxiv–xxvi; origin of, 15; tools and weapons of, xxiii–xxiv; mentioned, xxii, 28, 40, 97, 144, 171, 200, 207, 208, 209, 211, 213, 221, 224, 225, 228, 231, 238, 242, 248, 249, 250, 251, 255, 264, 271, 273, 274, 277, 282, 290, 291, 293, 295, 311, 316, 327, 328, 331, 335, 336, 339, 343, 346, 350, 351, 355, 357, 360, 371, 376, 379, 385, 387, 393, 394, 397, 401–12, 416, 419, 422, 425, 426
"Paleo Palate, The," 211
Palm Springs Desert Museum, 144
Palouse River Valley, 195
Pamunkey Indians, 426
Panamint Indians, 144
Panhandle culture, 248
Panhandle-Plains Historical Museum, 248